OXFORD
Illustrated
Children's
Dictionary

eggs

lips

OXFORD
UNIVERSITY PRESS

Great Clarendon Street, Oxford OX2 6DP

Oxford University Press is a department of the University of Oxford.
It furthers the University's objective of excellence in research, scholarship,
and education by publishing worldwide in

Oxford   New York

Auckland   Cape Town   Dar es Salaam   Hong Kong   Karachi
Kuala Lumpur   Madrid   Melbourne   Mexico City   Nairobi
New Delhi   Shanghai   Taipei   Toronto

With offices in

Argentina   Austria   Brazil   Chile   Czech Republic   France   Greece
Guatemala   Hungary   Italy   Japan   Poland   Portugal   Singapore
South Korea   Switzerland   Thailand   Turkey   Ukraine   Vietnam

Oxford is a registered trade mark of Oxford University Press
in the UK and in certain other countries

leaves

colours

cockroaches

British Library Cataloguing in Publication Data

Data available

ISBN: 978-0-19-9119936

3 5 7 9 10 8 6 4

Printed in India

clown

buzzard

film

The Publishers would like to thank Shutterstock and
Wikipedia for permission to use their material. Every care has
been taken to trace copyright holders. However, if there have
been unintentional omissions or failure to trace copyright
holders, we apologize, and will, if informed, endeavour to
make corrections in any future edition.

How to Use your Dictionary

Dictionary entries
The words defined are headwords, and they are arranged in alphabetical order. The words derived from each word (derivatives) are at the end of an entry, sometimes with short definitions, sometimes grouped together.
Words with the same spelling but with a different meaning or origin (homographs) are given separate entries and numbered with a raised figure, e.g. **lean**[1] (bend your body) and **lean**[2] (not fat).

Pronunciation
Help is given with pronouncing words when they are difficult in some way, when two words with the same spelling are pronounced differently (such as several words spelled **bow**), and when the same word is pronounced differently in its different word classes or parts of speech (as with **record**).

The pronunciation is given in brackets, introduced by '*rhymes with...*' (when possible) or '*say...*' followed by a simple scheme that uses ordinary letters, e.g.

frog

bow[1] noun (*rhymes with* **cow**)
apostrophe noun (say a-**pos**-tro-fi)

Words are divided into syllables, and the main stress is shown by bold type (thick black letters).

The following sounds should be noted:
oo shows the sound as in s**oo**n
uu shows the sound as in b**oo**k
th shows the sound as in **th**in
th shows the sound as in *th*is
zh shows the sound as in vi**si**on

Word classes
Word classes are printed in italics (e.g. *noun, adjective, adverb*) after the word and before its definition.

Inflections and plurals
The parts of verbs, plurals of nouns, and some comparatives and superlatives and adverbs are given after the word class when they are irregular, e.g.

break verb (**breaking, broke, broken**)
good adjective (**better, best**)

Meanings
Many words have more than one meaning. Each meaning is numbered separately.

Labels
Words or meanings that are only used informally or in spoken English are marked informal. Subject labels are given for certain meanings that are used in, say, grammar, mathematics, or science.

Examples
Examples of words in use are given in italic or sloping print *like this* to help make a meaning clearer.

Oxford Children's Corpus
All the text has been backed by the Oxford Children's English Language Corpus, which is a very large unique electronic database of language specifically aimed at children. It is resourced from a vast variety of children's literature and select websites, and consists of 30 million words and is growing!

Dictionary features

headword

alphabet tab

inflections

word class

plural

pronunciation help

label

word origin

---

guide ▷ hacksaw

Guide a member of the Girl Guides Association, an organization for girls

guide *verb* to guide someone is to show them the way or help them do something

guide dog *noun* a dog specially trained to lead a blind person

guidelines *plural noun* guidelines are rules and information about how to do something

guillotine *noun* (say **gil**-o-teen) 1 a machine once used in France for beheading people 2 a device with a sharp blade for cutting paper

guilt *noun* 1 guilt is an unpleasant feeling you have when you have done something wrong 2 a person's guilt is the fact that they have done something wrong • *Everyone was convinced of his guilt.*

guilty *adjective* (**guiltier, guiltiest**) 1 someone is guilty when they have done wrong 2 someone feels guilty when they know they have done wrong

guinea pig *noun* 1 a small furry animal without a tail, kept as a pet 2 a person who is used in an experiment

guitar *noun* a musical instrument played by plucking its strings

guitarist *noun* someone who plays the guitar

gulf *noun* a large area of sea partly surrounded by land

gull *noun* a seagull

gullet *noun* the tube from the throat to the stomach

gullible *adjective* someone is gullible when they can be easily fooled about something

gully *noun* (**gullies**) a narrow channel that carries water

gulp *verb* 1 to gulp something is to swallow it quickly or greedily 2 to gulp is to make a loud swallowing noise, especially out of fear

gulp *noun* a loud swallowing noise

gum¹ *noun* the firm fleshy part of the mouth that holds the teeth

gum² *noun* 1 a sticky substance used as glue 2 chewing gum **gummy** *adjective* sticky like gum

gum² *verb* (**gumming, gummed**) to gum something is to cover it or stick it with gum

gun *noun* 1 a weapon that fires shells or bullets from a metal tube 2 a pistol fired to signal the start of a race

gun *verb* (**gunning, gunned**) to gun someone down is to shoot them with a gun

gunfire *noun* gunfire is the firing of guns, or the noise they make

gunman *noun* (**gunmen**) a man armed with a gun

gunpowder *noun* gunpowder is a type of explosive

gurdwara *noun* a building where Sikhs worship

gurgle *verb* to gurgle is to make a bubbling sound • *Water gurgled down the pipe.*

guru *noun* 1 a Hindu religious teacher 2 a wise and respected teacher

Guru Granth Sahib *noun* the holy book of the Sikh religion

gush *verb* 1 to gush is to flow quickly 2 to gush is also to talk quickly and with excitement

gust *noun* a sudden rush of wind or rain **gusty** *adjective*

gut *noun* the lower part of the digestive system; the intestine

gut *verb* (**gutting, gutted**) 1 to gut a dead fish or animal is to remove its insides before cooking 2 to gut a place is to remove or destroy the inside of it • *The fire gutted the house.*

guts *plural noun* 1 the insides of a person or animal, especially the stomach and intestines 2 (*informal*) courage and determination

gutter *noun* a long narrow channel at the side of a street or along the edge of a roof, to carry away rainwater

guy¹ *noun* 1 a figure in the form of Guy Fawkes, burnt on or near 5 November in memory of the Gunpowder Plot to blow up Parliament in 1605 2 (*informal*) a man

guzzle *verb* to guzzle food or drink is to eat or drink it greedily

gym *noun* (say jim) (*informal*) 1 a gym is a gymnasium 2 gym is gymnastics

gymkhana *noun* (say jim-**kah**-na) a show of horse-riding contests and other events

gymnasium *noun* a place equipped for gymnastics

gymnast *noun* a person who does gymnastics

gymnastics *plural noun* gymnastics are exercises and movements that show the body's agility and strength

gypsy *noun* (**gypsies**) a member of a community of people, also called **travellers**, who live in caravans or similar vehicles and travel from place to place

gyroscope *noun* a device used in navigation, that keeps steady because of a heavy wheel spinning inside it

WORD ORIGIN
The word **gyroscope** comes from a Greek word *gyros* meaning 'a ring or circle'.

Hh

habit *noun* something that you do often and almost without thinking **habitual** *adjective* something is habitual when you do it regularly, as a habit **habitually** *adverb*

habitat *noun* an animal's or plant's habitat is the place where it naturally lives or grows

hack *verb* to hack something is to chop or cut it roughly

hacker *noun* someone who uses a computer to get access to a company's or government's computer system without permission

hacksaw *noun* a saw with a thin blade for cutting metal

112

4

haddock *noun* (**haddock**)
a sea fish used for food

hag *noun*
an ugly old woman

haggard *adjective*
looking ill or very tired

haggis *noun*
a Scottish food made from some of the inner parts of a sheep mixed with oatmeal

haggle *verb*
to haggle is to argue about a price or agreement

haiku *noun* (**haiku**) (*say* hy-koo)
a Japanese short poem, with three lines and 17 syllables in the pattern 5,7,5

hail¹ *noun*
frozen drops of rain

hail¹ *verb*
it hails or it is hailing when hail falls

hail² *verb*
to hail someone is to call out or wave to them to get their attention

hailstone *noun*
a piece of hail

hair *noun*
1 hair is the soft covering that grows on the heads and bodies of people and animals 2 a hair is one of the fine threads that makes up this soft covering

hairbrush *noun*
a brush for tidying your hair

haircut *noun*
cutting a person's hair when it gets too long; the style into which it is cut

hairdresser *noun*
someone whose job is to cut and arrange people's hair

hair-raising *adjective*
terrifying or dangerous

hairstyle *noun*
a way or style of arranging your hair

hairy *adjective* (**hairier, hairiest**)
having a lot of hair

Hajj *noun*
the Hajj is the journey to Mecca that all Muslims try to make at least once in their lives

hake *noun* (**hake**)
a sea fish used for food

halal *adjective*
halal meat is prepared according to Muslim law

half *noun* (**halves**)
each of the two equal parts that something is or can be divided into

half *adverb*
partly; not completely • *This meat is only half cooked.*

half-hearted *adjective*
not very enthusiastic

half-heartedly *adverb* not very enthusiastically

half-mast *noun*
a flag is at half-mast when it is lowered to halfway down its flagpole, as a sign that someone important has died

half-term *noun*
a short holiday from school in the middle of a school term

half-time *noun*
a short break in the middle of a game

halfway *adverb, adjective*
at a point half the distance or amount between two places or times

hall *noun*
1 a space or passage inside the front door of a house 2 a very large room for meetings, concerts, or other large gatherings of people 3 a large important building or house, such as a town hall

hallo *exclamation*
a word used to greet someone or to attract their attention

Hallowe'en *noun*
the night of 31 October, when people used to think that ghosts and witches might appear

hallucination *noun*
something you think you can see or hear when it isn't really there

halo *noun* (**haloes**)
a circle of light, especially one shown round the head of a saint or angel in a painting

halt *verb*
to halt is to stop

halt *noun*
to call a halt is to stop something to come to a halt is to stop

halter *noun*
a rope or strap put round a horse's head so that it can be controlled

halve *verb*
1 to halve something is to divide it into halves 2 to halve something is to reduce to half its size or amount • *If the shop had another checkout it would halve the queues.*

ham *noun*
ham is meat from a pig's leg

hamburger *noun*
a round flat cake of minced beef that is fried and usually eaten in a bread roll

hammer *noun*
a tool with a heavy metal head at the end of a handle, used for hitting nails in or beating out things

hammer *verb*
1 to hammer something is to hit it with a hammer 2 to hammer is to knock loudly • *We heard someone hammering on the door.* 3 (*informal*) to hammer someone in a game or contest is to defeat them completely

hammock *noun*
a bed made of a strong net or piece of cloth hung up above the ground or floor

hamper¹ *noun*
a large box-shaped basket with a lid

hamper² *verb*
to hamper someone or something is to get in their way or make it difficult for them to work

hamster *noun*
a small furry animal with cheek pouches, often kept as a pet

hand *noun*
1 the part of your body at the end of your arm 2 a pointer on a clock or watch 3 the cards held by one player in a card game 4 a worker, especially a member of a ship's crew 5 side or direction • *the right-hand side* • *on the other hand* at hand near or close by to give someone a hand is to help them on hand ready and available to get out of hand is to get out of control

hand *verb*
to hand something to someone is to give or pass it to them something is handed down when it is passed on from one generation to the next

handbag *noun*
a small bag for holding money, keys, and other personal items

handcuffs *plural noun*
a pair of metal rings joined by a chain, used for locking a person's wrists together

handful *noun*
1 as much as you can carry in one hand 2 a small number of people or things • *There were only a handful of people in the audience.* 3 (*informal*) a troublesome person

handicap *noun*
1 a disadvantage 2 a disability affecting a person

handicapped *adjective*
1 suffering from a disadvantage 2 suffering from a disability

handicraft *noun*
artistic work done with your hands, such as woodwork and pottery

a b c d e f g h i j k l m n o p q r s t u v w x y z

113

words with the same spelling but different meaning (homographs)

example sentence

numbered meanings

5

robots

Grammar

Words belong to various **word classes** (also called **parts of speech**). Knowing about word classes helps you to understand how words work and helps you to use them correctly and creatively.

nouns
Nouns are used to name people, places, or things and tell you who or what a sentence is about.
common nouns refer to people or things in general: for example, *dancer, lizard, sandwich,* and *television.* They can be divided into concrete nouns, which we can see, touch, taste, smell, or hear (e.g. *baby, penguin, explosion, aroma, telescope*), and abstract nouns, which describe ideas (e.g. *beauty, horror, mystery*).
proper nouns give the name of a specific person, place, or thing, for example *Shakespeare, Antarctica, Hallowe'en.* Proper nouns always begin with a capital letter.

verbs
A verb can describe an action or process (e.g. *dive, chew, heal, thaw*), a feeling or state of mind (e.g. *worry, think, know, believe*), or a state (e.g. *be, remain*). A sentence usually contains at least one verb.

adjectives
Adjectives give us more information about nouns e.g. *tall, pale, delicious, jagged, untrue.* They can come before a noun (e.g. a *tall* giraffe, a *jagged* cliff), or they can come after a verb like *be, become,* or *grow* (e.g. The soup will be *delicious*; My companion became *pale*; The weather grew *cold*). Some adjectives can only be used in one position: *afraid* can only be used after a verb, and *utter* only before a noun. You can say *The crew were afraid* but not *an afraid crew*; and you can say *It was an utter disaster* but not *The disaster was utter.*

adverbs
Adverbs answer questions such as *when?, where?, why?, how?,* and *how much?* A few adverbs modify adjectives: for example *The map is **very** old* tells you how old the map is, and *a **fairly** expensive car* describes a car that is quite (but not very) expensive. Most adverbs tells us more about verbs: for example, *The troll ate **ravenously*** tells you how the troll was eating, *It rains here **frequently*** tells you how often it rains, and *Hammering was heard **downstairs*** tells you where hammering was heard. Adverbs like these are often formed by adding *-ly* to an adjective e.g. *ravenously, frequently.* Notice that adverbs can also go with other adverbs: *Sam smiled **rather** sheepishly.*

pronouns
Pronouns are used to replace a noun or noun phrase in a sentence or clause, and help to avoid repeating words. There are several types of pronoun:
personal pronouns: *I, you, he, she, it, we, they, me, you, him, her, it, us, them*
reflexive prounouns: *myself, yourself, himself, herself, itself, ourselves, yourselves, themselves*
relative pronouns: *what, who, whom, whose, which, that*
interrogative pronouns: *what, who, whom, whose*
demonstrative pronouns: *this, that, these, those*

tarantula

prepositions

Prepositions show how a noun or pronoun relates to the other words in a sentence or clause. They can show:

• the position or direction of a person or thing:
*The spider scurried **along** the wall, **across** the carpet, **through** the doorway, **down** the stairs, **past** the cat, **up** the curtain, **out** of the window, and **into** the garden.*

• the time something happens or lasts:
*Can you come to my house **on** Tuesday **around** five o'clock?*
*We were in Athens **in** August, **during** the Olympics.*

• the connection between people of things:
*Inspector McBride was always grumbling **about** something.*
*Does this dress go better **with** the red shoes or the brown?*

conjunctions and connectives

Conjunctions are used to join words, phrases, or clauses in a sentence. *And, but, for, or, neither, nor, yet, although, because, if, until, unless, when, where, while,* and *whereas* are all conjunctions.

Connectives are used to link ideas in a piece of writing. They often occur at the start of a sentence and connect it with a previous sentence or paragraph. Common connectives are the words *moreover, nevertheless, finally, furthermore,* and *thus.*

beads

exclamations

These are words such as *ah!, oh!,* and *ouch!* that are typically written with an exclamation mark.

Punctuation

Punctuation is the use of special marks to make a piece of writing easier to read and understand. Punctuation marks show divisions and connections between sentences, clauses or individual words: for example, a full stop (.) marks the end of a sentence; a comma (,) separates clauses or items in a list; a question mark (?) indicates a question; and quotation marks (" ") show direct speech (the actual words someone speaks). Other types of punctuation are the use of capital letters at the start of a sentence or a proper noun, and the use of an apostrophe to show possession (the cat's bowl) or to indicate a missing letter (don't, I've).

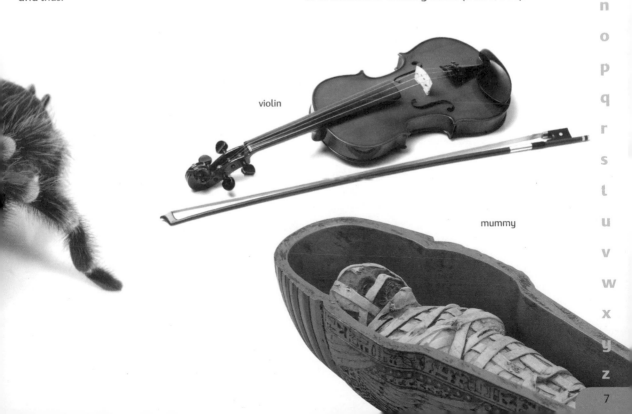
violin

mummy

Commonly misspelled words

i before e
chief
niece
pierce
priest
siege
yield
achievement
mischievous
wield

e before i
eight
height
seize
weird
deceive
foreign
receive

words including u
gauge
guard
juice
guarantee
nuisance
pronunciation
sausage

silent letters
knife
psychic
receipt
write

eed or ede
precede
proceed

double or single letters
accommodate
accommodation
address
aggressive
beginning
cassette
colossal
committee
disappear
disappearance
disappoint
disappointment
dissect
embarrass
embarrassment
exaggerate
harass
install
instalment
millennium
millionaire
necessary
parallel
questionnaire
recommend
skilful
threshold
unnecessary
withhold

other difficult spellings
answer
conscientious
cylinder
desperate
ecstasy
extraordinary
extravagant
February
government
length
library
responsible
rhythm
sandwich
scavenge
secretary
separate
sergeant
signature
strength
twelfth
unconscious
vengeance
Wednesday

leopard

Aa

a *adjective* (called the *indefinite article*)
1 one; any • *I would like a holiday.* **2** each; every • *I go there twice a month.*

aback *adverb*
to be taken aback is to be surprised and slightly shocked by something someone says or does • *We were taken aback by this silly idea.*

abacus *noun*
a frame with rows of beads that slide on wires, used for counting and doing sums

abacus

abandon *verb*
to abandon something or someone is to go away and leave them, without intending to go back for them • *Someone abandoned these poor kittens on the street.*
abandon ship passengers abandon a sinking ship when they get into the lifeboats to save their lives

abbey *noun*
a place where monks or nuns live and work

abbey

abbreviation *noun*
a word or group of letters that is a shorter form of something longer • *BBC is an abbreviation of 'British Broadcasting Corporation'.*

abdomen *noun*
1 the part of the human body where the stomach is **2** the back part of the body of an insect or spider

abide *verb*
you cannot abide something or someone when you don't like them at all • *I can't abide blackcurrants.*

ability *noun* (**abilities**)
1 ability is the skill or talent to do something • *They have a lot of ability at games.* **2** an ability is a special skill or talent • *a person of many abilities*

able *adjective*
1 having the power or skill or opportunity to do something • *They were not able to find our house.* **2** having a special talent or skill • *John is a very able musician.* **ably** *adverb* to do something ably is to do it well and use skill or talent

abnormal *adjective*
unusual or peculiar, not normal
abnormality *noun* something unusual or abnormal • *a physical abnormality*

aboard *adverb, preposition*
someone is aboard when they have got on a train, ship, or aircraft • *The passengers were now all aboard.* • *It's time to get aboard the train.*

abolish *verb*
to abolish a rule or custom is to get rid of it • *Some people would like to abolish homework.*

abolition *noun*
(*say* ab-o-**lish**-on)
getting rid of something

abominable *adjective*
very shocking, dreadful • *It was an abominable crime.*

aboriginal *noun*
one of the original inhabitants of a country. When **Aboriginal** refers to Australia you spell it with a capital A.

Aborigines *plural noun*
(*say* ab-er-**ij**-in-eez)
the people who lived in Australia before the European settlers arrived there

about *preposition*
1 to do with, connected with • *The story is about animals.* **2** approximately, roughly • *She's about five feet tall.*

about *adverb*
1 in various directions or places • *They were running about.* **2** somewhere near by • *There were wild animals about.* **to be about to do something** is to be just going to do it • *He was about to leave.*

above *preposition*
1 higher than, over • *There was a window above the door.* **2** more than • *The temperature was just above freezing.*

above *adverb*
at a higher point, or to a higher point • *Look at the stars above.*

abreast *adverb*
side by side • *They walked three abreast.*

abroad *adverb*
in a foreign country • *They live abroad now.*

abrupt *adjective*
1 sudden and unexpected • *The van came to an abrupt halt.* **2** rude and unfriendly • *He gave an abrupt reply.*

abscess *noun*
a painful swelling on the body containing pus

abseil *verb*
to abseil is to lower yourself down a steep cliff or rock by sliding down a rope

absence *noun*
not being in a place where you are expected, for example school or work

absent *adjective*
not present; away

absentee *noun*
someone who is away, for example not at school or work

absent-minded *adjective*
forgetting things easily
absent-mindedly *adverb*

absolute *adjective*
total, complete • *For a moment there was absolute silence.*

absolutely *adverb*
1 completely **2** (*informal*) definitely • *'Are you going to Beth's party?' 'Absolutely!'*

absorb *verb*
1 to absorb something like liquid is to soak it up **2** to be absorbed in something is to be interested in it and give it all your attention • *He was very absorbed in his book.*

absorbent *adjective*
an absorbent material soaks up liquid easily

abstract *adjective*
to do with ideas and not with physical things • *abstract patterns*

absurd *adjective*
silly or ridiculous • *It was an absurd thing to say.* **absurdity** *noun* something that is silly or ridiculous

abundant *adjective*
large in amount, plentiful
abundance *noun* a large amount, plenty • *There was an abundance of good things.*

abuse *verb* (*say* a-**bewz**)
1 to abuse something is to treat it badly and harm it **2** to abuse someone is to say unpleasant things about them **3** to abuse

someone also means to hurt them or treat them cruelly

abuse noun (say a-**bewss**)
1 treating something badly
2 unpleasant words said about someone • *She got a lot of abuse from her so-called friends.*
3 physical harm or cruelty done to someone

abusive adjective
saying unpleasant things about someone

academic adjective
to do with learning in a school or university • *an academic subject*

academy noun (**academies**)
a college or school

accelerate verb
to accelerate is to go faster
acceleration noun an increase in speed, going faster

accelerator noun
a pedal that you press down to make a motor vehicle go faster

accent noun
1 your accent is the way you pronounce words, which shows where you are from • *He has a Yorkshire accent.* **2** a special mark put over a letter, usually when it's a foreign word, to show its pronunciation • *The word 'resumé' has an accent on the second 'e'.*

accept verb
1 to accept something is to take it when someone offers it to you **2** to accept an invitation is to say 'yes' to it **3** to accept an idea or suggestion is to agree that it is true or worth thinking about **acceptance** noun taking something that someone offers you

acceptable adjective
good enough, satisfactory • *Their behaviour was not acceptable.*

access noun
a way to reach a place • *This road is the only access to the house.*

access verb
(in ICT) to access data is to find it on a computer and be able to use it

accessible adjective
easy to reach or approach

accident noun
something unexpected that happens, especially when something is broken, or someone is hurt or killed
by accident by chance, not intentionally

accidental adjective
something is accidental when it happens by chance and not

because someone wants it to happen • *accidental damage*
accidentally adverb to do something accidentally is to do it by mistake or without meaning to • *David accidentally dropped a tin on his foot.*

accommodate verb
to accommodate someone or something is to provide them with a place to stay or find space for them

accommodation noun
accommodation is a place to live or stay • *They were looking for cheap accommodation.*

accompaniment noun
the music played on a piano or another instrument while a singer sings

accompany verb (**accompanies, accompanying, accompanied**)
1 to accompany someone is to go somewhere with them
2 to accompany a singer is to play the piano or another instrument while they sing

accomplish verb
to accomplish something is to do it successfully
accomplished adjective good at doing something, skilful
accomplishment noun something you do well

accord noun
to do something of your own accord is to do it willingly and without being told to

accordingly adverb
1 consequently; therefore
2 in a way that is suitable • *You are older now and must behave accordingly.*

according to preposition
1 You say **according to someone** to show where a piece of information comes from • *According to Katie, there is a party tomorrow.* **2** You say **according to something** when you are comparing two things • *The shop has priced the apples according to their size.*

accordion noun
a portable musical instrument like a large concertina with a set of keys like a piano's at one end

accordion

account noun
1 a description or story about something that happened **2** an amount of money someone has

in a bank or building society
3 a statement of the money someone owes or has received, a bill **on account of something** because of it **to take something into account** is to consider it along with other things

account verb
to account for something is to be or give an explanation of it • *How do you account for these marks?*

accountant noun
a person whose job is to write and organize the money accounts of a person or organization **accountancy** noun accountancy is the job an accountant does

accumulate verb
1 to accumulate things is to collect them or pile them up
2 things accumulate when they form a heap or pile
accumulation noun

accuracy noun
accuracy is being exactly right or correct

accurate adjective
done exactly and carefully • *She does accurate work.*
accurately adverb to do something accurately is to do it carefully and exactly • *You have to measure the room accurately.*

accuse verb
to accuse someone is to say that they did something wrong
accusation noun a statement accusing someone of something

accustomed adjective
to be accustomed to something is to be used to it • *She was not accustomed to being treated so rudely.*

ace noun
1 the four aces in a pack of cards are the cards with an A in the corner and a large emblem of the suit in the centre
2 someone or something very clever or skilful

ache noun
a dull steady pain

ache verb
to ache is to feel a dull steady pain

achieve verb
to achieve something is to succeed in doing it or getting it
achievement noun something you succeed in doing • *Winning the prize was a fine achievement.*

acid noun
a substance that contains hydrogen and causes chemical change. Acids are the opposite of alkalis.

acid *adjective*
sour or bitter to taste **acidic** *adjective* containing a lot of acid **acidity** *noun* the level of acid in a substance

acid rain *noun*
rain that contains harmful acids because it has mixed with waste gases from the air

acknowledge *verb*
1 to acknowledge something is to admit that it is true 2 to acknowledge a letter is to say that you have received it 3 to acknowledge a debt or favour is to say you are grateful for it **acknowledgement** *noun*

acne *noun* (*say* **ak**-ni)
a skin disease with red pimples on the face

acorn *noun*
the seed of an oak tree. It is oval with a stem ending in the shape of a cup.

acoustics *plural noun* (*say* a-**koo**-stiks)
1 the acoustics of a place are the qualities that make it good or bad for sound 2 (*singular noun*) the science of sound

acquaint *verb*
1 to acquaint someone with something is to tell them something about it, so they know what it is 2 to be acquainted with someone is to know them slightly

acquaintance *noun*
someone you know slightly **to make someone's acquaintance** is to get to know them

acquire *verb*
to acquire something is to obtain it, usually with some effort or difficulty

acquit *verb* (**acquitting, acquitted**)
to acquit someone is to decide that they are not guilty of a crime, especially in a law trial

acre *noun* (*say* **ay**-ker)
an acre is the area of a piece of land containing 4,840 square yards

acrobat *noun* (*say* **ak**-ro-bat)
an entertainer who gives displays of jumping and balancing **acrobatic** *adjective* to do with an acrobat; like what an acrobat does • *They were amazed at her acrobatic skills.*

acrobatics *plural noun*
exercises of jumping and balancing that an acrobat does.

acronym *noun* (*say* **ak**-ro-nim)
a word or name that is formed from the first letters of other words, for example *UFO* is an acronym of *unidentified flying object*

across *adverb, preposition*
1 from one side of something to the other • *The table measures 1.5 metres across.* 2 to the other side of something • *How can we get across the busy road?*

act *noun*
1 something that someone does 2 an individual performance in a programme of entertainment, for example a juggling act or a comic act 3 one of the main sections of a play or opera 4 a new law that a government makes **to put on an act** is to show off or pretend to be something you are not

act *verb*
1 to do something useful or necessary • *We need to act straight away.* 2 to behave in a certain way • *She's been acting very strangely recently.* 3 to act in a play or film is to take part in it

action *noun*
1 an action is something that someone does 2 action is fighting in a battle • *He was killed in action.* **out of action** not working properly **to take action** is to do something decisive

activate *verb*
to activate a machine or device is to start it working

active *adjective*
1 busy, taking part in lots of activities 2 doing things, working • *an active volcano*

activity *noun* (**activities**)
1 activity is doing things 2 an activity is something special that someone does • *They enjoy outdoor activities.*

actor *noun*
someone who takes part in a play or film

actress *noun*
a girl or woman who takes part in a play or film

actual *adjective*
really there or really happening

actually *adverb*
really, in fact • *Actually, I think you are wrong.*

acupuncture *noun*
acupuncture is a way of curing disease or taking away pain by pricking parts of the body with needles

acute *adjective*
1 sharp or intense • *She has an acute pain.* 2 severe • *The explorers were suffering from an acute shortage of food.* 3 clever, quick to understand something 4 an acute accent is the mark put over a letter, as in resumé 5 an acute angle is an angle of less than 90 degrees

AD
short for *Anno Domini*, used with dates that come after the birth of Jesus Christ, for example AD 1492 is the year Columbus reached America

adapt *verb*
1 to adapt something is to change it so you can use it for something different 2 to adapt to something is to make yourself cope with it • *They adapted to life in the country very quickly.* **adaptation** *noun* an adaptation is something someone has adapted, for example a book they have made into a film

adaptor *noun*
a device for connecting different pieces of equipment

add *verb*
1 to add one number to another is to put them together to get a bigger number 2 to add one thing to another is to mix them together, for example the different things in a recipe **to add up** is what numbers do to make a bigger number, called a total **to add numbers up** is to make them into a bigger number

adder *noun*
a small poisonous snake

addict *noun*
someone with a habit they can't give up, for example taking drugs or drinking alcohol **addicted** *adjective* someone who is addicted to a habit can't give it up **addiction** *noun* a habit that someone can't give up

addition *noun*
1 addition is the process of adding numbers together, or adding other things 2 an addition is something or someone that has been added • *James is an addition to the class.* **in addition** also, as well

additional *adjective*
extra, added on

adder

acrobat

additive *noun*
something that is added to food, for example as a flavouring

address *noun*
1 the details of the place where someone lives • *My address is 29 High Street, Newtown.* **2** (*in computing*) a set of words and symbols that tells you where you can find something using a computer, for example on the Internet • *What's your email address?* **3** a speech

address *verb*
1 to address a letter or parcel is to write the address on it before sending it **2** to address a person or a group of people is to make an important remark or speech to them • *The judge addressed the prisoner.*

adenoids *plural noun*
your adenoids are the spongy flesh at the back of your nose, which can become swollen making it difficult to breathe

adequate *adjective*
enough, sufficient

adhesive *noun*
something such as glue that you use to stick things together

adhesive *adjective*
causing things to stick together

Adi Granth *noun*
(*say* ah-di **grunt**)
the holy book of the Sikhs

adjacent *adjective*
near or next to something • *Her house is adjacent to the shop.*

adjective *noun*
a word that describes a noun or adds to its meaning, for example *big, honest, red*

adjust *verb*
1 to adjust something is to change it slightly or change its position **2** to adjust to something is to try to get used to it • *They found it hard to adjust to life in the city.*

adjustment *noun* a small change you make to something

administration *noun*
administration is running a business or governing a country

administrator *noun* someone who helps to run a business or organization

admirable *adjective*
worth admiring; excellent • *You have done an admirable piece of work.* **admirably** *adverb* in an admirable way • *The note is written in admirably clear handwriting.*

admiral *noun*
an officer of the highest rank in the navy

admiration *noun*
admiration is a feeling you have for someone or something when you think they are very good or very beautiful • *He was filled with admiration for his sister.*

admire *verb*
1 to admire someone or something is to think they are very good or very beautiful **2** to admire something is also to look at it and enjoy it • *They went to the top of the hill to admire the view.* **admirer** *noun* • *Madonna has many admirers.*

admission *noun*
1 admission is being allowed to go into a place • *Admission to the show is by ticket only.* **2** an admission is something that someone admits or confesses • *He is guilty by his own admission.*

admit *verb* (**admitting, admitted**)
1 to admit someone is to let them come into a place **2** to admit something is to say that it has happened or that you have done it

admittance *noun*
admittance is being allowed to go into a private place

admittedly *adverb*
although it is true; without denying it • *Admittedly I was teasing the dog, but I didn't expect it to bite.*

ado *noun*
without more ado without wasting any more time

adolescent *noun*
a young person who is older than a child and not yet an adult, from about 15 to 18
adolescence *noun* the time between being a child and being an adult

adopt *verb*
1 to adopt a child is to take them into your family and bring them up as your own **2** to adopt a system or method is to start using it **adoption** *noun* adoption is adopting someone or something

adopted *adjective* an adopted child is one that someone has adopted **adoptive** *adjective* adoptive parents are parents who have adopted a child

adorable *adjective*
lovely, worth adoring

adore *verb*
to adore someone or something is to love them or admire them very much **adoration** *noun* adoration is adoring someone or something

adorn *verb*
to adorn something is to decorate it or make it pretty **adornment** *noun* adornment is making something pretty

adrenalin *noun*
a hormone that stimulates your nervous system and makes you feel ready to do something

adrift *adverb, adjective*
something such as a boat is adrift when it is loose and drifting about

adult *noun*
a fully grown person or animal

adultery *noun* (*say* a-**dul**-ter-i)
adultery is having a lover in addition to a husband or wife

advance *noun*
1 an advance is a forward movement **2** advance is improvement or progress **3** an advance of money is a loan **4** an advance warning is a warning given beforehand
in advance beforehand

advance *verb*
1 to advance is to move forward **2** to advance is also to make progress

advanced *adjective*
1 a long way forward **2** an advanced course or exam is one at a higher level

advantage *noun*
something useful or helpful **to take advantage of someone** is to treat them unfairly when they are not likely to complain **to take advantage of something** is to make good use of it

Advent *noun*
in the Christian Church, the period before Christmas

adventure *noun*
an adventure is an exciting, dangerous, or interesting event or journey
adventurous *adjective* an adventuorus person likes to do interesting or exciting things

adverb *noun*
a word that tells you how or when or where or why something happens. In these sentences, the words in italics are adverbs: They moved *slowly.* Come back *soon.* I *only* want a drink.

advert *noun*
(*informal*) an advertisement

advertise *verb*
to advertise something that you do or that you have made is to praise it in a newspaper or on television so that people will want it

a b c d e f g h i j k l m n o p q r s t u v w x y z

advertisement *noun*
a public notice or short television film that tries to persuade people to buy something

advice *noun*
advice is something you say to someone to help them decide what to do

advisable *adjective*
sensible, worth doing

advise *verb*
to advise someone is to tell them what you think they should do

aerial *noun*
a wire or metal rod for receiving or sending radio or television signals

aerial *adjective*
from or in the air, or from aircraft • *They showed us an aerial photograph of our school.*

aerobatics *plural noun*
an exciting display by flying aircraft **aerobatic** *adjective* to do with aerobatics • *They went to see an aerobatic display.*

aeroplane *noun*
a flying machine with wings

aeroplane

aerosol *noun*
a device that holds a liquid under pressure and lets it out in a fine spray

affair *noun*
1 something interesting that happens, an event 2 someone's affairs are their private business • *Keep your nose out of my affairs.*

affect *verb*
to affect someone or something is to cause them to change or to harm them • *The dampness might affect his health.*

affection *noun*
love or fondness • *I have a great affection for my nephew.* **affectionate** *adjective* showing love or fondness

afflict *verb*
to be afflicted by something unpleasant, like an illness, is to suffer from it **affliction** *noun* a great illness or problem that makes someone suffer

afford *verb*
1 to be able to afford something is to have enough

money to pay for it 2 to be unable to afford the time to do something is not to have enough time for it

afforestation *noun*
the process of covering an area of land with trees

afloat *adjective, adverb*
floating; on a boat • *Do you enjoy life afloat?*

afraid *adjective*
frightened **I'm afraid** I am sorry; I regret • *I'm afraid I've burnt the cakes.*

after *preposition, adverb*
meaning 'later' or 'later than' • *Come after dinner.* • *I'll do it after.*

afternoon *noun*
the time from midday or lunchtime until evening

afterwards *adverb*
at a later time

again *adverb*
1 once more; another time 2 as before • *You will soon be well again.* **again and again** lots of times

against *preposition*
1 touching or hitting • *He was leaning against the wall.* 2 opposed to, not liking • *Are you against smoking?*

age *noun*
1 your age is how old you are 2 an age is a period of history • *the Elizabethan age* **ages** (*informal*) a long time • *We've been waiting ages.*

age *verb*
to age is to become old

aged *adjective*
1 (*say* ayjd) having the age of • *The girl was aged 9.* 2 (*say* **ay**-jid) very old • *We saw an aged man.*

agent *noun*
1 someone whose job is to organize things for other people • *We booked our holiday with a travel agent.* 2 a spy • *He is a secret agent.* **agency** *noun* an agent's office or business

aggravate *verb*
1 to aggravate something is to make it worse 2 (*informal*) to aggravate someone is to annoy them **aggravation** *noun*

aggression *noun*
starting a war or attack; being aggressive **aggressor** *noun* someone who starts an attack

aggressive *adjective*
1 an aggressive person or group of people is one that is likely to attack or use violence 2 an

aggressive activity is one that people do with energy and that has a strong effect • *They began an aggressive sales campaign.*

agile *adjective*
able to move quickly and easily **agility** *noun* agility is being agile

agitated *adjective*
worried and anxious • *Why are you getting so agitated?* **agitation** *noun* agitation is getting worried or anxious • *He could not hide his agitation.*

ago *adverb*
in the past • *She died long ago.*

agonizing *adjective*
1 an agonizing pain is one that hurts terribly 2 an agonizing choice or decision is one that you find very difficult to make

agony *noun* (**agonies**)
severe pain or suffering

agree *verb*
1 to agree with someone is to think the same as them 2 to agree to do something is to say that you are willing to • *She agreed to go with him.* 3 something agrees with someone when it suits them or does them good • *Spicy food doesn't agree with her.*

agreeable *adjective*
1 willing to do something that someone suggests • *We shall go if you are agreeable.* 2 (*rather old use*) pleasant • *It is a very agreeable little place.*

agreement *noun*
1 agreement is thinking the same • *Are we in agreement?* 2 an agreement is an arrangement that people have agreed on

agriculture *noun*
agriculture is farming, or growing food on the land **agricultural** *adjective* to do with agriculture

aground *adverb*
stuck on the bottom of a river or the sea in shallow water • *The ship has run aground.*

ahead *adverb*
forwards, in front • *Sheila went ahead to show us the way.*

aid *noun*
1 aid is help you give someone 2 aid is also money or food or other help that a country sends to a poorer country 3 an aid is something that helps someone to do something better • *He was wearing a hearing aid.* **in aid of something** or **someone** so as to help them

aid *verb*
to aid someone is to help them
AIDS *noun*
a disease caused by a virus, which destroys the body's immunity to other diseases

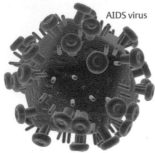
AIDS virus

ailment *noun*
a minor illness
aim *verb*
1 to aim a gun at someone or something is to point it at them so as to shoot them **2** to aim something like a ball is to throw it or kick it in a particular direction **3** to aim to do something is to try to do it
aim *noun*
1 a person's aim is what they intend to do **2** aim is also pointing a weapon in a particular direction
aimless *adjective*
not having any definite aim or purpose • *He led an aimless life.*
aimlessly *adverb*
air *noun*
1 air is the mixture of gases which surrounds the earth and which everyone breathes **2** an air is a tune **3** an air of mystery or secrecy is a feeling that things are mysterious or secret **to go by air** is to travel in an aeroplane **to be on the air** is to be on the radio or television
air *verb*
1 to air clothes or washing is to put them in a warm place to finish drying **2** to air a room is to let fresh air into it **3** to air views or opinions is to say them so that people know them
airborne *adjective*
1 flying in an aircraft **2** carried by the air • *an airborne virus*
aircraft *noun*
an aeroplane or a helicopter • *The two aircraft passed each other over the Atlantic.*
air force *noun*
the part of a country's fighting force that uses aircraft
airline *noun*
a company that takes people to places by aircraft

airliner *noun*
a large aircraft for carrying passengers
airlock *noun*
1 a bubble of air that forms in liquid and stops it flowing through a pipe **2** a compartment with airtight doors at each end
airmail *noun*
airmail is mail that is sent by air
airport *noun*
a place where aircraft land and take off, with passenger terminals and other buildings
air raid *noun*
an attack by bombs dropped from aircraft
airship *noun*
a large balloon with engines, designed to carry passengers or cargo
airtight *adjective*
not letting air get in or out
airy *adjective* (**airier, airiest**)
1 with plenty of fresh air
2 like air **airily** *adverb* to do something airily is to do it in a casual or light-hearted way • *He replied airily that he didn't want to know.*
aisle *noun* (**rhymes with mile**)
a passage between or beside rows of seats in a church, theatre, or cinema, or on an aeroplane
ajar *adverb, adjective*
slightly open • *Please leave the door ajar.*
alarm *verb*
to alarm someone is to make them frightened or anxious
alarm *noun*
1 a warning sound or signal
2 a feeling of fear or anxiety
• *He cried out in alarm.* **3** an alarm clock
alarm clock *noun*
a clock with a loud ring or bleep, which can be set to wake you up
alas *exclamation* (*old use*)
something you say when you are sad
albatross *noun*
a large seabird with long wings
album *noun*
1 a book in which you keep things like photographs or stamps or autographs **2** a collection of songs on a CD, record, or tape
alcohol *noun*
1 a colourless liquid made by fermenting sugar or starch **2** drinks containing this liquid (for example beer, wine, gin), which affects people's behaviour and can make them drunk if they have too much

alcoholic *adjective*
containing alcohol
alcoholic *noun*
someone who is constantly ill from drinking too much alcohol
alcove *noun*
a part of a room where the wall is set back from the main part
alert *adjective*
watching for something; ready to act
alert *verb*
to alert someone to a danger or problem is to warn them about it
alert *noun*
an alarm **on the alert** on the lookout for danger or attack
A level *noun*
a higher standard of examination that is taken after the GCSE, especially by pupils who want to go to university
algebra *noun* (*say* **al**-ji-bra)
mathematics in which letters and symbols are used to represent numbers

alias *noun* (*say* **ay**-li-as)
a false or different name that someone uses instead of their real name
alias *adverb*
also named • *Clark Kent, alias Superman*
alibi *noun* (*say* **al**-i-by)
evidence that someone accused of a crime was not there when the crime was committed
alien *noun* (*say* **ay**-li-en)
1 someone who is not a citizen of the country where they are living **2** in science fiction, a being from another world
alien *adjective*
1 foreign **2** not in keeping, quite unlike • *Lying was alien to his nature.*
alight *adjective*
on fire, burning
alike *adjective*
similar, like each other
alike *adverb*
in the same way • *He treats everybody alike.*
alive *adjective*
living, existing • *Is he alive?*
alkali *noun* (**alkalis**)
(*say* **al**-ka-ly)
a substance that neutralizes

a b c d e f g h i j k l m n o p q r s t u v w x y z

acids or that combines with acids to form salts **alkaline** *adjective* containing an alkili

all *adjective, adverb, noun* meaning 'everything' or 'everyone' • *That is all I know.* • *All my books are in the desk.* • *She was dressed all in white.*

Allah the Muslim name of God

allegation *noun* (say a-li-**gay**-shun) you make an allegation when you accuse someone of doing something wrong

allege *verb* (say a-**lej**) to allege that someone has done something is to accuse them of it, usually without proof • *He alleged that I stole his ring.*

allegiance *noun* (say a-**lee**-jans) loyalty shown to a person or organization

allergy *noun* a condition that some people have that makes their body react badly to things they eat or drink or touch or breathe in, for example dust, milk, or some kinds of food **allergic** *adjective* someone is allergic to something if they become ill or uncomfortable when they eat it or touch it • *She must be allergic to goat's milk.*

alley *noun* 1 a narrow street or passage 2 a place where you can play at skittles or tenpin bowling

alliance *noun* an agreement between countries to support each other and have the same enemies

allied *adjective* having an alliance; on the same side • *The allied countries declared war.*

alligator *noun* a large reptile like a crocodile

allotment *noun* a small rented piece of ground used for growing vegetables

allow *verb* 1 to allow someone to do something is to let them do it • *We will allow you to leave now.* • *Smoking is not allowed.* 2 to allow an amount of money is to provide it for some reason • *She was allowed £10 for books.*

allowance *noun* a sum of money given regularly to someone **to make allowances** is to be considerate • *We must make allowances for his age.*

alloy *noun* a metal formed from a mixture of other metals

all right *adjective* satisfactory; in good condition • *She fixed my bike, so it's all right.*

ally *noun* (**allies**) (say **al**-I) 1 a country in alliance with another country 2 a person who helps or cooperates with you

almighty *adjective* 1 having a lot of power 2 (*informal*) very great • *They were making an almighty din.*

almond *noun* (say **ah**-mond) an oval nut that you can eat

almost *adverb* very close to but not quite • *I am almost ready.*

alone *adjective, adverb* without any other people or other things; on your own • *He soon discovers that he is not alone on the island.*

along *preposition, adverb* 1 from one end of something to the other 2 on; onwards • *Move along, please!* 3 accompanying someone • *I have brought my brother along.*

alongside *preposition, adverb* next to something

aloud *adverb* in a voice that can be heard

alphabet *noun* the letters used in a language, usually arranged in a set order **alphabetical** *adjective* to do with the alphabet **alphabetically** *adverb* something is arranged alphabetically when it is in the order of the alphabet

alphabet

already *adverb* by or before now • *I've already told you once.*

also *adverb* as an extra, besides • *We also need some bread.*

altar *noun* a table or raised surface used in religious ceremonies

alter *verb* to alter something is to change it **alteration** *noun* a change you make to something

alternate *adjective* (say **ol**-ter-nat) 1 happening on every other one • *My sister and I take the dog for a walk on alternate days.* 2 coming in turns, one after the other • *alternate laughter and tears* **alternately** *adverb* one after the other in turn • *The weather was alternately fine and wet.*

alternate *verb* (say ol-ter-**nayt**) to alternate is to happen in turns

alternative *noun* (say ol-**ter**-na-tiv) something you can choose instead of something else • *If you don't like this book there is an alternative.*

alternative *adjective* for you to choose instead of something else • *The cafe has an alternative menu for vegetarians.*

although *conjunction* in spite of the fact that • *Although the sun was shining, it was still cold.*

altitude *noun* the height of something, especially above sea level

alto *noun* 1 a female singer with a low voice; also called a contralto 2 a male singer with a voice higher than a tenor's

altogether *adverb* 1 completely • *He is altogether wrong.* 2 on the whole • *Altogether, it wasn't a bad holiday.*

aluminium *noun* (Al) a silver-coloured metal that is light in weight

always *adverb* 1 all the time, at all times 2 often, constantly • *You are always crying.* 3 whatever happens • *You can always sleep on the floor.*

a.m. short for Latin *ante meridiem* which means 'before midday'

amateur *noun* (say **am**-a-ter) someone who does something because they like it, without being paid for it

amaze *verb* to amaze someone is to surprise them greatly **amazement** *noun* amazement is a feeling of great surprise

ambassador *noun* someone sent to a foreign country to represent their own government

amber *noun* 1 a hard, clear, yellowish

substance used for making ornaments **2** a yellowish colour, the one used in traffic lights as a signal for caution

ambiguous *adjective*
having more than one possible meaning, uncertain • *His reply was ambiguous.*

ambition *noun*
1 ambition is a strong desire to be successful in life **2** an ambition is something you want to do very much • *His ambition is to run his own airline.* **ambitious** *adjective* an ambitious person wants very much to be successful in life

amble *verb*
to amble along is to walk slowly

ambulance *noun*
a vehicle for carrying sick or injured people

ambush *noun*
a surprise attack from a hidden place

ambush *verb*
to ambush someone is to attack them suddenly from a hidden place

amend *verb*
to amend something like a piece of writing is to change or improve it **amendment** *noun* a change to a piece of writing or a law

amiable *adjective*
friendly, good-tempered **amiability** *noun* friendliness **amiably** *adverb*

amid or **amidst** *preposition*
in the middle of, among

ammonia *noun*
a gas or liquid with a strong smell, used to make cleaning liquids

ammunition *noun*
bullets, bombs, and other explosive objects used in fighting

amnesty *noun* (**amnesties**)
a decision to pardon people who have broken the law

amoeba *noun* (say a-**mee**-ba)
a tiny creature made of one cell. It can change shape and split itself in two.

among or **amongst** *preposition*
1 surrounded by, in the middle of • *She was hiding among the bushes.* **2** between • *Let's divide the money amongst ourselves.*

amount *noun*
a quantity or total

amount *verb*
to amount to something is to reach it as a total • *The bill amounted to £55.*

amphibian *noun*
an animal that can live on land and in water **amphibious** *adjective* an amphibious animal is able to live on land and in water

ample *adjective*
1 large, having plenty of space • *This car has an ample boot.* **2** more than enough • *We had ample provisions.* **amply** *adverb* generously; with as much as you need or even more • *They were amply rewarded.*

amplifier *noun*
an electronic device for making music or other sounds louder

amplify *verb* (**amplifies, amplifying, amplified**)
to amplify sounds is to make them louder or stronger **amplification** *noun* amplification is making voices or other sounds louder

amputate *verb*
to amputate an arm or a leg is to cut it off when it is diseased **amputation** *noun* amputation is cutting off an arm or a leg

amuse *verb*
1 to amuse someone is to make them laugh or smile **2** to amuse yourself is to find pleasant things to do

amusement *noun*
1 an amusement is something that amuses you **2** amusement is being amused; laughing or smiling

amusing *adjective*
making you laugh or smile • *It was an amusing story.*

an *adjective* (called the indefinite article)
a word used instead of **a** when the next word begins with a vowel-sound or a silent **h** • *Take an apple.* • *You can hire boats for £5 an hour.*

anaemia *noun* (say a-**nee**-mi-a)
a poor condition of the blood that makes someone look pale • *anaemic adjective* an anaemic person suffers from anaemia

anaesthetic *noun* (say an-iss-**thet**-ik)
a drug or gas that makes you unable to feel pain

anagram *noun*
a word or phrase made by rearranging the letters of another word or phrase, for example *carthorse* is an anagram of *orchestra*

analyse *verb*
1 to analyse something is to examine it carefully **2** to analyse a substance is to divide it into its parts **analysis** *noun* (**analyses**) a detailed study or examination of something

anarchy *noun*
1 anarchy is having no government or controls, leading to a breakdown in law and order **2** complete disorder or confusion **anarchist** *noun* someone who thinks that government and laws are bad and should be abolished

anatomy *noun*
the study of the parts of the body **anatomical** *adjective* to do with anatomy

ancestor *noun*
a person who lived in the past and was in the same family as someone alive now **ancestry** *noun* a person's ancestry is the list of all their ancestors

anchor *noun*
a heavy object joined to a ship by a chain or rope and dropped to the bottom of the sea to stop the ship from moving

ancient *adjective*
1 belonging to times that were long ago **2** very old • *They came from an ancient family.*

and *conjunction*
linking words and phrases • *We had cakes and lemonade.* • *Touch that and you'll get burnt.* • *Go and buy a pen.*

anecdote *noun*
a short amusing or interesting story about a real person or thing

anemone *noun* (say a-**nem**-on-i)
1 a small flower with the shape of a cup **2** a sea anemone

angel *noun*
1 a being that some people believe in, who is a messenger or attendant of God **2** a very kind or beautiful person

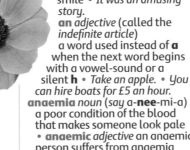
anemones

anger *noun*
a strong feeling that you do not like what someone has said or done, making you

want to quarrel or fight
with them

angle *noun*
1 the space between two lines
or surfaces that meet **2** a point
of view • *What is your angle on
this?*

angle *verb*
to angle something is to put it
in a slanting position

angler *noun*
someone who fishes with a
fishing rod **angling** *noun* the
sport of fishing with a fishing rod

angry *adjective* (**angrier,
angriest**)
feeling or showing anger
angrily *adverb*

anguish *noun*
great suffering or unhappiness
anguished *adjective* suffering
or unhappy

animal *noun*
a living thing that can move
and feel, such as a horse, snake,
fish, bird, or insect

animated *adjective*
an animated film is one made
by photographing a series of
still pictures and showing them
rapidly one after another,
so they appear to move
animation *noun* a way of
making films from still pictures
so they appear to move

aniseed *noun*
a seed with a strong sweet taste
like liquorice

ankle *noun*
the part of your leg where it is
joined to your foot

annihilate *verb* (*say* a-**ny**-il-ayt)
to annihilate something is
to destroy it completely
annihilation *noun* annihilation
is destroying something
completely

anniversary *noun*
(**anniversaries**)
a day when you remember
something special that
happened on the same date
in an earlier year

announce *verb*
to announce something is to
say it publicly **announcer**
noun someone who announces
something, especially on radio
or television

announcement *noun*
something that is made
known publicly, especially
in a newspaper or on radio or
television

annoy *verb*
to annoy someone is to give
them a feeling of not being
pleased

annoyance *noun*
1 annoyance is the feeling of
being annoyed **2** an annoyance
is something that annoys you
• *Wasps are a great annoyance
at a picnic.*

annual *adjective*
happening or coming every
year **annually** *adverb* once
every year • *A new book comes
out annually.*

annual *noun*
a children's book of stories or
comic strips that comes out
once a year

anonymous *adjective*
an anonymous book or letter is
one with the name of the writer
unknown **anonymously** *adverb*
with the name unknown

anorak *noun*
a thick warm jacket with a hood

anorexia *noun*
(*say* an-er-**eks**-ee-a)
an illness that makes someone
not want to eat **anorexic**
adjective an anorexic person
is suffering from anorexia
• *She has an anorexic daughter.*

another *determiner, pronoun*
a different person or thing
• *Have another look.* • *May I
have another?*

answer *noun*
1 an answer is what you say
when someone asks you a
question **2** the answer to a
problem is something that
solves it

answer *verb*
1 to answer someone is to give
them an answer **2** to answer a
telephone is to pick it up when
it rings **to answer back** is to
say something rude or cheeky
as an answer

ant *noun*
a tiny insect that lives in large
groups

antelope *noun*
an animal like a deer, that lives
in Africa and parts of Asia

antenna *noun*
1 (**antennae**) a long thin
feeler on the head of an
insect or shellfish
2 (**antennas**) an aerial

anthem *noun*
a religious or patriotic song,
usually sung by a choir or
group of people

anthology *noun* (**anthologies**)
a collection of poems, stories,
or songs in one book

antibiotic *noun*
a drug that kills bacteria.
Penicillin is an antibiotic.

anticipate *verb*
1 to anticipate something is

to expect it and be ready for it
• *The police were anticipating
trouble.* **2** to anticipate
someone is to act before they
do • *They anticipated us in
getting the early train.*

anticipation *noun*
looking forward to doing
something

anticlimax *noun*
a disappointing ending or result
after something exciting

anticlockwise *adverb, adjective*
moving in the opposite
direction to the hands of a clock

anticyclone *noun*
an area where air pressure
is high, usually causing fine
weather

antidote *noun*
something which takes away
the bad effects of a poison or
disease

antiquated *adjective*
old-fashioned

antique *noun* (*say* an-**teek**)
something that is valuable
because it is very old

antiseptic *noun*
a chemical that kills germs

antler *noun*
the horn of a deer, which
divides into several branches

antonym *noun* (*say* **ant**-o-nim)
a word that is opposite in
meaning to another • *'Soft' is
an antonym of 'hard'.*

anvil *noun*
a large block of iron on which
a blacksmith hammers metal
into shape

anxiety *noun* (**anxieties**)
1 anxiety is a feeling of
being worried **2** an anxiety
is something that worries
you

anxious *adjective*
1 worried and nervous **2** eager
to do something • *They were
anxious to help us.*

any *adjective*
1 one or some • *Have you
any wool?* **2** no matter which
• *Come any day you like.* **3** every
• *Any fool knows that!*

any *adverb*
at all; in some degree • *Is it any
good?*

anybody *noun, pronoun*
anyone

anyhow *adverb*
1 anyway **2** (*informal*)
carelessly, without much
thought • *Books were placed
anyhow on the shelves.*

anyone *noun, pronoun*
any person

anything *noun, pronoun*
any thing

ants

a
b
c
d
e
f
g
h
i
j
k
l
m
n
o
p
q
r
s
t
u
v
w
x
y
z

17

anyway adverb
whatever happens; whatever the situation may be • *If it rains, we'll go anyway.*

anywhere adverb
in any place or to any place

apart adverb
1 away from each other; separately • *Keep your desks apart.* **2** into pieces • *It fell apart.*

apartment noun
1 a set of rooms
2 (*in America*) a flat

ape noun
a monkey without a tail, such as a gorilla or a chimpanzee

ape

aphid or **aphis** noun (**aphids**)
a tiny insect that sucks juices from plants

apologetic adjective
saying you are sorry for something **apologetically** adverb in a way that shows you are sorry • *He replied apologetically.*

apologize verb
to apologize to someone is to tell them you are sorry

apology noun
a statement that you are sorry for doing something wrong

apostle noun
in Christianity, one of the twelve men sent out by Christ to tell people about God

apostrophe noun
(*say* a-**pos**-tro-fi)
a punctuation mark (') used to show that letters have been left out, as in *can't* and *he'll*. It is also used with *s* to show who owns something, as in *the boy's*

books (one boy), *the boys' books* (more than one boy).

appal verb (**appalling, appalled**)
to appal someone is to shock them a lot • *The violence appalled everyone.*

appalling adjective
dreadful, shocking • *The room was in an appalling mess.*

apparatus noun
an apparatus is a set of equipment for a special use

apparent adjective
1 clear, obvious • *He burst out laughing for no apparent reason.*
2 appearing to be true • *They were not put off by their apparent failure.*

apparently adverb
as it seems, so it appears
• *The door had apparently been locked.*

appeal verb
1 to appeal for something is to ask for it when you need it badly • *They are appealing for money to rebuild the church roof.*
2 to appeal to someone is to interest or attract them
• *The cover of the book really appeals to me.* **3** to appeal against a decision is to ask for it to be changed • *He decided to appeal against his prison sentence.*

appeal noun
1 an appeal is asking for something you need **2** appeal is what makes something interesting • *Adventure stories have a lot of appeal for older children.* **3** an appeal is asking for a decision to be changed

appear verb
1 to appear is to become visible **2** to appear is also to seem
• *They appeared very anxious.*
3 to appear in a film or play is to take part in it

appearance noun
1 coming into sight **2** taking part in a play, film, show, etc.
3 what someone looks like
4 what something seems to be

appendicitis noun
an inflammation or disease of the appendix

appendix noun
1 (**appendixes**) a small tube leading off from the intestines in the body
2 (**appendices**) an extra section at the end of a book

appetite noun
a desire for something, especially for food

appetizing adjective
looking good to eat

applaud verb
to applaud someone or something is to show that you like them, especially by clapping

applause noun
clapping or cheering after someone has given a speech or given a performance

apple noun
a round fruit with skin that is red, green, or yellow

appliance noun
a device or gadget

application noun
1 an application is a letter or form you use to ask for something important, such as a job **2** application is when you make a lot of effort to do something

applied adjective
used for something practical
• *Engineering is an applied science.*

apply verb (**applies, applying, applied**)
1 to apply something is to put it on something else • *You need to apply a patch to the puncture.*
2 to apply for a job is to write formally and ask for it **3** to apply to someone is to concern them • *These rules apply to everybody.* **4** to apply yourself to something is to give it all your attention

appoint verb
to appoint someone is to choose them for a job

appointment noun
1 an arrangement to meet or visit someone **2** a job or position

appreciate verb
1 to appreciate something is to enjoy or value it
2 to appreciate a fact is to understand it • *You don't seem to appreciate how lucky we are.*
3 to appreciate is to increase in value

appreciation noun
1 appreciation is showing that you enjoy or value something **2** appreciation is also an increase in the money value of something, such as a house or a work of art

appreciative adjective
an appreciative person or group shows how much they enjoy or value something
• *I enjoy playing to an appreciative audience.*

apprehension noun
nervous fear or worry
apprehensive adjective
nervous and worried

apprentice *noun*
someone who is learning a trade or craft **apprenticeship** *noun* the time when someone is an apprentice

approach *verb*
1 to approach a place is to come near to it **2** to approach someone is to go to them with a request or offer **3** to approach a problem or difficulty is to start solving it

approach *noun*
1 coming near to a place
2 a way of tackling a problem
3 a way or road leading up to a building • *The approach to the house had trees on each side.*
4 the final part of an aircraft's flight as it comes in to land

approachable *adjective*
friendly and easy to talk to

appropriate *adjective*
suitable

approval *noun*
thinking well of someone or something

approve *verb*
to approve of someone or something is to think they are good or suitable

approximate *adjective*
roughly correct but not exact • *The dates in brackets are approximate only.*
approximately *adverb*
roughly but not exactly
• *It will cost approximately twenty pounds.*

approximation *noun*
something that is a rough estimate and not exact

apricot *noun*
a juicy, orange-coloured fruit like a small peach, with a stone in it

apricots

April *noun*
the fourth month of the year

apron *noun*
a piece of clothing worn over the front of your body to protect your clothes

apt *adjective*
1 likely to do something
• *He is apt to be careless.*
2 suitable • *I need to find an apt quotation.*

aptitude *noun*
a natural ability to do something well

aquarium *noun*
a tank or building for keeping live fish

aquatic *adjective*
to do with water and swimming
• *They enjoy aquatic sports.*

aqueduct *noun*
a bridge that carries water across a valley

arabic figures or **arabic numerals** *plural noun*
the figures 1, 2, 3, 4, and so on (compare *Roman numerals*)

arable *adjective*
to do with the growing of crops

arbitrary *adjective*
(*say* **ar**-bi-trer-i)
done or chosen at random or without a proper reason
• *It was an arbitrary decision.*

arc *noun*
part of the circumference of a circle, a curve

arcade *noun*
a covered place to walk, with shops down each side

arch *noun*
a curved structure that helps to support a bridge or building

arch *verb*
to make a curved shape
• *The cat arched its back.*

archaeology *noun*
(*say* **ar**-ki-ol-o-ji)
the study of ancient people from the remains of their buildings **archaeological** *adjective* an archaeological site or discovery is one to do with people from the ancient past
archaeologist *noun* someone who studies archaeology

archbishop *noun*
the chief bishop of a region

archer *noun*
someone who shoots with a bow and arrows

archery *noun*
the sport of shooting with a bow and arrows

architect *noun* (*say* **ar**-ki-tekt)
someone whose work is to design buildings

architecture *noun*
1 the work of designing buildings **2** a style of building
• *Victorian architecture*

area *noun*
1 part of a country, place, surface, etc. **2** the space occupied by something
• *The area of this room is 20 square metres.*

arena *noun* (*say* a-**ree**-na)
a place where a sports event takes place

argue *verb*
1 to argue with someone is to quarrel with them **2** to argue is also to give reasons for something • *She argued that flying is safer than going by train.*

argument *noun*
1 a quarrel **2** a reason or set of reasons someone gives to try to convince someone about something

arise *verb* (**arising, arose, arisen**)
1 to arise is to appear or to come into existence • *All kinds of different problems arise through the story.* **2** (old meaning) to rise; to stand up

aristocracy *noun*
(**aristocracies**)
the aristocracy are the people from important families who often have titles like *Lord* and *Lady*

aristocrat *noun*
(*say* **a**-ris-to-krat)
a nobleman or noblewoman
aristocratic *adjective* to do with aristocrats

arithmetic *noun*
the study of using numbers and working things out with them **arithmetical** *adjective* to do with arithmetic, or using arithmetic

ark *noun*
1 in the Bible, the ship in which Noah and his family escaped the Flood **2** a model of Noah's ark

arm *noun*
1 the part of your body between your shoulder and your hand **2** the sleeve of a coat or dress **3** the side part of a chair, on which you can rest your arm

arm *verb*
1 to arm people is to give them weapons **2** to arm is to prepare for war

armada *noun* (*say* ar-**mah**-da)
a fleet of warships, especially the Spanish Armada which attacked England in 1588

armadillo *noun*
a South American animal whose body is covered with a shell of bony plates

armchair *noun*
a chair with parts on either side to rest your arms on

armed forces *plural noun*
the army, navy, and air force of a country

armistice *noun*
an agreement to stop fighting in a war or battle

a
b
c
d
e
f
g
h
i
j
k
l
m
n
o
p
q
r
s
t
u
v
w
x
y
z

armour noun
armour is a metal suit or covering to protect people or equipment in battle **armoured** adjective having armour

armpit noun
the hollow part under your arm at your shoulder

arms plural noun
weapons • Lay down your arms.

archer

army noun (**armies**)
1 a large number of soldiers ready to fight **2** a large group • They had an army of supporters.

aroma noun (say a-**roh**-ma)
a pleasant smell, for example of food

aromatic adjective having a pleasant smell

around adverb, preposition
1 round • They stood around the pond. **2** about • Stop running around.

arouse verb
1 to arouse someone is to make them wake up **2** to arouse feelings in someone is to cause them to have those feelings

arrange verb
1 to arrange things is to put them all in the position you want **2** to arrange a meeting or event is to organize it **3** to arrange to do something is to make sure someone does it

arrangement noun
1 arrangement is how you arrange or display something, for example flowers or a table setting **2** an arrangement is something you agree with someone else • We made an arrangement to meet at the clock tower.

arrest verb
to arrest someone is to take hold of them by the power of the law because they may have committed a crime

arrest noun
taking hold of someone by the power of the law

arrival noun
1 an arrival is when someone or something arrives at a place **2** an arrival is also someone who is new or has just arrived • Have you met the new arrivals?

arrive verb
1 to arrive at a place is to get there at the end of a journey **2** to arrive is also to happen • The great day arrived.

arrogant adjective
an arrogant person is unpleasantly proud and thinks they are more important than anyone else **arrogance** noun
a feeling someone has that they are more important than anyone else

arrow noun
arrows
1 a pointed stick shot from a bow **2** a sign used to show direction or position

arsenal noun
a place where bullets, shells, and weapons are made or stored

arsenic noun
a strong poison made from a metallic element and used in insecticides

arson noun
the crime of deliberately setting fire to a building

art noun
1 art is producing something by drawing or painting or sculpture **2** the arts are subjects such as history and languages, as distinct from the sciences such as physics and chemistry **3** an art is also a special skill in something, such as sewing or public speaking

artery noun (**arteries**)
a tube carrying blood from the heart to parts of the body

arthritis noun (say arth-**ry**-tiss)
a disease that makes joints in the body painful and stiff **arthritic** adjective (say arth-**rit**-ik) suffering from arthritis

article noun
1 an object or thing that you can touch or pick up **2** a piece of writing published in a newspaper or magazine **3** (in grammar) the word 'a' or 'an' (called the indefinite article) or the word 'the' (called the definite article)

articulate adjective (say ar-**tik**-yoo-lat)
an articulate person is able to speak clearly and fluently

articulated lorry noun (**articulated lorries**)
a large lorry with a cab that is connected to the main part by a joint that bends, so that it can turn more easily

artificial adjective
made by human beings and not by nature **artificially** adverb

artillery noun (**artilleries**)
1 artillery is a collection of large guns **2** the artillery is the part of the army that uses large guns

artist noun
1 someone who produces art, especially a painter **2** an entertainer **artistry** noun the skill of an artist • The carving showed great artistry. **artistic** adjective
1 to do with art and artists **2** showing skill and beauty • an artistic flower arrangement

as conjunction, adverb, preposition
linking words and phrases • As you were late, you had better stay behind. • Leave it as it is. • She slipped as she got off the bus. • It is not as hard as you think. • He was dressed as a sailor.

asbestos noun
a fireproof material that is made up of fine soft fibres

ascend verb
to ascend something like a hill or staircase is to go up it

ascent noun
an ascent is a climb, usually a hard or long one

ash[1] noun
ash is the powder that is left after something has been burned

ash[2] noun
an ash or ash tree is a tree with silvery bark and winged seeds

ashamed adjective
feeling guilty or upset about something you have done

ashore adverb
on the shore

aside adverb
to or at one side; away • Step aside and let them pass.

ask verb
1 to ask someone something is to speak to them so as to find out or get something **2** to ask someone to something like a party is to invite them

asleep adverb, adjective
sleeping

aspect *noun*
one way of looking at a problem or situation • *Perhaps the worst aspect of winter is the dark mornings.*

asphalt *noun* (say **ass**-falt)
a sticky black stuff like tar. It is mixed with gravel to make a surface for roads and areas such as playgrounds.

aspirin *noun*
a drug used to relieve pain or reduce fever

ass *noun*
a donkey

assassinate *verb*
to assassinate someone such as a ruler or leader is to murder them to stop them having power **assassin** *noun* a person who assassinates someone **assassination** *noun* the murder of a ruler or leader

assault *noun*
a violent or illegal attack on someone

assault *verb*
to assault someone is to attack them violently

assemble *verb*
1 to assemble people or things is to bring them together in one place **2** to assemble something is to make it by putting the parts together **3** to assemble is to come together in one place • *Please assemble in the playground.*

assembly *noun*
1 an assembly is when a lot of people come together and someone speaks to them, for example in a school **2** an assembly is also a group of people who meet together, such as a parliament **3** assembly of a machine or piece of furniture is putting the parts together to make it

WORD ORIGIN

The words **assemble** and **assembly** come from Latin words *ad* meaning 'to' or 'towards' and *simul* meaning 'together'.

assert *verb*
to assert something is to say it strongly and clearly **assertion** *noun* something you say clearly and strongly

assess *verb*
to assess someone or something is to decide how good or useful they are **assessment** *noun* an opinion about something after thinking about it carefully

asset *noun*
something useful or valuable to someone

assign *verb*
to assign something to someone is to give it to them as their share or duty • *A different teacher is assigned to each subject.*

assignment *noun*
a piece of work that someone is given to do

assist *verb*
to assist someone is to help them, usually in a practical way

assistance *noun*
help someone gets when they need information or support

assistant *noun*
1 someone whose job is to help another person in their work **2** someone who serves in a shop

associate *verb*
(say a-**soh**-shi-ayt)
to associate one thing with another is to connect them in your mind • *I associate Christmas with ice and snow.*

association *noun*
an association is an organization for people sharing an interest or doing the same work

assorted *adjective*
of various kinds; mixed and different

assortment *noun*
a mixture of different things or people

assume *verb*
to assume something is to think it is true or likely without being sure of it • *I assume you will be coming tomorrow.* **assumed** *adjective* an assumed name is one that is not the person's real name

assumption *noun*
something you assume or take for granted

assurance *noun*
1 an assurance is a promise or guarantee **2** assurance is confidence in yourself

assure *verb*
to assure someone is to tell someone something definite • *I can assure you that we will make every effort to help.*

asterisk *noun*
a star-shaped sign * used in printing and writing to draw attention to something

asteroid *noun*
one of the small planets found mainly between the orbits of Mars and Jupiter

asthma *noun* (say **ass**-ma)
a disease which makes breathing difficult

asthmatic *adjective*
suffering from asthma

asthmatic *noun*
someone who is suffering from asthma

astonish *verb*
to astonish someone is to surprise them very much **astonishment** *noun* a feeling of great surprise

astound *verb*
to astound someone is to amaze or shock them very much

astrology *noun*
astrology is studying how the planets and stars may affect people's lives **astrological** *adjective* to do with astrology **astrologer** *noun* someone who studies astrology

astronaut *noun*
someone who travels in a spacecraft

astronomical *adjective*
1 to do with astronomy **2** (informal) extremely large • *The cost of the party was astronomical.*

astronomy *noun*
astronomy is studying the sun, moon, planets, and stars **astronomer** *noun* someone who studies astronomy

at *preposition*
showing where someone or something is • *I was at the hospital.* • *They are looking at their new books.*

atheist *noun*
someone who does not believe in a God **atheism** *noun* a belief that there is no God

athlete *noun*
someone who is good at athletics or other sports

athletic *adjective*
1 to do with athletics • *an athletic competition* **2** good at sports; strong

athletics *plural noun*
physical exercises and sports such as running and jumping

atlas *noun*
a book of maps

WORD ORIGIN

Atlas was a Titan in Greek mythology who offended the gods and was punished by having to support the universe on his shoulders. A picture of him was often put at the beginning of old atlases, and this is how they got their name.

atmosphere *noun*
1 the earth's atmosphere is the air around it 2 an atmosphere is a feeling you get in a room or at a place • *The atmosphere of the house was cheerful and friendly.*
atmospheric *adjective*
1 to do with the earth's atmosphere 2 having a strong atmosphere
atom *noun*
the smallest possible part of a chemical element
atom bomb or **atomic bomb** *noun*
a bomb that uses atomic energy to make the explosion, and has nuclear fallout
atomic *adjective*
involving atoms; nuclear
atrocious *adjective*
(*say* a-**troh**-shus)
awful, terrible
attach *verb*
to attach one thing to another is to fix or fasten it
attached *adjective*
to be attached to someone is to be fond of them
attachment *noun*
1 an extra part you fix to a device so that it can do a special kind of work • *The garden hose has an attachment for washing cars.* 2 a fondness or friendship • *The boys felt a real attachment to their pet hamster.* 3 (*in computing*) a document that you send to someone with an email message
attack *noun*
1 an attempt to hurt someone with violence 2 an attempt to harm someone or something by using unfriendly words 3 a sudden illness or pain
attack *verb*
to attack someone is to try to hurt them with violence, or to harm them with unfriendly words
attain *verb*
to attain something is to reach or achieve it • *I have attained Grade 3 on the violin.*
attainment *noun* something you have achieved
attempt *verb*
to attempt to do something is to make an effort to do it
attempt *noun*
an attempt at something is making an effort to do it
attend *verb*
1 to attend something like a meeting or a wedding is to be there 2 to attend school or college is to be a pupil or

student there 3 to attend to someone is to look after them, especially when they are ill 4 to attend to something is to spend time dealing with it • *She had some business to attend to.*
attendance *noun*
1 attendance is being somewhere where you are supposed to be 2 the attendance at an event is the number of people who are there to see it
attendant *noun*
someone who helps or goes with another person
attention *noun*
giving care or thought to someone or something
to stand to attention is to stand with your feet together and your arms straight down, like soldiers on parade
attic *noun*
a room or space under the roof of a house
attitude *noun*
your attitude is the way you think or feel about something, and the way you behave
attract *verb*
1 to attract someone is to seem pleasant to them and get their attention or interest 2 to attract something unwelcome is to make it come • *Empty bottles of drink attract wasps.* 3 to attract something is also to pull it by a physical force like magnetism • *Magnets attract metal pins.*
attraction *noun*
1 attraction is the power to attract someone 2 an attraction is something pleasant that visitors to a place like to see, such as a fair or a museum
attractive *adjective*
1 pleasant, good-looking
2 interesting or welcome
• *They made us an attractive offer of a free holiday.*
auburn *adjective*
auburn hair is a reddish-brown colour
auction *noun*
a sale at which things are sold to the person who offers the most money for them
auctioneer *noun* an official in charge of an auction
audible *adjective*
loud enough to be heard
audience *noun*
the people who have come to see or hear an event like a concert or film

audition *noun*
a test to see if a performer is suitable to act in a play or sing in a choir
auditorium *noun*
(*say* aw-dit-**or**-i-um)
the part of a theatre or concert hall where the audience sits
August *noun*
the eighth month of the year
aunt *noun*
1 the sister of your mother or father 2 your uncle's wife
auntie or **aunty** *noun* (**aunties**)
(*informal*) an aunt
au pair *noun* (*say* oh-**pair**)
a person from another country, usually a girl or young woman, who works for a time in someone's home
authentic *adjective*
real, genuine **authenticity** *noun* being authentic
author *noun*
the writer of a book or something like a poem or story
authority *noun* (**authorities**)
1 authority is the power to give orders to other people 2 the authorities are the people who have the power to make decisions 3 an authority on a subject is an expert on it or it is a book that gives you reliable information about it
autistic *adjective*
having a disability that makes someone unable to communicate with other people **autism** *noun*
autobiography *noun* (**autobiographies**)
the story of someone's life that they have written themselves **autobiographical** *adjective* autobiographical writing is written by a person about their own life
autograph *noun*
the signature of a famous person
automatic *adjective*
1 an automatic process is one that works on its own, without needing attention or control by humans 2 an automatic action is one that you do without specially thinking about it **automatically** *adverb* by automatic means; without having to use controls all the time
automobile *noun*
(*in America*) a motor car
autumn *noun* (*say* **aw**-tum)
the season when leaves fall off the trees, between summer and winter

available *adjective*
able to be found or used • *The theme music is now available on a CD.* **availability** *noun* availability is how easily you can find or get something

avalanche *noun* (say **av**-a-lahnsh) a sudden heavy fall of snow and ice down the side of a mountain

avenue *noun* a wide street, usually with trees along each side

average *noun*
1 an average is the number you get by adding several amounts together and dividing the total by the number of amounts • *The average of 2, 4, 6, and 8 is 5.* 2 the average is the usual or ordinary standard • *Their work is well above the average.* **average** *adjective* of the usual or ordinary standard

average *verb*
to average is to have as an average • *In the rainforest the rainfall can average more than 2500mm a year.*

aviary *noun* (**aviaries**) a place where birds are kept

aviation *noun* aviation is flying in aircraft

avid *adjective* keen, eager • *She is an avid reader.*

avoid *verb*
1 to avoid something or someone is to keep yourself away from them • *She swerved in time to avoid a tree.* 2 to avoid something is also to find a way of not doing it • *They wanted to avoid extra homework.* **avoidance** *noun* avoidance is avoiding something

awake *adjective* not sleeping

awake *verb* (**awaking, awoke, awoken**) to awake is to wake up

award *noun* something such as a prize given to a person who has done something successful

award *verb* to award something to someone is to give it to them as an award

aware *adjective* to be aware of something is to know about it or realize it is there • *They soon became aware of the danger.* **awareness** *noun* awareness is knowing about something

away *adverb* at a distance or somewhere else • *I wish those people would go away.* • *The ice cream melted so I threw it away.*

away *adjective* an away match is one that is played at the opponents' ground

awe *noun* fear and wonder • *The mountains filled him with awe.* **awed** filled with fear and wonder

awful *adjective*
1 (*informal*) very bad; very great • *I've been an awful fool.* 2 causing fear or horror • *It was an awful sight.* **awfully** *adverb* (*informal*) very, extremely • *It's awfully hot in June.*

awhile *adverb* for a short time

awkward *adjective*
1 difficult to use or cope with • *The box was an awkward shape.* 2 embarrassed and uncomfortable • *She felt awkward and shy in his presence.*

axe *noun* a tool for chopping

axis *noun* (**axes**) a line through the centre of a spinning object • *The earth rotates on its axis once every 24 hours.*

axle *noun* the rod through the centre of a wheel, on which it turns

Bb

babble *verb*
1 to babble is to talk quickly, without making much sense 2 to babble is also to make a murmuring or bubbling sound • *They came across a babbling brook.*

baboon *noun* a large kind of monkey with a long muzzle and a tail

baby *noun* (**babies**) a very young child

babysit *verb* (**babysitting, babysat**) to babysit is to look after a child while its parents are out **babysitter** *noun* someone who babysits

bachelor *noun* a man who has not married

back *noun*
1 the part of your body between your shoulders and your bottom 2 the upper part of a four-legged animal's body 3 the part of a thing that is furthest away from the front • *The back of the house faces a river.*

back *adjective* placed at or near the back • *Let's sit in the back row.*

back *adverb*
1 backwards or towards the back • *Go back!* 2 to where someone or something was before • *When will you be coming back?* 3 to an earlier time • *Think back to when you were little.*

back *verb*
1 to back a vehicle is to move it backwards 2 to back someone is to support them or give them help **to back down** is to admit you were wrong about something **to back out** is to decide not to get involved in something

backbone *noun* your backbone is your spine

background *noun*
1 the background of a picture or view is the part that is farthest away from you, behind the main subject 2 the background to an event or situation is all the things that help to explain why it happened 3 a person's background is their family, education, and what they have done in their life

backing *noun*
1 backing is support or help • *Our firm will give you financial backing.* 2 the backing on a pop song is the music that is played or sung to

baboon

support the main singer
or tune

backstroke *noun*
a stroke you use when
swimming on your back

backward *adjective*
1 facing or aimed towards
the back • *She walked past
him without a backward
glance.* **2** slow in learning
or developing

backward *adverb*
backwards

backwards *adverb*
1 towards the back **2** with the
back end going first **3** in the
opposite order to the usual
one • *Can you say the alphabet
backwards?*

backyard *noun*
an open area at the back of a
building

bacon *noun*
smoked or salted meat from
the back or sides of a pig

bacteria *plural noun*
tiny organisms that can cause
diseases **bacterial** *adjective* to
do with bacteria

bad *adjective* (**worse, worst**)
1 not good or well done
• *We were watching a very
bad film on television.*
2 someone who is bad is wicked
or naughty **3** someone is bad
at something when they can't
do it very well • *Tracy is bad at
maths.* **4** harmful to your health
• *Eating fatty foods is bad for
you.* **not bad** fairly good, all
right

badge *noun*
a small piece of metal, plastic,
or cloth that you pin or sew
on your clothes to tell people
something about you

badger *noun*
a grey animal with a black
and white head, which lives
underground and comes out
at night to feed

badger *verb*
to badger someone is to
keep asking them to do
something • *He's been
badgering his mum for weeks
for a new bike.*

badly *adverb*
1 not well • *They did the work
badly.* **2** seriously • *He was
badly wounded.* **3** very much
• *I need a drink badly.* **badly
off** poor or unfortunate

badminton *noun*
a game in which players
use rackets to hit a light
object called a *shuttlecock*
backwards and forwards
across a high net

bad-tempered *adjective*
a bad-tempered person is one
who often becomes angry

baffle *verb*
to baffle someone is to puzzle
or confuse them completely

bag *noun*
a container made of soft
material, for holding or
carrying things **bags of
something** (*informal*) plenty
• *There's bags of room.*

bag *verb* (**bagging, bagged**)
to bag something is to get hold
of it or take it • *I bagged the best
seat.*

baggage *noun*
baggage is the suitcases and
bags you take on a journey

baggy *adjective* (**baggier,
baggiest**)
baggy clothes hang loosely
from your body

bagpipes *plural noun*
bagpipes are a musical
instrument you play by
squeezing air out of a bag
into a set of pipes

bail[1] *noun*
bail is money that has to be
paid or promised so that a
person accused of a crime will
not be kept in prison before
their trial

bail[2] *noun*
bails are the two small pieces
of wood placed on top of the
stumps in cricket

bail *verb*
to bail water out of a boat is to
scoop it over the side

Bairam *noun* (say **by**-ram)
either of two Muslim festivals,
one in the tenth month and
one in the twelfth month of the
Islamic year

Baisakhi *noun*
a Sikh festival held in April

bait *noun*
bait is a small
amount of food
put on a hook
or in a trap to
catch fish or
animals

bait *verb*
to bait a hook
or trap is to put
the bait on it or
in it, to catch fish
or animals

bake *verb*
1 to bake food is to cook
it in an oven, especially
bread or cakes **2** to bake
something like clay is to
make it hard by heating it in
an oven **3** to bake is to become
very hot, especially in the sun

baker *noun*
someone who makes or sells
bread and cakes

bakery *noun*
a place where bread is made
or sold

balance *noun*
1 a person's balance is their
feeling of being steady
• *He lost his balance and fell
over.* **2** a balance is a device for
weighing things, with two trays
hanging from the ends of a
horizontal bar **3** the balance of
a bank account is the difference
between the money paid into it
and the money taken out of it
4 a balance is also an amount
of money that someone owes
• *I will pay you the balance on
Saturday.*

balance *verb*
to balance something is to keep
it steady • *He was balancing a
tray on one hand.*

balcony *noun* (**balconies**)
1 a platform built out from the
wall of a building, with a railing
round it **2** the upstairs part of a
cinema or theatre

bald *adjective*
a bald person does not have
much hair or any hair on their
head

bale[1] *noun*
a large bundle of something
like hay or straw, usually tied
up tightly

bale[2] *verb*
to bale out is to jump out of an
aircraft with a parachute

ball *noun*
1 a round object used in many
games **2** anything that is made
into a round shape • *a ball of
string* **3** a grand or formal party
where people dance

ballad *noun*
a simple song or poem
that tells a story

ballerina *noun*
(say bal-e-**ree**-na)
a female ballet
dancer

ballet *noun*
(say **bal**-ay)
a form of
dancing in
which a group of
dancers perform
special steps and
movements to tell a
story to music

balloon *noun*
1 a small rubber pouch
that you fill up with air or
gas and use as a toy or
for decoration **2** a large
round or pear-shaped

balloon

bag filled with a light gas or hot air, so that it can carry people into the air **3** an outline in a strip cartoon containing the words the characters are saying

ballot noun (say **bal**-ot)
a method of voting in secret by making a mark on a piece of paper and putting it into a box

ballpoint noun
a pen with a tiny ball at the tip, round which the ink flows

ballroom noun
a large room where dances are held

balsa noun (say **bol**-sa)
a kind of lightweight wood used to make models

bamboo noun
a tall tropical plant with hard hollow stems, used for making furniture

ban verb (**banning, banned**)
to ban something is to forbid people to do it

bamboo

banana noun
a long curved fruit with a yellow skin

band noun
1 a group of people playing music together **2** an organized group of people doing something together **3** a circular strip of something

band verb
to band together is to join together to form an organized group

bandage noun (say **ban**-dij)
a strip of material that you wrap round a wound to protect it

bandit noun
a member of a gang of robbers who attack travellers

bandstand noun
a platform for a band playing music outdoors, usually in a park

bandy adjective (**bandier, bandiest**)
bandy legs curve outwards at the knees

bang noun
1 a sudden loud noise **2** a heavy blow or knock

bang verb
1 to bang something is to hit or shut it noisily • *Don't bang the door when you go out.* **2** to bang something is to knock it hard against something else • *She banged her knee on the desk.*

banish verb
to banish someone is to punish them by sending them away and ordering them not to return • *The emperor banished him to a remote island.* **banishment** noun banishment is being banished

banisters plural noun
banisters are a rail with upright supports at the side of a staircase

banjo noun
a musical instrument like a small guitar with a round body

bank noun
1 a business which looks after people's money **2** the ground beside a river or lake **3** a piece of raised or sloping ground **4** a place where something is stored and collected • *a blood bank* **5** a bank of clouds is a mass of them **6** a bank of lights or switches is a row of them

bank verb
1 to bank money is to put it in a bank **2** to bank is to lean over while changing direction • *The plane banked as it turned to land.*
to bank on something is to rely on it • *We're banking on the weather being good.*

bank holiday noun
a public holiday, when the banks are closed

bankrupt adjective
not able to pay your debts
bankruptcy noun bankruptcy is when a person or business can't pay their debts

banner noun
a large strip of cloth with writing on it, carried on a pole or between two poles in a procession or demonstration

banquet noun (say **bank**-wit)
a large formal dinner, often with speeches

baptism noun
baptism is the ceremony of baptizing someone

baptize verb
to baptize someone is to sprinkle them with water, or dip them in

water, in a ceremony welcoming them into the Christian Church

bar noun
1 a long piece of something hard **2** a counter or room where drinks and refreshments are served **3** one of the small equal sections into which music is divided • *A waltz has three beats in a bar.*

bar verb (**barring, barred**)
1 to bar something is to fasten it with a bar **2** to bar someone from something is to prevent them from taking part in it **3** to bar someone's way is to stop them getting past

barbarian noun
an uncivilized or savage person

barbaric or **barbarous** adjective
savage and cruel

barbarity noun savage cruelty

barbecue noun
1 a metal frame used for grilling food over a charcoal fire outdoors **2** a party at which food is cooked outdoors on a barbecue

barbed wire noun
wire with sharp twisted spikes on it, used to make fences

barber noun
someone whose job is to cut men's hair

bar code noun
a set of black lines that are printed on goods, library books, etc. so that they can be identified by a computer

bare adjective
1 not covered with anything • *The trees were bare.* **2** empty or almost empty • *The cupboard was bare.* **3** only just enough • *They just had the bare necessities of life.*

barely adverb
only just; with difficulty • *They were barely able to see in the fog.*

bargain noun
1 something that you buy cheaply **2** an agreement between two people to do something for each other • *I expect you to keep your side of the bargain.*

bargain verb
to bargain over something is to argue over its price

barge noun
a long flat-bottomed boat used especially on canals

barge verb
to barge into someone is to bump clumsily into them or push them out of the way

bark noun
1 a bark is the sound made by a dog or a fox **2** bark is the outer covering of a tree's branches or trunk

banjo

bark verb
1 a dog or fox barks when it makes its special sound 2 you can say a person barks when they speak loudly or sharply

barley noun
a kind of grain which is used for food and to make beer

bar mitzvah noun
a religious ceremony for Jewish boys who have reached the age of 13, when they accept some of the responsibilities of an adult. The ceremony for a girl is called a **bat mitzvah**.

barn noun
a building on a farm used to store things such as grain or hay

barnacle noun
a shellfish that attaches itself to rocks and the bottoms of ships

barometer noun (say ba-**rom**-it-er)
an instrument that measures air pressure, used in forecasting the weather

baron noun
a member of the lowest rank of noblemen

baroness noun
a female baron or a baron's wife

barracks noun
the buildings where soldiers live

barrage noun (say **ba**-rahzh)
1 heavy gunfire 2 a large amount of something • We received a barrage of complaints. 3 a dam or barrier built across a river to make the water deeper

barrel noun
1 a large container for liquids, with curved sides and flat ends 2 the metal tube of a gun, through which the shot is fired

barren adjective
barren land or plants cannot produce any crops or fruit

barricade noun
a barrier, especially one put up quickly to block a street

barricade verb
to barricade a place is to block or defend it with a barrier

barrier noun
a fence or wall put up to stop people getting past

barrister noun
a lawyer who argues legal cases in the higher courts

barrow noun
1 a small cart 2 an ancient mound of earth over a grave

barter verb
to barter is to exchange goods for other goods, without using money

base noun
1 the lowest part of something, or the part on which something stands 2 a place from which an organization like an army or business is controlled

base verb
to base one thing on another thing is to use the second thing as the starting point for the first • She based the story on an event in her own childhood.

baseball noun
1 baseball is an American game like rounders, in which the players hit a ball and run round a series of four 'bases' to score points 2 a baseball is the ball used in this game

basement noun
a room or part of a building below ground level

bash verb
(informal) to bash someone or something is to hit them hard

bashful adjective
shy

basic adjective
forming the first or most important part • He has a basic knowledge of French. • Food is a basic human need.

basically adverb
in the most important ways; essentially • She is basically lazy.

basin noun
1 a deep bowl for mixing food in 2 a large container to hold water for washing your face and hands in 3 a river basin is the area of land where the river's water comes from

basis noun (**bases**)
1 the basis of something is what you start from or add to • These players will be the basis of a new team. 2 a basis is the way in which something is arranged or organized • You will be paid on a monthly basis.

bask verb
to bask is to lie or sit comfortably warming yourself in the sun

basket noun
a container made of strips of wood, cane, or wire woven together

basketball noun
1 basketball is a team game in which players try to throw a large ball through a high net hanging from a hoop 2 a basketball is the ball used in this game

bass adjective (say bayss)
forming the lowest sounds in music

bass noun (say bayss)
a bass singer or instrument

bassoon noun
a woodwind instrument that plays low notes

bat¹ noun
a shaped piece of wood used to hit the ball in cricket, baseball, and other games

bat¹ verb (**batting, batted**)
to bat is to take a turn at using a bat in cricket, baseball, and other games

bat² noun
a flying mammal that looks like a mouse with wings. Bats come out at night to feed.

bat

batch noun
a set of things made at one time or dealt with together

bated adjective
with bated breath waiting anxiously

bath noun
1 a bath is a large container you fill with water and get into to wash yourself 2 a bath sometimes means the water in a bath • Your bath is getting cold. 3 the baths are also a public swimming pool

bath verb
1 to bath someone is to give them a bath 2 to bath is to have a bath

bathe verb
1 to bathe is to go swimming in the sea or a river 2 to bathe a sore part of your body is to wash it gently

bathe noun
a bathe is a swim

bathroom noun
a room for having a bath or wash in

bat mitzvah noun
a religious ceremony for Jewish girls who have reached the age of 12, when they accept some of the responsibilities of an adult. The ceremony for a boy is called a **bar mitzvah**.

baton noun
a short stick, especially one you use to conduct an orchestra or in a relay race

batsman noun (**batsmen**)
a player who uses a bat in cricket

batter *verb*
to batter someone or something is to hit them hard and often
• *The huge waves battered the rocks.*

batter *noun*
batter is a mixture of flour, eggs, and milk beaten together and used to make pancakes or to coat food before you fry it

battery *noun* (**batteries**)
1 a portable device for storing and supplying electricity
2 a series of cages in which animals are kept close together on a farm • *Free-range hens are not kept in batteries.* 3 a set of devices that are used together, especially a group of large guns

battle *noun*
1 a fight between two armies
2 a struggle

battlefield *noun*
a place where a battle is or was fought

battlements *plural noun*
the top of a castle wall, usually with gaps for firing arrows

battleship *noun*
a large warship armed with powerful guns

bawl *verb*
to bawl is to shout or cry loudly

bay *noun*
1 a place by the sea or a lake where the shore curves inwards
2 an area that is marked out to be used for parking vehicles, storing things, etc. **to keep someone at bay** is to prevent them from coming near you

bayonet *noun*
a steel blade that can be fixed to the end of a rifle and used for stabbing

bazaar *noun*
1 a sale held to raise money for charity 2 a covered market in an Eastern country

BC
short for *before Christ*, used with dates that come before the birth of Jesus Christ • *Julius Caesar came to Britain in 55 BC.*

be *verb* (**I am**; **you are**; **he, she,** or **it is**; **they are**; **I, he, she,** or **it was**, **you were**, **they were**; **I, you,** or **they have been**; **he, she,** or **it has been**)
1 to be is to exist or happen
• *There is a bus stop at the corner.*
• *The final is on Saturday.* 2 to be someone or something is to have that position or quality • *She is my teacher.* • *You are very tall.*

beach *noun*
the strip of pebbles or sand close to the sea

beacon *noun*
a light or fire used as a warning signal

bead *noun*
1 a small piece of glass, wood, or plastic with a hole through it, threaded on a string or wire to make a necklace or bracelet
2 a small drop of liquid • *She had beads of sweat on her face.*

beads

beady *adjective* (**beadier, beadiest**)
beady eyes are small and bright

beak *noun*
the hard, horny part of a bird's mouth

beaker *noun*
1 a tall drinking mug, usually without a handle 2 a glass container used for pouring liquids in a science laboratory

beam *noun*
1 a long, thick bar of wood or metal 2 a ray of light or other radiation

beam *verb*
1 to beam is to send out a beam of light or radio waves 2 you can say a person beams when they smile very happily

bean *noun*
1 a kind of plant with seeds growing in pods 2 the seed or pod of this kind of plant, eaten as food

bear[1] *verb* (**bore, born** or **borne**)
1 to bear something is to carry or support it 2 to bear something is to put up with it or suffer it
• *I can't bear all this noise.*
3 a woman bears children when she gives birth to them • *She has borne three sons.*

bear[2] *noun*
a large heavy animal with thick fur and sharp hooked claws

bearable *adjective*
something that is bearable is something you are able to put up with • *His toothache was hardly bearable.*

beard *noun*
hair on the lower part of a man's face **bearded** *adjective* a bearded man is a man with a beard

bearing *noun*
1 your bearing is the way you

stand and walk 2 the direction or position of something in relation to something else **to lose your bearings** is to forget where you are in relation to other things

beast *noun*
1 any large four-footed animal
2 (*informal*) a person you think is cruel or unkind

beat *verb* (**beating, beat, beaten**)
1 to beat someone or something is to hit them repeatedly, especially with a stick 2 to beat someone in a game or match is to do better than them and win it 3 to beat a cooking mixture is to stir it quickly so that it becomes thicker
4 to beat something is to shape or flatten it by hitting it many times 5 to beat is also to make regular movements like your heart does **to beat someone up** is to attack them very violently

beat *noun*
1 a regular rhythm or stroke, like your heart makes 2 a strong rhythm in pop music 3 the regular route of a police officer

beautiful *adjective*
very pleasing to look at or listen to **beautifully** *adverb*

beauty *noun* (**beauties**)
1 beauty is a quality that gives delight or pleasure, especially to your senses • *They enjoyed the beauty of the sunset.* 2 a beauty is a particularly beautiful person or thing

beaver *noun*
1 a brown furry animal with strong teeth and a long flat tail, which builds dams in rivers
2 a member of the most junior section of the Scout Association

because *conjunction*
for the reason that • *We were happy because it was a holiday.* **because of someone or something** for that reason; on account of them • *He limped because of his bad leg.*

beckon *verb*
to beckon to someone is to make a sign asking them to come to you

become *verb* (**becoming, became, become**)
to become is to start being something described
• *It gradually became darker.*

bed *noun*
1 a bed is a piece of furniture for sleeping on 2 bed is the place where you sleep • *I'm going to bed now.* 3 a bed is also a part of a garden where plants are grown

4 the bed of the sea or of a river is the bottom of it

bedclothes *plural noun*
sheets, blankets, and duvets for using on a bed

bedding *noun*
things for making a bed, such as sheets, blankets, and duvets

bedraggled *adjective*
(*say* bi-**drag**-uld)
wet and dirty

bedroom *noun*
a room where you sleep

bedside *noun*
the space beside a bed, especially the bed of someone who is ill • *He sat by his son's bedside all night.*

bedspread *noun*
a covering put over the top of a bed

bedtime *noun*
the time when you are supposed to go to bed

bee *noun*
a stinging insect that makes honey

beech *noun*
a tree with smooth bark and glossy leaves

beef *noun*
the meat of an ox, bull, or cow

beefburger *noun*
a hamburger

bees

beehive *noun*
a container for bees to live in

beer *noun*
beer is an alcoholic drink made from malt and hops

beet *noun* (**beet** or **beets**)
beet is a plant used as a vegetable or for making sugar

beetle *noun*
an insect with hard, shiny covers over its wings

beetroot *noun* (**beetroot**)
the dark red root of beet used as a vegetable

before *adverb, preposition*
1 earlier, or earlier than • *Have you been here before?* • *They came the day before yesterday.* **2** in front of • *He stood up before the whole school.*

beforehand *adverb*
earlier, or before something else happens • *She had tried to phone me beforehand.* • *Let me know beforehand if you want to come on the picnic.*

beg *verb* (**begging, begged**)
1 to beg is to ask people to give you money or food **2** to beg someone is to ask them seriously or desperately • *He begged me not to tell the teacher.*

beggar *noun*
someone who lives by begging in the street

begin *verb* (**beginning, began, begun**)
to begin something is to start doing it **beginner** *noun* someone who is just starting to learn or is still learning a subject

beginning *noun*
the start of something

behalf *noun*
on behalf of something to help a cause • *They were collecting money on behalf of cancer research.* **on someone's behalf** for them or in their name • *Will you accept the prize on my behalf?*

behave *verb*
1 to act in a certain way • *My sister has been behaving very strangely recently.* **2** to show good manners • *Why can't you behave?*

behaviour *noun*
1 your behaviour is the way you behave **2** animal behaviour is the way animals normally behave and treat one another

behind *adverb, preposition*
1 at or to the back • *The others are a long way behind.* • *She hid behind a tree.* **2** not making good progress • *He's behind the rest of the class in French.* **3** supporting or encouraging • *We're all behind you.* **behind someone's back** without them knowing about it

behind *noun*
your behind is your bottom • *He kicked me on the behind.*

beige *noun, adjective* (*say* bayzh)
a light yellowish-brown colour

being *noun*
a being is a person or creature of any kind

belch *verb*
1 to belch is to make a noise by letting air come up from your stomach through your mouth **2** a chimney or factory belches smoke or fumes when it sends out thick smoke or fumes into the air

belch *noun*
the act or sound of belching

belfry *noun* (**belfries**)
the top part of a tower or steeple, in which bells hang

belief *noun*
1 a belief is something you believe • *They have very few*
beliefs. **2** belief is when you believe something

believe *verb*
1 to believe something is to think that it is true **2** to believe someone is to think that they are telling the truth **3** to believe in something is to think it is real or important • *Do you believe in ghosts?*

bell

believable *adjective* something is believable when you are able to believe it

believer *noun* someone who believes in God

bell *noun*
a device that makes a ringing sound, especially a cup-shaped metal object that rings when it is struck

bellow *verb*
to bellow is to roar or shout loudly and deeply

bellows *plural noun*
bellows are a device for blowing out air, especially into a fire to make it burn more strongly

belly *noun* (**bellies**)
1 the abdomen or the stomach of a human **2** the part underneath the body of a four-legged animal

belong *verb*
1 to belong to someone is to be their property • *The pencil belongs to me.* **2** to belong to a club or group is to be a member of it • *We both belong to the tennis club.* **3** to belong somewhere is to have a special place where it goes • *The butter belongs in the fridge.*

belongings *plural noun*
your belongings are the things that you own

beloved *adjective*
(*say* bi-**luvd** or *say* bi-**luv**-id)
greatly loved

below *preposition*
lower than, under • *We have nice neighbours in the flat below us.*

below *adverb*
at a lower point, or to a lower point • *I'll have the top bunk, and you can sleep below.*

belt *noun*
1 a strip of material, often leather or cloth, that you wear round your waist **2** a long narrow area • *The path ran through a belt of woodland.*

belt *verb*
(*informal*) **1** to belt someone is to

hit them hard **2** to belt along is to move very fast

bench noun
1 a long seat **2** a long table for working at

bend verb (**bending, bent**)
1 to bend something is to make it curved or crooked **2** to bend is to become curved or crooked • The trees were bending in the wind. **3** to bend is also to move the top of your body downwards • She bent down to pick up the cat.

bend noun
a part where something curves or turns

beneath preposition, adverb
under • Beneath the soil there is clay.

benefit noun
1 a benefit is something that is useful or helpful • Television is one of the benefits of modern science. **2** benefit is money that the government pays to help people who are poor, sick, or out of work **to give someone the benefit of the doubt** is to believe them even though you cannot be sure

benefit verb
you benefit from something, or it benefits you, when it helps you

bent adjective
1 curved or crooked **2** (slang) dishonest

bequeath verb
(rhymes with **breathe**)
to bequeath something to someone is to leave it to them in a will

bequest noun
a gift of money or property that someone leaves to a person in their will

bereaved adjective
a bereaved person is someone with a close relative who has recently died **bereavement** noun someone suffers bereavement when a close relative dies

beret noun (say **bair**-ay)
a soft, round, flat cap

berry noun (**berries**)
a small, juicy fruit

berserk adjective
to go berserk is to become extremely angry or lose control • The man went berserk and started flinging things around.

berth noun
1 a sleeping place on a ship or train **2** a place where a ship is tied up

beside preposition
next to; close to • The little house stood beside a lake. **to be beside yourself** is to be very excited or

upset • He was beside himself with anger.

besides preposition
in addition to • Who came besides you?

besides adverb
also; in addition to this • The coat cost too much. Besides, it's the wrong colour.

besiege verb (say bi-**seej**)
to besiege a place is to surround it until the people inside surrender

best adjective
most excellent; most able to do something • She's the best swimmer in the class.

best adverb
1 in the best way; most • We'll do what suits you best. **2** most usefully; most wisely • He is best ignored.

best noun
the best person or thing, or the best people or things • She was the best at tennis. • These apples are the best you can buy. **to do your best** is to do as well as you can **to make the best of something** is to accept it and enjoy it as much as you can, even though it is not very good

best man noun
someone who helps the bridegroom at his wedding

best-seller noun
a book or other product that has sold in very large numbers

bet noun
1 an agreement that you will receive money if you are correct in choosing the winner of a race or in saying something will happen, and will lose money if you are not correct **2** the money you risk losing in a bet

bet verb (**betting, bet** or **betted**)
1 to bet, or to bet money, is to make a bet **2** (informal) to bet something is to say you are sure about it • I bet I'm right.

betray verb
1 to betray someone is to do them harm when they are expecting your support **2** to betray something you are trying to keep hidden is to reveal it • The look on her face betrayed her surprise.

betrayal noun betrayal is betraying someone

better adjective
1 more excellent • I need a better bike. **2** to be better is to feel well again after an illness • Are you better?

better noun
a better person or thing **to get the better of someone** is to defeat or outwit them

better adverb
in a better way • Try to do it better next time. **to be better off** is to be more fortunate in some way, for example by having more money

better verb
to better something is to improve on it • She hopes to better her own record time.

between preposition, adverb
within two or more points; among • Call me between Tuesday and Friday. • The train runs between London and Glasgow. • What is the difference between butter and margarine? • Divide the sweets between the children. • The two houses are side by side with a fence between.

beware verb (**beware**)
a warning to be careful • Beware of pickpockets.

bewilder verb
to bewilder someone is to puzzle them completely **bewilderment** noun bewilderment is being bewildered or puzzled

bewitch verb
to bewitch someone is to put a spell on them

beyond preposition, adverb
farther on • Don't go beyond the end of the street. • You can see the next valley and the mountains beyond.

bias noun
bias is a strong feeling in favour of one person or side and against another • The referee was accused of bias. **biased** adjective someone is biased when they show that they prefer one person or side over another

bib noun
a piece of cloth or plastic you put under a baby's chin during meals to protect its clothes from stains

Bible noun
the holy book of Christianity and Judaism **biblical** adjective to do with the Bible

bicycle noun
a two-wheeled vehicle that you ride by pushing down on pedals with your feet

bicycle

bid ▷ bladder

bid *noun*
1 offering an amount you will pay for something, especially at an auction **2** an attempt • *He will make a bid for the world record tomorrow.*

bid *verb* (**bidding, bid**)
to bid an amount of money is to offer it for something at an auction

bide *verb*
to bide your time is to wait, expecting something to happen that will help you

big *adjective* (**bigger, biggest**)
1 more than the normal size; large **2** important • *This is a big decision.* **3** elder • *Have you met my big sister?*

bike *noun*
(*informal*) a bicycle or motorcycle

bikini *noun*
a woman's two-piece swimsuit

bilingual *adjective*
speaking two languages well

bill¹ *noun*
1 a piece of paper that tells you how much money you owe for something **2** a plan for a new law in parliament **3** a poster

bill² *noun*
a bird's beak

billiards *noun*
a game played with long sticks (called cues) and three balls on a cloth-covered table

billion *noun*
a thousand million (1,000,000,000)
billionth *adjective, noun* a thousand-millionth

billow *verb*
to billow is to rise up or move like waves on the sea • *Her cloak billowed out behind her.*

bin *noun*
a large or deep container, especially one that you put rubbish or litter in

binary *adjective*
having two parts • *a binary star*

binary system *noun*
a system of expressing numbers by using the digits 0 and 1 only. For example, 21 is written 10101.

bind *verb* (**binding, bound**)
1 to bind things is to tie them up or tie them together **2** to bind something is to wrap a piece of material round it **3** to bind a book is to fasten the pages inside a cover **4** to bind someone is to make them do something or promise something

bingo *noun*
a game played with cards with numbered squares. These are covered or crossed out as the numbers are called out, and the first person to complete the card wins the game

binoculars *plural noun*
a device with lenses for both eyes, for making distant objects seem nearer

biodegradable *adjective*
able to be broken down by bacteria in the environment • *All our packaging is biodegradable.*

biography *noun* (**biographies**)
the story of a person's life
biographer *noun* someone who writes a biography
biographical *adjective* a biographical story or history is one that is about a person's life

biology *noun*
the science or study of living things **biological** *adjective* to do with biology **biologist** *noun* a person who studies biology

birch *noun*
a thin tree with shiny bark and slender branches

bird *noun*
a feathered animal with two wings, two legs, and a beak

bird of prey *noun*
a bird that feeds on animal flesh, such as an eagle or hawk

birth *noun*
birth is the beginning of a person's or animal's life, when they come out of their mother's body

birthday *noun*
the anniversary of the day on which you were born

birthmark *noun*
a coloured mark which has been on someone's skin since they were born

birthplace *noun*
the place where someone was born

biscuit *noun*
a small flat kind of cake that has been baked until it is hard

bishop *noun*
1 a senior priest in the Christian Church who is in charge of all the churches in a city or district **2** a chess piece shaped like a bishop's hat

bison *noun* (**bison**)
a wild ox with shaggy hair

bit *noun*
1 a small piece or amount of something **2** the part of a horse's bridle that is put into its mouth **3** the part of a tool that cuts or grips **4** (*in computing*) the smallest unit of data or memory **a bit** slightly • *I'm a bit worried.* **bit by bit** gradually

bitch *noun*
a female dog, fox, or wolf

bite *verb* (**biting, bit, bitten**)
1 to bite something is to cut it or hold it with your teeth **2** to sting or hurt • *a biting wind*

bite *noun*
1 to give a person or animal a bite is to bite them **2** a mark or spot made by biting • *He was covered in insect bites.* **3** a snack • *Would you like a bite?*

bitter *adjective*
1 tasting sour and unpleasant **2** feeling angry and resentful because you are disappointed about something • *She is very bitter about losing her place in the team.* **3** extremely cold • *There was a bitter wind.*

black *adjective* ●
1 of the darkest colour, like coal or soot **2** having dark skin **3** dismal; not hopeful • *The outlook is black.* **4** very dirty

black *noun*
1 a black colour **2** a person with dark skin

blackberry *noun* (**blackberries**)
a sweet black berry

blackberries

blackbird *noun*
a dark European songbird

blackboard *noun*
a dark board for writing on with chalk

blacken *verb*
1 to blacken something is to make it black **2** to blacken someone's name is to say bad things about them

black eye *noun*
an eye with heavy bruises round it

black hole *noun*
a region in space with such strong gravity that no light escapes

blackmail *verb*
to blackmail someone is to get money from them by threatening to tell people something that they want to keep secret

blackout *noun*
1 when a person becomes unconscious for a short time **2** a time when lights are kept hidden or turned off

blacksmith *noun*
someone who makes and repairs things made of iron, and fits shoes on horses

bladder *noun*
your bladder is the bag-like part of your body where urine collects

blade *noun*
1 the sharp part of a device for cutting, such as a knife or sword 2 the flat, wide part of an oar or propeller 3 a long narrow leaf of grass

blame *verb*
to blame someone is to say that they have done something wrong • *My brother broke the window but they blamed me.*

blame *noun*
to get the blame for something is to be blamed for it **to be to blame** is to be the person who has done something wrong

blancmange *noun* (*say* bla-**monj**)
blancmange is a pudding like a jelly made with milk

blank *adjective*
1 not written, drawn, or printed on • *The piece of paper was blank.* 2 showing no expression or interest • *His face looked blank.* **to go blank** is to suddenly forget everything • *When he asked me the way, my mind went blank.*

blank *noun*
1 an empty space 2 a cartridge for a gun which makes a noise but does not fire a bullet

blanket *noun*
a large piece of thick cloth, used as a warm covering for a bed

blare *verb*
to blare is to make a harsh, loud sound

blasphemous *adjective*
(*say* **blas**-fe-mus)
disrespectful about God or a religion **blasphemy** *noun* talking without respect about God or a religion

blast *noun*
1 a strong rush of wind or air 2 a sharp or loud noise • *The referee gave a long blast of his whistle.*

blast *verb*
to blast something is to blow it up with explosives

blast-off *noun*
the launch of a spacecraft

blaze *noun*
1 a very bright fire 2 a very bright colour or light

blaze *verb*
1 to blaze is to burn or shine brightly 2 to blaze with a feeling is to feel it very strongly • *He was blazing with anger.*

blazer *noun*
a kind of jacket, often with a badge on the front

bleach *noun*
a substance used to clean things or make clothes white

bleach *verb*
to bleach something is to make it white

bleak *adjective*
1 bare and cold • *No trees grew on this bleak hillside.* 2 dreary and miserable • *The future looks bleak.*

bleary *adjective* (**blearier, bleariest**)
bleary eyes are tired and do not see clearly

bleat *noun*
the cry of a sheep or goat

bleat *verb*
a sheep or goat bleats when it makes a bleat

bleed *verb* (**bleeding, bled**)
to bleed is to lose blood from your body, for example if you are injured

bleep *noun*
a small, high sound like the sound some digital watches make

blemish *noun*
1 a mark or stain on something 2 a fault or weakness

blend *verb*
to blend things is to mix them together smoothly or easily

blend *noun*
a smooth mixture

bless *verb*
1 to bless someone is to wish or bring them happiness 2 to bless someone is also to ask God to look after them

blessing *noun*
1 a prayer or act of blessing someone 2 something you are glad of or happy about • *It's a blessing that they are safe.*

blight *noun*
1 blight is a plant disease 2 a blight is a thing that spoils or damages something

blind *adjective*
1 not able to see 2 without thought or understanding

blind *verb*
1 to blind someone is to make them blind 2 a bright light blinds you when it makes you unable to see for a time

blind *noun*
a screen for a window

blindfold *noun*
a piece of cloth used to cover someone's eyes so that they cannot see

blindfold *verb*
to blindfold someone is to cover their eyes with a blindfold

blink *verb*
to blink is to shut and open your eyes quickly

bliss *noun*
bliss is great happiness **blissful** *adjective* very happy **blissfully** *adverb* very happily

blister *noun*
a swelling like a bubble on your skin

blitz *noun*
a sudden violent attack, especially from aircraft

blizzard *noun*
a severe snowstorm

bloated *adjective*
swollen or puffed out

blob *noun*
a small round lump of something like paint or ice cream

block *noun*
1 a solid piece of something hard such as wood 2 a large building or group of buildings with streets all around it 3 something that stops people getting through • *They came to a road block and had to turn back.*

block *verb*
1 to block something is to get in the way of it • *Tall buildings blocked our view.* 2 to block something like a pipe or drain is to prevent water flowing through it

blockade *noun*
when a city or port is surrounded to stop people or goods from getting in or out

blockage *noun*
1 something that stops up a pipe or drain 2 a blocked state • *Roadworks are causing blockages in the traffic.*

block capitals or **block letters** *plural noun*
large capital letters

blog *noun*
a website on which someone writes regularly about their own life or opinions

blond or **blonde** *adjective*
fair-haired

blonde *noun*
a fair-haired girl or woman

blood *noun*
the red liquid that flows through your veins and arteries

bloodhound *noun*
a large breed of dog which can track people over long distances by following their scent

bloodshed *noun*
bloodshed is the killing and injuring of people

bloodshot *adjective*
eyes are bloodshot when they are streaked with red from being strained or tired

a
b
c
d
e
f
g
h
i
m
n
p
q
r
s
t
u
v
w
x
y
z

31

bloodstream noun
the bloodstream is the blood flowing round your body

bloodthirsty adjective (**bloodthirstier, bloodthirstiest**)
enjoying killing and violence

bloody adjective
1 bleeding, or covered in blood 2 a bloody fight or battle is one in which a lot of people are killed or badly hurt

bloom verb
to bloom is to produce flowers • Look! The roses have bloomed!

bloom noun
a bloom is a flower **in bloom** trees and plants are in bloom when they are producing flowers

blossom noun
1 a blossom is a flower, especially on a fruit tree 2 blossom is a mass of flowers on a tree

blossom verb
1 a tree or bush blossoms when it produces flowers 2 to blossom is also to develop into something very fine or good • She has blossomed into a lovely singer.

blot noun
1 a spot or blob of ink 2 a flaw or fault

blot verb (**blotting, blotted**)
to blot something is to make a blot on it **to blot something out** is to remove it or make it invisible

blotch noun
an untidy patch of colour
blotchy adjective having lots of blotches

blouse noun
a loose piece of clothing like a shirt that girls and women wear

blow noun
1 a hard knock or hit 2 a shock or disappointment • The news came to her as a terrible blow. 3 the action of blowing

blow verb (**blowing, blew, blown**)
1 to blow is to force out air from your mouth or nose • He blew on his cold hands to warm them up. 2 to move in the wind • Her hat blew off. 3 to blow something is to form it by blowing • Let's blow bubbles. 4 to blow something such as a whistle is to make a sound with it **to blow something up**

blossom

is to destroy it with an explosion **to blow up** is to be destroyed in an explosion

blue adjective ●
1 of the colour of a bright cloudless sky 2 sad and miserable • I'm feeling blue.

blue noun
a blue colour **out of the blue** with no warning • My friend turned up out of the blue.

bluebottle noun
a large blue fly that makes a loud buzz

blues plural noun
blues is a type of music that is often sad **to get the blues** is to feel sad and miserable

bluff verb
to bluff someone is to make them think that you will do something that you don't intend to do or that you know something that you don't really know

bluff noun
a bluff is something that someone says or does to bluff someone else, for example an empty promise or threat • He said he'd report us, but that was just a bluff. **to call someone's bluff** is to challenge them to do what they have threatened to do

blunder noun
a careless mistake

blunt adjective
1 having an edge that is smooth and not good for cutting 2 saying what you mean without trying to be polite or tactful

blur verb (**blurring, blurred**)
to blur something is to make it unclear or smeared

blur noun
an unclear shape with no definite outline • Without her glasses on, everything was a blur.

blurt verb
to blurt something out is to say it suddenly, without thinking

blush verb
to blush is to have a strong pink tinge in your face because you are embarrassed or ashamed

bluster verb
to bluster is to boast or make threats that don't mean very much

boa or **boa constrictor** noun
a large South American snake that coils round its prey and crushes it

boar noun
1 a wild pig 2 a male pig

board noun
1 a board is a flat piece of wood, used in building 2 a board is also a flat piece of wood or cardboard used to play games with, for example a dartboard or a chess board 3 a board is also a group of people who run a company or organization 4 board is daily meals supplied in return for money or work • The price of the holiday includes full board. **on board** aboard a ship

board verb
1 to board a ship or train or aircraft is to get on it for a journey 2 to board is to get meals and accommodation **to board something up** is to cover it with boards

boarder noun
1 a child who lives at a boarding school during the term 2 a lodger

boarding school noun
a school in which the pupils live during the term

boast verb
to boast about something that you own or that you have done is to talk proudly about it, often in order to impress people

boastful adjective
a boastful person likes to talk a lot about the things they own or the things they have done **boastfully** adverb

boat noun
a vehicle designed to float and travel on water

bob verb (**bobbing, bobbed**)
to bob is to move gently up and down, like something floating on water

bobble noun
a small round ball of something soft such as wool, used as a decoration on a hat or clothing

bobsleigh or **bobsled** noun
a large sledge with two sets of runners

bodice noun
the upper part of a woman's dress

body noun (**bodies**)
1 the body is the flesh and bones and other parts of a person or animal 2 a body is a dead person or corpse 3 the body of something is the main part of it 4 a body of people is a group of them in one place 5 a body is a distinct object or piece of matter • Stars and planets are heavenly bodies.

bodyguard noun
a guard who protects someone from being attacked

bog *noun*
bog or a bog is an area of wet, spongy ground **boggy** *adjective* boggy ground is wet and spongy

bogus *adjective*
false; not real or genuine
• *He gave a name that turned out to be bogus.*

boil¹ *verb*
1 to boil a liquid is to heat it until it starts to bubble and give off vapour **2** to boil is to start bubbling, like water **3** to boil food is to cook it in boiling water **to be boiling** (*informal*) is to be very hot, like the weather • *It's boiling outside.*

boil² *noun*
a painful red swelling on the skin

boiler *noun*
a container for heating water or making steam

boiling point *noun*
the temperature at which something boils

boisterous *adjective*
noisy and lively

bold *adjective*
1 brave and adventurous
2 clear and easy to see

bollard *noun*
a short thick post put up on a road, used to keep out traffic

bolt *noun*
1 a sliding bar for fastening a door or window **2** a thick metal pin for fastening things together **3** a flash of lightning

bolt *verb*
1 to bolt a door or window is to fasten it with a bolt
2 to bolt is to run away in panic, as a horse does
3 to bolt food is to swallow it too quickly

bomb *noun*
a container with explosives, which blows up when it is detonated

bomb *verb*
to bomb a place is to attack it with bombs

bombard *verb*
1 to bombard a place is to attack it with heavy gunfire **2** to bombard someone with questions or complaints is to direct a large number of questions or complaints at them **bombardment** *noun* a heavy attack with guns

bomber *noun*
1 an aircraft built to drop bombs **2** a person who plants or sets off a bomb

bond *noun*
1 a shared experience or feeling that brings people close together

2 bonds are ropes or chains used to tie people up

bondage *noun*
bondage is being a slave

bone *noun*
a bone is one of the hard pieces of a skeleton

bonfire *noun*
a large fire lit out of doors

bonnet *noun*
1 the hinged cover over the front part of a car **2** a baby's or woman's hat with strings that tie under the chin

bonus *noun*
1 an extra payment that someone gets for their work
2 an extra advantage or reward

bony *adjective* (**bonier, boniest**)
1 bony people or animals have bones without much flesh on them **2** full of bones **3** thin and hard, like a bone

boo *verb*
to boo is to shout out that you don't like what someone has said or done, like an angry audience in a theatre

book *noun*
a set of sheets of paper, usually with printing or writing on, fastened together inside a cover

books

book *verb*
1 to book something such as a seat in a theatre or on a train, or a room in a hotel, is to arrange for it to be kept for you **2** to book something is to record it in a book or list

bookcase *noun*
a piece of furniture with shelves for holding books

booklet *noun*
a small book with paper covers

bookmaker *noun*
a person whose business is taking bets, especially bets made on horse races

bookmark *noun*
something you use to mark a place in a book

boom *noun*
1 a deep hollow sound **2** a time when people are well off **3** a long pole at the bottom of a sail to keep it stretched

boom *verb*
1 to boom is to make a deep hollow sound, like a heavy gun **2** to boom is also to speak in a loud deep voice **3** to boom is also to grow quickly or be prosperous
• *Business is booming.*

boomerang *noun*
a curved stick which moves in a curve and comes back to you when you throw it

boomerang

boost *verb*
to boost something is to increase its size or value or power
• *Being in the drama group has really boosted his confidence.*

booster *noun*

boot *noun*
1 a heavy shoe that covers the ankle and sometimes part of your leg **2** the space for luggage at the back of a car

boot *verb*
1 to boot someone is to kick them hard **2** to boot up a computer is to switch it on and start it

booth *noun*
a small compartment for a special purpose, such as making a telephone call or having your photo taken

border *noun*
1 the border between two countries is the line where they meet • *We're about to cross the Scottish border.* **2** an edge • *There is a black border around the poster.* **3** a flower bed

bore *verb*
1 to bore someone is to make them feel tired and uninterested **2** to bore a hole is to drill it through something

bore *noun*
a dull or uninteresting person or thing

boredom *noun*
a feeling of tiredness and lack of interest

boring *adjective*
dull and uninteresting
• *The book was really boring.*

born *adjective*
to be born is to start your life
• *My little brother was born on the 17th of December.*

borough *noun* (*say* **bu**-ro)
an important town or district with its own local council

borrow *verb*
to borrow something is to have

it for a time and then return it to its owner

bosom *noun*
a woman's breasts

boss *noun*
(*informal*) a person who is in charge of a business or group of workers

boss *verb*
(*informal*) to boss someone is to order them around

bossy *adjective* (**bossier, bossiest**)
(*informal*) a bossy person is fond of ordering people about

botany *noun*
botany is the study of plants
botanist *noun* someone who studies botany
botanical *adjective* to do with botany or plants

both *determiner, pronoun*
the two of them, not just one • *I want them both in the team.*

both *adverb*
you use **both** with **and** to say two things about something or someone • *He is both friendly and helpful.*

bother *verb*
1 to bother someone is to cause them trouble or worry **2** to be bothered to do something is to take trouble over it

bother *noun*
bother is trouble or worry

bottle *noun*
a glass or plastic container with a narrow neck for holding liquids

bottle *verb*
to bottle something is to put it in a bottle **to bottle something up** is to keep something you are worried about to yourself

bottle bank *noun*
a large tank or drum for putting glass bottles and jars in for recycling

bottom *noun*
1 the bottom of something is its lowest point **2** the bottom of a garden is the farther end of it, away from the house **3** your bottom is the part of you that you sit on, also called your buttocks

bough *noun* (*rhymes with* **cow**)
a large branch of a tree that reaches out from the trunk

boulder *noun*
a very large smooth stone

bounce *verb*
1 to bounce is to spring back when thrown against something, like a rubber ball **2** to bounce something like a ball is to throw it so that it bounces

bounce *noun*
1 a bounce is the action of

bouncing **2** bounce is liveliness, such as a young child or puppy has **bouncy** *adjective* a bouncy person is lively and full of energy

bound¹ *adjective*
to be bound for a place is to be travelling towards it • *This train is bound for London.* **to be bound to do something** is to have to do it or be likely to do it • *He is bound to come.*

bound² *verb*
to bound is to leap or to run with leaping steps

bound³ *noun*
a leaping movement

boundary *noun* (**boundaries**)
1 a line that marks a limit **2** a hit to the outer edge of a cricket field

bounds *plural noun*
a place that is **out of bounds** is somewhere you are not allowed to go • *The teachers' common room is out of bounds to pupils.*

bouquet *noun*
(*say* boo-**kay** *or say* boh-**kay**)
an attractively arranged bunch of flowers

bout *noun* (*say* bowt)
1 a period of illness • *I've just had a bout of flu.* **2** a boxing or wrestling fight

bow¹ *noun* (*rhymes with* **go**)
1 a knot made with loops **2** the stick used for playing a stringed musical instrument such as a violin or cello **3** a long curved piece of wood with a tight string joining its ends, used for shooting arrows

bow² *noun* (*rhymes with* **cow**)
the front part of a ship

bow³ *verb* (*rhymes with* **cow**)
to bow is to bend your body forwards to show respect or as a greeting

bow³ *noun* (*rhymes with* **cow**)
a movement of bowing your body • *The pianist stood up to take a bow.*

bowels *plural noun*
your bowels are the long tubes in your body that carry waste food for passing out of the body

bowl¹ *noun*
1 a deep round dish for eating from **2** a heavy ball used in the game of bowls or tenpin bowling

bowl² *verb*
(*in cricket*) **1** to bowl is to send the ball towards the batsman **2** to bowl someone

is to get them out by hitting the wicket with the ball

bowler *noun*
1 someone who bowls in cricket **2** a hat with a rounded top and a narrow brim

bowling *noun*
1 bowling is the game of bowls **2** bowling is also another game, in which you have to knock down skittles with a ball you roll down an alley **3** the action of throwing a cricket ball

bowls *plural noun*
a game played on a smooth piece of grass, in which you roll heavy balls towards a small target ball called the 'jack'

bow tie *noun*
a tie in the form of a bow, worn by men as part of formal dress

bounce

box *noun*
1 a container made of wood or cardboard, often with a lid **2** a small rectangle that you fill in on a form or computer screen **3** a special compartment or booth, such as a phone box or a witness box in a lawcourt

box *verb*
1 to box is to fight with the fists **2** to box something is to put it into a box

boxer *noun*
1 someone who boxes **2** a breed of dog that looks like a bulldog

Boxing Day *noun*
the first weekday after Christmas Day

box office *noun*
a place where you can buy seats for the theatre or cinema

boy *noun*
a male child **boyhood** *noun* the time when a man was a boy **boyish** *adjective* looking or behaving like a boy

boycott *verb*
to boycott something is to refuse to buy it or have anything to do with it • *They boycotted the buses when the fares went up.*

boyfriend *noun*
someone's boyfriend is the male friend they have a romantic relationship with

bra *noun*
a piece of underwear women wear to support their breasts

brace *noun*
1 a device for holding something in place **2** a wire device for straightening the teeth

bracelet *noun*
a small band or chain you wear round your wrist

braces *plural noun*
braces are a pair of stretching straps worn over the shoulders to hold trousers up

bracket *noun*
1 a kind of punctuation mark used in pairs round words or figures to separate them from what comes before and after. Brackets are round ( ) or square [ ]. **2** a support attached to a wall to hold up a shelf or light fitting

brag *verb* (**bragging, bragged**)
to brag is to boast

braid *noun*
1 a plait **2** a decorative ribbon or band

braille *noun*
braille is a system of writing or printing using raised dots, which blind people can read by touch

WORD ORIGIN

Braille is named after a French teacher called Louis Braille, who was blind from the age of three and invented the system. He died in 1852.

brain *noun*
1 your brain is the part inside the top of your head that controls your body **2** brain also means a person's mind or intelligence • *He's got a good brain.*

brainy *adjective* (**brainier, brainiest**)
(*informal*) clever, intelligent • *She's the brainiest child in the school.*

brake *noun*
a device for making a vehicle stop or slow down

bramble *noun*
a bramble is a blackberry bush or a prickly bush like it

branch *noun*
1 a part that sticks out from the trunk of a tree **2** a part of a railway or river or road that leads off from the main part **3** a part of a large organization

branch *verb*
to branch is to form a branch **to branch out** is to start doing something new

brand *noun*
a particular make or kind of goods • *Just get a cheap brand of tea.*

brand *verb*
to brand sheep or cattle is to mark them with a hot iron

brandish *verb*
to brandish something is to wave it about • *One of the guards*

stepped forward, brandishing his spear.

brand new *adjective*
completely new

brandy *noun*
brandy is a kind of strong alcoholic drink

brass *noun*
1 brass is an alloy made from copper and zinc **2** brass also means the wind instruments made of brass, such as trumpets and trombones

brass trumpet

brave *adjective*
ready to face danger or suffering

brave *noun*
a Native American warrior

bravery *noun*
bravery is being brave
bravely *adverb*

brawl *noun*
a noisy fight or quarrel

bray *verb*
to bray is to make a noise like a donkey

brazen *adjective*
shameless or cheeky

breach *noun*
1 the breaking of an agreement or rule **2** a gap or broken place in something like a wall

bread *noun*
bread is food made by baking flour and water, usually with yeast

breadth *noun*
a thing's breadth is its width from side to side

break *verb* (**breaking, broke, broken**)
1 to break something is to make it go into several pieces by hitting it or dropping it **2** to break is to stop working properly • *I think my watch must have broken.* **3** to break a law or rule or promise is to fail to keep it or observe it **4** the weather breaks when it changes after being hot **5** waves break over rocks when they fall and froth over them **6** a boy's voice breaks when it starts to go deeper at about the age of 14 **7** to break a record is to do better than the previous holder, for example in athletics **to break down** a machine or vehicle breaks down when it stops working properly **to break off** is to stop doing something for a time • *We broke off for lunch.*

to break out is to start and spread rapidly, like a disease or fighting **to break up 1** people break up when they leave one another after a long time together **2** is to finish school at the end of term

break *noun*
1 a broken place; a gap **2** a sudden dash or attempt to escape **3** a short rest from work

breakage *noun*
something that is broken • *All breakages must be paid for.*

breakdown *noun*
1 a sudden failure to work, especially by a car • *We had a breakdown on the motorway.* **2** a period of mental illness caused by anxiety or depression

breaker *noun*
a wave breaking on the shore

breakfast *noun*
breakfast is the first meal of the day

breakthrough *noun*
an important discovery or step forward, for example in medical research

breast *noun*
1 one of the two parts on the front of a woman's body where milk is produced after she has had a baby **2** a person's or animal's chest

breaststroke *noun*
a stroke you use when swimming on your front, by pushing your arms forward and bringing them round and back

breath *noun* (*say* breth)
the air that you take into your lungs and send out again **to be out of breath** is to gasp for air after exercise

breathe *verb* (*say* breeth)
to breathe is to take air into your lungs through your nose or mouth and send it out again

breathless *adjective*
short of breath

breathtaking *adjective*
extremely beautiful or delightful

breech *noun*
the part of a gun barrel where the bullets are put in

breed *verb* (**breeding, bred**)
1 to breed is to produce offspring **2** to breed animals is to keep them in order to get young ones from them **breeder** *noun* someone who breeds animals

breed *noun*
a variety of similar animals

breeze *noun*
a gentle wind

a
b
c
d
e
f
g
h
i
j
k
l
m
n
o
p
q
r
s
t
u
v
w
x
y
z

breezy adjective (**breezier, breeziest**)
1 slightly windy **2** bright and cheerful

brevity noun
brevity is being brief or short • *I was surprised by the brevity of her answer.*

brew verb
1 to brew beer or tea is to make it **2** to be brewing is to start or develop • *Trouble is brewing.*

brewery noun
a place where beer is made

bribe noun
a bribe is money or a gift offered to someone to make them do something

bribe verb
to bribe someone is to give them a bribe **bribery** noun bribery is offering someone a bribe

brick noun
1 a small hard block of baked clay used in building **2** a rectangular block of something

bricklayer noun
a worker who builds with bricks

bridal adjective
to do with brides

bride noun
a woman on her wedding day

bridegroom noun
a man on his wedding day

bride and bridegroom

bridesmaid noun
a girl or woman who helps the bride at her wedding

bridge noun
1 a bridge is a structure built over a river, railway, or road, to allow people to cross it **2** the bridge of a ship is the high platform above the deck, from where the ship is controlled **3** the bridge of your nose is the bony upper part of your nose **4** bridge is a card game rather like whist

bridle noun
the part of a horse's harness that fits over its head

bridle path noun
a path for people on horseback

brief adjective
lasting a short time or using only a few words **in brief** in a few words

briefcase noun
a flat case for keeping documents and papers in

briefs plural noun
short underpants

brigade noun
1 an army unit usually consisting of three battalions **2** a group of people in uniform, for example the fire brigade

bright adjective
1 giving out a strong light; shining **2** a bright colour is strong and vivid **3** clever • *He's a bright lad.* **4** cheerful

brighten verb
1 to brighten something is to make it brighter **2** to brighten is to become brighter

brilliance noun
1 brilliance is bright light • *the brilliance of the summer sky* **2** brilliance is also being very intelligent or clever

brilliant adjective
1 a brilliant person is very intelligent or clever **2** (*informal*) really good or enjoyable • *That was a brilliant film!* **3** very bright and sparkling

brim noun
1 the edge round the top of a container **2** the bottom edge of a hat that sticks out

brimming adjective
completely full **brimming over** overflowing

brine noun
brine is salty water

bring verb (**bringing, brought**)
to bring someone or something is to make them come with you to a place **to bring someone up** is to look after them and educate them as a child **to bring something about** is to make it happen **to bring something up** is to mention it in a conversation

brink noun
the edge of a steep or dangerous place

brisk adjective
quick and lively

bristle noun
a short, stiff hair **bristly** adjective having lots of bristles

British adjective
to do with Great Britain

Briton noun
someone born in Great Britain

brittle adjective hard but ikely tobreak or snap

broad adjective
1 wide and open • *They walked down a broad avenue.* **2** general, not detailed • *a broad outline*

broadband noun
a system for connecting computers to the Internet and sending information very quickly

broad bean noun
a large flat bean

broadcast noun
a radio or television programme

broadcast verb
to broadcast a radio or television programme is to transmit it or take part in it **broadcaster** noun a person who takes part in a radio or television programme

broaden verb
to broaden something is to make it broader

broadly adverb
in general terms • *They were broadly right.*

broccoli noun a vegetable with green or purple heads on green stalks

brochure noun
a booklet containing information, especially about a place

broke adjective (*informal*)
not having any money

broken adjective
1 broken English is English spoken with a strong foreign accent and lots of mistakes **2** a broken home is a home in which the parents have separated

bronchitis noun
(*say* brong-**ky**-tiss) bronchitis is a disease of the lungs

bronze noun
1 bronze is an alloy of copper and tin **2** bronze is also a yellowish-brown colour

brooch noun (*rhymes with* **coach**)
a piece of jewellery that can be pinned on to clothes

brooch

brood noun
a brood is a number of young birds hatched together
brood verb
1 birds such as chickens brood when they sit on eggs to hatch them 2 to brood over something is to keep on thinking and worrying about it
brook noun
a small stream
broom noun
1 a broom is a brush with a long handle, for sweeping 2 broom is a shrub with yellow, white, or pink flowers
broomstick noun
the handle of a broom
broth noun
broth is a thin kind of soup
brother noun
your brother is a man or boy who has the same parents as you
brother-in-law noun
a person's brother-in-law is the brother of their husband or wife, or the husband of their sister
brow noun
1 your brow is your forehead 2 your brows are your eyebrows 3 the brow of a hill is the top of it
brown adjective ●
of the colour of earth, wood, or toast
brown noun
a brown colour
Brownie noun
a junior member of the Guides
brownie noun
a small chocolate cake with nuts
browse verb
1 to browse is to read or look at something casually 2 animals browse when they feed on grass or leaves
bruise noun
a dark mark that appears on your skin when it is hit or hurt
bruise verb
to bruise your skin or a part of your body is to get a bruise on it
brunette noun
a woman with dark brown or black hair
brush noun
1 a tool with hairs or bristles for sweeping, painting, or arranging the hair 2 a fox's bushy tail
brush verb
1 to brush something is to use a brush on it • Have you brushed your hair yet? 2 to brush against someone is to touch them gently as you pass them
Brussels sprout noun
a green vegetable like a tiny cabbage
brutal adjective
savage and cruel

brutality noun brutality is savage cruelty **brutally** adverb with savage cruelty
brute noun
a cruel person
bubble noun
1 a thin transparent ball of liquid filled with air or gas 2 a small ball of air in a liquid or a solid
bubble verb
a liquid bubbles when it produces bubbles, as it does when it boils
bubbly adjective (**bubblier, bubbliest**)
1 full of bubbles, like fizzy water 2 a bubbly person is cheerful and lively
buccaneer noun
an old word for a pirate
buck noun
a male deer, rabbit, or hare
buck verb
a horse bucks when it jumps with its back arched
bucket noun
a container with a handle, for carrying liquids or something such as sand
buckle noun
a clip at the end of a belt or strap for fastening it
buckle verb
1 to buckle something is to fasten it with a buckle 2 to buckle is to bend or give way under a strain • The arm of the crane was beginning to buckle. **to buckle down** is to start work
bud noun
a flower or leaf before it has opened
Buddhism noun (say **buud**-izm)
Buddhism is a religion that started in Asia and follows the teachings of Buddha **Buddhist** noun someone who practises Buddhism
budding adjective
showing great promise • The new class had several budding musicians.
budge verb
to budge is to move slightly • The door was stuck and wouldn't budge.
budgerigar noun (say **bud**-jer-i-gar)
an Australian bird often kept as a pet in a cage
budget noun
1 the money

someone plans to spend on something 2 a plan for earning and spending money
budget verb
to budget is to plan how much you are going to spend
budgie noun
(informal) a budgerigar
buffalo noun (**buffalo** or **buffaloes**)
a wild ox with long curved horns
buffer noun
something that softens a blow or collision, especially a device on a railway engine or wagon or at the end of a railway line
buffet noun (say **buu**-fay)
1 a cafe or place for buying drinks and snacks 2 a meal where guests serve themselves
bug noun
1 a tiny insect 2 (informal) a germ that causes illness • I may have a tummy bug. 3 (informal) a hidden microphone 4 a fault or problem in a computer program that stops it working properly
bugle noun (say **byoo**-gul)
a brass instrument like a small trumpet **bugler** noun someone who plays the bugle
build verb (**building, built**)
to build something is to make it by putting the parts together **to build something up** is to make it larger or stronger • Regular exercise will build up your strength. **to build up** is to become larger or stronger • The traffic was starting to build up.
build noun
your build is the shape of your body
builder noun
someone who puts up buildings
building noun
a building is a structure that someone has built, such as a house or a block of flats
bulb noun
1 the glass part of an electric light which glows when you switch it on 2 an onion-shaped root which grows into a plant or flower when it is put in the ground
bulge noun
a part that sticks out; a swelling
bulge verb
to bulge is to stick out or swell
bulk noun
1 a thing's bulk is its size, especially when it is large 2 the bulk of something is most of it

budgerigar

a b c d e f g h i j k l m n o p q r s t u v w x y z

• *He spends the bulk of his time on the computer.* **in bulk** in large quantities

bulky *adjective* (**bulkier, bulkiest**)
taking up a lot of space

bull *noun*
1 the male of the cattle family
2 a male seal, whale, or elephant

bulldozer *noun*
a heavy vehicle with a wide metal blade in front, used to clear or flatten land

bullet *noun*
a piece of shaped metal shot from a rifle or pistol

bulletin *noun*
a short announcement of news on radio or television

bullfight *noun*
in Spain, a public entertainment in which people challenge bulls, and sometimes kill them

bullfighter *noun* someone who takes part in a bullfight

bullion *noun*
gold or silver in the form of bars

bullock *noun*
a young bull

bull's-eye *noun*
the centre of a target

bully *verb* (**bullies, bullying, bullied**)
to bully someone is to hurt or frighten them when they are weaker

bully *noun* (**bullies**)
someone who bullies people

bulrush *noun*
a tall reed which grows in water or on boggy land

bumble bee *noun*
a large kind of bee with a loud buzz

bump *verb*
to bump something is to knock against it accidentally **to bump into someone** (*informal*) is to meet them unexpectedly

bump *noun*
1 an accidental knock
2 a swelling or lump

bumper¹ *noun*
a bar along the front or back of a motor vehicle to protect it in collisions

bumper² *adjective*
unusually large or fine • *We had a bumper crop of apples this year.*

bumpy *adjective* (**bumpier, bumpiest**)
having lots of bumps

bun *noun*
1 a small round sweet cake
2 a round bunch of hair that some women make at the back of their head

bunch *noun*
a number of things joined or tied together, such as fruit or flowers

or keys • *He was eating a bunch of grapes.*

bundle *noun*
a number of things tied or wrapped loosely together, such as clothes or papers

bundle *verb*
1 to bundle things together is to tie or wrap them loosely 2 to bundle someone into a room or car is to push them there hurriedly • *They bundled him into the back of a taxi.*

bung *noun*
a stopper for a bottle or barrel

bungalow *noun*
a house with all the rooms on one floor

bungle *verb*
to bungle something is to do it badly and clumsily

bunk or **bunk bed** *noun*
a single bed with another bed above it or below it

bunker *noun*
1 a container for storing fuel such as coal 2 a hollow filled with sand, made as an obstacle on a golf course 3 an underground shelter

bunny *noun* (**bunnies**)
(*informal*) a rabbit

bunsen burner *noun*
a gas burner with a flame you can adjust, used in laboratories

buoy *noun* (*say* boi)
a floating object in the sea, used as a marker or warning sign

buoyant *adjective*
able to float **buoyancy** *noun* buoyancy is being able to float

bur *noun*
part of a plant that clings to your clothes or hair

burden *noun*
1 a heavy load 2 something troublesome that you have to put up with

bureau *noun* (**bureaux**) (*say* **bewr**-oh)
an office or department • *They will tell you at the Information Bureau.*

burger *noun*
a hamburger

burglar *noun*
someone who breaks into a building to steal things

burglary *noun* burglary is the crime of stealing things from a building

burgle *verb*
to burgle someone is to steal from their house

burial *noun*
putting a dead body in a grave

burly *adjective* (**burlier, burliest**)
a burly person is big and strong

burn¹ *verb* (**burning, burnt** or **burned**)
1 to burn something is to damage or destroy it by fire or strong heat 2 to burn is to be damaged or destroyed by fire or heat 3 to be burning is to be on fire 4 to be burning is also to feel very hot

burn¹ *noun*
1 an injury or mark caused by fire or strong heat 2 the firing of a spacecraft's rocket

burn² *noun*
(*in Scotland*) a small stream

burner *noun*
the part of a lamp or cooker that forms the flame

burp *verb*
to burp is to make a noise through your mouth by letting air come up from your stomach

burp *noun*
the act or sound of burping

burrow *noun*
a hole dug by an animal such as a rabbit or fox

burrow *verb*
1 an animal burrows when it digs a burrow 2 to burrow is also to dig or search deeply • *He burrowed in his pockets to find a pound coin.*

burst *verb* (**bursting, burst**)
1 to burst is to break apart suddenly 2 to burst something is to make it break apart 3 to be bursting with energy or excitement is to have a lot of energy or to be very excited **to burst in** is to rush in noisily or clumsily **to burst into tears** is to suddenly start crying **to burst out laughing** is to start laughing noisily

burst *noun*
1 a split caused by something bursting • *There's a burst in one of the pipes.* 2 something short and quick • *a burst of gunfire*

bury *verb* (**buries, burying, buried**)
1 to bury something is to put it under the ground 2 to bury someone is to put them in a grave when they are dead

bus *noun*
a large road vehicle for carrying passengers

bush *noun*
1 a bush is a plant like a small tree with a lot of stems or branches 2 the bush is wild land, especially in Australia or Africa

bushy *adjective* (**bushier, bushiest**)
thick and hairy • *His dad has bushy eyebrows.*

busily *adverb*
in a busy way

business noun (say **biz**-niss)
1 a business is an organization that makes money by selling goods or services • *His uncle worked in a garage business.* **2** business is what an organization does to make money • *She has made a career in business.* **3** a person's business is what concerns them and no one else • *Mind your own business.* **4** a business is also an affair or subject • *I am tired of the whole business.*

busker noun
someone who plays music in the street, hoping for money from people passing by

bus stop noun
a place where a bus regularly stops

bust[1] noun
1 a sculpture of a person's head and shoulders **2** a woman's breasts

bust[2] adjective (informal) **1** broken • *My watch is bust.* **2** bankrupt

bustle verb
to bustle is to be in a hurry or rushing about busily

busy adjective (**busier, busiest**)
1 a busy person is one with a lot to do **2** a busy place is one with a lot going on **3** a busy telephone line is one that someone is already using

busybody noun (**busybodies**)
someone who interferes in other people's affairs

but conjunction
you use **but** to join two words or statements that say different or opposite things • *I wanted to go but I couldn't.*

but preposition
except • *There's no one here but me.*

butcher noun
someone who runs a shop that cuts and sells meat

butler noun
a male servant in charge of other servants in a large private house

butt[1] noun
1 the thicker end of a weapon or tool **2** a large barrel **3** someone people often make fun of • *James always seems to be the butt of your jokes.*

butt[2] verb
to butt someone is to hit them hard with your head **to butt in** is to interrupt suddenly or rudely

butter noun
butter is a fatty yellow food made from cream

butterfly noun (**butterflies**)
1 an insect with a thin body and large white or brightly coloured wings **2** a stroke you use when swimming on your front, by raising both arms together over your head

butterflies

butterscotch noun
butterscotch is a kind of hard toffee

buttocks plural noun
your buttocks are the part of the body on which you sit, your bottom

button noun
1 a flat plastic or metal disc sewn on clothes and passed through a buttonhole to fasten them **2** a small knob you press to work an electric device

button verb
to button clothes or to button up clothes is to fasten them with buttons

buttress noun
a support built against a wall

buy verb (**buying, bought**)
to buy something is to get it by paying for it • *I bought a CD yesterday.* **buyer** noun someone who buys something

buy noun
something you buy • *That was a good buy.*

buzz noun
a sharp humming sound, like bees make

buzz verb
to buzz is to make a buzzing sound

buzzard noun
a bird of prey like a large hawk

buzzard

buzzer noun
an alarm or signalling device that makes a buzzing noise

by preposition, adverb
1 near, close • *Sit by me.* **2** using; by means of • *I fixed the tyre by sticking on a patch.* **3** before • *Do your homework by tomorrow.* **4** past • *She went by the window.* • *I can't get by.* **by and large** mostly, on the whole **by the way** a phrase you use to begin a new topic

bye noun
a run scored in cricket when the batsman has not touched the ball

bye-bye exclamation
(informal) goodbye

bypass noun
a road that takes traffic round the edge of a town or city rather than going through the centre

bystander noun
someone who sees something happening but takes no part in it

byte noun
(in computing) a unit that measures data or memory

Cc

c
1 short for Celsius or centigrade **2** 100 in Roman numerals

cab noun
1 a taxi **2** the place for the driver in a lorry, bus, train, or crane

cabbage noun
a large round green vegetable with layers of closely packed leaves

cabin noun
1 a hut or shelter **2** one of the small rooms on a ship for sleeping in **3** the part of an aircraft where the passengers sit

cabinet noun
1 a cupboard with shelves and doors, used for storing things **2** the group of chief ministers who run the government

cable noun
1 a thick rope, wire, or chain used for lifting heavy loads or tying up ships **2** a telegram sent overseas

cable television noun
a television system in which programmes are transmitted along underground cables into people's houses

cackle noun
1 a cackle is the clucking of a hen **2** a cackle is also a loud, silly laugh **3** cackle is stupid chattering

cactus noun (**cacti**)
a fleshy plant that is covered in prickles and grows in hot, dry places

caddie noun
someone whose job is to help a golfer by carrying the clubs and giving advice

cadet noun
a young person who is being trained for the armed forces or the police

cafe noun (say **kaf**-ay)
a place that sells hot and cold drinks and light meals

cafeteria noun (say kaf-e-**teer**-i-a)
a cafe where customers serve themselves from a counter

caffeine noun
caffeine is a substance in tea and coffee and some other drinks, which keeps you awake and makes you feel active

cage noun
an enclosure made of bars or wires, for keeping birds or animals so that they can't get away

cagoule noun
a lightweight waterproof jacket

cake noun
1 a sweet food made from a baked mixture of flour, eggs, fat, and sugar 2 something made into a lump rather like a cake, such as soap **a piece of cake** (informal) something very easy to do

caked adjective
covered with something that has dried hard, like mud

calamity noun (**calamities**)
a disaster **calamitous** adjective disastrous

calcium noun ⓒ
a greyish-white element contained in teeth, bones, and lime

calculate verb
to calculate something is to work it out by arithmetic or with a calculator **calculation** noun something you work out by using numbers or other information

calculator noun
a machine for adding up figures and doing other calculations with numbers

calendar noun
a chart or display that shows the days of the year

calf¹ noun (**calves**)
1 a young cow or ox 2 a young seal, whale, or elephant

calf² noun (**calves**)
the back part of your leg below your knee

call noun
1 a shout or cry • They heard a call for help. 2 a short visit • She decided to pay her father a call. 3 a telephone conversation with someone

call verb
1 to call is to shout out 2 to call someone is to telephone them • I'll call you at the weekend. 3 to call someone near you is to ask them to come to you 4 to call on someone is to visit them 5 to be called something is to have it as your name • His friend was called Damon. 6 to call something a certain thing is to describe it that way • You don't call that working, do you? **to call something off** is to cancel it

calling noun
someone's calling is their profession or trade

callipers plural noun
a device for measuring the width of tubes or of round objects

callous adjective
a callous person is very unkind and doesn't care about other people's feelings

calm adjective
1 quiet and still • a calm sea 2 someone is calm when they are not excited or agitated • Please keep calm. **calmly** adverb **calmness** noun

calorie noun
a unit for measuring the amount of heat or the energy produced by food

camcorder noun
a video camera that can record pictures and sound

camel noun
a large animal with a long neck and one or two humps on its back • Arabian camels have one hump, and Bactrian camels have two.

camera noun
a device for taking photographs, films, or television pictures

camouflage noun (say **kam**-o-flahzh)
a way of hiding things by making them look like part of their surroundings

camouflage verb
to camouflage something is to hide it by making it look like part of its surroundings

camp noun
a place where people live in tents or huts or caravans for a short time

camp verb
1 to camp or go camping is to have a holiday in a tent 2 to camp is also to put up a tent or tents • Let's camp here for the night. **camper** noun a person who goes to a camp

campaign noun
1 a planned series of actions, especially to get people

to support you or become interested in something • a campaign for human rights 2 a series of battles in one area or with one aim

campaign verb
to campaign is to carry out a plan of action to raise people's interest in something such as a good cause • They are campaigning to stop the destruction of the rainforests.

campsite noun
a place for camping

campus noun
the buildings of a college or university and the land around them

can¹ verb (present tense **can**; past tense **could**)
1 to be able to do something or to know how to do it • Can you lift this stone? • They can speak French. 2 to be allowed to do something • Can I go home?

can² noun
a sealed metal container holding food or drink

can² verb (**canning, canned**)
to can food is to put it into cans and seal it

canal noun
a long channel specially dug and filled with water for boats to travel alot

canary noun (**canaries**)
a small yellow bird that sings, often kept in a cage as a pet

canary

cancel verb (**cancelling, cancelled**)
1 to cancel something planned is to say that it will not be done or not take place after all 2 to cancel an order or instruction is to stop it 3 to cancel a stamp or ticket is to mark it so that it cannot be used again

cancellation noun
something that someone has cancelled, especially a theatre or travel booking that can then be sold to someone else

cancer noun
a serious disease in which a harmful growth forms in the body

candidate noun
1 someone who has applied for a job or position **2** someone who is taking an exam

candle noun
a stick of wax with a wick through it, giving light when it is burning

candlestick noun
a holder for a candle or candles

candy noun (**candies**)
1 candy is crystallized sugar **2** a candy is a sweet

candyfloss noun
candyfloss is a fluffy mass of sugar that has been spun into fine threads

cane noun
a cane is the hollow stem of a reed or tall grass

cane verb
to cane someone is to beat them with a cane

canine adjective
to do with dogs

cannibal noun
1 a person who eats human flesh **2** an animal that eats animals of its own kind
cannibalism noun cannibalism is eating other people, or animals of the same kind

cannon noun
a large gun that fires heavy balls made of metal or stone

cannon

cannonball noun
a heavy metal or stone ball fired from a cannon

cannot
can not • I cannot believe it.

canoe noun
a light narrow boat driven with paddles **canoeist** noun someone who uses a canoe

canopy noun (**canopies**)
a covering that hangs over something • The larger trees form a canopy over the roof of the forest.

can't
short for cannot • We can't see them.

canteen noun
a restaurant in a factory or office

or school, where the people working there can get a meal or snack

canter verb
a horse canters when it goes at a gentle gallop

canvas noun
1 canvas is strong, coarse cloth **2** a canvas is a piece of this kind of cloth used for painting on

canyon noun
a deep valley with a river running through it

cap noun
1 a soft hat without a brim but often with a peak **2** a cover or top

cap verb (**capping, capped**)
1 to cap something is to cover it

capable adjective
able to do something **capability** noun being able to do something **capably** adverb to do something capably is to do it well

capacity noun (**capacities**)
1 ability to do something • He has a great capacity for work. **2** the amount that something can hold

cape¹ noun
a piece of high land sticking out into the sea

cape² noun
a cloak

caper verb
to caper is to jump about playfully

capital noun
1 the capital of a country is the most important city in it **2** capital is money or property that can be used to make more wealth

capital letter noun
a large letter of the kind used at the start of a name or a sentence, such as A, B, C

capital punishment noun
capital punishment is when someone is killed as a punishment for a crime, such as murder or treason

capsize verb
to capsize is to overturn in a boat in the water

capsule noun
1 a hollow pill containing medicine **2** a small spacecraft that separates from a larger rocket

captain noun
1 an officer in charge of a ship or aircraft **2** an officer in the army or navy **3** the leader in a sports team

caption noun
the words printed beside a picture to describe it

captivate verb
to captivate someone is to charm them or make them interested
captivating adjective charming

and attractive

captive noun
a prisoner

captive adjective
imprisoned; unable to escape

captivity noun
1 captivity is being held prisoner **2** an animal in captivity is one kept in a zoo or wildlife park rather than living in the wild

capture verb
to capture an animal or person is to catch or imprison them

capture noun
catching or imprisoning an animal or person

car noun
1 a motor vehicle for about four or five people **2** a railway carriage • Does the train have a buffet car?

caramel noun
1 caramel is burnt sugar used to give a sweet taste to food **2** a caramel is a sweet made from butter, milk, and sugar

carat noun
1 a measure of weight for precious stones **2** a measure of the purity of gold

caravan noun
1 a vehicle towed by a car and used for living in, especially by people on holiday **2** a large number of people travelling together, especially across a desert

carbon noun ©
carbon is an element found in charcoal, graphite, diamonds, and other substances

carbon dioxide noun
a colourless gas made by humans and animals breathing

carbon monoxide noun
a colourless, poisonous gas found especially in the exhaust fumes of motor vehicles

carcass noun
the dead body of an animal or bird

card noun
1 card is thick stiff paper **2** a card is a folded piece of thick paper that you use to send greetings to someone, for example a birthday card **3** a card is also a playing card **4** a card is also a small piece of plastic that a bank or building society issues to a customer, with an electronic strip recording details of their account **cards** is a game with playing cards

cardboard noun
cardboard is thick stiff paper

cardigan noun
a knitted jumper fastened with buttons down the front

a
b
c
d
e
f
g
h
i
j
k
l
m
n
o
p
q
r
s
t
u
v
w
x
y
z

cardinal number *noun*
a number for counting things, for example 1, 2, 3
care *noun*
1 care is worry or trouble
• *She was free from care.*
2 care is also serious thought or attention • *Take more care with your homework.* **3** care is also protection or supervision • *You can leave your dog in my care.*
to take care is to be especially careful **to take care of someone or something** is to look after them • *Please could you take care of the cat while I'm away?*
care *verb*
to care about something or someone is to feel interested or concerned about them **to care for someone** is to look after them • *He cared for his wife when she was ill.* **to care for something** is to like it or want it • *I don't much care for fried food.*
career *noun*
a person's career is what they have been trained to do to earn a living and make progress during their lives
career *verb*
to career along or down somewhere is to rush along wildly
carefree *adjective*
not having any worries or responsibilities
careful *adjective*
making sure that you do something well without any mistakes and without causing any danger • *She is a careful driver.* • *He was careful to read the instructions first.*
carefully *adverb*
to do something carefully is to do it with a lot of care and attention
careless *adjective*
not taking care; clumsy
carelessly *adverb* to do something carelessly is to do it without much care and make a lot of mistakes
carelessness *noun*
carelessness is not taking care
caress *noun* (*say* ka-**ress**)
a gentle and loving touch
caress *verb*
to caress someone is to touch them gently and fondly
caretaker *noun*
someone who looks after a large building such as a church or school
cargo *noun*
the goods carried in a ship or aircraft

caricature *noun*
a drawing or description of someone that exaggerates their features and makes them look funny or ridiculous
carnation *noun*
a garden flower with a sweet smell
carnival *noun*
a festival or celebration with a procession of people in fancy dress
carnivore *noun*
an animal that eats meat
carnivorous *adjective* a carnivorous animal is one that eats meat
carol *noun*
a hymn or song that you sing at Christmas time
carpenter *noun*
someone who makes things, especially parts of buildings, out of wood **carpentry** making things from wood
carpet *noun*
a thick soft covering for a floor
carriage *noun*
1 a carriage is one of the separate sections of a train where passengers sit **2** a carriage is also a passenger vehicle pulled by horses
carriageway *noun*
the part of a road that vehicles travel on
carrier bag *noun*
a large bag for holding shopping
carrot *noun*   carrots
a long thin orange-coloured vegetable
carry *verb* (**carries, carrying, carried**)
1 to carry something is to lift it and take it somewhere **2** to carry something is also to have it with you
• *He is carrying a gun.*
3 a sound carries when it can be heard a long way away **to be carried away** is to become very excited **to carry on** is to continue doing something
• *They carried on chatting.*
to carry something out is to put it into practice • *The following night he carried out his plan.*
cart *noun*
a small vehicle for carrying loads
cart *verb*
(*informal*) to cart something somewhere is to carry or transport it, especially when it is heavy or tiring • *I've been carting these books around the school all afternoon.*

carthorse *noun*
a large heavy horse
cartilage *noun* (*say* **kar**-ti-lij)
cartilage is tough and flexible tissue attached to one of the bones in the nose or ear
carton *noun*
a lightweight cardboard or plastic box
cartoon *noun*
1 a drawing that is funny or tells a joke **2** a series of drawings that tell a story **3** an animated film
cartoonist *noun* someone who draws cartoons
cartridge *noun*
1 a container holding film to be put into a camera or ink to be put into a pen **2** the case containing the explosive for a bullet or shell
cartwheel *noun*
a somersault done sideways, with your arms and legs spread wide
carve *verb*
1 to carve wood or stone is to make something artistic by cutting it carefully **2** to carve meat is to cut it into slices
cascade *noun*
a waterfall or a series of waterfalls
cascade *verb*
to cascade is to tumble down like the water in a waterfall
case¹ *noun*
1 a container **2** a suitcase
case² *noun*
1 an example of something existing or happening • *We've had four cases of chickenpox.*
• *It's just a case of being patient.* **2** a crime or incident that the police or a lawcourt are investigating • *The next case was a murder.* **3** the facts or arguments used to support something • *She made a good case for getting some extra money.* **in any case** anyway **in case** because something may happen • *Take an umbrella in case it rains.*
cash *noun*
cash is coins and banknotes that you use to pay for something
cash *verb*
to cash a cheque is to exchange it for coins and banknotes
cash dispenser *noun*
a machine from which customers of a bank or building society can get money
cashier *noun*
someone in charge of the money in a bank, office, or shop

cash register noun
a machine that records and stores money received in a shop

casket noun
a small box for jewellery or other small objects

casserole noun
1 a covered dish in which food is cooked **2** the food cooked in a dish of this kind

cassette noun
a small sealed case containing recording tape or film on spools that turn when it is put in a tape recorder or camera

cast verb
1 to cast something is to throw it **2** to cast a vote is to make your vote in an election **3** to cast something made of metal or plaster is to make it in a mould **4** to cast a play or film is to choose the performers for it
to cast off is to untie a boat and start sailing in it

cast noun
1 a shape you make by pouring liquid metal or plaster into a mould **2** the performers in a play or film

castanets plural noun
two pieces of wood or ivory held in one hand and clapped together to make a clicking sound, as in Spanish dancing

castaway noun
someone who has been left in a deserted place, especially after a shipwreck

castle noun
1 a large old building with heavy stone walls and battlements, made to protect people in it from attack **2** a piece in chess, also called a rook

castor noun (say **kah**-ster)
a small wheel on the leg of a piece of furniture

castor sugar noun
finely ground white sugar

casual adjective
1 not deliberate or planned • It was just a casual remark. **2** casual clothes are informal clothes that you wear for leisure time **3** not regular or permanent • His dad was doing casual work.
casually adverb

casualty noun (**casualties**)
someone killed or injured in war or in an accident

cat noun
1 a small furry animal, usually kept as a pet and known for catching mice **2** a larger member of the same family, for example a lion, tiger, or leopard

catalogue noun
a list of goods for sale or of books in a library

catamaran noun
a sailing boat with two hulls fixed side by side

catapult noun
a small weapon made from a forked stick with elastic attached to each fork, used for shooting pellets or small stones

catastrophe noun
(say ka-**tas**-tro-fi)
a great or sudden disaster
catastrophic adjective
absolutely disastrous or dreadful • The tornado did catastrophic damage.

catch verb (**catching, caught**)
1 to catch something is to get hold of it, for example a ball that is coming towards you **2** to catch an animal is to capture it and not let it escape **3** to catch someone is to discover them doing something wrong • He was caught going home early. **4** to catch an illness is to get it from someone else **5** to catch a bus or train is to get on it before it leaves **6** to catch something someone says is to manage to hear it • I'm afraid I didn't catch your question. **7** to catch your clothes is to get them entangled in something • I've caught my sleeve on a bramble. **to catch fire** is to start burning **to catch on** (informal) is to become popular, as a craze or fashion does **to catch someone out** is to show that they are wrong or mistaken **to catch up with someone** is to reach them when they have been ahead of you

catch noun
1 catching something • Maya made a brilliant catch. **2** something you catch • They had a large catch of fish. **3** a hidden difficulty or snag • The car was so cheap there had to be a catch. **4** a device for fastening a door or window

catchment area noun
the area in which pupils go to a particular school

catchphrase noun
a phrase that someone famous has used and a lot of people now use

catchy adjective (**catchier, catchiest**)
pleasant and easy to remember, like a tune

category noun (**categories**)
a group or division of similar people or things • She was a runner-up in the 8-10 age category.

cater verb
to cater for someone or something is to give them what they need • The library caters for all ages.

caterer noun
someone whose job is to provide food for people, especially at an important party or occasion

caterpillar noun
a long, creeping creature that turns into a butterfly or moth

cathedral noun
a large and important church in a major city, with a bishop in charge of it

Catholic adjective
belonging to the Roman Catholic Church

Catholic noun
a member of the Roman Catholic Church

cattle plural noun
cattle are cows and bulls and other large grass-eating animals

cauldron noun
a large round iron cooking pot used especially by witches in stories

cauldron

cauliflower noun
a kind of cabbage with a large head of white flowers

cause noun
1 what makes something happen, a reason • The cause of the fire is still a mystery. **2** the aim or purpose that a group of people are working for • They were raising money for a good cause.

cause verb
to cause something is to make it happen

caution noun
1 caution is being careful to avoid danger or mistakes **2** a caution is a warning

cautious adjective
careful to avoid a risk or difficulty
cautiously adverb

cavalry noun
soldiers who fight on horseback or in armoured vehicles

cave noun
a large hole in the side of a hill or cliff, or under the ground

cave *verb*
to cave or go caving is to explore caves **to cave in** is to collapse

caveman or **cavewoman** *noun* (**cavemen** or **cavewomen**)
a person who lived in a cave in prehistoric times

cavern *noun*
a cave, especially a deep or dark cave

cavity *noun* (**cavities**)
a hollow or hole

CD
short for compact disc

CD-ROM
short for *compact disc read-only memory*, a system for storing information that can be viewed on a computer screen

cease *verb*
to cease doing something is to stop doing it

ceasefire *noun*
an agreement to stop using weapons, made by people who are fighting a war

cedar *noun*
an evergreen tree with hard sweet-smelling wood

ceiling *noun* (*say* **see**-ling)
the flat surface along the top of a room

celebrate *verb*
to celebrate a day or event is to do something special to show that it is important **celebration** *noun* a party or other special event to celebrate something

celebrity *noun* (**celebrities**)
a famous person, especially in show business or on television

celery *noun*
a vegetable with crisp white or green stems

cell *noun*
1 a small room, especially in a prison 2 a tiny part of a living creature or plant 3 a device for producing electric current chemically

cellar *noun*
an underground room for storing things

cello *noun* (*say* **chel**-oh)
a large stringed musical instrument, which you play by placing it upright between the knees and using a bow
cellist someone who plays the cello

cellulose *noun*
cellulose is a tissue that forms the main part of all plants and trees

Celsius *adjective*
using a scale for measuring temperature in which water freezes at 0 degrees and boils at 100 degrees

cement *noun*
1 cement is a mixture of lime and clay used in building to make floors and join bricks together 2 cement is also a strong glue

cemetery *noun* (**cemeteries**)
(*say* **sem**-e-tri) a place where dead people are buried

censor *verb*
to censor films, plays, or books is to look at them to make sure that they are suitable for people to see, and to take out any parts that do not seem suitable

censorship *noun*
the job or process of censoring films, plays, or books

census *noun*
an official count or survey of the number of people or the volume of traffic in a place

cent *noun*
a coin and unit of money in America and some other countries

centenary *noun* (**centenaries**)
the hundredth anniversary of something special or important

centigrade *adjective*
another word for Celsius

centimetre *noun*
one-hundredth of a metre, about four-tenths of an inch

centipede *noun*
a small, long creature with many pairs of legs

central *adjective*
1 at or near the centre of something 2 most important • *She will have a central role in our plans.*
centrally *adverb*
in a central position

central heating *noun*
central heating is a system of heating a building by sending hot water, hot air, or steam round it in pipes

centre *noun*
1 the middle of something 2 an important place • *Vienna is one of the great music centres of Europe.* 3 a building or place for a special purpose, such as a sports centre or a shopping centre

centurion *noun*
an officer in the ancient Roman army, originally commanding a hundred men

century *noun* (**centuries**)
1 a period of a hundred years 2 a hundred runs scored by one batsman in an innings at cricket

ceramics *plural noun*
ceramics is the art of making pottery

cereal *noun*
1 a grass that produces seeds which are used as food 2 a breakfast food made from seeds of this kind

ceremony *noun* (**ceremonies**)
(*say* **se**-ri-mo-ni)
1 ceremony is the formal actions carried out at a wedding, funeral, or other important occasion 2 a ceremony is a formal event such as a wedding or funeral **ceremonial** *adjective* a ceremonial event or duty is one to do with a ceremony

certain *adjective*
1 something is certain when it is definitely true or is going to happen 2 you are certain about something when you know it is definitely true 3 known but not named • *A certain person was here this morning.* **for certain** definitely, for sure **to make certain** is to make sure

certainly *adverb*
as a fact, without any doubt • *They were certainly here last night.*

certainty *noun* (**certainties**)
1 a certainty is something that is sure to happen 2 certainty is being sure

certificate *noun*
an official document that records an important event or achievement, such as someone's birth or passing an exam

centurion

CFC
short for *chlorofluorocarbon*, a chemical that can damage the earth's ozone layer, and was once used in refrigerators and aerosols

chaffinch *noun*
a small bird

chain *noun*
1 a row of metal rings fastened together 2 a line of people 3 a connected series of things • *The story told of a strange chain of events.*

chair *noun*
a seat with a back for one person

chalk noun
  1 a kind of soft white rock **2** a soft white or coloured stick of a similar rock, used for writing on blackboards **chalky** adjective white or powdery like chalk

challenge verb
  to challenge someone is to demand that they perform some feat or take part in a fight **challenger** noun a person who makes a challenge, especially for a sports title

challenge noun
  something difficult that someone has to do

chamber noun
  1 (old use) a room **2** a hall used for meetings of a parliament or council

chameleon noun
(say ka-**mee**-li-on)
  a small lizard that can change the colour of its skin to match its surroundings and appear almost invisible

chameleon

champagne noun
(say sham-**payn**)
  a bubbly white French wine

champion noun
  1 the person who has beaten all the others in a sport or competition **2** someone who supports a cause by fighting or speaking for it • *Martin Luther King was a champion of human rights.*

championship noun
  a contest to decide who is the best player or competitor in a game or sport

chance noun
  1 a chance is a possibility or opportunity • *This is your only chance to see them.* **2** chance is the way things happen accidentally • *It was pure chance that we met.* **by chance** accidentally, without any planning • *We found the place by chance.* **to take a chance** is to take a risk

chancellor noun
  1 an important government or legal official **2** the chief minister of the government in some European countries

Chancellor of the Exchequer noun
  the minister of the British government in charge of finances and taxes

chandelier noun
(say shan-de-**leer**)
  a light fitting that hangs from the ceiling and has a lot of bright bulbs

change verb
  1 to change something or someone is to make them different **2** to change is to become different • *My gran said I'd changed since she'd last seen me.* **3** to change one thing for another is to exchange them • *I'm going to change my bike for a new one.* **4** to change money is to give coins or notes of small values in exchange for higher value money • *Can you change a £5 note?* **5** to change trains or buses is to get off one and get on another • *Change at York for the train to Durham.*

change noun
  1 change is the process of changing **2** your change is the money you get back when you give more than the right money to pay for something **3** a change of clothes is a set of fresh clothes **to do something for a change** is to do it because it is different or unusual • *Let's walk home for a change.*

channel noun
  1 a stretch of water joining two seas, like the English Channel between Britain and France **2** a television or radio station **3** a way for water to flow along **4** the part of a river or sea that is deep enough for ships to sail on

chant noun
  a tune, especially one that is often repeated

chant verb
  to chant words is to say them or call them out in a special rhythm

chaos noun (say **kay**-oss)
  chaos is complete disorder or confusion • *The room was in chaos.*

chaotic adjective (say kay-**ot**-ik)
  completely confused or in a mess

chap noun
  (informal) a man or boy • *What a funny chap he is.*

chapatti noun
  a flat thin cake of Indian bread made without yeast

chapel noun
  1 a small church or part of a large church **2** a room in a large house, used for worship

chapped adjective
  having rough, cracked skin

chapter noun
  a section of a book

char verb (**charring, charred**)
  to char something is to scorch it or blacken it with fire

character noun
  1 the special nature and qualities of a person or thing **2** a person in a story or play

characteristic noun
  something that makes a person or thing noticeable or different from others

characteristic adjective
  typical, what you would expect of someone

charades noun (say sha-**rahdz**)
  charades is a game in which people have to guess a word or the title of a book or film when other people act it out

charcoal noun
  charcoal is a black substance made by burning wood slowly

charge noun
  1 the price asked for something **2** an accusation that someone committed a crime • *He is facing three charges of burglary.* **3** an attack in a battle **4** the amount of explosive needed to fire a weapon **5** the amount of an electric current **to be in charge of something or someone** is to be the one who decides what will happen to them

charge verb
  1 to charge a price for something is to ask people to pay it **2** to charge someone is to accuse them of committing a crime **3** to charge in a battle is to rush to attack the enemy

chariot noun
  a horse-drawn vehicle with two wheels, used in ancient times for fighting and racing **charioteer** noun someone who drove a chariot

charity noun (**charities**)
  1 charity is giving money and help to other people **2** a charity is an organization that helps those in need **charitable** adjective kind and generous

charm noun
  1 charm is being pleasant and attractive **2** a charm is a magic spell **3** a charm is also something small worn or carried to bring good luck

charm verb
  1 to charm someone is to give them pleasure or delight **2** to charm someone is also to put a spell on them

charming adjective
  pleasant and attractive

chart noun
  1 a large plan or map **2** a diagram or list with information set out in columns or rows **3** a list of the most popular CDs and records that are sold

charter noun
  an official document explaining people's rights or privileges

charter *verb*
to charter an aircraft or vehicle is to hire it for a special journey

chase *verb*
to chase someone is to go quickly after them to try to catch them up

chase *noun*
a chase is when you chase someone

chassis *noun* (**chassis**) (*say* **shass**-i)
the frame and wheels of a vehicle, which support the body

chat *noun*
a friendly or informal talk with someone

chat *verb* (**chatting, chatted**)
to chat to someone is to talk to them in a friendly or informal way **chatty** *adjective* liking to chat to people in a friendly way

château *noun* (**châteaux**) (*say* **shat**-oh)
a castle or large house in France

château

chatroom *noun*
a place on the Internet where people can have a conversation by sending messages to each other

chatter *verb*
1 to talk quickly or stupidly; to talk too much **2** to make a rattling noise • *She couldn't stop her teeth from chattering.*

chauffeur *noun* (*say* shoh-**fer**)
someone who is paid to drive a large smart car for someone important

cheap *adjective*
1 low in price; not expensive **2** not well made or of good quality

cheat *verb*
1 to cheat someone is to trick them so they lose something **2** to cheat is to try to do well in an examination or game by breaking the rules

cheat *noun*
someone who cheats

check *verb*
1 to check something is to make sure that it is correct or all right **2** to check someone or something is to make them stop or slow down **to check on something or check up on something** is to look at it carefully to see if it is correct or suitable

check *noun*
1 a check is when you check something **2** check in chess is when the king is threatened by another piece **3** a check is a pattern of squares

checkmate *noun*
checkmate in chess is when one side wins by trapping the other side's king

checkout *noun*
the place where you pay for your shopping in a supermarket or a large shop

check-up *noun*
a careful check or examination by a doctor or dentist

cheek *noun*
1 the side of your face below your eye **2** being rude or impolite

cheeky *adjective*
rude or impolite, without being unpleasant or nasty **cheekily** *adverb* in a rude or cheeky way

cheer *noun*
a shout praising or supporting someone

cheer *verb*
1 to cheer someone is to support them by cheering **2** to cheer someone is to comfort or encourage them **to cheer someone up** is to make them more cheerful **to cheer up** is to become more cheerful

cheerful *adjective*
happy and bright

cheese *noun*
a white or yellow food made from milk. Cheese can be hard or soft. **cheesy** *adjective* tasting or smelling like cheese

cheetah *noun*
a large spotted animal of the cat family, which can run very fast

chef *noun* (*say* shef)
the chief cook in a hotel or restaurant

chemical *noun*
a substance used in or made by chemistry

chemical *adjective*
to do with chemistry or made by chemistry

chemist *noun*
1 someone who makes or sells medicines **2** an expert in chemistry

chemistry *noun*
the study of the way substances combine and react with one another

cheque *noun*
a written form instructing a bank to pay money out of an account

cherish *verb*
to cherish something is to look after it lovingly

cherry *noun* (**cherries**)
a small bright red fruit with a large stone

chess *noun*
a game for two players played with sixteen pieces each on a board of 64 squares

chest *noun*
1 a chest is a large strong box **2** your chest is the front part of your body between your neck and your waist

chess

chestnut *noun*
1 a hard brown nut **2** the tree that produces this kind of nut

chest of drawers *noun*
a piece of furniture with drawers for holding clothes

chew *verb*
to chew food is to grind it into pieces between your teeth **chewy** *adjective* chewy food is tough and needs a lot of chewing

chewing gum *noun*
a sticky flavoured gum for chewing

chick *noun*
a young bird

chicken *noun*
1 a chicken is a young hen **2** chicken is the meat of a hen used as food

chicken *adjective* (*informal*)
cowardly

chicken *verb*
to chicken out of something (*informal*) is to avoid it because you are afraid

chicken

chickenpox *noun*
a disease that produces red itchy spots on your skin

chief *noun*
1 a leader or ruler **2** the most important person, the boss

chief *adjective*
1 having the highest rank or power **2** most important

chiefly *adverb*
mainly, mostly • *Peter is the one who is chiefly to blame.*

chieftain *noun*
the chief of a tribe or clan

child noun (**children**)
1 a young person, a boy or girl
2 someone's son or daughter
• Whose child is that?
childhood noun
the time when you are a child
childish adjective
silly and immature • Don't be childish!
childminder noun
a person who is paid to look after children while their parents are out at work
childproof adjective
not able to be opened or operated by small children
• The car has childproof door locks.
chill noun
1 chill is an unpleasant feeling of being cold 2 a chill is a cold that makes you shiver
chill verb
to chill something is to make it cold
chilli noun   chillies
the hot-tasting pod of a red pepper
chilly adjective (**chillier, chilliest**)
1 slightly cold 2 unfriendly
• They went to see the head and got a chilly reception.
chime noun
a ringing sound made by a bell
chime verb
to chime is to make a ringing sound • The clock chimes every quarter-hour.
chimney noun
a tall pipe or passage that carries away smoke from a fire
chimpanzee noun
an small African ape with black fur and large eyes
chin noun
your chin is the part of your face under your mouth
china noun
china is thin and delicate pottery
chink noun
1 a narrow opening • He looked through a chink in the curtains.
2 a clinking sound • They heard the chink of coins.
chip noun
1 a small piece of something
2 a place where a small piece has been knocked off something 3 a small piece of fried potato 4 a small counter used in gambling games 5 a silicon chip
chip verb
to chip something is to knock a small piece off it by accident

chirp verb
to chirp is to make short sharp sounds like a small bird
chisel noun
a tool with a sharp end for shaping wood or stone
chisel verb (**chiselling, chiselled**)
to chisel wood or stone is to shape or cut it with a chisel
chivalry noun
being ready to help people who are less strong than you are **chivalrous** adjective kind and helpful to people who are less strong
chlorine noun ⓐ
a chemical used to disinfect water
chlorophyll noun
the substance that makes plants green
chocolate noun
1 chocolate is a sweet brown food 2 a chocolate is a sweet made of or covered with chocolate 3 chocolate is also a sweet powder used for making drinks
choice noun
1 choice is the process of choosing or the power to choose
• I'm afraid we have no choice.
2 a choice is what someone chooses • Let me know your choice of book.
choir noun
a group of singers, especially in a church
choke verb
1 to choke on something is to be unable to breathe properly because it is stuck in your throat
2 to choke someone is to stop them breathing properly 3 to choke something is to block it up
cholera noun (say **kol**-er-a)
cholera is a severe infectious disease that affects the intestines
cholesterol noun
(say ko-**less**-te-rol)
cholesterol is a substance found in the cells of your body which helps to carry fat in the bloodstream
choose verb (**choosing, chose, chosen**)
to choose something or someone is to decide that you want them rather than any of the others
choosy adjective (**choosier, choosiest**)
(informal) a choosy person is fussy and difficult to please
chop verb (**chopping, chopped**)
1 to chop something up is to cut it into small pieces 2 to chop something is to cut or hit with a heavy blow

chop noun
1 a chopping blow 2 a small thick slice of meat
choppy adjective (**choppier, choppiest**)
a choppy sea is fairly rough with lots of small waves
chopsticks plural noun
a pair of thin sticks used for eating Chinese or Japanese food
choral adjective (say **kor**-al)
for a choir or chorus
chord noun (say kord)
a number of musical notes sounded together
chore noun (say chor)
a boring or difficult task
chorister noun (say **kor**-is-ter)
someone who sings in a choir
chorus noun (say **kor**-us)
1 a group of people singing or speaking together 2 a piece of music sung by a group of people 3 the words repeated after every verse of a song or poem
christen verb
to christen a child is to baptize it and give it a name
christening noun the ceremony at which a child is baptized
Christian noun
someone who believes in Jesus Christ
Christian adjective
to do with Christ or Christians
Christianity noun
the religion of Christians
Christmas noun
the time of celebrating the birth of Jesus Christ on 25 December
chrome or **chromium** noun ⓒ
a shiny silvery metal
chromosome noun
in living things, the part of a cell that contains the genes
chronic adjective
a chronic illness or problem is one that lasts for a long time **chronically** adverb to be chronically ill is to have a very long illness
chronicle noun
a list of events with their dates
chronological adjective
a chronological list of events is arranged in the order in which the events happened **chronologically** adverb in the order in which things happen
chrysalis noun   chrysalis
(say **kris**-a-lis)
the hard cover a caterpillar makes round itself before it turns into a butterfly or moth

47

chubby *adjective*
(**chubbier, chubbiest**)
plump and healthy

chuck *verb*
(*informal*) to chuck something is
to throw it roughly • *He chucked
a brick through the window.*

chuckle *verb*
to chuckle is to laugh quietly

chuckle *noun*
a quiet laugh

chum *noun*
(*informal*) a friend

chunk *noun*
a thick lump of something
chunky *adjective* big and thick

church *noun*
1 a church is a building where
Christians worship **2** a church
is also a particular Christian
religion, for example the Church
of England

churchyard *noun*
the ground round a church, used
as a graveyard

churn *noun*
1 a large container for milk
2 a machine for making butter

churn *verb*
to churn butter is to make it in a
churn **to churn something out**
(*informal*) is to produce lots of it
very quickly

chute *noun* (*say* shoot)
a steep channel for people or
things to slide down

chutney *noun*
a spicy mixture of fruit and
peppers in a sauce, eaten with
meat or cheese

cigarette *noun*
a small, thin roll of shredded
tobacco in thin paper for
smoking

cinder *noun*
a small piece of coal or wood
that is partly burned

cinema *noun*
a cinema is a place where people
go to see films

circle *noun*
1 a round flat shape, the shape of
a coin or wheel **2** a balcony in a
cinema or theatre

circle *verb*
1 to circle is to move in a circle
• *Vultures circled overhead.*
2 to circle a place is go round it
• *The space probe circled Mars.*

circuit *noun* (*say* **ser**-kit)
1 a circular line or journey
2 a racecourse **3** the path of
an electric current

circular *adjective*
round like a circle

circulate *verb*
to circulate is to move around
and come back to the beginning
• *Blood circulates in the body.*

circulation *noun*
1 the movement of blood around
your body **2** the number of copies
of each issue of a newspaper or
magazine that are sold

circumference *noun*
the line or distance round a circle

circumstance *noun*
a circumstance is a fact or event
that affects something • *He won
under difficult circumstances.*

circus *noun*
an entertainment with clowns,
acrobats, and sometimes
animals, usually performed
in a large tent

cistern *noun*
a water tank

citizen *noun*
a citizen of a place is someone
who was born there or who lives
there

citizenship *noun*
1 the citizenship of a country is
the right to live there and be a
citizen of it • *She has applied for
American citizenship.* **2** citizenship
is also the duties a person has
when they are the citizen of a
country • *The school has lessons
in citizenship.*

citrus fruit *noun*
citrus fruits are juicy fruits with
a tough skin, such as oranges,
lemons, limes, and grapefruit

city *noun* (**cities**)
a large or important town

civic *adjective*
to do with a city or its citizens

civil *adjective*
1 to do with the citizens of a
place **2** to do with the ordinary
people and not those who are in
the armed forces **3** a civil person
is polite and courteous to other
people

civilian *noun*
someone who is an ordinary
citizen and not in the armed forces

civilization *noun*
a civilization is a society or
culture at a particular time in
history • *They were learning
about the Bronze Age civilization.*

civilize *verb*
to civilize someone is to improve
their education and manners

civil rights *plural noun*
people's civil rights are their
rights as citizens to have freedom
and fair treatment, and to vote
in elections

civil service *noun*
the civil service is all the officials
who do the work the government
needs to do to run the country

civil war *noun*
a war fought between people of
the same country, such as the

English Civil War (1642–51) or
the American Civil War (1861–65)

clad *adjective*
clothed or covered • *The story
was about a knight clad in shining
armour.*

claim *verb*
1 to claim something is to ask for
it when you think it belongs to
you • *You can claim the money
for your train fare.* **2** to claim
something is to state or assert it
• *They claimed they had been at
home all evening.*

claim *noun*
1 an act of claiming
2 something claimed

clam *noun*
a large shellfish

clams

clamber *verb*
to clamber is to climb up or
over something difficult
using your hands and feet
• *We clambered over the
slippery rocks.*

clammy *adjective* (**clammier,
clammiest**)
damp and slimy

clamp *noun*
a device for holding things
together

clamp *verb*
to clamp something is to fit a
clamp on it

clan *noun*
a number of families with the
same ancestor • *The Scottish
clans include the Campbells and
the MacDonalds.*

clang *verb*
to clang is to make a loud ringing
sound

clap *verb* (**clapping, clapped**)
to clap is to make a noise by
hitting the palms of your hands
together, especially to show you
like something

clap *noun*
1 a round of clapping, especially
to show you like something
• *They gave the winners a loud
clap.* **2** a clap of thunder is a
sudden sound of loud thunder

clarify *verb* (**clarifies, clarifying,
clarified**)
to clarify something is to

explain it and make it easier to understand **clarification** noun
clarification is making something clear and easier to understand

clarinet noun
a woodwind instrument with a low tone
clarinettist noun
someone who plays the clarinet

clarity noun
clarity is a clear quality • *They spoke with clarity.*

clash verb
1 to clash is to make a loud sound like cymbals banging together **2** two events clash when they happen inconveniently at the same time • *My favourite TV programmes clash at 8 o'clock tonight.* **3** two or more people clash when they have a fight or argument • *Gangs of rival supporters clashed outside the ground.* **4** colours clash when they look ugly or unattractive together
clash noun
1 a clashing sound **2** a fight or argument

clasp verb
to clasp someone or something is to hold them tightly
clasp noun
1 a device for fastening things **2** a tight grasp

class noun
1 a class is a group of similar people, animals, or things **2** a class is also a division according to how good or important something is • *Send the letter by first class post.* **3** a class is also a group of children or students who are taught together, or a lesson **4** class is a system of different ranks in society
class verb
to class things is to put them in classes or groups

classic noun
a book, film, or story that is well known and thought to be very good and important
classic adjective
1 a classic story is one that most people think is very good and important **2** very typical or common • *They made the classic mistake of leaving things to the last moment.*

clarinet

classical adjective
1 to do with Greek and Latin literature **2** classical music is serious music, often written in the past and still played
classify verb (**classifies, classifying, classified**)
to classify things is to put them in classes or groups **classification** noun a system of classifying things or putting them into groups

classmate noun
your classmates are the people in the same class as you at school

classroom noun
a room where lessons are given at a school

clatter noun
a loud noise of things being rattled or banged
clatter verb
to clatter is to make a clatter

clause noun
1 (*in grammar*) a part of a sentence that has its own verb **2** a part of a contract, treaty, or law

claw noun
one of the hard sharp nails that some birds and animals have on their feet

clay noun
clay is a sticky kind of earth, and is used for making bricks and pottery

clean adjective
1 something is clean when it does not have any dirt or stains on it **2** fresh, not yet used • *Start on a clean page.* **3** not rude or offensive • *I hope your jokes are clean ones.*
clean verb
to clean something is to make it clean

cleaner noun
1 someone who cleans rooms or offices **2** something used for cleaning **the cleaners** a firm which cleans clothes

cleanliness noun (*say* **klen**-li-nes)
the practice of keeping things clean

cleanly adverb
neatly, exactly • *He cut the brick cleanly in two.*

cleanse verb (*say* klenz)
to cleanse something is to clean it and make it pure
cleanser noun something you use to make a thing clean

clear adjective
1 easy to see or hear or understand • *He spoke with a clear voice.* **2** easy to see through • *The window in the door has clear glass.* **3** free from things that get in the way or aren't wanted • *Make sure the table's clear for dinner.*

clear adverb
1 clearly • *Speak loud and clear.* **2** completely • *He got clear away.* **3** at a distance from something • *You'd better stand clear of the gates.*
clear verb
1 to clear something is to make it free of unwanted things • *They cleared a space on the floor to sit on.* **2** to clear is to become clearer • *After the storm, the sky slowly cleared.* **3** to clear someone is to find out that they are not to blame for something people thought they had done **4** to clear something is to jump over it without touching it **to clear something out** is to empty or tidy it **to clear up** is to make things tidy

clearing noun
an open space in a wood or forest

clearly adverb
1 in a clear way • *We could see the house clearly.* **2** obviously • *They were clearly going to win.*

clef noun
a sign that shows the pitch of a stave in music

clench verb
to clench your teeth or fingers is to close them tightly

clergy plural noun
the clergy are the priests and other officials of a Christian Church
clergyman noun
clergywoman noun

clerk noun (*say* klark)
someone who works in an office to keep records and accounts and file papers

clef

clever adjective
quick to learn and understand things; skilful

cliché noun (*say* **klee**-shay)
a phrase that people use a lot, so that it doesn't mean very much

click noun
a short sharp sound • *She heard a click as someone turned on the light.*

client noun
someone who gets help or advice from a professional person such as a lawyer or architect; a customer

cliff noun
a steep rock face, especially on the coast

climate noun
the usual sort of weather in a particular area **climatic** adjective to do with the climate

climax noun
the most important or exciting part of a story or series of events

climb verb
1 to climb or climb up something is go up it 2 to climb down something is to go down it 3 to climb is to grow or rise upwards, like a tall plant or a building

climb noun
an act of climbing • It's a long climb to the top of the hill.

climber noun
someone who climbs hills and mountains for sport

cling verb
to cling to someone or something is to hold on tightly • The child was clinging to its mother.

clinic noun
a place where people see doctors for treatment or advice

clink verb
to clink is to make a short ringing sound, like a coin being dropped

clip noun
a fastener for keeping things together

clip verb
1 to clip things together is to fasten them with a clip 2 to clip something is to cut it with shears or scissors

cloak noun
a piece of outdoor clothing, usually without sleeves, that hangs loosely from your shoulders

cloakroom noun
1 a place where you can leave coats and bags while you are visiting a building 2 a lavatory

clock noun
an instrument that shows what the time is

clockwise adverb, adjective
moving round a circle in the same direction as the hands of a clock

clockwork adjective
worked by a spring which you wind up

clog verb (**clogging, clogged**)
to clog something is to block it up accidentally

clog noun
a shoe with a wooden sole

cloister noun
a covered path that is open on one side and goes round a courtyard or along the side of a cathedral or monastery

clone noun
an animal or plant made from the cells of another animal or plant

clone verb
to clone something is to produce a clone of it

close[1] adjective (say klohss)
1 near, either in time or place • They were close to finding the answer. • The shops were quite close to their new house. 2 careful and detailed • Please pay close attention. 3 tight; with little empty space • They got the wardrobe in but it was a close fit. 4 having a strong relationship • The boys had been close friends for years. 5 a close race or finish is one in which competitors are nearly equal at the end 6 stuffy; without fresh air • It's very close in this room.

close[1] adverb (say klohss)
at a close distance • The children were following close behind.

close[1] noun (say klohss)
1 a street that is closed at one end 2 an enclosed area, especially round a cathedral

close[2] verb (say klohz)
1 to close something is to shut it 2 to close an event or meeting is to finish it **to close down** is to stop doing business • Several shops in the High Street have closed down recently. **to close in** is to get nearer • The police closed in around the house.

closely adverb (say **klohss**-li)
1 carefully, with attention • His friends were watching closely. 2 tightly • The box was closely packed with toys.

close-up noun (say **klohss**-up)
a photograph or film taken at short range

clot noun
a mass of thick liquid like blood or cream that has become nearly solid

clot verb (**clotting, clotted**)
to clot is to form into clots, like blood or cream

cloth noun
1 cloth is material woven from wool, cotton, or some other fabric 2 a cloth is a piece of this material 3 a cloth is also a tablecloth

clothe verb
to clothe someone is to put clothes on them

clothes plural noun
clothes are the things you wear to cover your body

clothing noun
clothing is the clothes you wear

cloud noun
1 a mass of water vapour floating in the air 2 a mass of smoke or something else dense in the air

cloud verb
to cloud or cloud over is to become full of clouds • In the afternoon the sky clouded over. **cloudless** adjective a cloudless sky does not have any clouds

cloudy adjective (**cloudier, cloudiest**)
1 full of clouds 2 hard to see through • The glass contained a cloudy liquid.

clout verb
to clout someone is to give them a hard blow

clove noun
the dried bud of a tropical tree used as a spice, especially to flavour apples

clover noun
a small wild plant, usually with leaves in three parts

clown noun
1 a circus performer who dresses up and wears bright face paint and does silly things to make people laugh 2 an amusing or silly person

clown verb
to clown is to behave like a clown

clown

club noun
1 a heavy stick 2 a stick for playing golf 3 a group of people who meet together because they are interested in the same thing 4 a playing card with a black clover-leaf printed on it

club verb (**clubbing, clubbed**)
to club someone is to hit them hard with a heavy stick **to club together** is to join with other people in doing something, especially raising money

cluck verb
to cluck is to make a noise like a hen

clue noun
something that helps you to solve a puzzle or a mystery

clump noun
a cluster of trees or plants

clumsy adjective (**clumsier, clumsiest**)
a clumsy person is careless and awkward, and likely to knock things over or drop things
clumsily adverb
clumsiness noun

cluster *noun*
a group of people or things close together

clutch¹ *verb*
to clutch something or clutch at something is to grab hold of it

clutch¹ *noun*
1 a tight grasp **2** a device for disconnecting the engine of a motor vehicle from its gears and wheels

clutch² *noun*
a set of eggs in a nest

clutter *verb*
to clutter a place up is to make it untidy or messy

clutter *noun*
clutter is a lot of things left around untidily

cm
short for centimetre or centimetres

Co.
short for company

coach *noun*
1 a comfortable single-deck bus used for long journeys **2** a carriage of a railway train **3** a carriage pulled by horses **4** a person who trains or instructs people in a sport or skill

coach *verb*
to coach someone is to instruct or train them in a sport or skill

coal *noun*
coal is a hard black mineral used as fuel

coarse *adjective*
1 rough, not delicate or smooth **2** rude or offensive • *You have a very coarse sense of humour.*

coast *noun*
the seashore and the land close to it

coast *verb*
to coast is to ride downhill without using power • *They stopped pedalling and coasted down the slope.*

coastal *adjective*
by the coast or near the coast

coastguard *noun*
someone whose job is to keep watch on coasts

coastline *noun*
the edge of the land by the sea

coat *noun*
1 a piece of clothing with sleeves that covers most of the body and is worn outdoors over other clothes **2** a layer of paint

coat *verb*
to coat something is to cover it with a coating

coating *noun*
a covering or layer, especially of paint

coat of arms *noun*
a design on a shield or building, representing a historic family or town

coax *verb*
to coax someone is to persuade them gently or patiently

cobbler *noun*
someone whose job is to mend shoes

cobbles *plural noun*
cobbles are a surface of cobblestones on a road
cobbled paved with cobbles

cobblestone *noun*
a small smooth and rounded stone sometimes used in large numbers to pave roads in towns

cobra *noun* (say **koh**-bra)
a poisonous snake

cobweb *noun*
a net of thin sticky threads that spiders spin to catch insects

cock *noun*
a male bird, especially a male fowl

cock *verb*
1 to cock your eye or ear is to turn it in a particular direction **2** to cock a gun is to make it ready to fire

cockerel *noun*
a young male fowl

cockle *noun*
an edible shellfish

cockney *noun*
1 a cockney is someone born in the East End of London **2** cockney is a kind of English spoken by people from this part of London

cockpit *noun*
the place in an aircraft where the pilot sits

cockroach *noun*
a dark brown insect

cocky *adjective*
(*informal*) conceite and cheeky

cocoa *noun*
1 a hot drink that tastes of chocolate **2** the powder from which you make this drink

cockroach

coconut *noun*
a large round nut containing a milky juice, that grows on palm trees

cocoon *noun*
the covering round a chrysalis

cod *noun*
a large edible sea fish

code *noun*
1 a set of signs and letters for sending messages secretly **2** a set of rules • *the Highway Code* • *a code of behaviour*

code *verb*
to code a message is to use special signs and letters, so that other people cannot understand it

co-education *noun*
the teaching of boys and girls together **co-educational** *adjective* a co-educational school or system is one that teaches boys and girls together

coffee *noun*
1 a hot drink made from the roasted and crushed beans of a tropical plant **2** the powder from which you make this drink

coffin *noun*
a long box in which a dead body is buried or cremated

cog *noun*
one of a number of pieces sticking out from the edge of a wheel and allowing it to drive another wheel

coil *noun*
a circle or spiral of rope or wire

coil *verb*
to coil something is to wind it into circles or spirals

coin *noun*
a piece of metal money

coin *verb*
to coin a new word is to invent it

coinage *noun*
a country's coinage is the system of money that it uses

coincide *verb*
to coincide is to happen at the same time as something else • *My birthday always seems to coincide with exams.*

coincidence *noun*
coincidence, or a coincidence, is when two things can happen by chance at the same time

coke *noun*
coke is a solid fuel made out of coal

cola *noun*
cola is a sweet brown fizzy drink

cold *adjective*
1 low in temperature, not hot or warm **2** a cold person is unfriendly and distant

cold *noun*
1 cold weather or temperature **2** a cold is an illness that makes your nose run and gives you a sore throat

coldly *adverb* to act coldly is to be very unfriendly

coldness *noun* coldness is being unfriendly

cold-blooded *adjective*
1 having blood that

changes temperature according to the surroundings **2** cruel, ruthless

coleslaw *noun*
a salad made of chopped cabbage covered in mayonnaise

collaborate *verb*
people collaborate when they work together or share their information **collaboration** *noun* working with someone or sharing information with them

collage *noun*
(*say* **kol**-ahzh *or say* kol-**ahzh**)
a picture made by arranging scraps of paper and other things on a card

collapse *verb*
1 to collapse is to fall or break into pieces because of too much weight **2** someone collapses when they fall from being very weak or ill

collapsible *adjective*
a collapsible piece of furniture or equipment can be folded up into a smaller space

collar *noun*
1 the part of a piece of clothing that goes round your neck **2** a band that goes round an animal's neck

colleague *noun*
someone's colleague is a person they work with

collect *verb*
1 to collect things is to get them together from various places, especially as a hobby • *She collects stamps, and I collect coins.* **2** to collect someone or something is to go and get them **collector** *noun* someone who collects things for a hobby

collection *noun*
1 things you have collected as a hobby **2** money given by people at a meeting or concert or service

college *noun*
a place where people continue to study after they have left school

collide *verb*
to collide with something is to hit it while moving • *The bicycle collided with the car.*

collision *noun*
a crash between moving vehicles • *There has been a collision on the motorway.*

colon *noun*
a punctuation mark (:) used to separate parts of a sentence or before items in a list

colonel *noun* (*say* **ker**-nel)
a senior army officer

colonial *adjective*
from or to do with a country's colonies abroad

colony *noun*
1 a country that another country governs and sends people out to live there **2** a group of people or animals living together

colossal *adjective*
huge, enormous

colour *noun*   colours
1 the quality of being red, green, blue, and so on, produced by rays of light of different wavelengths **2** the use of all colours, not just black and white • *Is this film in colour?* **3** the colour of someone's skin **4** a substance used to give colour to things

colour *verb*
to colour something is to give it a colour or colours with paints or crayons

colour-blind *adjective*
not able to see or distinguish between some colours, usually red and green

colourful *adjective*
1 having a lot of bright colours **2** lively • *The film was a colourful story of life on board a pirate ship.*

colt *noun*
a young male horse

column *noun*
1 a pillar **2** something long and narrow • *They could see a column of smoke in the distance.* **3** a strip of printing in a book or newspaper **4** a regular feature in a newspaper • *He always read the sports column.*

coma *noun* (*say* **koh**-ma)
someone is in a coma when they are unconscious for a long time

comb *noun*
1 a tool with teeth for making the hair tidy **2** the red, fleshy crest on a fowl's head

comb *verb*
1 to comb your hair is to tidy it with a comb **2** to comb an area is to search it carefully for something lost • *We combed the woods all day but couldn't find our dog.*

combat *noun*
a fight or contest

combat *verb*
to combat something bad or unpleasant is to fight it and try to get rid of it • *The police force combats crime.*

combination *noun*
1 combination is joining or mixing things **2** a combination is a group of things that have been joined or mixed together

combine *verb* (*say* kom-**byn**)
to combine things is to join them or mix them together

combine harvester *noun*
a machine that cuts and threshes the grain in the fields

combustion *noun*
combustion is what happens when something burns

come *verb* (**coming, came, come**)
1 to come is to move towards the person or place that is here, and is the opposite of **go** • *Do you want to come to my house?* • *Has that letter come yet?* **2** to come is also to occur or be present • *The pictures come at the end of the book.* **to come about** is to happen **to come to something** is to add up to it • *The bill came to £50.* **to come true** is to actually happen • *Their holiday was a dream come true.*

comedian *noun*
someone who entertains people with humour and jokes

comedy *noun* (**comedies**)
1 a comedy is a play or film that makes people laugh **2** comedy is using humour to make people laugh

comet *noun*
an object moving across the sky with a bright tail of light

comfort *noun*
1 comfort is a feeling of relief from worry or pain **2** your comforts are the things you have around you that you enjoy and that make life pleasant

comfort *verb*
to comfort someone is to make them feel happier when they are feeling sad or worried

comfortable *adjective*   comic
1 pleasant to use or wear • *a comfortable chair* **2** free from worry or pain • *The nurse made the patient comfortable.*
comfortably *adverb*

comic *noun*
1 a children's magazine that has stories with pictures **2** a comedian

comical *adjective*
funny, making people laugh
comically *adverb*

comic strip *noun*
a series of drawings that tell a story

comma *noun*
a punctuation mark (,) used to mark a pause in a sentence or between items in a list

command *noun*
1 a command is

an instruction telling someone to do something **2** command is authority or control • *Who has command of these soldiers?* **3** a command of a subject is the skill or ability to understand it • *She has a good command of Spanish.*

command *verb*
1 to command someone is to tell them to do something **2** to command a group of people is to be in charge of them • *A centurion commanded a hundred soldiers.*

commander *noun*
someone who commands, especially a senior naval officer

commandment *noun*
a sacred command, especially one of the Ten Commandments of Moses

commando *noun*
a soldier trained for making dangerous raids

commemorate *verb*
to commemorate a past event is to do something special so that people remember it **commemoration** *noun*

commence *verb*
to commence something is to begin it **commencement** *noun* the beginning of something

comment *noun*
a remark or opinion

commentary *noun* (**commentaries**)
a description of an event by someone who is watching it, especially for radio or television

commentator *noun*
a person who gives a commentary, especially of a sports event

commerce *noun*
commerce is trade, or buying and selling goods

commercial *adjective*
1 connected with trade and making money **2** paid for by advertising • *a commercial radio station*

commercial *noun*
an advertisement, especially on television or radio

commit *verb* (**committing, committed**)
to commit a crime is to do something against the law

commitment *noun*
1 commitment is being determined to do something **2** a commitment is something you have promised to do

committee *noun*
a group of people who meet to organize or discuss something

common *adjective*
1 ordinary or usual • *The dandelion is a common plant.*

2 happening or used often • *Traffic jams are common where we live.* **3** shared by many people • *The story was common knowledge.* • *Music was their common interest.*

common *noun*
a piece of open land that anyone can use

commonplace *adjective*
ordinary, familiar

commonwealth *noun*
a group of countries cooperating together **the Commonwealth** an association of Britain and various other countries, such as Canada, Australia, and New Zealand

commotion *noun*
an uproar • *Suddenly he could hear a commotion in the kitchen.*

commune *noun*
a group of people who live in the same house and share the money and work

communicate *verb*
to communicate news or information is to pass it on to other people **communicative** *adjective* a communicative person is willing to talk to people and give them information

communication *noun*
1 communication is giving people useful information and telling them about things that have happened **2** a communication is a message or piece of information that someone gives you **3** communication is also a form of technology for passing on information, for example television and text messaging

Communion *noun*
Communion is the Christian ceremony in which holy bread and wine are given to worshippers

communism *noun*
communism is a political belief that everyone should share the wealth of a country and the state should control its industry and resources **communist** *noun* someone who believes in communism

community *noun* (**communities**)
the people living in one area

commuter *noun*
someone who travels to work every day by train or bus **commute** *verb* to commute is to travel to work every day

compact *adjective*
small and neat

compact disc *noun*
a small plastic and metal disc on which music or information

is stored as digital signals and is read by a laser beam. Usually called CD.

companion *noun*
a companion is someone who spends a lot of time with you **companionship** *noun* companionship is being with someone and enjoying their friendship

company *noun* (**companies**)
1 a company is a group of people, especially a business firm **2** company is having people with you • *Jill was lonely and longed for some company.* **3** a company is an army unit consisting of two or more platoons

comparatively *adverb*
in comparison, relatively • *They all went to bed comparatively late.*

compare *verb*
1 to compare things is to see how they are similar • *Compare your answers.* **2** to compare with something is to be as good as it • *Our football pitch cannot compare with Wembley Stadium.*

comparison *noun*
comparison, or a comparison, is thinking about several things and seeing how they are similar or different

compartment *noun*
a special place or section where you can put something • *The coach had a luggage compartment under the floor.*

compass *noun*
an instrument with a magnetized needle that shows which direction you are facing **compasses** or **pair of compasses** a device for drawing circles

compassion *noun*
compassion is pity or mercy you show to people who are suffering **compassionate** *adjective* showing pity or mercy to people who are suffering

compass

compatible *adjective*
1 people are compatible when they are able to live or exist together without trouble **2** machines and devices are compatible when they can be used together

compel *verb* (**compelling, compelled**)
to compel someone to do something is to force them to do it

a b c d e f g h i j k l m n o p q r s t u v w x y z

compensate *verb*
to compensate someone is to give them something to make up for something they have lost or suffered **compensation** *noun* compensation is something given to someone to make up for a loss or injury

compete *verb*
to compete in a competition is to take part in it and try to win it

competent *adjective*
having the skill or knowledge to do something well • *He is not competent to teach French.* **competence** *noun* the ability to do something well

competition *noun*
a game or race in which you try to do better than other people **competitive** *adjective* a competitive person enjoys competing with other people **competitor** *noun* someone who competes in a game or race, or a rival in business

compile *verb*
to compile information is to collect and arrange it, especially in a book • *She compiled a collection of children's poems.* **compilation** *noun* a collection of information, stories, or poems that someone has compiled **compiler** *noun* someone who compiles something

complacent *adjective*
smugly satisfied with the way things are, without wanting to improve them

complain *verb*
to complain about something is to say that you are not pleased about it

complaint *noun*
1 you make a complaint when you are not pleased about something **2** you suffer from a complaint when you are slightly ill

complete *adjective*
1 having all its parts, with nothing missing • *I hope the tool kit is complete.* **2** finished, achieved • *By evening the jigsaw puzzle was complete.* **3** utter, total • *It came as a complete surprise.*

complete *verb*
to complete something is to finish it or make it complete **completion** *noun* the completing of something, the finish • *The work is nearing completion.*

completely *adverb*
totally, utterly • *You are completely wrong.*

complex *adjective*
difficult and complicated **complexity** *noun* being difficult or complicated

complex *noun*
a group of buildings, such as a sports centre

complexion *noun*
the colour or appearance of your skin

complicate *verb*
to complicate something is to make it difficult or awkward

complicated *adjective*
difficult to understand or cope with because it has so many parts or details

complication *noun*
a new problem that makes something else more difficult

compliment *noun*
words or actions that show you approve of a person or thing

complimentary *adjective*
1 praising someone or saying good things about them • *She liked Neil's work and was very complimentary about him.* **2** given to someone free of charge • *I enclose two complimentary tickets for our next production.*

component *noun*
one of the parts that a machine is made of

compose *verb*
1 to compose music or poetry is to write it **2** to be composed of several people or things is to be made up of them • *The class is composed of children up to the age of 8.* **composer** *noun* someone who writes music

composition *noun*
1 composition is composing or writing something **2** a composition is a piece of music or an essay

compost *noun*
compost is a mixture of decayed leaves, grass, and other natural refuse, and is used as manure

compost

compound[1] *noun*
1 a substance that is made of two or more parts or ingredients **2** (*grammar*) a word that is made from two or more other words, such as *bathroom* and *newspaper*

compound[2] *noun*
a fenced area containing buildings

comprehend *verb*
to comprehend something is to understand it

comprehension *noun*
1 comprehension is understanding **2** a comprehension is an exercise that tests or helps your understanding of a language

comprehensive school *noun*
a secondary school for children of all abilities

compress *verb*
1 to compress something is to press it or squeeze it together **2** to be compressed is to be forced into a small space **compression** *noun* compression is pressing or squeezing something

comprise *verb*
to comprise several people or things is to include them • *A football team comprises eleven players.*

compromise *verb*
(*say* **kom**-pro-myz)
to compromise is to accept less than you really wanted, especially so as to settle a disagreement

compromise *noun*
(*say* **kom**-pro-myz)
accepting less than you really wanted

compulsory *adjective*
something is compulsory when you have to do it • *Wearing seat belts is compulsory.*

computer *noun*
an electronic machine that does word processing and rapid calculations, sorts data, and can control other machines

comrade *noun*
a friend or companion **comradeship** *noun* enjoying other people's company, friendship

con *verb*
(**conning, conned**)
(*informal*) to con someone is to swindle them

concave *adjective*
a concave surface is curved

like the inside of a circle or ball. The opposite of convex.

conceal verb
to conceal something is to hide it carefully or cleverly **concealment** noun concealment is hiding something carefully

conceit noun
conceit is thinking a lot about how clever or attractive you are **conceited** adjective a conceited person thinks a lot of themselves and is vain and proud

conceive verb
1 to conceive an idea or plan is to form it in your mind **2** a woman conceives when she becomes pregnant

concentrate verb
1 to concentrate on something is to think hard about it **2** to concentrate people or things is to bring them together in one place **concentrated** adjective a liquid is concentrated when it is made stronger by having water removed from it

concentration noun
concentration is thinking hard about something

concept noun
a new idea about something

conception noun
1 conception is forming an idea in your mind **2** conception is also when a woman becomes pregnant

concern verb
1 to concern someone is to be important or interesting to them **2** to concern something is to be about a particular subject • This story concerns a shipwreck. **3** to worry someone

concern noun
1 something that matters to someone • I think that is my concern. **2** a business

concerning preposition
on the subject of; in connection with • Do you have any information concerning his disappearance?

concert noun
a performance of music

concertina noun
a portable musical instrument that you squeeze to push air past reeds

concerto noun (say kon-**cher**-toh)
a piece of music for a solo instrument and an orchestra • a violin concerto

concise adjective
giving a lot of information in a few words

conclude verb
1 to conclude something is to end it **2** to conclude something is

also to decide about it • The jury concluded that he was not guilty.

conclusion noun
1 the ending of something **2** a decision that you reach after a lot of thought

concrete noun
cement mixed with water and gravel or sand and used in building

concussion noun
a temporary injury to the brain that is caused by a hard knock and leaves you feeling dizzy or unconscious

condemn verb
1 to condemn someone or something is to say that you strongly disapprove of them **2** to condemn criminals is to sentence them to a punishment • He was condemned to death. **3** to condemn a building is to declare that it is not fit to be used **condemnation** noun condemnation is saying that you blame someone or something or do not approve of them

condensation noun
drops of liquid formed from vapour that has condensed

condense verb
1 to condense a piece of writing is to make it shorter **2** to condense is to change into water or other liquid • Steam condenses on cold windows.

condition noun
1 the state in which a person or thing is • This bike is in good condition. **2** something that must happen if something else is to happen • Learning to swim is a condition of going sailing. • You can come on condition that you bring your sister too.

conduct verb (say kon-**dukt**)
1 to conduct someone is to lead or guide them **2** to conduct something is to organize it or carry it out • I decided to conduct a little experiment. **3** to conduct an orchestra or band is to direct it in a piece of music **4** to conduct electricity or heat is to allow it to pass along • Copper conducts electricity well.

conduct noun (say **kon**-dukt)
a person's conduct is their behaviour

conduction noun
the conducting of electricity or heat

conductor noun
1 someone who conducts an orchestra or band **2** something that conducts electricity or heat **3** someone who collects the fares on a bus or coach

cone noun
1 an object which is circular at one end and pointed at the other end **2** an ice cream cornet **3** the fruit of a pine, fir, or cedar

confectionery noun
sweets that a shop sells

conference noun
a meeting for discussion

confess verb
to confess to something wrong or embarrassing is to admit that you have done it

confession noun
an act of admitting that you have committed a crime or done wrong • The burglar made a full confession.

confetti plural noun
tiny bits of coloured paper thrown at the bride and bridegroom after a wedding

confide verb
to confide in someone   confetti
is to tell them a secret

confidence noun
1 you have confidence when you are sure that you are right or can do something **2** confidence in someone is trusting or believing them **in confidence** as a secret • He told me all this in confidence.

confident adjective
1 being sure that you are right or can do something **2** certain that something will happen • We are confident it will be an enjoyable day.

confidential adjective
information is confidential when it has to be kept secret **confidentially** adverb in confidence, as a secret

confine verb
1 to confine something is to restrict or limit it • Please confine your comments to points of fact. **2** to confine someone is to lock them up or shut them in a place **confinement** noun confinement is being locked up or shut in

confirm verb
1 to confirm something is to say that it is true or to show that it is true **2** to confirm an arrangement is to make it definite • Please write to confirm your order.

confirmation noun
a fact or piece of information that shows something is true or has happened • You will receive confirmation of your booking by email.

confiscate verb
to confiscate something is to take it away from someone as a punishment **confiscation** noun confiscation is taking something from someone as a punishment

a b c d e f g h i j k l m n o p q r s t u v w x y z

conflict noun (say **kon**-flikt)
a fight or disagreement
• the conflict in the Middle East
• a conflict between the unions
and the bosses
conflict verb (say kon-**flikt**)
two things conflict when they
contradict or disagree with one
another • The two accounts of the
incident conflict.
conform verb
to conform is to follow other
people's rules or ideas about
something
confront verb
1 to confront someone is to
challenge them face to face for
a fight or argument • The police
decided to confront the criminals
there and then. **2** to confront a
problem or difficulty is to deal
with it firmly and positively
confrontation noun meeting
someone face to face for a fight
or argument
confuse verb
1 to confuse someone is to
make them puzzled or muddled
2 to confuse things is to mistake
one thing for another
confusing adjective difficult to
understand, muddling
confusion noun confusion is
being confused or muddled
congratulate verb
to congratulate someone is to
tell them how pleased you are
about something they have done
congratulations plural noun
congratulations are words that
tell someone how well they have
done
congregation noun
the people who take part in a
church service
congress noun
a large meeting or conference
Congress the parliament or
government of the USA
conical adjective
shaped like a cone
conifer noun (say **kon**-i-fer)
an evergreen tree with cones
coniferous adjective a coniferous
tree has cones
conjunction noun
a word that joins other words and
parts of a sentence, e.g. and, but,
and whether
conjure verb
to conjure is to perform tricks
that look like magic **conjurer**
noun someone who performs
magic tricks
conker noun
a hard and shiny
brown nut
that grows on a
horse chestnut

conkers

tree **conkers** a game played with
conkers threaded on pieces of
string
connect verb
to connect things is to join them
together
connection noun
1 a link between things **2** joining
together
conquer verb
to conquer a people or country
is to defeat them and take
them over • William I conquered
England. • He managed to
conquer all his fears. **conqueror**
noun someone who conquers a
country and takes it over
conquest noun
a victory over another country or
people
conscience noun (say **kon**-shens)
a feeling people have about what
is right or wrong
conscientious adjective
(say kon-shee-**en**-shus)
careful and hard-working
conscientiously adverb
conscious adjective (say **kon**-shus)
1 awake and knowing what is
happening **2** aware of something
• Are you conscious of the danger
you are in? **3** deliberate • She
has made a conscious effort to
improve. **consciously** adverb
consciousness noun being aware
of what is happening
conscription noun
conscription is a system of
making young people join the
army for a time
consecutive adjective
things are consecutive when they
come one after another in a list
or sequence
consent noun
consent is agreement or
permission
consent verb
to consent to something is to
agree to it or permit it
consequence noun
something which happens
because of an event or action
• His injury was the consequence of
an accident. **of no consequence**
not very important **to take
or suffer the consequences**
is to accept any unpleasant
results from something you do
consequently adverb as a result
conservation noun
conservation is keeping
buildings and natural
surroundings in
a good state
conservationist
noun someone who
takes an interest in
conservation

Conservative noun
someone who supports the
Conservative Party, a British
political party
conservative adjective
1 a conservative person doesn't
like change and wants things to
stay the same **2** a conservative
estimate or guess is a careful or
cautious one
conservatory noun
(**conservatories**)
a room built on the back or side
of a house, with glass walls and a
glass roof
conserve verb
to conserve something is to keep
it from being changed or spoilt
consider verb
1 to consider something is to
think carefully about it **2** to
consider something is also to
believe it • We consider that
people should be allowed to follow
their own religion.
considerable adjective
large or important • The
journey takes a considerable time.
considerably adverb very much
• Her new house is considerably
larger.
considerate adjective
kind and thoughtful towards
other people
consideration noun
1 consideration is careful
thought or attention **2** a
consideration is a serious thought
or reason • Money is a major
consideration in this plan. **to take
something into consideration**
is to think carefully about it
when you are making a decision
considering preposition
in view of • The car goes well,
considering its age.
consist verb
to consist of something is to
be made from it • The meal
consisted of pasta and cheese.
consistency noun (**consistencies**)
1 consistency is being the same
2 the consistency of a liquid is
how thick it is
consistent adjective
1 always the same, regular
2 always acting in the same
way **consistently** adverb in the
same way, without changing
• He consistently misspells
'accommodation'.
consolation noun
consolation is comfort or
sympathy given to someone
console verb
to console someone is to give
them comfort or sympathy
consonant noun
a letter that is not a vowel

The consonants in the English alphabet are b, c, d, f, g, h, j, k, l, m, n, p, q, r, s, t, v, w, x, y, z.

conspicuous *adjective*
something conspicuous stands out and is easy to see or notice

conspiracy *noun* (**conspiracies**)
a plot to do something bad or illegal **conspirator** *noun* someone who joins a conspiracy

constant *adjective*
1 not changing; continual 2 a constant person is loyal and faithful

constant *noun*
(*in science and mathematics*) a number or quantity that does not change **constancy** *noun* constancy is beng loyal and faithful **constantly** *adverb* continually, all the time • *They are constantly complaining.*

constellation *noun*
a group of stars that you can see in the sky at night

constellation

constipated *adjective*
someone is constipated when they cannot empty their bowels easily to get rid of the waste in their body **constipation** *noun* being constipated

constituency *noun* (**constituencies**)
a district of the country that chooses its own Member of Parliament

constitute *verb*
to constitute something is to form it or make it up • *50 states constitute the USA.*

constitution *noun*
1 the set of principles or laws by which a country is governed 2 a person's condition or state of health **constitutional** *adjective* to do with a constitution

construct *verb*
to construct something is to build it

construction *noun*
1 construction is the process of building 2 a construction is something that someone has built

constructive *adjective*
helpful and positive • *Their criticism was very constructive.*

consult *verb*
to consult a person or book is to look for information or advice **consultation** *noun* a meeting with someone for information or advice

consultant *noun*
1 a person who provides professional advice 2 a senior hospital doctor

consume *verb*
1 to consume food or drink is to eat or drink it 2 to consume something is to use it up or destroy it • *The building was consumed by fire.*

consumer *noun*
someone who buys goods or services

consumption *noun*
the using up of food or fuel • *The consumption of oil has increased.*

contact *noun*
1 contact is touching someone or something 2 contact is also communication • *I've lost contact with my uncle.* 3 a contact is a person to communicate with

contact *verb*
to contact someone is to get in touch with them

contact lens *noun*
a small plastic lens worn against the eyeball instead of glasses

contagious *adjective* (*say* kon-**tay**-jus)
you catch a contagious disease by having contact with people or things that are already infected with it

contain *verb*
to contain something is to have it inside • *This book contains a great deal of information.*

container *noun*
1 something that is designed to contain things 2 a large box-shaped container for taking goods abroad by sea

contaminate *verb*
to contaminate something is to make it dirty or impure **contamination** *noun* making something dirty or impure

contemplate *verb*
1 to contemplate something is to look hard at it or think about it 2 to contemplate doing something is to plan or intend to do it **contemplation** *noun* thinking hard and seriously about something

contemporary *adjective*
1 people or things are contemporary when they belong to the same time • *Florence*

Nightingale was contemporary with Queen Victoria. 2 modern or up to date • *The shop sells contemporary furniture.*

contempt *noun*
a feeling of strong disapproval when you despise someone or something **contemptible** *adjective* deserving contempt **contemptuous** *adjective* showing or feeling contempt

contend *verb*
1 to contend is to struggle or compete 2 to contend something is to state or claim it • *We contend that the company was guilty of negligence.* **contender** *noun* someone who takes part in a competition

content[1] *noun* (*say* **kon**-tent)
1 the amount of a substance that there is in something • *Drink milk with a low fat content.* 2 the content of a book, magazine, or piece of writing is what you read in it

content[2] *adjective* (*say* kon-**tent**)
happy and willing • *Are you content to stay behind?* **contentment** *noun* contentment is being happy

contented *adjective* (*say* kon-**tent**-id)
happy and satisfied • *After his big dinner he looked very contented.*

contents *plural noun* (*say* **kon**-tents)
1 the contents of a box or other container are what is inside it 2 the contents of a book or magazine are the things you read in it

contest *noun* (*say* **kon**-test)
a competition

contest *verb* (*say* kon-**test**)
to contest something is to argue about it • *After her death, relatives contested her will.*

contestant *noun* (*say* kon-**test**-ant)
someone who takes part in a contest or competition

continent *noun*
one of the main masses of land in the world. The continents are Africa, Antarctica, Asia, Australia, Europe, North America, and South America. **the Continent** the mainland of Europe from the point of view of people living in Britain

continual *adjective*
happening repeatedly • *I get fed up with his continual shouting.* **continually** *adverb* repeatedly, often

continue *verb*
to continue something, or to continue to do something, is to

go on doing it **continuation** *noun* continuing something

continuous *adjective*
going on all the time; without a break • *We could hear a continuous hum from the fridge.*
continuity *noun* the process of going on without any breaks or changes **continuously** *adverb* all the time

contour *noun*
1 the contour of something is its shape or outline 2 a line on a map joining points that are the same height above sea level

contract *noun* (say **kon**-trakt)
a written legal agreement
contract *verb* (say kon-**trakt**)
1 to contract is to become smaller • *Heated metal contracts as it cools.*
2 to contract to do something is to make a contract about it
3 to contract an illness is to catch it • *She contracted pneumonia.*
contraction *noun* contraction is getting smaller or shorter

contradict *verb*
to contradict someone or something is to say they are wrong or untrue **contradiction** *noun* saying that someone or something is wrong or untrue
contradictory *adjective* a contradictory statement says the opposite of what someone has just said

contraption *noun*
a clumsy or strange-looking device or machine

contrary *adjective*
1 (say **kon**-tra-ri) one thing is contrary to another when they are opposites or contradict one another • *Contrary to popular belief, Viking helmets didn't have horns.* 2 (say kon-**trair**-i) someone who is contrary is obstinate and difficult to deal with • *Mary, Mary, quite contrary.*
on the contrary the opposite is true • *Are you pleased? On the contrary, I'm very annoyed.*

contrast *verb* (say kon-**trahst**)
1 to contrast two things is to show they are different 2 one thing contrasts with another when it is clearly different
contrast *noun* (say **kon**-trahst)
a clear difference between things

contribute *verb*
1 to contribute to something is to give money to help it 2 to contribute to a result is to help cause it • *His tiredness contributed to the accident.* **contribution** *noun* money or help that someone gives towards something **contributor** *noun* someone who gives money or help

control *noun*
1 control is the power to make someone or something do what you want 2 the controls of a machine are the switches and levers that make it work
to be in control is to have power or control over people or things
control *verb* (**controlling, controlled**)
to control something or someone is to have power over what they do **controller** *noun* someone who controls or organizes something

controversial *adjective*
a controversial action or statement is one that is likely to cause people to have strong opinions and disagree about it
controversy *noun* (**controversies**) (say kon-**tro**-ver-si or say **kon**-trov-er-si)
a long argument or disagreement

conundrum *noun*
a riddle

convalescent *adjective*
recovering from an illness
convalescence *noun* a period of recovery after an illness

convenience *noun*
1 convenience is usefulness and comfort 2 a convenience is something that is useful, such as central heating 3 a convenience is also a public lavatory
to do something at your convenience is to do it when it suits you

convenient *adjective*
easy to use or reach
conveniently *adverb* in a convenient way

convent *noun*
a group of buildings where nuns live and work

conventional *adjective*
done in the accepted way; usual, traditional **conventionally** *adverb* in a conventional way, traditionally

converge *verb*
to converge is to come together from different directions • *The two roads converge at the pub.* • *Thousands of fans converged on the football ground.*

conversation *noun*
when you talk to someone for a while **conversational** *adjective* to do with conversation, like conversation • *Use a conversational style of writing.*

conversion *noun*
changing or converting something

convert *verb* (say kon-**vert**)
1 to convert something is to change it so it is suitable for

a new purpose 2 to convert someone is to persuade them to change their religion or beliefs
convert *noun* (say **kon**-vert)
someone who has changed their beliefs **convertible** *adjective* something is convertible when it can be changed from one form or shape to another

convex *adjective*
a convex surface is curved like the outside of a circle or ball. The opposite of concave.

convey *verb*
1 to convey someone or something is to take them somewhere 2 to convey a message or idea is to get someone to understand it

convict *noun* (say **kon**-vikt)
a criminal in a prison
convict *verb* (say kon-**vikt**)
to convict someone of a crime is to decide at their trial that they are guilty of it and punish them

conviction *noun*
1 being convicted of a crime 2 being convinced of something; a strong opinion

convince *verb*
to persuade someone that something is true or right

convoy *noun*
a group of ships or vehicles travelling together

cook *verb*
to cook food is to make it ready to eat by heating it
cook *noun*
someone who cooks, especially as their job

cooker *noun*
a device with an oven and hotplates for cooking food

cookery *noun*
the art or skill of cooking food

cool *adjective*
1 not very warm; fairly cold 2 a cool person is calm and not easily excited 3 (*informal*) good or fashionable • *He looks cool in those glasses.*
coolly *adverb* calmly
coolness *noun*
cool *verb*
1 to cool something is to make it cool 2 to cool is to become cool

coop *noun*
a cage for poultry

cooperate *verb*
to cooperate with people is to work helpfully with them
cooperation *noun* when people work together and help one another **cooperative** *adjective* someone who is cooperative is helpful and willing to do what people ask them

coordinate *verb*
(*say* koh-**or**-din-ayt)
to coordinate people or things
is to get them to work well
together **coordination** *noun*
the coordination of parts of
your body, for example your
hands and eyes, is making them
help each other and work well
together

cop *verb* (**copping, copped**)
(*informal*) to cop something is to
get or catch it, especially when
you don't want it • *Her brother
copped most of the blame.*
to cop it is to get into trouble

cop *noun*
(*informal*) a police officer

cope *verb*
to cope with something awkward
or difficult is to deal with it
successfully

copper *noun* Ⓒⓤ
1 copper is a reddish-brown
metal used for making wire and
pipes **2** a copper is a coin made of
copper or bronze

copy *noun* (**copies**)
1 something made to look
exactly like something else
2 something written out a
second time **3** one example of a
newspaper, magazine, or book
that is made in large numbers
• *We each have a copy of 'Alice
in Wonderland'.*

copy *verb* (**copies, copying,
copied**)
1 to copy something is to make
a copy of it **2** to copy someone is
to do the same as them **3** to copy
a computer file or piece of text is
to make another one exactly the
same **copier** *noun* a machine for
copying pages

coral *noun*
coral is a hard substance made of
the skeletons of tiny sea creatures

cord *noun*
a cord is a piece of thin rope

cordial *noun*
a sweet drink

corduroy *noun* (*say* **kor**-der-oi)
thick cotton cloth with ridges
along it

core *noun*
the part in the middle of
something

cork *noun*
1 cork is the lightweight bark of a
kind of oak tree **2** a cork is a piece
of this bark used to close a bottle

corkscrew *noun*
1 a device for removing corks
from bottles **2** a spiral

cormorant *noun*
a large black seabird

corn[1] *noun*
grain • *a field of corn*

corn[2] *noun*
a small, hard lump on your toe
or foot

corner *noun*
1 the point where two lines,
roads, or walls meet **2** a kick
from the corner of a football
field; a hit from the corner of
a hockey field

corner *verb*
1 to corner someone is to trap
them • *The police cornered the
escaped prisoner.* **2** to corner is
to go round a corner • *The car
cornered slowly and accelerated
up the road.*

cornet *noun*
1 a long cone-shaped biscuit
open at the top for ice cream
2 a musical instrument like a
trumpet

cornflakes *plural noun*
toasted maize flakes eaten
for breakfast

cornflour *noun*
fine flour used for making
puddings

corny *adjective* (**cornier, corniest**)
(*informal*) a corny joke is one that
is feeble and often repeated

coronation *noun*
the ceremony of crowning a king
or queen

coroner *noun*
an official who holds an inquiry
into the cause of an unnatural
death

corporal *noun*
a soldier just below sergeant
in rank

corporation *noun*
a group of people elected to
govern a town

corps *noun* (*say* kor)
1 a large unit of soldiers
2 a special army unit • *He is
in the Medical Corps.*

corpse *noun*
a dead body

correct *adjective*
1 true or accurate; without any
mistakes • *Your answers are all
correct.* **2** proper, suitable
• *Is that the correct way to talk to
your parents?* **correctly** *adverb* to
do something correctly is to do
it the right way and without any
mistakes

correct *verb*
to correct a piece of work is to
mark the mistakes in it, or to put
them right

correction *noun*
1 correction is correcting
something **2** a correction is a
change made to something in
order to make it right

correspond *verb*
1 to correspond with something
is to agree with it or match it
• *Your story corresponds with
what I heard.* **2** to correspond
with someone is to exchange
letters with them

correspondence *noun*
1 similarity or agreement
2 letters or writing letters

correspondent *noun*
1 someone who writes letters
2 a journalist who sends reports
to a newspaper or TV or radio
station • *Julie is our Moscow
correspondent.*

corridor *noun*
a long narrow passage from
which doors open into rooms
or compartments

corrode *verb*
to corrode is to wear away
by rust or chemical action
corrosion *noun* corrosion is the
process of corroding
corrosive *adjective* a corrosive
substance is likely to corrode

corrugated *adjective*
shaped into folds or ridges • *The
roof was made of corrugated iron.*

corrupt *adjective*
a corrupt person is dishonest in
carrying out their responsibilities
or duties, for example by taking
bribes

corrupt *verb*
to corrupt someone is to make
them dishonest, especially
when they have important
responsibilities

corruption *noun*
corruption is dishonest behaviour
by people who are in authority or
have important responsibilities

cosmetics *plural noun*
substances like lipstick and face
powder, for making the skin or
hair look attractive

cosmic *adjective* (*say* **koz**-mik)
to do with the universe

cost *verb*
to cost a certain amount is to
have that amount as its price
• *The book only cost £5 last year.*

cost *noun*
what you have to spend to do or
get something **at all costs** or
at any cost no matter what the
cost or difficulty may be

costly *adjective* (**costlier,
costliest**)
expensive

costume *noun*
clothes, especially for a

coral

a
b
c
d
e
f
g
h
i
j
k
l
m
n
o
p
q
r
s
t
u
v
w
x
y
z

particular purpose or of a
particular period

cosy *adjective* (**cosier, cosiest**)
warm and comfortable

cot *noun*
a baby's bed with high sides

cottage *noun*
a small house, especially in
the country

cottage cheese *noun*
soft white cheese made from
skimmed milk

cotton *noun*
1 a soft white substance covering
the seeds of a tropical plant
2 thread made from this
substance **3** cloth made from
cotton thread

couch *noun*
a long soft seat or sofa

cough *verb* (*say* kof)
to cough is to push air suddenly
out of your lungs with a harsh
noise

cough *noun*
1 the action or sound of coughing
2 an illness which makes you
cough a lot

could
past tense of **can**[1]

council *noun*
a group of people chosen to
organize or discuss something,
especially to plan the affairs of
a town

councillor *noun*
a member of a council

counsellor *noun*
someone who gives advice,
especially as their job

count[1] *verb*
1 to count is to use numbers to
find out how many people or
things there are in a place
2 to count or count out is to say
numbers in their proper order
3 to count someone or something
is to include them in a total
• *There are 30 in the class, counting
the teacher.* **4** to count is to have a
particular value or importance
• *Playing well counts a lot even if
you lose.* **to count on someone
or something** is to rely on them

count[1] *noun*
1 the total reached by counting
2 one of the things that someone
is accused of • *He was found
guilty on all counts.*

count[2] *noun*
a foreign nobleman

countdown *noun*
a counting down to 0, especially
before launching a rocket

counter *noun*
1 a long table where customers
are served in a shop or cafe
2 a small plastic disc used in
board games

counterfeit *adjective*
(*say* kown-ter-fit)
made as a copy of something
real, to deceive or swindle people
• *They were using counterfeit
money.*

countess *noun*
the wife or widow of a count or
earl; a female earl

countless *adjective*
too many to count; very many

country *noun* (**countries**)
1 a country is a part of the world
where a particular nation of
people lives **2** the country is the
countryside • *I wish we lived in
the country.*

countryside *noun*
an area with fields, woods, and
villages, away from towns

county *noun* (**counties**)
one of the areas that a country
is divided into, for example Kent
in England, Fife in Scotland, and
Powys in Wales

couple *noun*
a couple is two people or things

couple *verb*
to couple things is to join them
together

coupling *noun*
a link or fastening, especially for
vehicles

coupon *noun*
a piece of paper that gives
you the right to receive or do
something

courage *noun*
the ability to be brave and
overcome your fear

courageous *adjective*
ready to face danger or pain

courgette *noun*
a kind of vegetable like a small
marrow

course *noun*
1 the direction in which
something moves along • *The
ship's course was to the west.* **2** a
series of lessons or exercises in
learning something • *My Mum's
starting a cookery course at last.*
3 a part of a meal, such as the
meat course or the pudding
course **4** a racecourse or golf
course **of course** naturally;
certainly • *Of course they will help
us .* • *'Will you help us?' 'Of course!'*

court *noun*
1 a place where legal trials take
place; a lawcourt **2** an area
marked out for ball games like
tennis or netball **3** the place
where a king or queen lives
4 the people who are usually
at a king's or queen's court

court *verb*
to court someone is to try to win
their love or support

courteous *adjective* (*say* ker-ti-us)
friendly and polite towards other
people **courteously** *adverb*

courtesy *noun* courtesy is polite
behaviour towards other people

court martial *noun*
a trial of a soldier who is accused
of breaking a military law

courtship *noun*
courting someone, especially
a boyfriend or girlfriend

courtyard *noun*
a paved area surrounded by
walls or buildings

cousin *noun*
a son or daughter of your uncle
or aunt

cove *noun*
a small bay

cover *verb*
1 to cover something is to put
something else over it to hide or
protect it **2** to cover a distance is
to travel over it • *We managed
to cover ten miles a day.* **3** to
cover a subject is to deal with it
or include it • *This book covers
everything you need to know about
dinosaurs.* **4** to cover something
is to be enough money for it
• *I expect £2 will cover my fare.*
to cover something up is to
make sure no one knows about
something wrong or illegal

cover *noun*
1 a cover is something used for
covering something else; a lid or
wrapper **2** cover is a place where
someone can hide or take shelter

coverage *noun*
the amount of time or space
given to reporting an event
on radio, on television, or in
a newspaper

cow *noun*
a large female animal kept by
farmers for its milk and beef

coward *noun*
someone who has no courage
and runs away from danger
and difficulties **cowardice**
noun being a coward **cowardly**
adjective behaving like a coward

cowboy *noun*
a man who rides round looking
after the cattle on a large farm
in America

coy *adjective*
pretending to be shy or modest
coyly *adverb*

crab *noun*
a shellfish   crab
with a
pair of
pincers
and four
pairs of
legs

crack *noun*
1 a line on the surface of something where it has broken but not come completely apart; a narrow gap • *There's a crack in this cup.* **2** a sudden sharp noise • *They heard the crack of a pistol shot.* **3** a sudden sharp blow • *He got a crack on the head.*

crack *verb*
1 to crack something is to make a crack in it **2** something cracks when it splits without breaking • *The plate has cracked.* **3** to crack is to make a sudden sharp noise **4** to crack a joke is to tell it

cracker *noun*
1 a decorated paper tube with a small gift inside it, which bangs when two people pull it apart **2** a thin crisp biscuit

crackle *verb*
to crackle is to make small cracking sounds, like a fire

cradle *noun*
a cot for a baby

craft *noun*
1 a craft is an activity which needs skill with the hands **2** a boat

craftsman or **craftswoman** *noun* (**craftsmen** or **craftswomen**)
someone who is skilled at making things with the hands **craftsmanship** *noun* the skill of a craftsman or craftswoman

crafty *adjective* (**craftier, craftiest**)
cunning and clever **craftily** *adverb* **craftiness** *noun*

crag *noun*
a steep piece of rough rock **craggy** *adjective* steep and rocky

cram *verb* (**cramming, crammed**)
1 to cram things is to force them into a small space **2** to cram is to study very hard for an examination

cramp *noun*
pain caused by a muscle tightening suddenly

cramped *adjective*
in a space that is too small or tight • *We felt very cramped sleeping three in the same room.*

crane *noun*
1 a machine for lifting and moving heavy objects **2** a large bird with long legs and neck

crane *verb*
to crane your neck is to stretch it so that you can see something

crane-fly *noun* (**crane-flies**)
an insect with long thin legs

crank *noun*
1 an L-shaped rod used to turn or control something **2** a person with weird or unusual ideas

crank *verb*
to crank something like an engine is to turn it by using an L-shaped rod

cranny *noun* (**crannies**)
a crevice; a narrow hole or space

crash *noun*
1 the loud noise of something falling or breaking **2** a collision between road vehicles, causing damage

crash *verb*
1 to crash is to collide or fall violently **2** to crash a vehicle is to have a crash while driving it

crash helmet *noun*
a padded helmet worn by cyclists and motorcyclists

crate *noun*
a container in which goods are transported

crater *noun*
1 the mouth of a volcano **2** a hole in the ground made by a bomb

crave *verb*
to crave something is to want it very badly

crawl *verb*
1 to crawl is to move along on your hands and knees **2** to crawl is also to move slowly in a vehicle **3** to be crawling with something unpleasant is to be full of it or covered in it • *This room's crawling with cockroaches.*

crawl *noun*
1 a crawling movement **2** a powerful swimming stroke in which you bring each arm over your head in turn

crayon *noun*
a coloured pencil for drawing or writing

craze *noun*
a brief enthusiasm or fashion for something

crazy *adjective* (**crazier, craziest**)
mad or weird **crazily** *adverb* **craziness** *noun*

creak *noun*
a sound like the noise made by a stiff door opening

creak *verb*
to make a creak **creaky** *adjective* old and creaking

crane

cream *noun*
1 the rich fatty part of milk **2** yellowish-white colour

3 a food containing or looking like cream **4** something that looks like cream, for example face cream **creamy** *adjective* smooth and thick like cream

crease *noun*
1 a line made in something by folding or pressing it **2** a line on a cricket pitch showing where the batsman should stand

crease *verb*
to crease something is to make a crease in it

create *verb*
to create something is to make it exist **creation** *noun* creating something **creator** *noun* someone who creates something

creative *adjective*
showing imagination and thought as well as skill • *The older children have started some creative writing.* **creativity** *noun* the ability to use the imagination to create things

creature *noun*
a living animal or person

crèche *noun* (say kresh)
a place where babies or small children are looked after while their parents are busy

credible *adjective*
able to be believed; trustworthy **credibility** *noun* being credible **credibly** *adverb* in a credible way

credit *noun*
1 honour or approval • *You have to give her credit for trying.* **2** someone who brings honour or approval • *He is a credit to his family.* **3** a system of allowing someone to pay for something later on • *Do you want cash now or can I have it on credit?* **4** an amount of money in an account at a bank or building society **credits** the list of people who have helped to produce a film, television programme, etc.

credit card *noun*
a card allowing someone to buy goods and pay for them later

creep *verb* (**creeping, crept**)
1 to creep is to move along with the body close to the ground **2** to creep about is to move quietly or secretly **to creep up on someone** is to go up to them quietly from behind

creeper *noun*
a plant that grows close to the ground or up walls

creepy *adjective* (**creepier, creepiest**)
(*informal*) weird and slightly frightening

a b **c** d e f g h i j k l m n o p q r s t u v w x y z

cremate *verb*
to cremate a dead body is to burn it into fine ashes instead of burying it **cremation** *noun* the cremating of a dead body

crematorium *noun* (**crematoria**) (*say* krem-a-**tor**-i-um)
a place where dead bodies are cremated

crêpe *noun* (*say* krayp)
1 cloth or paper with a wrinkled surface **2** a kind of thin French pancake

crescent *noun*
1 a narrow curved shape, pointed at both ends, like a new moon **2** a curved street

cress *noun*
a green plant used in salads and sandwiches

crest *noun*
1 a tuft of hair, feathers, or skin on an animal's head **2** the top of a hill or wave **3** a badge or emblem

crevasse *noun*
a deep crack in a glacier

crevice *noun*
a crack in rock or in a wall

crew *noun*
the people who work on a ship or aircraft

crib *noun*
1 a baby's cot **2** a framework containing fodder for animals **3** something copied

crib *verb* (**cribbing, cribbed**)
to crib someone else's work is to copy it

cricket¹ *noun*
a game played outdoors by two teams with a ball, two bats, and two wickets **cricketer** *noun* someone who plays cricket

cricket² *noun*
an insect like a grasshopper

cricket

crime *noun*
an act that breaks the law

criminal *noun*
someone who has committed one or more crimes

criminal *adjective*
to do with crime or criminals

crimson *noun*, *adjective*
a dark red colour

crinkle *verb*
to crinkle something is to crease or wrinkle it **crinkly** *adjective* full of creases, wrinkled

cripple *noun*
someone who cannot walk properly

cripple *verb*
to cripple someone is to make them a cripple

crisis *noun* (**crises**) (*say* **kry**-sis)
a difficult or dangerous time or situation

crisp *adjective*
1 very dry so that it breaks easily **2** firm and fresh • *I'd like a nice crisp apple.* **3** cold and frosty • *We woke up to a crisp winter morning.*

crisp *noun*
a thin fried slice of potato, sold in packets

criss-cross *adjective, adverb*
with crossing lines

critic *noun*
1 a person who criticizes someone or something **2** someone who gives opinions on books, plays, films, music, or other performances

critical *adjective*
1 criticizing **2** to do with critics or criticism **3** serious, reaching a crisis **critically** *adverb* in a critical way; seriously

criticism *noun* (*say* **krit**-i-**si**-zum)
an opinion or judgement about something, usually pointing out its faults

criticize *verb* (*say* **krit**-i-syz)
to criticize something or someone is to give an opinion pointing out their faults

croak *noun*
a deep sound, like a frog makes

croak *verb*
to make a croak

crochet *noun* (*say* **kroh**-shay)
a kind of needlework done with a hooked needle

crockery *noun*
dishes, plates, and cups and saucers used for eating

crocodile *noun*
a large reptile living in hot countries, with a thick skin, long tail, and huge jaws

croissant *noun* (*say* **krwa**-sahn)
a crescent-shaped roll of rich pastry, first made in France and usually eaten for breakfast

crook *noun*
1 (*informal*) someone who cheats or robs people; a criminal **2** a shepherd's or bishop's stick with a curved end

crook *verb*
to crook something is to bend it into a hook shape

crooked *adjective* (*say* **kruuk**-id)
1 bent or twisted **2** (*informal*) dishonest or criminal

crop *noun*
1 something grown for food, especially in a field • *They had a good crop of wheat last year.* **2** a riding whip with a loop instead of a lash

crop *verb* (**cropping, cropped**)
to crop something is to cut or bite the top off it • *They could see sheep in a field, cropping the grass.* **to crop up** is to happen or appear unexpectedly

cross *noun*
1 a mark or shape like + or x **2** an upright post with another post across it, used in ancient times for crucifixions **3** an animal produced by mixing one breed with another • *A mule is a cross between a donkey and a horse.* **the Cross** the cross on which Christ was crucified, used as a symbol of Christianity

cross *verb*
1 to cross something is to go across it • *She crossed the road to meet him.* • *A bit further on the road crossed a river.* **2** to cross your fingers or legs is to put one over the other **to cross something out** is to draw a line across something because it is unwanted or wrong

cross *adjective*
angry or bad-tempered **crossly** *adverb* angrily **crossness** *noun* being cross

crossbar *noun*
a horizontal bar between two upright bars

crossbow *noun*
a kind of bow used for shooting arrows, held like a gun and fired by pulling a trigger

cross-country *noun*
a running race through fields and country

crossing *noun*
a place where people can cross a road or railway

crossroads *noun*
a place where two or more roads cross one another

cross-section *noun*
a drawing of something as if it has been cut through

crossword *noun*
a puzzle with blank squares in which you put the letters of words worked out from clues

crotchet *noun* (*say* **kroch**-it)
a musical note equal to half a minim, written ♩

a b c d e f g h i j k l m n o p q r s t u w x y z

crouch verb
to crouch is to lower your body, with your arms and legs bent

crow noun
a large black bird

crow verb
1 to make a noise like a cock 2 to boast; to be proudly triumphant

crowbar noun
an iron bar used as a lever

crowd noun
a large number of people in one place

crowd verb
to crowd or crowd round is to form a crowd

crow

crowded adjective
having too many people or things • The bus was a bit crowded, but we got on.

crown noun
1 a crown is an ornamental headdress worn by a king or queen 2 the crown is the king or queen of a country • This land belongs to the crown. 3 the top of something, such as a hill or a person's head

crown verb
1 to crown someone is to make them king or queen 2 to crown something is to form the top of it

crown

crucial adjective (say **kroo**-shal)
extremely important

crucifix noun
a model of Christ on the Cross

crucify verb (**crucifies, crucifying, crucified**)
to crucify someone is to execute them by fixing their hands and feet to a cross and leaving them to die. The Romans used this method of executing criminals.

crucifixion noun the execution of someone by crucifying them

crude adjective
1 natural; not purified • The country exported crude oil. 2 rough and simple • They stayed in a crude hut in the mountains. 3 rude or dirty • The boys were telling each other crude jokes.

cruel adjective (**crueller, cruellest**)
causing pain and suffering to

others • They were ruled by a cruel tyrant. **cruelly** adverb **cruelty** noun cruel acts or treatment

cruise noun
a holiday on a ship, usually visiting different places

cruise verb
1 to cruise is to sail or travel at a gentle speed 2 to cruise is also to have a cruise on a ship

crumb noun
a tiny piece of bread or cake

crumble verb
1 to crumble something is to break it into small pieces 2 to crumble is to be broken into small pieces • The cliff was slowly crumbling into the sea.

crumbly adjective soft and likely to crumble

crumpet noun
a soft flat cake made with yeast, toasted and eaten with butter

crumple verb
1 to crumple something is to make it creased 2 to crumple is to become creased

crunch noun
the noise made by chewing hard food or walking on gravel

crunch verb
to crunch something is to chew or crush it with a crunch

crunchy adjective making a crunching sound

crusade noun
1 a military expedition to Palestine made by Christians in the Middle Ages 2 a campaign against something that you think is bad

crusader noun someone who takes part in a crusade

crush verb
1 to crush something is to press it so that it gets broken or damaged 2 to crush an enemy is to defeat them

crush noun
1 a crowd; a crowded place 2 a fruit-flavoured drink 3 (informal) a sudden liking you have for someone

crust noun
1 the hard outside part of something, especially of a loaf 2 the rocky outer part of a planet

crustacean noun
(say krus-**tay**-shan)
a shellfish

crutch noun
a stick that fits under the arm, used as a support in walking

cry verb (**cries, crying, cried**)
1 to cry is to shout 2 to cry is also to let tears fall from your eyes

cry noun
1 a loud shout 2 a period of weeping

crypt noun
a large room underneath a church

crystal noun
1 a clear mineral rather like glass 2 a small solid piece of a substance with a symmetrical shape, such as snow and ice

crystallize verb
to crystallize is to form into crystals

cub noun
a young animal, especially a lion, tiger, fox, or bear
Cub a junior Scout

cube noun
1 an object that has six square sides, like a box or dice 2 the result of multiplying something by itself twice • The cube of 3 is 3 x 3 x 3 = 27.

cube verb
1 to cube a number is to multiply it by itself twice • 4 cubed is 4 x 4 x 4 = 64. 2 to cube something is to cut it into small cubes

cube root noun
a number that gives another number if it is multiplied by itself twice • 2 is the cube root of 8.

cubic adjective
a cubic metre or foot is the volume of a cube with sides that are one metre or foot long

cubicle noun
a small division of a room

cuckoo noun
a bird that makes a sound like 'cuck-oo', and lays its eggs in other birds' nests

cucumber noun
a long green vegetable, eaten raw

cud noun
half-digested food that a cow brings back from its first stomach to chew again

cuddle verb
to cuddle someone is to put your arms closely round them and squeeze them in a loving way
cuddly adjective a cuddly person is nice to cuddle

cue[1] noun
a word or signal that tells an actor when to start speaking or come on the stage

cue[2] noun
a long stick used to strike the ball in billiards or snooker

cuff noun
the end of a sleeve that fits round your wrist

cuff verb
to cuff someone is to hit them with the hand

a
b
c
d
e
f
g
h
i
j
k
l
m
n
o
p
q
r
s
t
u
v
w
x
y
z

cul-de-sac *noun*
a street that is closed at one end

culprit *noun*
someone who is to blame for something

cultivate *verb*
to cultivate land is to grow crops on it **cultivation** *noun*

culture *noun*
1 culture is the development of the mind by education and learning **2** a culture is the customs and traditions of a people • *They were studying Greek culture.* **cultural** *adjective* to do with culture **cultured** *adjective* well educated and knowledgeable

cunning *adjective*
clever at deceiving people

cup *noun*
1 a small container with a handle, from which you drink liquid **2** a prize in the form of a silver cup, usually with two handles

cup *verb*
(**cupping, cupped**)
to cup your hands is to form them into the shape of a cup

cup

cupboard *noun* (*say* **kub**-erd)
a compartment or piece of furniture with a door, for storing things

curator *noun* (*say* kewr-**ay**-ter)
someone in charge of a museum or art gallery

curb *verb*
to curb a feeling is to hold it back or hide it • *You must curb your anger.*

curd *noun*
a thick substance formed when milk turns sour

curdle *verb*
to curdle is to turn sour and form into curds

cure *verb*
1 to cure someone who is ill is to make them better **2** to cure something bad is to stop it **3** to cure food is to treat it so as to preserve it • *Fish can be cured in smoke.*

cure *noun*
something that cures a person or thing • *They are still trying to find a cure for cancer.*

curfew *noun*
a time or signal after which people must stay indoors until the next day

curiosity *noun* (**curiosities**)
1 curiosity is being curious **2** a curiosity is something strange or interesting

curious *adjective*
1 wanting to find out about things **2** strange or unusual **curiously** *adverb*

curl *noun*
a curve or coil, especially of hair

curl *verb*
to curl is to form into curls
to curl up is to sit or lie with your knees drawn up

curly *adjective*
full of curls

currant *noun*
1 a small black fruit made from dried grapes **2** a small juicy berry, or the bush that produces it

currency *noun* (**currencies**)
the money that is in use in a country • *You can pay with Russian currency.*

current *noun*
1 a flow of water or air **2** a flow of electricity through a wire
current *adjective* happening or used now **currently** *adverb* now, at the moment • *The admission charge is currently £10.*

curriculum *noun*
the subjects that you study in a school

curry *noun* (**curries**)
food cooked with spices that make it taste hot

curse *noun*
1 a call or prayer for someone to be harmed or killed **2** something very unpleasant **3** an angry word or words

curse *verb*
to curse someone is to use a curse against them

cursor *noun*
a flashing signal showing your position on a computer screen

curtain *noun*
a piece of material hung at a window or door, or at the front of a stage

curtsy *noun* (**curtsies**)
a bow made by bending the knees, done by women as a mark of respect

curtsy *verb* (**curtsies, curtsying, curtsied**)
to curtsy is to make a curtsy

curve *noun*
a line that bends smoothly

curve *verb*
to curve is to bend smoothly

cushion *noun*
a fabric cover filled with soft

material so that it is comfortable to sit on or rest against

custard *noun*
a sweet yellow sauce eaten with puddings

custom *noun*
1 the usual way of doing things • *It is the custom to go on holiday in the summer.* **2** regular business from customers • *That rude man at the corner shop won't get my custom any more.* **customs** are the group of officials at a port or airport whose job is to check what goods people are bringing into the country

customary *adjective*
something that is customary is usually done or done according to a custom

customer *noun*
someone who uses a shop, bank, or business

cut *verb* (**cutting, cut**)
1 to cut something is to divide it or make a slit in it with a knife or scissors **2** to cut something like prices or taxes is to reduce them **3** to cut a pack of playing cards is to divide it **4** to cut a corner is to go across it rather than round it **to cut someone off** is to interrupt them • *She cut me off before I could finish my sentence.* **to cut something out** (*informal*) is to stop doing it • *Cut out the talking!*

cut *noun*
1 an act of cutting; the result of cutting • *Your hair could do with a cut.* **2** a small wound caused by something sharp

cute *adjective*
(*informal*) attractive in a quaint or simple way

cutlass *noun*
a short sword with a wide curved blade

cutlery *noun*
knives, forks, and spoons used for eating

cutlet *noun*
a thick slice of meat still on the bone

cut-out *noun*
a design or shape cut out of paper or cardboard

cutlery

cutting *noun*
1 something cut from a newspaper or magazine **2** a piece cut off a plant to grow as a new plant **3** a deep passage cut through high ground for a railway or road

cycle *noun*
1 a bicycle 2 a series of events that are regularly repeated
• *Rainfall is part of the water cycle.*

cycle *verb*
to cycle is to ride a bicycle
cyclist *noun* someone who rides a bicycle

cyclone *noun*
a strong wind rotating round a calm central area

cygnet *noun* (*say* **sig**-nit)
a young swan

cylinder *noun*
1 an object with straight sides and circular ends 2 part of an engine in which a piston moves

cylindrical *adjective*
shaped like a cylinder

cymbal *noun*
a cymbal is a round, slightly hollowed metal plate that you hit to make a ringing sound in music

cymbals

cynical *adjective* (*say* **sin**-ik-al)
thinking that nothing is good or worthwhile **cynic** *noun* someone who doubts that anything is good or worthwhile **cynicism** *noun* being cynical

cypress *noun*
an evergreen tree with dark leaves

Dd

dab *noun*
a gentle touch with something soft

dab *verb* (**dabbing, dabbed**)
to dab something is to touch it gently with something soft
• *I dabbed my eyes with a handkerchief.*

dabble *verb*
1 to dabble something is to splash it about in water 2 to dabble in something is to do it as a hobby or not very seriously
• *She likes to dabble in photography.*

dad or **daddy** *noun* (**daddies**)
(*informal*) father

daddy-long-legs *noun*
a crane-fly

daffodil *noun*
a yellow flower that grows from a bulb

daft *adjective*
silly or stupid

dagger *noun*
a pointed knife with two sharp edges, used as a weapon

daily *adjective, adverb*
happening every day

dainty *adjective* (**daintier, daintiest**)
small and delicate **daintily** *adverb* **daintiness** *noun*

dairy *noun* (**dairies**)
a place where milk, butter, cream, and cheese are made or sold

daisy *noun* (**daisies**)
a small flower with white petals and a yellow centre

dale *noun*
a valley

dam *noun*
a wall built across a river to hold the water back

dam *verb* (**damming, dammed**)
to dam a river is to build a dam across it

damage *verb*
to damage something is to injure or harm it

damage *noun*
damage is injury or harm
• *The storm caused a lot of damage.*

damn *verb*
to damn something is to say it is bad or wrong

damp *adjective*
slightly wet; not quite dry

damp *noun*
wetness in the air or on something

dampen *verb*
1 to dampen something is to make it damp 2 to dampen sound or noise is to make it softer

dance *verb*
to dance is to move about in time to music

dance *noun*
1 a piece of music or set of movements for dancing 2 a party or gathering where people dance **dancer** *noun* someone who dances

dancer

dandelion *noun*
a yellow wild flower with jagged leaves

WORD ORIGIN

The word **dandelion** comes from the French words *dent-de-lion* meaning 'lion's tooth', because of the leaves having a jagged shape.

dandruff *noun*
dandruff is small white flakes of dead skin in a person's hair

danger *noun*
something that is dangerous

dangerous *adjective*
likely to harm you

dangle *verb*
to dangle is to swing or hang down loosely

dappled *adjective*
marked with patches of different colours

dare *verb*
1 to dare to do something is to be brave or bold enough to do it 2 to dare someone to do something is to challenge them to do it • *I dare you to climb that tree.*

dare *noun*
(*informal*) a challenge to do something risky

daredevil *noun*
a person who enjoys doing dangerous things

daring *adjective*
bold or brave

dark *adjective*
1 with little or no light 2 deep and rich in colour • *She wore a dark green coat.*

dark *noun*
1 dark or the dark is when there is no light • *Cats can see in the dark.* 2 dark is also the time when it becomes dark just after sunset
• *Be home before dark.*

darkness *noun* darkness is when there is no light **darken** *verb*
1 to darken something is to make it dark 2 to darken is to become dark • *The sky suddenly darkened.*

darling *noun*
someone who is loved very much

darn *verb*
to darn a hole is to mend it by sewing across it

dart *noun*
an object with a sharp point that you throw at a target called a dartboard in the game of **darts**

dash *noun*
1 a quick rush or a hurry • *They made a dash for the door.* 2 a dash of something is a small amount of it 3 a short line (–) used in writing or printing

dash *verb*
1 to dash somewhere is to rush there 2 to dash something is to hurl it and smash it • *In her anger she dashed the cup against the wall.*

dashboard *noun*
a panel with dials and controls in front of the driver of a car

data *noun* (*say* **day**-ta)
data is pieces of information

database *noun*
a store of information held in a computer

date¹ *noun*
1 the day of the month, or the year, when something happens or happened **2** an appointment to go out with someone

date¹ *verb*
1 to date something that happened is to give it a date **2** to date from a time is to have existed from then • *The church dates from the 15th century.* **3** to date is also to seem old-fashioned • *Some fashions date very quickly.*

date² *noun*
a sweet brown fruit that grows on a palm tree

daughter *noun*
a girl or woman who is someone's child

dawdle *verb*
to dawdle is to walk or do something too slowly

dawn *noun*
the time of the day when the sun rises

dawn *verb*
1 to dawn is to begin to become light in the morning **2** something dawns on you when you begin to realize it

day *noun*
1 the 24 hours between midnight and the next midnight **2** the light part of the day **3** a period in time • *Write about what it was like in Queen Victoria's day.*

daybreak *noun*
the first light of day; dawn

daydream *verb*
to daydream is to have pleasant thoughts about things you would like to happen

daylight *noun*
1 the light of day **2** dawn • *They left before daylight.*

daze *noun*
to be in a daze is to be unable to think or see clearly

dazed *adjective*
someone is dazed when they can't think or see clearly

dazzle *verb*
a light dazzles you when it shines so brightly in your eyes that you are blinded for a moment

dead *adjective*
1 no longer alive **2** no longer working or active • *The phone went dead.* **3** a dead place is not at all lively • *This town is dead at the weekend.*

deaden *verb*
to deaden pain or noise is to make it weaker

dead end *noun*
a road or passage that is closed at one end

dead heat *noun*
a race in which two or more winners finish exactly together

deadline *noun*
the time by which you must finish doing something

deadly *adjective* (**deadlier, deadliest**)
likely to kill • *The liquid in the glass was a deadly poison.*

deaf *adjective*
unable to hear **deafness** *noun* being deaf

deafen *verb*
to be deafening is to be very loud • *The noise from the party upstairs was deafening.*

deal *verb* (**dealing, dealt**)
1 to deal in something is to buy and sell it • *He deals in scrap metal.* **2** to deal playing cards is to give them to players in a card game **to deal with someone or something** is to spend time doing what needs to be done • *I'll deal with you later.* **to deal with something** is to be concerned with it • *This book deals with cacti.*

deal *noun*
1 an agreement or bargain **2** someone's turn to give out playing cards • *Whose deal is it?* **a good deal** or **a great deal** a large amount

dealer *noun*
1 someone who buys and sells things **2** the person dealing at cards

dear *adjective*
1 loved very much **2** you use dear as the usual way of beginning a letter • *Dear Mary* **3** expensive

death *noun*
dying; the end of life

debate *noun*
a formal discussion about a subject

debate *verb*
to debate is to discuss or argue about something

debris *noun* (*say* **deb**-ree)
debris is scattered pieces that are left after something has been destroyed

debt *noun* (*say* det)
something that someone owes
to be in debt is to owe money

début *noun*
(*say* **day**-bew *or say* **day**-boo) someone's first public appearance as a performer

decade *noun*
a period of ten years

decathlon *noun* (*say* dek-**ath**-lon)
an athletics competition in which you take part in ten different events

decay *verb*
to decay is to rot or go bad

decay *noun*
decay is going bad or rotting

deceased *adjective* (*say* di-**seest**)
a formal word for dead

deceit *noun* (*say* di-**seet**)
deceit is telling lies or doing something dishonest

deceitful *adjective* someone who is deceitful tells lies or does something dishonest **deceitfully** *adverb*

deceive *verb* (*say* di-**seev**)
to deceive someone is to make them believe something that is not true

December *noun*
the last month of the year

decent *adjective*
1 respectable and honest **2** of good enough quality • *Was it a decent film?* **decency** *noun* respectable and honest behaviour **decently** *adverb* in a respectable and honest way

deception *noun*
1 deception is making someone believe something that is not true **2** a deception is a trick or a lie

deceptive *adjective*
not what it seems to be • *The sunshine was deceptive and the wind made it very cold.*

decibel *noun*
a unit for measuring how loud a sound is

decide *verb*
1 to decide something is to make up your mind about it or make a choice **2** to decide a contest or argument is to settle it

deciduous *adjective*
a deciduous tree loses its leaves in autumn

decimal *adjective*
a decimal system uses tens or tenths to count things

decimal *noun*
a fraction with tenths shown as numbers after a dot (¼ is 0.25; 1 ½ is 1.5)

decimal point *noun*
the dot in a decimal fraction

decipher *verb* (*say* di-**sy**-fer)
to decipher writing is to work out what it means when it is in code or difficult to read

decision *noun*
a decision is what someone has decided

decisive *adjective*
1 ending or deciding something important • *The decisive battle of*

the war was fought here.
2 a decisive person decides things quickly and firmly **decisively** *adverb*

deck *noun*
a floor on a ship or bus

deckchair *noun*
a folding chair with a seat of canvas or plastic material

deckchair

declaration *noun*
an official or public statement

declare *verb*
1 to declare something is to say it clearly and openly **2** a cricket team declares when it ends its innings before all the batsmen are out **to declare war** is to announce a state of war with another country

decline *verb*
1 to decline is to become weaker or smaller **2** to decline an offer is to refuse it politely

decode *verb*
to decode something written in code is to work out its meaning

decompose *verb*
to decompose is to decay or rot **decomposition** *noun* when something decays or rots

decorate *verb*
1 to decorate something is to make it look more beautiful or colourful **2** to decorate a room or building is to put fresh paint or paper on the walls **decorative** *adjective* colourful and pretty

decoration *noun*
1 decorations are the paint, wallpaper, and ornaments that make a place look more attractive **2** decoration is making something look more attractive or colourful

decorator *noun*
a person whose job is to paint rooms and buildings and to put up wallpaper

decoy *noun* (*say* **dee**-koi or *say* **di**-koi)
something used to tempt a person or animal into a trap

decrease *verb* (*say* di-**kreess**)
1 to decrease something is to make it smaller or less **2** to decrease is to become smaller or less

decrease *noun* (*say* **dee**-kreess)
the amount by which something decreases

decree *noun*
an official order or decision

decree *verb*
to decree something is to give an official order that it must happen

decrepit *adjective* (*say* dik-**rep**-it)
old and weak

dedicate *verb*
1 to dedicate yourself or your life to something is to spend all your time doing it • *She dedicated her life to nursing.* **2** to dedicate a book to someone is to name them at the beginning, as a sign of friendship or thanks

dedication *noun*
1 dedication is hard work and effort **2** a dedication is a message at the beginning of a book in which you name someone as a sign of friendship or thanks

deduce *verb*
to deduce a fact or answer is to work it out from what you already know is true • *She deduced from my smile that I had won the prize.*

deduct *verb*
to deduct an amount is to subtract it from a total • *His Dad deducted 50 pence from his pocket money for breaking a window.*

deduction *noun*
1 something that you work out by reasoning **2** an amount taken away from a total

deed *noun*
1 something that someone has done **2** a legal document that shows who owns something

deep *adjective*
1 going down or back a long way from the top or front **2** measured from top to bottom or from front to back • *The hole was two metres deep.* **3** intense or strong • *The room was painted a deep blue.* **4** a deep voice is very low in pitch **deeply** *adverb* very, extremely • *She was deeply upset.*

deepen *verb*
to deepen is to become deeper • *The pool deepened to 2 metres half way along.*

deer *noun*
a fast-running, graceful animal. The male has antlers.

deface *verb*
to deface something is to spoil its appearance by writing or drawing on it

defeat *verb*
to defeat someone is to beat them in a game or battle

defeat *noun*
1 defeat is losing a game or battle **2** a defeat is a lost game or battle

defect *noun* (*say* **dee**-fekt)
a flaw or weakness

defect *verb* (*say* di-**fekt**)
to defect is to desert a country or cause and join the other side **defection** *noun* when someone deserts a country or cause and joins the other side **defector** *noun* someone who defects

defective *adjective*
something is defective when it has flaws or faults or doesn't work properly

defence *noun*
1 something that protects you • *High walls were built around the city as a defence against enemy attacks.* **2** protecting yourself or a place from an attack or from criticism • *In her defence, she thought she was acting for the best.* **3** the players whose job is to stop the other team scoring in football and other games

defenceless *adjective* someone who is defenceless can't protect themselves

defend *verb*
1 to defend someone or something is to protect them from an attack **2** to defend an idea, belief, or person is to argue in support of them **3** to defend an accused person is to try to prove that they are innocent **defender** *noun* someone who defends something

defendant *noun*
a person accused of something in a lawcourt

defensive *adjective*
1 used to defend something • *We need to take defensive measures.* **2** a defensive person is anxious about being criticized

defer *verb* (**deferring, deferred**)
to defer something is to put it off until later • *She deferred her departure until Saturday.*

defiant *adjective*
openly showing that you refuse to obey someone **defiance** *noun* when you openly show that you refuse to obey someone **defiantly** *adverb*

deficiency *noun* (**deficiencies**)
a lack or shortage **deficient** *adjective* to be deficient in something is not to have enough of it

define *verb*
1 to define a word is to explain what it means **2** to define an idea or problem is to show exactly what it is

definite *adjective*
fixed or certain • *Is it definite that we are going to move?*

definite article noun
the word the
definitely adverb, exclamation
certainly, without doubt
• We are definitely going to
the party.
definition noun
an explanation of what a word
means
deflect verb
to deflect something that is
moving is to make it go in a
different direction
deflection noun a deflection is
a sudden change in direction of
something that is moving
deforestation noun
the cutting down of a large
number of trees in an area
deformed adjective
not properly shaped **deformity**
noun a deformity is a part of
someone's body that is deformed
defrost verb
1 to defrost a refrigerator or
freezer is to remove the ice from
it 2 to defrost frozen food is to
thaw it out
deft adjective
skilful and quick **deftly** adverb
in a skilful and quick way
defuse verb
1 to defuse a bomb is to remove
its fuse so that it won't blow up
2 to defuse a situation is to make
it less dangerous or tense
defy verb (**defies, defying, defied**)
1 to defy someone is to refuse to
obey them 2 to defy something is
to prevent it happening • The door
defied all attempts to open it. 3 to
defy someone to do something is
to challenge them • I defy you to
find anything cheaper.
degree noun
1 a unit for measuring
temperature • Water boils
at 100 degrees centigrade,
or 100°C. 2 a unit for
measuring angles
• There are 90 degrees
(90°) in a right angle.
3 the level or amount
of something • I agree
with you to a large
degree. 4 an award
to someone at a
university or college
who has successfully
finished a course
• She has a degree
in English.
dehydrated adjective
dried up, with all the water
removed **dehydration**
noun someone suffers from
dehydration when they
lose too much water from
their body

deity noun (**deities**)
(say **dee**-i-ti or **day**-i-ti)
a god or goddess
dejected adjective
sad or depressed
dejection noun dejection is being
sad or depressed
delay verb
1 to delay someone is to make
them late 2 to delay something is
to put it off until later 3 to delay
is to wait before doing something
delay noun
1 delaying or waiting • Do it
without delay. 2 the period you
have to wait when something
happens late • There will be a
delay of 20 minutes.
delete verb
to delete something is to cross it
out or remove it **deletion** noun
a deletion is something that has
been crossed out or removed
deliberate adjective
(say di-**lib**-er-at)
1 done on purpose • It was a
deliberate lie. 2 slow and careful
• He has a deliberate way of
talking. **deliberately** adverb to
do something deliberately is to
do it on purpose
delicacy noun (**delicacies**)
1 delicacy is being delicate
2 a delicacy is something small
and tasty to eat
delicate adjective
1 fine and graceful • The cloth
had delicate embroidery. 2 fragile
and easily damaged 3 becoming
ill easily 4 a delicate situation
needs great care
delicately adverb
delicatessen noun
a shop that sells cooked or
prepared food such as meat and
cheese
delicious adjective
tasting or smelling very
pleasant **deliciously** adverb
in a delicious way • a
deliciously creamy sauce
delight verb
to delight someone is to
please them a lot
delight noun
great pleasure
delightful adjective
giving great pleasure
delightfully adverb
delinquent noun
a young person
who breaks the law
delinquency noun
delinquency is criminal
behaviour by young people
delirious adjective
1 in a confused state of mind
because you are ill or have a
high fever 2 extremely excited or

degrees

enthusiastic **deliriously** adverb
in a delirious way
deliver verb
1 to deliver letters, milk, or
newspapers is to take them to
a house or office 2 to deliver a
speech or lecture is to give it to
an audience 3 to deliver a baby
is to help with its birth
delivery noun (**deliveries**)
1 delivery is when letters or
goods are taken to a house or
office 2 a person's delivery is the
way they give a speech or lecture
3 giving birth to a baby
delta noun
a triangular area at the mouth
of a river where it spreads into
branches
deluge noun
1 a large flood 2 a heavy fall
of rain 3 something coming in
great numbers • After the speech
there was a deluge of questions.
deluge verb
to be deluged with something
is to get a huge amount of it
• We have been deluged with
replies.
de luxe adjective
of very high quality
demand verb
to demand something is to ask
for it forcefully
demand noun
1 a demand is a very firm request
for something 2 demand is
a desire to have something
• There's not much demand
for ice cream at this time of year.
to be in demand is to be wanted
or popular
demanding adjective
1 asking for many things
• Toddlers can be very demanding.
2 needing a lot of time or effort
• She has a demanding job.
democracy noun (**democracies**)
1 democracy is government by
leaders elected by the people
2 a democracy is a country
governed in this way
democrat noun
a person who believes in or
supports democracy
democratic adjective
a democratic idea or process
is one that involves ordinary
people and takes account of their
views **democratically** adverb
to do something democratically
is to take account of ordinary
people and their views
demolish verb
to demolish a building is to
knock it down and break it up
demolition noun the demolition
of a building is when it is knocked
down and broken up

demon *noun*
1 a devil or evil spirit 2 a fierce or forceful person

demonstrate *verb*
1 to demonstrate something is to show or prove it 2 to demonstrate is to take part in a demonstration
demonstrator *noun*

demonstration *noun*
1 showing how to do or work something 2 a march or meeting to show everyone what you think about something • *There will be a demonstration against the new motorway.*

den *noun*
1 the home of a wild animal • *a lion's den* 2 a hiding place, especially for children

denial *noun*
saying that something is not true

denim *noun*
strong cotton cloth, used to make jeans

denominator *noun*
the number below the line in a fraction • *In ¼ the 4 is the denominator.*

denounce *verb*
to denounce someone or something is to speak strongly against them, or accuse them of something • *They denounced him as a spy.*
denunciation *noun* denouncing someone or something

dense *adjective*
1 thick • *The fog was getting very dense.* 2 packed close together • *They walked through a dense forest.* 3 (informal) stupid **densely** *adverb* thickly, close together • *a densely populated area*

density *noun* (**densities**)
1 how thick or tightly packed something is 2 (in science) the proportion of mass to volume • *Water has greater density than air.*

dent *noun*
a hollow made in a surface by hitting it or pressing it

dent *verb*
to dent something is to make a dent in it

dental *adjective*
to do with the teeth or dentistry

dentist *noun*
a person who is trained to treat teeth, fill them or take them out, and fit false ones **dentistry** *noun* the work of a dentist

denture *noun*
a set of false teeth

deny *verb* (**denies, denying, denied**)
1 to deny something is to say that it is not true 2 to deny a request is to refuse it

deodorant *noun*
a powder or liquid that removes unpleasant smells

depart *verb*
to depart is to go away or leave
departure *noun* a departure is when someone or something leaves a place

department *noun*
one part of a large organization or shop

department store *noun*
a large shop that sells many different kinds of goods

depend *verb*
to depend on someone or something is to rely on them • *We depend on you for help.*
to depend on something is to be decided or controlled by it • *Whether we can have a picnic depends on the weather.*

dependable *adjective*
that you can depend on; reliable

dependant *noun*
a person who depends on someone else, especially for money • *She has two dependants, a son and a daughter.*

dependent *adjective*
depending or relying on someone • *He was dependent on his father.* • *She has two dependent children.* **dependence** *noun* dependence is being dependent on someone

depict *verb*
1 to depict something is to show it in a painting or drawing 2 to depict a scene is to describe it • *The story depicted a small village in Austria.*

deport *verb*
to deport someone is to send them out of a country
deportation *noun* deportation is when someone is sent out of a country

deposit *noun*
1 an amount of money you pay into a bank 2 a sum of money paid as a first instalment 3 a layer of solid matter in or on the earth

deposit *verb*
1 to deposit something is to put it down somewhere 2 to deposit money is to pay it into a bank

depot *noun* (say **dep**-oh)
1 a place where things are stored 2 a place where buses or trains are kept and repaired

depress *verb*
to depress someone is to make them very sad

depressed *adjective*
someone who is depressed feels very sad and without hope

depression *noun*
1 a feeling of great sadness and hopelessness 2 a long period when there is less trade and business than usual and many people have no work 3 a shallow hollow or dip in the ground 4 an area of low air pressure which may bring rain

deprive *verb*
to deprive someone of something is to take it away from them • *Prisoners are deprived of their freedom.*

deprived *adjective*
without all the things you need to live a happy and comfortable life, like enough food and good housing

depth *noun*
how deep something is • *What is the depth of the river here?* **in depth** thoroughly **out of your depth** 1 in water that is too deep to stand in 2 trying to do something that is too difficult for you

deputy *noun* (**deputies**)
a person who acts as a substitute or chief assistant for someone and does that person's job when they are away

derail *verb*
a train is derailed when something causes it to leave the track

derby *noun* (**derbies**)
a sports match between two teams from the same city or area

derelict *adjective* (say **de**-re-likt)
abandoned and left to fall into ruin • *The factory is now completely derelict.*

derision *noun*
scorn or ridicule • *They treated him with derision.*

derivation *noun*
where a word comes from

derive *verb*
to get something from another person or thing • *She derived a lot of pleasure from music.* • *Many English words are derived from Latin.*

derrick *noun*
1 a kind of large crane for lifting things 2 a tall framework that holds the machinery used for drilling an oil well

descant *noun*
a tune sung or played above another tune

descend *verb*
to descend something like a hill or staircase is to go down it **to be descended from someone** is to be in the same family as them but living at a later time

descendant *noun*
a person's descendants are the

people who are descended from them

descent noun
a descent is a climb down, usually a hard or long one

describe verb
to describe something or someone is to say what they are like

description noun
1 description is saying what someone or something is like • *She's a writer who's very good at description.* **2** a description is something you write or say that describes what someone or something is like • *He gave the police a description of the robbers.* **descriptive** adjective
a descriptive word or piece of writing describes someone or something • *a descriptive poem*

desert noun (say **dez**-ert)
a large area of very dry, often sandy, land

desert verb (say di-**zert**)
to desert someone or something is to leave them without intending to return **deserter** noun a soldier who runs away from the army **desertion** noun
desertion is when a soldier runs away from the army

deserted adjective
a place is deserted when there is nobody there

desert island noun
a tropical island where nobody lives

deserts plural noun (say di-**zerts**)
someone's deserts are what they deserve • *He got his deserts.*

deserve verb
to deserve something is to be worthy of it or to have a right to it **deservedly** adverb rightly, because it is deserved • *This restaurant is deservedly popular.*

design noun
1 the way that something is made or arranged **2** a drawing that shows how something is to be made **3** lines and shapes forming a pattern

design verb
to design something is to make a design or plan for it **designer** noun someone who designs things, especially clothes

desirable adjective
worth having or doing • *It is desirable for you to come with us.*

desire verb
to desire something is to want it very much

desire noun
a feeling of wanting something very much

desk noun
1 a piece of furniture with a flat top and drawers, used for writing, reading, or working at **2** a counter at which a cashier or receptionist sits

desktop adjective
small enough to use on a desk • *I've bought a desktop computer.*

desolate adjective
1 lonely and sad **2** a desolate place is empty, with no people living there • *It was now a dark and desolate land.* **desolation** noun feeling desolate

despair noun
despair is a complete loss of hope

despair verb
to despair is to lose hope completely

despatch noun (**despatches**), verb
a different spelling of *dispatch*

desperate adjective
1 extremely serious or hopeless • *We were in a desperate situation.* **2** ready to do anything to get out of a difficulty • *There are three desperate criminals at large.* **3** needing or wanting something very much • *She was desperate to go home.* **desperately** adverb seriously; recklessly **desperation** noun desperation is being desperate

despicable adjective
very unpleasant or evil

despise verb
to despise someone is to hate them and have no respect at all for them

despite preposition
in spite of • *They went out despite the rain.*

dessert noun (say di-**zert**)
fruit or a sweet food eaten at the end of a meal

destination noun
the place you are travelling to

destined adjective
intended by fate; meant to happen • *They felt they were destined to win.*

destiny noun (**destinies**)
your destiny is what is intended for you in the future; your fate • *His destiny was to travel the world.*

destroy verb
to destroy something is to ruin it or put an end to it **destruction** noun when something is destroyed **destructive** adjective causing a lot of damage

detach verb
to detach something is to remove it or separate it • *Detach the coupon from the bottom of the page.*

detached adjective
a detached house is one that is not joined to another house

detail noun
1 a small piece of information **2** a small part of a design or picture or piece of decoration **in detail** describing or dealing with everything fully

detain verb
1 to detain someone is to keep them in a place **2** to detain someone is also to keep them waiting • *I'll try not to detain you for long.*

detect verb
to detect something is to discover or notice it **detection** noun detection is detecting something **detector** noun a detector is a device that detects something

detective noun
a person, especially a police officer, who investigates crimes

detention noun
detention is when someone is made to stay in a place, especially made to stay late in school as a punishment

deter verb (**deterring**, **deterred**)
to deter someone is to put them off doing something

detergent noun
a kind of washing powder or liquid

deteriorate verb
to deteriorate is to become worse • *The weather was starting to deteriorate.* **deterioration** noun deterioration is when something becomes worse

determination noun
a strong intention to achieve something, even though it is difficult

determined djective
having your mind firmly made up

dessert

desert

deterrent *noun*
something that is meant to put people off doing something, such as a powerful weapon **deterrence** *noun* deterrence is being a deterrent

detest *verb*
to detest something is to dislike it very much
detestable *adjective* horrid

detonate *verb*
to detonate a bomb is to make it explode **detonation** *noun* detonation is making a bomb explode **detonator** *noun* a device that makes a bomb explode

detour *noun*
a less direct route you use instead of the normal route

deuce *noun*
a tennis score when each player has 40 points and needs two more points in a row to win the game

devastate *verb*
to devastate a place is to ruin or destroy it, making it impossible to live in **devastation** *noun* devastation is destruction of a place

devastated *adjective*
someone is devastated when they are extremely shocked and upset

develop *verb*
1 to develop something is to make it bigger or better **2** to develop is to become bigger or better **3** to develop photographic film is to treat it with chemicals so that pictures appear on it

developing country *noun* (**developing countries**)
a poor country that is building up its industry and trying to improve its living conditions

development *noun*
a development is something interesting that has happened • *Have there been any further developments since I last saw you?*

device *noun*
a piece of equipment used for a particular purpose **to leave someone to their own devices** is to leave them alone to do as they wish and not tell them what to do

devil *noun*
an evil spirit or person
devilish *adjective* cruel or wicked, like a devil

devious *adjective*
1 using unfair and dishonest methods • *He got rich by devious*

means. **2** not straight or direct • *The coach took us by a devious route to avoid the traffic jams.*

devise *verb*
to devise a plan or idea is to think it up

devolution *noun*
handing over power from a central government to a local or regional government

devote *verb*
to devote yourself or your time to something is to spend all your time doing it • *They devote all their free time to sport.*

devoted *adjective*
loving and loyal • *They are devoted parents.* **devotion** *noun* great love or loyalty

devour *verb*
to devour something is to eat or swallow it greedily

devout *adjective*
deeply religious

dew *noun*
tiny drops of water that form during the night on the ground and other surfaces out of doors **dewy** *adjective* wet with dew or like dew

diabetes *noun*
(*say* dy-a-**bee**-teez)
a disease in which there is too much sugar in a person's blood **diabetic** *noun* a person suffering from diabetes **diabetic** *adjective* suffering from diabetes

diabolical *adjective*
like a devil; very wicked

diagnose *verb*
to diagnose a disease is to find out what it is and what treatment is needed

diagnosis *noun*
a doctor makes a diagnosis when they decide what disease someone has

diagonal *noun*
a straight line joining opposite corners **diagonally** *adverb* across from one corner to another

diagram *noun*
a drawing or picture that shows the parts of something or how it works

dial *noun*
a circular piece of plastic or card with numbers or letters round it

dial *verb*
to dial a telephone number is to choose it by pressing numbered buttons

dialect *noun*
the form of a language used by people in one area of the country but not in the rest of the country

dialogue *noun*
talk between people, especially in a play, film, or book

diameter *noun*
1 a line drawn from one side of a circle to the other, passing through the centre **2** the length of this line

diamond *noun*
1 a very hard jewel that looks like clear glass **2** a shape which has four equal sides but which is not a square **3** a playing card with red diamond shapes on it

diarrhoea *noun*
(*say* dy-a-**ree**-a)
an illness that makes you have to keep going to the toilet and the waste matter you empty from your bowels is very watery

diary *noun*
(**diaries**)
a book with a separate space to write in for each day of the year, in which you write down what happens each day

diamond

dice *noun* (**dice**)
a small cube marked with one to six dots on each side, thrown to give a number in some games

dictate *verb*
1 to dictate something is to speak or read it aloud for someone else to write down **2** to dictate to someone is to give them orders in a bossy way **dictation** *noun* an exercise in writing down what someone reads out

dictator *noun*
a ruler who has complete power over the people of a country **dictatorship** *noun* a country ruled by a dictator

dictionary *noun* (**dictionaries**)
a book with words listed in alphabetical order, so that you can find out what a word means and how to spell it

die *verb* (**dying, died**)
to die is to stop living **to die down** is to gradually become less strong • *The wind died down at last.* **to die out** is to gradually disappear • *The tiger is beginning to die out.*

diesel *noun*
1 a diesel is an engine that works by burning oil in compressed air **2** diesel is fuel for this kind of engine

a
b
c
d
e
f
g
h
i
j
k
l
m
n
o
p
q
r
s
t
u
v
w
x
y
z

diet *noun*
1 a diet is a choice of food that someone eats to be healthy or to lose weight • *Mum's on a diet.* **2** someone's diet is the food they normally eat

diet *verb*
to diet is to keep to a special diet, especially in order to lose weight

differ *verb*
1 to differ from something is to be not the same as it **2** to differ is to disagree • *The two writers differ on this point.*

difference *noun*
1 the way in which something is different from something else **2** the amount between two numbers • *The difference between 8 and 3 is 5.*

different *adjective*
one person or thing is different from another when they are not the same **differently** *adverb* in a different way

difficult *adjective*
needing a lot of effort or skill; not easy

difficulty *noun* (**difficulties**)
1 difficulty is not being easy, trouble • *I had difficulty answering most of the questions.* **2** a difficulty is something that causes a problem • *She has learning difficulties.*

dig *verb* (**digging, dug**)
1 to dig soil or the ground is to break it up and move it **2** to dig a hole is to make it **3** to dig someone is to poke them • *He dug me in the ribs.* **digger** *noun* a machine for digging

dig *noun*
a sharp thrust or poke • *She gave me a dig in the ribs with her elbow.*

digest *verb*
to digest food is to soften and change it in the stomach and intestine so that the body can absorb it **digestible** *adjective* easy to digest **digestion** *noun* the way your body digests food

digestive *adjective*
to do with digesting food

digit *noun* (*say* **dij**-it)
1 any of the numbers from 0 to 9 **2** a finger or toe

digital *adjective*
1 a digital clock or watch has a row of digits to indicate numbers **2** a digital computer or recording stores the data or sound as a series of binary digits

dignified *adjective*
having dignity

dignity *noun*
a calm and serious manner

dike *noun*
1 a long wall or embankment

to hold back water and prevent flooding **2** a ditch for draining water from land

dilemma *noun*
an awkward choice between two possible actions, either of which would cause difficulties

dilute *verb*
to dilute a liquid is to make it weaker by mixing it with water **dilution** *noun* diluting a liquid

dim *adjective* (**dimmer, dimmest**)
only faintly lit and difficult to see **dimly** *adverb* to see something dimly is to find it hard to see clearly

dim *verb* (**dimming, dimmed**)
a light dims when it becomes less bright • *As the curtain rose, the lights dimmed.*

dimension *noun*
1 a measurement such as length, width, area, or volume • *What are the dimensions of the box?* **2** size or extent

diminish *verb*
1 to diminish something is to make it smaller **2** to diminish is to become smaller

dimple *noun*
a small hollow on a person's cheek or chin

din *noun*
a loud noise

dine *verb*
to dine is to have dinner **diner** *noun* someone eating a meal in a restaurant or hotel

dinghy *noun* (**dinghies**) (*say* **ding**-i)
a kind of small boat

dingy *adjective* (**dingier, dingiest**) (*say* **din**-ji)
shabby and dirty-looking

dinner *noun*
the main meal of the day, eaten either in the middle of the day or in the evening

dinosaur *noun*
a prehistoric reptile, often of enormous size

dip *verb* (**dipping, dipped**)
1 to dip something is to put it into a liquid and then take it out again • *Dip the brush in the paint.* **2** to dip is to go or slope downwards • *The road dips steeply after the hill.* **3** to dip a vehicle's headlights is to lower the beam so that they do not dazzle other drivers

dip *noun*
1 a downward slope **2** a quick swim **3** a mixture into which things are dipped

diploma *noun*
a certificate awarded for skill in a particular subject

diplomacy *noun*
1 the business of keeping friendly with other nations **2** dealing with other people without upsetting or offending them

diplomatic *adjective*
1 to do with diplomacy **2** tactful and courteous **diplomat** *noun* someone who works in diplomacy **diplomatically** *adverb* in a tactful and courteous way

dire *adjective*
dreadful or serious • *The refugees are in dire need of food and shelter.*

direct *adjective*
1 as straight or quick as possible **2** frank and honest **directness** *noun* directness is being frank and honest

direct *verb*
1 to direct someone is to show them the way **2** to direct a film or play is to decide how it should be made or performed

direction *noun*
1 a direction is the way you go to get somewhere **2** direction is directing something **directions** information on how to use or do something or how to get somewhere

directly *adverb*
1 by a direct route • *Go directly to the shop.* **2** immediately • *I want you to come directly.*

director *noun*
1 a person who is in charge of something, especially one of a group of people managing a company **2** a person who decides how a film or play should be made or performed

directory *noun* (**directories**)
a book containing a list of people with their telephone numbers and addresses

dinosaur

dirt noun
earth or soil; anything that is not clean

dirty adjective (**dirtier, dirtiest**)
1 covered with dirt; not clean
2 rude or offensive **3** unfair or mean • *That was a dirty trick.*
dirtily adverb **dirtiness** noun

disability noun
something that prevents someone from using their body in the usual way

disabled adjective
having a disease or injury that makes it difficult for someone to use their body properly

disadvantage noun
something that hinders you or makes things difficult

disagree verb
1 to disagree with someone is to have or express a different opinion from them **2** to disagree with someone is also to have a bad effect on them • *Rich food disagrees with me.*
disagreement noun when people don't agree about something or argue about it

disappear verb
1 to disappear is to become impossible to see; to vanish
2 to disappear is also to stop happening or existing • *Her nervousness soon disappeared.*
disappearance noun a person's or thing's disappearance is when they disappear

disappoint verb
to disappoint someone is to fail to do what they want
disappointing adjective causing someone to be disappointed
disappointment noun a feeling of being disappointed

disapprove verb
to disapprove of someone or something is to have a bad opinion of them **disapproval** noun having a bad opinion

disaster noun
1 a very bad accident or misfortune, often one where many people are killed or injured **2** a complete failure
• *The first night of the play was a disaster.* **disastrous** adjective causing great misfortune; going completely wrong
disastrously adverb

disc noun
1 a round flat object **2** a round, flat piece of plastic on which sound or data is recorded; a CD

discard verb
to discard something is to throw it away

disciple noun
a follower of a political or religious leader

discipline noun
1 training people to obey rules and punishing them if they don't
2 the control you have over how you behave • *You need lots of discipline to learn the piano.*

disc jockey noun
someone who introduces and plays records on the radio or at a club

disclose verb
to disclose information or a secret is to tell someone about it **disclosure** noun disclosure is telling people information that is secret

disco noun
a place or party where music is played for dancing

discomfort noun
being uncomfortable

disconnect verb
to disconnect something is to break its connection or detach it **disconnection** noun disconnecting something

discontented adjective
unhappy and not satisfied
discontent noun discontent is a feeling of being unhappy or not satisfied

discount noun
an amount by which a price is reduced

discourage verb
1 to discourage someone is to take away their enthusiasm or confidence **2** to discourage someone from doing something is to try to persuade them not to do it **discouragement** noun a feeling of being discouraged

discover verb
to discover something is to find it or learn about it, especially by chance or for the first time

discovery noun (**discoveries**)
1 finding or learning about something, especially by chance or for the first time • *Columbus is famous for the discovery of America.* **2** something that is found or learned about for the first time • *This drug was an important discovery in the history of medicine.*

discreet adjective
being careful in what you say and do, especially when you have a secret to keep
discreetly adverb

discriminate verb
1 to discriminate between things is to notice the differences between them, or to prefer one

thing to another **2** to discriminate between people is to treat them differently or unfairly because of their race, sex, or religion

discrimination noun
1 discrimination is treating people differently or unfairly because of their race, sex, or religion **2** discrimination is also the ability to notice the differences between things

discus noun (say **dis**-kuss)
a thick heavy disc thrown in an athletic contest

discuss verb (say dis-**kuss**)
to discuss a subject is to talk with other people about it or to write about it in detail

discussion noun
1 a conversation about a subject
2 a piece of writing in which the writer examines a subject from different points of view

disease noun
a disease is an illness or sickness
diseased adjective someone or something is diseased when they have a disease

disembark verb
to disembark is to get out of a boat or aircraft

disgrace noun
1 disgrace is shame • *You have brought disgrace to your family.*
2 a disgrace is a person or thing that is so bad that people should feel ashamed • *This room is an absolute disgrace.* **disgraceful** adjective so bad that people should feel ashamed about it
disgracefully adverb

disgrace verb
to disgrace someone or something is to bring them shame

disguise verb
to disguise someone or something is to make them look different so that other people won't recognize them
disguise noun
clothes or make-up you put on to change the way you look so that people won't recognize you

disguise

disgust noun
a strong feeling of dislike or contempt

disgust verb
to disgust someone is to make them feel disgust **disgusted** adjective disliking someone or something very much **disgusting** adjective very unpleasant; making you feel disgust

a
b
c
d
e
f
g
h
i
j
k
l
m
n
o
v
w
x
y
z

dish noun
1 a plate or bowl for food
2 food that has been prepared
for eating
dish verb
to dish something out
(informal) is to give it to people
dishonest adjective
not honest or truthful
dishonesty noun dishonesty
is being dishonest
dishwasher noun
a machine for washing dishes
automatically
disinfect verb
to disinfect something is to treat
it to kill all the germs in it
disinfectant noun
a liquid used to disinfect things
disintegrate verb
to disintegrate is to break up into
small pieces
disintegration noun the
disintegration of something is
when it disintegrates
disinterested adjective
not favouring one side more than
the other; impartial
disk noun
a disc, especially one used to
store computer data
dislike verb
to dislike someone or something
is not to like them
dislike noun
a feeling of not liking someone
or something
dislocate verb
to dislocate a bone or joint in
your body is to make it come out
of its proper place by accident
dislocation noun dislocating
something
dislodge verb
to dislodge something is to move
it from its place
disloyal adjective
not loyal
dismal adjective
gloomy and sad
dismally adverb
dismantle verb
to dismantle something is to take
it to pieces
dismay noun
a feeling of strong
disappointment and surprise
dismayed adjective disappointed
and surprised
dismiss verb
1 to dismiss someone is to tell
them that they have to leave,
especially to leave their job 2 to
dismiss an idea or suggestion is
to reject it **dismissal** noun losing
your job
dismount verb
to dismount is to get off a horse
or bicycle

disobey verb
to disobey someone is to refuse
to do what they tell you to do
disobedience noun disobedience
is refusing to obey someone
disobedient adjective someone
who is disobedient doesn't do
what someone tells them to do
disorder noun
1 disorder is confusion or
disturbance 2 a disorder is an
illness **disorderly** adjective
behaving in a wild and noisy way
dispatch noun
a report or message
dispatch verb
1 to dispatch something or
someone is to send them
somewhere 2 to dispatch
someone is to kill them
dispense verb
1 to dispense something is to give
it out to people • *The machine
dispenses drinks and snacks.* 2 to
dispense medicine is to prepare
it for patients **to dispense with
something** is to do without it
disperse verb
1 to disperse people is to send
them away in various directions
• *The police dispersed the crowd.*
2 to disperse is to go off in
various directions **dispersal**
noun dispersal is when people
go off in different directions
display verb
to display something is to
arrange it so that it can be
clearly seen
display noun
1 a show or exhibition 2 the
showing of information on a
computer screen
displease verb
to displease someone is to annoy
them
disposable adjective
something that is disposable is
made to be thrown away after it
has been used
disposal noun
getting rid of something **at your
disposal** ready for you to use
dispose verb
to dispose of something is to
get rid of it
disprove verb
to disprove something is to prove
that it is not true
dispute noun
a quarrel or disagreement
disqualify verb (**disqualifies,
disqualifying, disqualified**)
to disqualify someone is to
remove them from a race
or competition because
they have broken the rules
disqualification noun when
someone is disqualified

disregard verb
to disregard someone or
something is to take no notice
of them
disrespect noun
lack of respect; rudeness
disrespectful adjective showing
disrespect **disrespectfully**
adverb in a disrespectful way
disrupt verb
to disrupt something is to stop it
running smoothly or throw it into
confusion • *Floods have disrupted
local traffic.* **disruption** noun
when something stops running
smoothly **disruptive** adjective
causing so much disorder that a
meeting or lesson can't continue
dissatisfied adjective
not satisfied or pleased
dissatisfaction noun
dissatisfaction is being
dissatisfied
dissect verb
to dissect something is to cut
it up so that you can examine
it **dissection** noun dissecting
something
dissolve verb
1 to dissolve
something
is to mix
it with a
liquid so that
it becomes part
of the liquid 2 to
dissolve is to melt
or become liquid
dissuade verb
to dissuade
someone is to
persuade them not
to do something

dissolve

distance noun
the amount of space between
two places or things **in the
distance** a long way off but
able to be seen
distant adjective
1 far away 2 a person who
is distant is not friendly or
sociable
distil verb (**distilling, distilled**)
to distil a liquid is to purify it
by boiling it and then letting
it cool so that it becomes liquid
again
distillery noun (**distilleries**)
a place where whisky and
other alcoholic drinks are
produced
distinct adjective
1 easily heard or seen; clear
or definite • *You have made a
distinct improvement.* 2 clearly
separate or different • *A rabbit
is quite distinct from a hare.*
distinctly adverb clearly or
noticeably

distinction noun
1 a distinction is a clear difference between two things 2 distinction is excellence or honour • *She is a writer of distinction.*

distinctive adjective
clearly different from all the others and easy to recognize or notice • *The school has a distinctive blue football strip.*

distinguish verb
1 to distinguish things is to notice the differences between them 2 to distinguish something is to see or hear it clearly

distinguished adjective
famous, successful, and much admired by other people • *There was a distinguished writer staying at the same hotel.*

distort verb
1 to distort something is to change it into a strange shape • *His face was distorted with anger.* 2 to distort facts is to change them so that they are untrue or misleading **distortion** noun distortion is distorting something

distract verb
to distract someone is to take their attention away from what they are doing • *Don't distract the bus driver.* **distraction** noun when you are distracted

divers

distress noun
great sorrow, suffering or trouble **in distress** a ship or plane is in distress when it is in difficulty and needs help

distress verb
to distress someone is to make them feel very upset or worried

distribute verb
1 to distribute things is to give them out or deliver them • *The teacher distributed textbooks to the class.* 2 to distribute something is to share it among a number of people • *The money was distributed among all the local schools.* 3 to distribute something is also to spread or scatter it around • *Make sure your weight is evenly distributed.* **distribution** noun distribution is distributing things

district noun
part of a town or country

distrust noun
lack of trust; suspicion **distrustful** adjective not trusting people

distrust verb
to think that someone or something can't be trusted

disturb verb
1 to disturb someone is to interrupt them or spoil their peace 2 to disturb someone is also to worry or upset them 3 to disturb something is to move it from its right position **disturbance** noun a disturbance is something that disturbs someone

disused adjective
no longer used • *The house was next to a disused warehouse.*

ditch noun
a narrow trench to hold or carry away water

dither verb
to dither is to hesitate nervously

ditto noun
the same again. Ditto marks (″) are sometimes used in lists or bills to show where something is repeated

dive verb
1 to dive is to go into water head first 2 to dive is also to move downwards quickly • *The aeroplane then dived.*

diver noun
1 a swimmer who dives 2 someone who works under water using special breathing equipment

diverse adjective
very different from each other and of several different kinds • *He has a diverse collection of rocks.* **diversity** noun diversity is variety

diversion noun
1 a different way for traffic to go when the usual road is closed 2 something amusing or entertaining

divert verb
1 to divert something is to change the direction it is moving in 2 to divert someone is to amuse or entertain them

divide verb
1 to divide something is to separate it into smaller parts or shares 2 (in mathematics) to divide a number by another number is to find out how many times the second number is contained in the first • *Divide six by two and you get three (6÷2 = 3).*

divine adjective
1 belonging to God or coming from God 2 like a god 3 (informal) excellent; extremely beautiful **divinity** noun divinity is the fact

of being a god or like God

division noun
1 the process of dividing numbers or things 2 one of the parts into which something is divided

divisible adjective able to be divided exactly • *27 is divisible by 9.*

divorce noun
the legal ending of a marriage

divorce verb
a husband and wife divorce when they end their marriage by law

Diwali noun (say di-**wah**-li)
a Hindu festival held in October or November

DIY
short for do-it-yourself

dizzy adjective (**dizzier, dizziest**)
giddy and feeling confused **dizzily** adverb **dizziness** noun

DJ
short for disc jockey

do verb (**does, doing, did, done**)
1 to do something is to perform it or deal with it • *Are you doing your work?* • *I can't do this sum.* 2 to do well is to manage; to do badly is not to manage very well 3 you say that something will do when it is all right or suitable • *I'd really like some football boots but trainers will do.* 4 you also use **do** with other verbs in special ways • *Do you want this?* • *He does not want it.* • *I do like crisps.* • *We work as hard as they do.* **to do something up** is to fasten it • *Do up your coat.* **to do without something** is to manage without having it

docile adjective
gentle and obedient

dock¹ noun
a part of a harbour where ships are loaded, unloaded, or repaired

dock¹ verb
1 a ship docks when it comes into a dock 2 spacecraft dock when they join together in orbit

dock² noun
a place for the prisoner on trial in a lawcourt

dock³ verb
to dock an animal's tail is to cut it short

dock⁴ noun
a weed with broad leaves

docker noun
a person whose job is loading and unloading ships

doctor noun
a person trained to heal sick or injured people

document noun
1 an important written or printed piece of paper 2 something stored in a computer or on a disk, such as a piece of text or a picture

a
b
c
d
e
f
g
h
i
j
k
l
m
n
o
p
q
r
s
t
u
v
w
x
y
z

documentary noun
(**documentaries**)
a film or a television programme that tells you about real events or situations

dodge verb
to dodge something is to move quickly to avoid it

dodge noun
a trick; a clever way of doing something

dodgem noun
a small electrically driven car at a funfair, in which you drive round an enclosure, dodging and bumping other cars

doe noun
a female deer, rabbit, or hare

dog noun
a four-legged animal that barks, often kept as a pet

dog

dogged adjective
(say **dog**-id)
not giving up in spite of difficulties; obstinate
doggedly adverb

do-it-yourself adjective
suitable for anyone to make or use at home, rather than paying for someone else to do it

doldrums plural noun
the ocean regions near the equator, where there is little or no wind **in the doldrums** bored and unhappy

dole noun
(informal) money paid by the government to unemployed people

doll noun
a toy model of a person, especially a baby or child

dollar noun
a unit of money in the United States and some other countries

dolphin noun
a sea mammal like a small whale with a snout like a beak

dome noun
a roof shaped like the top half of a ball

domestic adjective
1 to do with the home **2** a domestic animal is tame and kept at home

dominant adjective
most powerful or important
dominance noun being dominant

dominate verb
to dominate people is to control

them by being the most powerful
domination noun dominating people

domino noun (**dominoes**)
a small flat oblong piece of wood or plastic with dots (1 to 6) or a blank space at each end, used in the game of **dominoes**

dominoes

donate verb
to donate something, especially money, is to give it to a charity or organization **donation** noun
a donation is something that is donated

donkey noun (**donkeys**)
an animal that looks like a small horse with long ears

donor noun
someone who gives something
• New blood donors are needed.

doodle noun
a quick drawing or scribble
doodle verb
to doodle is to draw a doodle

doom noun
a grim fate like ruin or death

doom verb
to be doomed to something is to have a grim fate you can't avoid

door noun
a movable panel that opens and closes the entrance to a room, building, or cupboard

doorway noun
the opening into which a door fits

dormitory noun (**dormitories**)
a room for several people to sleep in, especially in a school

dose noun
the amount of a medicine that you are meant to take at one time

dot noun
a tiny spot

dot verb (**dotting, dotted**)
to dot something is to mark it with dots **dotted** adjective
made of dots • Write on the dotted line.

double adjective
1 twice as much or twice as many **2** having two of something
• a double-barrelled shotgun
3 suitable for two people
• a double bed

double noun
1 double is twice the amount or cost **2** a double is someone who looks exactly like someone

else **3** you play doubles in tennis when you play with someone else against another pair of players

double verb
1 to double something is to make it twice as big **2** to double is to become twice as big **to double up** is to bend over because you are in pain or laughing so much

double bass noun
a musical instrument with strings, like a large cello

double-cross verb
to double-cross someone is to cheat or betray them when you are supposed to be supporting them

doubly adverb
twice as much • It's doubly important that you should go.

doubt noun
not feeling sure about something

doubt verb
to doubt something is to feel unsure about it • I doubt whether he is telling the truth.

doubtful adjective
1 having doubts • She looked doubtful. **2** making you feel doubt • Their story was very doubtful. **doubtfully** adverb

dough noun
a thick mixture of flour and water used for making bread or pastry
doughy adjective thick and sticky like dough

doughnut noun
a round or ring-shaped bun that has been fried and covered with sugar

doughnuts

dove noun
a kind of pigeon, often used as a symbol of peace

down[1] adverb, preposition
1 to or in a lower place • It fell down. • Run down the hill.
2 along • Go down to the shops.

down[2] noun
very soft feathers or hair • Ducks are covered with down. **downy** adjective covered in something very soft like feathers or hair

downcast adjective
sad or dejected

downfall noun
1 a person's downfall is their ruin or fall from power 2 a heavy fall of rain or snow

downhill adverb
down a slope

downpour noun
a heavy fall of rain

downright adjective, adverb
very, completely • I felt downright angry about it.

downs plural noun
grass-covered hills • Let's have a picnic on the downs.

downstairs adverb, adjective
to or on a lower floor

downstream adverb
in the direction that a river or stream flows

downward or **downwards** adverb
towards a lower place

doze verb
to doze is to sleep lightly
dozy adjective feeling sleepy

dozen noun
a set of twelve

Dr
short for **Doctor**

drab adjective (**drabber, drabbest**)
1 dull and without colour • His clothes were drab. 2 dreary and uninteresting

draft noun
a rough plan for something you are going to write

draft verb
to draft something you are going to write is to make a rough plan of it

drag verb (**dragging, dragged**)
to drag something heavy is to pull it along

drag noun
(informal) something annoying or tedious

dragon noun
a winged lizard-like monster that breathes fire in stories

dragonfly noun (**dragonflies**)
an insect with a long body and two pairs of transparent wings

dragonfly

drain noun
a pipe or ditch for taking away water or sewage

drain verb
1 to drain water is to take it away with drains 2 to drain is to flow or trickle away 3 to drain a glass or bottle is to empty liquid out of it 4 to drain someone is to exhaust them **drainage** noun a system of drains

drama noun
1 drama is writing or performing plays 2 a drama is a play 3 a drama is also a series of exciting events

dramatic adjective
1 to do with drama 2 exciting and impressive • A dramatic change has taken place.
dramatically adverb

dramatist noun
someone who writes plays

dramatize verb
1 to dramatize a story is to make it into a play 2 to dramatize an event is to exaggerate it • Why do you always dramatize everything? **dramatization** noun a dramatization is a play made from a story

drape verb
to drape something like cloth is to hang it loosely over something

drastic adjective
having a strong or violent effect
drastically adverb

draught noun (rhymes with **craft**)
a current of cold air indoors
draughty adjective a draughty room has lots of draughts

draughts noun
a game played with 24 round pieces on a chessboard

draw verb (**drawing, drew, drawn**)
1 to draw a picture or outline is to form it with a pencil or pen 2 to draw something is to pull it • She drew her chair up to the table. 3 to draw people is to attract them • The fair drew large crowds. 4 to draw is to end a game or contest with the same score on both sides • They drew 2-2 last Saturday. 5 to draw the curtains is to open or close them 6 to draw near is to come nearer • The ship was drawing nearer.

draw noun
1 a raffle or similar competition in which the winner is chosen by picking tickets or numbers at random 2 a game that ends with the same score on both sides 3 an attraction
drawback noun
a disadvantage

drawbridge noun
a bridge over a moat, hinged at one end so that it can be raised or lowered

drawer noun
a sliding box-like container in a piece of furniture

drawing noun
something you draw with a pencil or pen

drawing pin noun a short pin with a large flat top that you use for fixing paper to a surface

dread verb
to dread something is to fear it very much

dread noun
great fear

dreadful adjective
very bad • We've had dreadful weather. **dreadfully** adverb very badly

dreadlocks plural noun
hair in long tightly-curled ringlets, worn especially by Rastafarians

dream noun
1 things you picture happening while you are sleeping 2 something you would like to do or have very much • His dream is to be famous. **dreamy** adjective like a dream; not real

dream verb (**dreaming, dreamt** or **dreamed**)
1 to dream is to have a dream 2 to dream is also to want something badly • She dreams of being a ballet dancer. 3 to dream something is to think it may happen • I never dreamt she would leave.

dreary adjective (**drearier, dreariest**)
1 dull or boring 2 gloomy
drearily adverb
dreariness noun

dredge verb
to dredge something is to drag it up, especially mud from the bottom of water **dredger** noun a machine for clearing mud from the bottom of a river

drench verb
to drench someone or something is to soak them • They got drenched in the rain.

dress noun
1 a dress is a woman's or girl's piece of clothing, having a top and skirt in one 2 dress is clothes or costume • We have to wear fancy dress.

dress verb
1 to dress is to put clothes on 2 to dress a wound is to put a bandage or plaster it

dresser noun
a sideboard with shelves at the top

a b c d e f g h i j k l m n o p q r s t u v w x y z

a
b
c
d
e
f
g
h
i
j
k
l
m
n
o
p
q
r
s
t
u
v
w
x
y
z

dressing *noun*
1 a sauce of oil, vinegar, and spices for a salad **2** a bandage or plaster used to cover a wound
dressing gown *noun*
a loose light indoor coat you wear over pyjamas or a nightdress
dribble *verb*
1 to dribble is to let saliva trickle out of your mouth **2** to dribble with a ball is to kick it gently as you run along, so that it stays close to your feet
drier *noun*
a device for drying hair or washing
drift *verb*
1 to drift is to be carried gently along by water or air **2** to drift is also to live casually or wander about without any real plan or purpose
drift *noun*
1 a mass of snow or sand piled up by the wind **2** the general meaning of what someone says • *Do you get my drift?*
drill *noun*
1 a tool for making holes **2** repeated exercises in military training, gymnastics, or sport **3** a set way of doing something • *Do you know the drill?*
drill *verb*
1 to drill a hole is to make a hole with a drill **2** to drill is to do repeated exercises
drink *verb* (**drinking, drank, drunk**)
1 to drink is to swallow liquid **2** to drink can also mean to have a lot of alcohol • *Don't drink and drive.* **drinker** *noun* someone who drinks
drink *noun*
1 a liquid for drinking **2** an alcoholic drink
drip *verb* (**dripping, dripped**)
1 to drip is to fall in drops **2** to drip is also to let liquid fall in drops • *The tap was dripping.*
drip *noun*
a falling drop of liquid
drive *verb* (**driving, drove, driven**)
1 to drive a vehicle is to operate it **2** to drive someone or something is to make them move • *The farmer was driving his herd across the road.* **3** to drive someone into a state or feeling is to force them into it • *That music is driving me mad!* **driver** *noun* someone who drives a vehicle
drive *noun*
1 a drive is a journey in a vehicle **2** drive is energy and enthusiasm **3** a drive is a road leading to a house **4** a drive is a powerful stroke of the ball in cricket, golf, and other games
drizzle *noun*
gentle rain
drizzle *verb*
to rain gently
drone *verb*
1 to make a low humming sound **2** to talk in a boring voice
drone *noun*
1 a droning sound **2** a male bee
droop *verb*
to droop is to hang down weakly
drop *noun*
1 a tiny amount of liquid **2** a fall or decrease • *There has been a sharp drop in prices.*
droplet *noun* a small drop
drop *verb* (**dropping, dropped**)
1 to drop is to fall **2** to drop something is to let it fall **3** to drop is also to become less or lower • *The temperature suddenly dropped.* **to drop in** is to visit someone casually **to drop out** is to stop taking part in something
drought *noun* (*rhymes with* **out**)
a long period of dry weather
drown *verb*
1 to drown is to die from being under water and unable to breathe **2** to drown a person or animal is to kill them by forcing them to stay under water **3** to drown sounds is to make so much noise that they cannot be heard
drowsy *adjective* (**drowsier, drowsiest**)
sleepy **drowsily** *adverb*
drowsiness *noun*
drug *noun*
1 a substance that kills pain or cures a disease **2** a substance that people take because it affects their senses or their mind. Some drugs cause addiction or are illegal.
drug *verb* (**drugging, drugged**)
to drug someone is to make them unconscious with drugs
drum *noun*
1 a musical instrument made of a cylinder with a thin skin stretched over one end or both ends **2** a cylindrical container • *There was a row of oil drums along the side of the road.*

drums

drum *verb* (**drumming, drummed**)
1 to drum is to play a drum or drums **2** to drum on something is to tap it repeatedly • *He drummed his fingers on the table.*
drummer *noun* someone who plays the drums
drumstick *noun*
1 a stick used for hitting a drum **2** the lower part of a cooked bird's leg
drunk¹ *adjective*
not able to control your behaviour through drinking too much alcohol
drunk¹ *noun*
someone who is drunk **drunkard** *noun* a person who is often drunk
dry *adjective* (**drier, driest**)
1 not wet or damp **2** boring and dull • *The book I'm reading is rather dry.* **3** funny in a clever and sarcastic way • *He has a very dry sense of humour.* **drily** *adverb* you speak drily when you say something funny in a clever and sarcastic way **dryness** *noun*
dry *verb* (**dries, drying, dried**)
1 to dry is to become dry **2** to dry something is to make it dry
dry-cleaning *noun*
a method of cleaning clothes using chemicals rather than water
dual *adjective*
having two parts or aspects; double • *This building has a dual purpose.*
dual carriageway *noun*
a road with several lanes in each direction
dub *verb* (**dubbing, dubbed**)
1 to change or add new sound to the sound on a film • *It's a Japanese film but has been dubbed into English.* **2** to give someone a name or title
dubious *adjective*
1 feeling doubtful or uncertain • *I'm dubious about our chances of winning.* **2** probably not honest or not good
duchess *noun*
a duke's wife or widow
duck *noun*
1 a web-footed water bird with a flat beak **2** a batsman's score of nought at cricket
duck *verb*
1 to duck is to bend down quickly to avoid something **2** to duck someone is to push them under water quickly
duckling *noun*
a young duck
due *adjective*
1 expected to arrive • *The train is due in five minutes.* **2** needing to be paid • *Payment for the trip is*

due next week. **due to something or someone** because of something or someone • *The traffic jam was due to an accident.*

due *adverb*
directly • *The camp is due north.*

duel *noun*
a fight between two people, especially with pistols or swords

duet *noun*
a piece of music for two players or two singers

duke *noun*
a member of the highest rank of noblemen

dull *adjective*
1 not bright or clear; gloomy • *It was a dull day.* **2** boring • *What a dull programme.* **3** not sharp • *I had a dull pain.* **dully** *adverb* **dullness** *noun*

duly *adverb*
rightly; as expected • *They promised to come, and later they duly arrived.*

dumb *adjective*
1 unable to speak; silent **2** (*informal*) stupid

dumbfounded *adjective*
unable to say anything because you are so astonished

dummy *noun* (**dummies**)
1 a large doll or model made to look like a human being; an imitation **2** an imitation teat for a baby to suck

dump *noun*
1 a place where something, especially rubbish, is left or stored **2** (*informal*) a place you don't like

dump *verb*
1 to dump something is to get rid of it when you don't want it **2** to dump something somewhere is to put it down carelessly

dumpling *noun*
a lump of boiled or baked dough, usually eaten with a stew

dumpy *adjective* (**dumpier, dumpiest**)
short and fat

dune *noun*
a hill of loose sand formed by the wind

dung *noun*
solid waste matter from an animal

dungarees *plural noun*
trousers with a piece in front covering your chest, held up by straps over your shoulders

dungeon *noun* (*say* **dun**-jon)
an underground prison cell

dunk *verb*
to dunk something is to dip it into a liquid

duo *noun*
a pair of people, especially playing music

duplicate *noun* (*say* **dew**-pli-kat)
something that is exactly the same as something else; an exact copy

duplicate *verb* (*say* **dew**-pli-kayt)
to duplicate something is to make an exact copy of it **duplication** *noun* making an exact copy of something

durable *adjective*
lasting and strong **durability** *noun* something has durability when it is strong and lasts a long time

duration *noun*
the time something lasts

during *preposition*
while something else is going on • *Let's meet in the cafe during the interval.*

dusk *noun*
the time of the day just after sunset when it is starting to get dark

dust *noun*
a fine powder made up of tiny pieces of dry earth or other material

dust *verb*
1 to dust things is to clear the dust off them **2** to dust something is to sprinkle it with dust or powder • *You can dust the cake with sugar.*

dustbin *noun*
a bin kept outside a house for rubbish

duster *noun*
a cloth for dusting things

dustman *noun* (**dustmen**)
a person whose job is to empty dustbins

dustpan *noun*
a pan into which you brush dust

dusty *adjective* (**dustier, dustiest**)
covered with or full of dust

dutiful *adjective*
doing your duty; obedient **dutifully** *adverb*

duty *noun* (**duties**)
1 your duty is what you have to do, because it is right or part of your job **2** a duty is a kind of tax

duvet *noun* (*say* **doo**-vay)
a kind of quilt used instead of other bedclothes

DVD *noun*
short for *digital video disc* or *digital versatile disc*, a disc on which large amounts of sound and pictures can be stored, especially films

dwarf *noun* (**dwarfs** or **dwarves**)
a very small person or thing

dwarf *verb*
to dwarf something is to make it

seem very small • *The skyscraper dwarfs all the buildings round it.*

dwell *verb* (**dwelling, dwelt**)
to dwell in a place is to live there **to dwell on something** is to think or talk about it constantly

dwelling *noun*
a house or other place to live in

dwindle *verb*
to dwindle is to get smaller gradually • *Their food supplies were starting to dwindle.*

dye *verb*
to dye something is to change its colour by putting it in a special liquid

dye *noun*
a liquid used to dye things

dyke *noun*
another spelling of **dike**

dynamic *adjective*
energetic and active

dynamite *noun*
1 a powerful explosive **2** (*informal*) something that will make people angry or excited

dynamo *noun* (**dynamos**)
a machine that makes electricity

dynasty *noun* (**dynasties**) (*say* **din**-a-sti)
a series of kings and queens from the same family

dyslexia *noun* (*say* dis-**lek**-si-a)
special difficulty in being able to read and spell words **dyslexic** *adjective* someone is dyslexic when they have dyslexia

Ee

each *adjective, pronoun*
each person or thing in a group is every one of them when you think of them separately • *Each film lasts an hour.* • *You get ten marks for each of these questions.* • *We all knew each other.*

eager *adjective*
badly wanting to do something or to have something; enthusiastic **eagerly** *adverb* **eagerness** *noun*

eagle *noun*
a large bird of prey with strong eyesight

eagle

ear¹ *noun*
1 the part of your body that you hear with **2** an ear, or a good ear, for something is the ability to hear something clearly and understand it well • *She has an unusually good ear for music.*

ear² *noun*
the spike of seeds at the top of a stalk of corn

earache *noun*
a pain inside your ear

earl *noun*
a British nobleman

earlobe *noun*
the rounded part that hangs down at the bottom of your ear

early *adverb, adjective* (**earlier, earliest**)
1 arriving or happening before the usual or expected time • *Jane caught a bus and got home early.* **2** happening near the beginning • *The team was helped by an early goal.* • *The first murder comes early in the film.*

earn *verb*
1 to earn money is to get it by working for it **2** to earn a reward or praise is to do something good so that you deserve it

earnest *adjective*
serious about something you want to do or about something important **earnestly** *adverb*

earnings *plural noun*
earnings are money that someone earns

earphones *plural noun*
earphones are a set of two small flat speakers joined by a band that fits over your ears so that you can listen to music without other people hearing it

earring *noun*
an ornament worn on the ear

earshot *noun*
a sound is in earshot when it is close enough for you to be able to hear it

earth *noun*
1 the earth is the planet that we live on **2** earth is soil or the ground **3** an earth is a hole or burrow where a fox or badger lives you use **on earth** with words like *what, who,* and *where* to make the point stronger • *What on earth are you doing?*

earthly *adjective*
to do with life on earth

earthquake *noun*
a violent movement of part of the earth's surface caused by pressure that has built up underneath

earthworm *noun*
a common worm that is found in the soil

earwig *noun*
a crawling garden insect with pincers at the end of its body

ease *noun*
to do something with ease is to do it without any difficulty or trouble **to be at ease** is to be comfortable and relaxed • *She liked Tony and felt at ease with him.*

ease *verb*
1 to ease something unpleasant is to make it easier or less troublesome **2** a pain or problem eases when it becomes less severe or troublesome **3** to ease something is to move it gently into position

easel *noun*
a stand or frame for holding a blackboard or a painting

easily *adverb*
1 without difficulty; with ease • *Pencil marks can be easily rubbed out afterwards.* **2** by far • *This was easily the best victory of his career.* **3** very likely • *They could easily be wrong.*

east *noun*
1 the direction in which the sun rises **2** the part of a country or city that is in this direction

east *adjective, adverb*
1 towards the east or in the east **2** coming from the east • *An east wind made the day very cold.*

Easter *noun*
a Christian festival in spring, commemorating Christ's rising from the dead

eastern *adjective*
coming from or to do with the east

eastward or **eastwards** *adjective, adverb*
towards the east

easy *adjective* (**easier, easiest**)
something easy can be done or understood without trouble • *He started with easy questions.* • *The machine is easy to use.*

eat *verb* (**eating, ate, eaten**)
to eat food is to chew it and swallow it **to eat something up** or **eat something away** is to use it up or destroy it • *Acid rain has eaten away the forests.* • *The sun gradually ate up the mist.* • *Letter writing ate up most of her free time.*

eatable *adjective*
food is eatable when it is good and pleasant to eat

eaves *plural noun*
eaves are the overhanging edges of a roof

ebb *noun*
the movement of the tide when it is going out **to be at a low ebb** is to be in a poor or weak condition

ebb *verb*
1 the tide ebbs when it goes away from the land **2** a good feeling ebbs or ebbs away when it becomes much weaker • *When he saw his opponent his courage ebbed away.*

ebony *noun*
ebony is a hard black wood

eccentric *adjective* (say ik-**sen**-trik) behaving strangely **eccentricity** *noun* strange or unusual behaviour

echo *noun* (**echoes**)
a second sound that you hear when the original sound bounces back off something solid such as walls or high rocks

echo *verb*
1 to echo is to make an echo **2** to echo something said is to repeat it

éclair *noun* (say ay-**klair**)
a finger-shaped cake of pastry with a cream filling

eclipse *noun*
the blocking of light from the sun or moon, causing a short period of darkness. An eclipse of the sun happens when the moon comes between the sun and the earth and blocks out the light from the sun; and an eclipse of the moon happens when the earth comes between the moon and the sun and casts a dark shadow on the surface of the moon.

eclipse

ecology *noun* (say ee-**kol**-o-ji) ecology is the study of living creatures and plants in their surroundings **ecological** *adjective* to do with ecology

economic *adjective* (say eek-o-**nom**-ik or say ek-o-**nom**-ik)
1 to do with economics or the economy • *Coal no longer dominates the country's economic scene.* **2** making money, profitable • *It is not normally economic to get drinking water from the sea.*

economical *adjective* (say eek-o-**nom**-ik-al)
using money and resources carefully **economically** *adverb*

to do something economically is to use money and resources carefully when you do it

economics noun
(say eek-o-**nom**-iks or say ek-o-**nom**-iks)
economics is the study of how money is used and how goods and services are provided and used

economist noun (say i-**kon**-o-mist)
someone who studies economics

economize verb (say i-**kon**-o-myz)
to economize is to use money more carefully

economy noun (**economies**)
(say i-**kon**-o-mi)
1 an economy is a country's or family's income and the way it is spent **2** economy is being careful with money **3** economies are ways of saving money

ecstasy noun (**ecstasies**)
a feeling of great delight or joy
ecstatic adjective delighted and joyful about something

eczema noun (say **ek**-si-ma)
eczema is a skin disease that causes rough itching patches

edge noun
1 the part along the side or end of something **2** the sharp part of a knife or other cutting device
to be on edge is to feel nervous and irritable

edge verb
1 to edge is to move gradually and carefully • He edged a little closer to the door. **2** to edge something is to form a border to it • The lawn was edged with a brick path.

edgy adjective (**edgier**, **edgiest**)
nervous and irritable

edible adjective
an edible substance is one that you can eat, and is not poisonous

edit verb
1 to edit a book, newspaper, or magazine is to get it ready for publishing **2** to edit a film or tape recording is to choose parts of it and put them in the right order
editorial adjective to do with editing or editors

edition noun
1 the form in which something is published • There is a special illustrated edition of the book.
2 all the copies of a newspaper, magazine, or book issued at the same time

editor noun
1 someone who prepares a book, newspaper, or magazine for publishing **2** the person who manages a newspaper and is in charge of everything that is published in it

educate verb
to educate someone is to teach them and give them knowledge and skills

education noun
the process of teaching people and giving them knowledge and skills **educational** adjective to do with learning or teaching

eel noun
a long thin fish that looks like a snake

eerie adjective
weird and frightening • It was dark outside and there was an eerie silence. **eerily** adverb in an eerie way • Her voice echoed eerily in the cold air. **eeriness** noun

effect noun
1 something that happens because of something else • The drink had a strange effect on Alice.
2 a general impression • The lights made a cheerful effect.

effective adjective
producing what you want; successful • The program is much more effective if it is linked to the Internet. **effectively** adverb **effectiveness** noun

effervescent adjective
(say ef-er-**vess**-ent)
an effervescent liquid is fizzy and gives off bubbles
effervescence noun
effervescence is being fizzy or effervescent

efficient adjective
doing work well; effective
efficiency noun efficiency is being efficient and doing work well **efficiently** adverb

effort noun
1 effort is using energy or hard work **2** an effort is an attempt
effortless adjective not needing much work or effort • The team won another effortless victory.

e.g.
for example • There are lots of ways of finding out, e.g. ask a teacher.

egg¹ noun
1 an oval or round object with a thin shell that birds, fish, reptiles, and insects lay, and in which their young develop **2** a hen's or duck's egg used as food

eggs

egg² verb
to egg someone on is to encourage them with taunts or dares • He didn't want to dance but his friends egged him on.

Eid noun (say eed)
a Muslim festival that marks the end of the fast of Ramadan

eiderdown noun (say **I**-der-down)
a quilt stuffed with soft material

eight noun
the number 8

eighteen noun
the number 18
eighteenth adjective, noun 18th

eighth adjective, noun
the next after the seventh
eighthly adverb in the eighth place; as the eighth one

eighty noun (**eighties**)
the number 80
eightieth adjective, noun 80th

either determiner, pronoun
1 one or the other of two people or things • Either road will take us there. • Either of them might have seen the killer.
2 both of two things • The houses on either side were all boarded up.

either adverb
also; similarly • I don't like cabbage, and my brother doesn't either.

either conjunction
either … or … one thing or another, but not both • You can choose either a CD or a DVD.

eject verb
1 to eject something is to send it out with force **2** to eject someone is to make them leave
ejection noun ejection is ejecting something or someone

elaborate adjective
(say i-**lab**-er-at)
complicated or detailed

elastic noun
cord or material with strands of rubber in it so that it can stretch

elastic adjective
able to stretch and then return to its original shape or length

elated adjective
very pleased and excited

elbow noun
the joint in the middle of your arm, where it bends

elbow verb
to elbow someone is to push or prod them with your elbow

elder adjective
older • Josh is my elder brother.

elderly adjective
rather old

eldest adjective
oldest • Their eldest son George was born in 1660.

elect *verb*
to elect someone is to choose them by voting

election *noun*
the process of voting for people to be the government or to run an organization

electric or **electrical** *adjective*
to do with electricity, or worked by electricity **electrically** *adverb* by using electricity

electrician *noun*
someone whose job is to fit and repair electrical equipment

electricity *noun*
electricity is a kind of energy used to produce light and heat, and to make machines work

electrocute *verb*
to electrocute someone is to kill them when a large charge of electricity passes through them **electrocution** *noun* electrocution is electrocuting someone

electron *noun*
a particle of matter that is smaller than an atom and has a negative electric charge

electronic *adjective*
electronic equipment uses transistors and silicon chips which control electric currents **electronically** *adverb* by means of electronic devices

electronics *plural noun*
the use or study of electronic devices

elegant *adjective*
graceful and smart **elegance** *noun* elegance is being graceful and smart **elegantly** *adverb*

element *noun*
1 a substance that cannot be split up into simpler substances, for example copper and oxygen **2** a part of something **3** the elements of a subject are the basic facts to do with it, which you learn first **4** the elements are forces that make the weather, such as rain and wind **5** a wire or coil that gives out heat in an electric heater or cooker **to be in your element** is to be doing something you enjoy

elementary *adjective*
dealing with the simplest stages of something; easy

elephant *noun*
a very large animal found in Africa and India, with a thick grey skin, large ears, a trunk, and tusks

elevate *verb*
to elevate something is to lift it or raise it to a higher position

elevator *noun*
a lift for carrying people from one floor to another in a large building

eleven *noun*
1 the number 11 **2** a team of eleven people in cricket, football, and other sports
eleventh *adjective, noun* 11th

elf *noun* (**elves**)
a tiny mischievous fairy in stories

eligible *adjective*
a person is eligible for something when they are qualified or suitable for it
eligibility *noun* eligibility is being eligible for something

eliminate *verb*
to eliminate someone or something is to get rid of them **elimination** *noun* elimination is getting rid of someone or something

elk *noun* (**elk** or **elks**)
a large kind of deer

ellipse *noun*
an oval shape

elliptical *adjective*
oval-shaped

elm *noun*
a tall tree with large rough leaves

eloquent *adjective*
speaking well and expressing ideas clearly
eloquence *noun* eloquence is speaking well and clearly

else *adverb*
besides; instead • *Nobody else knows.* **or else** otherwise • *Run or else you'll be late.*

elsewhere *adverb*
somewhere else

elude *verb*
to elude someone is to escape from them or avoid being caught by them

elusive *adjective*
difficult to find or catch • *Deer are elusive animals.*

email *noun*
1 email is a system of sending messages from one person to another, using computers, it is short for *electronic mail* **2** an email is a message sent this way

email *verb*
to email someone is to send them an email

embankment *noun*
a long wall or bank of earth that holds back water or supports a road or railway

embark *verb*
to embark is to go on board a ship **to embark on something** is to begin something important
embarkation *noun* embarkation is going on board a ship

embarrass *verb*
to embarrass someone is to make them feel shy or awkward **embarrassment** *noun* embarrassment is feeling awkward or embarrassed

embassy *noun* (**embassies**)
a building where an ambassador from another country lives and has an office

embers *plural noun*
the embers of a fire are small pieces of coal or wood that keep glowing when the fire is going out

emblem *noun*
a symbol that stands for something • *The dove is an emblem of peace.*

embrace *verb*
to embrace someone is to hold them closely in your arms

embroider *verb*
to embroider cloth is to decorate it by stitching in designs or pictures **embroidery** *noun* embroidery is the art of embroidering

embroidery

embryo *noun* (**embryos**)
a baby or young animal that is growing in the womb

emerald *noun*
1 a green jewel **2** a bright green colour

emerge *verb*
to emerge is to come out or appear **emergence** *noun* the emergence of something is when it first appears

emergency *noun* (**emergencies**)
a sudden dangerous or serious

elephant

situation that needs to be dealt with very quickly

emigrant noun
someone who leaves their own country and goes to live in another country

emigrate verb
to emigrate is to leave your own country and go and live in another country **emigration** noun emigration is going to live in another country

eminent adjective
famous and respected • Britain's most eminent woman mountaineer died ten years ago. **eminence** noun eminence is being famous

emission noun
1 the action of sending something out 2 something that is emitted, for example smoke or fumes

emit verb (**emitting, emitted**)
to emit something such as smoke or fumes is to send it out

emotion noun
1 an emotion is a strong feeling in your mind, such as love or fear 2 emotion is being excited or upset • Tears of emotion flooded his eyes. **emotional** adjective showing emotion; to do with emotion **emotionally** adverb

emperor noun
the ruler of an empire

emphasis noun (**emphases**)
special importance given to something

emphasize verb
to emphasize something is to give it special importance, for example by saying it more loudly or by explaining it more fully

emphatic adjective
an emphatic statement or expression is one that you make very firmly or strongly • He agreed, with an emphatic nod of the head. **emphatically** adverb you say something emphatically when you are very firm and definite about it

empire noun
1 a group of countries ruled by one person or group of people 2 a large group of businesses or shops under the control of one person or group of people

employ verb
1 to employ someone is to pay them to work for you 2 to employ something is to use it

employee noun (say im-**ploi**-ee)
someone who works for another person or group of people

employer noun
a person or organization that has people working for them

employment noun
work for which you are paid

empress noun
a female emperor, or the wife of an emperor

empty adjective (**emptier, emptiest**)
an empty place or container has nothing or no one in it **emptiness** noun emptiness is being empty

empty verb (**empties, emptying, emptied**)
1 to empty something is to make it empty 2 to empty is to become empty • After the show the hall quickly emptied.

emu noun (say **ee**-mew)
a large Australian bird that cannot fly, like an ostrich but smaller

emulsion noun
1 emulsion is a creamy or slightly oily liquid 2 emulsion, or emulsion paint, a kind of water paint used for decorating buildings

enable verb
to enable someone to do something is to make it possible for them • A calculator will enable you to multiply and divide quickly.

emu

enamel noun
1 enamel is a shiny glassy substance that is baked on to metal or pottery to form a hard bright surface 2 enamel is also the hard shiny surface of teeth 3 an enamel paint is a hard glossy paint

enchant verb
1 to enchant someone is to delight or please them 2 to enchant someone is also to put a magic spell on them in stories **enchanted** adjective under a magic spell **enchanting** adjective beautiful or delightful **enchantment** noun a feeling of wonder or delight

enclose verb
1 to enclose an area is to put a fence or wall round it 2 to enclose something is to put it in an envelope or packet with a letter

enclosure noun
a piece of ground with a fence or wall round it

encore noun (say **on**-kor)
an extra item performed at a concert or show when the

audience has clapped or cheered the main items

encounter verb
1 to encounter someone is to meet them unexpectedly 2 to encounter something is to experience it • We have encountered a few problems.

encourage verb
1 to encourage someone is to give them confidence or hope • We were encouraged by your support. 2 to encourage someone to do something is to urge and help them to do it • They try to encourage schools to take part in these road safety schemes. **encouragement** noun encouragement is supporting someone or something in what they do • The crowd shouted their encouragement.

encyclopedia noun
a book or set of books containing a lot of information on a particular subject, or on many different subjects

encyclopedic adjective an encyclopedic book is one that gives you a lot of information

end noun
1 the end of something is the last part of it or the point where it stops • Holly stood at the end of the pier. • This is the end of our journey. 2 an end is an aim or purpose • They used the money for their own ends.
on end 1 upright • His hair stood on end. 2 continuously • She spoke for two hours on end.

end verb
1 to end something is to finish it 2 to end is to finish

endanger verb
to endanger someone or something is to cause them danger, especially of being injured

endangered species noun
a type of animal or plant that has become so rare that it is in danger of becoming extinct

endeavour verb
to endeavour to do something is to try hard to do it

ending noun
the last part of something • They all wanted a story with a happy ending.

endless adjective
never stopping • Top athletes need endless training. **endlessly** adverb without ending

endure verb
1 to endure pain or suffering is

a
b
c
d
e
f
g
h
i
j
k
l
m
n
o
p
q
r
s
t
u
v
w
x
y
z

to put up with it **2** to endure is to continue or last **endurance** *noun* endurance is suffering or putting up with something unpleasant

enemy *noun* (**enemies**)
1 someone who is opposed to someone else and wants to harm them **2** a nation or army that is at war with another country

energetic *adjective*
1 an energetic person has a lot of energy **2** an energetic activity needs a lot of energy • *They then performed an energetic dance.* **energetically** *adverb* with a lot of energy

energy *noun* (**energies**)
1 energy is the ability to do work or provide power, for example electrical energy **2** a person's energy is the strength they have to do things

enforce *verb*
to enforce a law or order is to make people obey it **enforcement** *noun* enforcement is making people obey laws

engage *verb*
1 to engage someone is to give them a job **2** to engage someone in conversation is to talk to them

engaged *adjective*
1 someone is engaged when they have promised to marry someone **2** a telephone line or lavatory is engaged when someone is already using it

engagement *noun*
1 a promise to marry someone **2** an appointment to meet someone or do something

engine *noun*
1 a machine that turns energy into motion **2** a vehicle that pulls a railway train

engineer *noun*
a person who designs and builds machines, roads, and bridges **engineering** *noun* engineering is the designing and building of machines, roads, bridges, and other large buildings

engrave *verb*
to engrave a surface is to carve figures or words on it **engraving** *noun* a print made by engraving a design

engine

engrossed *adjective*
to be engrossed in something is

to concentrate on it and ignore other things around you • *He was so engrossed in his work that he didn't hear her come in.*

engulf *verb*
to engulf something is to flow over it and swamp it • *The town was engulfed by smoke from a huge forest fire.*

enjoy *verb*
1 to enjoy something is to get pleasure from it **2** to enjoy yourself is to have a good time **enjoyable** *adjective* able to be enjoyed; pleasant **enjoyment** *noun* enjoyment is a feeling of great pleasure

enlarge *verb*
to enlarge something is to make it larger **enlargement** *noun* enlargement is making something larger

enormous *adjective*
very large; huge **enormously** *adverb* hugely; a lot • *I enjoyed the party enormously.*

enough *determiner, noun, adverb*
as much or as many as you need or can cope with

enquire *verb*
to enquire about something is to ask for information about it • *He enquired if I was well.* **enquiry** *noun* a question that asks for information

enrage *verb*
to enrage a person or animal is to make them very angry

enrol *verb* (**enrolling, enrolled**)
to enrol in a society or class is to become a member of it **enrolment** *noun* enrolment is becoming a member or making someone a member

ensure *verb*
to ensure that something happens or has happened is to make sure of it • *Please ensure that you leave the room tidy when you go.*

entangle *verb*
to entangle something is to get it tangled or caught up **entanglement** *noun* entanglement is becoming tangled

enter *verb*
1 to enter a place is to come into it or go into it **2** to enter something in a list or book is to write or record it there **3** to enter data in a computer is to key it in **4** to enter for a competition or examination is to take part in it

enterprise *noun*
1 enterprise is being bold and adventurous **2** an enterprise is a difficult or important task or project

enterprising *adjective*
an enterprising person or activity is one that is exciting or adventurous

entertain *verb*
1 to entertain someone is to amuse them or give them pleasure, as a singer or comedian does **2** to entertain people is to have them as guests and give them food and drink **entertainer** *noun* someone such as a singer or comedian who entertains people **entertainment** *noun* entertainment is something that entertains or amuses people

enthusiasm *noun*
1 enthusiasm is a feeling of excitement and interest you show for something **2** an enthusiasm is a strong liking or interest

enthusiastic *adjective*
full of enthusiasm • *She is very enthusiastic about breeding mice.* **enthusiastically** *adverb*

entire *adjective*
whole or complete • *The entire school gathered in the field for a photograph.* **entirely** *adverb* completely; in every way • *The brothers look entirely different.*

entitle *verb*
to entitle someone to something is to give them a right to it • *The voucher entitles you to a free drink with your pizza.* **entitlement** *noun* a right you have to something

entrance[1] *noun* (*say* en-transs)
1 the way into a place **2** coming into a room or on to a stage or arena • *Everyone clapped when the clowns made their entrance.*

entrance[2] *verb* (*say* in-**trahnss**)
to entrance someone is to delight or enchant them

entrant *noun*
someone who goes in for a competition or examination

entreat *verb*
to entreat someone is to ask them seriously or earnestly **entreaty** *noun* a serious or earnest request

entrust *verb*
to entrust someone with something, or to entrust something to someone, is to give it to them to look after

entry *noun* (**entries**)
1 an entrance **2** something written in a list or diary

envelop *verb* (*say* in-**vel**-op)
to envelop something is to cover or wrap it completely • *The mountain was enveloped in mist.*

envelope *noun*
(*say* **en**-ve-lohp or *say* **on**-ve-lohp)
a paper wrapper for a letter

envious *adjective*
you are envious of someone when they have something you would like to have too **enviously** *adverb*

environment *noun*
1 surroundings, especially as they affect people and other living things • *Some animals and plants can die out if their environment is damaged.* **2** the environment is the natural world of the land and sea and air **environmental** *adjective* to do with the environment

envy *noun*
an unhappy feeling you have when you want something that someone else has got

envy *verb* (**envies, envying, envied**)
to envy someone is to be envious of them

epic *noun*
1 a story or poem about heroes **2** an exciting or spectacular film

epidemic *noun*
a disease that spreads quickly among the people of an area

epilepsy *noun*
epilepsy is a disease of the nervous system, which causes fits **epileptic** *adjective* to do with epilepsy • *an epileptic fit*

epileptic *noun*
someone who suffers from epilepsy

epilogue *noun* (*say* **ep**-i-log)
words written or spoken at the end of a story or a play

episode *noun*
1 one event that is part of a series of happenings or forms part of a story **2** one programme in a radio or television serial

epitaph *noun*
words written on a tomb or describing a person who has died

equal *adjective*
things are equal when they are the same in amount, size, or value

equal *noun*
a person or thing that is equal to another • *He treated everyone as equals.*

equal *verb* (**equalling, equalled**)
to equal something is to be the same in amount, size, or value

equality *noun*
equality is being equal

equalize *verb*
to equalize things is to make them equal

equally *adverb*
in the same way or to the same extent • *You are all equally to blame.*

equation *noun* (*say* i-**kway**-zhon)
(*in mathematics*) a statement that two amounts are equal, for example 3 + 4 = 2 + 5

equator *noun* (*say* i-**kway**-ter)
an imaginary line round the earth at an equal distance from the North and South Poles **equatorial** *adjective* to do with the equator or near the equator

equestrian *adjective*
to do with horse-riding

equestrian

equilateral *adjective*
(*say* ee-kwi-**lat**-er-al)
an equilateral triangle has all its sides equal

equilibrium *noun* (**equilibria**)
(*say* ee-kwi-**lib**-ri-um)
equilibrium is a state of even balance

equinox *noun*
the time of year when day and night are equal in length (about 20 March in spring and about 22 September in autumn)

equip *verb* (**equipping, equipped**)
to equip someone or something is to supply them with what is needed • *Are you equipped for mountaineering?*

equipment *noun*
equipment is a set of things needed for a special purpose

equivalent *adjective*
things are equivalent when they are equal in value, importance, or meaning **equivalence** *noun* equivalence is being equivalent

era *noun* (*say* **eer**-a)
a long period of history

erase *verb*
1 to erase something written is to rub it out **2** to erase a recording on magnetic tape is to wipe it out **eraser** *noun* a piece of rubber or plastic for rubbing out writing

erect *adjective*
standing straight up

erect *verb*
to erect something is to set it up or build it **erection** *noun* something that has been built or erected

erode *verb*
to erode something is to wear it away • *Water has eroded the rocks.*

erosion *noun*
erosion is the wearing away of the earth's surface by the action of water and wind

errand *noun*
a short journey to take a message or fetch something

erratic *adjective* (*say* i-**rat**-ik)
not reliable or regular **erratically** *adverb*

error *noun*
a mistake **in error** by mistake

erupt *verb*
1 a volcano erupts when it shoots out lava **2** something powerful or violent erupts when it suddenly happens • *An argument erupted over a disputed goal.* **eruption** *noun* when a volcano erupts

escalate *verb*
to escalate is to become gradually greater or more serious • *The riots escalated into a war.* **escalation** *noun* when something becomes greater or more serious

escalator *noun*
a staircase with a revolving band of steps moving up or down

escape *verb*
1 to escape is to get free or get away **2** to escape something is to avoid it • *He escaped the washing-up.*

escape *noun*
an act or way of escaping • *What a lucky escape!* • *There was no escape.*

escort *noun* (*say* **ess**-kort)
1 a person or group who accompanies someone, especially to give protection **2** a group of vehicles, ships, or aircraft accompanying someone or something

escort *verb* (*say* i-**skort**)
to escort someone or something is to act as an escort to them

especially *adverb*
chiefly, more than anything else • *I like cheese, especially strong cheese.*

espionage *noun*
(*say* **ess**-pi-on-ahzh)
espionage is spying on other countries or people

essay *noun*
a short piece of writing on one subject

essence *noun*
1 the most important quality or ingredient of something **2** a concentrated liquid

essential *adjective*
something is essential when it is very important and you must have it or do it • *A car is essential*

a b c d e f g h i j k l m n o p q r s t u v w x y z

in the country.

essentially *adverb* basically; in many ways • *The two stories are essentially the same.*

essential *noun*
something you must have or do • *I've made a list of some essentials to pack.*

establish *verb*
1 to establish a business, government, or relationship is to start it on a firm basis **2** to establish a fact is to show that it is true • *He managed to establish his innocence.*

establishment *noun*
1 a place where people do business **2** establishing something

estate *noun*
1 an area of land with a set of houses or factories on it **2** a large area of land belonging to one person **3** everything that a person owns when they die

estate agent *noun*
someone whose business is selling or letting buildings and land

estimate *noun* (*say* **ess**-ti-mat)
a rough calculation or guess about an amount or value

estimate *verb* (*say* **ess**-ti-mayt)
to estimate is to make an estimate

estimation *noun*
1 estimation is making a rough estimate **2** a person's estimation is their opinion • *It is very good in my estimation.*

estuary *noun* (**estuaries**)
(*say* **ess**-tew-er-i)
the mouth of a large river where it flows into the sea

etc.
short for *et cetera*

et cetera
and other similar things; and so on

etch *verb*
to etch a picture is to make it by engraving on a metal plate with an acid **etching** *noun* a picture made by engraving

eternal *adjective*
lasting for ever; not ending or changing **eternally** *adverb* for ever **eternity** *noun* eternity is time that goes on for ever

ethnic *adjective*
belonging to a particular national or racial group

eucalyptus *noun*
(*say* yoo-ka-**lip**-tus)
an evergreen tree from which an oil is obtained

euphemism *noun*
a word or phrase which is used

instead of an impolite or less tactful one. 'Pass away' is a euphemism for 'die'.

euphemistic *adjective* using words that won't upset people

euro *noun* (**euros** or **euro**)
the single currency introduced in the European Union in 1999

euthanasia *noun*
(*say* yooth-an-**ay**-zi-a)
euthanasia is causing someone to die gently and without pain when they are suffering from an incurable disease

evacuate *verb*
to evacuate people is to move them away from a dangerous place

euro

evacuation *noun*
evacuation is moving people away, especially during a war or when there is a danger

evacuee *noun*
someone who is evacuated, especially during a war

evade *verb*
to evade someone or something is to make an effort to avoid them

evaporate *verb*
to evaporate is to change from liquid into steam or vapour

evaporation *noun* when a liquid changes into steam or vapour

evasive *adjective*
trying to avoid answering something; not honest or straightforward

eve *noun*
the day or evening before an important day, for example New Year's Eve

even *adjective*
1 level and smooth **2** calm and stable • *He has a very even temper.* **3** equal • *The scores were even.* **4** able to be divided exactly by two • *6 and 14 are even numbers.* **to get even with someone** is to take revenge on them

evenly *adverb* in an even way
• *Spread the varnish evenly over the surface.* • *The money will be shared out evenly.* **evenness** *noun*

even *verb*
1 to even something is to make it even **2** to even or even out is to become even

even *adverb*
used to emphasize another word
• *You haven't even started your work!* • *I ran fast, but she ran even faster.* **even so** although that is correct

evening *noun*
the time at the end of the day before night time

event *noun*
1 something that happens, especially something important **2** an item in an athletics contest
• *The next event will be the long jump.*

eventful *adjective*
full of happenings, especially remarkable or exciting ones
• *They had an eventful train journey across the USA.*

eventual *adjective*
happening at last or as a result
• *Many failures preceded his eventual success.*

eventually *adverb*
finally, in the end • *We eventually managed to get the door open.*

ever *adverb*
1 at any time • *It's the best present I've ever had.* **2** always
• *ever hopeful* **3** (*informal*) used for emphasis • *Why ever didn't you tell me?* **ever so** or **ever such** (*informal*) very much
• *I'm ever so pleased.*
• *She's ever such a nice girl.*

evergreen *adjective*
having green leaves all through the year

evergreen *noun*
an evergreen tree

everlasting *adjective*
lasting for ever or for a long time

every *adjective*
all the people or things of a particular kind; each • *Every child should learn to swim.* **every other** each alternate one; every second one • *Every other house had a garage.*

everybody *pronoun*
everyone

everyday *adjective*
happening or used every day; ordinary • *Everyday life has changed a lot in the last fifty years.*

everyone *pronoun*
every person; all people
• *Everyone likes her.*

everything *pronoun*
all things; all • *Everything you need is here.*

everywhere *adverb*
in all places

evict *verb*
to evict someone is to make them move out of their house **eviction** *noun* making someone move out of their house

evidence *noun*
evidence is facts and information that give people reason to believe something

evident *adjective*
obvious; clearly seen
• *It is evident that he is lying.*
evidently *adverb* clearly;
obviously • *His mother had
evidently changed her mind.*
evil *adjective*
an evil person or action is one
that is wicked and harmful
evil *noun*
something wicked or harmful
evolution *noun*
(*say* ee-vo-**loo**-shon)
the development of animals
and plants over many centuries
from earlier or simpler forms
of life
evolve *verb*
to develop gradually or
naturally
ewe *noun* (*say* yoo)
a female sheep

ewe

exact *adjective*
completely correct or accurate
exactly *adverb* in an exact way;
correctly **exactness** *noun* being
correct
exaggerate *verb*
to exaggerate something is
to make it seem bigger or
better or worse than it really
is **exaggeration** *noun* making
something seem more than it
really is
exam *noun*
(*informal*) an examination
examination *noun*
1 a test of someone's knowledge
or skill **2** a close inspection of
something
examine *verb*
to examine something is to look
at it closely or in detail
examiner *noun*
a person who sets and marks an
examination to test students'
knowledge
example *noun*
1 a single thing or event that
shows what others of the same
kind are like **2** a person or thing
that you should copy or learn
from **for example** as an example

exasperate *verb*
to exasperate someone is to
make them very annoyed
exasperation *noun* a feeling of
being very annoyed
excavate *verb*
to excavate a piece of land is to
dig in it, especially in building or
archaeology **excavation** *noun*
digging in land **excavator** *noun*
a machine that excavates
exceed *verb*
1 to exceed an amount or
achievement is to be more than
it or do better than it **2** to exceed
a rule or limit is to go beyond it
when you are not supposed to
• *The driver was exceeding the
speed limit.*
exceedingly *adverb*
extremely; very much
excel *verb* (**excelling, excelled**)
to excel at something is to be
very good at it, and better than
everyone else
excellent *adjective*
extremely good; of the best kind
excellence *noun* excellence is
being extremely good
except *preposition*
not including; apart from
• *Everyone got a prize except me.*
exception *noun*
1 something or someone that
does not follow the normal rule
2 something that is left out
exceptional *adjective*
unusual • *She has exceptional
skill.* **exceptionally** *adverb* to
an unusual degree
excerpt *noun*
a piece taken from a book or
story or film
excess *noun*
too much of something
• *We have an excess of food.*
excessive *adjective*
too much or too great
excessively *adverb* too; by too
much • *They are excessively
greedy.*
exchange *verb*
to exchange something is to give
it and receive something else
for it
exchange *noun*
1 changing one thing for another
2 a place where telephone lines
are connected to each other
when a call is made **3** a place
where company shares are
bought and sold
excite *verb*
to excite someone is to make
them eager and enthusiastic
about something • *The thought
of the outing excited them.*
excitable *adjective* easily
excited

excitement *noun*
excitement is being excited
exclaim *verb*
to exclaim is to shout or cry
out
exclamation *noun*
an exclamation is a word or
phrase you say out loud that
expresses a strong feeling such
as surprise or pain
exclamation mark *noun*
the punctuation mark (!) placed
after an exclamation
exclude *verb*
1 to exclude someone or
something is to keep them out
2 to exclude something is to
leave it out • *Do not exclude
the possibility of rain.*
exclusion *noun* exclusion is
keeping someone or something
out or leaving them out
exclusive *adjective*
1 not shared with others
• *Today's newspaper has an
exclusive report about the match.*
2 allowing only a few people
to be involved • *They joined an
exclusive club.* **exclusively** *adverb*
excrete *verb*
to excrete is to pass waste matter
out of your body **excretion** *noun*
excreting waste matter
excuse *noun* (*say* **iks**-kewss)
a reason you give to explain why
you have done something wrong
excuse *verb* (*say* iks-**kewz**)
1 to excuse someone is to forgive
them **2** to excuse someone
something is to allow them not
to do it • *Please may I be excused
swimming?* **excuse me** a polite
apology for interrupting or
disagreeing
execute *verb*
1 to execute someone is to put
them to death as a punishment
2 to execute something is to
perform or produce it • *She
executed the somersault perfectly.*
execution *noun* putting someone
to death **executioner** *noun*
someone who executes people
executive *noun*
a senior person in a business or
government organization
exercise *noun*
1 exercise is using your body to
make it strong and healthy **2** an
exercise is a piece of work done
for practice
exercise *verb*
1 to exercise is to do exercises
2 to exercise an animal is to give
it exercise
exercise book *noun*
a book for writing in
exert *verb*
to exert oneself or one's ability

a
b
c
d
e
f
g
h
i
j
k
l
m
n
o
p
q
r
s
t
u
v
w
x
y
z

is to make an effort to get something done • *He exerted all his strength to bend the bar.*
exertion *noun* exertion is making a big effort

exhale *verb*
to exhale is to breathe out
exhalation *noun* breathing out

exhaust *noun*
1 the waste gases from an engine **2** the pipe these gases are sent out through

exhaust *verb*
1 to exhaust someone is to make them very tired **2** to exhaust something is to use it up completely **exhaustion** *noun* great tiredness

exhibit *verb*
to exhibit something is to show it in public, especially in a gallery or museum

exhibit *noun*
something displayed in a gallery or museum

exhibition *noun*
a collection of things put on display for people to look at

exile *verb*
to exile someone is to send them away from their country

exile *noun*
1 exile is having to live away from your own country • *He was in exile for ten years.* **2** an exile is a person who is exiled

exist *verb*
1 to exist is to have life or be real • *Do ghosts exist?* **2** to exist is also to stay alive • *They existed on biscuits and water.*

existence *noun*
1 existing or being **2** staying alive • *It was a real struggle for existence.*

exit *noun*
1 the way out of a place **2** going out of a room or going off a stage or arena • *They decided it was time for a quick exit.*

exit *verb*
to exit is to leave a stage or arena

exotic *adjective*
unusual and colourful, especially because it comes from another part of the world

expand *verb*
1 to expand something is to make it larger **2** to expand is to become larger **expansion** *noun* expansion is becoming larger or making something larger

expanse *noun*
a wide area

expect *verb*
1 to expect something is to think that it will probably happen • *I expect it will rain.* **2** to be expecting someone is to be

waiting for them to arrive **3** to expect something is to think that it ought to happen • *She expects us to be quiet.* **expecting** *adjective* a woman is expecting when she is pregnant

expectant *adjective*
full of expectation or hope

expectation *noun*
1 expecting something or being hopeful **2** something you hope to get

expedition *noun*
a journey made in order to do something • *They are going on a climbing expedition.*

expel *verb* (**expelling, expelled**)
1 to expel something is to send or force it out • *The fan expels stale air and fumes.* **2** to expel someone is to make them leave a school or country • *He was expelled for bullying.*

expenditure *noun*
expenditure is when you spend money or use effort • *We must reduce our expenditure.*

expense *noun*
the cost of doing something

expensive *adjective*
costing a lot of money

experience *noun*
1 experience is what you learn from doing and seeing things **2** an experience is something that has happened to you

experience *verb*
to experience something is to have it happen to you

experienced *adjective*
having skill or knowledge from much experience

experiment *noun*
a test made in order to study what happens **experimental** *adjective* something is experimental when it is being tried out to see how good or successful it is **experimentally** *adverb* as an experiment

experiment *verb*
to experiment is to carry out experiments **experimentation** *noun* doing experiments

expert *noun*
someone who has skill or special knowledge in something

expert *adjective*
having great knowledge or skill

expertise *noun*
expert ability or knowledge

expire *verb*
1 to expire is to come to an end or to stop being usable • *My bus pass has expired.* **2** to expire is also to die **expiry** *noun* the time when something expires

explain *verb*
1 to explain something is to

make it clear to someone else **2** to explain a fact or event is to show why it happens • *That explains his absence.*

explanation *noun*
something you say that explains something or gives reasons for it

explode *verb*
1 to explode is to burst or suddenly release energy with a loud bang **2** to explode a bomb is to set it off **3** to explode is to increase suddenly or quickly • *The city's population exploded to 3 million in a year.*

exploit *noun* (say **eks**-ploit)
a brave or exciting deed

exploit *verb* (say iks-**ploit**)
1 to exploit resources is to use or develop them **2** to exploit someone is to use them selfishly or unfairly **exploitation** *noun* exploitation is exploiting something or someone

explore *verb*
1 to explore a place is to travel through it to find out more about it **2** to explore a subject is to examine it carefully • *We need to explore all the possibilities.*
exploration *noun* exploring a place **explorer** *noun* someone who explores a remote country to find out more about it

explosion *noun*
1 the exploding of a bomb or other weapon **2** a sudden and quick increase • *There was a population explosion after the war.*

explosive *noun*
a substance that can explode

explosive *adjective*
likely to explode; able to cause an explosion

export *verb* (say iks-**port**)
to export goods is to send them abroad to be sold **exporter** *noun* someone who exports goods

export *noun* (say **eks**-port)
something that is sent abroad to be sold

expose *verb*
1 to expose something is to reveal or uncover it **2** to expose someone is to show that they are to blame for something **3** to expose a photographic film is to let light reach it in a camera, so as to take a picture

exposure *noun*
1 exposure is being harmed by the weather when in the open without enough protection **2** an exposure is a single photograph or frame on a film

express *adjective*
going or sent quickly

express *noun*
a fast train stopping at only a few stations
express *verb*
to express an idea or feeling is to put it into words
expression *noun*
1 the look on a person's face that shows what they are thinking or feeling 2 a word or phrase 3 a way of speaking or performing music that expresses feelings **expressive** *adjective* an expressive look or statement is one that shows your feelings
expulsion *noun*
when someone is driven away or made to leave
exquisite *adjective*
very delicate or beautiful
exquisitely *adverb*
extend *verb*
1 to extend is to stretch out 2 to extend something is to make it longer or larger 3 to extend a greeting or welcome is to offer it
extension *noun*
1 extension is extending or being extended 2 an extension is something added on, especially to a building 3 an extension is also an extra telephone in an office or house
extensive *adjective*
covering a large area • *The bomb caused extensive damage.*
extensively *adverb* over a large area • *She travelled extensively*
extent *noun*
1 the area or length of something 2 an amount or level • *The extent of the damage was enormous.*
exterior *noun*
the outside of something
exterminate *verb*
to exterminate a people or breed of animal is to kill all the members of it
extermination *noun*
extermination is killing all the people or animals in a   place
external
adjective extinct dodo
outside
externally
adverb on
the outside
extinct
adjective
1 an animal or bird is extinct when there are no more examples of it alive like the dodo
2 a volcano is extinct when it is not burning or active any more **extinction** *noun* when something no longer exists or is no longer active

extinguish *verb*
to extinguish a fire or light is to put it out **extinguisher** *noun* a device for putting out a fire
extra *adjective*
more than usual; added • *There is a extra charge for taking a bicycle on the train.*
extra *noun*
1 an extra person or thing 2 someone acting as part of the crowd in a film or play
extract *noun* (*say* **eks**-trakt)
1 a short piece taken from a book, play, or film 2 something obtained from something else • *a plant extract*
extract *verb* (*say* iks-**trakt**)
to extract something is to remove it or take it out of something else
extraction *noun*
1 a person's extraction is the place or people they come from • *She is of Indian extraction.* 2 extraction is taking something out
extraordinary *adjective*
unusual or very strange **extraordinarily** *adverb* in an extraordinary way
extraterrestrial *adjective*
existing in or coming from another planet
extraterrestrial *noun*
a living thing from another planet, especially in science fiction
extravagant *adjective*
spending or using too much of something
extravagance *noun*
extravagance is being extravagant
extravagantly *adverb*
extreme *adjective*
1 very great or strong • *They were suffering from extreme cold.* 2 farthest away • *She lives in the extreme north of the country.*
extreme *noun*
1 something very great, strong, or far away 2 either end of something
extremely *adverb*
as much or as far as possible; very much • *They are extremely pleased.*
exuberant *adjective*
very cheerful or lively
exuberance *noun* exuberance is being exuberant

eye *noun*
1 the organ of your body used for seeing 2 the small hole in a needle 3 the centre of a storm
eye *verb* (**eyeing, eyed**)
to eye someone or something is to look at them closely
eyeball *noun*
the ball-shaped part of your eye, inside your eyelids
eyebrow *noun*
the curved line of hair growing above each eye
eyelash *noun*
one of the short hairs that grow on your eyelids
eyelid *noun*
the upper or lower fold of skin that can close over your eyeball
eyesight *noun*
a person's eyesight is their ability to see
eyesore *noun*
something that is ugly to look at
eyewitness *noun*
someone who actually saw something happen, especially an accident or crime

Ff

F
short for Fahrenheit
fable *noun*
a short story which teaches a lesson about how people should behave, often with animals as characters
fabric *noun*
cloth
fabulous *adjective*
1 very great • *The prince enjoyed fabulous wealth.* 2 (*informal*) wonderful; marvellous 3 belonging to fables and myths and not to real life • *Dragons are fabulous creatures.*
face *noun*
1 the front part of your head 2 the look on your face • *She had a friendly face.* 3 the front or upper side of something • *Put the cards face down.* 4 a surface • *A cube has six faces.* **face to face** looking directly at someone
facial *adjective* on or to do with your face • *He had some facial injuries.*
face *verb*
1 to face in a certain direction is to look there or have the front in that direction • *Please face*

the front. • *The church faces the school.* **2** to face a problem or danger is to accept that you have to deal with it

facility *noun* (**facilities**) (*say* fa-**sil**-i-ti) something that helps you to do things • *The youth club has facilities for dancing and sport.*

fact *noun* something that is true or certain **as a matter of fact** or **in fact** really

factor *noun* **1** something that helps to bring about a result or situation • *Hard work has been a factor in her success.* **2** a number by which a larger number can be divided exactly • *4 and 5 are factors of 20.*

factory *noun* (**factories**) a large building where machines are used to make things in large quantities

factual *adjective* based on or containing facts • *Write down a factual account of what happened.* **factually** *adverb*

fade *verb* **1** to fade is to lose colour, freshness, or strength **2** to fade or fade away is to disappear gradually

Fahrenheit *adjective* (*say* **fa**-ren-hyt) using a scale for measuring temperature that gives 32 degrees for freezing water and 212 degrees for boiling water

fail *verb* **1** to fail is to try to do something but not be able to do it **2** to fail an exam or test is not to pass it **3** to fail is also to become weak or useless or to come to an end • *The batteries are failing.* • *The crops failed last year.* **4** to fail to do something is not to do it when you should • *He failed to warn me of the danger.*

fail *noun* not being successful in an examination • *She has five passes and one fail.* **without fail** definitely or always • *I'll be there without fail.*

failing *noun* a fault or weakness

failure *noun* **1** failure is not being successful **2** a failure is someone or something that has failed

faint *adjective* **1** weak; not clear or distinct **2** nearly unconscious, often because you are exhausted or very hungry

faintly *adverb* weakly or not clearly **faintness** *noun*

faint *verb* to faint is to become unconscious for a short time

faint-hearted *adjective* not having much courage or confidence

fair[1] *adjective* **1** right or just; honest • *It was a fair fight.* **2** light in colour • *The sisters both had fair hair.* **3** quite good • *We've got a fair chance of winning.* **4** weather is fair when it is fine and not raining **fairness** *noun* fairness is being fair

fair[2] *noun* **1** an outdoor entertainment with rides, amusements, and stalls. Fairs move from town to town. **2** an exhibition or market • *a craft fair*

fairground *noun* a place where a fair is held

fairly *adverb* **1** quite or rather • *It is fairly hard.* **2** honestly; justly • *He promised to treat everyone fairly.*

fairy *noun* (**fairies**) an imaginary small creature with wings and magic powers

fairy story or **fairy tale** *noun* (**fairy stories**) a story about fairies or magic

faith *noun* **1** faith is strong belief or trust • *We have great faith in her.* **2** a faith is a religion

fairy

faithful *adjective* loyal and trustworthy **faithfully** *adverb* **faithfulness** *noun*

fake *noun* a copy of something made to deceive people into thinking it is real

fake *adjective* not real or genuine • *fake diamonds*

fake *verb* **1** to fake something is to make it look real in order to deceive people **2** to fake something is also to pretend to have it • *He was always faking illness so he could miss games.*

falcon *noun* a small kind of hawk **falconry** *noun* the sport of training falcons to hunt other birds

fall *verb* (**falling, fell, fallen**) **1** to fall is to come down quickly towards the ground **2** numbers or prices fall when they get lower or smaller **3** a city or stronghold falls when it is captured **4** soldiers fall when they die in battle **5** when silence falls it becomes quiet **6** to fall sick or ill is to become ill **7** a look or glance falls on someone when it is directed at them **to fall for someone** is to start loving them **to fall for something** is to be tricked into believing it **to fall in** is to collapse • *The roof fell in.* **to fall out** is to quarrel and stop being friends **to fall through** is to fail to happen • *Our plans have fallen through.*

fall *noun* **1** a time when a person or thing falls • *My grandma had a bad fall.* **2** (*in America*) autumn

fallout *noun* fallout is radioactive dust that is carried in the air after a nuclear explosion

fallow *adjective* land that is fallow has been ploughed but not sown with crops • *The field was left fallow every three years.*

falls *plural noun* a waterfall

false *adjective* **1** untrue or incorrect **2** faked; not genuine **3** treacherous or deceitful **falsely** *adverb* **falsehood** *noun* **1** falsehood is telling lies **2** a falsehood is a lie

falter *verb* **1** to falter is to hesitate when you move or speak **2** to falter is also to become weaker • *His courage began to falter.*

fame *noun* fame is being famous **famed** *adjective* a person or thing is famed when they are very well known

familiar *adjective* **1** well-known; often seen or experienced • *It was a familiar sight.* **2** knowing something well • *Are you familiar with this story?* **3** very friendly **familiarity** *noun* familiarity with something is being familiar with it

family *noun* (**families**) **1** parents and their children, sometimes including grandchildren and other relations **2** a group of animals, plants, or things that are alike in some way • *The tiger is a member of the cat family.*

family tree *noun* a diagram showing how people in a family are related

famine noun
a severe shortage of food that causes many people to die

famished adjective
extremely hungry

famous adjective
known to a lot of people • *Her uncle is a famous scientist.*

fan¹ noun
a device for making the air move about, in order to cool people or things

fan

fan¹ verb (**fanning, fanned**)
to fan something is to send a draught of air at it • *She fanned her face with her hand.* **to fan out** is to spread out in the shape of a fan

fan² noun
an enthusiastic follower or supporter of someone or something

fanatic noun (say fa-**nat**-ik)
someone who is too enthusiastic about something **fanatical** adjective too enthusiastic about something **fanatically** adverb

fanciful adjective
imagined rather than based on facts or reason

fancy noun (**fancies**)
1 fancy is imagination 2 a fancy is a liking or desire for something

fancy adjective (**fancier, fanciest**)
decorated; not plain

fancy verb (**fancies, fancying, fancied**)
1 to fancy something is to want or like it • *Does anyone fancy an ice cream?* 2 to fancy something unusual is to imagine or think of it • *Just fancy him riding a horse!*

fancy dress noun
unusual costume that you wear to a party or dance, often to make you look like someone else

fanfare noun
a short burst of music, often with trumpets and to announce something

fang noun
a long, sharp tooth

fantastic adjective
1 strange or unusual • *The blocks of ice had been carved into the most fantastic shapes.* 2 (informal) excellent **fantastically** adverb strangely or unusually

fantasy noun (**fantasies**)
1 something pleasant that you imagine but isn't likely to happen • *His fantasy is to play football for England.* 2 a very imaginative story

far adverb (**farther, farthest**)
1 a long way • *We didn't go far.* 2 much; by a great amount • *She's a far better singer than I am.*
so far up to now

far adjective (**farther, farthest**)
distant; opposite • *She swam to the far side of the river.*

farce noun
1 a far-fetched or absurd kind of comedy 2 a series of ridiculous events • *The trial was a complete farce.* **farcical** adjective absurd and ridiculous

fare noun
the money you pay to travel on a bus, train, ship, or aircraft

fare verb
to fare is to get on or make progress • *How did you fare in your exam?*

farewell exclamation
goodbye

far-fetched adjective
unlikely to be true; difficult to believe

farm noun
1 an area of land where someone grows crops and keeps animals for food 2 the buildings on land of this kind

farm verb
to farm is to grow crops and raise animals for food

farmer noun
someone who owns or looks after a farm

farmyard noun
the open area surrounded by farm buildings

farther adverb, adjective
at or to a greater distance; more distant • *She lives farther from the school than I do.*

farthest adverb, adjective
at or to the greatest distance; most distant

fascinate verb
to fascinate someone is to attract or interest them very much **fascinating** adjective very interesting **fascination** noun a feeling of being fascinated;

a great interest in something

fashion noun
1 the style of clothes or other things that most people like at a particular time 2 a way of doing something • *Please continue in the same fashion.*

fashion verb
to fashion something is to make it in a particular shape or style • *The ring had been fashioned from the finest gold.*

fashionable adjective
something is fashionable when it follows a style that is popular at a particular time

fast¹ adjective
1 moving or done quickly • *He's a fast runner.* 2 allowing fast movement • *This is a fast road.* 3 a watch or clock is fast when it shows a time later than the correct time 4 firmly fixed • *Make the boat fast.* 5 a fast colour is one that is not likely to fade

fast¹ adverb
1 quickly 2 firmly
fast asleep deeply asleep

fast² verb
to fast is to go without food

fasten verb
to fasten something is to join it firmly to something else

fastener or **fastening** noun a device used to fasten something

fat noun
1 the white greasy part of meat 2 an oily or greasy substance used in cooking

fat adjective (**fatter, fattest**)
1 having a very thick round body 2 thick • *What a fat book!* 3 fat meat is meat with a lot of fat

fatal adjective
1 causing someone's death • *There has been a fatal accident on the motorway.* 2 likely to have bad results • *He then made a fatal mistake.* **fatally** adverb someone is fatally injured or wounded when they die as a result of their injuries

fate noun
1 a power that is thought to make things happen 2 someone's fate is what has happened or will happen to them

father noun
your male parent

father-in-law noun
the father of your husband or wife

fatigue noun (say fa-**teeg**)
1 extreme tiredness 2 weakness in metals, caused by stress **fatigued** adjective extremely tired

fatten *verb*
1 to fatten something is to make it fat **2** to fatten is to become fat

fatty *adjective* (**fattier, fattiest**)
containing a lot of fat

fault *noun*
1 something wrong that spoils a person or thing; a flaw or mistake **2** the responsibility or blame for something • *It's my fault we are late.* **to be at fault** is to be in the wrong or responsible for a mistake **faultless** *adjective* something is faultless when it is perfect and has nothing wrong with it

fault *verb*
to fault something is to find faults in it

faulty *adjective* (**faultier, faultiest**)
having a fault or faults; not working properly

fauna *noun* (say **faw**-na)
the animals of an area or of a period of time

favour *noun*
1 a favour is something kind that you do for someone • *Will you do me a favour?* **2** favour is approval or goodwill • *The idea found favour with most people.* **to be in favour of someone or something** is to like or support them

favour *verb*
to favour someone or something is to like or support them, or prefer them to others

favourable *adjective*
1 helpful or advantageous **2** showing approval **favourably** *adverb*

favourite *adjective*
that you like best • *This is my favourite book.*

favourite *noun*
the person or thing that you like best • *This book is my favourite.*

favouritism *noun*
favouritism is when someone is unfairly kinder to one person than to others

fawn *noun*
1 a young deer **2** a light brown colour

fawn

fax *noun*
1 a machine that sends copies of documents by electronic means through a telephone line **2** a copy made by this process

fax *verb*
to fax a document is to send a copy of it using a fax machine

fear *noun*
fear, or a fear, is a feeling that something unpleasant may happen

fear *verb*
1 to fear someone or something is to be afraid of them **2** to fear something is also to be anxious or sad about it • *I fear we may be too late.*

fearful *adjective*
1 frightened **2** (*informal*) awful or horrid • *They had a fearful quarrel.* **fearfully** *adverb*

fearless *adjective*
having no fear **fearlessly** *adverb*

fearsome *adjective*
frightening

feasible *adjective*
able to be done; possible or likely

feast *noun*
a large and splendid meal for a lot of people

feast *verb*
to feast is to have a feast

feat *noun*
something brave or difficult that you do

feather *noun*
a bird's feathers are the very light coverings that grow from its skin **feathery** *adjective* soft or light like feathers

feature *noun*
1 your features are the different parts of your face • *He has rugged features.* **2** an important or noticeable part of something; a characteristic **3** a newspaper article or television programme on a particular subject

feature *verb*
1 to feature something is to make it an important part of something **2** to feature in something is to be an important part of it • *Sport features a lot in the Sunday papers.*

February *noun*
the second month of the year

fed up *adjective*
(*informal*) depressed or unhappy

fee *noun*
a payment or charge

feeble *adjective*
weak; not having much strength or force • *He uttered a feeble cry.* **feebly** *adverb*

feed *verb*
1 to feed a person or animal is to give them food **2** to feed on something is to eat it • *Sheep feed on grass.* **3** to feed a machine is to put coins or other things into it

feed *noun*
1 a feed is a meal **2** feed is food for animals

feel *verb* (**feeling, felt**)
1 to feel something is to touch it to find out what it is like **2** to feel a feeling or emotion is to experience it • *I feel very angry about it.* **to feel like something** is to want it

feel *noun*
what something is like when you touch it • *Her dress has a funny feel about it.*

feeler *noun*
an insect's feelers are the two long thin parts that extend from the front of its body and are used for feeling

feeling *noun*
1 feeling is the ability to feel or touch things • *She lost the feeling in her right hand.* **2** feeling is also what a person feels in the mind, such as love or fear • *I have hurt her feelings.* **3** a feeling is what you think about something • *My feeling is that he's right.*

feline *adjective*
to do with cats; like a cat

fell[1]
past tense of **fall** *verb*

fell[2] *verb*
1 to fell a tree is to cut it down **2** to fell someone is to knock them down

fell[3] *noun*
a hill or area of wild hilly country in the north of England

fellow *noun*
1 a friend or companion; someone who belongs to the same group **2** (*informal*) a man or boy • *He's a clever fellow.*

fellow *adjective*
of the same group or kind • *She arranged a meeting with her fellow teachers.*

fellowship *noun*
1 fellowship is friendship **2** a fellowship is a group of friends; a society

felt[1]
past tense and past participle of **feel**

felt[2] *noun*
felt-tip pens

thick woollen material

felt-tip pen or **felt-tipped pen** *noun*
a pen with a tip made of felt or fibre

female *adjective*
of the sex that can produce offspring
female *noun*
a female person or animal
feminine *adjective*
1 to do with women or like women; suitable for women **2** in some languages, belonging to the class of words that includes words referring to women
femininity *noun* being feminine
feminist *noun*
someone who believes that women should have the same rights and opportunities as men
feminism *noun* the belief that women should have the same rights and opportunities as men
fen *noun*
an area of low-lying marshy or flooded land
fence *noun*
a wooden or metal barrier round an area of land
fence *verb*
1 to fence something or to fence it in is to put a fence round it **2** to fence is to fight with long narrow swords called *foils*, as a sport **fencer** *noun* someone who fences **fencing** *noun* the sport of fighting with swords
fend *verb*
to fend for yourself is to take care of yourself **to fend someone or something off** is to keep them away from yourself when they are attacking you
fender *noun*
a low guard placed round a fireplace to stop coal from falling into the room
ferment *verb*
beer or wine ferments when it bubbles and changes chemically by the action of yeast or bacteria. This makes the sugar turn into alcohol.
fermentation *noun* the process of fermenting
fern *noun*
a plant with feathery leaves and no flowers
ferocious *adjective*
fierce or savage **ferociously** *adverb* **ferocity** *noun* fierceness
ferret *noun*
a small fierce animal with a long thin body, used for catching rabbits and rats
ferry *noun*
a boat that takes people or things across a river or other stretch of water
ferry *verb* (**ferries, ferrying, ferried**)
to ferry people or things is to take them from one place to

another, especially by boat or car
fertile *adjective*
1 land that is fertile is good for growing crops and plants **2** people or animals that are fertile can produce babies or young animals
fertility *noun* being fertile
fertilize *verb*
1 to fertilize the soil is to add chemicals or manure to it so that crops and plants grow better to fertilize an egg or plant is to put sperm or pollen into it so that it develops its young or seeds **fertilization** *noun* fertilizing the soil or an egg or plant
fertilizer *noun*
chemicals or manure added to the soil to make crops and plants grow better
fervent *adjective*
very enthusiastic or passionate about something • *He is a fervent supporter of reform.* **fervently** *adverb* **fervour** *noun* great enthusiasm or passion
festival *noun*
1 a time of celebration, especially for religious reasons **2** an organized set of concerts, shows, or other events, especially one that is arranged every year
festive *adjective*
to do with joyful celebrating **festivities** *noun* parties and other events held to celebrate something
fetch *verb*
1 to fetch something or someone is to go and get them **2** something fetches a particular price when it is sold for that price • *My old bike fetched £10.*
fête *noun* (*say* fayt)
an outdoor event with stalls, games, and things for sale, often held to raise money
fetters *plural noun*
fetters are chains put round a prisoner's ankles
feud *noun* (*say* fewd)
a bitter quarrel between two people or families that lasts a long time
feud *verb*
people feud when they keep up a quarrel for a long time
feudal *adjective* (*say* **few**-dal)
in the Middle Ages, the feudal system was a system in which people could farm land in exchange for working or fighting for the owner
feudalism *noun* the feudal system

fever *noun*
1 a person has a fever when their body temperature is higher than usual because they are ill **2** fever is excitement or agitation
feverish *adjective*
1 someone is feverish when they have a slight fever **2** excited or frantic • *There was feverish activity getting the hall ready for the show.* **feverishly** *adverb*
few *adjective*
not many
few *noun*
a small number of people or things **a good few** or **quite a few** a fairly large number
fez *noun* (**fezzes**)
a tall round hat with a flat top and a tassel, worn especially by Muslim men

fez

fiancé *noun*
(*say*-fee-**ahn**-say)
a woman's fiancé is the man who she is engaged to be married to
fiancée *noun* (*say* fee-**ahn**-say)
a man's fiancée is the woman who he is engaged to be married to
fiasco *noun* (**fiascos**)
(*say* fi-**ass**-koh)
a complete failure • *The party turned into a fiasco.*
fib *noun*
a lie about something unimportant
fib *verb* (**fibbing, fibbed**)
to fib is to tell a lie about something unimportant **fibber** *noun* someone who tells fibs
fibre *noun* (*say* **fy**-ber)
1 a fibre is a very thin thread **2** fibre is a substance made up of thin threads **3** fibre is also a substance in food that helps you to digest it **fibrous** *adjective* made up of lots of fibres
fibreglass *noun*
a kind of lightweight plastic containing glass fibres
fickle *adjective*
someone is fickle when they often change their mind or do not stay loyal to one person or group
fiction *noun*
fiction is writings about events that have not really happened; stories and novels
fictional *adjective* existing only in a story, not in real life
fictitious *adjective*
made up; not true

a
b
c
d
e
f
g
h
i
j
k
l
m
n
o
p
q
r
s
t
u
v
w
x
y
z

fiddle *noun*
1 a violin
2 (*informal*) a swindle
fiddle *verb*
1 to fiddle is to play the violin **2** to fiddle with something is to keep touching or playing with it with your fingers **3** (*informal*) to fiddle something is to be dishonest about it **fiddler** *noun* someone who plays the violin
fiddly *adjective* (*informal*) awkward to use or do because it involves handling small objects
• *Making the model of the ship was quite a fiddly job.*
fidelity *noun* (*say* fi-**del**-i-ti) being faithful or loyal
fidget *verb* to fidget is to make small restless movements because you are bored or nervous **fidgety** *adjective* someone is fidgety when they fidget a lot
field *noun*
1 a piece of land with crops or grass growing on it, often surrounded by a hedge or fence **2** an area of grass where people play a sport **3** a subject that someone is studying or interested in • *The book describes important developments in the field of science.* **4** all the people or animals that take part in a race
field *verb*
1 to field a ball in cricket or other games is to stop it or catch it **2** to be fielding in cricket is to be on the side that is not batting **fielder** *noun* a player who is fielding
fiend *noun* (*say* feend)
1 a devil or evil spirit **2** a wicked or cruel person
fiendish *adjective*
1 wicked or cruel **2** very difficult or complicated • *That was a fiendish puzzle.* **fiendishly** *adverb* to be fiendishly difficult or complicated is to be very difficult or complicated indeed
fierce *adjective*
1 angry and violent and likely to attack you **2** strong or intense • *The heat from the fire was fierce.* **fiercely** *adverb* **fierceness** *noun*
fiery *adjective*
1 full of flames or heat **2** easily made angry • *He had a fiery temper.*

fiddle

fifteen *noun* the number 15 **fifteenth** *adjective*, *noun* 15th
fifth *adjective*, *noun* the next after the fourth **fifthly** *adverb* in the fifth place; as the fifth one
fifty *noun* the number 50 **fiftieth** *adjective*, *noun* 50th
fifty-fifty *adjective*, *adverb* to share something fifty-fifty is to share it equally between two people or groups • *Let's split the money fifty-fifty.*
fig *noun* a soft fruit full of small seeds
fight *noun*
1 a struggle against someone, using hands or weapons **2** an attempt to achieve or overcome something • *We can all help in the fight against crime.*
fight *verb* (**fighting, fought**)
1 to fight someone is to have a fight with them **2** to fight something is to try to stop it • *They fought the fire all night.*
fighter *noun*
1 someone who fights **2** a fast military plane that attacks other aircraft

fighter

figure *noun*
1 one of the symbols that stand for numbers, such as 1, 2, and 3 **2** the shape of someone's body **3** a diagram or illustration in a book or magazine **4** a pattern or shape • *He drew a figure of eight.*
figure *verb*
1 to appear or take part in something • *His name does not figure in the list of entrants.* **2** to think that something is probably true • *I figure the best thing to do is to wait.* **to figure something out** is to work it out • *Can you figure out the answer?*
file¹ *noun* a metal tool with a rough surface that you rub on things to make them smooth or shape them
file¹ *verb* to file something is to make it smooth or shape it with a file
file² *noun*
1 a box or folder for keeping

papers in **2** (*in computing*) a set of data that has been stored under one name in a computer **to walk in single file** is to walk one behind the other
file² *verb*
1 to file a paper or document is to put it in a box or folder **2** to file is to walk one behind the other
fill *verb*
1 to fill something is to make it full **2** to fill is to become full • *The room was filling quickly.* **3** to fill a tooth is to put a filling in it **to fill in a form** is to write answers to all the questions on it **to fill something up** is to fill it completely
fill *noun* enough to make you full • *Eat your fill.*
fillet *noun* a piece of fish or meat without bones
filling *noun*
1 a piece of metal put in a tooth to replace a decayed part **2** food you put inside a pie, sandwich, or cake
filling station *noun* a place where petrol is sold
filly *noun* (**fillies**) a young female horse
film *noun*
1 a series of moving pictures that tells a story, such as those shown in a cinema or on television **2** a roll or piece of thin plastic coated with a chemical that is sensitive to light, that you put in a camera to take photographs **3** a very thin layer of something • *The table was covered in a film of grease.* **filmy** *adjective* thin and transparent
film *verb* to film a book or story is to make a film of it
filter *noun* a device for removing dirt or other unwanted things from a liquid or gas that passes through it
filter *verb*
1 to filter something is to pass it through a filter **2** to filter is to move gradually • *People started to filter into the hall.*
filth *noun* disgusting dirt **filthy** *adjective* extremely dirty
fin *noun*
1 a thin flat part that sticks out from a fish's body and helps it to swim **2** a small part that sticks out from an aircraft or rocket and helps it to balance
final *adjective*
1 coming at the end; last

2 a decision is final when it puts an end to argument or doubt • *You must not go, and that's final!*

final *noun*
the last of a series of contests, that decides the overall winner

finale *noun* (*say* fin-**ah**-li)
the last part of a show or piece of music

finalist *noun*
a person or team taking part in a final

finally *adverb*
1 after a long time, at last • *We finally got there around midnight.* **2** as the last thing • *Finally, I would like to thank my parents.*

finance *noun*
1 finance is the business of using and looking after money **2** someone's finances are the amount of money or funds they have

finance *verb*
to finance something is to provide money for it

financial *adjective*
to do with money

finch *noun*
a small bird with a short thick beak

find *verb* (**finding, found**)
1 to find something is to see or get it by chance or by looking for it **2** to find something is also to learn it by experience • *He found that digging is hard work.* **to find someone out** is to discover them doing wrong **to find something out** is to get information about it

finder *noun* someone who finds something

findings *plural noun*
things someone has found out

fine¹ *adjective*
1 of high quality; excellent **2** the weather is fine when it is sunny and not raining **3** very thin or delicate • *The curtains were made of a fine material.* **4** made of small particles • *The sand on the beach was very fine.* **finely** *adverb* into fine or small parts • *Slice the tomato finely.*

fine² *noun*
money that someone must pay as a punishment

fine² *verb*
to fine someone is to make them pay money as a punishment

finger *noun*
1 one of the long thin parts that stick out on your hand **2** something that is shaped like a finger

finger *verb*
to finger something is to touch it with your fingers

fingernail *noun*
the hard covering at the end of your finger

fingerprint *noun*
a mark made by the pattern of curved lines on the tip of your finger

fingerprint

finish *verb*
1 to finish something is to bring it to an end **2** to finish is to come to an end

finish *noun*
the end of something

fiord *noun* (*say* fi-**ord**)
in Norway, an inlet of the sea between high cliffs

fir *noun*
an evergreen tree with leaves like needles

fire *noun*
1 the flames, heat, and light that come from burning things **2** coal or wood burning in a grate or furnace to give heat **3** a device using electricity or gas to heat a room **4** the shooting of guns • *Hold your fire!* **to be on fire** is to be burning **to set fire to something** is to start it burning

fire *verb*
1 to fire a gun is to shoot it **2** (*informal*) to fire someone is to dismiss them from their job **3** to fire pottery or bricks is to bake them in an oven to make them hard

fire brigade *noun*
a team of people whose job is to put out fires and rescue people from fires

fire engine *noun*
a large vehicle that carries firefighters and equipment to fight fires

fire extinguisher *noun*
a metal cylinder containing water or foam for spraying over a fire to put it out

firefighter *noun*
someone whose job is to put out fires

fireplace *noun*
an open space for a fire in the wall of a room

fireproof *adjective*
something is fireproof when it can stand great heat without burning

fire station *noun*
the headquarters of a fire brigade

firework *noun*
a cardboard tube

fireworks

containing chemicals that give off coloured sparks and lights and sometimes make loud noises

firm *noun*
a business organization • *She works for a clothing firm.*

firm *adjective*
1 fixed or solid so that it will not move **2** definite and not likely to change • *She has made a firm decision to go.* **firmly** *adverb* in a strong or definite way

firmness *noun*

first *adjective*
1 coming before all others **2** the most important • *He plays football in the first team at school.*

first *adverb*
before everything else • *Finish your work first.*

first *noun*
a person or thing that is first **at first** at the beginning; to start with

first aid *noun*
simple medical treatment that is given to an injured person before a doctor comes

first-class *adjective*
1 belonging to the best part of a service • *Send the letter by first-class post.* **2** excellent

first-hand *adjective, adverb*
you get first-hand information directly, rather than from other people or from books

firstly *adverb*
as the first thing • *Firstly, let me tell you about our holiday.*

fish *noun* (**fish** or **fishes**)
an animal that lives and breathes in water

fish *verb*
to fish is to try to catch fish

fisherman *noun* (**fishermen**)
someone who tries to catch fish

fishmonger *noun*
a shopkeeper who sells fish

fishy *adjective* (**fishier, fishiest**)
1 smelling or tasting of fish **2** (*informal*) suspicious or doubtful • *His excuse was rather fishy.*

fist *noun*
a tightly closed hand with the fingers bent into the palm

fit¹ *adjective* (**fitter, fittest**)
1 healthy and strong because you get a lot of exercise **2** suitable or good enough • *It was a meal fit for a king.* **3** ready or likely • *They worked till they were fit to collapse.*

fit¹ *verb* (**fitting, fitted**)
1 to fit someone or something is to be the right size and shape for them **2** to fit something is to put it into place • *We need to fit a new lock on the door.* **3** to fit something is to be suitable for it • *Her speech fitted the occasion perfectly.* **to fit in** is to be suitable for something • *Does this fit in with your plans?*

fit¹ *noun*
the way something fits • *The coat is a good fit.*

fit² *noun*
1 a sudden illness, especially one that makes you move violently or become unconscious **2** (*informal*) a sudden outburst • *He rushed off in a fit of rage.* **in fits and starts** in short bursts; now and then

fitness *noun*
being healthy and strong because of doing a lot of exercise

fitting *adjective*
suitable or proper

fitting *noun*
fittings are pieces of furniture or equipment in a room or building

five *noun*
the number 5

fix *verb*
1 to fix something is to join it firmly to something else or to put it where it will not move **2** to fix something is also to decide or settle it • *We have fixed a date for the party.* **3** to fix something that is broken is to mend it • *He's fixing my bike.* **to fix something up** is to arrange or organize something

fix *noun*
(*informal*) an awkward situation • *I'm in a fix.*

fixture *noun*
1 a sports event planned for a particular day **2** something fixed in its place, like a cupboard or a washbasin

fizz *verb*
1 to fizz is to make a hissing or spluttering sound **2** liquid fizzes when it produces a lot of small bubbles **fizzy** *adjective* a fizzy drink has a lot of bubbles

fizzle *verb*
to fizzle is to make a slight hissing sound **to fizzle out** is to end in a disappointing or unsuccessful way

flabby *adjective* (**flabbier, flabbiest**)
fat and soft; not firm

flag *noun*
a piece of material with a coloured pattern or shape on it, often used as the symbol of a country or organization

flag *verb* (**flagging, flagged**)
to flag is to become weak or droop

flagship *noun*
the main ship in a navy's fleet, which has the commander of the fleet on board

flagstone *noun*
a flat slab of paving stone

flake *noun*
1 a very light thin piece of something **2** a piece of falling snow **flaky** *adjective* like flakes, or likely to break into flakes

flake *verb*
to flake is to come off in light thin pieces **to flake out** (*informal*) is to faint or fall asleep

flame *noun*
a bright strip of fire that flickers and leaps

flame *verb*
to flame is to produce flames or become bright red

flamingo *noun* (**flamingos**)
a large wading bird with long legs, a long neck, and pale pink feathers

flammable *adjective*
that can be set alight

flan *noun*
a pie without any pastry on top

flank *noun*
the side of something, especially an animal's body or an army

flannel *noun*
1 a flannel is a piece of soft cloth you use to wash yourself **2** flannel is a soft woollen material

flap *noun*
1 a part that hangs down from one edge of something, usually to cover an opening **2** the action or sound of flapping

flap *verb* (**flapping, flapped**)
1 to flap something is to move it up and down or from side to side • *The bird flapped its wings.* **2** to flap is to wave about • *The sails were flapping in the breeze.*

flapjack *noun*
a cake made from oats and syrup

flare *verb*
1 to flare is to burn with a sudden bright flame **2** to flare up is to become suddenly angry **3** things flare when they get gradually wider

flare *noun*
1 a bright light fired into the sky as a signal **2** a gradual widening, especially in skirts or trousers

flash *noun*
1 a sudden bright burst of light **2** a device for making a brief bright light when you take a photograph **3** a sudden display of anger or humour **in a flash** immediately or very quickly

flash *verb*
1 to flash is to make a sudden bright burst of light **2** to flash past or across is to approach and go past very fast • *The train flashed past into the distance.*

flashy *adjective* (**flashier, flashiest**)
showy and expensive

flask *noun*
1 a bottle with a narrow neck **2** a vacuum flask

flask

flat *adjective*
1 having no curves or bumps; smooth and level **2** spread out; lying at full length • *Lie flat on the ground.* **3** dull or uninteresting • *He spoke in a flat voice.* **4** a liquid is flat when it is no longer fizzy **5** a tyre is flat when it is punctured and has lost its air **6** below the proper musical pitch • *The clarinet was flat.*
flatness *noun*

flat *adverb*
exactly and no more • *He won the race in ten seconds flat.* **flat out** as fast as possible • *They all worked flat out to get everything ready in time.*

flat *noun*
1 a set of rooms for living in, usually on one floor of a building **2** (*in music*) the note that is a semitone lower than the natural note; the sign (#) that indicates this

flatly *adverb*
in a definite way, leaving no room for doubt • *They flatly refused to go.*

flatten *verb*
1 to flatten something is to make it flat **2** to flatten is to become flat

flatter *verb*
to flatter someone is to praise

them more than they deserve, often because you want to please them **flattery** noun too much praise

flavour noun
the taste and smell of something

flavour verb
to flavour something is to give it a particular taste and smell **flavouring** noun something added to food or drink to give it a particular flavour

flaw noun
a fault that stops a person or thing from being perfect • *The diamond had a flaw.* **flawed** adjective having a fault **flawless** adjective perfect, with no faults

flax noun
a plant that produces fibres from which cloth is made and seeds from which oil is obtained

flea noun
a small jumping insect that sucks blood

fled
past tense and past participle of **flee**

flee verb
to flee is to run away from something

flea

fleece noun
1 a sheep's fleece is the wool that covers its body 2 a piece of clothing made from a soft warm material **fleecy** adjective soft and warm like a fleece

fleet noun
a number of ships, aircraft, or vehicles owned by one country or company

fleeting adjective
very brief; passing quickly • *I caught a fleeting glimpse of him.*

flesh noun
the soft substance of the bodies of people and animals, made of muscle and fat **fleshy** adjective part of your body is fleshy when there is a lot of flesh on it

flex noun
flexible insulated wire for carrying an electric current

flex verb
to flex something is to move or bend it • *Try flexing your muscles.*

flexible adjective
1 easy to bend or stretch 2 able to be changed • *Our plans are flexible.* **flexibility** noun something that has flexibility can bend or stretch easily

flick noun
a quick light hit or movement

flick verb
to flick something is to hit or move it with a flick

flicker verb
to flicker is to burn or shine unsteadily

flight[1] noun
1 flight is the action of flying • *She looked up to see a flock of birds in flight.* 2 a flight is a journey in an aircraft or rocket 3 a flight is also a group of flying birds or aircraft 4 a flight of stairs is one set of stairs

flight[2] noun
running away; escape

flimsy adjective (**flimsier, flimsiest**)
light and thin; fragile

flinch verb
to flinch is to make a sudden movement because you are frightened or in pain

fling verb (**flinging, flung**)
to fling something is to throw it violently or carelessly

flint noun
1 flint is a very hard kind of stone 2 a flint is a piece of this stone or hard metal used to produce sparks

flip verb (**flipping, flipped**)
to flip something is to turn it over quickly • *We were flipping pancakes in the kitchen.*

flipper noun
1 a limb that water animals use for swimming 2 a flat rubber shoe shaped like a duck's foot, that you wear on your feet to help you swim

flit verb (**flitting, flitted**)
to flit is to fly or move lightly and quickly • *A moth flitted across the room.*

float verb
1 to float is to stay or move on the surface of a liquid or in the air 2 to float something is to make it stay on the surface of a liquid

float noun
1 a light object that is designed to float • *She learned to swim with the help of floats.* 2 a vehicle with a platform used for delivering milk or for carrying a display in a parade

flock noun
a group of sheep, goats, or birds

flock verb
to flock is to gather or move in a crowd

flog verb (**flogging, flogged**)
1 to flog someone is to beat them severely with a whip or stick

2 (slang) to flog something is to sell it

flood noun
1 a large amount of water spreading over a place that is usually dry 2 a great amount of something • *They received a flood of complaints.*

flood verb
1 to flood something is to cover it with a large amount of water 2 a river floods when it flows over its banks 3 to arrive in large amounts • *Offers of help came flooding in from all over the country.*

floodlight noun
a lamp that gives a broad bright beam, used to light up a public building or a sports ground at night **floodlit** adjective lit up by floodlights

floor noun
1 the part of a room that people walk on 2 all the rooms on the same level in a building • *The sports department is on the top floor.*

floorboard noun
one of the long flat boards in a wooden floor

flop verb (**flopping, flopped**)
1 to flop, or flop down, is to fall or sit down heavily 2 to flop is also to fall or hang loosely or heavily • *Her hair flopped over her eyes.* 3 (informal) to flop is to be a failure

flop noun
(informal) a failure or disappointment • *The play was a complete flop.*

floppy adjective (**floppier, floppiest**)
hanging loosely or heavily • *Our dog has huge floppy ears.*

flora noun (say **flor**-a)
the plants of an area or of a period of time

floral adjective
made of flowers or to do with flowers

florist noun
a shopkeeper who sells flowers

flounder verb
to flounder is to move or struggle clumsily because you are in difficulties • *For a moment the boy floundered about in the stream.*

flour noun
a fine powder made from corn or wheat and used for making bread, cakes, and pastry

flour

a b c d e f g h i j k l m n o p q r s t u v w x y z

floury adjective
powdery like flour

flourish verb
1 to flourish is to grow or develop strongly; to be successful
2 to flourish something is to wave it about

flow verb
1 to flow is to move along smoothly, like a river does
2 to flow is also to hang loosely • She had golden flowing hair.

flow noun
a continuous steady movement of something

flower noun
1 the part of a plant from which the seed or fruit develops
2 a plant with a flower

flower verb
a plant flowers when it produces flowers

flowerpot noun
a pot in which plants are grown

flowerpots

flu noun
influenza

fluent adjective
skilful at speaking, especially a foreign language **fluency** noun skill at speaking a language **fluently** adverb

fluff noun
fluff is the small soft bits that come off wool and cloth **fluffy** adjective soft like fluff

fluid noun
a substance that flows easily, like liquids and gases

fluke noun
a success that you achieve by unexpected good luck

fluorescent adjective
a fluorescent light or lamp is one that produces a bright light by means of radiation

fluoride noun
a chemical that is added to water and toothpaste to help prevent tooth decay

flush[1] verb
1 to flush is to go slightly red in the face 2 to flush something is to clean or remove it with a fast flow of liquid

flush[1] noun
1 a slight blush 2 a fast flow of water

flush[2] adjective
level; without any part sticking out • The doors are flush with the walls.

flustered adjective
nervous and confused

flute noun
a musical instrument which you hold sideways across your mouth and play by blowing across a hole in it at one end

flutter verb
1 to flutter is to move with a quick flapping of wings • A butterfly fluttered in through the window. 2 to flutter is to move or flap quickly and lightly • The flags fluttered in the breeze.

fly verb (**flies, flying, flew, flown**)
1 to fly is to move through the air with wings or in an aircraft 2 to fly is also to wave in the air • Flags were flying. 3 to fly something is to make it move through the air • They were flying model aircraft. 4 to fly is to move or pass quickly • The door flew open. • The weeks just flew by.

fly noun (**flies**)
1 a small flying insect with two wings 2 the front opening of a pair of trousers

flying saucer noun
a saucer-shaped flying object believed to come from outer space, especially in science fiction stories

flyover noun
a bridge that carries one road over another

foal noun
a young horse

foam noun
1 a mass of tiny bubbles on a liquid 2 a spongy kind of rubber or plastic **foamy** adjective a foamy liquid produces a mass of tiny bubbles

foam verb
to foam is to form a mass of tiny bubbles

focus noun (**focuses** or **foci**)
1 the distance at which something appears most clearly to your eye or in a lens 2 the part of something that people pay most attention to **to be in focus** is to appear clearly and not blurred **to be out of focus** is to appear blurred

focus verb
1 to focus your eye or a camera lens is to adjust it so that objects appear clearly 2 to focus your attention on something is to concentrate on it

fodder noun
fodder is food for horses and farm animals

foe noun
(old use) an enemy

foetus noun (say fee-tus)
a developing embryo, especially an unborn human baby

fog noun
thick mist which makes it difficult to see **foggy** adjective it is foggy when there is a lot of fog

foil[1] noun
a very thin sheet of metal

foil[2] noun
a long narrow sword you use in fencing

foil[3] verb
to foil someone or something is to prevent them from succeeding • Police foiled the kidnapping plan.

fold[1] verb
1 to fold something is to bend it so that one part lies over another part 2 to fold is to bend or move in this way • The table folds up when we are not using it.

fold[1] noun
a line where something has been folded

fold[2] noun
an enclosure for sheep

folder noun
1 a folding cardboard or plastic cover you use to keep loose papers in 2 (in computing) a place where a set of files are grouped together in a computer

foliage noun
the leaves of a tree or plant

folk plural noun
people

folklore noun
old beliefs and legends

folk song noun
a song in the traditional style of a country

follow verb
1 to follow someone or something is to go or come after them, or to do something after they do 2 to follow someone's instructions or advice is to obey them 3 to follow a road or path is to go along it 4 to follow a sport or team is to take an interest in them or support them • Which football team do you follow? 5 to follow someone is to understand them • Do you follow me? 6 to follow is to happen as a result • Who knows what trouble may follow? **follower** noun a person

who follows or supports someone or something

following *preposition*
after or as a result of • *Following the break-in we had new locks fitted.*

fond *adjective*
kind and loving • *She wished me a fond farewell.* **to be fond of someone or something** is to like them very much **fondly** *adverb*
fondness *noun*

font *noun*
a stone or wooden basin in a church, to hold water for baptism

food *noun*
anything that a plant or animal can take into its body to make it grow or give it energy

food chain *noun*
a series of plants and animals, each of which is eaten as food by the one above in the series

fool *noun*
1 a silly or stupid person **2** a jester or clown • *Stop playing the fool.* **3** a pudding of fruit mixed with custard or cream

fool *verb*
to fool someone is to trick or deceive them **to fool about** or **fool around** is to behave in a silly or stupid way

foolhardy *adjective* (**foolhardier, foolhardiest**)
bold but foolish; reckless
foolhardiness *noun* being foolhardy

foolish *adjective*
stupid or unwise **foolishly** *adverb*
foolishness *noun*

foolproof *adjective*
a plan or method is foolproof when it is easy to follow and can't easily go wrong

foot *noun*
1 the lower part of your leg below your ankle **2** the lowest part of something • *They met up at the foot of the hill.* **3** a measure of length, 12 inches or about 30 centimetres **on foot** walking

football *noun*
1 a game played by two teams which try to kick an inflated ball into their opponents' goal **2** the ball used in this game
footballer *noun* someone who plays football

footing *noun*
your footing is the position of your feet when you are standing firmly on something •
foot
He lost his footing and slipped.

footnote *noun*
a note printed at the bottom of the page

footpath *noun*
a path for people to walk along, especially one in the countryside

footprint *noun*
a mark made by a foot or shoe

footstep *noun*
the sound made each time your foot touches the ground when they are walking or running

for *preposition*
used to show **1** purpose or direction • *This letter is for you.* • *We set out for home.* • *Let's go for a walk.* **2** length of time or distance • *We've been waiting for hours.* • *They walked for three miles.* **3** price or cost • *She bought it for £2.* **4** an alternative • *New lamps for old!* **5** cause or reason • *He was rewarded for bravery.* • *I only did it for the money.* **6** support • *Are you for us or against us?* **for ever** always

for *conjunction*
because • *They paused, for they heard a noise.*

forbid *verb* (**forbidding, forbade, forbidden**)
1 to forbid someone to do something is to tell them that they must not do it **2** to forbid something is not to allow it • *Smoking is forbidden in this station.*

force *noun*
1 strength or power **2** (*in science*) an influence that pushes or pulls objects **3** an organized team of soldiers or police

force *verb*
1 to force someone to do something is to use your power or strength to make them do it **2** to force something is to break it open using your strength

forceful *adjective*
strong and effective
forcefully *adverb*

forceps *plural noun* (*say* **for**-seps)
a pair of pincers or tongs that a dentist or surgeon uses

ford *noun*
a shallow place where you can wade or drive across a river

forecast *noun*
a statement about what is likely to happen, especially what the weather is likely to be

forecast *verb* (**forecasting, forecast** or **forecasted**)
to forecast something is to say what is likely to happen • *The weather report forecasts snow for tomorrow.*

forefinger *noun*
the finger next to your thumb

foregone conclusion *noun*
a result that is certain to happen

foreground *noun*
the part of a picture or view that is nearest to you

forehead *noun*
(*say* **for**-hed or *say* **fo**-rid)
the part of your face above your eyes

foreign *adjective*
belonging to or coming from another country

foreigner *noun*
a person from another country

foremost *adjective*
most important

forename *noun*
a person's first name

foresee *verb* (**foreseeing, foresaw, foreseen**)
to foresee something is to realize that it is likely to happen **foreseeable** *adjective*
a foreseeable event is one that you should realize is likely to happen

foresight *noun*
the ability to realize that something is likely to happen in the future and prepare for it

forest *noun*
a large area of trees growing close together **forester** *noun* a worker in a forest

forestry *noun*
the science of planting forests and looking after them

foretell *verb* (**foretelling, foretold**)
to foretell something is to say it will happen

forever *adverb*
continually or always • *He is forever complaining.*

forfeit *noun*
something that you lose or have to pay as a penalty

forfeit *verb*
to forfeit something is to lose it as a penalty

forge *noun*
a place where metal is heated and shaped; a blacksmith's workshop

forge *verb*
1 to forge metal is to shape it by heating and hammering **2** to forge money or a signature is to copy it in order to deceive people

forgery *noun* (**forgeries**)
1 forgery is copying something in order to deceive people **2** a forgery is a copy of something made to deceive people

forget verb (**forgetting, forgot, forgotten**)
1 to forget something is to fail to remember it **2** to forget something is also to stop thinking about it • *Try to forget your worries.*
forgetful adjective
often forgetting things
forgetfulness noun
forget-me-not noun
a plant with small blue flowers
forgive verb (**forgiving, forgave, forgiven**)
to forgive someone is to stop being angry with them for something they have done
forgiveness noun
fork noun
1 a small tool with prongs for lifting food to your mouth **2** a large tool with prongs used for digging or lifting things **3** a place where a road or river divides into two or more parts
fork verb
1 to fork something is to dig or lift it with a fork **2** to fork is to divide into two or more branches • *The tunnel suddenly forked into two.*
fork-lift truck noun
a truck with two metal bars at the front for lifting and moving heavy loads
forlorn adjective
looking sad and lonely
form noun
1 a form is a kind or type of thing • *What is your favourite form of transport?*
2 the form of something is its shape and general appearance • *They could see a shadowy form in front of them.*
3 a form is also a class in a school
4 a form is also a piece of paper with printed questions and spaces for the answers
form verb
1 to form something is to shape or make it **2** to form is to come into existence or develop • *Icicles formed on the window sill.*
formal adjective
1 strictly following the accepted rules or customs; not casual • *She has a formal manner and never calls me by my first name.*
2 official or ceremonial • *The formal opening of the bridge takes place tomorrow.* **formally** adverb

fork-lift truck

formality noun (**formalities**)
1 formality is formal behaviour
2 a formality is something you do to obey a rule or custom
formation noun
1 the process of forming something • *This chapter is about the formation of ice crystals.*
2 something that is formed • *We were studying formations of rock.* **3** a special pattern or arrangement • *The aircraft were flying in formation.*
former adjective
earlier; in the past • *In former times the house had been an inn.* • *He is a former President of the US.* **the former** the first of two people or things just mentioned • *If it's a choice between a picnic or a swim I prefer the former.* See also **latter**
formerly adverb
once; previously
formidable adjective (say for-**mid**-a-bul)
1 deserving respect because of being so powerful or impressive
2 very difficult to deal with or do • *This is a formidable task.*
formidably adverb
something is formidably difficult when it is very difficult indeed
formula noun (**formulas** or **formulae**)
1 a set of chemical symbols showing what a substance consists of • *H_2O is the formula for water.* **2** a rule or statement expressed in symbols or numbers **3** a list of what you need to make something
forsake verb (**forsaking, forsook, forsaken**)
to forsake someone is to abandon them
fort noun
a building that has been strongly built against attack
forth adverb
forwards or onwards • *From that day forth they never fought again.*
fortification noun
a tower or wall that is built to help defend a place against attack
fortify verb (**fortifying, fortified**)
1 to fortify a place is to make it strong against attack **2** to fortify someone is to make them feel stronger • *A bowl of hot soup will fortify you.*
fortnight noun
a period of two weeks

fortnightly adverb every two weeks
fortress noun
a castle or town that has been strongly built against attack
fortunate adjective
lucky **fortunately** adverb luckily
fortune noun
1 fortune is luck or chance
2 a fortune is a large amount of money
fortune-teller noun
someone who tells you what will happen to you in the future
forty noun (**forties**)
the number 40
fortieth adjective, noun 40th
forward adjective
1 going towards the front
2 placed in the front **3** too eager or bold
forward adverb
forwards
forward noun
a player in an attacking position in a team at football, hockey, and other games
forwards adverb
to or towards the front; in the direction you are facing
fossil noun
the remains of a prehistoric animal or plant that has been in the ground for a very long time and become hardened in rock **fossilized** adjective a fossilized animal or plant has been formed into a fossil

fossil

foster verb
to foster someone is to look after someone else's child as if they were your own, but without adopting them
foster child noun
a child brought up by foster parents
foster parent noun
a parent who is fostering a child
foul adjective
1 disgusting; tasting or smelling unpleasant **2** breaking the rules of a game • *That was a foul shot.* **foulness** noun
foul noun
an action that breaks the rules of a game
foul verb
to foul a player in a game is to commit a foul against them
found¹ verb (**founding, founded**)
to found an organization or

society is to start it or set it up
• *When was the hospital founded?*

foundation *noun*
1 a building's foundations are the solid base under the ground on which it is built **2** the basis for something **3** the founding of something

founder¹ *noun*
someone who founds something
• *Guru Nanak was the founder of the Sikh religion.*

founder² *verb*
to founder is to fill with water and sink • *The ship foundered on the rocks.*

foundry *noun* (**foundries**)
a factory or workshop where metal or glass is made

fountain *noun*
an outdoor structure in which jets of water shoot up into the air

fountain pen *noun*
a pen that has a nib and can be filled with a cartridge or a supply of ink

four *noun*
the number 4 **to be on all fours** is to be on your hands and knees

fourteen *noun*
the number 14
fourteenth *adjective, noun* 14th

fourth *adjective, noun*
the next after the third
fourthly *adverb* in the fourth place; as the fourth one

fowl *noun* (**fowl** or **fowls**)
a bird, such as a chicken or duck, that is kept for its eggs or meat

fox *noun*
a wild animal that looks like a dog with a long furry tail

fox *verb*
to fox someone is to puzzle them

foxglove *noun*
a tall plant with flowers like the fingers of gloves

foyer *noun* (*say* **foi**-ay)
the entrance hall of a cinema, theatre, or hotel

fraction *noun*
1 a number that is not a whole number, for example ½ and 0.5 **2** a tiny part or amount of something

fracture *verb*
to fracture something, especially a bone, is to break it

fracture *noun*
the breaking of something, especially a bone

fragile *adjective* (*say* **fra**-jyl)
easy to break or damage
fragility *noun* being easy to break or damage

fragment *noun*
a small piece broken off something

fragrant *adjective* (*say* **fray**-grant)
having a sweet or pleasant smell **fragrance** *noun* a sweet or pleasant smell

frail *adjective*
weak or fragile
frailty *noun* being weak or fragile

frame *noun*
1 a set of wooden or metal strips that fit round the outside of a picture or mirror to hold it **2** a rigid structure that supports something
• *I've broken the frame of my glasses.*
3 a human body
• *He has a small frame.*
your frame of mind is the way you think or feel for a while • *Wait till he's in a better frame of mind.*

frame

frame *verb*
1 to frame a picture is to put a frame round it **2** (*informal*) to frame someone is to make them seem guilty of a crime by giving false evidence against them

framework *noun*
1 a structure that supports something **2** a basic plan or system

frank *adjective*
honest and saying exactly what you think • *I'll be frank with you.* **frankly** *adverb*
frankness *noun*

frank *verb*
to frank a letter or parcel is to mark it with a postmark

frantic *adjective*
wildly anxious or excited
frantically *adverb*

fraud *noun*
1 fraud is the crime of getting money by tricking people; a fraud is a swindle **2** a fraud is also someone who is not what they pretend to be **fraudulent** *adjective* dishonest

fraught *adjective*
someone is fraught when they are tense and upset

frayed *adjective*
1 frayed material is worn and ragged at the edge • *Your shirt collar is frayed.* **2** tempers or nerves are frayed when people feel strained or upset • *Tempers were becoming frayed.*

freak *noun*
a very strange or unusual person, animal, or thing

freckle *noun*
a small brown spot on someone's skin **freckled** *adjective* covered in freckles

free *adjective*
1 able to do what you want to do or go where you want to go **2** not costing any money
• *Entrance to the museum is free.*
3 available; not being used or occupied • *Is this seat free?* **4** not busy doing something • *Are you free tomorrow morning?*
5 generous • *She is very free with her money.* **to be free of something** is not to have it or be affected by it • *The roads are free of ice.* **freely** *adverb* to do something freely is to do it as you want, without anyone or anything stopping you

free *verb*
to free someone or something is to make them free **freedom** *noun* the right to go where you like or do what you like

freehand *adjective, adverb*
to draw something freehand is to do it without using a ruler or compasses

free-range *adjective*
1 free-range hens are allowed to move about freely in the open instead of being caged **2** free-range eggs are those laid by free-range hens

freewheel *verb*
to freewheel is to ride a bicycle without pedalling

freeze *verb*
1 to freeze is to turn into ice or another solid, or to become covered with ice • *The pond froze last night.* **2** to be freezing or to be frozen is to be very cold
• *My hands are frozen.* **3** to freeze food is to store it at a low temperature to preserve it **4** a person or animal freezes when they suddenly stand still with fright

freezer *noun*
a large refrigerator for keeping food frozen

freezing point *noun*
the temperature at which a liquid freezes

freight *noun* (*say* frayt)
goods carried by road or in a ship or aircraft

frenzy *noun* (**frenzies**)
to be in a frenzy is to be wildly excited or angry about something **frenzied** *adjective* wildly excited or angry about something

frequency noun (**frequencies**)
1 how often something happens
2 being frequent **3** the number of vibrations made each second by a wave of sound or light

frequent adjective (say **free**-kwent)
happening often
frequently adverb often

fresh adjective
1 newly made or produced; not old or used • We need fresh bread. **2** not tinned or preserved • Would you like some fresh fruit? **3** cool and clean • It's nice to be in the fresh air. **4** fresh water is water that is not salty
freshly adverb newly or recently • Here are some freshly made biscuits.
freshness noun

freshen verb
1 to freshen something is to make it fresh **2** to freshen is to become fresh

freshwater adjective
freshwater fish live in rivers or lakes and not the sea

fret verb (**fretting, fretted**)
to fret is to worry or be upset about something **fretful** adjective worried and upset

friar noun
a man belonging to a religious group that has vowed to live a life of poverty **friary** noun a place where friars live

friction noun
1 when one thing rubs against another **2** disagreement and quarrelling

Friday noun
the sixth day of the week

fridge noun
(informal) a refrigerator

friend noun
1 someone you like and who likes you **2** a helpful or kind person

friendly adjective (**friendlier, friendliest**)
kind and pleasant
friendliness noun

friendship noun
friendship, or a friendship, is being friends with someone

frieze noun (say freez)
a strip of designs or pictures along the top of a wall

fright noun
a sudden feeling of fear

frighten verb
to frighten someone is to make them afraid

frightful adjective
awful; very great or bad • It's a frightful shame.
frightfully adverb awfully or very • I'm frightfully sorry.

frill noun
a strip of pleated material used to decorate the edge of a dress or curtain **frilly** adjective decorated with frills

fringe noun
1 a straight line of short hair that hangs down over your forehead **2** a decorative edge of hanging threads on something like a piece of clothing or a curtain **3** the edge of something • We walked around on the fringe of the crowd.
fringed adjective having a fringe

frisk verb
(informal) to frisk someone is to search them by moving your hands over their body

frisky adjective (**friskier, friskiest**)
playful or lively **friskily** adverb
friskiness noun

fritter[1] noun
a slice of meat, potato, or fruit that is covered in batter and fried

fritter[2] verb
to fritter something or fritter it away is to waste it gradually • He frittered all his money on comics.

frivolous adjective
light-hearted and playful; not serious **frivolously** adverb

frizzy adjective (**frizzier, frizziest**)
frizzy hair has tight short curls

fro adverb
to and fro backwards and forwards

frog noun
a small jumping animal that can live both in water and on land **to have a frog in your throat** is to be hoarse

frolic verb (**frolicking, frolicked**)
to frolic is to spend time playing in a lively and cheerful way

from preposition
used to show **1** a beginning or starting point • She comes from London. • Buses run from 8 o'clock. **2** distance • We are a mile from home. **3** separation • Get the gun from him. **4** origin or source • Get water from the tap. **5** cause • I suffer from headaches. **6** difference • Can you tell margarine from butter?

front noun
1 the part of a person or thing that faces forwards • The front of the house is blue. **2** the part of a thing or place that is furthest forward • Go to the front of the class. **3** a wide road or path that runs alongside the seashore **4** the place where fighting is happening in a war • More troops were moved to the front.
in front at or near the front

front adjective
placed at or near the front • We sat in the front row.

frontier noun
the boundary between two countries or regions

frost noun
1 powdery ice that forms on things in freezing weather **2** weather with a temperature below freezing point

frost verb
to frost up is to become covered with frost

frostbite noun
harm done to a person's body by very cold weather **frostbitten** adjective suffering from frostbite

frosty adjective
1 so cold that there is frost • It was a frosty morning. **2** unfriendly • She gave us a frosty look.

froth noun
a white mass of tiny bubbles on or in a liquid **frothy** adjective a frothy liquid has froth on top

froth verb
to froth is to form a froth

frown verb
to frown is to wrinkle your forehead because you are angry or worried

frown noun
the wrinkling of your forehead when you frown

friends

frog

fruit noun
1 the part of a tree or plant that contains the seeds and is often used as food, such as apples, oranges, and bananas **2** the good result of doing something • *He lived to see the fruits of his efforts.*
fruitful adjective
something is fruitful when it is successful or has good results • *Their talks were fruitful.*
fruitfully adverb
fruitless adjective
something is fruitless when it is unsuccessful or has no results • *It was a fruitless search.*
fruitlessly adverb without success
fruity adjective (**fruitier, fruitiest**) tasting like fruit
frustrate verb
to frustrate someone is to prevent them from doing something or from succeeding in something, in a way that annoys them **frustration** noun the feeling of annoyance you have when you can't do what you want to do
fry verb (**fries, frying, fried**)
to fry food is to cook it in hot fat
frying pan noun
a shallow pan in which things are fried
fudge noun
a soft sweet made with milk, sugar, and butter
fuel noun
something that is burnt to make heat or power, such as coal and oil
fugitive noun (say **few**-ji-tiv)
a person who is running away from something, especially from the police
fulfil verb (**fulfilling, fulfilled**)
1 to fulfil something is to achieve it or carry it out • *She fulfilled her promise to come.* **2** to fulfil a prophecy is to make it come true **fulfilment** noun the feeling that you have achieved something
full adjective
1 containing as much or as many as possible • *The cinema was full.* **2** having many people or things • *You are full of ideas.* **3** complete • *Tell me the full story.* **4** the greatest possible • *They drove at full speed.* **5** fitting loosely; having many folds • *She's wearing a full skirt.*
in full not leaving anything out **fully** adverb completely
full moon noun
the moon when you can see the whole of it as a bright disc

full stop noun
the dot used as a punctuation mark at the end of a sentence or an abbreviation
full-time adjective, adverb
you do something full-time when you do it for all the normal working hours of the day
• *She has a full-time job.*
• *She works full-time.*
fumble verb
to fumble is to handle or feel for something clumsily • *He fumbled in the dark for the light switch.*
fume verb
1 to fume is to give off strong-smelling smoke or gas **2** to be fuming is to be very angry
fumes plural noun
strong-smelling smoke or gas
fun noun
amusement or enjoyment
to make fun of someone or something is to make them look silly or make people laugh at them
function noun
1 what someone or something does or ought to do • *The function of a doctor is to cure sick people.* **2** an important event or party **3** a basic operation of a computer or calculator
function verb
to function is to work properly or perform a function • *The chair also functions as a small table.*
fund noun
a fund is an amount of money collected or kept for a special purpose • *They started a fund for refugees.*
fundamental adjective
basic and necessary • *Let me explain the fundamental rules of the game.* **fundamentally** adverb basically
funeral noun
the ceremony where a person who has died is buried or cremated
fungus noun (**fungi**)
a plant without leaves or flowers that grows on other plants or on decayed material, such as mushrooms and toadstools

funnel noun
1 a tube that is wide at the top and narrow at the bottom, to help you pour things into bottles or other containers **2** a chimney on a ship or steam engine

funnel

funny adjective (**funnier, funniest**)
1 that makes you laugh or smile • *We heard a funny joke.* **2** strange or odd • *There's a funny smell in here.* **funnily** adverb
funny bone noun
part of your elbow which gives you a strange tingling feeling if you knock it
fur noun
1 the soft hair that covers some animals **2** animal skin with the hair on it, used for clothing; fabric that looks like animal skin with hair on it • *She was wearing a fur hat.*
furious adjective
very angry **furiously** adverb
furl verb
to furl a sail or flag or umbrella is to roll it up and fasten it
furnace noun
an oven in which great heat can be produced for making glass or heating metals
furnish verb
to furnish a room or building is to put furniture in it
furniture noun
tables, chairs, beds, cupboards, and other movable things that you need inside a building
furrow noun
1 a long cut in the ground made by a plough **2** a deep wrinkle on the skin
furry adjective (**furrier, furriest**)
1 soft and hairy like fur **2** covered with fur
further adverb and adjective
1 at or to a greater distance; more distant • *I can't walk any further.* **2** more • *We need further information.*
furthermore adverb
also; moreover
furthest adverb and adjective
at or to the greatest distance; most distant
furtive adjective
cautious, trying not to be seen • *He gave a furtive glance and helped himself to the biscuits.*
fury noun (**furies**)
violent or extreme anger
fuse[1] noun
a safety device containing a

fungi

short piece of wire that melts if too much electricity passes through it

fuse¹ *verb*
1 a piece of electrical equipment fuses when it stops working because a fuse has melted • *The lights have fused.* **2** to fuse things is to blend them together, especially through melting

fuse² *noun*
a device for setting off an explosive

fuselage *noun* (*say* **few**-ze-lahzh)
the main body of an aircraft

fuss *noun*
fuss, or a fuss, is unnecessary excitement or worry about something that is not important **to make a fuss of someone** is to pay a lot of attention to them in a kind way

fuss *verb*
to fuss is to be excited or worried about something that is not important

fussy *adjective* (**fussier, fussiest**)
worrying too much about something that is not important **fussily** *adverb* **fussiness** *noun*

futile *adjective* (*say* **few**-tyl)
useless or having no purpose **futility** *noun* being useless or having no purpose

futon *noun* (*say* **foo**-ton)
a seat with a mattress that you can roll out to form a bed

future *noun*
1 the time that will come **2** what is going to happen in the time that will come **in future** from now onwards

fuzzy *adjective* (**fuzzier, fuzziest**)
1 blurred or not clear **2** covered in something soft and hairy **fuzzily** *adverb* **fuzziness** *noun*

Gg

g
short for gram or grams

gabble *verb*
to gabble is to talk so quickly that it is difficult to hear the words

gable *noun*
the three-sided part of a wall between two sloping roofs

gadget *noun* (*say* **gaj**-it)
a small device or tool that helps you with a particular task

gag *noun*
1 something put over someone's mouth to stop them from speaking **2** (*informal*) a joke

gag *verb* (**gagging, gagged**)
to gag someone is to put a gag over their mouth

gain *verb*
1 to gain something is to get it when you did not have it before **2** a clock or watch gains when it goes ahead of the correct time **to gain on someone** is to come closer to them when you are following them

gain *noun*
something you have got that you did not have before; profit

gala *noun* (*say* **gah**-la)
1 a festival **2** a series of sports contests, especially in swimming

galaxy *noun* (**galaxies**) (*say* **gal**-ak-si)
a very large group of stars **galactic** *adjective* to do with a galaxy

gale *noun*
a very strong wind

gallant *adjective*
brave or courteous **gallantly** *adverb* **gallantry** *noun* gallantry is being gallant

galleon *noun*
a large Spanish sailing ship used in the 16th and 17th centuries

gallery *noun* (**galleries**)
1 a platform sticking out from the inside wall of a building **2** the highest set of seats in a cinema or theatre **3** a long room or passage **4** a building or room for showing works of art

galley *noun* (**galleys**)
1 an ancient type of long ship driven by oars **2** the kitchen in a ship

gallon *noun*
a measure of liquid, 8 pints or about 4.5 litres

gallop *noun*
1 the fastest pace that a horse can go **2** a fast ride on a horse

gallop *verb*
to gallop is to ride fast on a horse

gallows *plural noun*
gallows are a framework with a noose for hanging criminals

galore *adjective*
in large amounts • *There are bargains galore in the sale.*

gamble *verb*
to gamble is to play a betting game for money **gambler** *noun* someone who gambles

gamble *noun*
a risk • *We were taking a bit of a gamble on the weather being good.*

game *noun*
1 something that you can play, usually with rules **2** a section of a long game like tennis or whist **3** wild animals or birds hunted for sport or food **to give the game away** is to reveal a secret

gammon *noun*
gammon is a kind of ham or thick bacon

gander *noun*
a male goose

gang *noun*
1 a group of people who do things together **2** a group of criminals

gang *verb*
to gang up on someone is to form a group to fight them or frighten them

gangplank *noun*
a plank for walking on to or off a ship

gangster (*noun*)
a member of a gang of violent criminals

gangway *noun*
1 a gap left for people to move along between rows of seats or through a crowd **2** a movable bridge for getting on or off a ship

gaol *noun* and *verb*
a different spelling of jail

gaoler *noun*
a different spelling of **jailer**

gap *noun*
1 an opening or break in something **2** an interval

gape *verb*
1 to gape is to open your mouth wide **2** to gape is also to stare in amazement **gaping** *adjective* wide open • *There was now a gaping hole in the ice.*

garage *noun* (*say* **ga**-rahzh or *say* **ga**-rij)
1 a building for keeping motor vehicles in **2** a place where motor vehicles are serviced and repaired and where petrol is sold

garbage *noun*
garbage is household refuse or rubbish

garden *noun*
a piece of ground where flowers, fruit, or vegetables are grown

galleon

gardener *noun*
someone who looks after gardens, especially as a job

gardening *noun*
gardening is looking after a garden

gargle *verb*
to gargle is to wash your throat by holding liquid at the back of your mouth and breathing air through it

gargoyle *noun*
an ugly or comical carving of a face on a building, especially one that sticks out from a gutter and sends out rainwater through its mouth

garland *noun*
a wreath of flowers worn as a decoration

garlic *noun*
a plant with a bulb divided into sections (called cloves), which have a strong smell and taste and are used in cooking

garment *noun*
a piece of clothing

garnish *verb*
to garnish a dish of food is to decorate it with extra items such as salad

gas *noun*
1 a substance, such as oxygen, that can move freely and is not liquid or solid at normal temperatures **2** a gas that burns and is used for heating or cooking **gaseous** *adjective* in the form of a gas

gas *verb* (**gassing, gassed**)
to gas someone is to kill or injure them with a poisonous gas

gash *noun*
a long deep cut or wound

gasp *verb*
1 to gasp is to breathe in suddenly when you are shocked or surprised **2** to gasp is also to struggle to breathe when you are ill or tired **3** to gasp something is to say it in a breathless way

gate *noun*
1 a movable barrier, usually on hinges, used as a door in a wall or fence **2** a place where you wait before you board an aircraft **3** the number of people attending a football match

gateau *noun* (**gateaux**)
(*say* **gat**-oh)
a rich cream cake

gateway *noun*
an opening containing a gate

gather *verb*
1 to gather is to come together **2** to gather people or things is to collect them and bring them together **3** to gather a piece of information is to hear or read about it • *I gather you went to the same school as me?* **to gather speed** is to move gradually faster

gathering *noun*
an assembly or meeting of people; a party

gaudy *adjective* (**gaudier, gaudiest**)
very showy and bright

gauge *noun* (*say* gayj)
1 a measuring instrument, such as a fuel gauge **2** the distance between a pair of railway lines

gauge *verb*
to gauge something is to measure it or estimate it • *He looked down into the canyon, trying to gauge how deep it was.*

gaunt *adjective*
a gaunt person is thin and tired-looking

gauntlet *noun*
a glove with a wide covering for the wrist **to throw down the gauntlet** is to offer a challenge

gauze *noun*
gauze is thin transparent material

gaze *verb*
to gaze at something or someone is to look at them hard for a long time

gaze *noun*
a long steady look

GCSE
short for **General Certificate of Secondary Education**

gear *noun*
1 a gear is a set of toothed wheels working together in a machine, especially those connecting the engine to the wheels of a vehicle **2** gear is equipment or clothes • *He had left all his fishing gear behind by the river.* **in gear** with the gears connected **out of gear** with the gears no connected

Geiger counter *noun*
a device that detects and measures radioactivity

genie

gel *noun*
gel is a substance like jelly, especially one used to give a style to hair

gelatine *noun*
gelatine is a clear tasteless substance used to make jellies

gem *noun*
1 a precious stone or jewel **2** an excellent person or thing • *Her auntie's a real gem.*

gender *noun* (*say* **jen**-der)
the group to which a noun or pronoun belongs in some languages (masculine, feminine, and neuter)

gene *noun* (*say* jeen)
the part of a living cell that controls which characteristics (such as the colour of your hair or eyes) you inherit from your parents

general *adjective*
1 to do with most people or things • *The general feeling is that we should go to the beach.* **2** not detailed or special • *The website has lots of general information on marine life.* **in general** usually; to do with most people

general *noun*
an army officer of high rank

general election *noun*
an election of Members of Parliament for the whole country

generally *adverb*
usually; to do with most people

generate *verb*
to generate something is to produce or create it

generation *noun*
1 a single stage in a family • *Three generations were included: children, parents, and grandparents.* **2** all the people born about the same time • *He was one of the most famous film stars of his generation.*

generator *noun*
a machine for producing electricity

generous *adjective*
ready to give or share what you have **generosity** *noun* being generous and ready to give a lot **generously** *adverb*

genetic *adjective*
(*say* ji-**net**-ik)
to do with genes and with characteristics inherited from parents **genetically** *adverb* by means of genes

genetics *plural noun*
genetics is the study of genes and genetic behaviour

genie *noun*
a magical being in stories who can grant wishes

genius *noun*
1 an unusually clever person **2** an unusually great ability or talent

a b c d e f g h i j k l m n o p q r s t u v w x y z

gentle ▷ gist

gentle *adjective*
kind and quiet; not rough or severe **gentleness** *noun*
gently *adverb*
gentleman *noun* (**gentlemen**)
1 a man **2** a well-mannered or honest man • *He's a real gentleman.*
genuine *adjective*
1 something is genuine when it is real and not fake **2** a person is genuine when they are honest and sincere **genuinely** *adverb* really; in a genuine way
genus *noun* (**genera**)
(*say* **jee**-nus)
a group of similar animals or plants
geography *noun*
geography is the science or study of the world and its climate, peoples, and products **geographer** *noun* someone who studies geography **geographical** *adjective* a geographical area is a region of the earth that you can see on a map
geology *noun* (*say* ji-**ol**-o-ji)
geology is the study of the earth's crust and its layers **geologist** *noun* someone who studies geology **geological** *adjective* a geological era or period is a time in the past that you can see in the layers of the earth
geometry *noun*
geometry is the study of lines, angles, surfaces, and solids in mathematics **geometric** *adjective* a geometric shape or pattern has regular lines and angles **geometrical** *adjective*
gerbil *noun* (*say* **jer**-bil)
a small brown animal with long back legs
germ *noun*
a tiny living thing, especially one that causes a disease
germinate *verb*
a seed germinates when it starts growing and developing **germination** *noun* germination is the process of germinating
gesture *noun* (*say* **jes**-cher)
a movement or action which expresses what you feel
get *verb*
This word has many meanings, depending on the words that go with it **1** to get something is to obtain or receive it • *I got a new bike yesterday.* **2** to get (for example) angry or upset is to become angry or upset **3** to get to a place is to reach it • *We had to borrow money to get home.* **4** to get something (for example)

on or off is take it on or off • *I can't get my shoe on.* **5** to get (for example) a meal is to prepare it **6** to get an illness is to catch it • *I think she's got measles.* **7** to get someone to do something is to persuade or order them to do it • *Lara might get him to say yes.* **8** (*informal*) to get something is to understand it • *Do you get what I mean?* **to get by** is to manage **to get on** is to make progress, or to be friendly with someone **to get out of something** is to avoid having to do it **to get over something** is to recover from an illness or shock **to get your own back** is to have your revenge **to have got to do something** is to have no choice about it
getaway *noun*
an escape
geyser *noun*
(*say* **gee**-zer or *say* **gy**-zer)
a natural spring that shoots up columns of hot water
ghastly *adjective*
horrible; awful
ghetto *noun*
(*say* **get**-oh)
an area of a city, often a slum area, where a group of people live who are treated unfairly compared with other people
ghost *noun*
the spirit of a dead person seen by a living person **ghostly** *adjective* reminding you of a ghost • *The moon gave a ghostly light to the scene.*
ghoulish *adjective* (*say* **gool**-ish)
enjoying looking at things to do with death and suffering
giant *noun*
1 a creature in stories, like a huge man **2** something that is much larger than the usual size
giant *adjective*
huge
giddy *adjective*
feeling unsteady or dizzy **giddily** *adverb* **giddiness** *noun*
gift *noun*
1 a present **2** a talent • *She has a special gift for drawing.*
gifted *adjective*
a gifted person has a special talent or ability

gigantic *adjective*
huge; enormous
giggle *verb*
to giggle is to laugh in a silly way
giggle *noun*
1 a silly laugh **2** (*informal*) something amusing; a joke • *We did it for a giggle.* **the giggles** (*informal*) are a fit of giggling
gild *verb*
to gild something is to cover it with a thin layer of gold paint or gold
gills *plural noun*
the gills are the part of a fish's body that it breathes through
gimmick *noun*
something unusual done or used to attract people's attention
ginger *noun*
1 a hot-tasting tropical root, used as a flavouring for food **2** a reddish-yellow colour **gingery** *adjective*
gingerbread *noun*
a cake or biscuit flavoured with ginger
gingerly *adverb*
you do something gingerly when you do it carefully and cautiously because you are not sure about it • *She was walking very gingerly along the icy path.*

gingerbread

gipsy *noun*
a different spelling of **gypsy**
giraffe *noun*
a tall African animal with a very long neck
girder *noun*
a metal beam supporting part of a building or bridge
girl *noun*
1 a female child **2** a young woman **girlhood** *noun* the time when a woman was a girl **girlish** *adjective* looking or behaving like a girl
girlfriend *noun*
a person's regular female friend or lover
girth *noun*
1 the measurement round something **2** a band fastened round a horse's belly to keep its saddle in place
gist *noun* (*say* jist)
the main points or general meaning of a speech or conversation

give verb
1 to give someone something is to let them have it • *She gave me a sweet.* **2** to give (for example) a laugh or shout is to laugh or shout out **3** to give a performance is to present or perform something • *They gave a concert to raise money.* **4** something gives if it bends or goes down under a strain • *Will this branch give if I sit on it?* **to give in** is to surrender **to give up** is to stop doing or trying something **to give way** is to break or collapse **giver** noun a person who gives something

given adjective
stated or agreed in advance • *Work out how much you can do in a given time.*

glacial adjective (say **glay**-shal) made of ice or formed by glaciers

glacier noun (say **glas**-i-er) a mass of ice moving slowly along a valley

glad adjective
happy and pleased **to be glad of something** is to be grateful for it **gladly** adverb you do something gladly when you are pleased to do it **gladness** noun

gladden verb
to gladden someone is to make them glad

gladiator noun
a man who fought with a sword or other weapons at public shows in ancient Rome

glamorous adjective
attractive and exciting

glamour noun
1 the glamour of something is what makes it attractive or exciting • *Just think of the glamour of competing in the Olympics.* **2** a person's glamour is their beauty or attractiveness • *Most of her clothes were chosen for comfort rather than glamour.*

glance verb
1 to glance at something is to look at it quickly **2** to glance off something is to hit it and slide off • *The ball glanced off his bat.*

glance noun
a quick look

gland noun
an organ of the body that separates substances from the blood, so that they can be used or passed out of the body

glare verb
1 to glare is to shine with a bright or dazzling light **2** to glare at someone is to look angrily at them

glare noun
1 a strong light **2** an angry stare

glaring adjective
1 very bright **2** very obvious and embarrassing • *Fortunately there were no glaring mistakes in their work.*

glass noun
1 glass is a hard brittle substance that lets light through **2** a glass is a container made of glass, for drinking out of **3** a glass is also a mirror or a lens

glassy adjective (**glassier, glassiest**)
like glass • *He gave a glassy stare.*

glasses plural noun
a frame holding two lenses that you wear over your eyes to improve your sight; spectacles

glaze verb
1 to glaze something is to cover or fit it with glass **2** to glaze pottery is to give it a shiny surface

glaze noun
a shiny surface

gleam noun
1 a beam of soft light, especially one that comes and goes **2** a clear sign of something • *She could see the gleam of excitement in his eyes.*

gleam verb
to gleam is to shine with beams of soft light

glee noun
glee is when you feel happy and excited about something

gleeful adjective
happy and excited **gleefully** adverb

glen noun
a narrow valley, especially in Scotland

glide verb
1 to glide is to fly or move smoothly **2** to glide is also to fly without using an engine

glider noun
an aircraft that does not use an engine and floats on air currents

glimmer noun
a faint light

glimmer verb
to glimmer is to shine with a faint light

glimpse verb
to glimpse something is to see it briefly

glimpse noun
a brief view of something

glint verb
to glint is to shine with a flash of light

glint noun
a brief flash of light

glisten verb
to glisten is to shine like something wet or oily

glitter verb
to glitter is to shine with tiny flashes of light

gloat verb
to gloat is to be pleased in an unkind way that you have succeeded or that someone else has been hurt or upset

global adjective
to do with the whole world **globally** adverb all over the world

global warming noun
the gradual increase in the average temperature of the earth's climate, caused by the greenhouse effect

globe noun
1 a globe is something shaped like a ball, especially one with a map of the world on it **2** the globe is the world • *These stories come from all over the globe.*

gloom noun
gloom is a depressed condition or feeling

gloomy adjective (**gloomier, gloomiest**)
1 almost dark; not well lit **2** sad or depressed **gloomily** adverb **gloominess** noun

glorious adjective
splendid or magnificent

glory noun (**glories**)
1 glory is fame and honour **2** the glory of something is its splendour or beauty

gloss noun
the shine on a smooth surface

glossary noun (**glossaries**)
a list of words with their meanings explained

glossy adjective
smooth and shiny

glove noun
a covering for the hand, with a separate division for each finger

globe

a b c d e f g h i j k l m n o p q r s t u v w x y z

glow *noun*
1 a brightness and warmth without flames • *Her eyes glittered in the red glow of the fire.* **2** a warm or cheerful feeling • *Sarah felt a deep glow of satisfaction at her win.*

glow *verb*
to glow is to shine with a soft light

glower *verb* (rhymes with **flower**)
to glower is to stare with an angry look

glucose *noun*
glucose is a type of sugar found in fruits and honey

glue *noun*
glue is a thick liquid for sticking things together **gluey** *adjective* sticky like glue

glue *verb*
to glue something is to stick it with glue

glum *adjective* (**glummer, glummest**)
sad or depressed **glumly** *adverb*

glutton *noun*
someone who is greedy and enjoys eating too much **gluttonous** *adjective* greedy; eating too much **gluttony** *noun* when someone eats too much

gnarled *adjective* (say narld)
twisted and knobbly, like an old tree

gnash *verb* (say nash)
to gnash your teeth is to grind them together

gnat *noun* (say nat)
a tiny fly that bites

gnaw *verb* (say naw)
to gnaw something hard is to keep biting it

gnome *noun* (say nohm)
a kind of dwarf in fairy tales that usually lives underground

go *verb* (**going, went, gone**)
1 to go is to move or lead from one place to another • *Let's go in and see Mrs Cooper.* • *We'll have to go soon.* • *This road goes to Bristol.* **2** a machine or device goes when it is working • *My watch isn't going.* • *A car that doesn't go is not much use.* **3** you say that someone or something has gone when they are no longer there and you can't find them • *All her money had gone.* **4 Go** also has many special uses shown in these examples • *The milk went sour.* • *The plates go on that shelf.* • *The party went well.* • *The gun went bang.* **to be going to do something** is to be ready to do it **to go in for something** is to take part in it **to go off** is to explode **to go off someone** or **something** is to stop liking them

to go on is to happen or continue • *What's going on?*

go *noun* (**goes**)
1 a go is a turn or try • *May I have a go?* **2** (*informal*) go is energy or liveliness • *She's full of go.* **on the go** always working or moving

goal *noun* (**goals**)
1 the two posts that the ball must go between to score a point in football, hockey, and other games **2** a point scored in football, hockey, netball, and other games **3** something that you try to do or to achieve • *Her goal is to become a pilot.*

goalkeeper *noun*
the player who guards the goal in football and hockey

goalpost *noun*
each of the upright posts of a goal in sports

goat *noun*
an animal with horns, belonging to the same family as sheep

gobble *verb*
to gobble something is to eat it quickly and greedily

goblet *noun*
a drinking glass with a long stem and a base

goblin *noun*
an evil or mischievous fairy in stories

WORD ORIGIN

The word **goblin** comes from an Old French word *gobelin*, which may be related to a Greek word *kobalos* meaning 'a mischievous goblin'.

God *noun*
the creator of the universe in Christian, Jewish, and Muslim belief

goddess *noun*
a female being that is worshipped

goggles *plural noun*
goggles are large glasses that you wear to protect your eyes, for example when you are swimming

gold *noun* (Au)
1 gold is a precious yellow metal **2** gold is also a bright yellow colour

golden *adjective*
1 made of gold **2** coloured like gold **3** precious or excellent • *It was a golden opportunity.*

goldfinch *noun*
a small, brightly-coloured bird with yellow feathers in its wings

goldfish *noun* (**goldfish**)
a small red or orange fish, often kept as a pet

golf *noun*
golf is an outdoor game played on a prepared course by hitting a small ball into a series of small holes, using a club **golfer** *noun*

gondola *noun* (say **gon**-do-la)
a boat with high pointed ends, used on the canals in Venice **gondolier** *noun* a person who moves a gondola along with a pole

gong *noun*
a large metal disc that makes a deep hollow sound when it is hit

good *adjective* (**better, best**)
1 of the kind that people like, want, or praise • *They wanted to have a good time.* **2** kind • *It was good of you to come.* **3** well-behaved • *Be a good boy.* **4** healthy; giving benefit • *Exercise is good for you.* **5** thorough; large enough • *Let's give it a good clean.*

good *noun*
1 something good or right • *Do good to others.* **2** benefit or advantage • *I'm telling you for your own good.* **for good** for ever **no good** useless

goodbye *exclamation*
a word you use when you leave someone or at the end of a telephone call

Good Friday *noun*
the Friday before Easter, when Christians remember Christ's death on the Cross

good-looking *adjective*
attractive or handsome

good-natured *adjective*
kind

goodness *noun*
1 goodness is being good **2** a thing's goodness is the good it does

goods *plural noun*
goods are things that people buy and sell

goodwill *noun*
goodwill is a kindly and helpful feeling towards people

gooey *adjective*
sticky or slimy

goose *noun* (**geese**)
a water bird with webbed feet, larger than a duck

gooseberry *noun* (**gooseberries**)
a small green fruit that grows on a prickly bush

goose pimples *plural noun*
goose pimples are lots of tiny bumps

goose

you get on the skin when you are cold or afraid

gore verb
to gore a person or animal is to wound them savagely with a horn or tusk • *Several dogs had been gored by a wild boar.*

gorge noun
a narrow valley with steep sides

gorgeous adjective
magnificent; beautiful
gorgeously adverb

gorilla noun
a large strong African ape

gorse noun
gorse is a prickly bush with small yellow flowers

gory adjective (**gorier, goriest**)
having a lot of blood and violence

gosling noun
a young goose

gospel noun
1 the gospel is the teachings of Jesus Christ **2** gospel is something you can safely believe • *You can take what she says as gospel.*
the Gospels the first four books of the New Testament

gossip verb
to gossip is to talk a lot about other people

gossip noun
1 gossip is talk or rumours about other people **2** a gossip is someone who likes talking about other people

gouge verb (say gowj)
to gouge something is to press or scoop it out

govern verb
to govern a country or organization is to be in charge of it

government noun
the group of people who are in charge of a country

governor noun
someone who governs or runs a place

gown noun
a loose flowing piece of clothing

grab verb (**grabbing, grabbed**)
to grab something is to take hold of it firmly or suddenly

grace noun
1 grace is beauty, especially in movement **2** someone behaves with grace when they are kind and friendly to people

graceful adjective
beautiful and elegant in movement or shape
gracefully adverb

gracious adjective
1 kind and pleasant to other people **2** merciful **graciously** adverb in a kind and generous way

grade noun
a step in a scale of quality, value, or rank

grade verb
to grade things is to sort or divide them into grades

gradient noun (say **gray**-di-ent)
1 a slope **2** the amount that a road or railway slopes

gradual adjective
happening slowly but steadily
gradually adverb slowly or in stages

graduate noun (say **grad**-yoo-at)
someone who has a degree from a university or college

graffiti plural noun (say gra-**fee**-tee)
graffiti is words or drawings scribbled on a wall

WORD ORIGIN
The word **graffiti** is the plural of an Italian word *graffito* meaning 'a scratch'.

grain noun
1 grain is cereals when they are growing or after they have been harvested **2** a grain is the hard seed of a cereal **3** a grain of something is a small amount of it • *The story had a grain of truth in it.* **4** the grain on a piece of wood is the pattern of lines going through it

gram noun
a unit of weight in the metric system, a thousandth of a kilogram

grammar noun
1 grammar is the rules for using words **2** a grammar is a book that gives the rules for using words **grammatical** adjective following the rules of grammar

grammar school noun
a kind of secondary school

grand adjective
1 great or splendid **2** a grand total is one that includes everything **grandly** adverb in a grand way

grandchild noun (**grandchildren**)
a child of a person's son or daughter. A girl is a **granddaughter** and a boy is a **grandson**.

grandfather noun
the father of a person's mother or father

grandfather clock noun
a clock in a tall wooden case

grandmother noun
the mother of a person's mother or father

grandparent noun
a grandmother or grandfather

grandstand noun
a building at a racecourse or sports ground, that is open at the front with rows of seats for spectators

granite noun
granite is a very hard kind of rock

grant verb
to grant someone something is to give or allow them what they have asked for **to take something for granted** is to assume that it is true or will happen

grant noun
a sum of money given for a special purpose

grape noun
a small green or purple fruit that grows in bunches on a vine

grapefruit noun (**grapefruit**)
a large round yellow citrus fruit with a soft juicy pulp

graph noun
a diagram that shows how two amounts are related

graphic adjective
1 short and lively • *He gave a graphic account of the journey.* **2** to do with drawing or painting • *She wants to be a graphic artist.*
graphically adverb in a graphic way

grapefruit

graphics plural noun
graphics are diagrams, lettering, and drawings, especially pictures that are produced by a computer

graphite noun
graphite is a soft kind of carbon used for the lead in pencils

grapple verb
1 to grapple someone or grapple with someone is to fight them **2** to grapple something is to hold it tightly **3** to grapple with a problem is to try to deal with it

grasp verb
1 to grasp someone or something is to hold them tightly **2** to grasp something is to understand it

grasp noun
1 a firm hold **2** a person's grasp of a subject is how well they understand it

grass noun
1 grass is a green plant with thin stalks **2** a piece of grass is an area of ground covered with grass **grassy** adjective covered in grass

grasshopper *noun*
a jumping insect that makes a shrill noise

grate¹ *noun*
1 a metal framework that keeps fuel in the fireplace **2** a fireplace

grate² *verb*
1 to grate something is to shred it into small pieces **2** to grate is to make an unpleasant noise by rubbing something • *The chalk grated on the blackboard.*

grateful *adjective*
feeling glad that someone has done something for you **gratefully** *adverb*

grating *noun*
a framework of metal bars placed across an opening

gratitude *noun*
you show gratitude when you are grateful or thankful for something

grave¹ *noun*
the place where a dead body is buried

grave² *adjective*
serious or solemn • *We've had grave news.* **gravely** *adverb*
• *The man nodded gravely.*

gravel *noun*
gravel is small stones mixed with coarse sand, used to make paths

gravestone *noun*
a stone monument over a grave

graveyard *noun*
a place where dead bodies are buried

gravity *noun*
1 gravity is the force that pulls all objects in the universe towards each other **2** the earth's gravity is the force that pulls everything towards itself **3** gravity is also the seriousness or importance of something

gravy *noun*
a hot brown sauce made from meat juices

graze *verb*
1 to graze is to feed on growing grass **2** to graze your skin is to scrape it slightly against something rough

graze *noun*
a sore place where skin has been scraped

grease *noun*
grease is thick fat or oil **greasy** *adjective* oily like grease

great *adjective*
1 very large **2** very important or distinguished • *She was a great writer.* **3** (*informal*) very good or enjoyable • *It's great to see you again.* **4** older or younger by one generation, as in *great-grandmother* and *great-grandson* **greatly** *adverb* **greatness** *noun*

greed *noun*
greed is being greedy and wanting too much

greedy *adjective* (**greedier, greediest**)
wanting more food or money than you need **greedily** *adverb*

green *adjective* ●
1 of the colour of grass and leaves **2** concerned with protecting the natural environment

green *noun*
1 green is a green colour **2** a green is an area of grass

greenery *noun*
green leaves or plants

greenhouse *noun*
a glass building that is kept warm inside for growing plants

greenhouse effect *noun*
the warming of the earth's surface by gases (called **greenhouse gases**) such as methane and carbon dioxide, which trap heat in the earth's atmosphere

greet *verb*
1 to greet someone is to welcome them when they arrive • *His cat Moxie greeted him with a soft miaow.* **2** to greet something is to respond to it in a certain way • *They greeted the news with loud cheering.*

greeting *noun*
a greeting is the words or actions used to greet someone **greetings** are good wishes when you meet someone or talk to them

grenade *noun*
a small bomb, usually thrown by hand

grey *adjective* ●
of the colour between black and white, like ashes or dark clouds

grey *noun*
a grey colour

grid *noun*
a framework or pattern of bars or lines crossing each other

grief *noun*
grief is deep sadness or sorrow people feel when someone has died

grievance *noun*
something that people are unhappy or angry about

grieve *verb*
to grieve is to feel sad or sorrowful when someone has died

grill *noun*
1 a part of a cooker that sends heat downwards **2** grilled food **3** a grating

grill *verb*
1 to grill food is to cook it under

a grill **2** to grill someone is to question them closely and severely • *The police grilled him for several hours.*

grim *adjective* (**grimmer, grimmest**)
1 stern or severe **2** frightening or unpleasant • *They had a grim experience.* **grimly** *adverb*

grimace *noun*
a strange or twisted expression on your face

grime *noun*
grime is a layer of dirt on a surface **grimy** *adjective* very dirty

grin *noun*
a smile showing your teeth

grin *verb*
to grin is to smile showing your teeth

grind *verb* (**grinding, ground**)
1 to grind something is to crush it into a powder **2** to grind something hard is to sharpen or polish it by rubbing it on a rough surface **to grind to a halt** is to stop suddenly with a lot of noise **grinder** *noun* something that grinds things

grip *verb* (**gripping, gripped**)
1 to grip something is to hold it tightly **2** a story, film, game, or other activity grips you when you find it very interesting or exciting

grip *noun*
1 a firm hold on something **2** a handle

grisly *adjective* (**grislier, grisliest**)
disgusting or horrible • *The book is full of scary villains and grisly murders.*

gristle *noun*
gristle is the tough rubbery part of meat **gristly** *adjective* gristly meat is tough and full of gristle

grit *noun*
1 grit is tiny pieces of stone or sand **2** a person's grit is their courage and determination to do something difficult **gritty** *adjective* rough like grit

grit *verb* (**gritting, gritted**)
1 to grit your teeth is to clench them tightly when in pain or trouble **2** to grit a road or path is to put grit on it

grizzly bear *noun*
a large bear of North America

groan *verb*
to groan is to make a long deep sound when in pain or distress

groan *noun*
a long deep sound of pain or distress

grocer *noun*
someone who keeps a shop that sells food, drink, and other goods for the house

grocery noun (**groceries**)
a grocer's shop **groceries** goods sold by a grocer
groin noun
the flat part where your thighs join the rest of your body
groom noun
1 someone whose job is to look after horses 2 a bridegroom
groom verb
1 to groom a horse or other animal is to clean and brush it 2 to groom the hair or a beard is to make it neat and trim
groove noun
a long narrow channel cut in the surface of something
grope verb
to grope for something is to feel about for it when you cannot see it
gross adjective
1 fat and ugly 2 having bad manners; crude or vulgar 3 very bad or shocking • *They showed gross stupidity.* 4 total, without anything taken off **grossly** adverb extremely or too much • *That's grossly unfair!*
gross noun
a gross is twelve dozen or 144
grotesque adjective (say groh-**tesk**)
strange and ugly
grotesquely adverb
ground noun
1 the ground is the surface of the earth 2 a ground is a sports field
grounded adjective
1 aircraft are grounded when they are prevented from flying, for example because of the weather 2 (*informal*) someone is grounded when they are not allowed to go out
ground floor noun
in a building, the floor that is level with the ground
grounds plural noun
1 the reasons that explain or justify something • *There are grounds for suspecting that a crime has been committed.* 2 the gardens of a large house 3 bits of coffee at the bottom of a cup
group noun
a number of people, animals, or things that belong together in some way
group verb
to group people or things is to make them into a group
grouse noun
a large bird with feathered feet, that some people like to hunt as a sport
grove noun
a group of trees; a small wood

grovel verb (**grovelling, grovelled**)
1 to grovel is to crawl on the ground 2 to grovel is to be extremely humble and obedient towards someone, usually because you want something from them
grow verb (**growing, grew, grown**)
1 a person grows when they become bigger with age 2 a plant or seed grows when it develops in the ground 3 to grow something is to plant it in the ground and look after it • *She grows lovely roses.* 4 to grow is also to become • *By now it was growing dark on the moor.* • *He grew richer and richer.* **to grow out of something** is to become too big or too old for it **to grow up** is to become an adult **grower** noun someone who grows things
growl verb
to growl is to make a deep rough sound, like an angry dog
growl noun
a deep rough sound
grown-up noun
an adult
growth noun
1 growth is growing or development 2 a growth is something that has grown, especially something unwanted in the body such as a tumour
grub noun
1 a grub is a tiny creature that will become an insect; a larva 2 (*slang*) grub is food
grubby adjective (**grubbier, grubbiest**)
rather dirty
grudge noun
a dislike of someone because you think they have harmed you, or because you are jealous
grudge verb
to grudge someone something is to feel unwilling to let them have it **grudgingly** adverb you do something grudgingly when you don't really want to do it, and only do it because you have to
gruelling adjective
a gruelling test or journey or other experience is one that is very hard and tiring
gruesome adjective
horrible or disgusting to look at
gruff adjective
having a rough unfriendly voice or manner **gruffly** adverb
grumble verb
to grumble is to complain in a bad-tempered way **grumbler** noun someone who grumbles

grumpy adjective (**grumpier, grumpiest**)
bad-tempered **grumpily** adverb **grumpiness** noun
grunt verb
to grunt is to make a snorting sound like a pig
grunt noun
a snort like that of a pig
guarantee noun
a formal promise to do something, especially to repair something you have sold someone if it goes wrong
guarantee verb
to guarantee something is to make a promise to do it
guard verb
1 to guard something or someone is to keep them safe 2 to guard a prisoner is to prevent them from escaping **to guard against something** is to be careful to prevent it happening
guard noun
1 guard is protecting or guarding people or things • *Keep the prisoners under close guard.* 2 a guard is someone who protects or watches a person or place 3 a guard is also an official in charge of a railway train 4 a guard is a shield or device protecting people from the dangers of a fire or machinery **on guard** protecting; acting as a guard
guardian noun
1 someone who protects something 2 someone who is legally in charge of a child instead of the child's parents **guardianship** noun guardianship is being a guardian
guerrilla noun (say ge-**ril**-a)
a member of a small army or band that fights by means of surprise attacks
guess noun
an opinion or answer that you give without working it out in detail or being sure of it
guess verb
to guess is to make a guess
guest noun (say gest)
a person who is invited to a party or is staying at another person's house or at a hotel
guidance noun
guidance is giving help or information to someone, or telling them how to do something
guide noun
1 someone who shows people the way, helps them, or points out interesting sights 2 a book that tells you about a place

a
b
c
d
e
f
g
h
i
j
k
l
m
n
o
p
q
r
s
t
u
v
w
x
y
z

Guide a member of the Girl Guides Association, an organization for girls

guide *verb*
to guide someone is to show them the way or help them do something

guide dog *noun*
a dog specially trained to lead a blind person

guidelines *plural noun*
guidelines are rules and information about how to do something

guillotine *noun (say* gil-o-teen)
1 a machine once used in France for beheading people 2 a device with a sharp blade for cutting paper

guilt *noun*
1 guilt is an unpleasant feeling you have when you have done something wrong 2 a person's guilt is the fact that they have done something wrong
• *Everyone was convinced of his guilt.*

guilty *adjective* (**guiltier, guiltiest**)
1 someone is guilty when they have done wrong 2 someone feels guilty when they know they have done wrong

guinea pig *noun*
1 a small furry animal without a tail, kept as a pet 2 a person who is used in an experiment

guitar *noun*
a musical instrument played by plucking its strings
guitarist *noun* someone who plays the guitar

gulf *noun*
a large area of sea partly surrounded by land

gull *noun*
a seagull

gullet *noun*
the tube from the throat to the stomach

gullible *adjective*
someone is gullible when they can be easily fooled about something

gully *noun* (**gullies**)
a narrow channel that carries water

gulp *verb*
1 to gulp something is to swallow it quickly or greedily 2 to gulp is to make a loud swallowing noise, especially out of fear

gulp *noun*
a loud swallowing noise

gum¹ *noun*
the firm fleshy part of the mouth that holds the teeth

gum² *noun*
1 a sticky substance used as glue 2 chewing gum **gummy** *adjective* sticky like gum

gum² *verb* (**gumming, gummed**)
to gum something is to cover it or stick it with gum

gun *noun*
1 a weapon that fires shells or bullets from a metal tube 2 a pistol fired to signal the start of a race

gun *verb* (**gunning, gunned**)
to gun someone down is to shoot them with a gun

gunfire *noun*
gunfire is the firing of guns, or the noise they make

gunman *noun* (**gunmen**)
a man armed with a gun

gunpowder *noun*
gunpowder is a type of explosive

gurdwara *noun*
a building where Sikhs worship

gurgle *verb*
to gurgle is to make a bubbling sound • *Water gurgled down the pipe.*

guru *noun*
1 a Hindu religious teacher 2 a wise and respected teacher

Guru Granth Sahib *noun*
the holy book of the Sikh religion

gush *verb*
1 to gush is to flow quickly 2 to gush is also to talk quickly and with excitement

gust *noun*
a sudden rush of wind or rain
gusty *adjective*

gut *noun*
the lower part of the digestive system; the intestine

gut *verb* (**gutting, gutted**)
1 to gut a dead fish or animal is to remove its insides before cooking it 2 to gut a place is to remove or destroy the inside of it • *The fire gutted the house.*

guts *plural noun*
1 the insides of a person or animal, especially the stomach and intestines 2 (*informal*) courage and determination

gutter *noun*
a long narrow channel at the side of a street or along the edge of a roof, to carry away rainwater

guy¹ *noun*
1 a figure in the form of Guy Fawkes, burnt on or near 5 November in memory of the Gunpowder Plot to blow up Parliament in 1605 2 (*informal*) a man

guzzle *verb*
to guzzle food or drink is to eat or drink it greedily

gym *noun* (*say* jim) (*informal*)
1 a gym is a gymnasium 2 gym is gymnastics

gymkhana *noun* (*say* jim-**kah**-na)
a show of horse-riding contests and other events

gymnasium *noun*
a place equipped for gymnastics

gymnast *noun*
a person who does gymnastics

gymnastics *plural noun*
gymnastics are exercises and movements that show the body's agility and strength

gypsy *noun* (**gypsies**)
a member of a community of people, also called **travellers**, who live in caravans or similar vehicles and travel from place to place

gyroscope *noun*
a device used in navigation, that keeps steady because of a heavy wheel spinning inside it

gymnast

WORD ORIGIN

The word **gyroscope** comes from a Greek word *gyros* meaning 'a ring or circle'.

Hh

habit *noun*
something that you do often and almost without thinking **habitual** *adjective* something is habitual when you do it regularly, as a habit **habitually** *adverb*

habitat *noun*
an animal's or plant's habitat is the place where it naturally lives or grows

hack *verb*
to hack something is to chop or cut it roughly

hacker *noun*
someone who uses a computer to get access to a company's or government's computer system without permission

hacksaw *noun*
a saw with a thin blade for cutting metal

haddock *noun* (**haddock**)
a sea fish used for food

hag *noun*
an ugly old woman

haggard *adjective*
looking ill or very tired

haggis *noun*
a Scottish food made from some of the inner parts of a sheep mixed with oatmeal

haggle *verb*
to haggle is to argue about a price or agreement
haiku *noun* (**haiku**) (*say* **hy**-koo)
a Japanese short poem, with three lines and 17 syllables in the pattern 5,7,5

hail¹ *noun*
frozen drops of rain

hail¹ *verb*
it hails or it is hailing when hail falls

hail² *verb*
to hail someone is to call out or wave to them to get their attention

hailstone *noun*
a piece of hail

hair *noun*
1 hair is the soft covering that grows on the heads and bodies of people and animals 2 a hair is one of the fine threads that makes up this soft covering

hairbrush *noun*
a brush for tidying your hair

haircut *noun*
cutting a person's hair when it gets too long; the style into which it is cut

hairdresser *noun*
someone whose job is to cut and arrange people's hair

hair-raising *adjective*
terrifying or dangerous

hairstyle *noun*
a way or style of arranging your hair

hairy *adjective* (**hairier, hairiest**)
having a lot of hair

Hajj *noun*
the Hajj is the journey to Mecca that all Muslims try to make at least once in their lives

hake *noun* (**hake**)
a sea fish used for food

halal *adjective*
halal meat is prepared according to Muslim law

half *noun* (**halves**)
each of the two equal parts that something is or can be divided into

half *adverb*
partly; not completely • *This meat is only half cooked.*

half-hearted *adjective*
not very enthusiastic

half-heartedly *adverb* not very enthusiastically

half-mast *noun*
a flag is at half-mast when it is lowered to halfway down its flagpole, as a sign that someone important has died

half-term *noun*
a short holiday from school in the middle of a school term

half-time *noun*
a short break in the middle of a game

halfway *adverb, adjective*
at a point half the distance or amount between two places or times

hall *noun*
1 a space or passage inside the front door of a house 2 a very large room for meetings, concerts, or other large gatherings of people 3 a large important building or house, such as a town hall

hallo *exclamation*
a word used to greet someone or to attract their attention

Hallowe'en *noun*
the night of 31 October, when people used to think that ghosts and witches might appear

hallucination *noun*
something you think you can see or hear when it isn't really there

halo *noun* (**haloes**)
a circle of light, especially one shown round the head of a saint or angel in a painting

halt *verb*
to halt is to stop

halt *noun*
to call a halt is to stop something to come to a halt is to stop

halter *noun*
a rope or strap put round a horse's head so that it can be controlled

halve *verb*
1 to halve something is to divide it into halves 2 to halve something is to reduce to half its size or amount • *If the shop had another checkout it would halve the queues.*

ham *noun*
ham is meat from a pig's leg

hamburger *noun*
a round flat cake of minced beef that is fried and usually eaten in a bread roll

hammer *noun*
a tool with a heavy metal head at the end of a handle, used for hitting nails in or beating out things

hammer *verb*
1 to hammer something is to hit it with a hammer 2 to hammer is to knock loudly • *We heard someone hammering on the door.* 3 (*informal*) to hammer someone in a game or contest is to defeat them completely

hammock *noun*
a bed made of a strong net or piece of cloth hung up above the ground or floor

hamper¹ *noun*
a large box-shaped basket with a lid

hamper² *verb*
to hamper someone or something is to get in their way or make it difficult for them to work

hamster *noun*
a small furry animal with cheek pouches, often kept as a pet

hand *noun*
1 the part of your body at the end of your arm 2 a pointer on a clock or watch 3 the cards held by one player in a card game 4 a worker, especially a member of a ship's crew 5 side or direction • *the right-hand side* • *on the other hand* at hand near or close by to give someone a hand is to help them on hand ready and available to get out of hand is to get out of control

hand *verb*
to hand something to someone is to give or pass it to them something is handed down when it is passed on from one generation to the next

handbag *noun*
a small bag for holding money, keys, and other personal items

handcuffs *plural noun*
a pair of metal rings joined by a chain, used for locking a person's wrists together

handful *noun*
1 as much as you can carry in one hand 2 a small number of people or things • *There were only a handful of people in the audience.* 3 (*informal*) a troublesome person

handicap *noun*
1 a disadvantage 2 a disability affecting a person

handicapped *adjective*
1 suffering from a disadvantage 2 suffering from a disability

handicraft *noun*
artistic work done with your hands, such as woodwork and pottery

hang-glider

handiwork noun
something you have done or made with your hands

handkerchief noun
(say **hang**-ker-cheef)
a square piece of material for wiping your nose

handle noun
the part of a thing by which you can hold or control it or pick it up

handle verb
1 to handle something is to touch or feel it with your hands **2** to handle a task or problem is to deal with it • *I thought you handled the situation very well.*

handlebars plural noun
a bar with a handle at each end, used to steer a bicycle or motor cycle

handsome adjective
1 attractive or good-looking **2** large or generous • *They have made a handsome offer.*

handstand noun
an exercise in which you balance on your hands with your feet in the air

handwriting noun
writing done by hand; a person's style of writing **handwritten** adjective written by hand, not typed or printed

handy adjective (**handier, handiest**)
useful or convenient

hang verb (**hanging, hung**)
1 to hang something is to fix the top part of it to a hook or nail • *Hang your coat on one of the pegs.* **2** something hangs when it is supported from the top and does not touch the ground
• *The bat was hanging by its feet.*
3 to hang wallpaper is to paste it in strips on to a wall **4** to hang is to float in the air **5** (in this meaning, the past tense and past participle are **hanged**) to hang someone is to execute them by hanging them from a rope that tightens around their neck
• *He was hanged in 1950.* **to hang about** or **hang around** is to wait around doing nothing **to hang on** (informal) is to wait • *Hang on! I'm not ready yet.* **to hang on to**

something is to hold it tightly **to hang up** is to end a telephone conversation by putting back the receiver

hangar noun
a large shed where aircraft are kept

hanger noun
a curved piece of wood, plastic, or wire with a hook at the top, that you use to hang clothes up on

hang-glider noun
a frame like a large kite on which a person can glide through the air **hang-gliding** noun the sport of using a hang-glider

hanky noun (**hankies**)
(informal) a handkerchief

Hanukkah noun
Jewish festival held in December

haphazard adjective
(say **hap**-haz-erd)
done or chosen at random, with no particular order or plan
• *The books were arranged on the shelf in a haphazard way.*
haphazardly adverb

happen verb
to happen is to take place or occur **to happen to do something** is to do it by chance without planning it • *I happened to see him in the street.*

happening noun
something that happens; an unusual event

happy adjective (**happier, happiest**)
1 pleased or contented **2** satisfied that something is good • *My teacher is happy with my work this term.* **3** lucky or fortunate
• *By a happy coincidence, we met Jenny in town.* **happily** adverb
happiness noun

harass verb (say **ha**-ras)
to harass someone is to annoy or trouble them a lot
harassment noun

harbour noun
a place where ships can shelter or unload

hard adjective
1 firm or solid; not soft • *The ground was hard.* **2** difficult
• *These sums are quite hard.*
3 severe or harsh • *There has been a hard frost.* **4** energetic; using great effort • *She is a hard worker.* **hard up** short of money **hardness** noun being hard

hard adverb
1 with great effort • *We must work hard.* **2** with a lot of force
• *It was raining hard.*

hardboard noun
stiff board made of compressed wood pulp

hard disk noun
a disk fitted inside a computer, able to store large amounts of data

harden verb
1 to harden is to become hard • *Wait for the varnish to harden.*
2 to harden something is to make it hard • *What's the best way to harden a conker?*

hardly adverb
only just; only with difficulty
• *She was hardly able to walk.*

hardship noun
1 hardship is suffering or difficulty **2** a hardship is something that causes suffering

hardware noun
1 tools and other pieces of equipment you use in the house and garden **2** the machinery and electronic parts of a computer, not the software

hard-wearing adjective
able to stand a lot of wear

hardy adjective (**hardier, hardiest**)
able to endure cold or difficult conditions

hare noun
a fast-running animal like a large rabbit

harm verb
to harm someone or something is to hurt or damage them

harm noun
injury or damage
harmful adjective causing injury or damage **harmless** adjective safe; not at all dangerous

harmonica noun
a mouth organ

harmonious adjective
1 music is harmonious when it is pleasant to listen to **2** peaceful and friendly **harmoniously** adverb when people live or work harmoniously they do it in a friendly way without disagreeing

harmonize verb
to harmonize is to combine together in an effective or pleasant way

harmony noun (**harmonies**)
1 a pleasant combination of musical notes played or sung at the same time **2** agreement or friendship • *They live in perfect harmony.*

harness noun
the straps put over a horse's head and round its neck to control it

harness verb
1 to harness a horse is to put a harness on it **2** to harness something is to control it and make use of it • *They tried to harness the power of the wind to make electricity.*

harp noun
a musical instrument made of a frame with strings stretched across it that you pluck with your fingers
harpist noun
someone who plays the harp
harp verb
to harp on about something is to keep on talking about it in an annoying way • *He keeps harping on about all the work he has to do.*
harpoon noun
a spear attached to a rope, fired from a gun to catch whales and large fish
harpsichord noun
a musical instrument like a piano but with the strings plucked and not struck
harsh adjective
1 rough and unpleasant 2 cruel or severe **harshly** adverb **harshness** noun
harvest noun
1 the time when farmers gather in the corn, fruit, or vegetables they have grown 2 the crop that is gathered in
harvest verb
to harvest crops is to gather them in
hassle noun
(informal) something that is difficult or causes problems
haste noun
hurry or speed **to make haste** is to hurry
hasten verb
1 to hasten is to hurry 2 to hasten something is to speed it up
hasty adjective (**hastier, hastiest**)
hurried; done too quickly • *a hasty decision* **hastily** adverb in a hurried way **hastiness** noun
hat noun
a covering for the head
hatch[1] noun
an opening in a floor, wall, or door, usually with a covering
hatch[2] verb
1 to hatch is to break out of an egg • *The chicks hatched this morning.* 2 to hatch an egg is to keep it warm until a young bird hatches from it 3 to hatch a plan is to form it
hatchet noun
a small axe
hate verb
to hate someone or something is to dislike them very much
hate noun
1 hate is a feeling of great dislike 2 (informal) a hate is someone or

something that you dislike very much • *Sweetcorn is one of my hates.*
hateful adjective
hated; very nasty
hatefully adverb
hatred noun (say **hay**-trid)
a strong feeling of great dislike
hat trick noun
getting three goals, wickets, or victories one after another
haughty adjective (**haughtier, haughtiest**) (say **haw**-ti)
proud of yourself and looking down on other people
haughtily adverb **haughtiness** noun
haul verb
to haul something is to pull it using a lot of power or strength
haul noun
an amount that someone has won or gained • *The trawler brought home a large haul of fish.*
haunt verb
1 a ghost haunts a place or person when it appears often 2 an idea or memory haunts someone when they are always thinking of it **haunted** adjective a haunted place is one that people think is visited by ghosts
have verb (**has, having, had**)
This word has many meanings, depending on the words that go with it 1 to have something is to own or possess it • *We haven't any money.* 2 to have something in it is to contain it • *I thought this tin had biscuits in it.* 3 to have (for example) a party is to organize it 4 to have (for example) a shock or accident is to experience it • *I'm afraid she has had an accident.* 5 to have to do something is to be obliged or forced to do it • *We really have to go now.* 6 to have something (for example) mended or built is to get someone to mend or build it • *I'm having my watch mended.* 7 to have (for example) a letter is to receive it • *I had a letter from my cousin.* 8 The verb **have** can also be used to help make other verbs • *They have gone.* • *Has he seen my book?* • *We had eaten them.* **to have someone on** (informal) is to fool them
haven noun (say **hay**-ven)
1 a safe place 2 a harbour
hawk noun
a bird of prey with very strong eyesight and a hooked beak

hawthorn noun
a thorny tree with small red berries
hay noun
cut grass that is dried and used to feed to animals
hay fever noun
an allergy to pollen that makes you sneeze and makes your eyes water or itch
haystack noun
a large neat pile of stored hay
hazard noun
a risk or danger **hazardous** adjective dangerous or risky
haze noun
thin mist
hazel noun
1 a type of small nut tree 2 a nut from this tree 3 a light brown colour
hazy adjective (**hazier, haziest**)
1 misty • *hazy sunshine* 2 vague and unclear • *He has only a hazy memory of what happened.* **hazily** adverb **haziness** noun
he pronoun, noun
a male person or animal: used as the subject of a verb
head noun
1 the part of the body containing the brains, eyes, and mouth 2 brains or intelligence • *Use your head!* 3 the side of a coin on which someone's head is shown 4 a person • *It costs £3 per head.* 5 the top or front of something, such as a pin or nail 6 the person in charge • *She's the head of this school.* **to keep your head** is to stay calm **off the top of your head** (informal) without preparation or thinking carefully
head verb
1 to head a group or organization is to lead it or be the person in charge 2 to head a ball is to hit it with your head 3 to head in a particular direction is to start going there • *They headed for home.*
headache noun
1 a pain in your head that goes on hurting 2 (informal) a problem or difficulty
headdress noun
a decorative covering for the head
header noun
the act of hitting the ball with your head in football
heading noun
a word or words at the top of a piece of printing or writing
headlight noun
a strong light at the front of a vehicle
headline noun
a heading in a newspaper, printed in large type

harp

a b c d e f g h i j k l m n o p q r s t u v w x y z

a b c d e f g h i j k l m n o p q r s t u v w x y z

headlong *adverb, adjective*
1 falling with your head forward
2 in a hasty or thoughtless way
• *He's always rushing headlong into trouble.*

head-on *adverb, adjective*
with the front parts hitting each other • *They had a head-on collision.*

headphones *plural noun*
a listening device that fits over the top of your head

headquarters *noun*
the place from which an organization is controlled

headteacher *noun*
the person in charge of a school

heal *verb*
1 to heal someone is to make them healthy 2 a wound or injury heals when it gets better
• *The cut soon healed.*

healer *noun* someone who heals people who are ill

health *noun*
how well or ill a person is
• *His health is good for his age.*

health food *noun*
food that contains only natural substances and is thought to be good for your health

healthy *adjective* (**healthier, healthiest**)
1 free from illness; having good health 2 good for you • *Fresh air is healthy.* **healthily** *adverb* **healthiness** *noun*

heap *noun*
a pile, especially an untidy pile
heaps (*informal*) a large amount
• *We've got heaps of time.*

heap *verb*
1 to heap things is to pile them up 2 to heap something is to put large amounts on it • *She heaped his plate with food.*

hear *verb* (**hearing, heard**)
1 to hear is to take in sounds through your ears 2 to hear news or information is to receive it
3 you hear from someone when they write to you or phone you

hearing *noun*
1 the ability to hear 2 a chance to be heard • *Please give me a fair hearing.* 3 a trial in court

hearing aid *noun*
a device to help a deaf person to hear

hearse *noun*
a vehicle for taking a coffin to a funeral

heart *noun*
1 the part of the body inside your chest that pumps blood around your body 2 a person's feelings or emotions • *She has a kind heart.* 3 courage or enthusiasm • *We must take heart.*

4 the middle or most important part of something 5 a curved shape representing a heart, or a playing card with this shape on it **to break someone's heart** is to make them very unhappy **by heart** by using your memory

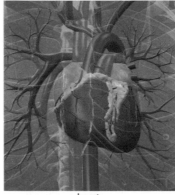
heart

heart attack *noun*
a sudden failure of the heart to work properly, causing pain and sometimes death

hearth *noun* (*say* harth)
the floor of a fireplace or the area near it

heartless *adjective*
cruel or without pity

hearty *adjective* (**heartier, heartiest**)
1 strong and healthy
2 enthusiastic or sincere
• *Hearty congratulations!*
3 a hearty meal is large and filling **heartily** *adverb* **heartiness** *noun*

heat *noun*
1 being hot; great warmth
2 a race or contest to decide who will take part in the final

heat *verb*
1 to heat something, or heat something up, is to make it hot
2 to heat, or heat up, is to become hot

heater *noun*
a device for heating a place, especially a room or a car

heath *noun*
wild flat land often covered with heather or bushes

heather *noun*
a low bush with small purple, pink, or white flowers

heatwave *noun*
a long period of hot weather

heave *verb*
1 to heave something is to lift or move it with great effort
2 (*informal*) to heave something is to throw it **to heave a sigh** is to sigh deeply

heaven *noun*
1 the place where, in some religions, good people are thought to go when they die and where God and the angels are thought to live 2 a very pleasant place or condition **the heavens** the sky

heavenly *adjective*
1 to do with the sky or in the sky
2 (*informal*) pleasing or delicious
• *The cake is heavenly.*

heavy *adjective* (**heavier, heaviest**)
1 weighing a lot; hard to lift or carry 2 you talk about how heavy something is when you are talking about how much it weighs 3 strong or severe
• *Heavy rain was falling.* 4 hard or difficult • *The climb up the hill was heavy going.* **heavily** *adverb* **heaviness** *noun*

Hebrew *noun*
the language of the ancient Jews, with a modern form used in Israel

hectare *noun* (*say* **hek**-tar)
a unit of area equal to 10,000 square metres or nearly 2½ acres

hectic *adjective*
very active or busy • *It's been a hectic morning.*

hedge *noun*
a row of bushes forming a barrier or boundary

hedgehog *noun*
a small animal covered with prickles

hedgerow *noun*
a row of bushes forming a hedge

heed *verb*
to heed something is to pay attention to it

heed *noun*
attention given to something
heedless *adjective* taking no notice of something

heel *noun*
1 the back part of your foot 2 the part of a sock or shoe round or under the back part of your foot

hefty *adjective* (**heftier, heftiest**)
big and strong

heifer *noun* (*say* **hef**-er)
a young cow

height *noun*
1 how high someone or something is 2 a high place
• *She's afraid of heights.* 3 the highest or most important part of something • *We shall be going at the height of the holiday season*

heighten *verb*
1 to heighten something is to make it higher or more intense
2 to heighten is to become higher or more intense • *Their excitement heightened as the kick-off approached.*

heir noun (say air)
someone who inherits money or a title **heiress** noun a girl or woman who inherits money or a title

helicopter noun
a kind of aircraft without wings, lifted by a large horizontal propeller on top

helicopter

helium noun (say **hee**-li-um) He
a colourless gas that is lighter than air and is sometimes used in balloons

hell noun
1 a place where, in some religions, wicked people are thought to be punished after they die and where the Devil is thought to live **2** a very unpleasant place or situation

hello exclamation
a word used to greet someone or to attract their attention

helm noun
the handle or wheel used to steer a ship

helmet noun
a strong hard hat or covering that you wear to protect your head

help verb
1 to help someone is to do something useful for them or make things easier for them **2** when you cannot help doing something, you cannot avoid doing it • I couldn't help sneezing. **3** to help someone to food is to give them some **helper** noun someone who helps another person

help noun
1 doing something useful for someone • Do you need any help? **2** someone who does something for someone • Thank you, you've been a great help.

helpful adjective
giving help; useful **helpfully** adverb

helping noun
a portion of food at a meal

helpless adjective
not able to do things or look after yourself **helplessly** adverb

hem noun
the edge of a piece of cloth that has been folded over and sewn down

hem verb (**hemming, hemmed**)
to hem material is to fold it over and sew down its edge **to hem someone in** is to surround them and stop them moving

hemisphere noun
each half of the earth, above or below the equator
• Australia is in the southern hemisphere.

hen noun
a female bird, especially a chicken

hence adverb
1 from this time on **2** therefore

her pronoun
a word used for she when it is the object of a verb, or when it comes after a preposition • I can see her. • He took the books from her.

her adjective
belonging to her • That is her book.

herald noun
1 an official who in the past used to make announcements or carry messages for a king or queen **2** someone or something that is a sign of things to come

herald verb
to herald something or someone is to say or show that they are coming

heraldry noun
the study of coats of arms **heraldic** adjective to do with heraldry

herb noun
a plant used for flavouring or for making medicines **herbal** adjective made from herbs or using herbs

herbivore noun
an animal that only eats plants

herd noun
a large group of animals, especially cattle

herd verb
to herd animals or people is to gather them together or move them in a large group

here adverb
in or to this place **here and there** in various places or directions

hereditary adjective
passed down to a child from a parent

heredity noun (say hi-**red**-i-ti)
the passing down of characteristics from parents to children through their genes

heritage noun
things that have been passed from one generation to another; a country's history and traditions • Music is part of our cultural heritage.

hermit noun
someone who lives alone and keeps away from people, often for religious reasons

hero noun (**heroes**)
1 a man or boy who has done something very brave **2** the most important man or boy in a story, film, or play **heroic** adjective very brave, like a hero **heroically** adverb bravely **heroism** noun being a hero; great bravery

heroine noun
1 a woman or girl who has done something very brave **2** the most important woman or girl in a story, film, or play

heron noun
a wading bird with long legs and a long neck

herring noun (**herring** or **herrings**)
a sea fish that swims in large groups and is used for food

hers pronoun
belonging to her • Those books are hers.

herself pronoun
she or her and nobody else, used to refer back to the subject of a verb • She has hurt herself. **by herself** on her own; alone • She did the work all by herself.

hesitant adjective
being slow or uncertain when you speak or move **hesitantly** adverb

hesitate verb
to hesitate is to be slow or uncertain when you speak or move **hesitation** noun when you hesitate; a pause

hexagon noun ◆
a flat shape with six sides **hexagonal** adjective having six sides

hibernate verb (say **hy**-ber-nayt)
animals hibernate when they sleep for a long time during cold weather **hibernation** noun hibernating

hiccup noun
a high gulping sound made when your breath is briefly interrupted

hiccup verb
to make this high gulping sound

hide verb (**hiding, hidden, hid, hidden**)
1 to hide is to get into a place where you cannot be seen or found • I hid behind a tree. **2** to hide someone or something is to keep them from being seen • The gold was hidden in a cave. **3** to hide information is to keep it secret • Are you hiding the truth from me?

hide-and-seek noun
a game in which one person looks for others who are hiding

hideous adjective
very ugly or unpleasant **hideously** adverb

a
b
c
d
e
f
g
h
i
j
k
l
m
n
o
p
q
r
s
t
u
v
w
x
y
z

hideout *noun*
a place where someone hides

hiding¹ *noun*
to go into hiding is to hide yourself so that people can't find you

hiding² *noun*
a thrashing or beating

hieroglyphics *plural noun* (*say* hyr-o-**glif**-iks)
pictures or symbols used in ancient Egypt to represent words

high *adjective*
1 reaching a long way up • *They could see a high building.* **2** far above the ground or above sea level • *The clouds were high in the sky.* **3** measuring from top to bottom • *The post is two metres high.* **4** above average in amount or importance • *They are people of a high rank.* • *Prices are high.* **5** lively; happy • *They are in high spirits.* **6** a high note is one at the top end of a musical scale

high *adverb*
1 far above the ground or a long way up • *She jumped high into the air.* **2** at a high level • *The temperature is going to rise even higher this week.* **it is high time to do something** when you should do it at once • *It's high time you started work.*

high jump *noun*
an athletic contest in which competitors jump over a high bar

highland *adjective*
in the highlands; to do with the highlands

highlands *plural noun*
mountainous country, especially in Scotland **highlander** *noun* someone who lives in the highlands

highlight *noun*
the most interesting part of something • *We watched the highlights of the match on the TV.*

highlight *verb*
to highlight something is to draw attention to it

highly *adverb*
extremely • *He is highly amusing.* **to think highly of someone** is to admire them very much

Highness *noun*
a title of a prince or princess • *His Royal Highness, the Prince of Wales*

high-pitched *adjective*
high in sound

highway *noun*
an important road or route

highwayman *noun* (**highwaymen**)
a man who in earlier times robbed travellers on highways

hijack *verb*
to hijack an aircraft or vehicle is to take control of it by force during a journey **hijacker** *noun* someone who hijacks an aircraft or vehicle

hike *noun*
a long walk in the countryside

hike *verb*
to hike is to go for a long walk in the countryside **hiker** *noun* someone who goes for long walks in the countryside

hilarious *adjective*
very funny **hilariously** *adverb* if something is hilariously funny it is extremely funny **hilarity** *noun* loud laughter

hill *noun*
a piece of ground that is higher than the ground around it **hillside** *noun* the side of a hill **hilly** *adjective* a hilly area has lots of hills

hilt *noun*
the handle of a sword or dagger **up to the hilt** completely

him *pronoun*
a word used for *he* when it is the object of a verb, or when it comes after a preposition • *I like him.* • *I gave it to him.*

himself *pronoun*
he or him and nobody else, used to refer back to the subject of a verb • *He has hurt himself.* **by himself** on his own; alone • *He did the work all by himself.*

hind¹ *adjective* (*say* hynd)
at the back • *The donkey had hurt one of its hind legs.*

hind² *noun* (*say* hynd)
a female deer

hinder *verb* (*say* **hin**-der)
to hinder someone is to get in their way, or to make it difficult for them to do something **hindrance** *noun* something that gets in your way, or makes it difficult for you to do something

Hindi *noun*
a language spoken in northern India

Hindu *noun*
someone who believes in **Hinduism**, one of the religions of India

hinge *noun*
a joining device on which a door, gate, or lid swings when it opens

hinged *adjective*
a hinged door, window, or lid is fixed on a hinge

hint *noun*
1 a slight indication or suggestion • *Give me a hint of what you want for your birthday.* **2** a useful piece of advice • *He was always giving us hints on model-making.*

hint *verb*
to hint is to suggest something without actually saying it • *She hinted that she'd like to have a puppy.*

hip *noun*
your hips are the bony parts at the side of your body between your waist and your thighs

hippo *noun* (**hippos**)
(*informal*) a hippopotamus

hippopotamus *noun*
a very large African animal that lives near water

hippopotamus

hire *verb*
to hire something is to pay to use it for a time

hire *noun*
something is for hire when you can hire it

his *adjective*
belonging to him • *That is his book.*

hiss *verb*
to hiss is to make a sound like a continuous *s*, as some snakes do

historian *noun*
someone who writes or studies history

historic *adjective*
famous or important in history

historical *adjective*
1 to do with history **2** that really happened in the past • *The story is based on historical events.*

history *noun* (**histories**)
1 what happened in the past **2** the study of past events **3** a description of important events

hit *verb* (**hitting, hit**)
1 to hit someone or something is to come up against them with force, or to give them a blow **2** something hits you when you suddenly realize or feel it • *The answer suddenly hit me.* **3** to hit a place or people is to have a bad effect on them • *Famine hit the poorer countries.* **4** to hit a note is to reach it when you are singing **to hit it off with someone** is to get on well with them when you

meet them **to hit on something** is to think of an idea suddenly

hit *noun*
1 a knock or stroke **2** a shot that hits the target **3** a successful song or show

hitch *verb*
1 to hitch something is to tie it up with a loop **2** (*informal*) to hitch a lift is to hitch-hike **to hitch something up** is to pull it up quickly or with a jerk • *He hitched up his trousers.*

hitch *noun*
a slight difficulty or delay

hitch-hike *verb*
to hitch-hike is to travel by getting lifts in other people's vehicles **hitch-hiker** *noun* someone who hitch-hikes

hitherto *adverb*
up to now

HIV
short for *human immunodeficiency virus*, a virus that weakens a person's resistance to disease and causes the disease Aids

hive *noun*
1 a beehive **2** a very busy place • *The office was a hive of activity.*

hoard *noun*
a hidden store of something valuable

hoard *verb*
to hoard things is to collect them and store them away **hoarder** *noun* someone who likes saving things and keeping them rather than throwing them out

hoarding *noun*
a tall fence covered with advertisements

hoarse *adjective*
having a rough or croaking voice • *He was hoarse from shouting.*

hoax *noun*
a trick played on someone in which they are told about something but it isn't true • *The bomb scare was hoax.*

hoax *verb*
to hoax someone is to trick them by telling them about something that isn't true

hobble *verb*
to hobble is to walk with unsteady steps, especially because your feet are sore

hobby *noun* (**hobbies**)
something that you enjoy doing in your spare time

hockey *noun*
an outdoor game played by two teams with long curved sticks and a small hard ball

hoe *noun*
a gardening tool with a long handle and a metal blade,
used for scraping up weeds and making soil loose

hog *noun*
1 a male pig **2** (*informal*) a greedy person

hog *verb* (**hogging, hogged**)
(*informal*) to hog something is to take more than your fair share of it

Hogmanay *noun*
New Year's Eve in Scotland

hoist *verb*
to hoist something is to lift it up using ropes or pulleys

hold *verb* (**holding, held**)
1 to hold something is to have it in your hands **2** to hold something is also to possess it or be the owner of it • *She holds the world high jump record.* **3** to hold a party, meeting, or event is to organize it • *The 2008 Olympic Games were held in Beijing.* **4** a container holds an amount when that is what you can put in it • *This jug holds a litre.* **5** to hold someone or something is to support them • *This plank won't hold my weight.* **6** to hold someone is to keep them and stop them getting away • *They held the thief until help arrived.* **7** something like the weather holds when it stays the same • *Will this good weather hold?* **8** to hold an opinion is to believe it **hold it** (*informal*) stop; wait a minute **to hold on** (*informal*) is to wait • *Hold on! I'm not ready yet.* **to hold out** is to last or continue **to hold someone up** is to rob them with threats of force **to hold someone or something up** is to hinder or delay them • *We were held up by the traffic.*

hold *noun*
1 holding something • *Don't lose hold of the rope.* **2** the part of a ship where cargo is stored **to get hold of someone** is to make contact with them • *I want to invite Jane to the party but I can't get hold of her.* **to get or take hold of something** is to grasp it

hold-up *noun*
1 a delay **2** a robbery with threats or force

hole *noun*
1 a gap or opening made in something **2** an animal's burrow • *a rabbit hole* **holey** *adjective* full of holes

Holi *noun*
a Hindu festival held in the spring

holiday *noun*
a day or time when you do not go to work or school; a time when you go away to enjoy yourself **to be on holiday** is to
be away from work or school enjoying yourself

hollow *adjective*
having an empty space inside; not solid

hollow *verb*
to hollow something is to make it hollow • *We always hollow out a pumpkin at Halloween.*

hollow *noun*
1 a hollow or sunken place **2** a small valley

holly *noun*
an evergreen bush with shiny prickly leaves and red berries

holster *noun*
a leather case for a pistol, usually attached to a belt

holy *adjective* (**holier, holiest**)
1 to do with God and treated with religious respect **2** a holy person is devoted to God or a religion **holiness** *noun*

home *noun*
1 the place where you live **2** the place where you were born or where you feel you belong **3** a place where people are looked after • *She went to a home for the elderly.* **to feel at home** is to feel comfortable and happy

home *adverb*
1 to or at the place where you live • *Go home!* • *Is she home yet?* **2** to the place aimed at • *Push the bolt home.* **to bring something home to someone** is to make them realize it

home *verb*
to home in on something is to aim for it

homeless *adjective*
not having a place to live

homely *adjective*
simple or ordinary

home-made *adjective*
made at home and not bought from a shop

homesick *adjective*
sad or upset because you are away from home **homesickness** *noun* the feeling of being homesick

homeward or **homewards** *adverb*
towards home

homework *noun*
school work that you have to do at home

honest *adjective*
truthful and able to be trusted; not stealing, cheating, or telling lies **honesty** *noun* being honest and truthful

honestly *adverb*
1 to say something honestly is to say it truthfully **2** to do something honestly is to do it without stealing or cheating

honey *noun*
a sweet sticky food made by bees

honeycomb *noun*
a wax framework made by bees
to hold their honey and eggs

honeycomb

honeymoon *noun*
a holiday that a newly-married
couple spend together

honour *noun*
1 honour is great respect or
reputation **2** an honour is
something given to a person who
deserves it because of the good
work they have done **3** an honour
is also something a person is
proud to do • *It is an honour to
meet you.*

honour *verb*
1 to honour someone is to show
you respect them or to give them
an honour **2** to honour a promise
or agreement is to keep it

honourable *adjective*
someone is honourable when
they can be trusted and
always try to do the right thing
honourably *adverb*

hood *noun*
1 a covering of soft material
for the head and neck, usually
part of a coat or sweatshirt
2 a folding roof or cover
hooded *adjective* having
or wearing a hood

hoof *noun* (**hoofs**)
the hard, bony part of the foot of
horses, cattle, or deer

hook *noun*
a piece of bent or curved metal
or plastic for hanging things on
or catching hold of something
hooked *adjective* having a curved
shape like a hook

hook *verb*
1 to hook something is to fasten
it with or on a hook **2** to hook a
fish is to catch it with a hook

hooligan *noun*
a rough or noisy person

hoop *noun*
a large ring made of metal,
wood, or plastic

hooray *exclamation*
a shout of joy or approval;
a cheer

hoot *noun*
1 a sound like the one made
by an owl or a car horn
2 a jeer

hoot *verb*
to hoot is to make a sound like an
owl or a car horn

hooter *noun*
a horn or other device that makes
a hoot

hop¹ *verb* (**hopping, hopped**)
1 to hop is to jump on one foot
2 animals hop when they move
in jumps **3** (*informal*) to hop is
also to move quickly • *Hop in
and I'll give you lift.*
hop it (*slang*) go away

hop¹ *noun*
a jump you make on one foot

hop² *noun*
a climbing plant used to give
beer its flavour

hope *noun*
1 the feeling of wanting
something to happen, and
thinking that it will happen
2 a person or thing that makes
you feel like this • *She is our big
hope for a gold medal.*

hope *verb*
to hope for something is to want
it and expect it to happen

hopeful *adjective*
1 having hope **2** likely to be good
or successful • *The future did not
seem very hopeful.*

hopefully *adverb*
1 in a hopeful way **2** I hope
that … • *Hopefully we can all go
to the sea tomorrow.*

hopeless *adjective*
1 without hope **2** very bad at
something • *I'm hopeless at
cricket.* **hopelessly** *adverb*

hopscotch *noun*
a game in which you hop into
squares drawn on the ground

horde *noun*
a large group or crowd

horizon *noun* (say ho-**ry**-zon)
the line where the sky appears
to meet the land or sea

horizontal *adjective*
(say ho-ri-**zon**-tal)
level or flat; going across from
left to right **horizontally** *adverb*
in a horizontal direction

hormone *noun*
a substance made in glands in
the body and sent directly into
the blood to make other organs
work in special ways

horn *noun*
1 a kind of pointed bone that
grows on the head of a bull,
cow, ram, and other animals
2 a brass musical instrument that
you blow **3** a device for making a
warning sound

hornet *noun*
a large kind of wasp

horoscope *noun*
an astrologer's forecast of future
events

horrible *adjective*
very unpleasant or nasty
horribly *adverb*

horrid *adjective*
nasty or unkind

horrific *adjective*
shocking or terrifying
horrifically *adverb*

horrify *verb* (**horrifying,
horrified**)
to horrify someone is to make
them feel shocked and disgusted

horror *noun*
1 horror is great fear or disgust
2 a horror is a person or thing
you really dislike

horse *noun*
1 a four-legged animal used for
riding on or pulling carts **2** a tall
box that you jump over when you
are doing gymnastics

horseback *noun*
to be on horseback is to be
riding a horse

horse chestnut *noun*
a large tree that produces dark
brown nuts called *conkers*

horsepower *noun* (**horsepower**)
a unit for measuring the power of
an engine, equal to 746 watts

horseshoe *noun* (**horseshoes**)
a U-shaped piece of metal nailed
as a shoe to a horse's hoof

hose *noun*
a long flexible tube through
which liquids or gases can travel

hospitable *adjective*
welcoming to people;
liking to give hospitality
hospitably *adverb*

hospital *noun*
a place where sick or injured
people are given medical
treatment

hospitality *noun*
welcoming people and giving
them food and entertainment

host¹ *noun*
someone who has guests and
looks after them

host² *noun*
a large number of people or
things

hostage *noun*
someone who is held prisoner
until the people who are holding
them get what they want

hostel *noun*
a building with rooms where
students or other people can
stay cheaply

hostess *noun*
a woman who has guests and
looks after them

hostile *adjective*
1 unfriendly and angry
• *The crowd outside was hostile.*
2 opposed to someone or something **hostility** *noun* unfriendliness and strong dislike

hot *adjective* (**hotter, hottest**)
1 having a high temperature; very warm **2** having a burning taste like pepper or mustard **3** excited or angry • *He has a hot temper.* **to be in hot water** (*informal*) is to be in trouble or difficulty

hot dog *noun*
a hot sausage in a bread roll

hotel *noun*
a building where people pay to stay for the night and have meals

hotly *adverb*
strongly or forcefully • *He hotly denied that he'd done it.*

hot-water bottle *noun*
a container that you fill with hot water to make a bed warm

hound *noun*
a dog used for hunting or racing

hound *verb*
to hound someone is to keep on chasing and bothering them • *The family was hounded by newspaper reporters.*

hour *noun*
1 one of the twenty-four parts into which a day is divided **2** a particular time • *Why are you up at this hour?*

hourglass *noun*
an old-fashioned device for telling the time, with sand running from one half of a glass container into the other through a narrow middle part

hourly *adjective, adverb*
every hour; done once an hour

house *noun* (*say* howss)
1 a building where people live, usually designed for one family **2** a building used for a special purpose • *They passed the opera house.* • *We visited the Houses of Parliament.* **3** one of the divisions in some schools for sports competitions and other events

house *verb* (*say* howz)
to house someone or something is to provide a house or room for them

household *noun*
all the people who live together in the same house

house-trained *adjective*
an animal that is house-trained is trained to be clean in the house

housewife *noun* (**housewives**)
a woman who stays at home to look after her children and do the

housework rather than doing a paid job

housework *noun*
the work like cooking and cleaning that has to be done in a house

hover *verb*
1 to hover is to stay in one place in the air **2** to hover round someone is to wait near them to watch what they do

hovercraft *noun* (**hovercraft**)
a vehicle that travels just above the surface of water or land, supported by a strong current of air sent downwards by its engines

how *adverb*
1 in what way • *How did you do it?* **2** to what extent • *How much do you want?* **3** in what condition • *How are you?* **how about ...** would you like ... ? • *How about a game of football?* **how do you do?** a more formal greeting when you meet someone

however *adverb*
1 no matter how; in whatever way • *You will never catch him, however hard you try.*
2 nevertheless • *It was snowing; however, he went out.*

however *conjunction*
in any way • *You can do it however you like.*

howl *noun*
a long loud cry like an animal in pain

howl *verb*
to howl is to make a long loud cry like an animal in pain, or to weep loudly

HQ
short for headquarters

hub *noun*
the centre of a wheel

huddle *verb*
to huddle is to crowd together with other people for warmth or comfort

hue *noun*
a colour or tint

huff *noun*
to be in a huff is to be annoyed or offended

hug *verb* (**hugging, hugged**)
1 to hug someone is to clasp them tightly in your arms **2** to hug something is to keep close to it • *The ship hugged the shore.*

hug *noun*
clasping someone tightly in your arms

huge *adjective*
extremely large
hugely *adverb* greatly; very

hulk *noun*
1 the remains of an old decaying ship **2** a large clumsy person or thing **hulking** *adjective* large, heavy, and clumsy

hull *noun*
the main part or framework of a ship

hum *verb* (**humming, hummed**)
1 to hum is to sing a tune with your lips closed **2** to hum is also to make a low continuous sound like a bee

hum *noun*
a humming sound

human *noun*
a man, woman, or child; a human being

human *adjective*
to do with humans

human being *noun*
a man, woman, or child; a human

humane *adjective* (*say* hew-**mayn**)
showing kindness and a wish to cause as little suffering or pain as possible **humanely** *adverb* in a way that causes as little suffering or pain as possible

humanity *noun*
1 all the people in the world **2** kindness and sympathy to other people

humble *adjective*
modest and not proud
humbly *adverb*

humid *adjective* (*say* **hew**-mid)
damp and warm in the air
humidity *noun* how damp it is in the air

humiliate *verb*
to humiliate someone is to make them feel ashamed or foolish in front of other people **humiliation** *noun*

humility *noun*
being humble

hummingbird *noun*
a small tropical bird that makes a humming sound by beating its wings rapidly

a
b
c
d
e
f
g
h
i
j
k
l
m
n
o
p
q

hummingbird

v
w
x
y
z

humorous *adjective*
amusing or funny

humour *noun*
1 being amusing; what makes people laugh **2** being able to enjoy things that are funny • *He has a good sense of humour.* **3** a person's mood • *Keep him in a good humour.*

humour *verb*
to humour someone is to keep them happy by doing what they want

hump *noun*
1 a rounded lump or mound **2** a lump on a person's back

hump *verb*
to hump something heavy is to carry it with difficulty on your back

hunch¹ *noun*
a feeling that you can guess what will happen • *I have a hunch that she won't come.*

hunch² *verb*
to hunch your shoulders is to bring them up and forward so that your back is rounded

hunchback *noun*
someone with a hump on their back **hunchbacked** *adjective* having a hunchback

hundred *noun*
the number 100
hundredth *adjective*, *noun* 100th

hundredweight *noun*
a unit of weight equal to 112 pounds or 50.8 kilograms

hunger *noun*
the feeling you get when you want or need to eat

hungry *adjective* (**hungrier, hungriest**)
you are hungry when you want or need to eat **hungrily** *adverb*

hunk *noun*
a large piece or chunk of something

hunt *verb*
1 to hunt animals is to chase and kill them for food or sport **2** to hunt for something is to look hard for it

hunt *noun*
1 a time when a group of people chase and kill animals for food or sport **2** a group of people who go hunting **3** a search

hunter or **huntsman** *noun*
someone who hunts for sport

hurdle *noun*
1 an upright frame that runners jump over in an athletics race **2** a problem or difficulty

hurl *verb*
to hurl something is to throw it as far as you can

hurrah or **hurray** *exclamation*
a shout of joy or approval; a cheer

hurricane *noun*
a severe storm with a strong wind

hurry *verb* (**hurries, hurrying, hurried**)
1 to hurry is to move or act quickly **2** to hurry someone is to try to make them be quick
hurriedly *adverb* in a hurry • *We hurriedly got dressed.*

hurry *noun*
moving quickly; doing something quickly **in a hurry** hurrying or impatient • *They were in a hurry to catch their train.*

hurt *verb*
1 to hurt a person or animal is to harm them or cause them pain **2** part of your body hurts when you feel pain there **3** to hurt someone is also to upset them by doing or saying something unkind

hurt *noun*
pain or injury **hurtful** *adjective* a hurtful remark upsets someone because it is unkind

hurtle *verb*
to hurtle is to move quickly or dangerously • *A mass of snow and rocks hurtled down the mountain.*

husband *noun*
the man that a woman is married to

hush *verb*
to hush someone is to make them be quiet

hush *noun*
silence or quiet • *Let's have a bit of hush.*

husk *noun*
the dry outer covering of a seed

husky¹ *adjective* (**huskier, huskiest**)
you say a voice is husky when it is deep and rough • *She has a husky voice.*
huskily *adverb* with a husky voice **huskiness** *noun*

husky² *noun* (**huskies**)
a large strong dog used in the Arctic for pulling sledges

hustle *verb*
1 to hustle is to hurry **2** to hustle someone is to push them rudely

hut *noun*
a small roughly made house or shelter

hutch *noun*
a box or cage for a rabbit or other pet animal

hybrid *noun*
an animal or plant that combines two different species • *A mule is a hybrid of a donkey and a mare.*

hydrant *noun*
an outdoor water-tap connected to the main water supply, for fixing a hose to

hydraulic *adjective*
worked by the movement of water or other liquid

hydroelectric *adjective*
using water-power to make electricity

hydrofoil *noun*
a boat designed to skim over the surface of the water

hydrogen *noun* Ⓗ
a very light gas which with oxygen makes water

hyena *noun* (*say* hy-**ee**-na)
a wild animal that looks like a wolf and makes a shrieking howl

hyena

hygiene *noun* (*say* **hy**-jeen)
keeping clean and healthy and free of germs

hygienic *adjective*
clean and healthy and free of germs **hygienically** *adverb*

hymn *noun*
a Christian religious song, especially one that praises God

hypermarket *noun*
a very large supermarket, usually outside a town

hyphen *noun*
a short dash used to join words or parts of words together, for example in *red-handed*

hypnosis *noun* (*say* hip-**noh**-sis)
to be under hypnosis is to be in a condition like a deep sleep in which a person follows the instructions of another person

hypnotism *noun* (*say* **hip**-no-tizm)
hypnotizing people
hypnotist *noun* someone who hypnotizes people

hypnotize *verb*
to hypnotize someone is to put them to sleep by hypnosis

hypocrite *noun* (*say* **hip**-o-krit)
someone who pretends to be a

better person than they really are **hypocrisy** *noun* being a hypocrite **hypocritical** *adjective* someone is being hypocritical when they are pretending to be a better person than they really are

hypodermic *adjective* (*say* hy-po-**der**-mik) a hypodermic needle or syringe is one used to inject something under the skin

hypotenuse *noun* (*say* hy-**pot**-i-newz) the side opposite the right angle in a right-angled triangle

hypothermia *noun* a person suffers from hypothermia when they become so cold that their body temperature falls well below normal

hysteria *noun* wild uncontrollable excitement or emotion

hysterical *adjective* 1 extremely excited or emotional 2 (*informal*) very funny **hysterically** *adverb*

hysterics *plural noun* a fit of hysteria **to be in hysterics** (*informal*) is to be laughing a lot

Ii

I *pronoun* a word used by someone to speak about himself or herself

ice *noun* 1 ice is frozen water 2 an ice is an ice cream

ice *verb* 1 to ice or ice up is to become covered in ice 2 to ice a cake is to put icing on it

ice age *noun* a time in the past when ice covered large areas of the earth's surface

iceberg *noun* a large mass of ice floating in the sea, with most of it under water

ice cream *noun* 1 ice cream is a sweet creamy frozen food 2 an ice cream is a portion of this

ice hockey *noun* ice hockey is a game like hockey played on ice

ice cream

ice lolly *noun* (**ice lollies**) a piece of flavoured ice on a stick

ice-skating *noun* moving on ice wearing special boots with blades on the bottom

icicle *noun* a thin pointed piece of hanging ice formed from dripping water

icing *noun* a sugary substance for decorating cakes

icon *noun* 1 a small picture or symbol standing for a program on a computer screen 2 a painting of a holy person

ICT short for *information and communication technology*

icy *adjective* (**icier, iciest**) 1 an icy road has ice on it 2 an icy wind is very cold 3 very unfriendly; hostile • *He gave them an icy stare.* **icily** *adverb* in an unfriendly way

idea *noun* something that you have thought of; a plan **to have no idea** is to not know something

ideal *adjective* exactly what you want; perfect **ideally** *adverb* if things were perfect • *Ideally, I'd like to live by the sea.*

ideal *noun* something that is perfect or the best thing to have; a very high standard

identical *adjective* exactly the same • *Daniel and Sammy are identical twins.* **identically** *adverb* in exactly the same way • *They were identically dressed.*

identification *noun* 1 identification is any document, such as a passport, that proves who you are 2 identification is the process of discovering who someone is or what something is

identify *verb* (**identifies, identifying, identified**) to identify someone or something is to discover who or what they are • *The police have identified the car used in the robbery.*

identity *noun* (**identities**) who someone is or what something is • *Can you discover the identity of our mystery guest?*

idiom *noun* (*say* **id**-i-om) a phrase or group of words that together have a special meaning that is not obvious from the words themselves, for example *to be in hot water* means to be in trouble or difficulty

idiot *noun* (*informal*) a stupid or foolish

person **idiotic** *adjective* stupid or foolish **idiocy** *noun* foolish behaviour

idle *adjective* 1 a person is idle when they are lazy or doing nothing 2 a machine is idle when it is not being used 3 idle talk or gossip is talk that is silly or pointless

idle *verb* a machine or engine idles when it is working slowly **idly** *adverb* in a lazy way

idol *noun* 1 a famous person who is admired by a lot of people 2 a statue or image that people worship as a god

idolize *verb* to idolize someone is to admire them very much

i.e. short for the Latin *id est*, which means 'that is', used to explain something • *The world's highest mountain (i.e. Mount Everest) is in the Himalayas.*

if *conjunction* 1 on condition that • *I'll tell you what happened if you promise to keep it secret.* 2 although; even though • *I'll finish this job if it kills me!* 3 whether • *Do you know if lunch is ready?* **if only ...** I wish ... • *If only I could go with you!*

igloo *noun* a round house made of blocks of hard snow, built by the Inuit people of the Arctic

WORD ORIGIN

The word **igloo** comes from an Inuit word *iglu* meaning 'house'.

ignite *verb* 1 to ignite something is to set fire to it 2 to ignite is to catch fire

ignition *noun* 1 igniting 2 ignition is the system in a motor engine that starts the fuel burning

ignorant *adjective* not knowing about something; knowing very little **ignorance** *noun* someone shows ignorance when they don't know about something or know very little

ignore *verb* to ignore someone or something is to take no notice of them

ill *adjective* 1 not well; in bad health 2 bad or harmful • *There were no ill effects.*

illegal *adjective* something is illegal when it is against the law **illegally** *adverb*

illegible *adjective* (*say* i-**lej**-i-bul) illegible writing is not clear enough to read **illegibly** *adverb*

illegitimate *adjective*
(*say* il-i-**jit**-i-mat)
(*old use*) someone is illegitimate when they are born to parents who are not married to each other

illiterate *adjective* (*say* i-**lit**-er-at)
unable to read or write
illiteracy *noun* illiteracy is not being able to read or write

illness *noun*
1 illness is being ill **2** an illness is something that makes people ill; a disease

illogical *adjective*
not logical or having any good reason **illogically** *adverb* in a way that is not logical

illuminate *verb*
to illuminate a place or street is to light it up or decorate it with lights **illuminations** *plural noun* lights put up to decorate a place or street

illusion *noun*
1 something that you think is real or happening but is not **2** an idea or belief you have that isn't true

illustrate *verb*
1 to illustrate something is to show it with pictures or examples **2** to illustrate a book is to put pictures in it

illustration *noun*
a picture in a book

illustrator *noun*
a person who produces the illustrations in a book

image *noun*
1 a picture or statue of a person or thing **2** what you see in a mirror or through a lens **3** a picture you have in your mind **4** the way that people think of a person or thing

imaginary *adjective*
not real; existing only in your mind

imagination *noun*
your ability to form pictures and ideas in your mind

imaginative *adjective*
showing that you are good at thinking of new and exciting ideas • *Her stories are always very imaginative.*

imagine *verb*
to imagine something or someone is to form a picture of them in your mind **imaginable** *adjective* that you can imagine

imam *noun*
a Muslim religious leader

imitate *verb*
to imitate someone or something is to do the same as them **imitation** *noun* copying someone or something

imitator *noun* someone who copies someone or something else

immature *adjective*
1 not fully grown or developed **2** behaving in a silly or childish way **immaturity** *noun* being immature

immediate *adjective*
1 happening or done without any delay **2** nearest; with nothing or no one between • *The Smiths are our immediate neighbours.*

immediately *adverb*
without any delay; at once • *You must come immediately.*

immense *adjective*
huge **immensely** *adverb* extremely **immensity** *noun* immensity is being immense

immerse *verb*
1 to immerse something is to put it completely into a liquid **2** to be immersed in something is to be very interested or involved in it **immersion** *noun* the immersion of something is when you put it into a liquid

immigrant *noun*
someone who has come into a country to live there

immigrate *verb*
to immigrate is to come into a country to live there **immigration** *noun* people coming into a country to live

immobile *adjective*
not moving **immobility** *noun* being immobile

immoral *adjective*
not following the usual standards of right and wrong **immorality** *noun* behaviour that does not follow the usual standards of right and wrong

immortal *adjective*
someone who is immortal lives for ever and never dies **immortality** *noun* living for ever

immune *adjective*
someone is immune to a disease if they cannot catch it **immunity** *noun* protection against a disease

immunize *verb*
to immunize someone is to make them safe from a disease, usually by giving them an injection

immunization *noun*
immunization is immunizing someone

imp *noun*
1 a small devil **2** a naughty child **impish** *adjective* naughty or mischievous

impact *noun*
1 the force of one thing hitting another **2** a strong influence or effect • *The Internet is having a big impact on our lives.*

impair *verb*
to impair something is to harm or weaken it • *The accident has impaired his health.*

impartial *adjective*
fair and not supporting one side more than the other • *A referee must be impartial.*
impartiality *noun* someone shows impartiality when they are fair and do not support one side more than the other **impartially** *adverb*

impatient *adjective*
annoyed because you can't wait for something to happen **impatience** *noun* annoyance because you can't wait for something to happen **impatiently** *adverb*

imperative *adjective*
essential • *Speed is imperative.*

imperceptible *adjective*
too small or gradual to be noticed • *The change in the weather was imperceptible.*
imperceptibly *adverb*

imperfect *adjective*
not perfect or complete **imperfection** *noun* being imperfect

imperial *adjective*
belonging to an empire or its rulers

impersonal *adjective*
not showing friendly human feelings • *The letter was a bit impersonal.*

impersonate *verb*
to impersonate someone is to pretend to be them **impersonation** *noun* an act in which you impersonate someone **impersonator** *noun* a person who impersonates someone else

impertinent *adjective*
rude to someone and not showing them respect **impertinence** *noun* being impertinent

implement *noun*
a tool or device you use to do something

implication *noun*
1 an implication is something that someone suggests without actually saying it **2** an implication is also a possible effect or result

implore *verb*
to implore someone to do something is to beg them to do it

imply *verb* (**implies, implying, implied**)
to imply something is to suggest it without actually saying it • *Are you implying that I'm lazy?*

impolite *adjective*
not having good manners;

not respectful and thoughtful towards other people

import verb (say im-**port**)
to import goods is to bring them in from another country to sell them **importer** noun
someone who imports goods

import noun (say **im**-port)
something brought in from another country to be sold

important adjective
1 needing to be taken seriously; having a great effect • *This is an important decision.* **2** an important person is powerful or influential **importance** noun being important

importantly adverb seriously • *Try to win the match but, more importantly, don't lose.*

impossible adjective
1 not possible **2** (informal) very annoying • *He is impossible!* **impossibility** noun something that is not possible

impossibly adverb

impostor noun
someone who is not what he or she pretends to be

impractical adjective
1 impractical people are not good at making or doing things **2** not likely to work or be useful • *Their ideas are impractical.*

impress verb
1 to impress someone is to make them admire you **2** to impress something on someone is to make them realize or remember it

impression noun
1 a vague idea that you have about something • *I had the impression that he was waiting for me to speak.* **2** the effect that something has on your mind or feelings • *The book left a strong impression on me.* **3** an imitation of a person or a sound

impressive adjective
something is impressive when it makes you admire it **impressively** adverb

imprison verb
to imprison someone is to put them in prison **imprisonment** noun being put in prison

improbable adjective
unlikely **improbability** noun being improbable

improper adjective
1 not proper; wrong **2** rude or indecent

improve verb
1 to improve something is to make it better **2** to improve is to become better **improvement** noun something that is better or makes a thing better

improvise verb
1 to improvise is to do something without any rehearsal or preparation, especially to play music without rehearsing **2** to improvise something is to make it quickly with what is to hand **improvisation** noun improvisation is improvising something

impudent adjective
not respectful; rude **impudence** noun being impudent

impulse noun
a sudden desire to do something

impulsive adjective
doing things suddenly without much thought **impulsively** adverb

impure adjective
not pure **impurity** noun something in a substance that makes it not pure

in preposition, adverb
1 showing position at or inside something • *They live in London.* • *Please come in.* • *She fell in the water.* • *Then the others fell in.* **2 In** also has some special uses, shown by the following examples • *We came in April.* • *I paid in cash.* • *The serial was in four parts.* • *He is in the army.* • *We knocked on the door but no one was in.* **in all** including everything • *The bill comes to £120 in all.* **to be in for something** is to be likely to get it • *You're in for a shock.*

inability noun
inability is being unable to do something

inaccessible adjective
an inaccessible place is impossible to reach

inaccurate adjective
not accurate **inaccuracy** noun inaccuracy is being inaccurate **inaccurately** adverb

inactive adjective
not working or doing anything **inactivity** noun inactivity is being inactive

inadequate adjective
not enough **inadequacy** noun inadequacy is being inadequate **inadequately** adverb

inanimate adjective
(say in-**an**-im-at)
not living or moving

inappropriate adjective
not appropriate or suitable **inappropriately** adverb

inaudible adjective
not able to be heard **inaudibly** adverb so quietly that it cannot be heard

incapable adjective
not able to do something • *They*

are incapable of understanding the problem.

incapacity noun
incapacity is inability or disability

incense noun (say in-senss)
incense is a substance that makes a spicy smell when it is burnt

incense verb (say in-**senss**)
to incense someone is to make them very angry

incentive noun
something that encourages a person to do something or to work harder

incessant adjective
going on without stopping, usually in an annoying way • *They were bothered by the incessant noise.* **incessantly** adverb

inch noun
a measure of length, one twelfth of a foot or about 2½ centimetres

incident noun
an event, usually a strange or unusual one

incidental adjective
happening along with something else; not so important **incidentally** adverb by the way

incinerator noun
a bin or container for burning rubbish

inclination noun
a feeling that makes you want to do something • *He suddenly had an inclination to look through the keyhole.*

incline verb (say in-**klyn**)
to incline is to lean or bend **to be inclined to do something** is to feel like doing it • *I'm inclined to wait until later.*

incline noun (say **in**-klyn)
a slope

include verb
to include something or someone is to make or consider them as part of a group of things • *Did you include Peter in the party?* **inclusion** noun being included

inclusive adjective
including everything; including all the things mentioned • *We want to stay from Monday to Thursday inclusive.*

income noun
the money that a person earns regularly for their work

incompatible *adjective*
1 not able to live or exist together without trouble 2 machines and devices are incompatible when they cannot be used together
incompetent *adjective*
unable to do something properly **incompetence** *noun* the inability to do something properly **incompetently** *adverb*
incomplete *adjective*
not complete **incompletely** *adverb* not completely
incomprehensible *adjective*
not able to be understood
incongruous *adjective*
(*say* in-**kong**-roo-us)
not suitable and out of place
inconsiderate *adjective*
not thinking of other people
inconsistent *adjective*
not consistent **inconsistency** *noun* being inconsistent **inconsistently** *adverb*
inconspicuous *adjective*
not easy to see or notice
inconvenient *adjective*
not convenient; awkward **inconvenience** *noun* when something is inconvenient • *Sorry for the inconvenience.*
incorporate *verb*
to incorporate something is to include it as a part of something else
incorrect *adjective*
not correct; wrong **incorrectly** *adverb* wrongly
increase *verb* (*say* in-**kreess**)
1 to increase something is to make it bigger 2 to increase is to become bigger **increasingly** *adverb* more and more • *They were becoming increasingly angry.*
increase *noun* (*say* **in**-kreess)
1 increasing 2 the amount by which something increases
incredible *adjective*
hard to believe; unbelievable **incredibly** *adverb*
incredulous *adjective*
finding it difficult to believe someone
incubate *verb*
to incubate eggs is to hatch them by keeping them warm **incubation** *noun* incubation is the hatching of eggs
incubator *noun*
1 a specially heated container for keeping newly born babies warm and well supplied with oxygen 2 a container for hatching eggs
indecent *adjective*
not decent; improper **indecency** *noun* **indecently** *adverb*
indeed *adverb*
used for emphasis • *He was very wet indeed.*

indefinite *adjective*
not definite; vague and unclear
indefinite article *noun*
the word *a* or *an*
indefinitely *adverb*
for an indefinite or unlimited time
independent *adjective*
1 free from the control of another person or country 2 not needing help from other people **independence** *noun* being independent **independently** *adverb* without help from other people
index *noun*
a list of names or topics, usually in alphabetical order at the end of a book
index finger *noun*
the finger next to the thumb
indicate *verb*
to indicate something is to point it out or show that it is there **indication** *noun* a sign of something
indicator *noun*
1 something that tells you what is happening 2 a flashing light on a vehicle, to show that it is turning left or right
indifferent *adjective*
1 you are indifferent to something when you have no interest in it at all 2 not very good; ordinary • *He is an indifferent tennis player.* **indifference** *noun* you show indifference when you have no interest at all in something **indifferently** *adverb*
indigestible *adjective*
not easy to digest
indigestion *noun*
indigestion is pain that you get when food is hard to digest
indignant *adjective*
angry at something that seems wrong or unjust **indignantly** *adverb* **indignation** *noun* indignation is a feeling of being indignant
indirect *adjective*
not direct or straight **indirectly** *adverb*
indispensable *adjective*
essential; that you have to have
indistinct *adjective*
not clear **indistinctly** *adverb*
individual *adjective*
1 of or for one person 2 single or separate **individually** *adverb* separately; one by one
individual *noun*
an individual is one person
indoctrinate *verb*
to indoctrinate someone is to fill their mind with particular ideas or beliefs, so that

they accept them without thinking **indoctrination** *noun* indoctrination is indoctrinating someone
indoor *adjective*
placed or done inside a building • *We like indoor sports.*
indoors *adverb*
inside a building • *We'd better go indoors.*
induce *verb*
to induce someone to do something is to persuade them to do it **inducement** *noun* something given or done to persuade someone to do something
indulge *verb*
to indulge someone is to let them have or do what they want **to indulge in something** is to have or do something that you really like
indulgent *adjective*
kind and allowing people to do what they want **indulgence** *noun* indulgence is being indulgent
industrial *adjective*
to do with industry
industrious *adjective*
hard-working **industriously** *adverb*
industry *noun*
1 industry is making or producing goods to sell, especially in factories 2 an industry is a branch of this, such as the motor industry 3 industry is also working hard
ineffective *adjective*
not effective; not working well **ineffectively** *adverb*
inefficient *adjective*
not working well and wasting time or energy **inefficiency** *noun* being inefficient **inefficiently** *adverb*
inequality *noun* (**inequalities**)
inequality is not being equal
inevitable *adjective*
something is inevitable when it can't be avoided **inevitability** *noun* being inevitable **inevitably** *adverb*
inexhaustible *adjective*
that you cannot use up completely; never-ending
inexpensive *adjective*
not expensive; cheap **inexpensively** *adverb* cheaply
inexperience *noun*
inexperience is lack of experience **inexperienced** *adjective* someone is inexperienced when they don't have much experience
inexplicable *adjective*
impossible to explain

inexplicably *adverb* in a way that is impossible to explain

infallible *adjective*
1 never wrong **2** that never fails • *They have an infallible way of winning the lottery.* **infallibility** *noun* infallibility is being infallible **infallibly** *adverb*

infamous *adjective* (*say* **in**-fa-mus) well-known for being bad or wicked **infamy** *noun* being infamous

infant *noun*
a baby or young child
infancy *noun* the time when someone is a baby or young child

infantile *adjective*
childish and silly

infantry *noun*
infantry are soldiers trained to fight on foot

infect *verb*
to infect someone is to pass on a disease to them

infection *noun*
1 infection is infecting someone **2** an infection is an infectious disease

infectious *adjective*
1 an infectious disease is one that can spread from one person to another **2** something like laughter or fear is infectious when it spreads to other people

infer *verb* (**inferring, inferred**)
to infer something is to work it out from what someone says or does • *I inferred from his words that he did not really want to come.* **inference** *noun* something that you can work out from what someone says or does

inferior *adjective*
not as good or important as something else; lower in position or quality **inferiority** *noun* being inferior

inferior *noun*
a person who is lower in position or rank than someone else

inferno *noun* (**infernos**)
(say in-**fer**-noh)
a fierce fire

infested *adjective*
a place is infested with (for example) insects or rats when it is full of them

infinite *adjective* (*say* **in**-fi-nit)
endless; too large to be measured or imagined **infinitely** *adverb* to an infinite extent

infinitive *noun* (say in-**fin**-i-tiv)
the basic form of a verb. In English it often comes after *to*, as in *to go* and *to hit.*

infinity *noun* (say in-**fin**-i-ti)
infinity is an infinite number or distance

infirm *adjective*
someone is infirm when they are weak because they are ill or old **infirmity** *noun* being infirm

infirmary *noun* (**infirmaries**)
a place for sick people; a hospital

inflame *verb*
1 a part of the body is inflamed when it has become red and sore **2** to inflame someone is to make them angry

inflammable *adjective*
an inflammable material can be set alight

inflammation *noun*
a painful swelling or sore place on the body

inflate *verb*
1 to inflate something is to fill it with air or gas so that it swells up **2** a claim or statement is inflated when it is exaggerated **inflatable** *adjective* something is inflatable when it can be filled with air to make it swell up

inflation *noun*
inflation is a general rise in prices

inflexible *adjective*
that you cannot bend or change • *There are a lot of inflexible rules.* **inflexibility** *noun* being inflexible **inflexibly** *adverb*

inflict *verb*
to inflict something on someone is to make them suffer it • *She inflicted a severe blow on him.*

influence *noun*
the power to affect someone or something

influence *verb*
to influence someone or something is to have an effect on what they are or do • *The tides are influenced by the moon.*

influential *adjective*
having a big influence; important

influenza *noun* (*say* in-floo-**en**-za)
an infectious disease that causes fever, catarrh, and pain. It is more usually called **flu.**

inform *verb*
to inform someone of something is to tell them about it **to inform against or on someone** is to give information about them, especially to the police

informal *adjective*
not formal; casual and relaxed **informality** *noun* informality is being informal
informally *adverb*

information *noun*
information is facts or what someone tells you

information technology *noun*
information technology is ways of storing, arranging, and giving out information, especially the use of computers and telecommunications

informative *adjective*
(*say* in-**form**-a-tiv)
containing a lot of helpful information

informed *adjective*
you are informed about something when you know about it

informer *noun*
a person who tells the police about someone else

infrequent *adjective*
not frequent **infrequently** *adverb* only now and then

infuriate *verb*
to infuriate someone is to make them very angry

ingenious *adjective*
1 clever at doing things **2** cleverly made or done **ingeniously** *adverb*
ingenuity *noun*
cleverness or skill in doing things

ingot *noun*
a lump of gold or silver that has been cast in the form of a brick

ingots

ingratitude *noun*
ingratitude is not showing that you are grateful for something that someone has done for you

ingredient *noun*
(*say* in-**greed**-i-ent)
1 one of the parts of a mixture **2** one of the things used in a recipe

inhabit *verb*
to inhabit a place is to live in it **inhabitant** *noun* one of the people who live in a place

inhale *verb*
1 to inhale is to breathe in **2** to inhale something is to breathe it in

inhaler *noun*
a device for taking medicine by inhaling it

inherit *verb*
1 to inherit money, property, or a title is to receive it when its previous owner dies **2** to inherit qualities or characteristics is to get them from your parents or ancestors **inheritance** *noun* something you inherit
inheritor *noun* a person who inherits something

inhospitable *adjective*
(*say* in-hos-**pit**-a-bul or *say* in-**hos**-pit-a-bul)
1 unfriendly to visitors **2** an inhospitable place is difficult to live in because it gives no shelter • *They reached an inhospitable rocky island.*

inhuman *adjective*
cruel; without pity or kindness
inhumanity *noun* cruel behaviour

initial *noun*
the first letter of a word or name, especially of someone's forename

initial *adjective*
first; of the beginning • *the initial stages of the work* **initially** *adverb* at the beginning

initiate *verb* (*say* in-ish-i-ayt)
1 to initiate something is to start it **2** to initiate someone is to admit them as a member of a society or group, often with special ceremonies **initiation** *noun* making someone a new member of a society or group

initiative *noun* (*say* in-ish-a-tiv)
1 the action that starts something • *She took the initiative in planning the party.* **2** initiative is the ability or power to start things or to get them done on your own

inject *verb*
to inject someone is to put a medicine or drug through their skin using a hollow needle **injection** *noun* injecting someone with medicine

injure *verb*
to injure someone is to harm or hurt them

injury *noun* (**injuries**)
harm or damage done to someone

injustice *noun*
unfairness in the way someone is treated

ink *noun*
ink is a black or coloured liquid used for writing and printing **inky** *adjective* inky fingers or pages are covered in ink

inkling *noun*
a slight idea or suspicion • *I had an inkling that we'd find them in here.*

inland *adverb*
away from the coast

inn *noun*
a hotel or public house, especially in the country **innkeeper** *noun* someone who runs an inn

inner *adjective*
inside; nearer the centre **innermost** *adjective* furthest inside

innings *noun*
the time when a cricket team or player is batting

innocence *noun*
1 when someone is not guilty of doing something wrong **2** lack of experience of the world and the evil things in it

innocent *adjective*
1 not guilty of doing something wrong **2** not knowing much about the world and the evil things in it **innocently** *adverb*

innovation *noun*
1 innovation is inventing or using new things **2** an innovation is something new that you have just invented or started using **innovative** *adjective* new or original

innumerable *adjective*
too many to be counted

inoculate *verb*
to inoculate someone is to inject them to protect them against a disease **inoculation** *noun* inoculation is being inoculated

input *noun*
what you put into something, especially data put into a computer

input *verb* (**inputting, input**)
(*in computing*) to input data or programs is to put them into a computer

inquest *noun*
an official investigation to decide why someone died

inquire *verb*
1 to inquire about something is to ask about it **2** to inquire into something is to make an official investigation of it

inquiry *noun* (**inquiries**)
an official investigation

inquisitive *adjective*
always trying to find out things, especially about other people **inquisitively** *adverb*

insane *adjective*
not sane; mad **insanely** *adverb* **insanity** *noun* insanity is being insane

insanitary *adjective*
dirty and unhealthy

inscribe *verb*
to inscribe something is to write or carve it on a surface

inscription *noun*
words written or carved on a monument, stone, or coin, or written in the front of a book

insect *noun*
a small animal with six legs and a body divided into three parts

insects

insecticide *noun*
a poisonous chemical used for killing insects

insecure *adjective*
1 not safe or protected properly **2** not feeling safe or confident **insecurely** *adverb* not firmly or safely **insecurity** *noun* insecurity is not feeling safe or confident

insensitive *adjective*
not sensitive or thinking about the feelings of other people **insensitively** *adverb* **insensitivity** *noun* being insensitive

inseparable *adjective*
1 unable to be separated **2** people are inseparable when they are very good friends and always together • *The two girls were inseparable during the summer.* **inseparably** *adverb* two things are inseparably linked when they are so closely linked that they can't be separated

insert *verb*
to insert something is to put it into something else **insertion** *noun* the insertion of something is when it is inserted into something else

inside *noun*
1 the middle or centre of something; the part nearest to the middle **2** (*informal*) your insides are your stomach or abdomen **inside out** with the inside turned so that it faces outwards

inside *adjective*
placed on the inside of something • *Stick the picture on an inside page.*

inside *adverb, preposition*
in or to the inside of something • *Come inside.* • *It's inside that box.*

insignificant *adjective*
not important or influential **insignificance** *noun* being insignificant

insincere *adjective*
not sincere **insincerely** *adverb* **insincerity** *noun* not being sincere

insist *verb*
to insist something is to be very firm in saying it • *He insisted that he was innocent.* **to insist on something** is to demand it • *We insist on seeing the manager.*

insistent *adjective*
insisting on doing or having something **insistence** *noun* being insistent

insolent *adjective*
very rude and insulting **insolence** *noun* speaking to someone rudely and without respect

insomnia noun (say in-**som**-ni-a)
insomnia is being unable to sleep
inspect verb
to inspect something or
someone is to look carefully
at them, especially to check
them **inspection** noun a close
or careful look at something to
check it
inspector noun
1 someone whose job is to
inspect things or people
2 a police officer next in rank
above a sergeant
inspire verb
to inspire someone is to fill
them with ideas or enthusiasm
inspiration noun a person or
thing that encourages you and
fills you with ideas
install verb
to install something is to put it in
position ready for use
• *We want to install central
heating.* **installation** noun being
installed
instalment noun
one of the parts into which
something is divided so that it
is spread over a period of time
• *He is paying for his bike in
monthly instalments.* • *The
story was in three instalments.*
instance noun
an example **for instance** for
example
instant adjective
1 happening immediately
• *It has been an instant success.*
2 that can be made very quickly
• *Do you like instant coffee?*
instant noun
a moment • *I don't believe it for
an instant.* **this instant** at once
• *Come here this instant!*
instantaneous adjective
happening or done in an
instant, or without any delay
instantaneously adverb in an
instant; immediately
instantly adverb
to do something instantly is to
do it without any delay
instead adverb
in place of something else; as
a substitute • *There were no
potatoes, so we had rice instead.*
instep noun
the top of your foot between the
toes and the ankle
instinct noun
a natural tendency to do or feel
something without being taught
• *Spiders spin webs by instinct.*
instinctive adjective done by
instinct **instinctively** adverb in
an instinctive way • *He knew
instinctively that something was
wrong.*

institute noun
an organization set up to study
something or for some other
purpose, or the building used
by it
institution noun
1 a large organization
2 something that is an
established habit or custom
• *Going for a swim on Sunday
was a family institution.*
instruct verb
1 to instruct someone is to
teach them a subject or skill
2 to instruct someone is also
to give them information or
orders
instruction noun
1 instruction is teaching a
subject or skill **2** an instruction
is an order or piece of information
• *Follow the instructions carefully.*
instrument noun
1 a device for making musical
sounds **2** a device for delicate or
scientific work
instrumental adjective
instrumental music uses musical
instruments without any singing
insufficient adjective not enough
insulate verb
to insulate something is to
cover it to stop heat, cold, or
electricity from passing in or
out **insulation** noun insulation
is insulating something
insult verb (say in-**sult**)
to insult someone is to speak
or behave in a rude way that
offends them
insult noun (say **in**-sult)
a rude remark or action that
offends someone
insurance noun
a business agreement to receive
money or compensation if you
suffer a loss or injury, in return
for a regular payment called a
premium
insure verb
to insure yourself or your
goods is to protect them with
insurance
intact adjective
complete and undamaged
• *Despite the storm our tent was
still intact.*
intake noun
the number of people or things
taken in • *The school had a high
intake of pupils this year.*
integer noun (say **in**-ti-jer)
a whole number, such as 0, 1, 24,
and not a fraction
integrate verb (say **in**-ti-grayt)
1 to integrate different things
or parts is to make them into
a whole **2** to integrate people,
especially of different origins,

is to bring them together into a
single community
integration noun integration is
being integrated
integrity noun (say in-**teg**-ri-ti)
integrity is being honest and
behaving well
intellect noun
the ability to think and work
things out with your mind
intellectual adjective
1 involving the mind and thinking
2 able to think effectively;
keen to study and learn
intellectually adverb
intellectual noun
an intellectual person
intelligence noun
your intelligence is your
ability to think and learn
intelligent adjective
good at thinking and learning
intelligently adverb
intelligible adjective
able to be understood
• *The message was barely
intelligible.* **intelligibility** noun
being intelligible **intelligibly**
adverb in a way that can be
understood
intend verb
to intend to do something is to
have it in mind as a plan • *She
was intending to go swimming.*
intense adjective
1 very strong or great • *The heat
was intense.* **2** having or showing
strong feelings **intensely** adverb
very strongly **intensity** noun
how strong or great something is
intensive adjective
using a lot of effort; thorough
• *We have made an intensive
search.* **intensively** adverb
intent adjective
showing a lot of attention
and interest **to be intent on
something** is to be eager or
determined to do it **intently**
adverb with a lot of attention
and interest
intent noun
a person's intent is what they
intend to do
intention noun
what you intend to do; a plan
intentional adjective
done on purpose; deliberate
intentionally adverb on
purpose; deliberately
interactive adjective
allowing information to be
sent in either direction,
especially between a computer
system and its user
intercept verb
to intercept someone or
something is to stop them going
from one place to another

129

interception *noun* interception is intercepting someone or something

interchange *noun* a place where traffic moves from one main road or motorway to another

interchangeable *adjective* things are interchangeable when they can be changed or swapped round

intercom *noun* a device by which people in different rooms or places can communicate with one another

interest *verb* to interest someone is to make them want to look or listen or take part in something

interest *noun*
1 interest is being interested
2 an interest is a thing that interests you • *Jane's main interest is music.* **3** interest is also money a borrower has to pay regularly for a loan

interfere *verb*
1 to interfere in something is to become involved in it when it has nothing to do with you
2 to interfere is to get in the way • *I hope the weather won't interfere with our picnic.*

interference *noun*
1 interfering in something
2 a crackling or distorting of a radio or television signal

interior *noun* the inside of something

interjection *noun* an exclamation, such as *oh!*

interlock *verb* to interlock is to fit into one another • *The gearwheels interlocked.*

interlude *noun* an interval

intermediate *adjective* coming between two things in place, order, or time

interminable *adjective* (say in-**ter**-min-a-bul) seeming to go on for ever **interminably** *adverb*

interlock

internal *adjective* of or in the inside of something **internally** *adverb* on the inside

international *adjective* to do with more than one country • *Interpol is an international police organization.*

internationally *adverb* for or in more than one country

Internet *noun* the Internet is a computer network that allows people all over the world to share information and send messages

interpret *verb*
1 to interpret something is to explain what it means **2** to interpret a foreign language is to translate it into another language **interpretation** *noun* an explanation or translation of something **interpreter** *noun* a person who translates what someone says into another language

interrogate *verb* to interrogate someone is to question them closely in order to get information **interrogation** *noun* when someone is interrogated

interrupt *verb*
1 to interrupt someone is to stop them talking
2 to interrupt something is to stop it continuing **interruption** *noun* when someone or something is interrupted

intersect *verb* to intersect something is to cross or divide it • *The cloth had a design of intersecting lines.*

intersection *noun* a place where lines or roads cross each other

interval *noun* a time between two events or between two parts of a play or film **at intervals** with some time or distance between each one; not continuously

intervene *verb*
1 to intervene is to come between two events • *During the intervening years they went abroad.* **2** to intervene in an argument or fight is to interrupt it in order to stop it or affect the result **intervention** *noun* an intervention is when someone intervenes in something

interview *noun* a meeting with someone to ask them questions or discuss something

interview *verb* to interview someone is to have an interview with them **interviewer** *noun* a person who interviews someone, especially on radio or television

intestine *noun* the long tube along which food passes after leaving your stomach

intimate *adjective* (say **in**-ti-mat)
1 very friendly with someone

2 intimate thoughts are thoughts that are private or personal **3** detailed • *They have an intimate knowledge of the town.* **intimacy** *noun* closeness or friendship **intimately** *adverb*

intimidate *verb* to frighten a person with threats into doing something **intimidation** *noun* intimidation is intimidating someone

into *preposition*
1 to the inside of something • *Go into the house.* **2 into** also has some special uses, shown by the following examples • *He got into trouble.* • *She went into acting.* • *3 into 12 goes 4 times.*

intolerable *adjective* unbearable • *The noise outside was intolerable.* **intolerably** *adverb* to an intolerable degree

intolerant *adjective* not willing to accept people or ideas that are different in some way **intolerance** *noun* intolerance is being intolerant **intolerantly** *adverb*

intonation *noun* the way you use the pitch of your voice to alter the meaning of what you are saying, for example when asking a question

intoxicate *verb* a person is intoxicated when they are drunk **intoxication** *noun* being drunk

intrepid *adjective* brave or fearless **intrepidly** *adverb*

intricate *adjective* an intricate pattern or design is detailed and complicated **intricacy** *noun* intricacy is being intricate **intricately** *adverb*

intrigue *verb* (say in-**treeg**) to intrigue someone is to interest them very much and make them curious **intriguing** *adjective* very interesting because it is unusual

introduce *verb*
1 to introduce someone is to make them known to other people **2** to introduce something is to get it into general use **3** to introduce a radio or television programme is to say a few words to explain it

introduction *noun*
1 introducing someone or something **2** a piece at the beginning of a book, explaining what it is about

introductory *adjective* coming at the beginning of something

intrude *verb* to intrude is to come in or join in without being wanted

intrusion noun coming in where you are not wanted

intruder noun
someone who forces their way into a place where they are not supposed to be

intuition noun (say in-tew-**ish**-on)
the power to know or understand things without having to think hard **intuitive** adjective using intuition

invade verb
to invade a country or place is to attack and enter it **invaders** plural noun people who invade a place

invalid[1] noun (say **in**-va-leed or **in**-va-lid)
someone who is ill or weakened by a long illness

invalid[2] adjective (say in-**val**-id)
not valid • This passport is invalid.

invaluable adjective
very valuable

invariable adjective
never changing; always the same **invariably** adverb always

invasion noun
when an army or a large number of people attack and enter a place

invent verb
1 to invent something is to be the first person to make it or think of it **2** to invent a story or excuse is to make it up **invention** noun something invented **inventor** noun a person who invents things

invertebrate noun
(say in-**vert**-i-brat)
an animal without a backbone, such as a worm or an amoeba

inverted commas plural noun
punctuation marks (" ") or (' ') that you put round spoken words and quotations

invertebrate

invest verb
to invest money is to use it to earn interest or make a profit **investor** noun someone who invests money

investigate verb
to investigate something or someone is to find out as much as you can about them • Police are investigating the robbery **investigation** noun a careful

search for information

investigator noun a person who investigates someone or something

investment noun
1 money someone invests **2** something someone invests money in • Houses are a safe investment.

invincible adjective
not able to be defeated

invisible adjective
not visible; not able to be seen **invisibility** noun being invisible **invisibly** adverb

invitation noun
a request for someone to do something, such as come to a party

invite verb
to invite someone is to ask them to come to a party or do something special

inviting adjective
attractive or tempting **invitingly** adverb

invoice noun
a bill that you get when someone has sold you something or done a job for you

involuntary adjective
not deliberate; done without thinking

involve verb
1 to involve something is to need it or result in it • The job involved a lot of effort. **2** to be involved in something is to take part in it • The police think he may have been involved in the robbery. **involvement** noun being involved in something

involved adjective
long and complicated

inward adjective
on the inside, or facing the inside

inward adverb
inwards

inwardly adverb
in your thoughts; privately • He kept his face severe but inwardly he was smiling.

inwards adverb
towards the inside

iodine noun ⓘ
(say **I**-o-deen or **I**-o-dyn)
iodine is a chemical used to kill germs

IQ noun
a measure of someone's intelligence, calculated from the results of a test. **IQ** stands for intelligence quotient.

iris noun
1 the coloured part of your eyeball **2** a flower with long pointed leaves

iron noun ⒡
1 iron is a strong heavy metal

2 an iron is a device that you heat up and press on clothes to make them smooth **3** an iron is also a tool made of iron

iron verb
to iron clothes is to smooth them with an iron **to iron something out** is to solve a difficulty gradually and carefully

ironic or **ironical** adjective
(say I-**ron**-ik or say I-**ron**-ikal)
1 an ironic situation is strange because the opposite happens to what you might expect **2** you are being ironic when you say the opposite of what you mean **ironically** adverb

irony noun (**ironies**) (say **I**-ro-ni)
1 irony is saying the opposite of what you mean in order to emphasize it or be funny, for example What a lovely day when it is pouring with rain **2** an irony is an unexpected or strange event or situation • The irony is that she had sold all her jewels the day before the burglars broke in.

irregular adjective
1 not regular; not usual **2** against the rules **irregularity** noun being irregular or unusual **irregularly** adverb

irrelevant adjective
(say i-**rel**-i-vant)
not relevant; not having anything to do with what is being discussed **irrelevance** noun something irrelevant

irresistible adjective
too strong or attractive or tempting to resist

irresponsible adjective
not thinking enough about the effects of your actions **irresponsibility** noun someone shows irresponsibility when they act without thinking enough about the effects of their actions **irresponsibly** adverb

irreverent adjective
not respectful **irreverence** noun lack of respect **irreverently** adverb

irrigate verb
to irrigate land is to supply it with water so that crops can grow **irrigation** noun irrigating land

irritable adjective
easily annoyed; bad-tempered **irritability** noun crossness; bad temper **irritably** adverb

irritate verb
1 to irritate someone is to annoy them **2** to irritate a part of your body is to make it itch or feel sore

irritation noun
1 irritation is being annoyed **2** an irritation is something that annoys you

Islam noun (say **iz**-lahm)
Islam is the religion of Muslims **Islamic** adjective to do with Islam

island noun
a piece of land surrounded by water **islander** noun someone who lives on an island

isle noun
an island

isolate verb
to isolate someone or something is to keep them apart from others • Patients with the disease need to be isolated. **isolation** noun being isolated or alone

issue verb
1 to issue something is to send it or give it out to people • They issued blankets to the refugees. **2** to issue a book or piece of information is to publish it **3** to issue is to come out of something • Smoke was issuing from the chimney.

issue noun
1 an issue is a subject that people are discussing • What are the most important issues? **2** an issue of a magazine or newspaper is the edition sold on a particular day • There's a good poster in this week's issue of my football magazine.

it pronoun
1 the thing being talked about, used as the subject or object of a verb • When the tree fell it hit the greenhouse. **2** used to say things about the weather or the time • It is raining. • Is it lunch time yet?

italics plural noun (say it-**al**-iks)
letters printed with a slant, like this

itch noun
a tickling feeling in your skin that makes you want to scratch it **itchy** adjective a part of your body is itchy when it makes you want to scratch it

itch verb
a part of your body itches when it makes you want to scratch it

item noun
one thing in a list or group of things

itinerary noun (**itineraries**) (say I-**tin**-er-er-i)
a list of places to be visited on a journey

its adjective, pronoun
of it; belonging to it • The cat hurt its paw.

it's
short for it is and (before a verb in the past tense) it has • It's raining. • It's been raining.

itself pronoun
it and nothing else, used to refer back to the subject of a verb • I think the cat has hurt itself. **by itself** on its own, alone • The house stands by itself in a wood.

ivory noun
the hard creamy-white substance that forms elephants' tusks

ivy noun
a climbing evergreen plant with shiny leaves

ivy

Jj

jab verb (**jabbing, jabbed**)
1 to jab someone or something is to poke them roughly **2** to jab something is to push it roughly into something else

jab noun
1 a quick hit with something pointed or a fist **2** (informal) an injection

jabber verb
to jabber is to chatter a lot or to speak quickly and not clearly

jack noun
1 a piece of equipment for lifting something heavy off the ground, especially a car **2** a playing card with a picture of a young man

jack verb
to jack something is to lift it with a jack

jackal noun
a wild animal rather like a dog

jacket noun
1 a short coat covering the top half of the body **2** a paper cover for a book

jackpot noun
an amount of prize money that increases until someone wins it

jade noun
jade is a hard green stone which is carved to make ornaments

jagged adjective (say **jag**-id)
having an uneven edge with sharp points

jaguar noun
a large fierce South American animal of the cat family rather like a leopard

jail noun
a prison

jail verb
to jail someone is to put them in prison

jailer noun
a person in charge of a jail

jam noun
1 a sweet food made of fruit boiled with sugar until it is thick **2** a lot of people or cars or other things crowded together so that it is difficult to move **to be in a jam** (informal) is to be in a difficult situation

jam verb (**jamming, jammed**)
1 to jam something is to make it stuck and difficult to move **2** to jam is to become stuck • The door has jammed. **3** to jam something is to push or squeeze it with force • I jammed on the brakes.

jamboree noun
1 a large party or celebration **2** a rally of Scouts

jangle verb
to jangle is to make a harsh ringing sound

January noun
the first month of the year

jar[1] noun
a container made of glass or pottery

jar[2] verb (**jarring, jarred**)
1 to jar is to give you an unpleasant shock or jolt • I jarred every bone in my body. **2** to jar is also to make a harsh sound • All that shrieking really jars on my ears.

jaundice noun
jaundice is a disease that makes your skin turn yellow

jaunt noun
a short trip for fun

jaunty adjective (**jauntier, jauntiest**)
lively and cheerful **jauntily** adverb **jauntiness** noun

javelin noun
a light spear used for throwing in athletics competitions

jaw noun
1 one of the two bones that hold the teeth **2** the lower part of the face; the mouth and teeth of a person or animal **3** the part of a tool that grips something

jay noun
a noisy brightly-coloured bird

jazz noun
jazz is a kind of music with strong rhythm **jazzy** adjective bright and colourful

jealous *adjective*
  1 unhappy or resentful because you feel that someone is better or luckier than you **2** upset because you think that someone you love is loved by someone else more **jealously** *adverb*
jealousy *noun* the feeling of being jealous

jeans *plural noun*
  casual trousers made of denim

jeep *noun*
  (*trademark*) a small strong vehicle that can be driven over rough ground

jeer *verb*
  to jeer is to laugh rudely at someone and shout insults at them

jelly *noun* (**jellies**)
  1 a soft sweet food with a fruit flavour **2** any soft slippery substance

jellyfish *noun* (**jellyfish**)
  a sea animal with a body like jelly and tentacles that can sting

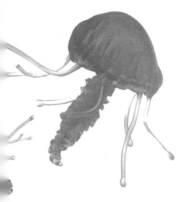

jellyfish

jerk *verb*
  1 to jerk is to make a sudden sharp movement **2** to jerk something is to pull it suddenly
jerk *noun*
  a sudden sharp movement
jerky *adjective* (**jerkier, jerkiest**)
  moving with sudden sharp movements **jerkily** *adverb*
jersey *noun* (**jerseys**)
  a pullover with sleeves
jest *noun*
  a joke
jest *verb*
  to jest is to make jokes to say something **in jest** is to be joking
jester *noun*
  a professional entertainer at a royal court in the Middle Ages
jet¹ *noun*
  a stream of liquid, gas, or flame

forced out of a narrow opening **2** a narrow opening from which a jet comes out **3** an aircraft driven by jet engines
jet¹ *verb* (**jetting, jetted**)
  1 to jet is to come out in a strong stream **2** (*informal*) to jet around is to travel a lot in jet aircraft
jet² *noun*
  1 a hard black mineral **2** a deep glossy black colour
jet engine *noun*
  an engine that drives an aircraft forward by sending out a powerful jet of hot gas at the back
jetty *noun* (**jetties**)
  a small pier or landing stage for boats
jewel *noun*
  1 a precious stone **2** an ornament containing precious stones
jeweller *noun*
  someone who sells or makes jewellery
jewellery *noun*
  jewels or ornaments that people wear, such as rings and necklaces
Jewish *adjective*
  being of Jewish faith; to do with Judaism
jig *noun*
  a lively jumping dance
jig *verb* (**jigging, jigged**)
  to jig is to move up and down with quick jerks
jigsaw *noun*
  1 a jigsaw puzzle **2** a saw that can cut curved shapes
jigsaw puzzle *noun*
  a puzzle made of differently shaped pieces that you fit together to make a picture
jingle *verb*
  to jingle is to make a tinkling or clinking sound
jingle *noun*
  1 a tinkling or clinking sound **2** a simple tune or song that is used in an advertisement
job *noun*
  1 work that someone does regularly to earn a living • *He got a job as a postman.* **2** a piece of work that needs to be done • *We'll have tea when we've finished this job.* **3** (*informal*) a difficult task • *You'll have a job to lift that box.*
jockey *noun* (**jockeys**)
  someone who rides horses in races
jodhpurs *plural noun*
  (*say* **jod**-perz)
  jodhpurs are trousers for riding a horse, fitting closely from the knee to the ankle
jog *verb* (**jogging, jogged**)
  1 to jog is to run slowly, especially for exercise

2 to jog someone is to give them a slight knock or push
  to jog someone's memory is to help them remember something
jogger *noun* someone who goes jogging
join *verb*
  1 to join things together, or join one thing to another, is to put or fix them together **2** two or more things join when they come together **3** to join a society or group is to become a member of it **to join in** is to take part in something
join *noun*
  a place where things join
joiner *noun*
  someone whose job is to make furniture and other things out of wood **joinery** *noun* the work of making furniture and other things out of wood
joint *noun*
  1 a place where things are fixed together **2** the place where two bones fit together **3** a large piece of meat
joint *adjective*
  shared or done by two or more people or groups • *The song was a joint effort.* **jointly** *adverb*
joist *noun*
  a long beam supporting a floor or ceiling
joke *noun*
  something that you say or do to make people laugh
joke *verb*
  to joke is to make jokes, or to talk in a way that is not serious
joker *noun*
  1 someone who makes jokes **2** an extra playing card with a picture of a jester on it
jolly *adjective*
  happy and cheerful
jolly *adverb*
  (*informal*) very • *It's jolly cold!*
jolt *verb*
  1 to jolt something or someone is to hit them or move them suddenly and sharply **2** to jolt is to make a sudden sharp movement • *The bus jolted to a halt.*
jolt *noun*
  1 a sudden sharp movement • *The plane landed with a jolt.* **2** a surprise or shock
jostle *verb*
  to jostle someone is to push them roughly
jot *verb*
  to jot something down is to write it quickly
journal *noun*
  1 a newspaper or magazine **2** a diary

journalist noun
someone whose job is to write news stories for a newspaper or magazine or on television or radio **journalism** noun the job of writing news stories for a newspaper or magazine or on television or radio

journey noun
1 going from one place to another 2 the distance or time you take to travel somewhere • *The town is a day's journey away.*

journey verb
to journey is to go from one place to another

joust verb
to joust is to fight on horseback with lances, as knights did in medieval times

jovial adjective
cheerful and jolly **joviality** noun cheerfulness **jovially** adverb

joy noun
1 joy is great happiness or pleasure 2 a joy is something that gives happiness

joyful adjective
very happy **joyfully** adverb

joystick noun
1 (*informal*) the lever that controls the movement of an aircraft 2 a lever for controlling the cursor on a screen, especially in computer games

jubilant adjective (*say* **joo**-bi-lant)
very happy because you have won or succeeded **jubilantly** adverb **jubilation** noun rejoicing because you have won or succeeded

jubilee noun
a special anniversary of an important event. A **silver jubilee** is the 25th anniversary, a **golden jubilee** is the 50th anniversary, and a **diamond jubilee** is the 60th anniversary

Judaism noun (*say* **joo**-day-izm)
Judaism is the religion of the Jewish people

judge noun
1 someone who hears cases in a lawcourt and decides what should be done 2 someone who decides who has won a contest or competition 3 someone who is good at forming opinions or making decisions about things • *She's a good judge of musical ability.*

judge verb
1 to judge something is to act as judge in a law case or a competition 2 to judge an amount is to estimate or guess what it is 3 to judge something is to form an opinion about it

judgement noun
1 judgement is acting as judge for a law case or a contest 2 a judgement is the decision made by a lawcourt 3 judgement is also the ability to make decisions wisely 4 someone's judgement is their opinion • *In my judgement, you're making a big mistake.*

judo noun (*say* **joo**-doh)
judo is a Japanese form of unarmed combat for sport

jug noun
a container for pouring liquids, with a handle and lip

juggernaut noun
a very large articulated lorry

juggle verb
to juggle objects is to keep tossing and catching them so that you keep them moving in the air without dropping any **juggler** noun someone who juggles at a fair or circus

juice noun
the liquid from fruit, vegetables, or other food **juicy** adjective juicy fruit or meat is full of juice

jukebox noun
a machine that automatically plays a record of your choice when you put a coin in

July noun
the seventh month of the year

jumble verb
to jumble things is to mix them up in a confused way

jumble noun
a confused mixture of things; a muddle

jumble sale noun
a sale of second-hand clothes and other goods to raise money

jump verb
1 to jump is to move suddenly from the ground into the air 2 to jump a fence or other obstacle is to go over it by jumping 3 to jump up or out is to move quickly or suddenly • *He jumped out of his seat.* 4 to jump in or out of a vehicle is to get in or out quickly **to jump at something** (*informal*) is to accept it eagerly **to jump the queue** is to go in front of people before it is your turn

jump noun
1 a sudden movement into the air 2 an obstacle to jump over

jumper noun
a pullover with sleeves

junction noun
a place where roads or railway lines join

June noun
the sixth month of the year

jungle noun
a thick tangled forest, especially in tropical countries

junior adjective
1 younger 2 for young children • *She goes to a junior school.* 3 lower in rank or importance

junior noun
1 a younger person • *Peter is my junior.* 2 a person of lower rank or importance

junk[1] noun
useless or worthless things that should be thrown away • *The garage is full of junk.*

junk[2] noun
a Chinese sailing boat

junk food noun
food that contains a lot of sugar and starch and is not good for you

jury noun
a group of people (usually twelve) chosen to make a decision about a case in a lawcourt, especially whether a person accused of a crime is innocent or guilty **juror** noun a member of a jury

just adjective
1 fair and right; giving proper thought to everybody 2 deserved • *He got his just reward.* **justly** adverb in a just or fair way

just adverb
1 exactly • *It's just what I wanted* 2 only; simply • *I just wanted another cake.* 3 barely; by only a short amount • *The ball hit her just below the knee.* 4 a short time ago • *They had just gone.* 5 now; immediately • *I'm just leaving.*

justice noun
1 justice is being just or having fair treatment 2 justice is also the actions of the law • *They were tried in a court of justice.*

justify verb
to justify something is to show that it is reasonable or necessary • *Do you think that you were justified in taking such a risk?* **justifiable** adjective easy to justify **justification** noun a good reason for doing something

jut verb
to jut, or to jut out, is to stick out

juvenile adjective (*say* **joo**-vi-nyl)
to do with young people

juvenile noun
a young person who is not yet an adult

Kk

kaleidoscope noun
(say kal-**I**-dos-kohp)
a tube that you
look through to see
brightly-coloured
patterns which
change as you turn
the end of the tube

kangaroo noun
an Australian
animal that moves
by jumping on its
strong back legs

karaoke noun
(say ka-ri-**oh**-ki)
a party
entertainment
in which people
sing songs with
a recorded
background played
from a special
machine

karate noun
(say ka-**rah**-ti)
karate is a
Japanese
method
of self-defence
using the hands,
arms, and feet

kangaroo

kayak noun (say **ky**-ak)
a small canoe with a covering
that fits round the canoeist's
waist

kebab noun
small pieces of meat or
vegetables grilled on a skewer

keel noun
the long piece of wood or metal
along the bottom of a boat

keel verb
to keel over is to fall sideways
or overturn

keen adjective
1 enthusiastic or eager • She
is keen on swimming. • We are
keen to go. **2** strong or sharp
• The knife had a keen edge.
• There was a keen wind.

keenly adverb a keenly fought
contest is one in which people
are competing very hard

keenness noun being keen

keep verb (**keeping, kept**)
1 to keep something is to have
it and not get rid of it **2** to keep
something in a place is to put
it there when you aren't using
it **3** to keep (for example) well
or still is to continue to be well
or still **4** to keep someone (for
example) warm or happy is to
cause them to continue to be

warm or happy **5** something
keeps when it lasts without
going bad • Will the milk keep
until tomorrow? **6** to keep doing
something is to continue to
do it • They kept laughing
at her. **7** to keep your word
or promise is to honour it
and not break it **8** to keep
animals or pets is to have
them and look after them
to keep something up is to
continue doing it • Keep up the
good work! **to keep up with
someone** is to go as fast as
them

keep noun
1 someone's keep is the
food or money they
need to live • They have
to earn their keep.
2 a keep is a strong
tower in a castle **for
keeps** (informal) to
keep; permanently
• Is this football mine for
keeps?

keeper noun
1 someone who looks
after the animals in a
zoo **2** a goalkeeper

keeping noun
something is in your
keeping when you are looking
after it • The diaries are in safe
keeping.

keg noun
a small barrel

kennel noun
a shelter for a dog

kerb noun
the edge of a pavement

kernel noun
the part inside the shell of a nut

ketchup noun
ketchup is a thick sauce made
from tomatoes

kettle noun
a container with a spout and
handle, used for boiling water in

key noun
1 a piece of metal shaped so
that it opens a lock **2** a small
lever that you press with your
finger, on a piano or keyboard
3 a device for winding up a
clock or clockwork toy
4 a scale of musical notes
• It is played in the key of C
major. **5** something that solves
a problem or mystery
• Police think they have found
the key to the crime.

keyboard noun
a set of keys on a piano,
typewriter, or computer

keyhole noun
the hole through which you put
a key into a lock

kg
short for kilogram or kilograms

khaki noun (say **kah**-ki)
a dull yellowish-brown colour,
often used for army uniforms

kick verb
1 to kick someone or something
is to hit them with your foot
2 to kick is to move your legs
about vigorously **to kick off**
is to start a football match,
or (informal) to start doing
something **to kick someone
out** is to get rid of them **to kick
up a fuss or row** (informal) is to
make a loud fuss or noise

kick noun
a kicking movement **to get
a kick out of something**
(informal) is to enjoy it very
much

kick-off noun
the start of a football match

kid noun
1 a young goat
2 (informal) a child

kid verb (**kidding, kidded**)
(informal) to kid someone is to
deceive or tease them

kidnap verb (**kidnapping,
kidnapped**)
to kidnap someone is to capture
them by force, usually to get
a ransom **kidnapper** noun a
person who kidnaps someone

kidney noun (**kidneys**)
each of two organs in your body
that remove waste products
from your blood and send them
as urine to your bladder

kill verb
to kill a person or animal is to
make them die **killer** noun a
person who kills someone

kiln noun
an oven for hardening or drying
pottery or bricks

kilo noun
a kilogram

kilobyte noun
(in computing) a unit that
measures data or memory,
equal to 1,024 bytes

kilogram noun
a unit of weight equal to
1,000 grams or about 2.2 pounds

kilometre noun
(say **kil**-o-mee-ter
or say kil-**om**-i-ter)
a unit of length equal to 1,000
metres or about ⅔ of a mile

kilowatt noun
a unit of electrical power equal
to 1,000 watts

kilt noun
a kind of pleated skirt worn
by men as part of traditional
Scottish dress **kilted** adjective
wearing a kilt

a
b
c
d
e
f
g
h
i
j
k
l
m
n
o
p
q
r
s
t
u
v
w
x
y
z

kin *noun*
a person's family or relatives
your next of kin is your closest relative

kind¹ *noun*
a type or sort of something
• *What kind of food do you like?*

kind² *adjective*
helpful and friendly
kindness *noun*

kindergarten *noun*
(say **kin**-der-gar-ten)
a school or class for very young children

kind-hearted *adjective*
kind and generous

kindle *verb*
1 to kindle something is to get it to burn **2** to kindle is to start burning

kindly *adverb*
1 in a kind way • *He spoke kindly to the little boy.* **2** please
• *Kindly close the door.*

kindly *adjective* (**kindlier, kindliest**)
kind • *She gave a kindly smile.*
kindliness *noun* kindliness is being kindly

king *noun*
1 a man who has been crowned as the ruler of a country **2** a piece in chess that has to be captured to win the game **3** a playing card with a picture of a king on it **kingly** *adjective* like a king

kingdom *noun*
a country that is ruled by a king or queen

kingfisher *noun*
a brightly-coloured bird that lives near water and catches fish

king-size or **king-sized** *adjective*
larger than the usual size

kink *noun*
a short twist in a rope, wire, or piece of hair

kiosk *noun*
(say **kee**-osk)
1 a telephone box **2** a small hut or stall where you can buy newspapers, sweets, and drinks

kiss *noun*
touching someone with your lips as a sign of affection or greeting

kiss *verb*
1 to kiss someone is to give them a kiss

kingfisher

kit *noun*
1 equipment or clothes that you need to do a sport, a job, or some other activity **2** a set of parts sold to be fitted together to make something • *a model aircraft kit*

kitchen *noun*
a room where food is prepared and cooked

kite *noun*
a light frame covered with cloth or paper that you fly in the wind at the end of a long piece of string

kitten *noun*
a very young cat

kitty¹ *noun* (**kitties**)
1 an amount of money that you can win in a card game **2** an amount of money that you put aside for a special purpose

kiwi *noun* (say **kee**-wee)
a New Zealand bird that cannot fly

kiwi fruit *noun*
a fruit with thin hairy skin, soft green flesh, and black seeds

km
short for kilometre or kilometres

knack *noun*
a special skill or talent • *There's a knack to putting up a deckchair.*

knapsack *noun*
a bag carried on the back by hikers or soldiers

knead *verb*
to knead dough is to press and stretch it with your hands, to make it ready for baking

knee *noun*
the joint in the middle of your leg

kneecap *noun*
the bony part at the front of your knee

kneel *verb* (**kneeling, knelt**)
to kneel is to bend your legs so you are resting on your knees

knickers *plural noun*
underpants worn by women or girls

knife *noun* (**knives**)
a cutting instrument made of a short blade set in a handle

knife *verb*
to knife someone is to stab them with a knife

knight *noun*
1 a man who has been given the honour that lets him put 'Sir' before his name **2** a warrior who had been given the rank of a nobleman, in the Middle Ages **3** a piece in chess, with a horse's head **knighthood** *noun* a man receives a knighthood when he is made a knight

knight *verb*
to knight someone is to make them a knight

knit *verb* (**knitting, knitted**)
to knit something is to make it by looping together threads of wool or other material, using long needles or a machine

knitting *noun*
1 knitting is the activity of making things by knitting **2** knitting is also something that is being made this way

knitting needle *noun*
a long large needle used in knitting

knob *noun*
1 the round handle of a door or drawer **2** a control to adjust a radio or television set **3** a lump of something
knobbly *adjective* having a lumpy or bumpy surface

knock *verb*
1 to knock something is to hit it hard or bump into it • *Oops, I knocked the vase over.* **2** to knock is to hit something with your hand or fist • *Who's knocking at the door?* **to knock someone out** is to hit them so that they become unconscious

knock *noun*
the act or sound of hitting something

knocker *noun*
a device for knocking on a door

knot

knockout *noun*
1 knocking someone out **2** a game or contest in which the loser in each round has to drop out

knot *noun*
1 a fastening made by tying or looping two ends of string, rope, or ribbon together **2** a round spot on a piece of wood where a branch once joined it **3** a unit for measuring the speed of ships and aircraft, 1,852 metres (or 2,025 yards) per hour **4** a knot of people is a small group of them standing close together

knot verb (**knotting, knotted**)
to knot something is to tie or fasten it with a knot

knotty adjective
1 full of knots **2** difficult or puzzling • *It's a knotty problem.*

know verb (**knowing, knew, known**)
1 to have something in your mind that you have learned or discovered • *Do you know the answer?* **2** to know a person or place is to recognize it or be familiar with it • *I've known him for years.*

knowledge noun (say **nol**-ij)
knowledge is what someone or everybody knows

knowledgeable adjective (say **nol**-ij-a-bul)
knowing a lot about something **knowledgeably** adverb

knuckle noun
a joint in your finger

koala noun (say koh-**ah**-la)
a furry Australian animal that looks like a small bear

Koran noun (say kor-**ahn**)
the holy book of Islam, believed by Muslims to contain the words of Allah

kosher adjective (say **koh**-sher)
kosher food is food prepared according to Jewish religious law

kung fu noun (say kuung-**foo**)
kung fu is a Chinese method of self-defence rather like karate

Ll

short for learner

label noun
a piece of paper, cloth, or metal fixed on or beside something to show what it is or to give other information about it such as its price

label verb (**labelling, labelled**)
to label something is to put a label on it

laboratory noun (**laboratories**) (say la-**bo**-ra-ter-i)
a room or building equipped for scientific work

laborious adjective
needing a lot of effort; very hard **laboriously** adverb

labour noun
1 labour is hard work **2** labour is also the movements of a woman's womb when a baby is born **Labour** the Labour Party, one of the main British political parties

labourer noun
someone who does hard work with their hands, especially outdoors

labyrinth noun
a complicated set of passages or paths; a maze • *She disappeared into the labyrinth of small streets.*

lace noun
1 lace is thin material with decorative patterns of holes in it **2** a lace is a piece of thin cord used to tie up a shoe or boot **lacy** adjective like lace or made of lace

lace verb
to lace up a shoe or boot is to fasten it with a lace

lack noun
there is a lack of something when there isn't any of it or there isn't enough of it • *The trip was cancelled because of lack of interest.*

lack verb
to lack something is to be without it • *He lacks courage.*

lacquer noun
lacquer is a kind of varnish

lacrosse noun
lacrosse is a game using a stick with a net on it (called a crosse) to catch and throw a ball

lad noun
a boy or young man

ladder noun
1 a device to help you climb up or down something, made of upright pieces of wood, metal, or rope with crosspieces called rungs **2** a run of damaged stitches in tights or a stocking

laden adjective
carrying a heavy load

ladle noun
a large deep spoon with a long handle, which you use for serving soup or other liquids

lady noun (**ladies**)
1 a polite name for a woman **2** a well-mannered woman, or a woman who is high up in society **Lady** the title of a noblewoman or the wife of a knight

ladybird noun
a small flying beetle, usually red with black spots

ladylike adjective
polite and quiet, as a lady is supposed to be

ladybirds

lag¹ verb (**lagging, lagged**)
to lag is to go too slowly and not keep up with others • *The little boy was lagging behind.*

lag² verb (**lagging, lagged**)
to lag pipes or boilers is to wrap

them with insulating material to keep in the heat

lager noun (say **lah**-ger)
a light beer

lagoon noun
a lake separated from the sea by sandbanks or reefs

lair noun
the place where a wild animal lives

lake noun
a large area of water completely surrounded by land

lama noun
a Buddhist priest or monk in Tibet and Mongolia

lamb noun
1 a lamb is a young sheep **2** lamb is the meat from young sheep

lame adjective
1 not able to walk normally **2** weak and not very convincing • *What a lame excuse.* **lamely** adverb **lameness** noun

lamp noun
a device for producing light from electricity, gas, or oil

lamp-post noun
a tall post in a street or public place, with a lamp at the top

lampshade noun
a cover for the bulb of an electric lamp, to soften the light

lance noun
a long spear once used by soldiers on horseback

land noun
1 land or the land is all the dry parts of the world's surface **2** land is an area of ground **3** a land is a country or nation

land verb
1 to land is to come down to the ground from the air • *Where did the arrow land?* **2** to land is also to arrive in a ship or aircraft **3** to land someone or something is to bring them to a place by means of a ship or aircraft

landing noun
the floor at the top of a flight of stairs

landlady noun (**landladies**)
1 a woman who owns a house or rooms that people can rent **2** a woman who looks after a pub
landlord noun
1 a person who owns a house or rooms that people can rent **2** a person who looks after a pub

landmark noun
an object on land that you can easily see from a distance

landowner noun
a person who owns a large amount of land

a
b
c
d
e
f
g
h
i
j
k
l
m
n
o
p
q
r
s
t
u
w
x
y
z

landscape *noun*
1 a view of a particular area of town or countryside 2 a picture of the countryside

landslide *noun*
a landslide is when earth or rocks slide down the side of a hill

lane *noun*
1 a narrow road, especially in the country 2 a strip of road for a single line of traffic 3 a strip of track or water for one runner or swimmer in a race

language *noun*
1 language is the use of words in speech and writing 2 a language is the words used in a particular country or by a particular group of people 3 a language is also a system of signs or symbols giving information, especially in computing

lanky *adjective* (**lankier, lankiest**)
awkwardly tall and thin
lankiness *noun*

lantern *noun*
a transparent case for holding a light and shielding it from the wind

lap¹ *noun*
1 the flat area from the waist to the knees, formed when a person is sitting down 2 going once round a racecourse

lap¹ *verb* (**lapping, lapped**)
to lap someone in a race round a track is to be so far ahead of them that you pass them from behind

lap² *verb* (**lapping, lapped**)
1 to lap liquid is to drink it with the tongue, as a cat or dog does 2 waves lap when they make a gentle splash on rocks or the shore

lapel *noun* (*say* la-**pel**)
the flap folded back at each front edge of a coat or jacket

lapse *noun*
1 a slight mistake or fault 2 the passing of time • *After a lapse of three months work began again.*

lapse *verb*
1 to lapse into a state is to pass gradually into it • *He lapsed into unconsciousness.* 2 a contract or document lapses when it is no longer valid • *My passport has lapsed.*

laptop *noun*
a computer small enough to be held and used on your lap, especially while you are travelling

lard *noun*
lard is white greasy fat from pigs, used in cooking

larder *noun*
a cupboard or small room for storing food

large *adjective*
more than the ordinary or average size; big **to be at large** is to be free and dangerous • *The escaped prisoners were still at large.* **largeness** *noun*

largely *adverb*
mainly; mostly • *His success is largely a matter of hard work.*

lark¹ *noun*
a small sandy-brown bird; a skylark

lark² *noun*
(*informal*) something amusing; a bit of fun • *They just did it for a lark.*

lark² *verb*
to lark about is to have fun or play tricks

larva *noun* (**larvae**)
an insect in the first stage of its life, after it comes out of the egg

lasagne *noun* (*say* la-**zan**-ya)
lasagne is pasta in the form of flat sheets, cooked with minced meat or vegetables and a white sauce

laser *noun* (*say* **lay**-zer)
a device that makes a very strong narrow beam of light

lash *noun*
1 an eyelash 2 a stroke with a whip

lash *verb*
1 to lash someone or something is to hit them with a whip or like a whip • *Rain lashed the window.* 2 to lash something is to tie it tightly • *During the storm they lashed the boxes to the mast.* **to lash out** is to speak or hit out angrily

lass *noun*
a girl or young woman

lasso *noun* (**lassos**) (*say* la-**soo**)
a rope with a loop at the end which tightens when you pull the rope, used for catching cattle

last¹ *adjective*
1 coming after all the others; final • *Try not to miss the last bus.* 2 most recent or latest • *Where were you last night?*

last¹ *adverb*
at the end; after everything or everyone else • *He came last in the race.*

last¹ *noun*
a person or thing that is last • *I think I was the last to arrive.*
at last finally; at the end

last² *verb*
1 to continue • *The journey lasts for two hours.* 2 to go on without being used up

• *Our supplies won't last much longer.*

lastly *adverb*
in the last place; finally

latch *noun*
a small bar fastening a gate or door

late *adjective, adverb*
1 after the proper or expected time 2 near the end of a period of time • *They came late in the afternoon.* 3 recent • *Have you heard the latest news?* 4 no longer alive • *They saw the tomb of the late king.* **lateness** *noun*

lately *adverb*
recently • *She has been very tired lately.*

lathe *noun* (*say* layth)
a machine for holding and turning pieces of wood or metal while you shape them

lather *noun*
the thick foam you get when you mix soap with water

Latin *noun*
Latin is the language of the ancient Romans

latitude *noun*
the distance of a place north or south of the equator, measured in degrees

latter *adjective*
later • *We'd like a holiday in the latter part of the year.* **the latter** the second of two people or things just mentioned • *If it's a choice between a picnic or a swim I prefer the latter.* see also **former**

laugh *verb*
to laugh is to make sounds that show you are happy or that you think something is funny

laugh *noun*
1 the sound you make when you laugh 2 (*informal*) something that is fun or amusing • *Yesterday's party was quite a laugh.*

laughter *noun*
laughter is laughing or the sound of laughing

launch¹ *verb*
1 to launch a ship is to send it into the water for the first time 2 to launch a rocket is to send it into space 3 to launch a new idea or product is to make it available for the first time

launch¹ *noun*
the launching of a ship or spacecraft

launch² *noun*
a large motor boat

launderette *noun*
a shop with washing machines that people pay to use

laundry *noun* (**laundries**)
1 laundry is clothes to be washed **2** a laundry is a place where clothes are sent or taken to be washed

laurel *noun*
an evergreen bush with smooth shiny leaves

lava *noun*
lava is molten rock that flows from a volcano, or the solid rock formed when it cools

lavatory *noun* (**lavatories**)
a toilet

lavender *noun*
1 lavender is a shrub with pale purple flowers that smell very sweet **2** a pale purple colour

lavish *adjective*
1 generous • *They are lavish with their gifts.* **2** plentiful • *What a lavish meal!*

law *noun*
1 a rule or set of rules that everyone must keep **2** something that always happens, for example the law of gravity

lawcourt *noun*
a room or building where a judge and jury or a magistrate decide whether someone has broken the law

lawful *adjective*
allowed or accepted by the law **lawfully** *adverb*

lawn *noun*
an area of mown grass in a garden

lawnmower *noun*
a machine you use for cutting grass

lawyer *noun*
a person whose job is to help people with the law

lax *adjective*
not strict; tolerant • *Discipline was very lax.*

lay *verb* (**laying, laid**)
1 to lay something somewhere is to put it down in a particular place or in a particular way **2** to lay a table is to arrange things on it for a meal **3** to lay an egg is to produce it **to lay someone off** is to stop employing them **to lay something on** is to supply or provide it **to lay something out** is to arrange or prepare it

layer *noun*
something flat that lies on or under something else • *The cake had a layer of icing on top and a layer of jam inside.*

layout *noun*
the arrangement or design of something

laze *verb*
to laze is to spend time in a

lazy way

lazy *adjective* (**lazier, laziest**)
not wanting to work; doing as little as possible **lazily** *adverb* **laziness** *noun*

lb.
short for pound or pounds in weight

lead[1] *verb* (**leading, led**) (*say* leed)
1 to lead a person or animal is to guide them, especially by going in front **2** to lead an activity is to be in charge of it **3** to lead in a race or contest is to be winning it **4** a road or path leads somewhere when it goes in that direction • *This road leads to the beach.* **to lead to something** is to cause it • *Their carelessness led to the accident.*

lead[1] *noun* (*say* leed)
1 the first or front place or position • *Who's in the lead now?* **2** help or guidance • *Just follow my lead.* **3** a strap or cord for leading a dog **4** an electric wire • *Don't trip over that lead.*

lead[2] *noun* (*say* led)
1 lead is a soft heavy grey metal **2** a lead is the writing substance (graphite) in the middle of a pencil

leader *noun*
someone who leads or is in charge **leadership** *noun* the ability to be a good leader

leaf *noun* (**leaves**)
1 a flat and usually green growth on a tree or plant, growing from its stem **2** a page of a book **3** a very thin sheet of metal, such as gold leaf **4** a flap that makes a table larger **to turn over a new leaf** is to make a fresh start and improve your behaviour **leafy** *adjective* having a lot of leaves or trees

leaf

leaflet *noun*
a piece of paper printed with information

league *noun* (*say* leeg)
1 a group of teams that play matches against each other **2** a group of countries that have agreed to work together for a particular reason

leak *noun*
a hole or crack through which liquid or gas escapes **leaky** *adjective* a leaky pipe or tap has a leak

leak *verb*
1 something leaks when it lets something out through a hole or crack • *The sink is leaking.*

2 liquid or gas leaks out when it escapes from a container
leakage *noun* an escape of liquid or gas from a container

lean[1] *verb* (**leaning, leaned** or **leant**)
1 to lean is to bend your body towards something or over it **2** to lean something is to put it into a sloping position • *Do not lean bicycles against the window.* **3** to lean against something is to rest against it

lean[2] *adjective*
1 lean meat has little fat **2** a lean person is thin

leap *noun*
1 a high or long jump **2** a sudden increase or advance

leap *verb* (**leaping, leapt** or **leaped**)
1 to leap is to jump high or a long way **2** to leap is also to increase or advance suddenly

leap year *noun*
a year with an extra day in it, on 29 February

learn *verb*
to learn something is to find out about it and gain knowledge or skill in it • *She's learning to play the guitar.*

learned *adjective* (*say* **ler**-nid)
clever and knowledgeable

learner *noun*
someone who is learning something, for example how to drive a car

lease *noun*
an agreement to let someone use a building or land for a fixed period in return for a payment

leash *noun*
a strap or cord for leading a dog

least *adjective, adverb*
smallest; less than all the others • *I'll get the least expensive bike.* • *I like this one least.* **at least 1** not less than what is mentioned • *It will cost at least £50.* **2** anyway • *He's at home; at least I think he is.*

least *noun*
the smallest amount

leather *noun*
a strong material made from animals' skins **leathery** *adjective* tough, like leather

leave *verb* (**leaving, left**)
1 to leave a person, place, or group is to go away from them **2** to leave something is to let it stay where it is or remain as it is • *You can leave your bags by the door.* **3** to leave something to someone is to give it to them in a will **to leave something or**

someone out is not to include them to be left over is to remain when other things have been used

leave *noun*
permission, especially to be away from work

lecture *noun*
1 a talk about a subject to an audience or a class 2 a long or serious warning given to someone • *We got a lecture about closing the windows.*

lecture *verb*
to lecture is to give a lecture **lecturer** *noun* someone who gives a lecture

ledge *noun*
a narrow shelf

leek *noun*
a long green and white vegetable like an onion with broad leaves

leer *verb*
to leer at someone is to look at them in an unpleasant or evil way

left *adjective, adverb*
on or towards the west if you think of yourself as facing north

left *noun*
the left side

left-hand *adjective*
on the left side of something

left-handed *adjective*
using the left hand more than the right hand

leftovers *plural noun*
food that has not been eaten by the end of a meal

leg *noun*
1 one of the parts of a human's or animal's body on which they stand or move 2 one of the parts of a pair of trousers that cover your leg 3 each of the supports of a chair or other piece of furniture 4 one part of a journey 5 each of a pair of matches between the same teams in a competition

legacy *noun* (**legacies**)
something given to someone in a will

legal *adjective*
1 allowed by the law 2 to do with the law or lawyers **legality** *noun* the legality of something is whether it is legal or not **legally** *adverb*

legalize *verb*
to legalize something is to make it legal

legend *noun* (*say* **lej**-end)
an old story handed down from the past **legendary** *adjective* to do with legends; very famous • *the legendary knight Sir Galahad*

legible *adjective*
clear enough to read • *Make sure your writing is legible.* **legibility** *noun* how easily you can read something **legibly** *adverb*

legion *noun*
1 a division of the ancient Roman army 2 a group of soldiers, or men who used to be soldiers

legitimate *adjective* (*say* li-**jit**-i-mat)
1 allowed by a law or rule 2 (*old use*) born of parents who were married to each other **legitimacy** *noun* whether or not something is allowed by a law or rule **legitimately** *adverb*

leisure *noun*
leisure is free time, when you can do what you like

leisurely *adjective*
done with plenty of time, without hurrying • *They took a leisurely stroll down to the river.*

lemon *noun*
1 a yellow citrus fruit with a sour taste 2 a pale yellow colour

lemon

lemonade *noun*
a drink with a lemon flavour

lend *verb* (**lending, lent**)
1 to lend something to someone is to let them have it for a short time 2 to lend someone money is to give them money which they must pay back plus an extra amount called interest

length *noun*
1 how long something is 2 a piece of something cut from a longer piece, for example rope, wire, or cloth 3 the distance of a swimming pool from one end to the other **at length** after a while; eventually

lengthen *verb*
1 to lengthen something is to make it longer 2 to lengthen is to become longer

lengthy *adjective* (**lengthier, lengthiest**)
going on for a long time • *He gave a lengthy speech.*

lenient *adjective* (*say* **lee**-ni-ent)
not as strict as expected, especially when punishing someone **leniency** *noun* when someone is not as strict as expected **leniently** *adverb*

lens *noun*
1 a curved piece of glass or plastic used to focus the light in a camera or a pair of glasses 2 the transparent part of the eye, behind the pupil

Lent *noun*
Lent is a period of about six weeks before Easter when some Christians give up something they enjoy

lentil *noun*
a kind of small bean

leopard *noun* (*say* **lep**-erd)
a large spotted wild animal of the cat family

leopard

leotard *noun* (*say* **lee**-o-tard)
a close-fitting piece of clothing worn by acrobats and dancers

less *adjective, adverb*
smaller; not so much • *Make less noise.* • *It is less important.*

less *noun*
a smaller amount • *I have less than you.*

lessen *verb*
1 to lessen something is to make it smaller or not so much 2 to lessen is to become smaller or not so much

lesser *adjective*
the smaller or less great of two things • *This is the lesser evil.*

lesson *noun*
  1 the time when someone is teaching you **2** something that you have to learn **3** a passage from the Bible read aloud as part of a church service

let *verb* (**letting, let**)
  1 to let someone do something is to allow them to do it **2** to let something happen is to cause it or not prevent it • *Don't let your bike slide into the ditch.* **3** to let a house or room or building is to allow someone to use it in return for payment **4** to let someone in or out is to allow them to go in or out **to let someone down** is to disappoint them **to let someone off** is to excuse them from a punishment or duty **to let something off** is to make it explode

lethal *adjective*
  something that is lethal can kill you

let's *verb*
  (*informal*) shall we? • *Let's go to the park.*

letter *noun*
  1 one of the symbols used for writing words, such as a, b, or c **2** a written message sent to another person

letter box *noun*
  a box or slot into which letters are delivered or posted

lettering *noun*
  lettering is letters drawn or painted

lettuce *noun*
  a green vegetable with crisp leaves used in salads

leukaemia *noun*
  (*say* lew-**kee**-mi-a)
  a disease in which there are too many white cells in the blood

level *adjective*
  1 flat or horizontal • *The ground is level near the house.* **2** at the same height or position • *Are these pictures level?* **3** equal or even • *After half an hour the scores were still level.*

level *verb* (**levelling, levelled**)
  1 to level something is to make it flat or horizontal **2** to level, or to level out, is to become horizontal

level *noun*
  1 height or position • *Fix the shelf at eye level.* **2** a standard or grade of achievement • *She has reached level 3 in gymnastics.* **3** a device that shows if something is horizontal

level crossing *noun*
  a place where a road crosses a railway at the same level

lever *noun*
  a bar that is pushed or pulled to lift something heavy, force something open, or make a machine work

liable *adjective*
  1 likely to do or get something • *They are liable to forget things.* **2** responsible for something • *If there is any damage you will be liable.*

liar *noun*
  someone who tells lies

liberal *adjective*
  1 tolerant of other people's point of view **2** generous • *She is liberal with her money.*

liberally *adverb* in large amounts or generously • *Pour the cream on liberally.*

liberate *verb*
  to liberate someone is to set them free **liberation** *noun* setting someone free

liberty *noun* (**liberties**)
  liberty is freedom

librarian *noun*
  someone who looks after a library or works in one

library *noun* (**libraries**)
  a place where books are kept for people to use or borrow

lice
  plural of **louse**

licence *noun*
  an official document allowing someone to do or use or own something

license *verb*
  to license someone to do something is to give them a licence to do it • *We are not licensed to sell alcoholic drinks.*

lichen *noun* (*say* **ly**-ken)
  a dry-looking plant that grows on rocks, walls, trees, and other surfaces

lick *verb*
  to lick something is to move your tongue over it

lick *noun*
  the act of moving your tongue over something

lid *noun*
  1 a cover for a box or jar **2** an eyelid

lie¹ *verb* (**lying, lay, lain**)
  1 to lie is to be in or get into a flat position, especially to rest with your body flat as it is in bed • *He lay on the grass.* • *The cat has lain here all night.* **2** to lie is also to be or remain a certain way • *The castle was lying in ruins.* • *The valley lay before us.*

lie² *verb* (**lying, lied**)
  to lie is to say something that you know is not true

lie² *noun*
  something you say that you know is not true

lieutenant *noun* (*say* lef-**ten**-ant)
  an officer in the army or navy

life *noun* (**lives**)
  1 a person's or animal's life is the time between their birth and death **2** life is being alive and able to grow **3** life is also all living things • *Is there life on Mars?* **4** life is also liveliness • *She is full of life.*

lifebelt *noun*
  a large ring that will float, used to support someone's body in water

lifeboat *noun*
  a boat for rescuing people at sea

life cycle *noun*
  the series of changes in the life of a living thing • *The diagram shows the life cycle of a frog.*

lifeguard *noun*
  someone whose job is to rescue swimmers who are in difficulty

life jacket *noun*
  a special safety jacket that will help a person to float in water

lifeless *adjective*
  1 without life **2** unconscious

lifelike *adjective*
  looking exactly like a real person or thing

lifespan *noun*
  how long a person or animal or plant lives

lifetime *noun*
  the period of time during which someone is alive

lift *verb*
  1 to lift something is to pick it up or move it to a higher position **2** to lift is to rise or go upwards • *The fog was beginning to lift.*

lift *noun*
  1 a movement upwards **2** a device for taking people or goods from one floor to another in a building **3** a ride in someone else's car or other vehicle

lift-off *noun*
  the vertical take-off of a rocket or spacecraft

light¹ *noun*
  1 light is the form of energy that makes things visible, the opposite of darkness • *There was not enough light to see the garden.* **2** a light is something that provides light or a flame, especially an electric lamp • *Switch on the light.*

light¹ *adjective*
1 full of light; not dark
2 pale • *The house was painted light blue.*

light¹ *verb* (**lighting, lit** or **lighted**)
1 to light something is to start it burning 2 to light is to begin to burn • *The fire won't light.* 3 to light a place is to give it light • *The streets were lit by gaslamps.*

light² *adjective*
1 not heavy; weighing little
2 not large or strong • *There is a light wind.* 3 not needing much effort • *They were doing some light work in the garden.* 4 pleasant and entertaining rather than serious • *We prefer light music.* **lightly** *adverb* gently or only a little • *He kissed her lightly on the cheek.* • *It began to snow lightly.*

lighten *verb*
1 to lighten something is to make it lighter or brighter 2 to lighten is to become lighter

lighter *noun*
a device for lighting something like a cigarette or a fire

light-hearted *adjective*
1 cheerful; free from worry
2 not serious **light-heartedly** *adverb* **light-heartedness** *noun*

lighthouse *noun*
a tower with a bright light at the top to guide ships and warn them of danger

lightning *noun*
lightning is a flash of bright light in the sky during a thunderstorm

light year *noun*
the distance that light travels in one year (about 9.5 million million kilometres or 6 million million miles)

like¹ *verb*
to like someone or something is to think they are pleasant or satisfactory **should like** or **would like** to want • *I should like to see him.*

like² *preposition*
1 resembling; similar to; in the manner of • *She looks like her mother.* • *He cried like a baby.*
2 such as • *We need things like knives and forks.* 3 typical of • *It was like her to forgive him.*

likeable *adjective*
pleasant and easy to like

likely *adjective* (**likelier, likeliest**)
probable; expected to happen or to be true or suitable • *It's likely that it will rain this afternoon.*

likeness *noun*
a resemblance

likewise *adverb*
similarly; in the same way

liking *noun*
a feeling that you like something or someone • *She has a great liking for chocolate.* **to be to someone's liking** is to be what they like • *These shoes are not to my liking.*

lily *noun* (**lilies**)
a trumpet-shaped flower grown from a bulb

limb *noun*)
a leg or an arm

lime¹ *noun*
a green fruit like a small round lemon

lime

lime² *noun*
a tree with yellow blossom

lime³ *noun*
a white chalky powder used in making cement or as a fertilizer

limelight *noun*
to be in the limelight is to get a lot of publicity and attention

limerick *noun* (*say* **lim**-er-ik)
an amusing poem with five lines and a strong rhythm

limestone *noun*
limestone is rock from which lime (the chalky powder) is made, used in building and in making cement

limit *noun*
a line or point that you cannot or should not pass • *You must obey the speed limit.*

limit *verb*
to limit something or someone is to keep them within a limit • *You are limited to one choice each.* **limitation** *noun* something that limits what you can do

limited *adjective*
kept within limits; not great • *The choice was limited.*

limp¹ *verb*
to limp is to walk with difficulty because something is wrong with your leg or foot

limp¹ *noun*
a limping movement

limp² *adjective*
not stiff or firm; without much strength • *He gave me a limp*

handshake. **limply** *adverb* something hangs limply when it does so in a limp way • *Her hair hung limply over her forehead.*

limpet *noun*
a small shellfish that clings firmly to rocks

line¹ *noun*
1 a long thin mark made on a surface 2 a row or series of people or things 3 a length of something long and thin like rope, string, or wire 4 a number of words together in a play, film, poem, or song 5 a railway or a length of railway track
in line 1 forming a straight line 2 obeying or behaving well

line¹ *verb*
1 to line something is to mark it with lines 2 to line a place is to form an edge or border along it • *People lined the streets to watch the race.* **to line up** is to form lines or rows • *The children lined up in the playground.* **to line things up** is to set them up in a line or row

line² *verb*
to line material or a piece of clothing is to put a lining in it

linen *noun*
1 linen is cloth made from flax, used to make shirts, sheets, tablecloths, and so on 2 linen is also things made of this cloth

liner *noun*
a large passenger ship or aircraft

linesman *noun*
an official in football, tennis, and other games who decides whether the ball has crossed a line

linger *verb*
to linger is to stay for a long time or be slow to leave • *The smell of her perfume lingered in the room.*

linguist *noun*
an expert in languages, or someone who can speak several languages well **linguistic** *adjective* to do with languages

lining *noun*
a layer of material covering the inside of something

link *noun*
1 one of the rings in a chain
2 a connection between two things

link *verb*
to link things is to join them together **to link up** is to become connected

lino *noun*
lino is linoleum

linoleum *noun*
(*say* lin-**oh**-li-um)
linoleum is a stiff shiny floor covering

lint *noun*
lint is a soft material for covering wounds

lion *noun*
a large strong flesh-eating animal found in Africa and India

lioness *noun*
a female lion

lip *noun*
1 each of the two fleshy edges of the mouth **2** the edge of something hollow such as a cup or a crater **3** the pointed part at the top of a jug or saucepan, for pouring from

lips

lip-read *verb*
to lip-read is to understand what someone is saying by watching the movements of their lips, not by hearing their voice

lipstick *noun*
a stick of a waxy substance for colouring the lips

liquid *noun*
a substance (such as water or oil) that can flow but is not a gas

liquid *adjective*
in the form of a liquid; flowing freely

liquidizer *noun*
a device for making food into a pulp or a liquid

liquor *noun* (*say* **lik**-er)
liquor is strong alcoholic drink

liquorice *noun*
(*say* **lik**-er-iss)
liquorice is a soft black sweet with a strong taste, which comes from the root of a plant

lisp *noun*
a way of speaking, in which *s* and *z* are pronounced like *th*

lisp *verb*
to lisp is to speak with a lisp

list¹ *noun*
a number of names or figures or items written or printed one after another

list¹ *verb*
to list things is to write or say them one after another

list² *verb*
a ship lists when it leans over to one side in the water

listen *verb*
to listen to someone or something is to pay attention so that you can hear them
• *Listen to me.* • *I like listening to music.* **listener** *noun* someone who is listening

literacy *noun* (*say* **lit**-er-a-si)
the ability to read and write

literal *adjective*
1 meaning exactly what it says **2** word for word • *Write out a literal translation.*

literally *adverb*
really; exactly as the words say
• *The noise made me literally jump out of my seat.*

literary *adjective* (*say* **lit**-er-er-i)
to do with literature; interested in literature

literate *adjective* (*say* **lit**-er-at)
able to read and write

literature *noun*
literature is books or writings, especially the best or most famous

litmus *noun*
litmus is a blue substance used to show whether something is an acid or an alkali

litre *noun* (*say* **lee**-ter)
a measure of liquid, 1,000 cubic centimetres or about 1¾ pints

litter *noun*
1 litter is rubbish or untidy things left lying about **2** a litter is a number of young animals born to one mother at one time

litter *verb*
to litter a place is to make it untidy with litter

little *adjective* (**less** or **littler**, **least** or **littlest**)
1 small; not great or not much
• *She brought a little boy.* • *We have very little time.* **2** a small amount of something • *Have a little sugar.* **little by little** gradually

little *adverb*
not much • *They go swimming very little now.*

live¹ *verb* (rhymes with **give**)
1 to live is to be alive **2** to live in a particular place is to have your home there • *She is living in Glasgow.* **3** to live in a certain way is to pass your life in that way • *He lived as a hermit.*
to live on something is to have it as food or income • *The islanders lived mainly on fish.*
• *No one can live on £50 a week.*

live² *adjective* (rhymes with **hive**)
1 alive **2** carrying electricity **3** broadcast while it is actually happening, not from a recording

livelihood *noun* (*say* **lyv**-li-huud) a person's livelihood is the way in which they earn a living

lively *adjective* (**livelier**, **liveliest**)
full of life and energy; cheerful **liveliness** *noun*

liver *noun*
1 a large organ in the body that helps keep the blood clean **2** an animal's liver used as food

livestock *noun*
farm animals

livid *adjective*
1 very angry **2** of a dark blue-grey colour, like bruised skin

living *noun*
1 the way that a person lives
• *They have a good standard of living.* **2** a means of earning money • *She makes a living selling jewellery.*

living room *noun*
a room for sitting and relaxing in

lizard *noun*
a reptile with a scaly skin, four legs, and a long tail

llama *noun* (*say* **lah**-ma)
a South American animal that has woolly fur and looks like a small camel without a hump

load *noun*
1 something large or heavy that has to be carried
2 (*informal*) a large amount
• *It's a load of nonsense.*

load *verb*
1 to load something is to put things into it so they can be carried • *I'll go and load the back of the car.* **2** to load someone with something is to give them large amounts of it
• *They loaded him with gifts.* **3** to load a gun is to put a bullet or shell into it **4** to load a machine is to put something it needs into it, such as a film in a camera **5** to load a computer is to enter programs or data on it

loaf¹ *noun* (**loaves**)
a shaped mass of bread baked in one piece

loaf² *verb*
to loaf or loaf about is to loiter or waste time **loafer** *noun* someone who loafs about

loan *noun*
something that has been lent to someone, especially money **on loan** being lent • *The books are on loan from the library.*

loan *verb*
to loan something is to lend it

loathe *verb* (rhymes with **clothe**)
to loathe something or someone is to dislike them very much

loathsome *adjective*
making you feel disgusted; horrible

lob *verb* (**lobbing**, **lobbed**)
to lob something is to throw or hit it high into the air

lobby *noun* (**lobbies**)
an entrance hall

a
b
c
d
e
f
g
h
i
j
k
l
m
n
o
p
q
r
s
t
u
v
w
x
y
z

143

lobe *noun*
the rounded part at the bottom of your ear

lobster *noun*
a large shellfish with eight legs and two claws

lobster

local *adjective*
1 belonging to a particular place or area • *Where is your local library?* **2** affecting a certain part of the body • *You'll need a local anaesthetic.* **locally** *adverb* nearby, in the area where you are • *Do you live locally?*

local *noun*
(*informal*) someone who lives in a particular district

locate *verb*
1 to locate something is to discover where it is • *I have located the fault.* **2** to be located in a place is to be situated there • *The cinema is located in the High Street.*

location *noun*
the place where something is • *What is the exact location of the submarine?* When a film is filmed **on location** it is filmed in natural surroundings, not in a studio.

loch *noun*
a lake in Scotland

lock¹ *noun*
1 a device for fastening a door or window or container, needing a key to open it **2** a section of a canal or river with gates at each end, so that the level of water can be raised or lowered to allow boats to pass from one level to another

lock¹ *verb*
1 to lock a door or window or lid is to fasten it with a lock **2** to lock something somewhere is to put it in a safe place that can be fastened with a lock

3 to lock is to become fixed in one place, or to jam

lock² *noun*
a few strands of hair formed into a loop

locker *noun*
a small cupboard for keeping things safe, often in a changing room

locket *noun*
a small case holding a photograph or lock of hair, worn on a chain round the neck

locomotive *noun*
a railway engine

locust *noun*
an insect like a large grasshopper, that flies in swarms which eat all the plants in an area

lodge *noun*
a small house, often at the entrance to a large house or building

lodge *verb*
1 to lodge is to become fixed or get stuck somewhere • *The ball lodged in the branches.* **2** to lodge somewhere is to stay there as a lodger

lodger *noun*
someone who pays to live in someone else's house

lodgings *plural noun*
a room or set of rooms that a person rents in someone else's house

loft *noun*
the room or space under the roof of a house

lofty *adjective* (**loftier, loftiest**)
1 high or tall **2** noble and proud • *They have lofty ideas.* **loftily** *adverb*

log *noun*
1 a large piece of a tree that has fallen or been cut down **2** a detailed record of what happens each day, especially on a journey or voyage

log *verb* (**logging, logged**)
to log information is to put it in a log **to log in** or **to log on** is to gain access to a computer **to log out** or **to log off** is to finish using a computer

logic *noun*
a way of thinking and working out ideas that makes sense

logical *adjective*
using logic or worked out by logic **logically** *adverb*

logo *noun*
a printed symbol used by a business company or other organization as its emblem

loiter *verb*
to loiter is to stand about not doing anything

lollipop *noun*
a hard sticky sweet on the end of a stick

lolly *noun* (**lollies**)
1 (*informal*) a lolly is a lollipop or an ice lolly **2** (*slang*) lolly is money

lone *adjective*
on its own; solitary • *a lone rider*

lonely *adjective* (**lonelier, loneliest**)
1 unhappy because you are on your own **2** far from other inhabited places; not often used or visited • *They passed through a lonely village.* **loneliness** *noun*

long¹ *adjective*
1 measuring a lot from one end to the other • *They walked up a long path.* **2** taking a lot of time • *I'd like a long holiday.* **3** measuring from one end to the other • *A cricket pitch is 22 yards long.*

long¹ *adverb*
1 for a long time • *Have you been waiting long?* **2** a long time before or after • *They left long ago.* **as long as** or **so long as** provided that; on condition that • *I'll come as long as I can bring my dog.*

long² *verb*
to long for something is to want it very much

longitude *noun*
(*say* **long**-i-tewd *or* **lon**-ji-tewd) longitude is the distance of a place east or west, measured in degrees from an imaginary line that passes through Greenwich in London

long jump *noun*
an athletic contest of jumping as far as possible along the ground with one leap

long-sighted *adjective*
able to see things clearly when they are at a distance but not when they are close

look *verb*
1 to look is to use your eyes to see something, or to turn your eyes towards something **2** to look in a particular direction is to face it • *Look right and left before you cross.* **3** to look (for example) happy or sad is to appear that way **to look after something** or **someone** is to protect them or take care of them **to look down on someone** is to despise them **to look for something** or **someone** is to try to find them **to look forward to something** is

to be waiting eagerly for it
to happen **to look out** is to
be careful **to look up to
someone** is to admire or
respect them
look noun
1 a look is the act of looking
• *Take a look at this.* **2** the
expression on someone's face
• *She gave me a surprised look.*
3 the look of someone or
something is their appearance
• *I don't like the look of that dog.*
looking-glass noun
(*old use*) a glass mirror
lookout noun
1 a place from which you
watch for something
2 someone whose job is
to keep watch **3** watching
or being watchful • *Keep a
lookout for snakes.*
loom¹ noun
a machine for weaving cloth
loom² verb
to loom or loom up is to appear
large and threatening • *An
iceberg loomed out of the fog.*
loop noun
the shape made by a curve
crossing itself; a piece of string,
ribbon, or wire made into this
shape
loop verb
to loop something is to make it
into a loop
loophole noun
a way of getting round a law or
rule without quite breaking it
loose adjective
1 not tight or firmly fixed
• *a loose tooth* **2** not tied up
or shut in • *The dog got loose.*
to be at a loose end is to
have nothing to do **to be on
the loose** is to be free after
escaping **loosely** adverb in a
way that is not firm or tight
• *She tied the scarf loosely round
her waist*
loosen verb
1 to loosen something is to
make it loose **2** to loosen is
to become loose
loot noun
loot is stolen things
loot verb
to loot a place is to rob it
violently, especially during
a war or riot **looter** noun
someone who loots a place
lopsided adjective
uneven, with one side lower
than the other • *She had a
lopsided smile.*
lord noun
1 a nobleman, especially one
who is allowed to use the title
'Lord' in front of his name

2 (*old use*) a master or ruler
Lord a name used by Christians
for God or Jesus Christ
lordly adjective
1 relating to a lord **2** proud;
haughty
lorry noun (**lorries**)
a large motor vehicle for
carrying goods
lose verb (**losing, lost**)
1 to lose something is to no
longer have it, especially
because you can't find it • *I've
lost my hat.* **2** to lose a contest
or game is to be beaten in it
• *We lost last Friday's match.* **3** a
clock or watch loses time when
it gives a time that is earlier
than the correct time **to lose
your way** is not to know where
you are **loser** noun someone
who loses a game, or who often
loses or fails at things
loss noun
1 losing something
2 something you have lost
to be at a loss is to be puzzled
or unable to do something
lost adjective
1 not knowing where you are
or not able to find your way
• *I think we're lost.* **2** missing
or strayed • *a lost dog*
lot noun
1 a lot is a large number of
people or things **2** a lot can also
mean very much • *Thanks a lot.*
to draw lots is to choose one
person or thing from a group
by a method that depends on
chance **the lot** or **the whole
lot** everything
lotion noun
a liquid that you put on your
skin to clean or soothe it
lottery noun (**lotteries**)
a game in which prizes are
given to people who have
winning tickets that are chosen
by a draw
loud adjective
1 noisy; easily heard **2** bright or
gaudy • *The room was painted in
loud colours.*
loudly adverb
loudness noun
loudspeaker noun
the part of a radio or music
system that produces the sound
lounge noun
a room in a house, hotel,
or airport for sitting in and
relaxing
lounge verb
to lounge is to sit or stand in a
relaxed or lazy way
louse noun (**lice**)
a small insect that sucks the
blood of humans or animals

love noun
1 love is a feeling of liking
someone or something very
much; great affection or
kindness **2** someone's love
is a person that they love
3 in games, love is a score
of nothing **to be in love**
is to love another person
very deeply
love verb
to love someone or something
is to like them very much
lovable adjective easy to love
lovingly adverb in a way that
shows love
lovely adjective (**lovelier,
loveliest**)
1 beautiful **2** (*informal*)
very pleasant or enjoyable
loveliness noun
low¹ adjective
1 only reaching a short way
up; not high **2** below average in
amount or importance • *They
are people of a low rank.* • *Prices
are low.* **3** unhappy • *I'm feeling
low.* **4** a low note is one at the
bottom end of a musical scale
low² verb
to low is to make a sound like
a cow
lower verb
1 to lower something is to move
it down **2** to lower a sound is to
make it less loud • *Please lower
your voices.*
lowly adjective (**lowlier,
lowliest**)
humble **lowliness** noun
loyal adjective
always true to your friends;
faithful **loyally** adverb in a
faithful way **loyalty** noun
being true to your friends
lozenge noun
a small sweet tablet, especially
one that contains medicine
lubricant noun
oil or grease for lubricating
machinery
lubricate verb
to lubricate something like
machinery is to put oil or grease
on it so that it moves smoothly
lubrication noun putting oil or
grease on something so that it
moves smoothly
luck noun
1 luck is the way things happen
by chance, without being
planned **2** luck is also good
fortune
luckily adverb
by a lucky chance; fortunately
• *Luckily it stayed warm all day.*
lucky adjective (**luckier,
luckiest**)
having or bringing good luck

a b c d e f g h i j k l m n o p q r s t u v w x y z

ludicrous adjective
(say **loo**-di-krus)
extremely silly or absurd
ludicrously adverb
lug verb (**lugging, lugged**)
to lug something heavy is to
carry it or drag it
with difficulty
luggage noun
luggage is
the suitcases
and bags you
take on a
journey
lukewarm
adjective
1 slightly
warm **2** not
very keen or
enthusiastic
• They got
a lukewarm
response.
lull verb
to lull
someone is to
soothe or calm
them
lull noun
a short period of quiet or
rest • There was a lull in
the fighting.
lullaby noun (**lullabies**)
a song that you sing to send a
baby to sleep
lumber verb
1 to lumber is to move along
clumsily and heavily • A black
bear came lumbering through the
woods. **2** (informal) to lumber
someone is to leave them
with something unpleasant
or difficult to do
lumberjack noun
someone whose job is to cut
down trees and transport them
luminous adjective
(say **loo**-mi-nus)
shining or glowing in the dark
luminosity noun luminosity is
being luminous
lump noun
1 a solid piece of something
2 a swelling **lumpy** adjective
having lots of lumps
lump verb
to lump different things
together is to put them
together in the same group
lunacy noun (**lunacies**)
(say **loo**-na-si)
lunacy is madness
lunar adjective
to do with the moon
lunatic noun (say **loo**-na-tik)
an insane person
lunch noun
a meal eaten in the middle of
the day

luggage

lung noun
each of the two
organs in your chest
that you use for
breathing
lunge verb
to lunge is to make a
sudden movement
forwards
lurch[1] verb
to lurch is to stagger
or lean suddenly
lurch[1] noun
a sudden staggering
or leaning
movement
lurch[2] noun
**to leave someone
in the lurch** is
to desert them
when they are in
difficulty
lure verb
to lure a person or
animal is to tempt
them into a trap or
difficulty
lurk verb
to lurk is to wait
threateningly where you
can't be seen
luscious adjective (say **lush**-us)
tasting or smelling delicious
• The bushes were heavy with
luscious fruit.
lush adjective
growing thickly and healthily
• The moist climate helps to
cover the countryside with
lush grass.
lustre noun (say **lus**-ter)
a thing's lustre is its brightness
or brilliance **lustrous** adjective
shining brightly
lute noun
a musical instrument rather like
a guitar but with a deeper and
rounder body. It was used a lot
in the Middle Ages.
luxury noun (**luxuries**)
1 a luxury is something
expensive that you enjoy but
don't really need **2** luxury is
having a very comfortable
and expensive way of life
• They led a life of luxury.
luxurious adjective very
comfortable and expensive
lynch verb
to lynch someone is to
execute them without a
proper trial
lyre noun
an ancient musical instrument
like a small harp
lyrical adjective
sounding like a song or a poem
lyrics plural noun
the words of a popular song

Mm

m
short for metre, metres, miles,
or millions
mac noun
(informal) a mackintosh
macaroni noun
macaroni is pasta in the form of
short tubes

WORD ORIGIN

The word **macaroni** comes from an
Italian word maccaroni, which in turn
comes from a Greek word makaria
meaning 'food made from barley'.

machine noun
a piece of equipment made
of moving parts that work
together to do a job
machine-gun noun
a gun that can keep firing
bullets quickly one after
another
machinery noun
1 machinery is machines
generally • farm machinery
2 machinery is also the moving
parts of a machine • The lift's
machinery is faulty.
mackerel noun (**mackerel**)
a sea fish used as food
mackintosh noun
a raincoat
mad adjective (**madder,
maddest**)
1 having something wrong
with your mind; not sane **2** very
foolish **3** very keen • She's mad
about rock music. **4** (informal)
very excited or annoyed **like
mad** (informal) with great
speed, energy, or enthusiasm
madness noun
madam noun
a word sometimes used
when speaking or writing
politely to a woman, instead
of her name • Can I help
you, madam?
madden verb
to madden someone is to make
them mad or angry
madly adverb
extremely; very much • They
are madly in love.
magazine noun
1 a paper-covered publication
with articles or stories, which
comes out regularly **2** the
part of a gun that holds
the cartridges **3** a store for
weapons and ammunition or
for explosives **4** a device that

holds film for a camera or slides for a projector

maggot noun
the larva of some kinds of fly

magic noun
1 magic is the power to make impossible things happen
2 magic is also performing clever tricks

magical adjective
1 done by magic or as if by magic 2 wonderful; marvellous
magically adverb by magic or as if by magic

magician noun
1 someone who does magic tricks 2 a man with magic powers; a wizard

magistrate noun
a judge in a local court who deals with some less serious cases

magnesium noun (Mg)
magnesium is a silvery-white metal that burns with a very bright flame

magnet noun
a piece of metal that can attract iron or steel and that points north and south when it is hung in the air **magnetism** noun the attraction of a magnet

magnetic adjective
having or using the powers of a magnet

magnetize verb
to magnetize something is to make it into a magnet

magnificent adjective
1 looking splendid or impressive 2 excellent
• We had a magnificent meal.
magnificence noun being magnificent
magnificently adverb

magnify verb (**magnifies, magnified**)
to magnify something is to make it look bigger than it really is **magnification** noun magnification is making something look bigger than it really is

magnifying glass noun
a lens that magnifies things

magnitude noun
magnitude is how large or important something is

magpie noun (**magpies**)
a black and white bird with a long tail, which likes to collect bright objects

mahogany noun
(say ma-**hog**-a-ni)
mahogany is a hard brown wood used for making furniture

maid noun
1 a female servant in a hotel or private house 2 (old use) a girl

maiden noun
(old use) a girl

maiden name noun
a woman's family name before she gets married

maiden voyage or **maiden flight** noun
a ship's first voyage or an aircraft's first flight

mail¹ noun
1 mail is letters and parcels sent by post 2 mail is also electronic mail

mail¹ verb
to mail something is to send it by post or by electronic mail

mail² noun
armour made of metal rings joined together

maim verb
to maim someone is to injure them so badly that part of their body is damaged for life

main adjective
largest or most important

mains noun
the main pipe or cable in a system carrying water, gas, or electricity to a building

mainland noun
the mainland is the main part of a country or continent, not the islands around it

mainly adverb
chiefly or usually; almost completely

maintain verb
1 to maintain something is to keep it in good condition 2 to maintain a belief is to have it or state it • I maintain that animals should not be hunted. 3 to maintain someone is to provide money for them

maintenance noun
maintenance is keeping something in good condition

maize noun
maize is a tall kind of corn with large seeds

majestic adjective
stately and dignified
majestically adverb

majesty noun
(**majesties**)
1 the title of a king or queen
2 majesty is the quality of being stately and dignified

major adjective
more important; main • The major roads are shown in red on the map.

maize

major noun
an army officer above captain in rank

majority noun (**majorities**)
(say ma-**jo**-ri-ti)
1 the greatest part of a group of people or things; more than half • The majority of the class wanted a quiz. 2 the amount by which the winner in an election beats the loser • She had a majority of 25 over her opponent.

make verb (**making, made**)
1 to make something is to build or produce it • They are making a raft out of logs. 2 to make someone or something do something is to cause it to happen • The bang made him jump. 3 to make money is to get it or earn it • She makes £30,000 a year. 4 in a game, to make a score is to achieve it • He has made 20 runs so far. 5 to make a certain point is to reach it • The swimmer just made the shore. • Do you think we can make the 7 o'clock train? 6 to make something is to estimate it or reckon it • What do you make the time? 7 several numbers make a total when they add up to it • 4 and 6 make 10. 8 to make (for example) a suggestion or promise is to give it to someone 9 to make a bed is to tidy it or arrange it for use **to make someone's day** is to cause them to be happy or successful **to make do** is to manage with something that is not what you really want **to make for a place** is to go towards it **to make off** is to leave quickly **to make something** or **someone out** is to manage to see or hear or understand them **to make something up** is to invent a false story or excuse **to make up** is to be friendly again after a disagreement **to make up for something** is to give or do something in return for a loss or difficulty **to make up your mind** is to decide

make noun
a brand of goods; something made by a particular firm • What make of car is that?

make-believe noun
make-believe is pretending or imagining things

makeshift *adjective*
used because you have nothing better • *We'll use the bed as a makeshift table.*

make-up *noun*
make-up is creams and powders for making your skin look beautiful or different

malaria *noun* (*say* ma-**lair**-i-a)
a tropical disease spread by mosquito bites, that causes fever

male *adjective*
of the sex that produces young by fertilizing the female's egg cells

male *noun*
a male person or animal

malevolent *adjective*
(*say* ma-**lev**-o-lent)
wanting to harm other people **malevolence** *noun*
malevolence is wanting to harm people
malevolently *adverb*

malice *noun*
malice is a desire to harm other people

malicious *adjective*
intending to do harm • *He had a malicious glint in his eye.*
maliciously *adverb*

mall *noun*
a large covered shopping centre

mallet *noun*
a large wooden hammer

malnutrition *noun*
malnutrition is bad health caused by not having enough food **malnourished** *adjective*
suffering from malnutrition

malt *noun*
malt is dried barley used in brewing and making vinegar

mammal *noun*
any animal of which the female gives birth to live young and can feed them with her own milk

mammoth *noun*
an extinct kind of hairy elephant with long curved tusks

mammoth *adjective*
huge

man *noun* (**men**)
1 a man is a grown-up male human being **2** a man is also any individual person • *No man is perfect.* **3** man is all the people in the world • *Look what harm man is doing to the environment.* **4** a man is one of the pieces used in a board game

man *verb* (**manning, manned**)
to man something is to supply people to work it • *Man the pumps!*

manage *verb*
1 to manage something is to be able to do it although it is difficult **2** to manage a shop or factory or other business is to be in charge of it

manageable *adjective*
able to be managed or done

management *noun*
1 management is being in charge of something **2** the management of a business is the people in charge of it

manager *noun*
a person who manages a business or part of it

manageress *noun*
a woman manager of a shop or restaurant

mane *noun*
the long hair along the back of the neck of a horse or lion

manger *noun* (*say* **mayn**-jer)
a trough in a stable for animals to feed from

mangle *verb*
to mangle something is to crush or twist it so it is badly damaged

mango *noun* (**mangoes**)
a juicy tropical fruit with yellow flesh

manhole *noun*
a hole, usually with a cover, through which a person can get into a sewer or boiler to inspect or repair it

mania *noun*
1 mania is violent madness **2** a mania is a strong enthusiasm • *They have a mania for sport.*

maniac *noun*
a person who acts in a violent and wild way

manic *adjective*
manic behaviour is busy and excited

manipulate *verb*
1 to manipulate something is to handle it skilfully
2 to manipulate someone is to get them to do what you want by treating them cleverly **manipulation** *noun*
manipulating something or someone **manipulator** *noun*
a person who manipulates something or someone

mankind *noun*
mankind is all the people in the world • *This is a discovery for the good of all mankind.*

manly *adjective* (**manlier, manliest**)
1 strong or brave **2** suitable for a man or like a man
manliness *noun*

manner *noun*
the way that something happens or is done

manners *plural noun*
a person's manners are how they behave with other people; behaving politely

manoeuvre *noun*
(*say* ma-**noo**-ver)
a skilful or clever action

manoeuvre *verb*
1 to manoeuvre something is to move it skilfully into position **2** to manoeuvre is to move skilfully or cleverly
manoeuvrable *adjective* easy to move into position

manor *noun*
a large important house in the country

mansion *noun*
a grand house

manslaughter *noun*
(*say* **man**-slaw-ter)
manslaughter is the crime of killing someone without meaning to

mantelpiece *noun*
a shelf above a fireplace

manual *adjective*
manual work is work you do with your hands; manual equipment is equipment used with your hands
manually *adverb* you do something manually when you use your hands to do it

manual *noun*
a handbook or book of instructions

manufacture *verb*
to manufacture things is to make them with machines, usually in a factory
manufacturer *noun* a business that manufactures things

manure *noun*
animal dung added to the soil to make it more fertile

manuscript *noun*
something written or typed before it has been printed

many *adjective* (**more, most**)
large in number • *There were many people at the party.* • *How many potatoes do you want?*

many
a large number of people or things • *Many of them wanted to stay.*

Maori *noun* (*say* **mow**-ri)
1 a member of the aboriginal people of New Zealand **2** their language

map *noun*
a diagram of part or all of the earth's surface, showing features such as towns, mountains, and rivers

map *verb* (**mapping, mapped**)
to map an area is to make a map of it

maple *noun*
a tree with broad leaves

mar *verb* (**marring, marred**)
to mar something is to spoil it

marathon *noun*
a long-distance running race on roads, usually 26 miles (42 kilometres) long

marble *noun*
1 a marble is a small glass ball used in games **2** marble is a hard kind of limestone that is polished and used for building or sculpture

marbles

March *noun*
the third month of the year

march *verb*
1 to march is to walk with regular steps **2** to march someone is to make them walk somewhere • *He marched them up the hill.*

march *noun*
1 a march is a large group of people marching, sometimes to protest about something **2** a march is also a piece of music suitable for marching to

mare *noun*
a female horse or donkey

margarine *noun*
(*say* mar-ja-**reen**)
margarine is a soft creamy food used like butter, made from animal or vegetable fats

margin *noun*
1 the empty space between the edge of a page and the writing or pictures **2** the small difference between two scores or prices • *She won by a narrow margin.*

marine *adjective* (*say* ma-**reen**)
to do with the sea

marine *noun*
a soldier trained to serve on land and sea

marionette *noun*
a puppet that you work by strings or wires

mark *noun*
1 a spot, dot, line, or stain on something **2** a number or letter put on a piece of work to show how good it is **3** a special feature or sign of something • *They kept a minute's silence as a mark of respect.* **4** the place from which you start a race • *On your marks, get set, go!*

mark *verb*
1 to mark something is to put a mark on it **2** to mark a piece of work is to give it a number or letter to show how good it is **3** in football or hockey, to mark a player on the other team is to keep close to them to stop them getting the ball **4** to mark something said is to take note of it • *Mark my words!*

market *noun*
1 a place where things are bought and sold, usually from stalls in the open air **2** a demand for goods • *There is hardly any market for typewriters now.*

marksman *noun* (**marksmen**)
an expert in shooting at a target **marksmanship** *noun* the skill of shooting at a target

marmalade *noun*
jam made from oranges or lemons

maroon *verb*
to maroon someone is to abandon them in a place far away from other people • *He was shipwrecked and marooned on a desert island.*

marquee *noun* (*say* mar-**kee**)
a large tent used for a party or exhibition

marriage *noun*
1 marriage is the state of being married **2** a marriage is a wedding

marrow *noun*
1 a marrow is a large green or yellow vegetable with a hard skin **2** marrow is the soft substance inside your bones

marry *verb* (**marries, marrying, married**)
1 to marry someone is to become their husband or wife **2** to marry two people is to perform a marriage ceremony

marsh *noun*
a low-lying area of very wet ground **marshy** *adjective* marshy ground is low-lying and very wet

marshal *noun*
1 an official who supervises a contest or ceremony **2** a law officer in the USA

marshmallow *noun*
marshmallow is a soft spongy sweet

marsupial *noun*
(*say* mar-**soo**-pi-al)
an animal such as a kangaroo, wallaby, or koala. The female has a pouch for carrying her young.

martial arts *plural noun*
martial arts are fighting sports such as karate and judo

martyr *noun* (*say* **mar**-ter)
someone who is killed or suffers because of their beliefs **martyrdom** *noun* when someone is killed or suffers because of their beliefs

marvel *noun*
a wonderful thing

marvel *verb* (**marvelling, marvelled**)
to marvel at something is to be filled with wonder or astonishment by it

marvellous *adjective*
wonderful **marvellously** *adverb*

marzipan *noun*
marzipan is a soft sweet food made from almonds and sugar, sometimes put on the top of cakes

mascot *noun*
a person, animal, or object that people think will bring them good luck

masculine *adjective*
1 to do with men or like men; suitable for men **2** in some languages, belonging to the class of words that includes words referring to men **masculinity** *noun* being masculine

mash *verb*
to mash something is to crush it into a soft mass

mash *noun*
(*informal*) mashed potatoes

mask *noun*
a covering that you wear over your face to disguise or protect it

mask *verb*
1 to mask your face is to cover it with a mask **2** to mask something is to hide it

masks

mason *noun*
someone who builds or works with stone

masonry *noun*
masonry is the stone parts of a building

149

Mass noun
the Communion service in a Roman Catholic church

mass noun
1 a large amount of something **2** a lump or heap **3** (in science) the amount of matter in an object, measured in grams
the masses the ordinary people

mass verb
to mass is to collect into a mass • People were massing in the square.

massacre verb (say **mas**-a-ker)
to massacre people is to kill a large number of them

massacre noun
the killing of a large number of people

massage verb (say **mas**-ahzh)
to massage the body is to rub and press it to make it less stiff or less painful

massage noun
massaging someone's body

massive adjective
very big; large and heavy
massively adverb hugely

mast noun
a tall pole that holds up a ship's sails or a flag or aerial

master noun
1 a man who is in charge of something **2** a male teacher **3** someone who is very good at what they do, such as a great artist or composer **4** something from which copies are made
Master (old use) a title put before a boy's name

master verb
1 to master a subject or skill is to learn it completely **2** to master a fear or difficulty is to control it • She succeeded in mastering her fear of heights.

mastermind noun
1 a very clever person **2** someone who organizes a scheme or crime

masterpiece noun
1 an excellent piece of work **2** someone's best piece of work

mastery noun
mastery is complete control or knowledge of something • He has a complete mastery of the art of fencing.

mat noun
1 a small piece of material that partly covers a floor **2** a small piece of material put on a table to protect the surface

match¹ noun
a small thin stick with a small amount of chemical at one end that gives a flame when rubbed on something rough

match² noun
1 a game or contest between two teams or players **2** one person or thing that is equal or similar to another • Can you find a match for this sock? **3** a marriage

match² verb
1 to match another person or thing is to be equal to them **2** one thing matches another when it goes well with it • Your jacket matches your shoes.

mate¹ noun
1 a friend or companion **2** one of a pair of animals that produce young together **3** one of the officers on a ship

mate¹ verb
animals mate when they come together in order to have offspring

mate² noun
checkmate in chess

material noun
1 anything used for making something else **2** cloth or fabric

maternal adjective
to do with a mother; motherly

maternity noun
maternity is having a baby; motherhood

mathematician noun
(say math-em-a-**tish**-an)
an expert in mathematics

mathematics noun
mathematics is the study of numbers, measurements, and shapes
mathematical adjective
to do with mathematics

maths noun (informal)
maths is mathematics

matinee noun (say **mat**-i-nay)
an afternoon performance at a theatre or cinema

matrimony noun
(say **mat**-ri-mo-ni)
matrimony is marriage
matrimonial adjective to do with marriage

matt adjective
not shiny • The wall was decorated with matt paint.

matted adjective
tangled

matter noun
1 something you need to think about or do • It is a serious matter. **2** a substance • Peat consists mainly of vegetable matter. **a matter of fact** something true **no matter** it is not important **what's the matter?** what is wrong?

matter verb
to matter is to be important

mattress noun
a thick layer of soft or springy

material covered in cloth and used on a bed

mature adjective
1 fully grown or developed **2** behaving in a sensible adult manner
maturity noun maturity is being fully grown or behaving in a sensible adult manner

mature verb
to become fully grown or developed

maximum noun (**maxima**)
the greatest number or amount possible • The maximum is 10.

maximum adjective
the greatest possible
• The maximum speed is 60 miles per hour.

May noun
the fifth month of the year

may verb (past tense **might**)
1 may means to be allowed to • May I have a sweet? **2** may also means that something will possibly happen or has possibly happened • He may come tomorrow. • He might have missed the train.

maybe adverb
perhaps

mayonnaise noun
(say may-on-**ayz**)
mayonnaise is a creamy sauce made from eggs, oil, and vinegar, and used on salads

mayor noun
the person in charge of the council in a town or city

mayoress noun
a woman who is a mayor

maze noun
a complicated arrangement of paths or lines to follow your way through as a game or puzzle

me pronoun
a word used for I, usually when it is the object of a sentence, or when it comes after a preposition • She likes me. • She gave it to me.

meadow noun
a field of grass

meagre adjective (say **meeg**-er)
very little; barely enough
• They had already used up their meagre savings.

meal noun
a meal is the food eaten at one time, such as breakfast, lunch, or dinner

mean¹ verb (**meaning, meant**)
1 to mean something is to have that as its explanation or equivalent, or to convey that as its sense • What does this word mean? **2** to mean to do something is to intend to do it • I meant to tell him, but I forgot.

mean² *adjective*
1 not generous; selfish • *What a mean man.* **2** unkind or spiteful • *That was a mean trick.* **meanly** *adverb* **meanness** *noun*
mean³ *adjective*
(*in mathematics*) average • *Work out the mean temperature.*
meaning *noun*
what something means **meaningless** *adjective* having no meaning or purpose
means *noun*
a means of doing something is a way or method of doing it **by all means** certainly **by means of something** using something or with something **by no means** not at all
means *plural noun*
money or other resources for doing things
meantime *noun*
in the meantime meanwhile
meanwhile *adverb*
while something else is happening • *I'll cut the cake up. Meanwhile, you get the plates out.*
measles *plural noun*
measles is an infectious disease that causes small red spots on the skin
measure *verb*
1 to measure something is to find out how big it is **2** to measure (for example) six feet is to be six feet long
measure *noun*
1 a unit used for measuring something **2** a device used for measuring **3** the size of something **4** something done for a particular purpose; a law or rule • *We are bringing in new measures to deal with bullies.*
measurement *noun*
1 a measurement is the size or length of something **2** measurement is when you measure something
meat *noun*
meat is animal flesh that is cooked as food **meaty** *adjective* full of meat or like meat
mechanic *noun*
someone who maintains and repairs machinery
mechanical *adjective*
1 to do with machines **2** done without thinking about it **mechanically** *adverb* you do something mechanically when you do it without thinking about it
mechanism *noun*
1 the moving parts of a machine **2** the way a machine works

medal

medal
noun
a piece of metal shaped like a coin, star, or cross, given to someone for bravery or for achieving something • *She won two Olympic gold medals.*
medallist *noun*
a winner of a medal
meddle *verb*
to meddle in something is to interfere in it **meddler** *noun* someone who interferes with something **meddlesome** *adjective* always interfering
media *plural noun* (*say* mee-di-a)
the plural of **medium²** **the media** newspapers and radio and television, which provide information about current events to the public
medical *adjective*
to do with the treatment of disease **medically** *adverb* by medical means
medicine *noun*
1 a medicine is a substance, usually swallowed, used to try to cure an illness **2** medicine is the treatment of disease and injuries **medicinal** *adjective* something is medicinal when it helps to cure an illness
medieval *adjective*
(*say* med-i-**ee**-val)
to do with the Middle Ages
mediocre *adjective*
(*say* meed-i-**oh**-ker)
only fairly good **mediocrity** *noun* being mediocre
meditate *verb*
to meditate is to think deeply and seriously, usually in silence **meditation** *noun* when someone meditates
medium¹ *adjective*
average; of middle size
medium² *noun*
1 (**media**) a thing in which something exists, moves, or is expressed • *Air is the medium in which sound travels.* • *Local radio is a good medium for traffic information.* **2** (**mediums**) someone who claims to communicate with the dead
meek *adjective*
quiet and obedient **meekly** *adverb* quietly and obediently **meekness** *noun*
meet *verb* (**meeting, met**)
1 to meet is to come together

from different places • *We all met in London.* • *There is a statue where the two roads meet.* **2** to meet someone is to come face to face with them, especially for the first time or by an arrangement • *I met her at a party.* • *I'll meet you at the station.* **3** to meet a bill or cost is to be able to pay it • *He is finding it difficult to meet all his debts.*
meeting *noun*
a time when people come together for a special purpose, often to discuss something
megabyte *noun*
(*in computing*) a unit that measures data or memory, roughly equal to one million bytes
megaphone *noun*
a funnel-shaped device for making someone's voice sound louder
melancholy *adjective*
sad and gloomy
mellow *adjective*
having a soft rich sound or colour
melody *noun* (**melodies**)
a tune, especially one that is pleasant to listen to **melodic** *adjective* having a tune that is pleasant to listen to
melon *noun*
a large juicy fruit with yellow or green skin
melt *verb*
1 to melt something solid is to make it liquid by heating it **2** to melt is to become liquid by heating **3** to melt, or to melt away, is to go away or disappear slowly • *The crowd gradually melted away.*
member *noun*
someone who belongs to a society or group **membership** *noun* being a member of a society or group
Member of Parliament *noun*
someone who has been elected by the people of an area to speak for them in Parliament
memorable *adjective*
1 worth remembering • *It was a memorable holiday.* **2** easy to remember • *He has a memorable name.* **memorably** *adverb*
memorial *noun*
something set up to remind people of a person or an event • *They passed a war memorial in the High Street.*
memorize *verb*
to memorize something is

to learn it and remember it exactly

memory noun (**memories**)
1 memory is the ability to remember things **2** a memory is something that you remember, usually something interesting or special **3** a computer's memory is the part where information is stored **to do something in memory of someone** or **something** is to do it in order to remind people of a person or an event

menace verb
to menace someone is to threaten them with harm or danger

menace noun
1 something that threatens people with harm or danger **2** an annoying person or thing

mend verb
to mend something that is broken or damaged is to make it as good as it was before

menstruation noun
menstruation is the natural flow of blood from a woman's womb, normally happening every 28 days **menstrual** adjective to do with menstruation

mental adjective
1 to do with the mind • mental arithmetic. **2** (informal) mad or crazy **mentally** adverb in your head or mind

mention verb
to mention someone or something is to speak about them briefly

mention noun
when someone or something is mentioned • Our school got a mention in the local paper.

menu noun (**menus**)
(say **men**-yoo)
1 a list of the food that is available in a restaurant or served at a meal **2** (in computing) a list of possible actions, displayed on a screen, from which you choose what you want a computer to do

mercenary noun (**mercenaries**)
a soldier hired to fight for a foreign country

merchandise noun
merchandise is goods for buying or selling

merchant noun
someone involved in trade

merciful adjective
showing mercy
mercifully adverb

merciless adjective
showing no mercy; cruel
mercilessly adverb

mercury noun (Hg)
mercury is a heavy silvery metal that is usually liquid, used in thermometers

mercy noun (**mercies**)
1 mercy is kindness or pity shown towards someone instead of harming them or punishing them **2** a mercy is something to be thankful for • Thank God for small mercies.

mere adjective
not more than • He's a mere child.

merely adverb
only; simply • I was merely repeating what he told me.

merge verb
1 to merge things is to combine or blend them **2** to merge is to be combined

meringue noun (say mer-**rang**)
a crisp cake made from the whites of eggs mixed with sugar and baked

merit noun
something that deserves praise • I can see the merits of this argument.

mermaid noun
in stories, a sea creature with a woman's body and a fish's tail instead of legs

merry adjective (**merrier, merriest**)
happy and cheerful **merrily** adverb **merriment** noun being happy and cheerful

merry-go-round noun
a large roundabout with horses and other things to ride on

mesh noun
mesh is material made like a net, with open spaces between the wire or threads

mess noun
1 something untidy or dirty **2** a difficult or confused situation **3** a place where soldiers or sailors eat their meals **to make a mess of something** is to do it very badly

mess verb
to mess about is to waste time behaving stupidly or doing things slowly • Stop messing about and give me a hand.
to mess something up is to do it very badly

message noun
a piece of information that one person sends to another

messenger noun
someone who carries a message

messy adjective (**messier, messiest**)
1 untidy or dirty **2** difficult or complicated • I'm

afraid it's a messy situation.
messily adverb

metal noun
a hard substance that melts when it is heated, such as gold, silver, copper, and iron **metallic** adjective like metal, especially sounding like it or shining like it

meteor noun (say **meet**-i-er)
a piece of rock or metal that moves through space and burns up as it enters the earth's atmosphere

meteorite noun (say **meet**-i-er-ryt)
the remains of a meteor that has landed on the earth

meteorology noun (say meet-i-er-**ol**-o-ji)
meteorology is the study of the weather **meteorological** adjective to do with meteorology **meteorologist** noun an expert on the weather

meter noun
a device for measuring something, especially for measuring how much of something has been used

method noun
a method is a way of doing something

methodical adjective (say mi-**thod**-i-kal)
done carefully and in a logical way **methodically** adverb

meticulous adjective
very careful and precise **meticulously** adverb

metre noun (say **meet**-er)
1 the main unit of length in the metric system, equal to 100 centimetres or about 39½ inches **2** a particular type of rhythm in poetry

metric system noun
a measuring system based on decimal units (the metre, litre, and gram)

mew verb
to make a sound like a cat

miaow verb (say mee-**ow**)
to make a sound like a cat

microbe noun (say **my**-krohb)
a tiny organism that you need a microscope to see

microchip noun
a very small piece of silicon working as an electric circuit, used in computers

microchip

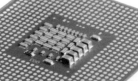

microphone noun
an electrical device that picks up sound waves for recording them or making them louder

microscope noun
(say **my**-kro-skohp)
a device with lenses that make tiny objects appear larger so you can study them

microscopic adjective
(say my-kro-**skop**-ik)
too small to be seen without a microscope; tiny

microwave noun
a kind of oven which heats things quickly by using energy in very short waves

microwave verb
to microwave food is to cook it in a microwave

mid adjective
in the middle of • The holiday is from mid-July to mid-August.

midday noun
the middle of the day; noon

middle noun
1 the middle of something is the place or part that is at the same distance from all its sides or edges or from both its ends 2 someone's waist

middle adjective
placed in the middle

middle-aged adjective
aged between about forty and sixty

Middle Ages noun
the period in history from about AD 1100 to 1500

Middle East noun
the countries to the east of the Mediterranean Sea, from Egypt to Iran

middle school noun
a school for children aged from about 9 to 13

midge noun
a small insect like a gnat

midnight noun
twelve o'clock at night

midst noun
to be in the midst of something is to be in the middle of it

midsummer noun
the middle of summer, when the days are longest

midway adverb
halfway

midwife noun (**midwives**)
a person trained to look after a woman who is giving birth to a baby

might[1]
past tense of **may**

might[2] noun
great power or strength

mighty adjective (**mightier, mightiest**) very strong or

powerful **mightily** adverb very much indeed • I was mightily relieved to see her.

migraine noun (say **mee**-grayn)
a severe kind of headache

migrant noun (say **my**-grant)
1 a person who moves from one place to another, usually to find work 2 a bird or animal that moves from one region to another

migrate verb (say my-**grayt**)
1 to migrate is to move from one place to another, usually to find work 2 birds migrate when they fly to a warmer region for the winter

migration noun migrating to another country

mild adjective
gentle; not harsh or severe

mildly adverb slightly
• She looked mildly surprised.

mildness noun

mile noun
a measure of distance, equal to 1,760 yards or about 1.6 kilometres

mileage noun
the number of miles you have travelled

milestone noun
1 a stone of a kind that used to be placed beside a road to mark the distance between towns 2 an important event in history or in a person's life

military adjective
to do with soldiers or the armed forces

milk noun
milk is a white liquid that female mammals produce in their bodies to feed to their young

milk verb
to milk a cow or other animal is to get milk from it

milkman noun (**milkmen**)
a person who delivers milk to people's houses

milk shake noun
a frothy drink of milk mixed with a sweet fruit flavouring

milky adjective (**milkier, milkiest**)
1 like milk; white 2 made with a lot of milk

mill noun
1 a building with machinery for grinding corn to make flour 2 a factory for making materials, such as a paper mill or a steel mill 3 a machine for grinding something such as coffee or pepper

mill verb
1 to mill something is to grind or crush it in a mill 2 people

mill or mill about when they move in a confused crowd

millennium noun
a period of 1,000 years

miller noun
someone who runs a flour mill

milligram noun
one thousandth of a gram

millilitre noun
one thousandth of a litre

millimetre noun
one thousandth of a metre

million noun
a thousand thousands (1,000,000) **millionth** adjective, noun 1,000,000th

millionaire noun
an extremely rich person who has at least a million pounds or dollars

mime verb
to mime is to tell a story by using movements of the body without speaking

mime noun
mime is the art of telling a story by using movements of the body without speaking

mimic verb
to mimic someone is to imitate them, especially to make people laugh **mimicry** noun imitating someone to make people laugh

mimic noun
a person who is good at imitating other people

minaret noun
a tall tower on a mosque

WORD ORIGIN

The word **minaret** comes from an Arabic word manara meaning 'lighthouse'.

mince noun
mince is meat that has been cut up into very small pieces

mince verb
to mince food is to cut it up into very small pieces **mincer** noun
a device for mincing food

mincemeat noun
mincemeat is a sweet mixture of currants, raisins, and chopped fruit, used in pies

mince pie noun
a pie containing mincemeat

mind noun
the ability of your brain to think, feel, understand, and remember; your thoughts and feelings to change your mind is to have a new opinion or make a different decision about something to have a good mind to do something is to intend to do it

mind verb
1 to mind something is to be bothered or upset about it • *I don't mind missing the party.* 2 to mind someone or something is to look after them for a time • *He was minding the baby.* 3 to mind, or to mind out, is to be careful or watch out for something • *Mind you don't trip on the step.*

mindless adjective
done without thinking; stupid or pointless

mine¹ adjective, pronoun
belonging to me • *That book is mine.*

mine² noun
1 a place where coal, metal, or precious stones are dug out of the ground 2 a type of bomb hidden under the ground or in the sea that explodes when anything touches it

mine² verb
1 to mine something is to dig it from a mine 2 to mine a place is to lay explosives in it

minefield noun
an area where explosive mines have been laid

miner noun
someone who works in a mine

mineral noun
1 a hard substance that can be dug out of the ground, such as coal and iron ore 2 a cold fizzy drink

mineral water noun
mineral water is water that comes from a natural spring. It can be fizzy or still.

mingle verb
1 things mingle when they become mixed together 2 to mingle things is to mix or blend them

miniature adjective
(say **min**-i-cher)
very small; made in a much smaller size than usual

minibus noun
a small bus with seats for about ten people

minim noun
a musical note equal to two crotchets or half a semibreve, written ♩

minimum noun (**minima**)
the smallest number or amount possible • *We want the minimum of fuss.*

minimum adjective
least or smallest
• *The minimum charge is £5.*

minister noun
1 a member of the government who is in charge of a department 2 a member of the clergy

ministry noun (**ministries**)
1 a government department • *the Ministry of Defence* 2 the work of a minister in the church

mink noun
1 a mink is a small animal rather like a stoat 2 mink is this animal's valuable brown fur

minnow noun
a tiny freshwater fish

minor adjective
not very important, especially when compared to something else

minority noun (**minorities**)
(say myn-**o**-ri-ti)
1 the smaller part of a group of people or things • *There was a minority who wanted to leave.* 2 a small group that is different from others

minstrel noun
a travelling singer and musician in the Middle Ages

mint¹ noun
1 mint is a green plant with strong-smelling leaves used for flavouring 2 a mint is a sweet flavoured with peppermint

mint² noun
a place where a country's coins are made **to be in mint condition** is to be new, as if it had just been made

mint² verb
to mint coins is to make them

minus preposition
1 less; with the next number taken away • *Eight minus two equals six (8-2 = 6).* 2 less than zero • *The temperature is minus 5 degrees.*

minute¹ noun (say **min**-it)
1 one-sixtieth of an hour 2 (*informal*) a short time • *I'll be ready in a minute!*

minute² adjective (say my-**newt**)
1 tiny • *The insect was minute.* 2 very detailed • *He gave it a minute examination.* **minutely** adverb in a very detailed way

miracle noun
a wonderful or magical happening that cannot be explained **miraculous** adjective wonderful or magical **miraculously** adverb

mirage noun (say **mi**-rahzh)
something that seems to be visible but is not really there, like a lake in a desert

mirror noun
a sheet of glass painted with silver on the back so that it reflects things clearly

WORD ORIGIN

The word **mirror** comes from a Latin word *mirare* meaning 'to look at'.

mirth noun
mirth is laughter or cheerfulness

misbehave verb
to misbehave is to behave badly **misbehaviour** noun when someone behaves badly

miscarriage noun
a woman has a miscarriage when she gives birth to a baby before it is old enough to survive

miscellaneous adjective
(say mis-el-**ay**-ni-us)
a miscellaneous group is one that is made up of different kinds of thing

miscellany noun (**miscellanies**)
(say mis-**el**-an-ee)
a mixture of different things

mischief noun
mischief is naughty or troublesome behaviour

mischievous adjective
naughty or troublesome; full of mischief

miser noun
someone who stores money away and spends as little as they can **miserly** adjective hating to spend money

miserable adjective
1 very unhappy • *He felt miserable.* 2 unpleasant • *What miserable weather!* **miserably** adverb

misery noun (**miseries**)
1 misery is great unhappiness or suffering 2 (*informal*) a misery is someone who is always unhappy or complaining

misfire verb
1 a gun misfires when it fails to fire 2 a plan or idea or joke misfires when it goes wrong

misfit noun
someone who does not fit in well with other people

misfortune noun
1 a misfortune is an unlucky event or an accident 2 misfortune is bad luck

mishap noun (say **mis**-hap)
an unfortunate accident

misjudge verb
to misjudge someone or something is to form a wrong idea or opinion about them

mislay verb (**mislaying, mislaid**)
to mislay something is to lose it for a short time

mislead verb
to mislead someone is to give them a wrong idea or impression deliberately

misprint noun
a mistake in printing, such as a spelling mistake

Miss noun
a title you put before the name of a girl or unmarried woman

miss verb
1 to miss something is to fail to hit, reach, catch, see, hear, or find it • *The bullet missed him by inches.* • *I missed the last episode.* **2** to miss someone or something is to be sad because they are not with you • *I missed my sister when she was in hospital.* **3** to miss a train, bus, or plane is to arrive too late to catch it **4** to miss a lesson or other activity is to fail to attend it • *How many classes have you missed?* **5** to miss something is also to notice that it isn't where it should be • *When did you first miss your wallet?*

miss noun
not hitting, reaching, or catching something • *Was that shot a hit or a miss?*

missile noun
1 a weapon that is fired a long distance and explodes when it lands **2** an object thrown at someone

missing adjective
something is missing when it is lost or not in the proper place

mission noun
1 an important job that someone is sent to do or that someone feels they must do **2** a place or building where missionaries work

missionary noun (**missionaries**)
someone who goes to another country to spread a religious faith

misspell verb (**misspelling, misspelt** or **misspelled**)
to misspell a word is to spell it wrongly

mist noun
1 damp cloudy air like a thin fog **2** condensed water vapour on a window or mirror

mistake noun
something done or said wrongly

mistake verb (**mistaking, mistook, mistaken**)
to mistake one person or thing for another is to confuse them • *I'm sorry, I mistook you for someone else.*

mistaken adjective
to be mistaken is to be incorrect or wrong • *You are mistaken if you believe that.*
mistakenly adverb

mistletoe noun
mistletoe is a plant with green leaves and white berries in winter

mistreat verb
to mistreat someone is to treat them badly or unfairly
mistreatment noun treating someone badly or unfairly

mistress noun
1 a woman who is in charge of something **2** a woman who teaches in a school **3** the woman owner of a dog or other animal

mistrust verb
to mistrust someone or something is not to trust them

misty adjective (**mistier, mistiest**)
1 if it is misty outside there is a lot of mist **2** misty eyes are full of tears

misunderstand verb (**misunderstanding, misunderstood**)
to misunderstand something is to get a wrong idea or impression about it • *You misunderstood what I said.*
misunderstanding noun a wrong idea or impression

misuse verb (say mis-**yooz**)
to misuse something is to use it in the wrong way or treat it badly

misuse noun (say mis-**yooss**)
misuse is using something in the wrong way

mite noun
1 a tiny insect found in food **2** a small child

mitten noun
a kind of glove without separate parts for the fingers

mix verb
1 to mix different things is to stir or shake them together to make one thing **2** to mix is to get on well with other people • *She mixes well.* **to mix up people** or **things** is to confuse them **mixer** noun a machine for mixing food

mixed adjective
containing two or more kinds of things or people • *a bag of mixed nuts*

mixture noun
something made of different things mixed together

mix-up noun
a muddle or confused situation, especially one that ruins a plan

mm
short for millimetre or millimetres

moan noun
1 a long low sound, usually of suffering **2** a complaint or grumble

moan verb
1 to moan is to make a long low sound **2** to moan is also to complain or grumble

moat noun
a deep ditch round a castle, usually filled with water

mob noun
1 a large crowd of people who are hard to control **2** a gang

mob verb (**mobbing, mobbed**)
people mob someone when they crowd round them • *The singer was mobbed by her fans.*

mobile adjective
able to be moved or carried about easily **mobility** noun the ability to move easily from place to place

mobile noun
1 a decoration made to be hung up from threads so that it moves about in the air **2** (*informal*) a mobile phone

mobile phone noun
a telephone you can carry around with you

mock verb
to mock someone or something is to make fun of them **mockery** noun making fun of someone or something

mock adjective
not real or genuine • *They fought a mock battle.*

mode noun
the way that something is done • *Flying is the fastest mode of transport.*

model noun
1 a small copy of an object • *He makes models of aircraft.* **2** a particular version or design of something • *We saw the latest models at the motor show.* **3** someone who displays clothes by wearing them or who poses for an artist or photographer **4** someone or something worth copying or imitating

model adjective
1 being a small copy of something • *I'd like a model railway.* **2** being a good example for people to follow • *She was a model pupil.*

model verb (**modelling, modelled**)
1 to model something is to make it out of a material such as clay **2** to model one thing on another is to use the second thing as a pattern for the first • *The building is modelled on an Egyptian temple.* **3** to model, or to model clothes, is to work as an artist's model or a fashion model

modem noun
(*in computing*) a piece of

equipment that links a
computer to a telephone line

moderate *adjective*
(*say* **mod**-er-at)
a moderate amount or level is
not too little and not too much
moderately *adverb* fairly but
not very **moderation** *noun*
being moderate, not too little
and not too much

modern *adjective*
belonging to the present day or
recent times

modest *adjective*
1 not thinking or talking too
much about how good you are
2 quite small in amount • *Their
needs were modest.* **modestly**
adverb **modesty** *noun* being
modest

modify *verb* (**modifies,
modifying, modified**)
to modify something is to
change it slightly
modification *noun* a slight
change in something

module *noun* (*say* **mod**-yool)
a separate section or part of
something larger, such as a
spacecraft or building

moist *adjective*
slightly wet

moisten *verb* (*say* **moi**-sen)
to moisten something is to
make it slightly wet

moisture *noun*
moisture is tiny drops of water
in the air or on a surface

mole *noun*
1 a small furry animal that
digs holes under the ground
2 a small dark spot on the skin

molecule *noun* (*say* **mol**-i-kewl)
(*in science*) the smallest part
into which a substance can be
divided without changing its
chemical nature; a group of
atoms

molehill *noun*
a small pile of earth thrown
up by a mole **to make a
mountain out of a molehill**
is to give something too much
importance

mollusc *noun*
an animal with a soft body and
usually a hard shell, such as a
snail or an oyster

molten *adjective*
molten rock or metal has been
made into liquid by great heat
• *Molten lava flowed down the
side of the volcano.*

moment *noun*
1 a very short period of time
• *Wait a moment.* **2** a particular
time • *At that moment, all the
lights went out.*
at the moment now

momentous *adjective*
(*say* moh-**ment**-us)
very important

momentum *noun*
(*say* moh-**ment**-um)
momentum is the force
developed by something
moving • *The stone gained
momentum as it rolled down
the hill.*

monarch *noun*
a king, queen, emperor, or
empress ruling a country

monarchy *noun* (**monarchies**)
1 monarchy is rule by a
monarch **2** a monarchy is a
country ruled by a monarch

monastery *noun* (**monasteries**)
(*say* **mon**-a-ster-i)
a building where monks live
and work **monastic** *adjective* to
do with monks or monasteries

Monday *noun*
the second day of the week

money *noun*
money is coins and notes used
by people to buy things

mongrel *noun* (*say* **mung**-rel)
a dog of mixed breeds

monitor *noun*
1 a device used for checking
how something is working **2** a
computer or television screen

monitor *verb*
to monitor something or
someone is to watch or test
them to see how they are
working

monk *noun*
a member of a religious
community of men

monkey *noun* (**monkeys**)
1 an animal with long arms,
hands with thumbs, and a
tail **2** a mischievous person,
especially a child

monopolize *verb*
to monopolize something is
to keep it to yourself without
letting other people use it

monopoly *noun* (**monopolies**)
a situation where one person
or group is the only one to
sell something that people
need

monotonous *adjective*
(*say* mon-**ot**-on-us)
boring because it does not
change • *This is monotonous
work.* **monotonously** *adverb*

monotony *noun* when
something is boring because
it does not change; dullness

monsoon *noun*
a strong wind in and around the
Indian Ocean, bringing heavy
rain in summer

monster *noun*
a huge frightening creature

monstrous *adjective*
1 like a monster; huge **2** very
shocking or cruel • *It was a
monstrous crime.* **monstrosity**
noun a monstrous thing

month *noun*
one of the twelve parts into
which a year is divided

monthly *adjective, adverb*
something happens monthly
when it happens every month

monument *noun*
a statue, building, or column
put up to remind people of
some person or event

moo *verb*
to make the sound of a cow

mood *noun*
the way someone feels at a
particular time • *She is in a
cheerful mood.*

moody *adjective* (**moodier,
moodiest**)
1 gloomy or bad-tempered
2 likely to have sudden changes
of mood **moodily** *adverb*
moodiness *noun*

moon *noun*
1 the natural satellite which
orbits the earth and shines
in the sky at night **2** a similar
object which orbits another
planet

moonlight *noun*
moonlight is the light reflected
from the moon **moonlit**
adjective a moonlit night is
one that is lit by the moon

moor[1] *noun*
an area of rough land covered
with bracken and bushes

moor[2] *verb*
to moor a boat is to tie it up to
the land

moorhen *noun*
a small water bird

moose *noun* (**moose**)
a North American elk

mop *noun*
a piece of soft material on the
end of a stick, used for cleaning
floors or dishes

mop *verb* (**mopping, mopped**)
to mop something is to clean it
with a mop **to mop something
up** is to clear away spilt liquid

mope *verb*
to mope is to be miserable
and not interested in doing
anything

moped *noun* (*say* **moh**-ped)
a kind of small motorcycle with
pedals

moral *adjective*
1 to do with people's behaviour
and what is right and wrong
2 being or doing good and what
is right • *We are expected to lead
moral lives.* **morality** *noun* how

moral someone or something is **morally** adverb

moral noun
a lesson taught by a story or event

morale noun (say mo-**rahl**)
morale is confidence or courage

morals plural noun
standards of behaviour

morbid adjective
thinking about gloomy or unpleasant things such as death **morbidly** adverb

more adjective
greater in number or amount
• We need more money. • She is more beautiful.

more noun
a larger number or amount
• I want more.

more adverb
1 to a greater extent • You must work more. **2** again • I'll tell you once more. **more or less** almost; approximately • I've more or less finished the work. • The repairs cost £100, more or less.

morning noun
the early part of the day before noon or before lunchtime

morphine noun (say **mor**-feen)
morphine is a drug made from opium, used to relieve pain

morris dance noun
a traditional English dance performed by people in costume with ribbons and bells

Morse code noun
a code for sending messages by radio, using dots and dashes to represent letters and numbers

morsel noun
a small piece of food

mortal adjective
1 certain to die • All men are mortal. **2** causing death
• He received a mortal wound.
mortality noun being certain to die **mortally** adverb
someone who is mortally wounded or ill is certain to die from their wounds or illness

mortar noun
1 mortar is a mixture of sand, cement, and water used in building to stick bricks together **2** a mortar is a small cannon

mortgage noun (say **mor**-gij)
an arrangement to borrow money to buy a house, repaid over many years

mortuary noun (**mortuaries**)
a place where dead bodies are kept before they are buried or cremated

mosaic noun (say moh-**zay**-ik)
a picture or design made from small coloured pieces of glass or stone

mosque noun (say mosk)
a building where Muslims worship

mosquito noun (**mosquitoes**) (say mos-**kee**-toh)
an insect that sucks blood and carries disease

moss noun
a plant that grows in damp places and has no flowers **mossy** adjective covered in moss

mosquito

most adjective
greatest in number or amount
• Most people came by bus.

most noun
the greatest number or amount
• They've eaten most of the food.

most adverb
1 more than any other
• I liked this book most.
2 very; extremely
• It was most amusing.

mostly adverb
mainly

motel noun (say moh-**tel**)
a hotel for people travelling by road, with parking near the rooms

moth noun
an insect rather like a butterfly, that usually flies around at night

mother noun
your female parent

mother-in-law noun
the mother of your husband or wife

motherly adjective
kind or tender like a mother

motion noun
a way of moving; movement

motionless adjective
not moving; still

motive noun
a person's motive is what makes them do something

motor noun
a machine that provides power to drive machinery

motorbike noun
(informal) a motorcycle

motorcycle noun
a two-wheeled vehicle with a petrol engine and a saddle for the rider
motorcyclist noun someone who rides a motorcycle

motorist noun
someone who drives a car

motorway noun
a wide road with two or more lanes for fast long-distance traffic

mottled adjective
marked with spots or patches of colour

motto noun (**mottoes**)
1 a short saying used as a guide for behaviour
• His motto was 'Do your best'.
2 a short verse or riddle found inside a cracker

mould¹ noun
a mould is a container for making liquid things like jelly or plaster form a special shape when they harden

mould¹ verb
to mould something is to make it have a particular shape or character

mould² noun
mould is a furry growth that appears on some damp surfaces or stale food

mouldy adjective (**mouldier, mouldiest**)
something is mouldy when it has mould on it

moult verb (say mohlt)
animals or birds moult when they lose hair or feathers

mound noun
a pile of earth or stones; a small hill

mount verb
1 to mount a horse or bicycle is to get on it so that you can ride it **2** to mount is to increase in amount • The excitement was mounting. **3** to mount a picture or photograph is to put it in a frame or album in order to display it

mount noun
1 a mountain, especially in names such as Mount Everest
2 something on which a picture or photograph is mounted **3** an animal for someone to ride on

mountain noun
1 a very high hill **2** a large amount • We've got a mountain of work to do. **mountainous** adjective a mountainous place has a lot of mountains

mountaineer noun
someone who climbs mountains
mountaineering noun the sport of climbing mountains

mourn verb
to mourn is to be sad, especially because someone has died **mourner** noun
mourners are the people who go to a funeral, especially the family and friends of the person who has died

157

mournful *adjective*
sad and sorrowful
mournfully *adverb*
mouse *noun* (**mice**)
1 a small animal with a long tail and a pointed nose 2 a small device that you move around with your hand to control the movements of a cursor on a computer screen
mousse *noun* (*say* mooss)
1 a creamy pudding flavoured with chocolate or fruit 2 a frothy creamy substance that you use to style your hair
moustache *noun* (*say* mus-**tahsh**)
a strip of hair that a man grows above his upper lip
mouth *noun*
1 the part of the face that opens for eating and speaking 2 the place where a river flows into the sea 3 an opening or outlet
mouthful *noun*
an amount of food you put in your mouth
mouth organ *noun*
a small musical instrument you play by blowing and sucking while passing it along your lips
mouthpiece *noun*
the part of a musical instrument or other device that you put to your mouth
movable *adjective*
able to be moved
move *verb*
1 to move something is to take it from one place to another 2 to move is to go from one place to another 3 to move someone is to affect their feelings • *Their story moved us deeply.*
move *noun*
1 a movement 2 a player's turn in a game **to get a move on** (*informal*) is to hurry up **to be on the move** is to be moving or making progress
movement *noun*
1 movement is moving or being moved 2 a movement is a group of people working together to achieve something 3 a movement is also one of the main parts of a long piece of classical music such as a symphony
movie *noun*
a cinema film

moving *adjective*
making you feel strong emotion, especially sadness or pity
mow *verb* (**mowing, mowed, mown**)
to mow grass is to cut it with a machine **to mow people down** is to knock them down and kill them **mower** *noun* a machine for mowing grass
MP
short for *Member of Parliament*
m.p.h.
short for *miles per hour*
Mr *noun* (*say* **mis**-ter)
a title you put before a man's name
Mrs *noun* (*say* **mis**-iz)
a title you put before a married woman's name
Ms *noun* (*say* miz)
a title you put before a woman's name, whether or not she is married
much *adjective*
existing in a large amount • *There is much work to do.*
much *noun*
a large amount of something • *£5 is not very much.*
much *adverb*
greatly; considerably • *They came, much to my surprise.*
muck *noun*
1 muck is farmyard manure 2 (*informal*) muck is dirt or filth
muck *verb*
(*informal*) **to muck about** or **muck around** is to behave stupidly or idly **to muck something up** is to do it very badly
mucky *adjective* (**muckier, muckiest**)
dirty or messy
mud *noun*
mud is wet soft earth **muddy** *adjective* covered with mud
muddle *verb*
1 to muddle things is to mix them up 2 to muddle someone is to confuse them
muddle *noun*
a confusion or mess • *I've got these papers in a bit of a muddle.*
mudguard *noun*
a curved cover fixed over a bicycle wheel to stop mud and water being thrown up on to the rider
muesli *noun* (*say* **mooz**-li)
muesli is a breakfast food made of cereals, nuts, and dried fruit

muffle *verb*
1 to muffle something is to cover or wrap it to protect it or keep it warm 2 to muffle a sound is to make it quieter by covering the place that it is coming from
mug *noun*
a large cup, usually used without a saucer
mug *verb* (**mugging, mugged**)
to mug someone is to attack and rob them in the street **mugger** *noun* a person who attacks and robs someone in the street
muggy *adjective* (**muggier, muggiest**)
a muggy day is unpleasantly warm and damp
mule *noun*
an animal that is the offspring of a male donkey and a female horse
multiple *adjective*
having many parts
multiple *noun*
a number that can be divided exactly by another number • *30 and 50 are multiples of 10.*
multiply *verb* (**multiplies, multiplying, multiplied**)
1 to multiply a number is to add it to itself a certain number of times • *Five multiplied by four equals twenty (5 x 4 = 20).* 2 to multiply is to increase or become many • *His doubts started to multiply.* **multiplication** *noun* multiplication is when you multiply numbers
multiracial *adjective* (*say* mul-ti-**ray**-shal)
a multiracial area has people living there of many different races
multitude *noun*
a very large number of people or things
mum *noun*
(*informal*) mother
mumble *verb*
to mumble is to speak softly and unclearly
mummy *noun* (**mummies**)
in ancient Egypt, a dead body wrapped in cloth and treated with oils for burial

mummy

mumps *noun*
mumps is an infectious disease that makes your neck swell painfully
munch *verb*
to munch food is to chew it noisily
mural *noun*
a picture painted on a wall
murder *verb*
to murder someone is to kill them deliberately
murderer *noun* someone who commits murder
murder *noun*
murder is the deliberate killing of someone
murky *adjective* (**murkier, murkiest**)
dark and gloomy
murmur *noun*
a low or soft continuous sound, especially of people speaking
murmur *verb*
to murmur is to speak softly with a low continuous sound
muscle *noun*
a bundle of fibres that can stretch or tighten to make a part of your body move
muscular *adjective*
having strong muscles
museum *noun*
a place where interesting old or valuable objects are displayed for people to see
mushroom *noun*
a fungus with a dome-shaped top, especially the kind that you can eat
music *noun*
1 music is pleasant or interesting sounds made by instruments or by the voice **2** music is also a system of printed or written symbols for making this kind of sound
musical *adjective*
1 to do with music **2** good at music or interested in it
musically *adverb*
musical *noun*
a play or film with music and songs
musician *noun*
someone who plays a musical instrument, especially for a living
musket *noun*
an old type of rifle
Muslim *noun* (*say* **muuz**-lim)
someone who follows religious teachings of Muhammad, as set out in the Koran
muslin *noun*
fine cotton cloth
mussel *noun*
a black shellfish, often found sticking to rocks

must *verb*
a word used with another verb to show **1** that someone has to do something • *I must go home soon.* **2** that something is certain • *You must be joking!*
mustard *noun*
mustard is a yellow paste or powder used to give food a hot taste
muster *verb*
to muster something is to assemble or gather it together • *He put all the enthusiasm he could muster into his voice.*
musty *adjective* (**mustier, mustiest**)
smelling or tasting mouldy or stale **mustiness** *noun*
mute *adjective*
not speaking or able to speak
mutely *adverb* without speaking
mutilate *verb*
to mutilate something is to damage it by breaking or cutting off part of it **mutilation** *noun* when someone damages something by breaking or cutting off part of it
mutiny *noun* (**mutinies**) (*say* **mew**-tin-i)
a rebellion by sailors or soldiers against their officers
mutinous *adjective* rebellious; taking part in a mutiny
mutiny *verb* (**mutinies, mutinying, mutinied**) (*say* **mew**-tin-i)
to mutiny is to take part in a mutiny
mutter *verb*
to mutter is to speak in a low quiet voice that is difficult to understand
mutton *noun*
mutton is meat from an adult sheep
mutual *adjective* (*say* **mew**-tew-al)
given or done to each other • *They have mutual respect for one another.*
mutually *adverb* equally to two or more people • *Let's arrange a mutually convenient time to meet.*
muzzle *noun*
1 an animal's nose and mouth **2** a cover put over an animal's nose and mouth so that it cannot bite **3** the open end of a gun
muzzle *verb*
to muzzle an animal is to put a muzzle on it
my *adjective*
belonging to me • *This is my book.*

myself *pronoun*
me and nobody else, used to refer back to the person who is speaking • *I have hurt myself.*
by myself on my own; alone • *I did the work all by myself.*
mysterious *adjective*
full of mystery; strange and puzzling **mysteriously** *adverb*
mystery *noun* (**mysteries**)
something strange or puzzling • *Exactly why the ship sank is a mystery.*
mystify *verb* (**mystifies, mystifying, mystified**)
to mystify someone is to puzzle them very much
mystification *noun*
mystification is being mystified
myth *noun*
1 an old story about gods and heroes in ancient times **2** an untrue story or belief • *It is a myth that carrots make you see better.*
mythical *adjective*
imaginary; only found in myths
mythology *noun*
mythology is a collection of myths or the study of myths
mythological *adjective*
mythological creatures or characters are found in myths

Nn

nab *verb* (**nabbing, nabbed**)
(*informal*) to nab someone is to catch or grab them
nag *verb* (**nagging, nagged**)
to nag someone is to keep criticizing them or complaining to them
nail *noun*
1 the hard covering on the end of one of your fingers or toes **2** a small, sharp piece of metal used to fix pieces of wood together
nail *verb*
to nail something is to fasten it with a nail or nails
naked *adjective* (*say* **nay**-kid)
without any clothes or coverings on **to look at something with the naked eye** is to look at it with your eyes without the help of a telescope or microscope
nakedness *noun*
name *noun*
what you call a person or thing
name *verb*
1 to name someone or something is to give them a

a
b
c
d
e
f
g
h
i
j
k
l
m
n
o
p
q
r
s
t
u
v
w
x
y
z

name 2 to name someone or something is to say what they are called • *Can you name these plants?*

nameless *adjective*
1 not having a name **2** not named or identified • *The culprit shall be nameless.*

namely *adverb*
that is to say • *I will invite two friends, namely Vicky and Tom.*

nanny *noun* (**nannies**)
1 a woman whose job is to look after small children **2** (*informal*) a grandmother

nap *noun*
a short sleep

napkin *noun*
a piece of cloth or paper to keep your clothes clean or wipe your lips at meals

nappy *noun* (**nappies**)
a piece of cloth or a paper pad put round a baby's bottom

narrate *verb*
to narrate a story or experiences is to tell them to someone • *She narrated her adventures in South America.*
narration *noun* telling a story

narrative *noun*
a story or account that someone tells

narrator *noun*
the person who is telling a story

narrow *adjective*
1 not wide **2** with only a small margin of error or safety • *We all had a narrow escape.*
narrowly *adverb* only just • *She narrowly escaped injury.*

narrow-minded *adjective*
not liking or understanding other people's ideas or beliefs

nasal *adjective*
to do with the nose

nasty *adjective* (**nastier, nastiest**)
not pleasant; unkind **nastily** *adverb* **nastiness** *noun*

nation *noun*
1 a large number of people who have the same history, language, and customs, and live in the same part of the world • *The Czechs are a very musical nation.* **2** a country and the people who live there • *Athletes from 16 nations took part in the tournament.*

national *adjective*
belonging to a nation or country **nationally** *adverb* over the whole of a country

nationality *noun* (**nationalities**)
the nation someone belongs to • *What is her nationality?*

nationwide *adjective, adverb*
over the whole of a country

native *noun*
a person born in a particular place • *He is a native of Sweden.*

native *adjective*
of the country where you were born • *English is my native language.*

Native American *noun*
one of the original inhabitants of North or South America

Nativity *noun* (*say* na-**tiv**-i-ti)
the Nativity is the birth of Jesus Christ

natural *adjective*
1 made or done by nature, not by people or machines **2** normal; not surprising • *It was only natural that she was nervous.* **3** belonging to someone from birth • *He has plenty of natural ability.* **4** in music, not sharp or flat

natural *noun*
1 a natural note in music; a sign (♮) that shows a note is natural **2** someone who is naturally good at something • *She's a natural at juggling.*

natural history *noun*
natural history is the study of plants and animals

naturalist *noun*
someone who studies natural history

naturally *adverb*
1 in a natural way • *The gas is produced naturally.* **2** as you would expect • *Naturally I will pay your train fare.*

nature *noun*
1 nature is everything in the world that was not made by people, such as plants, animals, mountains, and rivers **2** a person's or thing's nature is the qualities or characteristics they have • *She has a loving nature.* **3** a nature is a kind or sort of thing • *He likes things of that nature.*

nature reserve *noun*
an area of land set aside to keep wild life

naughty *adjective* (**naughtier, naughtiest**)
not behaving as you should; disobedient or rude
naughtily *adverb*
naughtiness *noun*

nausea *noun*
nausea is a feeling of sickness or disgust **nauseous** *adjective* feeling sick

nautical *adjective*
to do with ships or sailors

naval *adjective*
to do with a navy

nave *noun*
the main central part of a church

navel *noun*
the small hollow at the front of your stomach, where the umbilical cord was attached

navigate *verb*
to navigate is to make sure that an aircraft, ship, or vehicle is going in the right direction
navigation *noun* making sure that an aircraft, ship, or vehicle is going in the right direction
navigator *noun* a person who navigates

navy *noun* (**navies**)
1 a fleet of ships and the people trained to use them **2** dark blue

near *adverb, adjective*
not far away **near by** at a place not far away • *They live near by.*

near *preposition*
not far away from something • *She lives near the town.*

near *verb*
to near a place is to come close to it • *The ships were nearing the harbour.*

nearby *adjective*
near; not far away • *We live in a nearby town.*

nearly *adverb*
almost • *It was nearly midnight.* **not nearly** not at all • *There is not nearly enough food.*

neat *adjective*
1 tidy and carefully arranged **2** skilfully done • *That was a neat goal.* **3** without water added • *They were drinking neat orange juice.* **neatly** *adverb* **neatness** *noun*

necessarily *adverb*
for certain; definitely • *It won't necessarily cost you a lot.*

necessary *adjective*
needed very much; essential

necessity *noun* (**necessities**)
1 necessity is need • *There is no necessity for you to come too.* **2** a necessity is something needed • *We have brought all the necessities for a picnic.*

neck *noun*
1 the part of the body that joins the head to the shoulders **2** a narrow part of something, especially of a bottle **to be neck and neck** is to be almost exactly together in a race or contest

neckerchief *noun*
a square of cloth worn round the neck, for example by Scouts and Cubs

necklace *noun*
a piece of jewellery you wear round your neck

nectar *noun*
nectar is a sweet liquid collected by bees from flowers

nectarine *noun*
a kind of peach with a smooth skin

need *verb*
1 to need something is to be without it when you should have it **2** to need to do something is to have to do it • *I needed to get a haircut.*

need *noun*
1 a need is something that you need **2** need is a situation in which something is necessary • *There's no need to shout.* **to be in need** is to need money or help **needless** *adjective* unnecessary

needle *noun*
1 a very thin pointed piece of metal used for sewing **2** something long, thin, and sharp, such as a knitting needle or a pine needle **3** the pointer of a meter or compass

needlework *noun*
needlework is sewing or embroidery

needy *adjective* (**needier, neediest**)
needy people are very poor and don't have what they need to live properly

negative *adjective*
1 a negative statement or answer is one that says 'no' **2** not definite or helpful **3** a negative number is one that is less than nought **4** a negative electric charge is one that carries electrons **negatively** *adverb*

negative *noun*
1 something that means 'no' **2** a photograph or film with the dark parts light and the light parts dark, from which prints are made

neglect *verb*
1 to neglect something or someone is to fail to look after them or deal with them **2** to neglect to do something is to fail to do it

neglect *noun*
neglect is failing to look after someone or do something

negotiate *verb*
(say nig-**oh**-shi-ayt)
1 to negotiate is to try to reach an agreement about something by discussing it **2** to negotiate an obstacle or difficulty is to get past it or over it

negotiation *noun* negotiations are discussions people have to try to reach an agreement about something **negotiator** *noun* one of the people involved in negotiations

neigh *verb*
to make a high-pitched cry like a horse

neigh *noun*
the sound of a horse neighing

neighbour *noun*
someone who lives next door or near to you **neighbouring** *adjective* the neighbouring house or family is the one next door

neighbourhood *noun*
the area you live in

neighbourly *adjective*
someone is neighbourly when they are friendly and helpful to people who live near them

neither *adjective, pronoun*
(say **ny**-ther or say **nee**-ther)
not either • *Neither light was working.* • *Neither of them likes cabbage.*

neither *conjunction*
neither ... nor ... not one thing and not the other • *I neither know nor care.*

neon *noun* (say **nee**-on) Ne
neon is a gas that glows when electricity passes through it, used in street lighting and signs

nephew *noun*
the son of a person's brother or sister

nerve *noun*
1 a nerve is one of the fibres inside your body that carry messages to and from your brain, so that parts of your body can feel and move **2** nerve is courage and calmness in a dangerous situation • *Don't lose your nerve.* **3** (informal) nerve is cheek or rudeness • *He had the nerve to ask for more.* **to get on someone's nerves** is to irritate them **nerves** nervousness • *I always suffer from nerves before an exam.*

nervous *adjective*
1 easily upset or agitated; timid **2** to do with the nerves **nervously** *adverb* in a way that shows you are nervous • *He smiled nervously.* **nervousness** *noun*

nest *noun*
1 the place where a bird lays its eggs and feeds its young **2** a warm place where some small animals live

nest *verb*
birds or animals nest when they make or have a nest • *Gulls were nesting on the cliffs.*

nestle *verb*
to nestle is to curl up comfortably

net *noun*
1 net is material made of pieces of thread, cord, or wire joined together in a criss-cross pattern with holes between **2** a net is a piece of this material • *a fishing net* **3** the net is the Internet

netball *noun*
netball is a game in which two teams try to throw a ball through a high net hanging from a ring

nettle *noun*
a wild plant with leaves that sting when you touch them

network *noun*
1 a criss-cross arrangement of lines **2** a system with many connections or parts, such as a railway or broadcasting or computer system

neuter *adjective* (say **new**-ter)
1 neither male nor female **2** in some languages, belonging to the class of words that are neither masculine nor feminine

neuter *verb* (say **new**-ter)
to neuter an animal is to remove its sexual organs so that it cannot breed

neutral *adjective* (say **new**-tral)
1 not supporting either side in a war or quarrel **2** not distinct or distinctive • *The room was painted in neutral colours.* **3** a neutral gear is one that is not connected to the driving parts of an engine **neutrality** *noun* neutrality is not supporting either side in a war or quarrel

neutralize *verb*
to neutralize something is to take away its use or effect

neutron *noun*
a particle of matter with no electric charge

never *adverb*
at no time; not ever; not at all

nevertheless *conjunction, adverb*
in spite of this; although that is a fact

new *adjective*
1 not existing before; just bought, made, or received • *Do you like my new shoes?* **2** different or unfamiliar • *They've moved to a new area.* **newly** *adverb* recently **newness** *noun*

newcomer *noun*
someone who has recently arrived in a place

new moon *noun*
the moon at the beginning of its cycle, when it appears as a thin crescent

a b c d e f g h i j k l m **n** o p q r s t u v w x y z

news noun
1 news is new information about people or recent events • *I've got some good news.*
2 news is also a radio or television report about important events

newsagent noun
a shopkeeper who sells newspapers and magazines

newspaper noun
1 a newspaper is a daily or weekly publication of large sheets of printed paper folded together, containing news reports and articles
2 newspaper is the paper these are printed on • *Wrap it in newspaper.*

newt noun
a small animal rather like a lizard, that lives near or in water

next adjective
the nearest; following immediately after

next adverb
1 in the nearest place 2 at the nearest time • *What comes next?*

nib noun
the pointed metal part at the end of a pen

nibble verb
to nibble something is to take small or gentle bites at it

nice adjective
pleasant or kind **nicely** adverb in a nice way • *Ask me nicely and I might say yes.*
niceness noun

nick noun
a small cut or notch **in the nick of time** only just in time

nick verb
1 to nick something is to make a small cut in it 2 (*slang*) to nick something is to steal it

nickel noun Ⓝ
a silvery-white metal

nickname noun
an informal name given to someone instead of their real name

nicotine noun (*say* **nik**-o-teen)
nicotine is a poisonous substance found in tobacco

niece noun
the daughter of a person's brother or sister

night noun
the time when it is dark, between sunset and sunrise

nightfall noun
nightfall is the time when it becomes dark just after sunset

nightingale noun
a small brown bird that sings sweetly

nightly adjective
happening every night

nightmare noun
1 a frightening or unpleasant dream 2 a terrifying experience
nightmarish adjective terrifying

nil noun
nothing • *We lost three-nil.*

nimble adjective
moving quickly or easily
nimbly adverb

nine noun
the number 9

nineteen noun
the number 19
nineteenth adjective, noun 19th

ninety noun
the number 90
ninetieth adjective, noun 90th

ninth adjective, noun
the next after the eighth
ninthly adverb in the ninth place; as the ninth one

nip verb (**nipping, nipped**)
1 to nip someone is to pinch or bite them sharply 2 (*informal*) to nip somewhere is to go quickly there • *I'll just nip into the supermarket.*

nip noun
1 a quick pinch or bite
2 a cold feeling • *There's a nip in the air.*

nipple noun
one of the two small parts that stick out at the front of a person's chest

nit noun
a louse or its egg

nitrogen noun (*say* **ny**-tro-jen) Ⓝ
nitrogen is a gas that makes up about four-fifths of the air

no exclamation
a word you use to refuse something or say that you don't agree

no adjective, adverb
not any • *We have no money.* • *She is no better.*

nobility noun
1 the nobility is the nobles or the aristocracy 2 nobility is being noble

noble adjective
1 coming from the highest class in society; aristocratic
2 having a good and generous nature • *He is a noble king.*
3 grand or impressive • *It was a noble building.*
nobly adverb

noble noun
a person who comes from a noble family, for example a duke or an earl

nobleman or **noblewoman** noun (**noblemen** or **noblewomen**)

a man or woman from the highest class in society

nobody pronoun
no person; not anyone • *Nobody knows.*

nocturnal adjective (*say* nok-**ter**-nal)
happening or active at night • *Badgers are nocturnal animals.*

nod verb (**nodding, nodded**)
to nod, or nod your head, is to move your head up and down as a way of agreeing with someone or as a greeting

noise noun
a loud sound, especially one that is unpleasant or unwanted

noisy adjective
making a lot of noise
noisily adverb

nomad noun (*say* **noh**-mad)
a member of a tribe that moves from place to place
nomadic adjective nomadic people move around from place to place

no man's land noun
the land between two armies in a war

nominate verb
to nominate someone is to suggest that they should be a candidate in an election or should be given a job or award **nomination** noun when someone is nominated for a job or award

none pronoun
not any; not one • *None of us went.*

none adverb
not at all • *He's none too pleased.*

nonetheless conjunction, adverb
in spite of this; nevertheless

non-existent adjective
not existing

non-fiction noun
writings that are not fiction; books about real things and true events

nonsense noun
1 nonsense is words that do not mean anything or make any sense 2 nonsense is also absurd or silly ideas or behaviour
nonsensical adjective not making any sense

non-stop adverb, adjective
1 not stopping • *They talked non-stop all morning.*
2 not stopping until the end of a journey • *There's a non-stop train to London.*

noodles *plural noun*
pasta made in narrow
strips, used in soups
and stir-fries

noon *noun*
twelve o'clock
midday

no one *pronoun*
no person; not
anyone

noose *noun*
a loop in a rope
that gets smaller
when the rope
is pulled

noodles

nor *conjunction*
and not • *She
cannot do it; nor can I.*

normal *adjective*
1 usual or ordinary • *It's normal
to want a holiday.* **2** natural and
healthy; not suffering from
an illness **normality** *noun*
a situation where things are
normal

normally *adverb*
1 usually • *The journey
normally takes an hour.* **2** in
the usual way • *Just breathe
normally.*

north *noun*
1 north is the direction to the
left of a person facing east
2 north is also the part of a
country or city that is in this
direction

north *adjective, adverb*
1 towards the north or in the
north **2** coming from the north
• *A north wind was blowing.*

north-east *noun, adjective, adverb*
midway between north and east

northern *adjective*
from or to do with the north

northerner *noun*
someone who lives in the north
of a country

northward or **northwards**
adjective, adverb
towards the north

north-west *noun, adjective,
adverb*
midway between north and
west

nose *noun*
1 the part of your face that you
use for breathing and smelling
2 the front part of something,
especially a vehicle or aircraft

nose *verb*
to nose forward or through is to
make progress cautiously • *The
ship nosed through the ice.*

nostalgia *noun* (*say* nos-**tal**-ja)
you feel nostalgia when you
fondly remember something
that made you happy in the past

nostalgic *adjective* making you
long for something in the past

nostril *noun*
each of the two
openings in your
nose

nosy *adjective*
(**nosier,
nosiest**)
(*informal*)
always wanting
to know other
people's business

nosiness *noun*

not *adverb*
a word you use to change
the meaning of something
to its opposite

notable *adjective*
remarkable or famous **notably**
adverb especially or remarkably

notch *noun*
a small V-shaped cut or mark

note *noun*
1 something you write down
as a reminder or help **2** a short
letter **3** a single sound in music
4 a sound or tone that indicates
something • *There was a note
of anger in his voice.* **5** a piece of
paper money • *Have you got a
five-pound note?* **to take note of
something** is to listen to it and
understand it

note *verb*
to note something is to pay
attention to it, or to write it
down as a reminder or help

notebook *noun*
a book in which you write
things down

notepaper *noun*
notepaper is paper for writing
letters

nothing *noun*
nothing is not anything

notice *noun*
1 a notice is something written
or printed and displayed for
people to see **2** to take notice of
something is to pay attention
to it • *It escaped my notice.*
3 a warning that something is
going to happen

notice *verb*
to notice something is to see it
or become aware of it

noticeable *adjective*
easy to see or notice
noticeably *adverb*

noticeboard *noun*
a board on which notices can
be displayed

notion *noun*
an idea, especially one that
is vague or uncertain • *The
notion that the earth is flat was
disproved long ago.*

notorious *adjective*
(*say* noh-**tor**-i-us)
well-known for doing

something bad • *He was a
notorious criminal.* **notoriety**
noun being well-known
for doing something bad
notoriously *adverb*

nougat *noun* (*say* **noo**-gah)
nougat is a chewy sweet made
from nuts and sugar or honey

nought *noun* (*say* nawt)
the figure 0

noun *noun*
a word that stands for a person,
place, or thing

nourish *verb*
to nourish someone is to give
them enough good food to keep
them alive and well

nourishment *noun*
nourishment is the food
someone needs to keep them
alive and well

novel *noun*
a long story that fills a whole
book

novel *adjective*
unusual • *What a novel idea.*

novelist *noun* (*say* **nov**-el-ist)
someone who writes novels

novelty *noun* (**novelties**)
1 novelty is being new or
unusual • *The novelty of living in
a cave soon wore off.* **2** a novelty
is something new and unusual
3 a novelty is also a cheap toy
or ornament

November *noun*
the eleventh month of the year

novice *noun*
a beginner

now *adverb*
1 at this time • *I am now
living in Glasgow.*
2 without any delay • *Do it
now!* **for now** until a later time
• *Goodbye for now.* **now and
again** or **now and then**
occasionally; sometimes

now *conjunction*
since or as • *I do remember,
now you mention it.*

now *noun*
this moment • *They should be
home by now.*

nowadays *adverb*
at the present time

nowhere *adverb*
not anywhere; in no place
or to no place

nozzle *noun*
the part at the end of a hose
or pipe from which something
flows

nuclear *adjective* (*say* **new**-kli-er)
1 to do with a nucleus,
especially of an atom
2 using the energy that is
created by the splitting of
atoms • *nuclear weapons*

a
b
c
d
e
f
g
h
i
j
k
l
m
n
o
p
q
r
s
t
u
v
w
x
y
z

nucleus noun (**nuclei**)
(say **new**-kli-us)
1 the central part of an atom or cell **2** the part in the centre of something, round which other things are grouped • *The queen bee is the nucleus of the hive.*

nude adjective
not wearing any clothes

nude noun
a nude person, especially in a work of art **nudity** noun nudity is not wearing any clothes

nudge verb
to nudge someone is to touch or push them with your elbow

nugget noun
a rough lump of gold from the ground

nuisance noun
an annoying person or thing

numb adjective
part of your body is numb when you can't feel anything in it **numbness** noun

number noun
1 a symbol or word that tells you how many of something there are **2** a quantity of people or things • *Do you know the number of bones in your body?* **3** a person's number is their telephone number **4** a song or piece of music

number verb
1 to number things is to count them or mark them with numbers • *Please number the pages of your essay.* **2** to number a certain amount is to reach it • *The crowd numbered 10,000.*

numeracy noun
numeracy is the ability to understand and work with numbers

numeral noun
a symbol or figure that stands for a number

numerical adjective
to do with numbers

numerous adjective
many • *There are numerous kinds of cat.*

nun noun
a member of a religious community of women

nurse noun
a person trained to look after people who are ill or injured

nurse verb
to nurse someone is to look after them when they are ill or injured

nursery noun (**nurseries**)
1 a place where young children are looked after or play **2** a place where young plants are grown and usually offered for sale

nursery rhyme noun
a simple poem or song that young children like

nursery school noun
a school for very young children

nurture verb
to nurture children is to look after them and educate them

nut noun
1 a fruit with a hard shell **2** the eatable part of this kind of fruit **3** a hollow piece of metal for screwing on to a bolt **nutty** adjective tasting of nuts or full of nuts

nutcrackers plural noun
pincers for cracking the shells of nuts

nutmeg noun
a hard seed that is made into a powder and used as a spice

nutrition noun
(say new-**trish**-on)
nutrition is the food someone needs to keep them alive and well

nutcrackers

nutritious adjective
(say new-**trish**-us)
nutritious food helps you to grow and keep well • *They ate a nutritious meal.*

nuzzle verb
to nuzzle someone is to rub gently against them with the nose, in the way that some animals do • *The kitten nuzzled her leg.*

nylon noun
nylon is a lightweight synthetic cloth or fibre

nymph noun
in myths, a young goddess who lives in trees or rivers or the sea

Oo

oak noun
a large tree that produces seeds called acorns

oar noun
a pole with a flat blade at one end, used for rowing a boat

oasis noun (say oh-**ay**-sis)
a fertile place with water and trees in a desert

oath noun
1 a solemn promise **2** a swear word

oats plural noun
a cereal used to make food for humans and animals

obedient adjective
doing what someone tells you to do; willing to obey **obedience** noun obedience is doing what you are told **obediently** adverb

obey verb
1 to obey someone is to do what they tell you **2** to obey a rule or law is to do what it says

object noun (say **ob**-jikt)
1 something that can be seen or touched **2** the purpose of something **3** (in grammar) the word naming the person or thing that the action of the verb affects, for example *him* in the sentence *I chased him*

object verb (say ob-**jekt**)
to object to something or someone is to say that you do not like them or do not agree with them

objection noun
1 objection is objecting to something **2** an objection is a reason for objecting • *I have three objections to your plan.*

objective noun
what you are trying to reach or do; an aim

obligation noun
a duty

obligatory adjective
something is obligatory when you must do it because of a rule or law • *Games are obligatory.*

oblige verb
1 to oblige someone to do something is to force them to do it **2** to oblige someone is to help and please them • *Will you oblige me by closing the window?* **to be obliged to someone** is to be grateful to them for helping you

oblong noun
a four-sided shape with right angles that is longer than it is wide

oblong adjective
having the shape of an oblong

obnoxious adjective
really horrible

oboe noun (say **oh**-boh)
a high-pitched woodwind instrument

oboist noun
a person who plays the oboe

obscure adjective
1 difficult to see or understand; very unclear **2** not well-known **obscurely** adverb **obscurity** noun obscurity is being not well-known

a b c d e f g h i j k l m n o p q r s t u v w x y z

observant *adjective*
quick at noticing things
observantly *adverb*

observation *noun*
1 observation is noticing or watching something carefully **2** an observation is a comment or remark • *He made a few observations about the weather.*

observatory *noun*
(**observatories**)
(*say* ob-**zerv**-a-ter-i)
a building equipped with telescopes for looking at the stars or weather

observe *verb*
1 to observe someone or something is to watch them carefully **2** to observe something is to notice it **3** to observe a law or custom is to obey it or keep it **4** to observe a fact is to state it • *She observed that she did not like ice in her drinks.* **observer** *noun* someone who watches something

obsessed *adjective*
always thinking about something • *He is obsessed with his work.*
obsession *noun* something that you think about too much

obsolete *adjective*
not used any more; out of date

obstacle *noun*
something that gets in your way or makes it difficult for you to do something

obstinate *adjective*
not willing to change your ideas or ways, even though they may be wrong **obstinacy** *noun* obstinacy is being obstinate **obstinately** *adverb*

obstruct *verb*
to obstruct someone or something is to stop them from getting past, or to hinder them **obstruction** *noun* something causing a blockage

obtain *verb*
to obtain something is to get it or be given it
obtainable *adjective* able to be bought or got

obtuse *adjective*
1 slow to understand; stupid **2** an obtuse angle is an angle of between 90 and 180 degrees **obtusely** *adverb*

obvious *adjective*
easy to see or understand
obviously *adverb*
it's obvious that; clearly • *Obviously we don't want to lose.*

occasion *noun*
1 the time when something happens • *On this occasion, we will not take any action.*
2 a special event • *The wedding was a marvellous occasion.*

occasional *adjective*
happening from time to time, but not often and not regularly **occasionally** *adverb* something happens occasionally when it happens from time to time

occupation *noun*
1 a person's occupation is their job or profession **2** the occupation of a country or territory is when an army captures it and stays there

occupy *verb* (**occupies, occupying, occupied**)
1 to occupy a place or building is to live in it **2** to occupy a space or position is to fill it **3** in a war, to occupy territory is to capture it and keep an army in it **4** to occupy someone is to keep them busy or interested

occur *verb* (**occurring, occurred**)
1 an event occurs when it happens or takes place • *An earthquake occurred on the island in 1953.* **2** something occurs when it exists or is found somewhere • *These plants occur in ponds.* **3** something occurs to you when it suddenly comes into your mind • *Just then an idea occurred to me.*

occurrence *noun*
something that happens or exists

ocean *noun*
1 the ocean is the area of salt water surrounding the land of the earth **2** an ocean is a large part of this water, such as the Pacific Ocean

o'clock *adverb*
used with numbers to show an exact hour • *Lunch is at one o'clock.*

octagon *noun* ⬤
a flat shape with eight sides
octagonal *adjective* having eight sides

octave *noun*
1 the interval between one musical note and the next note of the same name above or below it **2** these two notes played together

October *noun*
the tenth month of the year

octopus *noun*
a sea creature with eight arms (called *tentacles*)

WORD ORIGIN

The word **octopus** comes from a Greek word *oktopous*, which in turn comes from the words *okto* meaning 'eight' and *pous* meaning 'foot'.

odd *adjective*
1 strange or unusual **2** an odd number is one that cannot be divided by 2, such as 5 or 31 **3** left over or spare • *I've got an odd sock.* **4** of various kinds; occasional • *He's doing odd jobs.* **oddity** *noun* something that is odd or strange **oddly** *adverb*
oddness *noun*

odds *plural noun*
1 the chances that something will happen **2** the proportion of money that you will win if a bet is successful • *When the odds are 10 to 1, you will win £10 if you bet £1.* **odds and ends** small things of various kinds

odour *noun*
a smell, usually an unpleasant one

of *preposition*
1 belonging to • *She is the mother of the child.* **2** coming from • *He is a native of Italy.* **3** about; concerning • *Is there any news of your father?* **4** from; out of • *The house is built of stone.*

off *adverb*
1 not on; away • *His hat blew off.* **2** not working or happening • *The heating is off.* • *The match is off because of snow.* **3** beginning to go bad • *I think the milk is off.*

off *preposition*
1 not on; away or down from • *He fell off his chair.* **2** not taking or wanting • *She is off her food.* **3** taken away from • *There is £5 off the normal price.*

offence *noun*
1 an offence is a crime or something illegal • *When was the offence committed?* **2** offence is a feeling of annoyance or hurt **to cause offence** is to hurt someone's feelings **to take offence** is to be upset by what someone has said or done

offend *verb*
1 to offend someone is to hurt their feelings or be unpleasant to them **2** to offend is to break a law or do something wrong **offender** *noun* someone who breaks a law or does something wrong

offensive *adjective*
1 insulting or causing offence **2** used for attacking • *He was arrested for carrying an offensive weapon.* **offensively** *adverb*

offer *verb*
1 to offer something is to hold it out so that someone can take

it if they want it **2** to offer to do something is to say that you are willing to do it **3** to offer a sum of money is to say how much you are willing to pay for something

offer noun
1 the action of offering something • *Thank you for your offer of help.* **2** an amount of money that you are willing to pay for something

offhand adjective
1 said without much thought **2** rude or abrupt

office noun
1 a room or building where people work, often at desks **2** a place where you can go for tickets, information, or some other purpose • *a lost property office* **3** an important job or position • *He was honoured to hold the office of President.*

officer noun
1 someone who is in charge of other people, especially in the armed forces **2** a policeman or policewoman

official adjective
1 done or said by someone with authority **2** connected with the job of someone in a position of authority • *The prime minister will make an official visit to Australia next month.*
officially adverb

official noun
someone who has power or makes decisions as part of their job

off-licence noun
a shop with a licence to sell alcoholic drinks for people to take away

offside adjective
(*in sport*) in a position which is not allowed by the rules

offspring noun
a child or young animal

often adverb
many times; in many cases

ogre noun
1 a cruel giant in stories **2** a frightening person

oil noun
1 an oil is a thick slippery liquid that does not mix with water **2** oil is a thick sticky liquid that is found underground and used to make petrol and other fuels and to keep machinery working smoothly

oil verb
to oil something is to put oil on it to make it work smoothly

oil painting noun
a painting done using paints made with oil

oil rig noun
a structure set up to support the equipment for drilling for oil

oil well noun
a hole drilled in the ground or under the sea to get oil

oily adjective
like oil or covered in oil

ointment noun
a cream that you put on sore skin and cuts

OK adverb, adjective
(*informal*) all right

old adjective
1 not new; born or made a long time ago **2** of a particular age • *I'm ten years old.* **3** former or original • *I liked my old school better than the one I go to now.*

old age noun
old age is the time when a person is old

old-fashioned adjective
of a kind that was usual a long time ago; out of date

olive noun
1 an evergreen tree with a small bitter fruit **2** the black or green fruit of this tree, used for eating and to make olive oil

olives

omelette noun (*say* **om**-lit)
eggs beaten together and fried, often with a filling or flavouring

omen noun
an event that some people see as a sign that something is going to happen

ominous adjective
suggesting that trouble is coming • *There was an ominous rumble from inside the tunnel.*
ominously adverb

omission noun
something left out or not done

omit verb (**omitting, omitted**)
1 to omit something is to leave it out • *Several names have been omitted from the list.* **2** to omit to do something is to fail to do it • *I omitted to lock the back door.*

omnivorous adjective
an omnivorous animal is one that eats plants as well as meat

on preposition
1 at or over the top or surface of something • *Sit on the floor.* **2** at the time of • *Come on Monday.* **3** about; concerning • *We went to a talk on snakes.* **4** towards or near • *They advanced on the town.*

on adverb
1 so as to be on something • *Put your hat on.* **2** forwards • *Move on.* **3** working; in action • *Is the heater on?*

once adverb
1 at one time • *I once lived in Leeds.* **2** one time only • *I've only met him once.*

once conjunction
as soon as • *We can get out once I open this door.*
at once immediately

one noun
the smallest whole number, 1

one pronoun
a person or thing on their own • *One likes to help.* • *One of my friends is ill.*
one another each other

one adjective
single • *I have one packet left.*

oneself pronoun
one's own self; yourself • *One should not always think of oneself.*

one-way adjective
a one-way street is one where traffic is only allowed to go in one direction

onion noun
a round vegetable with a strong flavour

online adjective, adverb
connected to a computer

only adjective
being the one person or thing of a kind • *He's the only person we can trust.*

only adverb
no more than • *There are only three cakes.*

only conjunction
but then; however • *I want to come, only I'm very busy.*

onto preposition
to a position on • *They fell onto the floor.*

onward or **onwards** adverb
forward or forwards

ooze verb
a thick liquid oozes when it flows out slowly, especially through a narrow opening • *Blood oozed from his wound.*

opaque adjective (*say* oh-**payk**)
something that is opaque doesn't allow light through and so can't be seen through

open *adjective*
1 allowing people or things to pass through; not shut • *The door is open.* • *The bottles need to be open.* **2** not enclosed • *There were miles of open land.* **3** not folded; spread out • *She greeted us with open arms.* **4** honest; not secret or secretive • *They were quite open about what they had done.* **5** not settled or finished • *That is still an open question.* **in the open air** outdoors; not inside a house or building

open *verb*
1 to open something is to make it open **2** to open is to become open **3** to open is also to start • *The jumble sale opens at 2 o'clock.* **4** a shop opens when it starts business for the day • *What time do you open?*

opener *noun*
a device for opening a bottle or can

opening *noun*
1 a space or gap in something **2** the beginning of something

openly *adverb*
to do something openly is to do it for all to see, not secretly

open-minded *adjective*
ready to listen to other people's ideas and opinions; not having fixed ideas

opera *noun*
a form of drama in which the characters sing all or most of the words, with an orchestra **operatic** *adjective* to do with opera

operate *verb*
1 to operate something is to make it work **2** to operate is to work or be in action **3** to operate on someone is to perform a surgical operation on them

operation *noun*
1 something done to a patient's body by a surgeon to remove or repair a part of it **2** a carefully planned activity **to be in operation** is to be working • *The new rules are now in operation.*

operator *noun*
someone who works something, especially a telephone switchboard or exchange

opinion *noun*
what you think of something; a belief or judgement

opponent *noun*
someone who is against you in a contest, war, or argument

opportunity *noun*
a good time or chance to do something

oppose *verb*
to oppose someone or something is to be against them or disagree with them **to be opposed to something** is to disagree strongly with it • *We are opposed to parking in the town centre.*

opposite *adjective, adverb*
1 on the other side; facing • *She lives on the opposite side of the road to me.* • *I'll sit opposite.* **2** completely different • *They went in opposite directions.*

opposite *noun*
something that is completely different from something else • *'Happy' is the opposite of 'sad'.*

opposition *noun*
opposition is opposing something; resistance **the Opposition** the chief political party opposing the one that has formed the government

oppress *verb*
1 to oppress people is to govern them or treat them cruelly or unjustly **2** to oppress someone is to trouble them with worry or sadness **oppression** *noun* treating people cruelly or unjustly **oppressor** *noun* someone who treats people cruelly or unjustly

oppressive *adjective*
1 harsh and cruel • *He was an oppressive ruler.* **2** hot and tiring • *The weather can be very oppressive in July.*

opt *verb*
to opt for something or to do something is to choose it • *I opted for the cash prize.* • *We opted to go abroad.* **to opt out of something** is to decide not to join in with it

optical *adjective*
to do with sight or the eyes **optically** *adverb* as far as sight or the eyes are concerned

optician *noun* (*say* op-**tish**-an)
someone who tests your eyesight and makes and sells glasses and contact lenses

optimist *noun*
someone who usually expects things to turn out well **optimism** *noun* the feeling that things will turn out well

optimistic *adjective*
expecting things to turn out well **optimistically** *adverb*

option *noun*
1 one of the things that you can choose • *Your options are to travel by bus or by train.* **2** the

right to choose; choice • *You have the option of staying.*

optional *adjective*
something is optional when you can choose whether to do it or not • *You have to study French, but German is optional.*

or *conjunction*
used to show that there is a choice or alternative • *Do you want a cake or a biscuit?*

oral *adjective*
1 spoken, not written **2** to do with the mouth or using your mouth **orally** *adverb* by speaking or using your mouth • *This medicine must not be taken orally.*

orange *noun*
1 a round juicy fruit with thick reddish-yellow peel **2** a reddish-yellow colour

orange *adjective* ●
reddish-yellow

orang-utan *noun*
(*say* o-**rang**-u-tan)
a large kind of ape found in Borneo and Sumatra

orbit *noun*
the curved path taken by something moving round a planet or other body in space

orbit *verb*
to orbit a planet or other body in space is to move round it • *The satellite orbited the earth.*

orchard *noun*
a piece of ground with fruit trees

orchestra *noun*
a group of musicians playing various instruments together **orchestral** *adjective* orchestral music is written to be played by an orchestra

orchid *noun* (*say* **or**-kid)
a type of brightly coloured flower

orchid

ordeal *noun*
a difficult or unpleasant experience

order *noun*
1 a command **2** a request for something to be supplied • *The waiter took our order.* **3** the way things are arranged • *The words are in alphabetical order.* **4** obedience or good behaviour • *Can we have some order please?*

a b c d e f g h i j k l m n o p q r

5 tidiness or neatness **6** a group of religious monks, priests, or nuns **in order that** or **in order to** for the purpose of **to be out of order** is to be broken or not working

order *verb*
1 to order someone to do something is to tell them to do it **2** to order something is to ask for it to be supplied to you

orderly *adjective*
1 arranged tidily or well; methodical **2** well-behaved; obedient

ordinary *adjective*
normal or usual; not special **ordinarily** *adverb* normally or usually

ore *noun*
rock with metal in it, such as iron ore

organ *noun*
1 a musical instrument from which sounds are produced by air forced through pipes, played by keys and pedals **2** a part of your body which does a particular job, for example the liver which cleans the blood

organic *adjective*
1 organic food is grown or produced without using artificial chemicals **2** made by or found in living things

organism *noun*
a living animal or plant

organist *noun*
someone who plays the organ

organization *noun*
1 an organization is a group of people who work together to do something **2** organization is planning or arranging things such as getting people together to do something

organize *verb*
1 to organize people is to get them together to do something **2** to organize something is to plan or arrange it • *We organized a picnic.* **3** to organize things is to put them in order **organizer** *noun* someone who organizes something

oriental *adjective*
to do with the countries east of the Mediterranean Sea, especially China and Japan

orienteering *noun*
(*say* or-i-en-**teer**-ing) orienteering is the sport of finding your way across rough country with a map and compass

origin *noun*
the start of something; the point where something began

• *a book about the origins of life on earth*

original *adjective*
1 existing from the start; earliest • *They were the original inhabitants.* **2** new; not a copy or an imitation • *It is an original design.* **3** producing new ideas; inventive • *She was an original thinker.* **originality** *noun* originality is being original or inventive **originally** *adverb* in the beginning

originate *verb*
1 to originate something is to create it or develop it **2** to originate is to start in a certain way • *Supermarkets originated in America.* **originator** *noun* someone who originates something

ornament *noun*
an object you wear or display as a decoration **ornamental** *adjective* used to decorate something • *an ornamental fountain*

ornithology *noun*
(*say* or-ni-**thol**-o-ji) ornithology is the study of birds **ornithological** *adjective* to do with birds **ornithologist** *noun* a person who studies birds

orphan *noun*
a child whose parents are dead

orphanage *noun*
a home for orphans

orthodox *adjective*
having beliefs that are correct or generally accepted

ostrich *noun*
a large long-legged bird that can run fast but cannot fly

other *determiner*
not the same as this; different • *Play some other tune.* • *Try the other shoe.* **every other day** every second day, for example Monday, Wednesday, and Friday **other than** except • *They have no belongings other than what they are carrying.* **the other day** or **the other week** a few days or weeks ago

ostrich

other *noun*
the other person or thing • *Where are the others?*

otherwise *adverb*
1 if you do not; if things happen differently • *Write it down, otherwise you'll forget it.* **2** in other ways • *It rained a lot but otherwise the holiday was good.* **3** differently • *We could not do otherwise.*

otter *noun*
an animal with thick fur, webbed feet, and a flat tail, that lives near water

otter

ought *verb*
used with other words to show **1** what you should or must do • *You ought to do your music practice.* **2** what is likely to happen • *With all these dark clouds it ought to rain.*

ounce *noun*
a unit of weight equal to $\frac{1}{16}$ of a pound or about 28 grams

our *adjective*
belonging to us • *This is our house.*

ours *pronoun*
belonging to us • *This house is ours.*

ourselves *pronoun*
us and nobody else, used to refer back to the subject of a verb • *We have hurt ourselves.* **by ourselves** on our own; alone • *We did the work all by ourselves.*

out *adverb*
1 away from a place or not in it; not at home **2** into the open or outdoors • *Are you going out today?* **3** not burning or working • *The fire has gone out.* **4** loudly • *She cried out.* **5** completely • *They were tired out.* **6** dismissed from a game • *Another batsman is out.*

to be out of something is to have no more of it left **out of date** old-fashioned; not used any more **out of doors** in the open air **out of the way** remote or distant

outback *noun*
the remote inland areas of Australia

outbreak *noun*
the sudden start of a disease, war, or show of anger

outburst *noun*
the sudden beginning of anger or laughter

outcast *noun*
someone who has been rejected by family, friends, or society

outcome *noun*
the result of what happens or has happened

outcry *noun* (**outcries**)
a strong protest from many people • *There was an outcry over the rise in bus fares.*

outdated *adjective*
out of date

outdoor *adjective*
done or used outside • *You'll need your outdoor clothes.*

outdoors *adverb*
in the open air • *It is cold outdoors.*

outer *adjective*
nearer the outside; external

outer space *noun*
outer space is the universe beyond the earth's atmosphere

outfit *noun*
1 a set of clothes you wear together **2** a set of things you need for doing something

outgrow *verb* (**outgrowing, outgrew, outgrown**)
1 to outgrow something such as clothes or a habit is to grow too big or too old for them **2** to outgrow someone is to grow faster or taller than them

outing *noun*
a trip or short journey you make for pleasure

outlaw *noun*
a robber or bandit who is hiding to avoid being caught and is not protected by the law

outlaw *verb*
to outlaw something is to make it illegal

outlet *noun*
1 a way for something to get out • *The tank has an outlet at the bottom.* **2** a place to sell goods • *We need to find fresh outlets for our products.*

outline *noun*
1 a line round the outside of something; a line showing the shape of a thing **2** a summary

outline *verb*
1 to outline something is to draw a line round it to show its shape **2** to outline a story or account is to summarize or describe it briefly

outlook *noun*
1 a person's outlook is the way that they look at and think about things • *She has an odd outlook on life.* **2** what seems likely to happen in the future • *The outlook is bright.*

outnumber *verb*
to outnumber something else is to be greater in number than it • *The girls outnumber the boys in our team.*

outpatient *noun*
a patient who visits a hospital for treatment but does not stay there overnight

output *noun*
1 the amount produced, especially by a factory or business **2** information produced by a computer

output *verb*
to output information is to get it from a computer

outrage *noun*
1 outrage is the anger you feel when something shocking happens **2** an outrage is something very shocking or cruel

outrage *verb*
to outrage someone is to make them very shocked and angry

outrageous *adjective*
shocking or dreadful

outright *adverb*
1 completely • *We won outright.* **2** all at once; in one go • *They were able to buy their house outright.*

outside *noun*
the outer side or surface of a thing; the part furthest from the middle

outside *adjective*
1 on or coming from the outside **2** slight or remote • *There is an outside chance of snow.*

outside *adverb, preposition*
on or to the outside of something • *Go outside.* • *It's outside the house.*

outsider *noun*
1 someone who is not a member of a particular group of people **2** a horse or person that people think has no chance of winning a race or contest

outskirts *plural noun*
the parts on the outside edge of an area, especially of a town or city

outspoken *adjective*
speaking frankly even though it might offend people

outstanding *adjective*
1 extremely good or distinguished • *She is an outstanding athlete.* **2** not yet dealt with • *What are your outstanding debts?*

outward *adjective*
1 going outwards **2** on the outside

outwardly *adverb*
on the outside; for people to see • *They were outwardly calm.*

outwards *adverb*
towards the outside

outwit *verb* (**outwitting, outwitted**)
to outwit someone is to deceive or defeat them by being more clever

oval *adjective*
shaped like an egg or a number 0

oval *noun*
an oval shape

oven *noun*
a closed space, often part of a cooker, in which things are cooked or heated

over *adverb*
1 down or sideways; out and down from the top or edge • *He fell over.* **2** across to a place • *We walked over to the house.* **3** so that a different side shows • *Turn the sheet over.* **4** finished • *The lesson is over.* **5** left or remaining • *There are a few apples over.* **6** through or thoroughly • *Think it over.*
over and over repeatedly; many times

over *preposition*
1 above or covering • *There's a light over the door.* • *I'll put a cloth over the table.* **2** across • *They ran over the road.* **3** more than • *The house is over a mile away.* **4** concerning; about • *They quarrelled over money.* **5** during • *We can talk over dinner.*

over *noun*
in cricket, a series of six balls bowled by one person

overall *adjective, adverb*
including everything; total • *What is the overall cost?*

overalls *plural noun*
clothes that you wear over your other clothes to protect them when you are working

overboard *adverb*
to fall or jump overboard is to go over the side of a boat into the water

a
b
c
d
e
f
g
h
i
j
k
l
m
n
o
p
q
r
s
t
u
v
w
x
y
z

overcast *adjective*
covered with cloud • *The sky is grey and overcast.*

overcoat *noun*
a warm outdoor coat

overcome *verb* (**overcomes, overcoming, overcame, overcome**)
1 to overcome a problem or difficulty is to succeed in dealing with it or controlling it • *He overcame injury to win a gold medal.* **2** to be overcome by something is to become helpless from it • *She was overcome by the fumes.* **3** to overcome someone is to beat them

overdose *noun*
too large a dose of a drug or medicine

overdue *adjective*
something is overdue when it is later than it should be • *The train is overdue.*

overflow *verb*
to overflow is to flow over the edges or limits of something

overgrown *adjective*
a place is overgrown when it is thickly covered with weeds or unwanted plants

overhaul *verb*
to overhaul a machine or vehicle is to check it thoroughly and repair it if necessary

overhead *adjective, adverb*
above your head; in the sky

overhear *verb*
to overhear something is to hear it accidentally or without the speaker knowing

overlap *verb* (**overlapping, overlapped**)
one thing overlaps another when it lies across part of it • *The carpet overlapped the fireplace.*

overlook *verb*
not to notice it **2** to overlook a mistake or offence is not to punish it **3** to overlook a place is to have a view over it • *The hotel overlooks the sea.*

overnight *adverb, adjective*
of or during a night • *We stayed overnight in a hotel.* • *There will be an overnight stop in Paris.*

overpower *verb*
to overpower someone is to defeat them because you are stronger **overpowering** *adjective* very strong

overrun *verb* (**overrunning, overran, overrun**)
1 to overrun an area is to spread harmfully over it • *The place is overrun with mice.* **2** something overruns when it goes on longer than it should • *The programme*

overran by ten minutes.

overseas *adverb*
abroad • *They travelled overseas.*

overseas *adjective*
from abroad; foreign • *We met some overseas students.*

oversight *noun*
a mistake you make by not noticing something

oversleep *verb* (**oversleeping, overslept**)
to sleep longer than you meant to

overtake *verb* (**overtaking, overtook, overtaken**)
to overtake a moving vehicle or person is to catch them up or pass them in the same direction

overthrow *verb* (**overthrowing, overthrew, overthrown**)
to overthrow a government is to remove it from power by force

overthrow *noun*
the overthrow of a government is when it is forced out of power

overtime *noun*
time someone spends working outside their normal hours

overture *noun*
a piece of music played at the start of a concert, opera, or ballet

overturn *verb*
1 to overturn something is to make it turn over or fall over **2** to overturn is to turn over • *The car went out of control and overturned.*

overweight *adjective*
too heavy

overwhelm *verb*
1 to overwhelm someone is to have a very strong effect on them • *I was overwhelmed by everyone's kindness.* **2** to overwhelm someone is to defeat them completely

owe *verb*
1 to owe something, especially money, is to have a duty to pay or give it to someone • *I owe you a pound.* **2** to owe something to someone is to have it thanks to them • *They owed their lives to the pilot's skill.* **owing to something** because of it • *The train was late owing to leaves on the line.*

owl

owl *noun*
a bird of prey with large eyes and a short beak, usually flying at night

own *adjective*
belonging to yourself or itself **to get your own back** (*informal*) is to have your revenge **on your own** by yourself; alone • *I did it all on my own.* • *I sat on my own in the empty room.*

own *verb*
to own something is to have it as your property **to own up to something** (*informal*) is to admit that you did it

owner *noun*
the person who owns something **ownership** *noun* ownership is owning something

ox *noun* (**oxen**)
a male animal of the cow family, used for pulling loads

oxygen *noun* ⊙
oxygen is one of the gases in the air that people need to stay alive

oyster *noun*
a kind of shellfish whose shell sometimes contains a pearl

ozone *noun*
ozone is a strong-smelling gas that is a form of oxygen

ozone layer *noun*
a layer of ozone high in the atmosphere, which protects the earth from the sun's radiation

Pp

p
short for penny or pence

pace *noun*
1 one step in walking, marching, or running **2** speed • *He set a fast pace.*

pace *verb*
to pace is to walk up and down with slow or regular steps • *He was pacing across the room as he spoke.*

pacifist *noun* (*say* pas-i-fist)
someone who believes that war is always wrong **pacifism** *noun* the belief that war is always wrong

pacify *verb* (**pacifies, pacifying, pacified**) (*say* pas-i-fy)
to pacify someone is to calm them down

pack *noun*
1 a bundle or collection of things wrapped or tied together 2 a set of playing cards 3 a strong bag carried on your back 4 a group of hounds, wolves, or other animals 5 a group of people, especially a group of Brownies or Cub Scouts

pack *verb*
1 to pack a suitcase or bag is to put things in it so that you can store them or take them somewhere 2 to pack a room or building is to fill it • *The hall was packed.*

package *noun*
1 a parcel or packet 2 a number of things offered or accepted together

package holiday *noun*
a holiday in which all the travel and accommodation is arranged and included in the price

packet *noun*
a small parcel

pad¹ *noun*
1 a number of sheets of blank or lined paper joined together along one edge 2 a piece of soft material used to protect or shape something 3 a piece of soft material that you wear to protect your leg in cricket and other games 4 a flat surface from which helicopters take off or rockets are launched

pad¹ *verb* (**padding, padded**)
to pad something is to put a piece of soft material on it or into it in order to protect or shape it

pad² *verb* (**padding, padded**)
to pad is to walk softly

padding *noun*
padding is soft material used to protect something or make it more comfortable

paddle *verb*
1 to paddle is to walk about with bare feet in shallow water 2 to paddle a boat is to move it along with a short oar

paddle *noun*
1 a time spent paddling in water 2 a short oar with a broad blade

paddock *noun*
a small field for keeping horses

paddy *noun* (**paddies**)
a field where rice is grown

padlock *noun*
padlock
a lock with a metal loop that you can use to fasten a gate or lock a bicycle

page¹ *noun*
a piece of paper that is part of a book or newspaper; one side of this piece of paper

page² *noun*
a boy who acts as an attendant or runs errands

pageant *noun* (*say* **paj**-ent)
1 a play or entertainment about historical events and people 2 a procession of people in costume

pageantry *noun* pageantry is elaborate display that is part of a ceremony or procession

pagoda *noun* (*say* pa-**goh**-da)
a Buddhist tower or Hindu temple in the Far East

pail *noun*
a bucket

pain *noun*
1 pain or a pain is an unpleasant feeling caused by injury or disease • *Are you in pain?* 2 pain is also mental suffering **to take pains** is to make a careful effort or take trouble over something

painful *adjective*
causing you pain • *My ankle is too painful to walk on.* **painfully** *adverb* to be (for example) painfully thin or painfully slow is to be extremely thin or slow

painstaking *adjective*
making a careful effort

paint *noun*
a liquid substance put on something to colour or cover it

paint *verb*
1 to paint something is to put paint on it 2 to paint a picture is to make it with paints 3 to paint someone or something is to make a picture of them using paint

paintbrush *noun*
a brush used in painting

paintbrushes

painter *noun*
1 an artist who paints pictures 2 a person whose job is painting walls and houses

painting *noun*
1 painting is using paints to make a picture • *She likes painting.* 2 a painting is a painted picture

pair *noun*
1 two things or people that go together or are the same kind • *I need a new pair of shoes.* 2 something made of two parts joined together • *Have you got a pair of scissors?*

palace *noun*
a large and splendid house where a king or queen or other important person lives

palate *noun* (*say* **pal**-at)
the roof of your mouth

pale *adjective*
1 almost white • *He had a pale face.* 2 not bright in colour; faint • *The sky was a pale blue.* **paleness** *noun*

palette *noun* (*say* **pal**-it)
a board on which an artist mixes colours

pallid *adjective*
pale, especially because of illness

palm *noun*
1 the inner part of your hand, between your fingers and wrist 2 a tropical tree with large leaves and no branches

paltry *adjective*
not very much or not very valuable • *His reward was a paltry 50 pence.*

pamper *verb*
to pamper someone is to go to a lot of trouble to make them feel comfortable and let them have whatever they want

pamphlet *noun*
a thin book with a paper cover

WORD ORIGIN

The word **pamphlet** comes from *Pamphilet*, the name of a 12th-century Latin love poem about someone called Pamphilus.

pan *noun*
1 a pot or dish with a flat base, used for cooking 2 something shaped like an open dish

pancake *noun*
a flat round cake of batter fried on both sides

panda *noun*
a large black and white bear-like animal found in China

pandemonium *noun*
you say there is pandemonium when there is a loud noise or disturbance • *Suddenly pandemonium broke loose.*

a b c d e f g h i j k l m n o **p** q r s t u v w x y z

pane *noun*
a sheet of glass in a window

panel *noun*
1 a long flat piece of wood, metal, or other material that is part of a door, wall, or piece of furniture **2** a group of people chosen to judge a competition or take part in a television quiz

pang *noun*
a sudden feeling of pain or strong emotion

panic *noun*
panic is sudden fear that makes you behave wildly **panicky** *adjective* feeling or showing panic

panic *verb* (**panicking, panicked**)
to panic is to be overcome with fear or anxiety and behave wildly

panorama *noun*
a view or picture of a wide area

pansy *noun* (**pansies**)
a small brightly-coloured garden flower

pant *verb*
you pant when you take short quick breaths, usually after running or working hard

panther *noun*
a leopard

pantomime *noun*
a Christmas show with dancing and songs, based on a fairy tale

pantry *noun* (**pantries**)
a cupboard or small room for storing food

pants *plural noun*
1 (*informal*) underpants or knickers **2** (*in America*) trousers

paper *noun*
1 paper is a thin substance made in sheets and used for writing or printing or drawing on, or for wrapping things **2** a paper is a newspaper **3** papers are documents

paper *verb*
to paper a wall or room is to cover it with wallpaper

paperback *noun*
a book with thin flexible covers

papier mâché *noun*
(*say* **pap**-yay **mash**-ay)
papier mâché is a mixture of paper pulp and glue you use to make models or ornaments

papyrus *noun* (**papyri**)
(*say* pa-**py**-rus)
papyrus is a kind of paper made from the stems of reeds, used in ancient Egypt

parable *noun*
a story told to teach people

something, especially one of the stories told by Jesus Christ

parachute *noun*
an umbrella-shaped device on which people or things can float slowly down to the ground from an aircraft **parachutist** *noun* someone who uses a parachute

parade *noun*
1 a line of people or vehicles moving forward through a place as a celebration **2** soldiers are on parade when they assemble for an inspection or drill

parade *verb*
1 to parade is to move forward through a place as a celebration **2** soldiers parade when they assemble for an inspection or drill

paradise *noun*
1 paradise is heaven or, in the Bible, the Garden of Eden **2** you can describe a wonderful or perfect place as a paradise

paraffin *noun*
paraffin is a kind of oil used as fuel

paragraph *noun*
one of the group of sentences that a piece of writing is divided into, beginning on a new line

parallel *adjective*
parallel lines are lines that are the same distance apart for their whole length, like railway lines

parallelogram *noun*
a four-sided figure with its opposite sides parallel to each other and equal in length

paralyse *verb*
to paralyse someone is to make them unable to feel anything or to move

paralysis *noun* (*say* pa-**ral**-i-sis)
paralysis is the loss of the ability to move or feel anything

parapet *noun*
a low wall along the edge of a balcony, bridge, or roof

parasite *noun*
an animal or plant that lives in or on another and gets its food from it **parasitic** *adjective* a parasitic animal or plant lives as a parasite on another

parasol *noun*
a lightweight umbrella you use to shade yourself from the sun

paratroops *plural noun*
troops trained to be dropped from aircraft by parachute

paratrooper *noun* a soldier in the paratroops

parcel *noun*
something wrapped up in paper for sending in the post

parched *adjective*
very dry or thirsty

parchment *noun*
parchment is a kind of heavy paper originally made from animal skins

pardon *verb*
to pardon someone is to forgive or excuse them

pardon *noun*
1 forgiveness; when someone is pardoned **2** used as an exclamation to mean 'I didn't hear or understand what you said', or 'I apologize'

parent *noun*
your parents are your father and mother **parental** *adjective* to do with parents

parish *noun*
a district that has its own church **parishoner** *noun* a person who regularly goes to a particular church

park *noun*
a large area with grass and trees, for public use

park *verb*
to park a vehicle is to leave it somewhere for a time

parliament *noun*
the group of people that make a country's laws **parliamentary** *adjective* to do with a parliament
• *a parliamentary election*

parole *noun* (*say* pa-**rohl**)
parole is letting someone out of prison before they have finished their sentence, on condition that they behave well
• *He was on parole.*

parrot *noun*
a brightly-coloured bird with a curved beak, that can learn to repeat words or sounds

parrot

parsley noun
parsley is a plant with crinkled green leaves used to flavour and decorate food

parsnip noun
a pale yellow vegetable

parson noun
a member of the Christian clergy, especially a vicar

part noun
1 some but not all of a thing or a number of things; anything that belongs to something bigger **2** the character played by an actor or actress; the words spoken by a character in a play • *She has a good part in the school play.*

part verb
1 to part people or things is to separate them or divide them **2** to part is to separate **3** to part hair is to divide it so that it goes in two different directions **to part with something** is to give it away or get rid of it

partial adjective
1 not complete or total • *There will be a partial eclipse of the sun.* **2** unfairly showing more support for one person or side than another
to be partial to something is to like it **partially** adverb partly or not completely

participate verb
to participate in something is to take part in it **participant** noun someone who takes part in something **participation** noun taking part in something

participle noun
a word formed from a verb and used as part of the verb or as an adjective, for example 'going', 'gone', 'sailed', 'sailing'

particle noun
a very small piece or amount

particular adjective
1 only this one and no other; special; individual • *Are you looking for a particular book?* **2** fussy; hard to please • *He is very particular about his clothes.*
in particular especially; chiefly **particularly** adverb you can say something is (for example) particularly good or useful when it is especially good or useful

parting noun
1 leaving or separation **2** the line where hair is combed in different directions

partition noun
a thin wall that divides a space into separate areas

partly adverb
not completely; in some ways

partner noun
1 one of a pair of people who do something together, especially dancing, running a business, or playing a game **2** someone's partner is the person they are married to or live with **partnership** noun partnership is being partners

part of speech noun
each of the groups (also called **word classes**) into which words can be divided in grammar: noun, adjective, verb, pronoun, adverb, preposition, conjunction, interjection

partridge noun
a bird with brown feathers that some people shoot as a sport

part-time adjective, adverb
working for only some of the normal hours

party noun (**parties**)
1 a time when people get together to enjoy themselves • *Come to my birthday party.* **2** a group of people working or travelling together • *They organized a search party.* **3** an organized group of people with similar political beliefs • *The Labour Party won the election.*

pass verb
1 to pass something or someone is to go past them **2** to pass in a certain direction is to move or go that way • *They passed over the bridge.* **3** to pass something to someone is to give it or hand it to them • *Can you pass the butter, please?* **4** to pass an examination is to be successful in it **5** to pass time is to use time doing something **6** to pass is to finish or no longer be there • *His opportunity passed.* **7** to pass a law or rule is to approve or accept it

pass noun
1 when a ball is kicked, hit, or thrown from one player to another in a game **2** a success in an examination • *She got several GCSE passes.* **3** a card or ticket that allows you to go in or out of a place

passage noun
1 a corridor or narrow space between two walls **2** a section of a piece of writing or music **3** a journey by sea or air **4** passing • *the passage of time*

passageway noun
a passage or way through, especially between buildings

passenger noun
someone who is driven in a car or travels by public transport

passer-by noun (**passers-by**)
someone who happens to be going past when something happens

passion noun
1 passion is strong feeling or emotion **2** a passion is a great enthusiasm for something

passionate adjective
full of passion or strong feeling **passionately** adverb

passive adjective
not active; not resisting or fighting against something **passively** adverb

Passover noun
Passover is a Jewish religious festival, celebrating the escape of the ancient Jews from slavery in Egypt

passport noun
an official document that allows you to travel abroad

password noun
a secret word or phrase that you need to know to be allowed to go somewhere or to use a computer system

passport

past noun
1 the time that has gone by • *Try to forget the past.* **2** the form of a verb used to describe an action that happened at a time before now, for example *came* in the sentence *My uncle came to visit us*

past adjective
of the time gone by • *He was thinking about his past achievements.*

past preposition
1 beyond • *Go past the school and turn right.* **2** later than • *It is past midnight.*

pasta noun
pasta is an Italian food made as a dried paste of flour, water, and often eggs, formed into various shapes such as spaghetti and lasagne

paste noun
a soft and moist or gluey substance

paste verb
to paste something is to stick it to a surface with paste

pastel noun
1 a crayon that is like a slightly greasy chalk **2** a light delicate colour

pasteurize verb
(say **pahs**-cher-ryz)
to pasteurize milk is to purify it by heating and

then cooling it **pasteurization** *noun* the process of pasteurizing milk

pastime *noun*
something you do to pass time pleasantly; a hobby or game

past participle *noun*
a form of a verb used after *has, have, had, was, were,* to describe an action that happened at a time before now, for example *done, overtaken,* and *written*

pastry *noun* (**pastries**)
1 pastry is dough made from flour, fat, and water rolled flat and baked **2** a pastry is a cake made from this dough

pasture *noun*
land covered with grass where cattle, sheep, or horses can feed

pasty[1] *noun* (**pasties**)
(*say* **pas**-ti)
a pastry filled with meat and vegetables, like a small pie

pasty[2] *adjective* (**pastier, pastiest**) (*say* **pay**-sti)
looking pale and unhealthy

pat *verb* (**patting, patted**)
to pat something or someone is to tap them gently with your open hand or with something flat

pat *noun*
a patting movement or sound **a pat on the back** congratulations or praise

patch *noun*
1 a piece of material put over a hole or damaged place **2** an area that is different from its surroundings • *We have a black cat with a white patch on its chest.* **3** a small area of land **4** a small piece of something • *There are patches of ice on the road.*

patch *verb*
to patch something is to put a piece of material on it to repair it **to patch something up** is to repair it roughly

patchwork *noun*
patchwork is small pieces of different cloth which are sewn together

patchy *adjective* (**patchier, patchiest**)
occurring in some areas but not others; uneven • *There may be some patchy rain.*

paternal *adjective*
to do with a father, or like a father

path *noun*
1 a narrow way to walk or ride along **2** the line along which something moves • *They were tracing the path of the meteor.*

pathetic *adjective*
1 sad and pitiful **2** sadly or comically weak or useless • *He made a pathetic attempt to climb the tree.*
pathetically *adverb*

patience *noun* (*say* **pay**-shens)
1 patience is the ability to stay calm, especially when you have to wait for a long time **2** patience is also a card game that you play by yourself

patient *adjective* (*say* **pay**-shent)
1 able to wait for a long time without getting anxious or angry **2** able to bear pain or trouble **patiently** *adverb*

patient *noun* (*say* **pay**-shent)
a person who is getting treatment from a doctor or dentist

patio *noun* (**patios**)
(*say* **pat**-i-oh)
a paved area beside a house

WORD ORIGIN

The word **patio** is a Spanish word, and in Spanish it means 'a courtyard'.

patriot *noun* (*say* **pay**-tri-ot or *say* **pat**-ri-ot)
someone who loves and supports their country
patriotic *adjective* loyal to your country **patriotism** *noun* patriotism is loving and supporting your country

patrol *verb* (**patrolling, patrolled**)
to walk or travel regularly round a place or a thing to guard it and make sure that all is well

patrol *noun*
1 a group of people or vehicles patrolling a place **2** a group of Scouts or Guides **to be on patrol** is to be patrolling a place

patron *noun* (*say* **pay**-tron)
1 someone who supports a person or cause with money or encouragement **2** a regular customer of a shop or business

patter *noun*
a series of light tapping sounds

patter *verb*
to patter is to make light tapping sounds • *The rain was pattering on the glass roof.*

pattern *noun*
1 a decorative arrangement of lines or shapes **2** a thing that you copy so that you can make something, such as a piece of clothing

pause *noun*
a short stop before continuing with something

pause *verb*
1 to pause is to make a short stop before continuing with something **2** to pause (for example) a DVD player or CD player is to make it stop for a short time

pave *verb*
to pave a road or path is to put a hard surface on it **to pave the way** is to prepare for something

pavement *noun*
a path with a hard surface, along the side of a street

pavilion *noun*
a building at a sports ground for players and spectators to use

paw *noun*
an animal's foot

paw *verb*
an animal paws something when it touches or scrapes it clumsily with its paw

pawn *noun*
one of the sixteen pieces in chess that are at the front on each side and are the least valuable

pawn *verb*
to pawn something is to leave it with a pawnbroker in exchange for money • *He had to pawn his watch.*

pawnbroker *noun*
a shopkeeper who lends money to people in return for objects that they leave and which are later sold if the money is not paid back

pay *verb* (**paying, paid**)
1 to pay for something is to give money in return for it • *Have you paid for your lunch?* **2** to pay someone is to give them money for something they have done • *Wash my car and I'll pay you £5.* **3** to pay is to be profitable or worthwhile • *It pays to be honest.* **4** to pay (for example) attention or a compliment is to give someone your attention or make them a compliment **5** to pay for something you have done wrong is to suffer for it • *I'll make you pay for this!* **to pay someone back 1** is to pay money that you owe them **2** is to get revenge on them

pay *noun*
pay is the money you earn when you work

payment *noun*
1 payment is when you pay someone or are paid for something **2** a payment is money you pay

PC
short for personal computer, police constable

PE
short for *physical education*

pea *noun*
a small round green seed of a climbing plant, growing inside a pod and used as a vegetable

peace *noun*
1 peace is a time when there is no war or violence • *At last the country was at peace.*
2 peace is also quietness and calm

peaceful *adjective*
1 quiet and calm **2** not involving violence **peacefully** *adverb*

peach *noun*
a soft round juicy fruit with a slightly furry skin and a large stone

peacock *noun*
a large male bird with a long brightly coloured tail that it can spread out like a fan. The female is called a peahen.

peak *noun*
1 the top of a mountain **2** the highest or best point of something • *Traffic reaches its peak at 5 o'clock.* **3** the part of a cap that sticks out in front **peaked** *adjective* a peaked hat or cap is one with a peak

peal *verb*
bells peal when they make a loud ringing sound

peal *noun*
a loud ringing sound made by bells

peanut *noun*
a small round nut that grows in a pod in the ground

pear *noun*
a juicy fruit that gets narrower near the stalk

pearl *noun*
a small shiny white ball found in the shells of some oysters and used as a jewel
pearly *adjective* pearly white teeth are as white and shiny as a pearl

peasant *noun*
a person who works on the land, especially in poor areas of the world or in the Middle Ages **peasantry** *noun* the peasants of a region or country

peat *noun*
peat is rotted plant material that can be dug out of the ground and used as fuel or fertilizer

pebble *noun*
a small round stone found on the beach **pebbly** *adjective* a pebbly beach is one with lots of pebbles

peck *verb*
when a bird pecks something, it bites it or eats it with its beak

peck *noun*
1 a short sharp bite with a bird's beak **2** (*informal*) a quick kiss

peckish *adjective*
(*informal*) slightly hungry

peculiar *adjective*
strange or unusual **to be peculiar to someone** or **something** is to belong to a particular people or place • *This species of bird is peculiar to Asia.* **peculiarly** *adverb* more than usually; strangely • *He is peculiarly fond of brightly coloured socks.*

pedal *noun*
a lever that you press with your foot to operate a bicycle, car, or machine, or to play some musical instruments

pedal *verb* (**pedalling, pedalled**)
to pedal is to push or turn the pedals of a bicycle or other device

pedestal *noun*
the base that supports a statue or pillar

pedestrian *noun*
someone who is walking in the street

pedigree *noun*
a list of a person's or animal's ancestors, especially to show how well an animal has been bred

peel *noun*
the skin of some fruit and vegetables

peel

peel *verb*
1 to peel a piece of fruit or a vegetable is to remove the peel or covering from it **2** to peel is to lose a covering or skin • *The paint on the walls was peeling.*

peep *verb*
1 to peep is to look quickly or secretly, or through a narrow opening **2** to peep or peep out is to come slowly or briefly into view • *The moon peeped out through the clouds.*

peep *noun*
a quick look

peer¹ *verb*
to peer at something or someone is to look at them closely or with difficulty

peer² *noun*
1 a nobleman or noblewoman **2** your peers are the people who are the same age as you

peg *noun*
a clip or pin for fixing things in place or for hanging things on

peg *verb* (**pegging, pegged**)
to peg something is to fix it with pegs • *We pegged out the tent.*

pelican *noun*
a large bird with a pouch in its long beak for storing fish

pellet *noun*
a tiny ball of metal, food, wet paper, or other substance

pelt¹ *verb*
1 to pelt someone with things is to throw a lot of things at them • *We pelted him with snowballs.* **2** it pelts down when it is raining very hard **3** to pelt is to run fast

pelt² *noun*
an animal skin, especially with the fur or hair still on it

pen¹ *noun*
a device with a metal point for writing with ink

pen² *noun*
an enclosure for cattle or other animals

penalize *verb*
1 to penalize someone is to punish them **2** in a game, to penalize someone is to award a penalty against them

penalty *noun* (**penalties**)
1 a punishment **2** a point or advantage given to one side in a game when a member of the other side breaks a rule

pence *plural noun*
pennies

pencil *noun*
a device for drawing or writing, made of a thin stick of graphite or coloured chalk inside a cylinder of wood or metal

pendulum *noun*
a weight hung at the end of a rod so that it swings to and fro, especially to keep a clock working

penetrate *verb*
to penetrate something is to find a way through it or into it **penetration** *noun* penetrating something

penfriend *noun*
someone in another country you write to, usually without meeting them

penguin *noun*
an Antarctic sea bird that cannot fly but uses its wings as flippers for swimming

penguins

penicillin *noun*
penicillin is a drug that kills bacteria, used to cure infections

peninsula *noun*
a long piece of land that is almost surrounded by water

penis *noun*
the part of the body with which a male person or animal urinates and has sexual intercourse

penknife *noun* (**penknives**)
a small folding knife

penniless *adjective*
having no money; very poor

penny *noun* (**pennies** or **pence**)
a British coin worth a hundredth of a pound

pension *noun*
an income of regular payments made to someone who has retired or been widowed **pensioner** *noun* someone who is receiving a pension

pentagon *noun* ⬟
a flat shape with five sides

pentathlon *noun*
(*say* pent-**ath**-lon)
a sports competition that has five different events

people *plural noun*
1 people are human beings; men, women, and children
2 the people of a particular country or area are the men, women, and children who live there

people *noun*
a people is a community or

nation • *They are a peaceful people.*

pepper *noun*
1 pepper is a hot-tasting powder used to flavour food
2 a pepper is a bright green, red, or yellow vegetable **peppery** *adjective* peppery food is hot-tasting like pepper

peppermint *noun*
1 peppermint is a kind of mint used for flavouring
2 a peppermint is a sweet flavoured with this mint

per *preposition*
for each • *The charge is £2 per person.*

perceive *verb*
to perceive something is to see or notice it or understand it

per cent *adverb*
for every hundred • *We pay interest at 5 per cent (5%).*
• *Fifty per cent of the pupils walk to school.*

percentage *noun*
an amount or rate expressed as a proportion of 100

perceptible *adjective*
able to be seen or noticed **perceptibly** *adverb* in a perceptible way • *It was perceptibly warmer.*

perception *noun*
perception is the ability to see, notice, or understand something

perceptive *adjective*
quick to notice or understand things • *It was very perceptive of you to spot that.*

perch[1] *noun*
a place where a bird sits or rests

perch[1] *verb*
to perch is to sit or stand on the edge of something or on something small • *She was perched on a tall stool at the kitchen table.*

perch[2] *noun*
a freshwater fish used for food

percussion *noun*
percussion is musical instruments that you play by hitting them or shaking them, such as drums and cymbals **percussionist** *noun* someone who plays percussion instruments

perennial *adjective*
lasting or occurring for many years • *It is a perennial problem.*

perennial *noun*
a plant that lives for many years **perennially** *adverb* year after year

perfect *adjective* (*say* **per**-fikt)
1 so good that it cannot be made any better; without any

faults **2** complete • *The man is a perfect stranger.* **perfection** *noun* when something is perfect

perfect *verb* (*say* **per**-fekt)
to perfect something is to make it perfect

perfectly *adverb*
1 completely • *She stood perfectly still.* **2** without any faults • *The toaster works perfectly now.*

perforate *verb*
to perforate something is to make tiny holes in it, especially so that it can be torn off easily **perforation** *noun* perforations are the tiny holes made in something so that it can be torn off easily

perform *verb*
1 to perform something is to present it in front of an audience • *They performed a play in the school hall.*
2 to perform something is also to carry it out or complete it • *The surgeon performed the operation on Tuesday.* **performer** *noun* someone who performs an entertainment

performance *noun*
the showing of something in front of an audience

perfume *noun*
1 a sweet-smelling liquid that people put on their skin
2 a sweet or pleasant smell

perhaps *adverb*
it may be; possibly

peril *noun*
peril is danger • *She was in great peril.* **perilous** *adjective* dangerous • *It was a perilous climb.* **perilously** *adverb* dangerously • *We came perilously close to disaster*

perimeter *noun*
(*say* per-**im**-it-er)
1 a boundary • *A fence marks the perimeter of the airfield.*
2 the distance round the edge of something

period *noun*
1 a length of time **2** the time every month when a woman or girl bleeds from her womb in menstruation

periodical *noun*
a magazine published regularly, for example once a month

periscope *noun*
a device with a tube and mirrors that lets you see things at a higher level, used for example in submarines

perish *verb*
1 to perish is to die or be destroyed • *Many sailors*

perished in the shipwreck.
2 to perish is also to rot • *The tyres have perished.* **3** (*informal*) to be perished is to feel extremely cold • *I was perished after the long walk in the hills.*
perishable *adjective* perishable food is likely to go off quickly
permanent *adjective*
lasting for ever or for a long time • *Will there be any permanent damage?*
permanently *adverb* for ever or for a long time
permission *noun*
you have permission to do something when you are allowed to do it
permissive *adjective*
letting people do what they wish; tolerant or liberal
permit *verb* (**permitting, permitted**) (*say* per-**mit**)
1 to permit someone to do something is to allow them to do it **2** to permit something is to allow it to be done
permit *noun* (*say* **per**-mit)
a written or printed statement that says you are allowed to do something
perpendicular *adjective*
standing upright, or at a right angle to a line or surface
perpetual *adjective*
lasting for ever or for a long time **perpetually** *adverb* continually
perplex *verb*
to perplex someone is to puzzle them very much
perplexity *noun* feeling puzzled and confused
persecute *verb*
to persecute someone is to be continually cruel to them, especially because you disagree with their beliefs
persecution *noun* when someone is being persecuted
persecutor *noun* the person who is persecuting someone
persevere *verb*
to persevere is to go on with something even though it is difficult **perseverance** *noun*
you show perseverance when you go on with something even though it is difficult
persist *verb*
1 to persist is to keep on firmly or obstinately doing something • *She persists in breaking the rules.* **2** to persist is also to last for a long time • *The rain persisted all afternoon.*
persistent *adjective*
1 refusing to give up **2** lasting for a long time • *The rain was*

persistent. **persistence** *noun*
you show persistence when you keep on doing something without giving up
persistently *adverb*
person *noun* (**people** or **persons**)
a human being; a man, woman, or child
personal *adjective*
1 belonging to, done by, or concerning a particular person • *The stars of the film will be making a personal appearance at the première.* **2** private • *I can't tell you about that because it's personal.*
personal computer *noun*
a small computer designed to be used by one person
personality *noun* (**personalities**)
1 your personality is your nature and character • *She has a cheerful personality.* **2** a well-known person • *There were several TV personalities at the party.*
personally *adverb*
1 in person; being actually there • *The head thanked me personally.* **2** as far as I am concerned • *Personally, I'd rather stay here.*
personnel *noun* (*say* per-so-**nel**)
the personnel in a business or organization are the people who work there
perspective *noun*
1 perspective is the impression of depth and space in a picture or scene **2** your perspective on a situation is your point of view **in perspective** giving a balanced view of things • *Try to see the problem in perspective.*
perspire *verb*
to perspire is to sweat
perspiration *noun* sweat
persuade *verb*
to persuade someone is to get them to agree about something or do something, by giving them reasons
persuasion *noun* when you persuade someone to do or believe something **persuasive** *adjective* good at persuading people
pessimist *noun*
someone who usually expects things to turn out badly **pessimism** *noun* the feeling that things will turn out badly
pessimistic *adjective*
expecting things to turn out badly **pessimistically** *adverb*

pest *noun*
1 a destructive insect or animal, such as a locust or a mouse **2** an annoying person; a nuisance
pester *verb*
to pester someone is to annoy them with frequent questions or interruptions
pet *noun*
1 a tame animal that you keep at home **2** a person treated as a favourite • *She seems to be teacher's pet.*
petal *noun*
each of the separate coloured outer parts of a flower
petition *noun*
a written request for someone in authority to do something, usually signed by a large number of people
petrify *verb* (**petrifies, petrifying, petrified**)
to petrify someone is to make them so terrified that they cannot move or act
petrol *noun*
petrol is a liquid made from oil, used as a fuel for engines
petticoat *noun*
a piece of women's clothing worn under a skirt or dress
petty *adjective* (**pettier, pettiest**)
1 minor and unimportant • *There are some petty regulations.* **2** mean and selfish about small things **pettily** *adverb* **pettiness** *noun*
pew *noun*
one of the long wooden seats in a church
pewter *noun*
pewter is a grey alloy of tin and lead
pH *noun*
a measure of how much acid or alkali a solution contains. Acids have a pH between 0 and 7, and alkalis have a pH between 7 and 14.
phantom *noun*
a ghost
pharmacy *noun* (**pharmacies**)
a shop that sells medicines
phase *noun*
a stage in the progress or development of something
pheasant *noun* (*say* **fez**-ant)
a bird with a long tail that some people shoot as a sport
phenomenal *adjective* (*say* fin-**om**-in-al)
amazing or remarkable
phenomenon *noun* (**phenomena**)
an event or fact, especially one that is remarkable or unusual

a
b
c
d
e
f
g
h
i
j
k
l
m
n
o
p
q
r
s
t
u
v
w
x
y
z

philosophical *adjective*
1 to do with philosophy
2 calmly accepting disappointment or suffering • *He was philosophical about losing.* **philosophically** *adverb*

philosophy *noun* (**philosophies**) (*say* fil-**os**-o-fi)
1 philosophy is the study of what life and human behaviour is all about 2 a philosophy is a way of thinking or a system of beliefs
philosopher *noun* someone who studies philosophy

phobia *noun* (*say* **foh**-bi-a) a great or unusual fear of something

phone *noun*
a telephone

phone *verb*
to phone someone is to telephone them

phone-in *noun*
a radio or TV programme in which people telephone the studio and take part in a discussion

phosphorescent *adjective* shining or glowing in the dark **phosphorescence** *noun* phosphorescence is being phosphorescent

phosphorus *noun* Ⓟ phosphorus is a yellowish substance that glows in the dark

photo *noun*
(*informal*) a photograph

photocopier *noun*
a machine that makes photocopies

photocopy *noun*
a copy of a document or page made by a machine that photographs it on special paper

photocopy *verb* (**photocopies, photocopying, photocopied**)
to photocopy a document is to make a copy of it with a photocopier

photograph *noun*
a picture made on film, using a camera

photograph *verb*
to photograph someone or something is to take a photograph of them **photographer** *noun* someone who takes photographs

photography *noun*
photography is taking photographs with a camera **photographic** *adjective* to do with photography

phrase *noun*
1 a group of words that do not make a complete sentence, for example *in the garden* in the sentence *The Queen was in the garden* 2 a short section of a tune

physical *adjective*
1 to do with the body rather than the mind or feelings 2 to do with things you can touch or see **physically** *adverb* in a way that is connected with the body rather than the mind or feelings

physical education *noun*
physical education is gymnastics or other exercises that you do to keep your body healthy

physics *noun*
physics is the study of matter and energy, including movement, heat, light, and sound **physicist** *noun* an expert in physics

pianist *noun*
someone who plays the piano

piano *noun*
a large musical instrument with a row of black and white keys on a keyboard

piccolo *noun*
a small high-pitched flute

pick¹ *verb*
1 to pick something or someone is to choose them • *Pick a card from this pack.* 2 to pick flowers or fruit is to cut or pull them off the plant or tree 3 to pick someone's pocket is to steal from it 4 to pick a lock is to open it without using a key 5 to pick bits off or out of something is to pull them away from it **to pick on someone** is to keep criticizing or bothering them **to pick someone up** is to give them a lift in a vehicle **to pick something up** 1 is to take it from the ground or a surface 2 is to collect it • *I'll pick up my bags from the station.*

pick¹ *noun*
1 a choice • *Take your pick.* 2 the best part of something

pick² *noun*
a pickaxe

pickaxe *noun*
a heavy pointed tool with a long handle, used for breaking up concrete or hard ground

picket *noun*
a group of workers on strike who try to persuade other people not to go into the place where they work

pickle *noun*
a strong-tasting food made of vegetables preserved in vinegar

pickle *verb*
to pickle food is to preserve it in vinegar or salt water

pickpocket *noun*
a thief who steals from people's pockets or bags

picnic *noun*
a meal eaten in the open air away from home

picnic *verb* (**picnicking, picnicked**)
to picnic is to have a picnic **picnicker** *noun* someone having a picnic

pictorial *adjective*
with or using pictures **pictorially** *adverb*

picture *noun*
1 a painting, drawing, or photograph 2 a film at the cinema **to be in the picture** is to know about something

picture *verb*
1 to picture someone or something is to show them in a picture 2 to picture someone or something in your mind is to imagine them

picturesque *adjective* (*say* pik-cher-**esk**)
a picturesque place is attractive or charming • *We drove through a picturesque village.*

pie *noun*
a baked dish of meat or fruit covered with pastry

piece *noun*
1 a part of something; a bit 2 a work of art or writing or music • *They played a piece of piano music.* 3 one of the objects you use on a board to play a game • *You've dropped a chess piece.* 4 a coin • *a 20p piece* **piece by piece** gradually; one bit at a time

piece *verb*
to piece things together is to join them to make something

pier *noun*
a long structure built out into the sea for people to walk on

pierce *verb*
to pierce something is to make a hole through it

piercing *adjective*
1 a piercing sound is loud nd high-pitched • *We heard a piercing shriek.* 2 something piercing seems to go right through you • *The wind was cold and piercing.*

piccolo

pig *noun*
1 a fat animal with short legs and a blunt snout, kept for its meat **2** (*informal*) you can describe someone as a pig when they are greedy, dirty, or unpleasant

pigeon *noun*
a common grey bird with a small head and large chest

piggyback *noun*
a ride on someone's back

piglet *noun*
a young pig

pigment *noun*
a substance that colours something

pigmy *noun* (**pigmies**)
another spelling of **pygmy**

pigsty *noun* (**pigsties**)
1 a place for keeping pigs **2** (*informal*) you can describe a very untidy room or place as a pigsty

pigtail *noun*
a single plait of hair worn hanging at the back of the head

pike *noun*
1 a large fish that lives in rivers and lakes **2** a heavy spear

pilchard *noun*
a small sea fish

pile *noun*
a number of things on top of one another; a large amount of something

pile *verb*
to pile things is to put them into a pile

pilgrim *noun*
someone who goes on a journey to a holy place

pilgrimage *noun*
a journey to a holy place

pill *noun*
a small piece of medicine that you swallow **the pill** a special kind of pill taken by a woman to prevent her from becoming pregnant

pillar *noun*
a tall stone post supporting part of a building

pillion *noun*
a seat for a passenger behind the driver's seat on a motorcycle

pillow *noun*
a cushion to rest your head on in bed

pillowcase *noun*
a cloth cover for a pillow

pilot *noun*
1 someone who flies an aircraft **2** someone who helps to steer a ship in and out of a port or through a difficult stretch of water

pilot *verb*
to pilot an aircraft is to be the pilot of it

pimple *noun*
a small round swelling on your skin **pimply** *adjective* having pimples

pin *noun*
a short piece of metal with a sharp point and a rounded head, used to fasten pieces of paper or cloth together **pins and needles** a tingling feeling in the skin

pin *verb* (**pinning, pinned**)
to pin something is to fasten it with a pin

pincer *noun*
the claw of a shellfish such as a lobster

pincers *plural noun*
a tool for gripping and pulling things, especially for pulling out nails

pinch *verb*
1 to pinch something is to squeeze it tightly between two things, especially between the finger and thumb **2** (*informal*) to pinch something is to steal it

pinch *noun*
1 a firm squeezing movement **2** the amount you can pick up between the tips of your finger and thumb • *Take a pinch of salt.* **at a pinch** if it is really necessary

pine¹ *noun*
an evergreen tree with leaves shaped like needles

pine² *verb*
1 to pine for someone or something is to feel a strong longing for them **2** to pine, or pine away, is to become weak or ill through sorrow or yearning

pineapple *noun*
a large tropical fruit with yellow flesh and prickly leaves and skin

ping-pong *noun*
ping-pong is table tennis

pineapple

pink *adjective* ●
pale red

pink *noun*
1 a sweet-smelling garden flower **2** a pink colour

pint *noun*
a measure of liquid, an eighth of a gallon or about 568 millilitres

pioneer *noun*
one of the first people to go to a place or do something new

pious *adjective*
very religious or devout
piously *adverb*

pip *noun*
a small hard seed of a fruit such as an apple, orange, or pear

pipe *noun*
1 a tube for carrying water, gas, or oil from one place to another **2** a short tube with a small bowl at one end, used to smoke tobacco **3** a musical instrument in the shape of a small tube

pipe *verb*
1 to pipe something is to send it along pipes or wires **2** to pipe is to play music on a pipe or the bagpipes **to pipe up** (*informal*) is to start saying something

pipeline *noun*
a pipe for carrying oil, water, or gas over a long distance

piper *noun*
someone who plays a pipe or the bagpipes

piping *adjective*
high-pitched; shrill
piping hot very hot, ready to eat

pirate *noun*
a sailor who attacks and robs other ships

piracy *noun*
piracy is robbing ships

pistol *noun*
a small gun held in the hand

piston *noun*
a disc that moves up and down inside a cylinder in an engine or pump

pit *noun*
1 a deep hole or hollow **2** a coal mine **3** the part of a race circuit where cars are refuelled and serviced during a race

pirate

pitch¹ *noun*
1 a pitch is a piece of ground marked out for cricket, football, or another game **2** pitch is how high or low a

a
b
c
d
e
f
g
h
i
j
k
l
m
n
o
v
w
x
y
z

voice or musical note is **3** the pitch of something is also its intensity or strength • *Excitement was at a high pitch.*

pitch¹ *verb*
1 to pitch something is to throw or fling it **2** to pitch a tent is to set it up **3** to pitch is to fall heavily • *He tripped over the doorstep and pitched forward.* **4** a ship pitches when it moves up and down on a rough sea

pitch² *noun*
pitch is a black sticky substance like tar

pitch-black or **pitch-dark** *adjective*
completely black or dark, with no light at all

pitcher *noun*
a large jug, usually with two handles

pitchfork *noun*
a large fork with two prongs for lifting hay

pitfall *noun*
a hidden danger or difficulty

pitiful *adjective*
1 making you feel pity • *It was a pitiful sight.* **2** inadequate; feeble • *He made a pitiful attempt to make us laugh.* **pitifully** *adverb*

pitiless *adjective*
having or showing no pity **pitilessly** *adverb*

pitta bread *noun*
pitta bread is a flat, round piece of bread that you can open and fill with food

pity *noun*
1 pity is the feeling of being sorry because someone is suffering or in trouble • *I feel pity for the homeless people.* **2** a pity is something that you regret • *It's a pity they can't come.* **to take pity on someone** is to help someone who is in trouble

pity *verb* (**pities, pitying, pitied**)
to pity someone is to feel sorry for them

pivot *noun*
a point on which something turns or balances

pixie or **pixy** *noun*
a small fairy or elf

pizza *noun* (*say* **peet**-sa)
an Italian food made as a layer of dough covered with cheese, vegetables, and spices and baked

placard *noun*
a large poster or notice, especially one carried at a demonstration

place *noun*
1 a particular part of space, especially where something belongs; an area or position

2 a position in a race or competition **3** a seat • *Save me a place.* **in place** in the proper position **in place of something** or **someone** instead of them **out of place 1** in the wrong position **2** unsuitable • *Jeans and sandals are out of place in a smart restaurant.* **to take place** is to happen

place *verb*
to place something somewhere is to put it in a particular place

placid *adjective*
calm and gentle; peaceful • *a placid horse.* **placidly** *adverb*

plague *noun*
1 a dangerous illness that spreads very quickly **2** a large number of pests • *The crops were devastated by a plague of locusts.*

plague *verb*
to plague someone is to pester or annoy them continuously • *They have been plagued with complaints.*

plaice *noun* (**plaice**)
a flat sea fish used for food

plain *adjective*
1 simple; not decorated **2** not pretty **3** easy to understand or see **4** frank; straightforward • *I'll be quite plain with you.* **plainness** *noun*

plain *noun*
a large area of flat country without trees

plainly *adverb*
1 clearly or obviously • *The clock tower was plainly visible in the distance.* **2** simply • *She was plainly dressed.*

plait *noun* (*say* plat)
a length of hair or rope made by twisting several strands together

plait *verb* (*say* plat)
to plait hair or rope is to make it into a plait

plan *noun*
1 a way of doing something that you think out in advance **2** a drawing showing how the parts of something are arranged **3** a map of a town or district

plan *verb* (**planning, planned**)
1 to plan something is to think out in advance how you are going to do it **2** to plan to do something is to intend to do it **planner** *noun* someone who plans things

plane¹ *noun*
1 an aeroplane **2** a tool for making wood smooth **3** a flat or level surface

plane¹ *verb*
to plane wood is to smooth it with a plane

plane² *noun*
a tall tree with broad leaves

planet *noun*
one of the bodies that move in an orbit round the sun. The main planets of the solar system are Mercury, Venus, Earth, Mars, Jupiter, Saturn, Uranus and Neptune.

plank *noun*
a long flat piece of wood

plankton *noun*
plankton is made up of tiny creatures that float in the sea and lakes

plant *noun*
1 a living thing that grows out of the ground, including flowers, bushes, trees, and vegetables **2** a factory or its equipment

plant *verb*
1 to plant something such as a tree or flower is to put it in the ground to grow **2** to plant something is also to put it firmly in place • *He planted his feet on the ground and took hold of the rope.* **3** to plant something is to secretly put it somewhere, usually to cause trouble • *A bomb was planted on a train.*

plantation *noun*
an area of land where a crop such as tobacco, tea, or rubber is planted

plaque *noun* (*say* plak or plahk)
1 a plaque is a metal or porcelain plate fixed on a wall as a memorial or an ornament **2** plaque is a substance that forms a thin layer on your teeth, allowing bacteria to develop

plaster *noun*
1 a plaster is a small covering you put over your skin around a cut or wound to protect it **2** plaster is a mixture of lime, sand, and water, used to cover walls and ceilings

plaster *verb*
1 to plaster a wall or ceiling is to cover it with plaster **2** to plaster a surface with something is to cover it thickly • *His clothes were plastered with mud.* **plasterer** *noun* someone who plasters walls and ceilings

plastic *noun*
a strong light synthetic substance that can be moulded into different shapes

plastic *adjective*
made of plastic • *I need a plastic bag.*

Plasticine *noun*
(*trademark*) Plasticine is a soft and easily shaped substance used for making models

a b c d e f g h i j k l m n o **p** q r s t u v w x y z

plastic surgery *noun*
plastic surgery is work done by a surgeon to change or mend parts of someone's body

plate *noun*
1 a dish that is flat or almost flat, used for eating **2** a thin flat sheet of metal, glass, or other hard material **3** an illustration on a separate page in a book

plate *verb*
to plate metal is to cover it with a thin layer of gold, silver, tin, or other soft metal

plateau *noun* (**plateaux**) (*say* **plat**-oh)
a flat area of high land

platform *noun*
1 a flat raised area along the side of the line at a railway station **2** a raised area for speakers or performers in a hall

platinum *noun* (Pt)
platinum is a silver-coloured metal that does not lose its brightness

platoon *noun*
a small unit of soldiers

platypus *noun*
an Australian animal with a beak and feet like those of a duck

play *verb*
1 to play, or play a game, is to take part in a game or other amusement **2** to play music, or a musical instrument, is to make music or sound with it **3** to play a part in a film or play is to perform it **4** to play a CD, DVD, or tape is to put it in a machine and listen to it or watch it **to play about** or **around** is to have fun or be mischievous **to play someone up** is to tease or annoy them

player *noun* someone who plays a game or a musical instrument

play *noun*
1 a play is a story acted on a stage or broadcast on radio or television **2** play is playing or having fun

playful *adjective*
1 wanting to play; full of fun **2** not serious **playfully** *adverb* **playfulness** *noun*

playground *noun*
a place out of doors where children can play

playgroup *noun*
a place where very young children can play together and are looked after by parents and other helpers

playing card *noun*
each of a set of cards (usually 52) used for playing games

playing field *noun*
a grassy field for outdoor games

playtime *noun*
the time when young schoolchildren go out to play

playwright *noun*
someone who writes plays

plea *noun*
1 a request or appeal **2** a statement of 'guilty' or 'not guilty' made in a lawcourt by someone accused of a crime

plead *verb*
to plead with someone is to beg them to do something **to plead guilty or not guilty** is to state in a lawcourt that you are guilty or not guilty of a crime

pleasant *adjective*
pleasing or enjoyable or friendly **pleasantly** *adverb* in a pleasant way • *I was pleasantly surprised.*

please *verb*
1 to please someone is to make them happy or satisfied **2** used when you want to ask something politely • *Please shut the door.*

pleasure *noun*
1 pleasure is a feeling of being pleased **2** a pleasure is something that pleases you **with pleasure** gladly; willingly

pleat *noun*
a fold made in cloth by pressing or sewing it **pleated** *adjective*

pledge *noun*
a solemn promise

pledge *verb*
to pledge something is to promise it

plentiful *adjective*
large in amount **plentifully** *adverb*

plenty *noun*
to have plenty of something is to have a lot of it or more than enough • *We have plenty of chairs.*

pliers *plural noun*
pincers with flattened jaws for gripping something or for breaking wire

plight *noun*
a difficult and sad situation • *They were stranded for several days before anyone knew of heir plight.*

plod *verb* (**plodding, plodded**)
to plod is to walk slowly and with heavy steps • *We plodded back through the rain.*

plop *noun*
the sound of something dropping into a liquid

plop *verb* (**plopping, plopped**)
to plop is to fall into a liquid with a plop

plot *noun*
1 a secret plan, especially to do something illegal or bad **2** what happens in a story, film, or play **3** a piece of land for a house or garden

plot *verb* (**plotting, plotted**)
1 to plot is to make a secret plan to do something **2** to plot a chart or graph is to make it, marking all the points on it **plotter** *noun* plotters are people who take part in a plot

plough *noun* (*say* plow)
a large farm tool pulled by a tractor or animal, used for turning over the soil

plough *verb*
to plough the soil is to turn it over with a plough

ploughman *noun* (**ploughmen**)
someone who uses a plough

pluck *verb*
1 to pluck a bird is to pull the feathers off it to prepare it for cooking **2** to pluck a flower or fruit is to pick it **3** to pluck something is to pull it or pull it out • *She plucked a book from the shelf.* **4** in music, to pluck a string is to pull it and let it go again **to pluck up courage** is to be brave and overcome fear

pluck *noun*
pluck is courage or bravery

plucky *adjective* (**pluckier, pluckiest**)
brave or courageous **pluckily** *adverb*

plug *noun*
1 something used to stop up a hole, especially in a sink or bath **2** a device that is used to connect a piece of electric equipment to a socket

plug *verb* (**plugging, plugged**)
1 to plug a hole is to stop it up **2** (*informal*) to plug an event or product is to publicize it **to plug something in** is to connect it to an electric socket with a plug

plum *noun*
a soft juicy red or purple fruit with a stone in the middle

plum

plumage noun (say **ploo**-mij)
a bird's plumage is its feathers

plumber noun
someone who fits and mends water pipes in a building

plumbing noun
1 plumbing is the work of a plumber **2** the plumbing in a building is all the water pipes and water tanks

plume noun
1 a large feather **2** something shaped like a feather • *We saw a plume of smoke in the distance.*

plump adjective
rounded or slightly fat

plump verb
to plump for something or **someone** is to choose them

plunder verb
to plunder a place or an enemy is to rob them violently, especially in a time of war or disorder **plunderer** noun someone who plunders a place

plunder noun
1 plunder is plundering a person or place **2** plunder is also goods taken by plundering

plunge verb
1 to plunge into water is to jump or dive into it with force **2** to plunge something into a liquid or something soft is to put it in with force

plunge noun
a sudden fall or dive

plural noun
the form of a word meaning more than one person or thing, such as *cakes* and *children*

plural adjective
in the plural; meaning more than one • *'Mice' is a plural noun.*

plus preposition
with the next number or thing added • *2 plus 2 equals 4 (2 + 2 = 4).*

p.m.
short for Latin *post meridiem* which means 'after midday'

pneumatic adjective
(say new-**mat**-ik)
filled with air or worked by compressed air • *a pneumatic tyre* • *a pneumatic drill*

pneumonia noun
(say new-**moh**-ni-a)
pneumonia is a serious disease of the lungs

poach verb
1 to poach food, especially fish or an egg taken out of its shell, is to cook it in or over boiling water **2** to poach animals is to hunt them illegally on someone else's land
poacher noun someone who

hunts animals illegally on someone else's land

pocket noun
part of a piece of clothing shaped like a small bag, for keeping things in

pocket adjective
small enough to carry in your pocket • *Use a pocket calculator.*

pocket verb
to pocket something is to put it in your pocket

pocket money noun
pocket money is money given to a child to spend

pod noun
a long seed-container on a pea or bean plant

podgy adjective (**podgier, podgiest**)
short and fat

poem noun
a piece of writing arranged in short lines, often with a particular rhythm and sometimes rhyming

poet noun
someone who writes poetry

poetry noun
poetry is poems as a form of literature • *Do you write poetry?*

point noun
1 the narrow or sharp end of something • *Don't hold the knife by its point.* **2** a written dot • *Put in a decimal point.* **3** a single mark in a game or quiz • *How many points did I get?* **4** a particular place or time • *They gave up at this point.* **5** something that someone says during a discussion • *That's a very good point.* **6** a detail or special feature • *He has some good points.* **7** purpose or advantage • *There's no point in hurrying.* **8** the points on a railway line are the movable parts that allow trains to change from one track to another **to come to the point** is to mention the thing you really want to say

point verb
1 to point to something is to show where it is, especially by holding out your finger towards it **2** to point something is to aim it or direct it • *She pointed a gun at us.* **to point something out** is to show it or explain it

point-blank adjective, adverb
1 close to the target **2** directly and completely • *He refused point-blank.*

pointed adjective
having a point at the end

pointer noun
a stick or device you use to point at something

pointless adjective
something is pointless when it has no purpose or meaning
pointlessly adverb

point of view noun (**points of view**)
a way of looking or thinking of something

poise noun
poise is a dignified and self-confident manner

poise verb
1 to poise something is to balance it or keep it steady **2** to be poised to do something is to be ready to do it

poison noun
a substance that can kill or harm living things if they eat or absorb it

poison verb
1 to poison someone is to kill or harm them with poison **2** to poison something is to put poison in it **poisoner** noun a person who kills someone using poison

poisonous adjective
1 a poisonous chemical, gas, or plant can kill or harm you if you swallow it or breathe it in **2** poisonous animals or insects can kill or harm you with poison if they bite you • *a poisonous snake*

poke verb
to poke something or someone is to push or jab them hard with your finger or a pointed object **to poke out** is to stick out

poke noun
a prod or jab

poker noun
1 a poker is a metal rod for stirring a fire **2** poker is a card game in which the players bet on who has the best cards

polar adjective
to do with the North or South Pole, or near one of them

polar bear noun
a powerful white bear living near the North Pole

pole[1] noun
a long thin piece of wood or metal

pole[2] noun
1 each of the two points on the earth that are furthest from the equator, the **North Pole** and the **South Pole** **2** each end of a magnet

pole vault noun
the pole vault is an athletic contest in which you jump over a high bar with the help of a long springy pole

police noun
the police are the people whose

job is to catch criminals and make sure that people obey the law

policeman or **policewoman** noun (**policemen** or **policewomen**)
a man or woman member of the police

police officer noun
a member of the police

policy noun (**policies**)
the aims or plans of a person or group of people

polio noun (say **poh**-li-oh)
a disease that paralyses the body

polish verb (say **pol**-ish)
to polish something is to make its surface shiny or smooth
to polish something off (informal) is to finish it quickly

polish noun (say **pol**-ish)
1 polish is a substance used in polishing **2** a polish is a shine got by polishing • He gave his shoes a good polish.

polite adjective
having good manners; respectful and thoughtful towards other people **politely** adverb **politeness** noun

political adjective
to do with the governing of a country **politically** adverb in a way that is to do with politics

politician noun
someone who is involved in politics

politics noun
politics is political matters; the business of governing a country

poll noun
1 a round of voting at an election **2** a survey of what people think about something

pollen noun
pollen is yellow powder found inside flowers, containing male seeds for fertilizing other flowers

pollinate verb
to pollinate a flower or plant is to put pollen into it so that it becomes fertilized
pollination noun the process of pollinating a flower or plant

pollute verb
to pollute a place or thing is to make it dirty or impure

pollution noun
pollution is the process of making the air, water, and soil dirty or impure

polo noun
polo is a game rather like hockey, with players on horseback using long mallets

poltergeist noun (say pol-ter-**gyst**)
a noisy mischievous ghost that moves things or throws them about

polygon noun
a figure or shape with many sides, such as a hexagon or octagon

polythene noun (say **pol**-i-theen)
polythene is a lightweight plastic used to make bags and wrappings

pomp noun
pomp is the dignified and solemn way in which an important ceremony is carried out

pompous adjective
someone is being pompous when they are thinking too much of their own importance

pond noun
a small lake

ponder verb
to ponder something is to think carefully and seriously about it

pony noun
a small horse

ponytail noun
a bunch of long hair tied at the back of the head

poodle noun
a dog with long curly hair

pool¹ noun
1 a pond **2** a puddle **3** a swimming pool

pool² noun
1 a group of things shared by several people **2** the fund of money that can be won in a gambling game **3** pool is a game similar to snooker but played on a smaller table **the pools** a system of gambling on the results of football matches

poor adjective
1 having very little money • He came from a poor family. **2** not good or adequate • This is poor work. **3** unfortunate • Poor fellow!

poorly adverb
not adequately; badly • She did poorly in the test.

poorly adjective
unwell • I'm feeling poorly today.

pop¹ noun
1 a pop is a small sharp bang **2** pop is a fizzy drink

pop¹ verb (**popping, popped**)
1 to pop is to make a small sharp bang **2** (informal) to pop somewhere is to go there

quickly • I'm just popping out to the shops. **3** to pop something somewhere is to put it there quickly • Will you pop the potatoes in the oven?

pop² noun
pop is modern popular music

popcorn noun
a snack made from grains of maize heated till they burst and form light fluffy balls

Pope noun
the Pope is the leader of the Roman Catholic Church

poppy noun (**poppies**)
a plant with large red flowers

popular adjective
liked or enjoyed by a lot of people **popularity** noun being liked or enjoyed by a lot of people

populated adjective
a place is populated when it has people living there • The land is thinly populated.

population noun
the population of a particular place is all the people who live there; the total number of people who live there • What's the population of London?

porcelain noun (say **por**-se-lin)
porcelain is a fine kind of china

porch noun
a covered area in front of the door of a building

porcupine noun
a small animal covered with long prickles

WORD ORIGINS
The word **porcupine** comes from old French words meaning 'prickly pig'.

porcupine

pore noun
one of the tiny openings in your skin which sweat can pass through

pork noun
pork is meat from a pig

porous *adjective*
something is porous when it allows liquid or air to pass through • *Sandy soil is porous.*

porpoise *noun* (*say* **por**-pus)
a sea animal rather like a small whale

porridge *noun*
porridge is a food made by boiling oatmeal to make a thick paste

port¹ *noun*
1 a port is a harbour **2** a port is also a city or town with a harbour **3** port is the left-hand side of a ship or aircraft when you are facing forward

port² *noun*
port is a strong red Portuguese wine

portable *adjective*
able to be carried easily

portcullis *noun*
a heavy grating that can be lowered to block the gateway to a castle

porter *noun*
1 someone whose job is to carry luggage or goods **2** someone whose job is to look after the entrance to a large building

porthole *noun*
a small round window in the side of a ship or aircraft

portion *noun*
1 a part or share given to someone **2** an amount of food for one person

portly *adjective* (**portlier, portliest**)
rather fat

portrait *noun*
a picture of a person

portray *verb*
to portray something or someone is to describe or show them in a certain way • *The play portrays the king as a kind man.* **portrayal** *noun* how a person or thing is described or shown

pose *noun*
a way of standing or sitting for a portrait or photograph to be made of you • *Just hold that pose for a second.*

pose *verb*
1 to pose is to put your body into a special position **2** to pose someone is to put them in a particular position to be painted or photographed **3** to pose as someone is to pretend to be them • *The man posed as a police officer.* **4** to pose a question or problem is to present it • *Icy weather always poses a problem to motorists.*

posh *adjective*
(*informal*) very smart or high-class • *They stayed at a posh hotel.* • *She spoke with a posh accent.*

position *noun*
1 the place where something is or should be **2** the way in which someone or something is placed or arranged • *He was sleeping in an uncomfortable position.* **3** a person's place in a race or competition **4** a regular job

positive *adjective*
1 sure or definite • *I am positive I saw him.* • *We need positive proof.* **2** agreeing or saying 'yes' • *We received a positive answer.* **3** a positive number is one that is greater than nought **4** a positive electric charge is one that does not carry electrons **positively** *adverb*

positive *noun*
a photographic print made from a negative, with light and dark parts as in real life

posse *noun* (*say* **poss**-i)
a group of people who help a sheriff in the USA

possess *verb*
to possess something is to own or have it **possessor** *noun* a person who owns or has something

possessed *adjective*
someone is possessed when they are behaving as if they are controlled by an outside force • *He fought like a man possessed.*

possession *noun*
something that you own

possessive *adjective*
you are being possessive when you want to get and keep things for yourself

possibility *noun* (**possibilities**)
1 possibility is being possible • *Is there any possibility of changing your mind?* **2** a possibility is something that is possible • *There are many possibilities.*

possible *adjective*
able to exist, happen, be done, or be used

possibly *adverb*
1 in any way • *That cannot possibly be right.* **2** perhaps • *I will arrive at six o'clock, or possibly earlier.*

post¹ *noun*
1 an upright piece of wood, concrete, or metal fixed in the ground **2** the starting point or finishing point of a race • *He was left at the post.*

post² *noun*
1 the post is the collecting and delivering of letters and parcels **2** post is letters and parcels carried by post; mail **3** a post is a collection or delivery of mail at a particular time • *The last post is at 4 p.m.*

post² *verb*
to post a letter or parcel is to send it to someone by post

post³ *noun*
1 a regular job **2** the place where a sentry stands

post³ *verb*
to be posted somewhere is to be sent there for a time as part of your job

postage *noun*
postage is the cost of sending a letter or parcel by post

postal *adjective*
to do with the post; by post

postbox *noun*
a box into which you put letters to be sent by post

postcard *noun*
a card that you can write a message on and post without an envelope

postcode *noun*
a group of letters and numbers put at the end of an address to help in sorting the post

poster *noun*
a large public notice having information or advertising something

postman *noun* (**postmen**)
someone who collects and delivers letters and parcels

postmark *noun*
an official mark stamped on something sent by post, showing when and where it was posted

post office *noun*
a place where you can post letters and parcels and buy stamps and other official documents

postpone *verb*
to postpone a meeting or event is to arrange for it to take place later than was originally planned • *The match has been postponed for two weeks.* **postponement** *noun* when something is arranged to take place later than was originally planned

posture *noun*
the way that a person stands, sits, or walks

posy *noun* (**posies**)
a small bunch of flowers

pot *noun*
1 a deep round container **2** a flowerpot **pots of money** (*informal*) a lot of money

pot *verb* (**potting, potted**)
1 to pot a plant is to put it into a flowerpot **2** to pot a ball in a game such as snooker or pool is to hit it into a pocket

potassium *noun* Ⓚ
potassium is a soft silvery-white metallic substance that living things need

potato *noun* (**potatoes**)
a vegetable that grows underground

potent *adjective*
powerful **potency** *noun* the potency of something is how powerful it is **potently** *adverb*

potential *adjective*
possible or capable of happening in the future • *She is a potential star.* **potentially** *adverb* as a possibility in the future • *He is potentially one of our best players.*

potential *noun*
to have potential is to be capable of becoming important or useful in the future

pothole *noun*
1 a deep natural hole in the ground **2** a hole in a road

potion *noun* (say **poh**-shon)
a drink containing medicine or poison

potter *noun*
someone who makes pottery

pottery *noun* (**potteries**)
1 pottery is pots, cups, plates, and other things made of baked clay **2** pottery is also the craft of making pottery

potty *noun* (**potties**)
(*informal*) a small bowl used by young children as a toilet

pouch *noun*
1 a small bag or pocket **2** a fold of skin in which a kangaroo keeps its young

poultry *noun*
poultry are birds such as chickens, geese, and turkeys, kept for their eggs and meat

pounce *verb*
to pounce on someone or something is to jump on them or attack them suddenly

pound[1] *noun*
1 a unit of money, in Britain equal to 100 pence **2** a unit of weight equal to 16 ounces or about 454 grams

pound[2] *verb*
1 to pound something is to hit it repeatedly to crush it **2** to pound, or pound along, is to walk with heavy steps **3** your heart is pounding when it beats heavily, making a dull thumping sound • *My heart was pounding with the excitement.*

pour *verb*
1 to pour a liquid is to make it flow out of a container
2 to pour is to flow in a large amount • *Blood was pouring from the wound on her leg.*
3 it is pouring when it is raining heavily **4** to pour in or out is to come or go in large numbers or amounts
• *After the programme, letters of complaint poured in.* • *The fans poured out of the stadium.*

pout *verb*
you pout when you stick out your lips because you are annoyed or sulking

poverty *noun*
poverty is being poor

powder *noun*
1 a mass of tiny pieces of something dry, like flour or dust **2** make-up in the form of powder **powdery** *adjective* like powder

powder *verb*
to powder something is to put powder on it • *She powdered her face.* **powdered** *adjective* made into a powder • *powdered milk*

power *noun*
1 power is strength or great energy **2** power is also control over other people **3** the power to do something is the ability to do it • *Humans have the power of speech.* **4** a power is a powerful country **5** power is also electricity or another form of energy **6** (*in mathematics*) the power of a number is the result obtained by multiplying the number by itself one or more times • *27 is the third power of 3 (3 x 3 x 3 = 27).*
powered *adjective* a device is (for example) electric-powered or solar-powered when it is worked by electricity or by the sun's energy

powerful *adjective*
having a lot of power or influence **powerfully** *adverb*

powerless *adjective*
someone is powerless if they are unable to act or control things

power station *noun*
a building where electricity is produced

practical *adjective*
1 someone is practical when they are able to do or make useful things • *She is a very practical person.* **2** something is practical when it is likely to be useful • *That is a practical idea.* **3** concerned with doing or making things • *He has had practical experience.*

practical *noun*
a lesson or examination in which you actually do or make something rather than reading or writing about it

practical joke *noun*
a trick played on someone

practically *adverb*
1 in a practical way • *He is practically skilled.* **2** almost • *It's practically ready now.*

practice *noun*
1 practice is doing something often and regularly so that you get better at it • *I must do my piano practice.* **2** practice is also actually doing something rather than thinking or talking about it • *It's time to put this theory of yours into practice.*
• *I hope my plan works in practice.* **3** a practice is the business of a doctor or lawyer

practise *verb*
1 to practise something is to do it often so that you get better at it **2** to practise an activity or custom is to do it regularly • *She practises yoga.*
3 to practise (for example) medicine or law is to work as a doctor or lawyer

prairie *noun*
a large area of flat grass-covered land in North America

praise *verb*
to praise someone or something is to say that they are good or have done well

praise *noun*
praise is words that praise someone or something

pram *noun*
a small open carriage for a baby, pushed by a person walking

prance *verb*
to prance is to jump about in a lively or happy way

prank *noun*
a trick played on someone for mischief

prawn *noun*
a shellfish like a large shrimp, used for food

pray *verb*
1 to pray is to talk to God **2** to pray is also to ask earnestly or hope for something • *We are praying for good weather.*

prayer *noun*
1 prayer is praying **2** a prayer is what you say when you pray

preach *verb*
to preach is to give a talk about religion or about right and wrong **preacher** *noun* someone who preaches

precarious adjective
(say pri-**kair**-i-us)
not at all safe or secure • *That vase is in a precarious position.*
precariously adverb

precaution noun
something you do to prevent trouble or danger in the future • *I took the precaution of bringing my umbrella.*

precede verb
one thing precedes another when it comes or goes in front of the other thing • *The film was preceded by a short cartoon.*

precinct noun (say **pree**-sinkt)
a part of a town where traffic is not allowed • *The town has a large shopping precinct.*

precious adjective
very valuable or loved

precipice noun
the steep face of a mountain or cliff

precise adjective
1 clear and accurate • *I gave them precise instructions.*
2 exact • *At that precise moment, the doorbell rang.*
precisely adverb accurately and carefully **precision** noun being exact or accurate

predator noun (say **pred**-a-ter)
an animal that hunts other animals **predatory** adjective hunting other animals

predict verb
to predict something is to say that it will happen in the future **predictable** adjective likely or expected • *His angry reaction was predictable.*
prediction noun something that you predict

preen verb
a bird preens when it smoothes and cleans its feathers using its beak

preface noun (say **pref**-ass)
an introduction at the beginning of a book

prefect noun
an older pupil in some schools who is given authority to help to keep order

prefer verb (**preferring**, **preferred**)
to prefer one thing to another is to like it better than the other thing **preference** noun what you prefer

prefix noun
a group of letters joined to the front of a word to change or add to its meaning, as in *disorder*, *overflow*, and *unhappy*

pregnant adjective
a pregnant woman has an unborn baby growing inside

her womb **pregnancy** noun a time of being pregnant

prehistoric adjective
belonging to a very long time ago, before written records were kept **prehistory** noun prehistoric times

prejudice noun
a prejudice is when you make up your mind that you don't like someone or something without a good reason or without thinking about it **prejudiced** adjective having a prejudice

preliminary adjective
coming before something or preparing for it

prelude noun (say **prel**-yood)
an introduction to a play, poem, or event

premature adjective
happening or coming before the proper time • *a premature baby*

première noun (say **prem**-yair)
the first public performance of a play or showing of a film

premises plural noun
an organization's or business's premises are the building and land it uses

premium noun
(say **pree**-mi-um)
an amount paid regularly to an insurance company

preparation noun
1 preparation is getting something ready
2 preparations are things you do in order to get ready for something • *We were making last-minute preparations.*

prepare verb
to prepare something is to get it ready **to be prepared to do something** is to be ready or willing to do it

preposition noun
a word you put in front of a noun or pronoun to show how the noun or pronoun is connected with another word, for example *on* in the sentence *Put the flowers on the table* and *with* in the sentence *I'd like some sauce with my food.*

prescribe verb
to prescribe a medicine for a patient is to instruct them to take it and give them a prescription for it

prescription noun
a doctor's written order for a chemist to prepare a medicine for a patient

presence noun
your presence somewhere is the fact that you are there • *Your presence is expected.*
in the presence of someone

while they are there, in the same place

present[1] adjective (say **prez**-ent)
1 in a particular place; here • *Nobody else was present.*
2 existing or happening now • *Who is the present Queen?*

present[1] noun (say **prez**-ent)
1 the present is the time now • *Our teacher is away at present.*
2 the form of a verb that describes something that is happening now, for example *likes* in the sentence *He likes swimming.*

present[2] noun (say **prez**-ent)
something that you give to someone or receive from them

presents

present[2] verb (say pri-**zent**)
1 to present something to someone is to give it to them, especially with a ceremony • *Who will present the prizes this year?* **2** to present a play or other entertainment is to perform it or arrange for it to be performed **3** to present a radio or television programme is to introduce it to the audience **4** to present something you have done or made is to show it formally to people • *We are here to present our latest products.*

presentation noun
1 a formal talk showing or demonstrating something
2 a ceremony in which someone is given a gift or prize • *I'd like to make a little presentation.*

presenter noun
someone who presents something, especially a radio or television programme

presently adverb
soon; in a while • *They will be here presently.*

present participle noun
a form of a verb that ends in -ing and describes something that is or was happening, for example *watching* in the sentences *I am watching television* and *They were watching television.*

preservative noun
a substance added to food to preserve it

preserve *verb*
to preserve something is to keep it safe or in good condition **preservation** *noun* preserving something

president *noun*
1 the head of a country that is a republic **2** the person in charge of a society, business, or club **presidency** *noun* the job of being a president **presidential** *adjective* to do with a president

press *verb*
1 to press something is to push it firmly or squeeze it • *Press the red button.* **2** to press clothes is to make them flat and smooth with an iron **3** to press someone for something is to urge them to do or give it • *She's pressing me for a decision.*

press *noun*
1 the action of squeezing or pushing on something • *Give the bell another press.* **2** the press are newspapers and journalists **3** a machine for printing things

pressure *noun*
1 pressure is continuous pushing or squeezing • *Apply pressure to the cut to stop it bleeding.* **2** pressure is also the force with which a liquid or gas pushes against something **3** there is pressure on you when someone is trying to persuade or force you to do something

prestige *noun* (say pres-**tee**zh)
prestige is the respect something has because it is important or of a high quality

presumably *adverb*
probably; I suppose

presume *verb*
1 to presume something is to suppose it • *I presumed that he was dead.* **2** to presume to do something is to dare to do it • *I wouldn't presume to advise you.*

pretence *noun*
a pretence is an attempt to pretend something

pretend *verb*
1 to pretend is to behave as if something untrue or imaginary is true **2** to pretend something is to claim it dishonestly • *They pretended they were policemen.*

pretty *adjective* (**prettier, prettiest**)
pleasant to look at or hear; attractive **prettily** *adverb* **prettiness** *noun*

pretty *adverb* (*informal*) quite; moderately • *It's pretty cold outside.*

prevent *verb*
1 to prevent something is to stop it from happening or make it impossible **2** to prevent someone is to stop them from doing something **prevention** *noun* stopping something bad from happening **preventive** *adjective* meant to help prevent something • *preventive medicine*

preview *noun*
a showing of a film or play before it is shown to most people

previous *adjective*
coming before this; preceding • *I was in London the previous week.* **previously** *adverb* before or earlier

prey *noun* (say pray)
an animal that is hunted or killed by another animal for food

prey *verb* (say pray)
to prey on something is to hunt and kill an animal for food • *Owls prey on mice and other small animals.*

price *noun*
1 the amount of money for which something is sold **2** what you have to give or do to get something • *Giving up this land was a small price to pay for peace.* **at any price** at any cost **pricey** *adjective* expensive

priceless *adjective*
very valuable

prick *verb*
1 to prick something is to make a tiny hole in it **2** to prick someone is to hurt them with something sharp or pointed **to prick up your ears** is to start listening suddenly

prickle *noun*
a sharp point on a plant or animal **prickly** *adjective* covered in prickles or feeling like prickles

prickle *verb*
to prickle is to make your skin feel as though lots of little sharp points are sticking into it • *This jumper is prickling me.*

pride *noun*
1 pride is a feeling of being very pleased with yourself or with someone else who has done well • *My heart swelled with pride.* **2** pride is also being too satisfied because of who you are or what you have done **3** a pride is something that makes you feel proud • *This stamp is the pride of my collection.* **4** a pride is also a group of lions

priest *noun*
1 a member of the clergy **2** someone who performs religious ceremonies; a religious leader

priesthood *noun* the position of being a priest

priestess *noun*
a female priest in a non-Christian religion

prim *adjective* (**primmer, primmest**)
liking things to be correct, and easily shocked by anything rude **primly** *adverb*

primary *adjective*
first; most important **primarily** *adverb* mainly; most importantly

primary colour *noun*
one of the colours from which all other colours can be made by mixing: red, yellow, and blue (of paint), and red, green, and violet (of light)

primary school *noun*
a first school for children from the age of 5 onwards

prime *adjective*
1 chief or most important • *The weather was the prime cause of the accident.* **2** of the best quality

prime minister *noun*
the leader of a government

prime number *noun*
a number that can only be divided exactly by itself and the number one, for example 2, 3, 5, 7, and 11

primitive *adjective*
1 at an early stage of development or civilization • *Primitive humans were hunters rather than farmers.* **2** basic or simple • *Our accommodation was fairly primitive.*

prince *noun*
1 the son of a king or queen **2** a man or boy in a royal family **princely** *adjective* a princely sum is a large or generous amount of money

princess *noun*
1 the daughter of a king or queen **2** a woman or girl in a royal family **3** the wife of a prince

principal *adjective*
chief or most important • *Name the principal cities of Britain.* **principally** *adverb* chiefly or mainly

principal *noun*
the head of a college or school

principle *noun*
1 a general rule or truth • *She taught me the principles of geometry.* **2** someone's principles are the basic rules and beliefs they have about how they should behave **in principle** in general, not in detail • *I agree with your plan in principle.*

print *verb*
1 to print words or pictures is to put them on paper with a machine **2** to print letters is to write them separately and not joined together **3** to print a photograph is to make it from a negative

printer's letters

print *noun*
1 print is printed words or pictures **2** a print is a mark made by something pressing on a surface • *Her thumb left a print on the glass.* **3** a print is also a photograph made from a negative

printer *noun*
1 a machine that prints on paper from data in a computer **2** someone who prints books or newspapers

printout *noun*
the information printed on paper from data in a computer

priority *noun* (**priorities**)
(*say* pry-**o**-ri-ti)
1 a priority is something that is more urgent or important than other things and needs to be dealt with first • *Repairing the roof is a priority.* **2** priority is the right to go first or be considered before other things • *People in need of urgent medical help will have priority.*

prise *verb*
to prise something open is to force or lever it open • *He prised open the lid with a screwdriver.*

prism *noun*
a piece of glass that breaks up light into the colours of the rainbow

prison *noun*
a place where people are locked up as a punishment for crimes

prisoner *noun*
someone who is kept in a prison or who is a captive

privacy *noun*
privacy is being private or away from other people • *Our new garden fence will give us more privacy.*

private *adjective*
1 belonging to a particular person or group of people • *This is a private road.* **2** meant to be kept secret • *These letters are private.* **3** away from other people • *Is there a private place to swim?* **in private** where only particular people can see or hear; not in public
privately *adverb* separately; not with other people • *Can we speak privately?*

private *noun*
a soldier of the lowest rank

privilege *noun*
a special right or advantage given to one person or group of people **privileged** *adjective* having special advantages that other people don't have

prize *noun*
something you get for winning a game or competition, or for doing well in an examination

prize *verb*
to prize something is to value it highly

probable *adjective*
likely to be true or to happen **probability** *noun* the probability of something is how likely it is to happen **probably** *adverb*

probation *noun*
probation is a time when someone is tried out in a new job to make sure they are suitable for the work **on probation** being supervised by a probation officer

probe *noun*
1 a long thin instrument used to look closely at something such as a wound **2** an investigation

probe *verb*
to probe is to investigate or look at something closely

problem *noun*
something that is difficult to answer or deal with

procedure *noun*
a fixed or special way of doing something

proceed *verb* (*say* pro-**seed**)
to proceed is to go on or continue

proceedings *plural noun*
things that happen; activities

proceeds *plural noun*
(*say* **proh**-seedz)
the proceeds of a sale or event are the money made from it

process *noun*
a series of actions for making or doing something **to be in the process of doing something** is to be in the middle of doing it

process *verb*
to process something is to treat it or deal with it by a process so that it can be used • *He took the film to the chemist to be processed.*

procession *noun*
a number of people or vehicles moving steadily forwards

proclaim *verb*
to proclaim something is to announce it officially or publicly **proclamation** *noun* a public announcement

prod *verb* (**prodding, prodded**)
to prod something or someone is to poke or jab them

produce *verb* (*say* pro-**dewss**)
1 to produce something is to make or create it **2** to produce something that is hidden or put away is to bring it out so that people can see it **3** to produce a play or film or other entertainment is to organize the performance of it

produce *noun*
(*say* prod-**yewss**)
produce is things produced, especially by farmers **producer** *noun* someone who produces a play or film

product *noun*
1 something someone makes or produces for sale **2** the result of multiplying two numbers • *12 is the product of 4 and 3.*

production *noun*
1 production is the process of making or creating something • *The factory is equipped for car production.* **2** a production is a version of a play or film

productive *adjective*
producing a lot of good or useful things **productivity** *noun* the rate at which someone works or produces things

profession *noun*
a type of work for which you need special knowledge and training, for example medicine, law, or teaching

professional *adjective*
1 doing a certain type of work to earn money • *He became a professional tennis player.* **2** to do with a profession **3** done with great skill and to a high standard **professionally** *adverb*

professional *noun*
someone doing a certain type of work to earn money

professor *noun*
a teacher of the highest rank in a university

proficient *adjective*
(*say* pro-**fish**-ent)
to be proficient at something

is to be able to do it well

proficiency noun the ability to do something well

proficiently adverb

profile noun
1 a person's profile is a side view of their face 2 a short description of a person's life or character

profit noun
1 the extra money you get by selling something for more than it cost to buy or make 2 an advantage or benefit

profit verb
to profit from something is to get an advantage from it

profitable adjective
making a profit; bringing in money

profound adjective
1 very deep or intense • His death had a profound effect on us all. 2 showing or needing great knowledge or thought • The poem she wrote was quite profound. **profoundly** adverb

program noun
a series of instructions for a computer to carry out

program verb (**programming, programmed**)
to program a computer is to prepare or control it by means of a program

programme noun
1 a show, play, or talk on radio or television 2 a list of a planned series of events 3 a leaflet or pamphlet that gives details of a play, concert, or other event

progress noun (say **proh**-gress)
1 progress is forward movement • The procession made slow progress. 2 progress is also development or improvement • You have made a lot of progress this term.

progress verb (say pro-**gress**)
1 to progress is to move forward 2 to progress is also to develop or improve **progression** noun when something develops or moves forward

prohibit verb
to prohibit something is to forbid it, especially by law • Smoking is prohibited. **prohibition** noun forbidding something

project noun (say **proj**-ekt)
1 a task in which you find out as much as you can about something and write about it 2 a plan or scheme

project verb (say pro-**jekt**)
1 to project is to stick out 2 to project your voice is to speak

loudly and clearly so that it carries a long way 3 to project a picture or film is to show it with a projector on a screen

projection noun 1 something that sticks out 2 showing a picture or film on a screen

projector noun
a machine for showing films or photographs on a screen

prologue noun (say **proh**-log)
an introduction to a poem or play or long story

prolong verb
to prolong something is to make it last longer

promenade noun (say prom-en-**ahd**)
a wide path for walking beside the sea

prominent adjective
1 easily seen; standing out • She has prominent teeth. 2 important **prominence** noun being prominent **prominently** adverb

promise noun
1 a promise is a statement that you will definitely do or not do something 2 something shows promise when it shows signs that it will be successful in the future

promise verb
to promise to do something is to say that you will definitely do it

promising adjective
likely to be good or successful • We have several promising pupils.

promote verb
1 to be promoted is to be given a more senior or more important job or rank 2 a sports team is promoted when it moves to a higher division or league 3 to promote a product or cause is to make people more aware of it • He has done much to promote the cause of peace.

promotion noun
1 promotion is when someone is given a more senior or more important job or rank 2 promotion is also when a sports team moves to a higher division or league 3 a promotion is a piece of publicity or advertising

prompt adjective
happening soon or without delay • We need a prompt reply. **promptly** adverb without delay

prompt verb
1 to prompt someone to do something is to cause or encourage them to do it

2 to prompt an actor is to remind them of their words if they forget them during a play

prone adjective
lying face downwards to be prone to something is to be likely to do it or suffer from it • He is prone to lose his temper.

prong noun
one of the pointed spikes at the end of a fork

pronoun noun
a word used instead of a noun, such as he, her, it, them, those

pronounce verb
1 to pronounce a word is to say it in a particular way • 'Too' and 'two' are pronounced the same. 2 to pronounce something is to declare it formally • I now pronounce you man and wife.

pronunciation noun (say pro-**nun**-si-ay-shon)
the way a word is pronounced

proof noun
proof is a fact which shows that something is true or exists • There is no proof that she stole the money.

proof adjective
giving protection against something • They wore bullet-proof jackets.

prop¹ noun
a support, especially one made of a long piece of wood or metal

prop¹ verb (**propping, propped**)
to prop something somewhere is to lean it there so that it doesn't fall over • The ladder was propped up against the wall.

prop² noun
a piece of furniture or other object used on stage in a theatre

propaganda noun
propaganda is information, especially false information, that is spread around to make people believe something

propel verb (**propelling, propelled**)
to propel something is to send it rapidly forward

propeller noun
a set of blades on a hub that spin round to drive an aircraft or ship

propeller

proper *adjective*
1 suitable or right • *This is the proper way to hold a bat.* **2** respectable • *You must behave in a proper fashion.* **3** (*informal*) complete; real • *I haven't had a proper meal for days.* **properly** *adverb* in a way that is correct or suitable

proper noun *noun*
the name given to one person or thing, such as *Mary* and *Tokyo*, and usually written with a capital first letter

property *noun* (**properties**)
1 a person's property is a thing, or all the things, that belong to them **2** a property is buildings or land belonging to someone **3** a property is also a quality or characteristic that something has • *People thought the berries had healing properties.*

prophecy *noun* (**prophecies**)
(say **prof**-i-si)
something that someone has said will happen in the future

prophesy *verb* (**prophesies, prophesying, prophesied**)
(say prof-i-**sy**)
to prophesy something is to say that it will happen in the future

prophet *noun*
1 someone who makes prophecies **2** a religious teacher who is believed to speak the word of God **the Prophet** a name for Muhammad, the founder of the Muslim faith

prophetic *adjective*
saying or showing what will happen in the future

proportion *noun*
1 a fraction or share of something • *Water covers a large proportion of the earth's surface.* **2** the proportion of one thing to another is how much there is of one compared to the other • *What is the proportion of oil to vinegar in this salad dressing?* **3** the correct relationship between the size, amount, or importance of two things • *You've drawn the head out of proportion with the body.* **proportions** size or scale • *It is a ship of large proportions.*

proportional or **proportionate** *adjective*
in proportion; according to a ratio **proportionally, proportionately** *adverb* in proportion

proposal *noun*
1 a suggestion or plan **2** when someone asks another person to marry them

propose *verb*
1 to propose an idea or plan is to suggest it **2** to propose to someone is to ask them to marry you

proprietor *noun*
(say pro-**pry**-et-er)
the owner of a shop or business

propulsion *noun*
propulsion is propelling something or driving it forward

prose *noun*
prose is writing that is like ordinary speech, not poetry or verse

prosecute *verb*
to prosecute someone is to make them go to a lawcourt to be tried for a crime **prosecution** *noun* the process of prosecuting someone **prosecutor** *noun* an official who prosecutes people

prospect *noun* (say **pros**-pekt)
a possibility or hope; what may happen in the future • *There's not much prospect of the weather improving.*

prosper *verb*
to prosper is to be successful or do well

prosperous *adjective*
successful or rich **prosperity** *noun* being successful or rich

protect *verb*
to protect someone or something is to keep them safe **protection** *noun* keeping someone or something safe **protector** *noun* a person who protects someone or something

protective *adjective*
1 a person is protective when they want to protect someone or something **2** a thing is protective when it is meant to protect something

protein *noun* (say **proh**-teen)
protein is a substance found in some types of food which your body needs to help you grow and be healthy

protest *noun* (say **proh**-test)
something you say or do because you disapprove of someone or something

protest *verb* (say pro-**test**)
to protest about something is to say publicly that you think it is wrong **protester** *noun* someone who protests about something

Protestant *noun*
(say **prot**-is-tant)
a member of a western Christian Church other than the Roman Catholic Church

proton *noun*
a particle of matter with a positive electric charge

protractor *noun*
a device in the shape of a semicircle, used for measuring and drawing angles on paper

protractor

proud *adjective*
1 very pleased with yourself or with someone else who has done well • *I am proud of my sister.* **2** too satisfied because of who you are or what you have done • *They were too proud to ask for help.* **proudly** *adverb*

prove *verb*
1 to prove something is to show that it is true **2** to prove to be something is to turn out to be that way • *The forecast proved to be correct.*

proverb *noun*
a short well-known saying that gives advice or says something about life, for example *many hands make light work*

proverbial *adjective*
1 occurring in a proverb **2** familiar or well-known

provide *verb*
1 to provide something is to supply it **2** to provide for something is to prepare for it • *They have provided for all possible disasters.* **provided** or **providing** on condition; on condition that • *You can come providing you bring some food.*

province *noun*
a region or division of a country

provision *noun*
provision is providing something • *the provision of free meals for old people*

provisional *adjective*
arranged or agreed on for the time being, but not yet definite • *21 July is the provisional date for the summer fair.*

provisions *plural noun*
supplies of food and drink

provocative *adjective*
likely to make someone angry • *That was a provocative remark.*

provoke *verb*
1 to provoke someone is to deliberately make them angry **2** to provoke a feeling is to arouse or cause it • *His remarks provoked a great deal of criticism.* **provocation** *noun* saying or doing something to deliberately make someone angry

prow *noun*
the front end of a ship

prowl *verb*
to prowl is to move about quietly and secretly, as some

animals do when they are hunting **prowler** noun someone who prowls threateningly

proximity noun
to be in the proximity of something is to be near it

prudent adjective (say **proo**-dent) wise and careful; not taking risks **prudence** noun being wise and careful **prudently** adverb

prune[1] noun
a dried plum

prune[2] verb
to prune a tree or bush is to cut off unwanted parts from it

pry verb (**pries, prying, pried**)
to pry is to be nosy or inquisitive about someone else's business

PS
something you write at the end of a letter when you want to add something else to it. **PS** is short for Latin post meridiem which means 'after midday'.

psalm noun (say sahm)
a religious song from the Bible

pseudonym noun (say **s'yoo**-do-nim)
a name used by an author instead of their real name

psychiatrist noun (say sy-**ky**-a-trist)
a doctor who treats mental illness

psychiatry noun (say sy-**ky**-a-tree)
psychiatry is the treatment of mental illness **psychiatric** adjective to do with psychiatry

psychic adjective (say **sy**-kik)
someone is psychic when they can tell the future or read other people's minds

psychologist noun (say sy-**kol**-o-jist)
someone who studies how the mind works

psychology noun
psychology is the study of the mind and the way people behave **psychological** adjective to do with psychology

pub noun
(informal) a building where people can buy and drink alcoholic drinks

puberty noun (say **pew**-ber-ti)
puberty is the time when a young person starts to become an adult and their body starts to change

public adjective
1 belonging to everyone or able to be used by everyone • I often use public transport. **2** to do with people in general • Newspapers can influence public opinion.

publicly adverb in public

public noun
the public is people in general **in public** openly; where anyone can see or take part

publication noun
1 a publication is a book or magazine that is printed and sold **2** publication is printing and selling books or magazines

publicity noun
publicity is information or advertising that makes people know about someone or something

public school noun
a secondary school that charges fees

publish verb
1 to publish books or magazines is to print and sell them **2** to publish information is to make it known publicly **publisher** noun a person or company that publishes books or magazines

puck noun
a hard rubber disc used in ice hockey

pudding noun
1 a hot sweet cooked food • rice pudding **2** a savoury food made with flour or suet • Yorkshire pudding **3** the sweet course of a meal • What's for pudding?

puddle noun
a small pool, especially of rainwater

puff verb
1 to puff smoke or steam is to blow it out **2** you puff when you breathe with difficulty • She was puffing when she got to the top of the hill. **3** to puff something, or to puff it out, is to inflate or swell it • He puffed out his chest.

puff noun
a small amount of breath, wind, smoke, or steam • He vanished in a puff of smoke.

puffin noun
a seabird with a large striped beak

puma

pull verb
1 to pull something is to get hold of it and make it come towards you or follow behind you **2** to pull is to move with an effort • She tried to grab the boy but he pulled away. **to pull a face** is to twist your face into a strange expression **to pull in 1** a car pulls in when it stops at the side of the road **2** a train pulls in when it comes into a station and stops **to pull out** is to decide to stop taking part in something • He had to pull out of the race after he twisted his ankle. **to pull someone's leg** is to tease them **to pull something off** is to achieve it **to pull through** is to recover from an illness **to pull up** is to stop • A car pulled up and two men got out. **to pull yourself together** is to become calm or sensible

pull noun
a pull is an action of pulling • Give the handle a good pull.

pulley noun (**pulleys**)
a wheel with a groove round it to take a rope, used for lifting heavy things

pullover noun
a knitted piece of clothing for the top half of your body, that you put on over your head

pulp noun
a soft wet mass of something, especially for making paper

pulpit noun
a raised platform in a church, from which the priest or minister speaks to the congregation

pulse[1] noun
1 your pulse is the regular beat as your heart pumps your blood through your arteries. You can feel your pulse in your wrist or neck. **2** a regular vibration or movement • The music had a throbbing pulse.

pulse[2] noun
pulses are the edible seeds of certain plants, such as peas, beans, and lentils

puma noun
a large wild cat of North America

a b c d e f g h i j k l m n o p q r s t u v w x y

pumice noun (say **pum**-iss)
pumice is a kind of soft sponge-like stone rubbed on hard surfaces to clean or polish them

pump noun
1 a device that forces air or liquid into or out of something, or along pipes **2** a lightweight shoe • *She took off her pumps.*

pump verb
to pump air or liquid is to force it into or out of something with a pump **to pump something up** is to fill something like a balloon or tyre with air or gas

pumpkin noun
a large round fruit with a hard yellow skin

pun noun
a joke made by using a word with two different meanings, or two words that sound the same, as in *Choosing where to bury him was a grave decision.*

punch¹ verb
1 to punch someone is to hit them with your fist **2** to punch a hole is to make a hole in something • *The guard checked and punched our tickets.* • *The builder punched a hole in the wall.*

punch¹ noun
1 a punch is a blow or hit with the fist **2** a punch is also a device for making holes in paper, metal, or other things

punch² noun
punch is a hot alcoholic drink

punchline noun
the last part of a joke or story, that makes it funny

punctual adjective
you are punctual when you arrive exactly on time, not late **punctuality** noun how punctual someone is **punctually** adverb in good time

punctuate verb
to punctuate a piece of writing is to put the commas, full stops, and other punctuation in it

punctuation noun
punctuation is the set of marks such as commas, full stops, and brackets put into a piece of writing to make it easier to understand

puncture noun
a small hole made in a tyre by accident

punish verb
to punish someone is to make them suffer in some way because they have done something wrong **punishment** noun a way of punishing someone

puny adjective (**punier, puniest**) (say **pew**-ni)
small and weak

pup noun
a puppy

pupa noun (**pupae**) (say **pew**-pa)
an insect at the stage of development between a larva and an adult insect; a chrysalis

pupil noun
1 someone who is being taught by a teacher **2** the opening in the centre of your eye

puppet noun
a kind of doll that can be made to move by fitting it over your fingers or hand or by pulling strings or wires attached to it

puppy noun (**puppies**)
a young dog

purchase verb
to purchase something is to buy it **purchaser** noun someone who buys something

purchase noun
1 a purchase is something you have bought **2** purchase is the fact of buying something • *Keep the receipt as proof of purchase.*

pure adjective
1 not mixed with anything else • *Use pure olive oil.* **2** clean or clear • *They washed in a pure cold mountain stream.*

purely adverb
only, simply • *They did it purely for the money.*

purify verb (**purifies, purifying, purified**)
to purify something is to make it pure **purification** noun purification is purifying something

purity noun
purity is the state of being pure

purple noun and adjective ●
a deep reddish-blue

purpose noun
the reason why you do something; what something is for **to do something on purpose** is to do it deliberately

purposely adverb
on purpose

purr verb
a cat purrs when it makes a gentle murmuring sound because it is pleased

purse noun
a small bag for holding money

pursue verb
1 to pursue someone or something is to chase them **2** to pursue an activity is to continue to do it or work at it • *She pursued her studies at college.* **pursuer** noun a person who chases someone

pursuit noun
1 pursuit is the action of chasing someone **2** a pursuit is something you spend a lot of time doing

pus noun
pus is a thick yellowish substance produced in boils and other sore places on your body

push verb
1 to push something is to move it away from you by pressing against it **2** to push something is also to press it in • *Try pushing the button.*

push noun
a pushing movement

pushchair noun
a small folding chair with wheels, in which a child can be pushed along

puss or **pussy** noun (**pusses** or **pussies**)
(*informal*) a cat

put verb (**putting, put**)
1 to put something in a place is to move it there • *Put the shopping down here.* • *Where shall I put it?* **2** to put also means to affect someone or something in a particular way • *They've put me in a bad mood.* **3** to put an idea in a certain way is to express it in words of a special kind • *She put it very tactfully.* **to put someone off** is to make them less keen on something • *Seeing you eat so much has put me off my food.* **to put something off** is to decide to do it later instead of now • *We'll have to put off the party if you're ill.* **to put something on 1** is to switch on an electrical device, for example a light or a television **2** is to start wearing a piece of clothing • *I'll just put on my coat.* **to put something out** is to stop something like a fire or light from burning or shining **to put someone up** is to give them a place to sleep • *Can we put them up for the night?* **to put something up** is to raise it or make it upright • *Let's put up the tent.* **to put up with something** is to be willing to accept it without complaining

putty noun
putty is a soft paste that sets hard, used by builders to fit windows in their frames

puzzle noun
1 a tricky game that you have to solve **2** a difficult question; a problem

puzzle verb
1 to puzzle someone is to give them a problem that is hard

to understand **2** to puzzle over something is to think hard about it

pygmy noun (**pygmies**) (say **pig**-mi)
an unusually small person or animal

pyjamas plural noun
a loose lightweight set of jacket and trousers that you wear in bed

pylon noun
a metal tower for supporting electric cables

pyramid noun
1 an object with a square base and four sloping sides coming to a point **2** a massive ancient Egyptian monument shaped like this

python noun
a large snake that crushes its prey

Qq

quack noun
the harsh loud sound made by a duck

quack verb
a duck quacks when it makes a harsh loud sound

quad noun
(informal) **1** a quadrangle **2** a quadruplet

quadrangle noun
a rectangular courtyard with large buildings round it

quadrant noun
a quarter of a circle

quadrilateral noun
a flat shape with four straight sides

quadruple adjective
1 four times as much or as many **2** having four parts

quadruplet noun
each of four children born to the same mother at one time

quail[1] noun
a bird that looks like a small partridge

quail[2] verb
to quail is to feel or show fear

quaint adjective
attractive in an unusual or old-fashioned way

quake verb
to quake is to tremble or shake

qualification noun
1 a skill or ability to do a job **2** an examination you have passed or a course you have completed that shows you have a skill or ability

qualify verb (**qualifies, qualifying, qualified**)
1 to qualify for something such as a job is to be suitable for it or show you have gained the abilities you need to do it
• She qualified as a doctor last year. **2** to qualify for a competition is to reach a high enough standard to take part in it

quality noun (**qualities**)
1 the quality of something is how good or bad it is **2** what something is like • The paper had a shiny quality.

quantity noun
how much there is of something, or how many things there are of one sort

quarantine noun
(say **kwo**-ran-teen)
quarantine is a period when a person or animal is kept apart from others to prevent a disease from spreading

quarrel noun
a strong or angry argument

quarrel verb (**quarrelling, quarrelled**)
to quarrel with someone is to argue fiercely with them

quarrelsome adjective
fond of quarrelling or often quarrelling

quarry noun (**quarries**)
1 a place where stone or slate is dug out of the ground **2** an animal that is being hunted

quart noun (say kwort)
a measure of liquid, a quarter of a gallon or about 1.136 litres

quarter noun
1 each of four equal parts into which something is divided or can be divided **2** three months, one-fourth of a year • We get a phone bill every quarter. **at close quarters** close together • They fought at close quarters.

quarters plural noun
where someone lives for a time; lodgings

quartet noun (say **kwor**-tet)
a group of four musicians or singers

quartz noun (say kworts)
quartz is a hard mineral, used in making accurate electronic watches and clocks

quaver verb
to quaver is to tremble
• He spoke in a quavering voice.

quaver noun
1 a trembling sound **2** a musical note equal to half a crotchet, written ♪

quay noun (say kee)
a harbour wall or pier where ships can be tied up for loading and unloading

queasy adjective (**queasier, queasiest**)
you feel queasy when you feel slightly sick

queen noun
1 a woman who has been crowned as the ruler of a country **2** a king's wife **3** a female bee or ant that produces eggs **4** a piece in chess, the most powerful on the board **5** a playing card with a picture of a queen on it

queer adjective
1 strange or odd **2** ill or unwell • I feel a bit queer.

quench verb
1 to quench your thirst is to drink until you aren't thirsty any more **2** to quench a fire is to put it out

query noun (**queries**)
(say **kweer**-i)
a question

query verb (**queries, querying, queried**)
to query something is to question whether it is true or correct

quest noun
a long search, especially for something precious or valuable

question noun
1 something you ask • I will try to answer your question. **2** a problem or subject for discussion **to be out of the question** is to be impossible or not even worth considering

question verb
1 to question someone is to ask them questions **2** to question something is to be doubtful about it **questioner** noun someone who asks a question

question mark noun
the punctuation mark (?) put at the end of a question

quartz

a b c d e f g h i j k l m n o **p** **q** r s t

a b c d e f g h i j k l m n o p q r s t u v w x y z

questionnaire *noun*
(*say* kwes-chon-**air**)
a set of questions asked to get
information for a survey

queue *noun* (*say* kew)
a line of people or vehicles
waiting for something

queue *verb* (*say* kew)
people queue, or queue up,
when they wait in a queue

quiche *noun* (*say* keesh)
an open tart with a savoury
filling

quick *adjective*
1 taking only a short time
• *You were quick.* **2** done in a
short time • *She gave a quick
answer.* **3** able to learn or
think fast **quickly** *adverb*
in a short time; fast

quicken *verb*
1 to quicken
something is to
make it quicker
• *She quickened her
pace.* **2** to quicken
is to become
quicker

quicksand *noun*
quicksand is an
area of loose wet
sand that sucks
in anything that
falls into it

quiet *adjective*
1 silent **2** not
loud • *He spoke
in a quiet voice.*
3 calm and
peaceful • *They
lead a quiet life.*
quietly *adverb*

quiet *noun*
quiet is a time
when it is calm and
peaceful • *Let's have
a bit of quiet now.*

quieten *verb*
1 to quieten something
or someone is to make
them quiet **2** to quieten
is to become quiet

quill *noun*
a pen made from
a large feather

quilt *noun*
a thick soft cover
for a bed

quintet *noun*
a group of five
musicians or singers

quit *verb* (**quitting,
quitted** or **quit**)
1 to quit something is
to leave or abandon
it **2** (*informal*) to quit
doing something is
to stop it
• *Quit teasing him!*

quill

quite *adverb*
1 rather or fairly • *He's quite a
good swimmer.* **2** completely
or entirely • *I haven't quite
finished.*

quiver[1] *verb*
to quiver is to tremble • *He was
quivering with excitement.*

quiver[2] *noun*
a long container for arrows

quiz *noun*
a series of questions, especially
as an entertainment or
competition

quota *noun* (*say* **kwoh**-ta)
a fixed share or amount
• *Each school has its quota
of equipment.*

quotation *noun*
an interesting sentence or set
of words taken from a book
or speech

quotation marks *plural
noun*
inverted commas, used to
mark a quotation (" ")

quote *verb*
to quote words is to use
them in a quotation

quotient *noun*
(*say* **kwoh**-shent)
the result of dividing one
number by another • *The
quotient of 12 divided by 3 is 4.*

Rr

rabbi *noun* (*say* **rab**-I)
a Jewish religious leader

rabbit *noun*
a furry animal with long
ears that digs burrows

rabies *noun* (*say* **ray**-beez)
rabies is a fatal disease
which causes madness
in dogs and cats and
can be passed
to humans

raccoon *noun*
a small North
American
meat-eating animal
with greyish-brown fur
and a bushy, striped tail

rabbit

race[1] *noun*
a competition to be the first to
reach a particular place or to
do something

race[1] *verb*
1 to race someone is to have a
race against them **2** to race is to
move very fast • *The train raced
along the track.* **racer** *noun* a
competitor in a race

race[2] *noun*
a large group of people who
have the same ancestors, and
share certain physical features
such as the colour of their skin
and hair

racecourse *noun*
a place where horse races
are run

racial *adjective*
to do with a person's race or
with different races
racially *adverb*

racism *noun* (*say* **ray**-sizm)
racism is believing that one
race of people is better than
all the others and treating
people unfairly because they
belong to a different race

racist *noun* someone who
practises racism
racist *adjective* showing racism

rack *noun*
1 a framework used as a shelf
or container • *a plate rack*
2 an ancient device for torturing
people by stretching them

rack *verb*
to rack your brains is to think
hard to remember something
or solve a problem

racket[1] *noun*
a bat with strings stretched
across a frame, used in tennis
and similar games

racket[2] *noun*
1 to make a racket is to make
a loud noise **2** (*informal*) a
dishonest way of making
money

radar *noun* (*say* **ray**-dar)
radar is a system that uses
radio waves to show the
position of ships or aircraft
which cannot be seen
because of distance or
poor visibility

radiant *adjective*
1 radiating light or
heat **2** you can
say someone is
radiant when
they look happy
and beautiful
radiance *noun*
brightness
radiantly *adverb*

radiate *verb*
1 to radiate heat, light, or
other energy is to send it
out in rays **2** to radiate is to
spread out like the spokes
of a wheel • *The city's streets
radiate from the central
square.*

radiation *noun*
1 radiation is heat, light, or
other energy given out by
something **2** radiation is also

energy or particles sent out by something radioactive

radiator *noun*
1 a device that gives out heat, especially a metal container through which steam or hot water flows 2 a device that cools a car's engine

radical *adjective*
1 thorough and complete; going right to the roots of something • *The new government made radical changes.* 2 wanting to make changes or reforms • *He is a radical politician.* **radically** *adverb* to be radically different is to be completely different

radio *noun*
1 radio is sending or receiving sound by means of electrical waves 2 a radio is an apparatus for receiving broadcast sound programmes, or for receiving and sending messages

radioactive *adjective*
radioactive substances have atoms that break up and give out dangerous radiation **radioactivity** *noun* the state of being radioactive

radish *noun*
a small hard red vegetable with a hot taste, eaten raw in salads

radius *noun* (**radii**)
1 a straight line from the centre of a circle to the circumference 2 the length of this line

raffle *noun*
a way of raising money by selling numbered tickets, some of which win prizes

raffle *verb*
to raffle something is to give it as a prize in a raffle

raft *noun*
a floating platform of logs or barrels tied together

rafter *noun*
each of the long sloping pieces of wood that hold up a roof

rag *noun*
1 an old or torn piece of cloth 2 to be dressed in rags is to be wearing very old, torn clothes

rage *noun*
great or violent anger

rage *verb*
1 to rage is to be very angry 2 to rage is also to be violent or noisy • *The storm was raging outside.*

ragged *adjective* (*say* **rag**-id)
1 torn or frayed 2 wearing torn or old clothes • *a ragged beggar*

raid *noun*
1 a sudden attack 2 an unexpected visit from police

to search a place or arrest people

raid *verb*
to raid a place is to make a raid on it **raider** *noun* raiders are people who attack a place in a raid

rail *noun*
1 a bar or rod that you can hang things on or that forms part of a fence or banisters 2 a long metal strip that is part of a railway track **by rail** on a train

railings *plural noun*
a fence made of metal bars

railway *noun*
1 a system of transport with trains running on rails 2 the parallel metal strips that trains travel on

rain *noun*
rain is drops of water that fall from the sky

rain *verb*
1 to fall as rain • *It is still raining.* • *Do you think it will rain this afternoon?* 2 to rain is to come down like rain • *After the explosion fragments of glass rained on them from above.* 3 to rain something is to send it down like rain • *They rained blows on him.*

rainbow *noun*
a curved band of colours that you can sometimes see in the sky when the sun shines through rain

raincoat *noun*
a waterproof coat

raindrop *noun*
a single drop of rain

rainfall *noun*
rainfall is the amount of rain that falls in a particular place or time

rainforest *noun*
a dense tropical forest in an area of very heavy rainfall

raise *verb*
1 to raise something is to move it to a higher place or to an upright position 2 to raise money is to succeed in collecting it • *They raised £1,000 for the appeal.* 3 to raise your voice is to speak loudly 4 to raise a subject or idea is to mention it for people to think about 5 to raise young children is to bring them up and educate them 6 to raise animals is to breed them

raisin *noun*
a dried grape

rake *noun*
a gardening tool with a row of short spikes fixed to a long handle

rain

rake *verb*
to rake something is to move it or smooth it with a rake

rally *noun* (**rallies**)
1 a large public meeting 2 a competition to test skill in driving 3 a series of strokes and return strokes of the ball in tennis or squash

rally *verb* (**rallies, rallying, rallied**)
1 to rally people is to bring them together for a special effort 2 to rally, or rally round, is to come together to support someone 3 to rally is to recover after an illness or setback • *The team rallied when they realized they could win.*

ram *noun*
a male sheep

ram *verb* (**ramming, rammed**)
to ram something is to push one thing hard against another

Ramadan *noun* (*say* **ram**-a-dan)
Ramadan is the ninth month of the Muslim year, when Muslims do not eat or drink during the daytime

ramble *noun*
a long walk in the country

ramble *verb*
1 to ramble is to go for a long walk in the country 2 to ramble is also to say a lot without keeping to a subject **rambler** *noun* someone who goes rambling in the country

ramp *noun*
a slope joining two different levels

rampage *verb* (*say* **ram**-payj)
to rampage is to rush about wildly or violently

ranch *noun*
a large cattle-farm in America

random *noun*
at random by chance; without any purpose or plan

random *adjective*
done or taken at random • *They took a random sample.*

range *noun*
1 a collection of different things of the same type • *The shop sells a wide range of games and puzzles.* 2 the limits of something, from the highest to the lowest • *Most of the children here are in the 8–11 age range.* 3 a line of hills or mountains 4 the distance that a gun can shoot, or an aircraft can fly, or a sound can be heard 5 a place with targets for shooting practice 6 a kitchen fireplace with ovens

range *verb*
1 to range between two limits is to extend from one to the other • *Prices ranged from £1 to £50.* **2** to range people or things is to arrange them in a line • *Crowds were ranged along the streets, hoping to see the Queen go by.* **3** to range is to wander or move over a wide area • *Hens ranged all over the farm.*

Ranger *noun*
a senior member of the Guides

ranger *noun*
1 someone who looks after a park or forest **2** a mounted police officer in a remote area

rank *noun*
1 a position in a series of people or things • *He was promoted to the rank of captain.* **2** a line of people or things

rank *verb*
to rank is to have a certain rank or place • *She ranks among the greatest writers.*

ransack *verb*
to ransack a place is to search it thoroughly, looking for something to steal, and leave it in a mess

ransom *noun*
money paid so that someone who has been kidnapped can be set free **to hold someone to ransom** is to keep them prisoner and demand a ransom

rap *verb* (**rapping, rapped**)
to rap is to knock quickly and loudly

rap *noun*
1 a rap is a rapping movement or sound **2** rap is a kind of pop music in which you speak words rapidly in rhythm

rapid *adjective*
moving or working at speed **rapidity** *noun* speed **rapidly** *adverb* very quickly

rapids *plural noun*
part of a river where the water flows very fast over rocks

rare *adjective*
unusual; not often found or experienced • *She died of a rare disease.* **rarely** *adverb* not very often **rarity** *noun* something that is rare

rascal *noun*
a dishonest or mischievous person

rash¹ *adjective*
you are rash when you do something too quickly without thinking properly about it • *He tends to be rash.* • *It was a rash decision.* **rashly** *adverb*

rash² *noun*
an outbreak of red spots or patches on the skin

rasher *noun*
a slice of bacon

raspberry *noun* (**raspberries**)
a small soft red fruit

Rastafarian *noun*
(*say* ras-ta-**fair**-i-an)
a member of a religious group that started in Jamaica

rat *noun*
an animal like a large mouse

rate *noun*
1 how fast or how often something happens • *The train moved at a great rate.* **2** a charge or payment • *What is the rate for a letter to Italy?* **at any rate** anyway **at this rate** if this is typical or true

rate *verb*
to rate something or someone is to regard them in a certain way or as having a certain value • *Drivers rate the new car very highly.* • *He rated me among his best friends.*

rather *adverb*
1 slightly; somewhat • *It was rather dark.* **2** you would rather do one thing than another thing if you would prefer to do it • *I think I'd rather do this later.* **3** more truly or correctly • *He lay down, or rather fell, on the bed.*

ratio *noun* (**ratios**)
(*say* **ray**-shi-oh)
the relationship between two numbers; how many times one number goes into another • *In a group of 2 girls and 10 boys, the ratio of girls to boys is 1 to 5.*

ration *noun* (*say* **rash**-on)
the amount of something one person is allowed to have

ration *verb* (*say* **rash**-on)
to ration something is to give it out in fixed amounts because there is not a lot of it to share

rational *adjective*
(*say* **rash**-o-nal)
reasonable or sensible • *No rational person would do such a thing.* **rationally** *adverb*

rattle *verb*
1 to rattle is to make a series of short sharp hard sounds **2** to rattle something is to make it rattle

rattle *noun*
1 a rattling sound **2** a baby's toy that rattles when you shake it

rattle

rattlesnake *noun*
a poisonous American snake that makes rattling sounds with its tail

rave *verb*
1 to be raving is to be talking wildly **2** to rave about something is to talk very enthusiastically about it

rave *noun*
a big party held in a large building with loud electronic music to dance to

raven *noun*
a large black bird

raven

ravenous *adjective*
(*say* **rav**-e-nus)
very hungry **ravenously** *adverb*

ravine *noun*
(*say* ra-**veen**)
a very deep narrow gorge

ravioli *noun*
ravioli is small squares of pasta filled with meat and served with a sauce

raw *adjective*
1 raw food is not cooked **2** raw (for example) cotton or sugar is in its natural state before being processed • *What raw materials do you need?* **3** you can say someone is raw when they don't have any experience • *They are just raw beginners.* **4** with the skin removed • *He had a raw wound on his leg.* **5** cold and damp • *There was a raw wind.*

ray¹ *noun*
a thin line of light, heat, or other energy

ray² *noun*
a large sea fish with a flat body and a long tail

razor *noun*
a device with a very sharp blade, used for shaving

reach *verb*
1 to reach a place is to go as far as it and arrive there **2** to reach, or reach out, is to stretch out your hand to get or touch something **3** to reach something is to be long enough to touch it • *The carpet doesn't reach the wall.*

reach *noun*
1 the distance you can reach with your hand **2** a distance that you can easily travel • *I'd like to live within reach of the sea.*

react *verb*
to react is to act in response to another person or thing

reaction noun
what you feel or say or do when something happens, or when someone does something
reactor noun an apparatus for producing nuclear power
read verb (**reading, read**)
1 to read something written or printed is to look at it and understand it or say it aloud **2** a gauge or instrument reads a certain amount when that is what it shows • *The thermometer reads 20°.*
reader noun
1 someone who reads **2** a book that helps you learn to read
readily adverb
1 willingly or eagerly • *She readily agreed to help.* **2** quickly and without any difficulty • *All the ingredients you need are readily available.*
reading noun
1 reading is the action of reading a book, magazine, or newspaper **2** a reading is an amount shown on a gauge or instrument
ready adjective (**readier, readiest**)
1 prepared so that you can do something straight away; able or willing to do something • *Are you ready to leave?* **2** prepared for use • *Is dinner ready?* **at the ready** ready for action or ready to be used **readiness** noun readiness is being ready for something
real adjective
1 true or existing; not imaginary **2** genuine; not a copy • *Are those pearls real?*
realistic adjective
1 true to life • *It is a very realistic painting.* **2** seeing things as they really are • *She is realistic about her chances of winning.* **realistically** adverb
reality noun (**realities**) reality is what is real
realize verb
to realize something is to understand it or accept that it is true **realization** noun when you realize something
really adverb
truly; certainly; in fact
realm noun (*say* relm)
1 a kingdom **2** an area of knowledge or activity

reap verb
1 to reap corn is to cut it down and gather it in when it is ripe **2** to reap a benefit is to gain it **reaper** noun someone who reaps corn
reappear verb
to reappear is to appear again **reappearance** noun a time when someone or something appears again
rear[1] adjective
placed or found at the back • *I was looking out of the rear window.*
rear[1] noun
the back part of something
rear[2] verb
1 to rear young children or animals is to bring them up or help them grow **2** a horse or other animal rears, or rears up, when it rises up on its hind legs so that its front legs are in the air
reason noun
1 the reason for something is why it happens **2** reason is thinking in a clear and logical way • *He wouldn't listen to reason.*
reason verb
1 to reason is to think in a logical way **2** to reason with someone is to try to persuade them of something
reasonable adjective
1 sensible or logical **2** fair or moderate • *These are reasonable prices for what you get.*
reasonably adverb
1 in a reasonable way; sensibly • *They were behaving quite reasonably.* **2** fairly; somewhat • *She can swim reasonably well.*
reassure verb
to reassure someone is to take away their doubts or fears **reassurance** noun something you say that reassures someone
rebel verb (**rebelling, rebelled**) (*say* ri-**bel**)
to rebel is to refuse to obey someone in authority, especially the government
rebel noun (*say* **reb**-el)
someone who refuses to obey or fights against people who are in charge
rebellion noun
1 rebellion is when people refuse to obey or fight against people in charge **2** a rebellion is a fight against someone in authority, especially the government
rebellious adjective
someone is rebellious when

they refuse to obey people in charge or are likely to rebel
rebound verb
to rebound is to bounce back after hitting something
rebuild verb (**rebuilding, rebuilt**)
to rebuild something is to build it again after it has been destroyed
recall verb
1 to recall someone or something is to remember them **2** to recall someone is to tell them to come back
recap verb (**recapping, recapped**)
(*informal*) to recap is to summarize what has been said
recapture verb
to recapture something or someone is to capture them again, especially after they have escaped
recede verb
1 to recede is to go back • *The floods have receded.* **2** a man's hair is receding when he starts to go bald at the front
receipt noun (*say* ri-**seet**)
a written statement saying that a payment has been received or goods have been delivered
receive verb
1 to receive something is to get it when it is given or sent to you **2** to receive visitors is to greet them formally • *The President was received at Buckingham Palace.*
receiver noun
1 the part of a telephone that you hold to your ear **2** a radio or television set
recent adjective
made or happening a short time ago **recently** adverb only a short time ago
receptacle noun
a container used for holding something
reception noun
1 the sort of welcome that someone gets • *We were given a friendly reception.* **2** a formal party to receive guests • *a wedding reception* **3** a place in a hotel or office where visitors report or check in **4** the quality of the signals your radio or television set receives • *We don't get good reception here.*
receptionist noun
someone in an office or hotel who deals with visitors and answers the telephone

a
b
c
d
e
f
g
h
i
j
k
l
m
n
o
p
q
r
s
t
u
v
w
x
y
z

recession *noun*
a time when a country is not trading well and a lot of people can't find jobs

recipe *noun* (say **ress**-i-pi)
a list of ingredients and instructions for preparing or cooking food

recital *noun* (say ri-**sy**-tal)
a performance of music or poetry by a small number of people

recite *verb*
to recite something such as a poem is to say it aloud

reckless *adjective*
someone is reckless when they do things without thinking or caring about what might happen **recklessly** *adverb* **recklessness** *noun*

reckon *verb*
1 to reckon something is to calculate or count it 2 to reckon something is to think it or have an opinion about it • *I reckon it's about to rain.*

recline *verb*
to recline is to lean or lie back

recognize *verb*
1 to recognize someone or something is to know who they are because you have seen them before 2 to recognize a fault or mistake is to admit to it • *We recognize that we may have acted unfairly.* **recognition** *noun* recognizing someone or something **recognizable** *adjective* able to be recognized

recoil *verb*
to recoil is to move backwards suddenly • *He recoiled in horror.*

recollect *verb*
to recollect something is to remember it **recollection** *noun* a memory of something; being able to remember something

recommend *verb*
1 to recommend something is to suggest it because you think it is good or suitable • *I recommend the strawberry ice cream.* 2 to recommend an action is to advise someone to do it • *We recommend that you wear strong shoes on the walk.* **recommendation** *noun* something that you recommend

reconcile *verb*
1 to be reconciled with someone is to become friendly with them again after quarrelling or fighting with

them 2 you are reconciled to something when you are persuaded to put up with it • *He soon became reconciled to wearing glasses.* **reconciliation** *noun* becoming friendly with someone again after quarrelling or fighting with them

reconstruction *noun*
1 reconstruction is building something up again 2 a reconstruction is acting out an event that took place in the past • *The police did a reconstruction of the bank robbery.*

record *noun* (say **rek**-ord)
1 a disc with recorded sound on it 2 the best performance in a sport or the most remarkable event of its kind • *She broke the record for swimming 100 metres.* 3 a set of facts or information about something that you write down and keep • *Keep a record of all the birds you see in the garden.*

records

record *verb* (say ri-**kord**)
1 to record music or sound or a television programme is to store it on a tape or disc 2 to record things that have happened is to put them down in writing

recorder *noun*
1 a wooden musical instrument that you play by blowing into one end and covering holes with your fingers 2 a tape recorder, video recorder, or other machine for recording sounds and pictures

recount *verb*
to tell someone about something true that has happened • *We recounted our adventures.*

recover *verb*
1 to recover is to get better after being ill 2 to recover something is to get it back after losing it **recovery** *noun* getting better after being ill; getting something back after it was lost

recorder

recreation *noun*
something you do for fun

or enjoyment **recreational** *adjective* to do with recreation

recruit *noun*
someone who has just joined the armed forces or a business or club

recruit *verb*
to recruit someone is to get them to join something you belong to

rectangle *noun*
a shape with four straight sides and four right angles **rectangular** *adjective* in the form of a rectangle

recuperate *verb*
to recuperate is to get better after you have been ill

recur *verb*
something recurs when it happens again **recurrence** *noun* a recurrence of something is when it happens again

recycle *verb*
to recycle waste material is to treat it so that it can be used again • *Waste paper can be recycled to make cardboard.*

red *adjective* (**redder**, **reddest**) ●
1 of the colour of blood 2 red hair is orangey-brown in colour

red *noun*
a red colour **to see red** is to become suddenly angry

redden *verb*
to redden is to become red • *He reddened with embarrassment.*

red-handed *adjective*
to catch someone red-handed is to catch them while they are actually committing a crime or doing something wrong

redhead *noun*
a person with reddish-brown hair

reduce *verb*
1 to reduce something is to make it smaller or less 2 to be reduced to something is to be forced to do it • *He was reduced to asking for more money.*

reduction *noun*
1 there is a reduction in something when it becomes smaller or less 2 the amount by which something is reduced • *They gave us a reduction of £5.*

redundant *adjective*
1 to be redundant is to be no longer needed 2 someone is

made redundant when they
lose their job because it is no
longer needed

redundancy *noun* when
someone loses their job
because it is no longer needed

reed *noun*
1 a plant that grows in or near
water **2** a thin strip that vibrates
to make the sound in some
wind instruments, such as a
clarinet, saxophone, or oboe

reedy *adjective* a reedy voice
or sound is high and not very
pleasant

reef *noun*
a line of rocks or sand just
below the surface of the sea

reek *verb*
to reek is to have a strong
unpleasant smell

reel *noun*
1 a round device on which
cotton or thread is wound
2 a lively Scottish dance

reels

refer *verb* (**referring, referred**)
1 to refer to someone or
something is to mention them
or speak about them **2** to refer
to (for example) a dictionary
or encyclopedia is to look at it
so that you can find something
out **3** to refer a question or
problem to someone else is
to give it to them to deal with

referee *noun*
someone who makes sure
that people keep to the rules
of a game

referee *verb*
to referee a game is to act as
referee in it

reference *noun*
1 a mention of something
2 a place in a book or file
where information can be
found **3** a letter or note
about how well someone
has done their work, used
especially when they are
applying for a job

reference book *noun*
a book that gives
information, such as a
dictionary or encyclopedia

referendum *noun*
(*say* ref-er-**en**-dum)
a vote on an important matter
by all the people in a country

refill *verb*
to refill something is to fill
it again

refill *noun*
a container used to replace
something that has been used
up • *My pen needs a refill.*

refine *verb*
to refine something is to purify
or improve it

refined *adjective*
1 refined (for example) sugar
or oil has been made pure by
taking other substances out of
it **2** someone is refined when
they have good manners and
are well educated

refinement *noun*
1 refinement is the process
of refining something **2** a
refinement is something special
that improves a thing

refinery *noun* (**refineries**)
a factory for refining a product,
such as oil

reflect *verb*
1 something reflects light or
heat or sound when it sends
them back from a surface **2** a
mirror or other shiny surface
reflects something when it
forms an image of it **3** you
reflect on something when you
think seriously about it

reflection *noun*
the image you can see in a
mirror or other shiny surface

reflex *noun* (*say* **ree**-fleks)
a movement or action that
you do without any conscious
thought

reform *verb*
1 to reform a person or thing
is to improve them by getting
rid of their faults **2** someone
reforms when they improve
their behaviour

reform *noun*
1 reform is changing something
to improve it **2** a reform is a
change in a system or law

reformer *noun* someone who
tries to change a system

refrain¹ *verb*
to refrain from something is to
keep yourself from doing it
• *Please refrain from talking.*

refrain² *noun*
the chorus of a song

refresh *verb*
to refresh someone who is tired
is to make them feel fresh and
strong again

refreshments *plural noun*
food and drink

refrigerator *noun*
a cabinet in which you can
store food at a low temperature
to keep it fresh

refuel *verb* (**refuelling,
refuelled**)
to refuel a ship or aircraft is to
supply it with more fuel

refuge *noun*
a place where someone can go
to be safe from danger

refugee *noun* (*say* ref-yoo-**jee**)
someone who has had to
leave their home or country
because of war or persecution
or disaster

refund *verb* (*say* ri-**fund**)
to refund money is to pay it
back

refund *noun* (*say* **ree**-fund)
money that is paid back to you

refuse *verb* (*say* ri-**fewz**)
to refuse something, or to do
something, is to say that you
will not accept it or do it
• *They refuse to help.*

refusal *noun* when someone
refuses something

refuse *noun* (*say* **ref**-yooss)
rubbish or waste material

regain *verb*
to regain something is to get
it back

regard *verb*
1 to regard someone or
something as something is to
think of them in a certain way
• *I regard her as a friend.* **2** to
regard someone or something
is also to look at them closely

regard *noun*
with regard to something
about it; in connection with it

regarding *preposition*
to do with; about • *There are
rules regarding use of the library.*

regardless *adjective, adverb*
paying no attention to
something • *Buy it, regardless of
the cost.* • *We asked her to stop,
but she carried on regardless.*

regards *plural noun*
kind wishes you send in a
message • *Give your parents my
regards.*

regatta *noun* (*say* ri-**gat**-a)
a meeting for boat or yacht
races

reggae *noun* (*say* **reg**-ay)
reggae is a West Indian style of
music with a strong beat

regiment *noun*
a large army unit

regimental *noun* to do with or
belonging to a regiment

region *noun*
1 a part of a country **2** a part
of the world • *These plants
only grow in tropical regions.*

regional *adjective* belonging to a particular region

register *noun*
an official list of names or information, especially of people present each day at a school

register *verb*
1 to register something or someone is to put their name on an official list **2** a gauge or instrument registers a certain amount when that is what it shows • *The thermometer registered 25°.* **3** to register a letter or parcel is to have it officially recorded for sending with special care **registration** *noun* making an official record of something

regret *noun*
you feel regret when you feel sorry or sad about something

regret *verb* (**regretting, regretted**)
to regret something is to feel sorry or sad about it

regrettable *adjective*
you say something is regrettable when you wish it hadn't happened

regular *adjective*
1 always happening at certain times • *You need regular meals.* **2** even or symmetrical • *She has beautiful regular teeth.* **3** normal or correct • *Do you want a regular or large coffee?* **regularity** *noun* being regular **regularly** *adverb*

regulate *verb*
to regulate something is to adjust or control it

regulation *noun*
a regulation is a rule or law

rehearse *verb*
to rehearse (for example) a play or piece of music is to practise it before you perform it **rehearsal** *noun* when you practise something before performing it

reign *verb*
to reign is to rule as a king or queen

reign *noun*
the time when someone is king or queen

rein *noun*
a strap used by a rider to guide a horse

reindeer *noun*
a kind of deer that lives in Arctic regions

reinforce *verb*
to reinforce something is to strengthen it

reinforcement *noun*
a thing that strengthens something **reinforcements** extra troops sent to strengthen a military force

reject *verb* (*say* ri-**jekt**)
1 to reject something or someone is to refuse to accept them • *They have rejected my offer of help.* **2** to reject something is to get rid of it • *Faulty parts are rejected at the factory.* **rejection** *noun* being rejected

reject *noun* (*say* **ree**-jekt)
a thing that is got rid of, especially because it is faulty or poorly made

rejoice *verb*
to rejoice is to be very happy or pleased

relate *verb*
1 things relate to each other when there is a connection between them **2** to relate one thing with another is to compare them **3** to relate a story is to tell it

related *adjective*
1 two people are related when they belong to the same family **2** two things are related when they are connected or linked in some way

relation *noun*
a relation is someone who is related to you

relationship *noun*
1 the way people or things are connected with each other **2** the way people get on with one another • *There is a good relationship between the teachers and the children.* **3** a close friendship or connection between two people

relative *noun*
your relatives are the people who are related to you

relative *adjective*
1 connected or compared with something **2** compared with the average • *They live in relative comfort.*

relatively *adverb*
compared with other people or things; more or less • *Books are relatively cheap.*

relax *verb*
1 to relax is to become less anxious or worried **2** to relax is also to rest or stop working **3** to relax a part of you is make it less stiff or tense • *Try to relax your arm.* **relaxation** *noun* relaxing

relay *verb*
to relay a message or broadcast is to pass it on

relay *noun*
1 a race between two teams in which each member of the team runs part of the distance **2** a fresh group taking the place of another • *The firemen worked in relays.*

release *verb*
1 to release something or someone is to set them free or unfasten them **2** to release a film or record is to make it available to the public

release *noun*
1 release is being released **2** a release is something released, especially a new film or record

relegate *verb* (*say* **rel**-i-gayt)
1 a sports team is relegated when it goes down into a lower division of a league **2** to relegate something is to put it into a lower group or position than before **relegation** *noun* when a sports team is relegated

relent *verb*
to relent is to be less angry or severe than you were going to be

relentless *adjective*
never stopping or letting up • *Their criticism was relentless.* **relentlessly** *adverb*

relevant *adjective*
(*say* **rel**-i-vant)
connected with what you are discussing or dealing with **relevance** *noun* the relevance of something is how relevant it is

reliable *adjective*
able to be trusted or depended on **reliability** *noun* how reliable something is **reliably** *adverb*

relic *noun*
something that has survived from an ancient time

reindeer

relief noun
1 a good feeling you get because something unpleasant has stopped or is not going to happen • *It was such a relief when we reached dry land.* 2 relief is the ending or lessening of pain or suffering 3 aid or help given to people in need • *The charity is involved in famine relief.* 4 relief is also a method of making a map or design that stands out from a flat surface • *The model shows hills and valleys in relief.*

relieve verb
to relieve pain or suffering is to end or lessen it

relieved adjective
feeling good because something unpleasant has stopped or is not going to happen

religion noun
what people believe about God or gods, and how they worship

religious adjective
1 to do with religion 2 believing in a religion

reluctant adjective
you are reluctant to do something when you don't want to do it
reluctance noun not wanting to do something
reluctantly adverb you do something reluctantly when you would prefer not to be doing it

rely verb (**relies, relying, relied**)
to rely on someone or **something** is to trust them or need them to help or support you

remain verb
1 to remain is to continue in the same place or condition • *It will remain cloudy all day.* 2 to remain is also to be left over • *A lot of food remained after the party.*

remainder noun
1 something left over 2 (*in mathematics*) the amount that is left over when you divide one number into another

remains plural noun
1 something left over 2 ruins or relics 3 a dead body

remark verb
to remark on something is to say something that you have thought or noticed

remark noun
something you say

remarkable adjective
so unusual or impressive that you notice or remember it

remarkably adverb unusually or noticeably

remedy noun (**remedies**)
a cure for an illness or problem

remember verb
1 to remember something is to keep it in your mind, or bring it into your mind when you need to 2 to remember someone is to be thinking about them

remembrance noun you do something in remembrance of someone or something when you do it as a way of remembering them

remind verb
to remind someone is to help or make them remember something • *The girl in that painting reminds me of you.*

reminder noun something that makes you think about or remember a person or thing

remnant noun
a small piece of something left over

remorse noun
remorse is deep regret for something wrong you have done **remorseful** adjective feeling remorse

remote adjective
1 far away • *He lived on a remote island.* 2 unlikely or slight • *Their chances of winning were remote.* **remotely** adverb **remoteness** noun

remote control noun
1 remote control is controlling something from a distance, usually by means of radio or electricity 2 a remote control is a device for doing this

removal noun
removing or moving something

remove verb
to remove something is to take it away or take it off

rendezvous noun
(**rendezvous**) (say **ron**-day-voo)
an arrangement to meet someone

renew verb
to renew something is to make it as it was before or replace it with something new
renewal noun when something begins again or is replaced with something new

renewable adjective
able to be renewed or replaced; never completely used up • *Wind is a renewable source of energy.*

renowned adjective
famous • *She is renowned for her generosity.*

rent noun
a regular payment for using

something, especially a house or flat

rent verb
to rent something is to pay money to use it

repair verb
to repair something is to mend it

repair noun
1 repair is mending something • *The car is in for repair.* 2 a repair is a mended place • *You can hardly see the repair.* **to be in good repair** is to be in good condition

repay verb (**repaying, repaid**)
1 to repay money is to pay it back 2 to repay someone's kindness is to do something for them in return **repayment** noun paying money back

repeat verb
to repeat something is to say it or do it again

repeat noun
something that is repeated, especially a television programme

repeatedly adverb
several times; again and again

repel verb (**repelling, repelled**)
1 to repel someone or something is to drive or force them away or apart 2 to repel someone is to make them disgusted **repellent** adjective disgusting

repent verb
to repent is to be sorry for what you have done **repentance** noun repentance is being sorry for what you have done **repentant** adjective sorry for what you have done

repetition noun
1 repeating or doing something again 2 something repeated

repetitive adjective
something is repetitive when it is repeated too much and so becomes boring

replace verb
1 to replace something is to put it back in its place 2 to replace someone or something is to take their place 3 to replace something is to put a new thing in the place of it • *I promise I'll replace the book I lost.*

replacement noun
1 replacement is when something or someone is replaced for another 2 a replacement is something used or given in place of another

replay noun
1 a football match played for a second time after the first match has ended in a draw 2 the playing or showing again of a recording

a
b
c
d
e
f
g
h
i
j
k
l
m
n
o
p
q
r
s
t
u
v
w
x
y
z

replica noun (say **rep**-li-ka)
an exact copy

reply noun (**replies**)
what you say or write when someone asks or says something

reply verb (**replies, replying, replied**)
to reply is to give a reply

report verb
1 to report something is to describe something that has happened or something you have studied **2** to report someone is to complain about them to those in charge of them **3** to report to someone is to tell them you have arrived or are available

report noun
1 a description or account of something **2** a regular statement of how someone has worked or behaved, especially at school **3** an explosive sound • We heard the report of a gun.

reporter noun
someone whose job is to collect news for a newspaper or for radio or television

represent verb
1 to represent something or someone is to be a picture or model or symbol of them • The dotted lines represent county boundaries. **2** to represent someone else is to speak or act on their behalf • She was chosen to represent her school in the competition.

representation noun a representation of a thing is something that shows or describes it

representative noun
a person who acts or speaks for other people

representative adjective
typical of a group

reprieve noun (say ri-**preev**)
someone is given a reprieve when their punishment is postponed or cancelled, especially the death penalty

reprieve verb
to reprieve someone is to cancel or postpone their punishment

reprimand verb
to reprimand someone is to scold them or tell them off

reprimand noun
a telling-off

reprisal noun (say ri-**pry**-zal)
an act of revenge

reproach verb
to reproach someone is to blame them for something and show you are disappointed with them

reproach noun
reproach is blame or criticism • His behaviour was beyond reproach.

reproduce verb
1 to reproduce something is to make it be heard or seen again • CDs can reproduce sound. **2** to reproduce something is also to copy it **3** animals and people reproduce when they produce offspring

reproductive adjective to do with producing offspring

reproduction noun
1 reproduction is the process of producing offspring **2** a reproduction is a copy of something

reptile noun
a cold-blooded animal that creeps or crawls, such as snakes and lizards

reptile

republic noun
a country ruled by a president and government that are chosen by the people

repulsive adjective
disgusting

reputation noun
what most people think about a person or thing • He has a reputation for being honest.

request verb
to request something is to ask politely or formally for it

request noun
what someone asks for

require verb
1 to require something is to need or want it **2** you are required to do something when you have to do it • Pedestrians are required to walk on the pavements. **requirement** noun something that is needed

rescue verb
to rescue someone is to save them from danger or capture

rescue noun
when someone is rescued **rescuer** noun a person who rescues someone

research noun
research is careful study or investigation to learn more about a subject
researcher noun someone who does research

resemblance noun
there is a resemblance between two or more things when they are similar

resemble verb
to resemble someone or something is to look or sound like them

resent verb
to resent something is to feel angry about it because you think it is unfair **resentful** adjective angry about something that you think is unfair **resentment** noun a feeling of resenting something

reservation noun
1 arranging for (for example) a restaurant table or seat on a train to be kept for you **2** an area of land kept for a special purpose **3** you have reservations about something when you feel doubtful or uneasy about it • I had reservations about the excuses he made.

reserve verb
to reserve something is to keep it or order it for a particular person or for a special use

reserve noun
1 a person kept ready to be used if necessary, especially an extra player in a sports team **2** an area of land kept for a special purpose • This island is a nature reserve.

reserved adjective
1 kept for someone • These seats are reserved. **2** someone is reserved when they are shy or unwilling to show their feelings

reservoir noun (say **rez**-er-vwar)
an artificial lake where water
is stored

residence noun
a place where someone lives

resident noun
someone who lives in a
particular place

resign verb
to resign is to give up your job
or position **to resign yourself
to something** is to accept a
difficulty without complaining
or arguing

resignation noun
1 resignation is accepting a
difficulty without complaining
2 a resignation is a letter saying
you are resigning a job or
position

resin noun (say **rez**-in)
resin is a sticky substance that
comes from plants or is made
artificially

resist verb
1 to resist someone or
something is to oppose them or
try to stop them 2 you cannot
resist something when you
cannot stop yourself doing it
• I can't resist telling her what
happened.

resistance noun fighting
back or taking action against
someone or something

resistant adjective to be
resistant to something is not to
be affected or damaged by it

resolute adjective
(say rez-o-loot) determined
or firm

resolutely adverb

resolution noun
1 resolution is being
determined or firm 2 a
resolution is something
you have decided to do

resolve verb
1 to resolve to do something is
to decide to do it 2 to resolve
doubts or disagreements is to
deal successfully with them

resort noun
a place where people go for a
holiday, especially by the sea
the last resort the only thing
you can do when everything
else has failed

resort verb
to resort to something is to
make use of it, especially when
everything else has failed • In
the end they resorted to violence.

resource noun
resources are things that you
have and are able to use • The
land is rich in natural resources.

respect noun
1 respect is admiration for

someone's good qualities or
achievements 2 respect is also
consideration or concern • Have
respect for people's feelings. 3 a
respect is a detail or aspect • In
some respects, he is like his sister.
with respect to something
concerning something

respect verb
to respect someone is to have
respect for them

respectable adjective
1 a respectable person
has good manners and
character 2 something
respectable is of a good size
or standard **respectability**
noun respectability is being
respectable **respectably**
adverb **respectful** adjective
showing respect; polite
respectfully adverb

respective adjective
belonging to each one of
several • We went to our
respective rooms.

respectively adverb
in the same order as the people
or things already mentioned
• Emma and I went to London
and Paris respectively.

respiration noun
respiration is breathing
respiratory adjective to do with
breathing

respirator noun
a mask or machine for helping
with people's breathing

respond verb
to respond to
someone or something is to
reply or react to them

response noun
how you reply or react to
something

responsibility noun
(**responsibilities**)
1 responsibility is being
responsible for something
2 a responsibility is something
for which you are responsible

responsible adjective
1 looking after something
and likely to take the blame
if anything goes wrong 2 able
to be trusted 3 important
and needing trust • She has
a responsible job. 4 to be
responsible for something is to
be the cause of it • Faulty wiring
was responsible for the fire.
responsibly adverb in a way
that shows you can be trusted

rest¹ noun
1 a time when you can sleep or
relax 2 a support for something

rest¹ verb
1 to rest is to sleep or relax 2 to
rest on or against something

is to lean on it • The ladder is
resting against the wall. 3 to rest
something is to lean or support
it somewhere • Rest the ladder
on the roof.

rest² noun
the rest the part that is left;
the others

restaurant noun
a place where you can buy a
meal and eat it

restless adjective
you are restless when you
can't relax or keep still
restlessly adverb
restlessness noun

restore verb
to restore something is to put
it back as it was or make it new
again **restoration** noun when
something is put back as it was
or made new again

restrain verb
to restrain someone or
something is to hold them or
keep them tightly controlled
restraint noun self-control

restrict verb
to restrict someone or
something is to keep them
within certain limits or stop
them from acting freely
restriction noun something
that restricts you

result noun
1 a thing that happens because
something else has happened
2 the score or situation at the
end of a game or competition
or race 3 the answer to a sum
or problem

result verb
to result is to happen as a result
to result in something is to
have it as a result • The game
resulted in a draw.

retain verb
1 to retain something is to
keep it • Retain your tickets
for inspection. 2 to retain
something is to hold it in place

retina noun (say **ret**-i-na)
a layer at the back of your
eyeball that is sensitive
to light

retire verb
1 someone retires when they
give up regular work at a
certain age 2 to retire is also to
retreat or withdraw, or to go
to bed • He was so exhausted
he had to retire from the race.
retirement noun the time
when someone gives up
regular work

retort verb
to retort is to reply quickly
or angrily

a
b
c
d
e
f
g
h
i
j
k
l
m
n
o
p
q
r
s
t
u
v
w
x
y
z

203

retort *noun*
a quick or angry reply

retrace *verb*
to retrace your steps is to go back the way you came

retreat *verb*
to retreat is to go back when you are attacked or defeated

retrieve *verb*
to retrieve something is to get it back or find it again
retrieval *noun* retrieval is retrieving something

return *verb*
1 to return is to come or go back to a place **2** to return something is to give it or send it back

return *noun*
1 when you come back to a place **2** something that is given or sent back **3** a ticket for a journey to a place and back again • *Do you want a single or return?*

reunion *noun*
a meeting of people who have not met for some time

rev *verb* (**revving, revved**)
(*informal*) to rev an engine is to make it run quickly

reveal *verb*
to reveal something is to show it or make it known
revelation *noun* a surprising fact that is made known

revenge *noun*
revenge is harming someone because they have done harm to you

revenue *noun* (*say* **rev**-e-nyoo)
revenue is money that a business or organization receives

revere *verb* (*say* ri-**veer**)
to revere someone or something is to respect them deeply or religiously

reverence *noun*
reverence is great respect or awe, especially towards God or holy things
reverent *adjective* feeling or showing awe or respect

Reverend *noun*
the title of a member of the clergy • *This is the Reverend John Smith.*

reverse *noun*
1 the opposite way or side **2** the gear used to drive a vehicle backwards **in reverse** going in the opposite direction

reverse *verb*
1 to reverse something is to turn it round **2** to reverse is to go backwards in a vehicle **3** to reverse a decision is to change or cancel it **reversal** *noun*

when something is reversed
reversible *adjective* reversible clothing can be worn with either side on the outside

review *noun*
1 a published description and opinion of a book or film or play, or a piece of music **2** an inspection or survey of something

review *verb*
1 to review a book or play or film, or a piece of music, is to write a review of it **2** to review something is to inspect or survey it **reviewer** *noun* someone who writes a review

revise *verb*
1 before you do an examination, you revise when you go over work that you have already done **2** to revise something is to correct or change it

revision *noun*
a change or correction; learning work before you do an examination

revive *verb*
1 to revive something is to start using it again • *The village has revived a number of traditional customs.* **2** to revive someone is to make them conscious again after fainting **revival** *noun* when something improves or becomes popular again

revolt *verb*
1 to revolt is to rebel **2** something revolts you when it disgusts or horrifies you **revolting** *adjective* very unpleasant or disgusting

revolt *noun*
a rebellion

revolution *noun*
1 a rebellion that overthrows the government **2** a complete change **3** one turn of a wheel or engine

revolutionary *adjective*
1 to do with a revolution **2** completely new or original

revolve *verb*
something revolves when it goes round in a circle

revolver *noun*
a pistol that has a revolving store for bullets so that it can be fired several times without having to be loaded again

reward *noun*
something given to a person in return for something they have done

reward *verb*
to reward someone is to give them a reward

rewarding *adjective*
satisfying and worth doing

rewrite *verb* (**rewriting, rewrote, rewritten**)
to rewrite something is to write it again or differently

rheumatism *noun*
(*say* **roo**-ma-tizm)
rheumatism is a disease that causes pain and stiffness in the joints and muscles

rhinoceros *noun* (**rhinoceroses** or **rhinoceros**)
(*say* ry-**noss**-er-os)
a large heavy animal with a horn or two horns on its nose

rhombus *noun* ◆
a shape with four equal sides and no right angles, like a diamond on a playing card

rhubarb *noun*
rhubarb is a plant with pink or green stalks that you can cook and eat

rhyme *noun*
1 similar sounds in the endings of words, as in *bat* and *mat*, *batter* and *matter* **2** a short rhyming poem

rhinoceros

rhyme *verb*
1 a poem rhymes when it has rhymes at the ends of its lines **2** one word rhymes with another word when it forms a rhyme with it • *Bat rhymes with hat.*

rhythm *noun*
a regular pattern of beats, sounds, or movements in music and poetry **rhythmic** or **rhythmical** *adjective* having a rhythm **rhythmically** *adverb*

rib *noun*
your ribs are the curved bones above your waist

ribbon *noun*
a strip of nylon, silk, or other material

ribbon

rice *noun*
rice is white seeds from a cereal plant, used as food
rich *adjective*
1 someone is rich when they have a lot of money or property **2** something is rich when it is full of goodness, quality, or strength • *Fruit is rich in vitamins.* **3** costly or luxurious • *The house has rich furnishings.*
richness *noun*
riches *plural noun*
wealth
richly *adverb*
thoroughly, completely • *They richly deserved their punishment.*
rickety *adjective*
unsteady and likely to break or fall down • *a rickety chair*
rickshaw *noun*
a two-wheeled carriage pulled by one or more people, used in the Far East

WORD ORIGIN

The word **rickshaw** is from Japanese, and is a shorter form of *jinriksha* which means 'person-power vehicle'.

ricochet *verb* (say **rik**-o-shay)
to ricochet is to bounce off something • *The bullets ricocheted off the wall.*
rid *verb* (**ridding, rid**)
to rid a person or place of something unwanted is to free them from it • *He rid the town of rats.* **to get rid of something** or **someone** is to cause them to go away • *I wish I could get rid of these spots.*
riddance *noun*
good riddance used to show that you are glad that something or someone has gone
riddle *noun*
a puzzling question, especially as a joke
ride *verb* (**riding, rode, ridden**)
1 to ride a horse or bicycle is to sit on it and be carried along on it **2** to ride is to travel in a vehicle **rider** *noun* someone who rides a horse
ride *noun*
a journey on a horse or bicycle, or in a vehicle
ridge *noun*
a long narrow part higher than the rest of something • *a mountain ridge*
ridicule *verb*
to ridicule someone or something is to make fun of them

ridiculous *adjective*
extremely silly or absurd
ridiculously *adverb*
rifle *noun*
a long gun that you hold against your shoulder when you fire it
rift *noun*
1 a crack or split **2** a disagreement or a break in a friendship
rig *verb* (**rigging, rigged**)
1 to rig a ship is to fit it with rigging, sails, and other equipment **2** to rig an election or competition is to control the result dishonestly **to rig something up** is to make it quickly
rigging *noun*
rigging is the ropes that support a ship's masts and sails
right *adjective*
1 on or towards the east if you think of yourself as facing north **2** correct • *Is this sum right?* **3** fair or honest • *It's not right to cheat.*
right *adverb*
1 on or towards the right • *Turn right.* **2** completely • *Turn right round.* **3** exactly • *She stood right in the middle.* **4** straight; directly • *Go right ahead.* **right away** immediately
right *noun*
1 the right side **2** what is fair or just; something that people ought to be allowed • *They fought for their rights.* • *He had no right to talk to you like that.*
right *verb*
to right something is to put it right • *The fault might right itself.*
right angle *noun*
an angle of 90 degrees, like angles in a rectangle
rightful *adjective*
deserved or proper • *The bike was returned to its rightful owner.*
right-hand *adjective*
on the right side of something
right-handed *adjective*
using the right hand more than the left hand
rightly *adverb*
correctly or fairly
rigid *adjective* (say **rij**-id)
1 firm or stiff **2** strict or harsh • *The rules are rigid.*
rigidity *noun* how rigid something is **rigidly** *adverb*
rim *noun*
the outer edge of a cup or wheel or other round object
rind *noun*
the tough skin on bacon, cheese, or fruit

ring¹ *noun*
1 something in the shape of a circle • *The children sat in a ring around the clown.* **2** a thin circular piece of metal you wear on a finger **3** the place where a boxing match or other contest is held **4** the space where a circus performs
ring¹ *verb*
to ring something is to put a ring round it • *Ring the answer that you think is the right one.*
ring² *verb* (**ringing, rang, rung**)
1 to ring a bell is to make it sound **2** a bell rings when it makes a clear musical sound **3** to ring someone is to telephone them • *She rang her brother last night.*
ring² *noun*
a ringing sound **to give someone a ring** (*informal*) is to telephone them
ringleader *noun*
someone who leads other people in doing wrong or in rebellion
ringlet *noun*
a long curled piece of hair
ringmaster *noun*
the person who is in charge of a performance in the circus ring
ring road *noun*
a road that takes traffic round a town rather than through it
rink *noun*
a place made for skating
rinse *verb*
to rinse something is to wash it in clean water without soap
rinse *noun*
a wash in clean water without soap
riot *noun*
wild or violent behaviour by a crowd of people in a public place
riot *verb*
people riot when they run wild and behave violently in a public place
rip *verb* (**ripping, ripped**)
to rip something is to tear it roughly
rip *noun*
a torn place
ripe *adjective*
ready to be harvested or eaten **ripeness** *noun*
ripen *verb*
1 to ripen something is to make it ripe **2** to ripen is to become ripe

ripple *noun*
a small wave on the surface of water

ripple *verb*
water ripples when it forms small waves on the surface

rise *verb* (**rising, rose, risen**)
1 to rise is to go upwards
• *Smoke was rising from the fire.*
• *The sun rises in the east.* **2** to rise is also to get larger or more
• *Prices rose this year.*
3 a person rises when they get up from sleeping or sitting
• *They all rose as she came in.*
4 people rise, or rise up, when they rebel • *The army rose against the government.*

rise *noun*
1 an increase, especially in wages **2** an upward slope

risk *verb*
to risk something is to take a chance of damaging or losing it
• *They risked their lives during the rescue.*

risk *noun*
a chance that something bad will happen • *There's a risk that the river might flood.* **risky** *adjective*
dangerous; involving risk

rite *noun*
a ceremony or ritual

ritual *noun*
a regular ceremony or series of actions

rival *noun*
a person or thing that competes with another or tries to do the same thing **rivalry** *noun* when two people compete against each other

rival *verb* (**rivalling, rivalled**)
to rival someone or something is to be as good as they are
• *Nothing can rival the taste of home-made ice cream.*

river *noun*
a large natural stream of water that flows into the sea or into a lake

rivet *noun*
a strong metal pin for holding pieces of metal together

rivet *verb*
1 to rivet something is to fasten it with rivets **2** to rivet someone is to hold them still
• *She stood riveted to the spot.*
3 to be riveted by something is to be fascinated by it • *The children were riveted by his story.*
riveting *adjective* fascinating; holding your attention

roam *verb*
to roam is to wander • *They roamed about the city.*

roar *noun*
a loud deep sound of the kind that a lion makes

roar *verb*
to roar is to make a loud deep sound

roast *verb*
1 to roast food is to cook it in an oven or over a fire **2** you say you are roasting when you are very hot

rob *verb* (**robbing, robbed**)
to rob someone or a place is to steal something from them
• *He robbed me of my watch.* • *The bank's been robbed.* **robber** *noun*
someone who steals something

robbery *noun* when something is stolen

robe *noun*
a long loose piece of clothing

robin *noun*
a small brown bird with a red breast

robot *noun*
a machine that imitates the movements of a person or does the work of a person

robot

robust *adjective*
tough and strong

rock¹ *noun*
1 a rock is a large stone **2** rock is a large mass of stone **3** rock is also a hard sweet usually shaped like a stick and sold at the seaside

rock² *verb*
1 to rock is to move gently backwards and forwards or from side to side **2** to rock something is to make it do this

rock² *noun*
rock music

rockery *noun* (**rockeries**)
part of a garden where people grow flowers between rocks

rocket *noun*
1 a firework that shoots high into the air **2** a pointed tube-shaped vehicle propelled into the air by hot gases, especially as a spacecraft or weapon

rocking chair *noun*
a chair which can be rocked by the person sitting in it

rock music *noun*
rock music is popular music with a heavy beat

rocky *adjective* (**rockier, rockiest**)
1 a rocky place is full of rocks **2** unsteady or shaky

rod *noun*
1 a long thin stick or bar **2** a rod with a line attached for fishing

rode
past tense of **ride** *verb*

rodent *noun*
an animal that has large front teeth for gnawing things, such as a rat, mouse, or squirrel

rodeo *noun* (**rodeos**)
(*say* roh-**day**-oh or *say* **roh**-di-oh)
a display or contest in which cowboys show their skills in riding and in controlling cattle

rogue *noun*
a dishonest or mischievous person **roguish** *adjective* a roguish smile is a mischievous one

role *noun*
1 the part that an actor plays in a play, film, or story
2 the purpose something has
• *Computers have a role in language learning.*

roll *verb*
1 to roll is to move along by turning over and over, like a ball or wheel **2** to roll something is to make it do this
3 to roll something, or roll something up, is to form it into the shape of a cylinder or ball
4 to roll something soft is to flatten it by moving a round heavy object over it **5** a ship rolls when it sways from side to side **6** drums roll when they make a long rumbling sound

roll *noun*
1 a cylinder made by rolling something up **2** a small loaf of bread shaped like a bun **3** a list of names **4** the rumbling sound of drums or thunder

roller *noun*
a cylinder-shaped object, especially one used for flattening things

roller skate *noun*
roller skates are boots with two pairs of wheels fitted underneath, so that you can move smoothly over the ground

rolling pin *noun*
a heavy cylinder you roll over pastry to flatten it

rocket

Roman Catholic noun
a member of the Church with
the Pope in Rome at its head
romance noun
1 romance is experiences and
feelings connected with love
2 a romance is a love affair or
a love story
Roman numerals plural noun
letters that represent numbers,
as used by the ancient Romans
(compare arabic figures): I = 1, V
= 5, X = 10, L = 50, C = 100, and
M = 1000
romantic adjective
to do with love or romance
romantically adverb
romp verb
to romp is to play in a lively
way
rompers plural noun
a piece of clothing for a
young child, covering the
body and legs
roof noun
1 the part that covers the top of
a building, shelter, or vehicle
2 the upper part of your mouth
rook noun
1 a black bird that looks like
a crow 2 a piece in chess, also
called a castle
room noun
1 a room is a part of a building
with its own walls and ceiling
2 room is space for someone
or something • Is there room
for me?
roomy adjective (**roomier,
roomiest**)
somewhere is roomy when
there is plenty of room or
space inside
roost noun
the place where a bird rests
root noun
1 the part of a plant that grows
under the ground 2 a source or
basis of something • People say
that money is the root of all evil.
3 a number that gives another
number when multiplied by
itself • 9 is the square root of 81.
to take root is to grow roots or
to become established
• The custom never took root
in other countries.
root verb
1 to root is to take root in the
ground 2 to root someone is to
fix them firmly • Fear rooted him
to the spot. **to root something
out** is to find it and get rid of it
rope noun
a strong thick cord made
of strands twisted together
to show someone the ropes
is to show them how to do
a job

rose noun
a scented flower with
a long thorny stem
rosy adjective (**rosier,
rosiest**)
1 pink 2 hopeful
or cheerful
• The future
looks rosy.
rot verb (**rotting, rotted**)
to rot is to go soft or bad
so that it is useless
• This wood has rotted.
rot noun
rot is decay
rota noun
a list of tasks to be done and
the people who have to
do them
rotate verb
1 to rotate is to go round like
a wheel 2 to rotate is to take
turns at something • The job
of treasurer rotates.
rotation noun
1 rotation, or a rotation, is
when something goes round
like a wheel 2 rotation is also
taking turns to do something
rotor noun
the part of a machine that
goes round, especially the
large horizontal blade on
top of a helicopter
rotten adjective
1 rotted or decayed
• There was rotten
fruit on the ground.
2 (informal) nasty
or very bad
• We had rotten
weather.
rough adjective
1 not smooth; uneven
2 violent; not gentle
• He is a rough boy.
3 not exact; done quickly
• It's only a rough guess.
roughness noun
roughen verb
to roughen something is to
make it rough
roughly adverb
1 approximately; not exactly
• There were roughly a hundred
people there. 2 in a rough way;
not gently • She pushed him
roughly out of the way.
round adjective
1 shaped like a circle or ball or
cylinder 2 a round trip is one
that returns to the start
round adverb
1 in a circle or curve; by a
longer route • Go round to the
back of the house. 2 in every
direction or to every person
• Hand the cakes round. 3 in a
new direction • Turn your chair

rose

rotten

round. 4 to someone's
house or place of work
• Come round at lunchtime.
round preposition 1 on all
sides of • We'll put a fence
round the field. 2 in a curve
or circle about • The earth
moves round the sun.
3 to every part of
• Show them round
the house.
round noun
1 each stage in a
competition • The
winners go on to the
next round. 2 a series of visits
or calls made by a doctor,
postman, or other person
3 a whole slice of bread, or a
sandwich made from two whole
slices of bread 4 a shot or series
of shots from a gun; a piece of
ammunition 5 a song in which
people sing the same words but
start at different times
round verb
to round a place is to travel
round it • A large car rounded
the corner. **to round a number
down** is to decrease it to the
nearest lower number
• 123.4 may be rounded down
to 123. **to round a number up**
is to increase it to the nearest
higher number • 123.7 may
be rounded up to 124. **to
round something off** is
to finish it **to round up
people or things** is to
gather them together
roundabout noun
1 a road junction at which
traffic has to pass round a
circular island 2 a merry-go-
round
roundabout adjective
not using the shortest or most
direct way • We went by a
roundabout route.
rounders noun
rounders is a game in which
players try to hit a ball and
run round a circuit
roundly adverb
thoroughly or severely
• We were roundly told off
for being late.
rouse verb
to rouse someone is to wake
them up or make them excited
rout verb (say rowt)
to rout an enemy is to defeat
them and chase them away
route noun (say root)
the way you have to go to get
to a place
routine noun (say roo-**teen**)
a regular or fixed way of
doing things

rove *verb*
to rove is to roam or wander
• *Her eyes roved around the classroom.* **rover** *noun* someone who roves

row¹ *noun* (rhymes with **go**)
a line of people or things

row² *verb* (rhymes with **go**)
to row a boat is to use oars to make it move
rower *noun* someone who rows a boat

row³ *noun* (rhymes with **cow**)
1 a great noise or disturbance **2** a noisy quarrel or argument

row³ *verb*
people row when they have a noisy argument

rowdy *adjective* (**rowdier, rowdiest**)
noisy and disorderly
rowdily *adverb* **rowdiness** *noun*

rowing boat *noun*
a small boat that you move forward by using oars

royal *adjective*
to do with a king or queen
royalty *noun* the members of a royal family

rub *verb* (**rubbing, rubbed**)
to rub something is to move it backwards and forwards while pressing it on something else
• *He rubbed his hands together.*
to rub something off or out is to make it disappear by rubbing it

rub *noun*
when you rub something
• *Give it a quick rub.*

rubber *noun*
1 rubber is a strong elastic substance used for making tyres, balls, hoses, and other things **2** a rubber is a piece of rubber or soft plastic for rubbing out pencil marks
rubbery *adjective* soft and easy to stretch

rubbish *noun*
1 things that are not wanted or needed **2** nonsense

rubble *noun*
rubble is broken pieces of brick or stone

ruby *noun* (**rubies**)
a red jewel

rucksack *noun*
a bag with shoulder straps that you carry on your back

rudder *noun*
a flat hinged device at the back of a ship or aircraft, used for steering it

ruddy *adjective* (**ruddier, ruddiest**)
red and healthy-looking
• *He had a ruddy face.*

rude *adjective*
1 not polite; not showing respect for other people • *It was rude of me to push in.* **2** indecent or improper • *a rude joke*
rudely *adverb* **rudeness** *noun*

ruffian *noun*
a rough violent person

ruffle *verb*
1 to ruffle something is to make it untidy or less smooth • *The bird ruffled its feathers.* **2** to ruffle someone is to annoy them or upset them

rug *noun*
1 a thick piece of material that partly covers a floor **2** a thick blanket

rugby or **rugby football** *noun*
rugby is a kind of football game using an oval ball that players may kick or carry

rugby ball

rugged *adjective* (say **rug**-id)
something rugged has a rough or uneven surface or outline
• *His face was rugged.* • *It has a rugged coastline.*

ruin *verb*
to ruin something is to spoil it or destroy it completely

ruin *noun*
1 a ruin is a building that has been so badly damaged that it has almost all fallen down **2** ruin is when something is ruined or destroyed **to be in ruins** is to be destroyed
• *My plans were in ruins.*
ruinous *adjective* leading to ruin

rule *noun*
1 a rule is something that people have to obey **2** rule is ruling or governing
• *The country used to be under French rule.* **as a rule** usually; normally

rule *verb*
1 to rule people is to govern them; to rule is to be a ruler **2** to rule something is to make a decision • *The referee ruled that it was a foul.* **3** to rule a line is to draw a straight line with a ruler or other straight edge

ruler *noun*
1 someone who governs a country **2** a strip of wood, plastic, or metal with straight edges, used for measuring and drawing straight lines

ruler

ruling *noun*
a judgement or decision
• *I will give my ruling tomorrow.*

rum *noun*
rum is a strong alcoholic drink made from sugar cane

rumble *verb*
to rumble is to make a deep heavy sound like thunder
• *His stomach was rumbling.*

rumble *noun*
a long deep heavy sound
• *There was a rumble of thunder in the distance.*

rummage *verb*
to rummage is to turn things over or move them about while looking for something

rummy *noun*
rummy is a card game in which players try to form sets or sequences of cards

rumour *noun*
something that a lot of people are saying, although it may not be true

rump *noun*
the back part of an animal, above its hind legs

run *verb* (**running, ran, run**)
1 to run is to move with quick steps and with both feet off the ground for a time **2** to run is also to move or go or travel
• *Tears ran down his cheeks.*
3 a tap or your nose runs when liquid flows from it **4** an engine or machine runs when it is working or functioning • *The engine was running smoothly.*
5 to run something is to manage it or organize it
• *She runs a corner shop.* **6** to run someone somewhere is to give them a lift there **to run a risk** is to take a chance **to run away** is to leave a place quickly or secretly **to run into someone** is to meet them unexpectedly **to run out of something** is to have used up a supply of it **to run someone over** is to knock them down with a car or bicycle

run *noun*
1 a spell of running • *Let's go for a run.* **2** a point scored in cricket or baseball **3** a series of damaged stitches in a pair of

tights or other piece of clothing **4** a continuous series of events • *They've had a run of good luck.* **5** a place with a fence round it for keeping animals **to be on the run** is to be running away, especially from the police

runaway *noun*
someone who has run away from home

rung *noun*
each of the short crossbars on a ladder

runner *noun*
1 a person or animal that runs in a race **2** the part of a sledge that slides along the ground

runner bean *noun*
a kind of climbing bean

runner-up *noun*
someone who comes second in a race or competition

runny *adjective* (**runnier, runniest**)
flowing or moving like liquid

runway *noun*
a long strip with a hard surface for aircraft to take off and land

rural *adjective*
to do with the countryside; in the country

rush¹ *verb*
1 to rush is to move or go very quickly • *When the doorbell rang I rushed to see who it was.* **2** to rush someone is to make them hurry • *I'm trying not to rush you.* **3** to rush someone is also to attack or capture them by surprise

rush¹ *noun*
a rush is a hurry • *I can't stop – I'm in a rush.*

rush² *noun*
rushes are plants with thin stems that grow in wet or marshy places

rusk *noun*
a kind of hard dry biscuit for babies to chew

rust *noun*
rust is a red or brown substance formed on metal that is exposed to air and dampness

rust *verb*
metal rusts when it develops rust

rustle *verb*
1 to rustle is to make a gentle sound like dry leaves being blown by the wind **2** to rustle horses or cattle is to steal them

rusty *adjective*
1 coated with rust **2** not as good as it used to be because you have not had enough practice • *My French is a bit rusty.*

rut *noun*
a deep groove made by wheels

in soft ground **to be in a rut** is to have a dull life with no changes

ruthless *adjective*
someone is ruthless when they are determined to get what they want and don't care if they hurt other people **ruthlessly** *adverb* **ruthlessness** *noun*

rye *noun*
rye is a cereal used to make bread and biscuits

Ss

sabbath *noun*
the sabbath is the weekly day for rest and prayer, Saturday for Jews, Sunday for Christians

sabotage *noun* (*say* **sab**-o-tahzh)
sabotage is deliberately damaging machinery or equipment

sabotage *verb*
to sabotage machinery or equipment is to deliberately damage it **saboteur** *noun* someone who commits sabotage

sac *noun*
any bag-like part of an animal or plant

sachet *noun* (*say* **sash**-ay)
a small sealed packet of something such as shampoo or sugar

sack *noun*
a large bag made of strong material **to get the sack** (*informal*) is to be dismissed from your job

sack *verb*
(*informal*) to sack someone is to dismiss them from their job

sacred *adjective*
to do with God or a god; holy

sacrifice *noun*
1 giving up a thing that you value so that something good may happen • *If you want to save some money you might have to make a few sacrifices.* **2** killing an animal or person as an offering to a god **sacrificial** *adjective* offered as a sacrifice

sacrifice *verb*
1 to sacrifice something is to give it up so that something good may happen **2** to sacrifice an animal or person is to kill them as an offering to a god

sad *adjective* (**sadder, saddest**)
unhappy; showing sorrow or causing it **sadly** *adverb* in a sad way • *He shook his head sadly.*

sadness *noun*

sadden *verb*
something saddens you when it makes you sad or unhappy

saddle *noun*
1 a seat that you put on the back of a horse or other animal so that you can ride it **2** the seat of a bicycle

saddle *verb*
to saddle an animal is to put a saddle on its back

safari *noun* (*say* sa-**far**-i)
an expedition to see wild animals or hunt them

WORD ORIGIN

The word **safari** comes from an Arabic word *safara* meaning 'to travel'.

safari park *noun*
a large park where wild animals can roam around freely and visitors can watch them from their cars

safe *adjective*
1 free from danger; protected **2** not causing danger • *Drive at a safe speed.* **safely** *adverb* without risk or danger • *The plane landed safely.*

safe *noun*
a strong cupboard or box in which valuable things can be locked away to keep them safe

safeguard *noun*
something that protects you against danger

safeguard *verb*
to safeguard something is to protect it from danger

safety *noun* safety is being safe; protection • *We listened to a talk on road safety.*

safety belt *noun*
a belt to hold someone securely in a seat

safety pin *noun*
a curved pin made with a clip that closes to cover the point

sag *verb* (**sagging, sagged**)
something sags when it sinks slightly in the middle because something heavy is pressing on it

saga *noun*
a long story with many adventures

safety pins

sail *noun*
1 a large piece of strong cloth attached to a mast to make a boat move **2** a short voyage • *We went for a sail around the island.* **3** an arm of a windmill **to set sail** is to start on a voyage in a ship

sail *verb*
1 to sail somewhere is to travel there in a ship **2** a ship or boat sails when it starts out on a

a
b
c
d
e
f
g
h
i
j
k
l
m
n
o
p
q
r
x
y
z

voyage • *What time does the ferry sail?* **3** to sail a ship or boat is to control it

sailor noun
1 a member of a ship's crew
2 someone who sails

saint noun
a holy or very good person
saintly adjective very good or holy

sake noun
for the sake of something in order to do it or get it • *He'll do anything for the sake of money.* **for someone's sake** in order to help them or please them • *She went to a lot of trouble for his sake.*

salad noun
a mixture of vegetables eaten cold and often raw

salami noun
salami is a kind of strong spicy sausage

salary noun
a regular wage, usually paid every month

sale noun
1 the selling of something
2 a time when a shop sells things at reduced prices **for sale** or **on sale** able to be bought

salesperson noun
someone whose job is to sell things **salesman** noun
saleswoman noun

saliva noun (*say* sa-**ly**-va)
saliva is the natural liquid in your mouth

salmon noun (**salmon**)
a large fish with pink flesh, used for food

salon noun
a room or shop where a hairdresser or a beauty specialist works

salt noun
salt is the white substance that gives sea water its taste and is used for flavouring food **salty** adjective tasting of salt

salmon

salt verb
to salt food is to use salt to flavour or preserve it

salute verb
to salute is to raise your hand to your forehead as a sign of respect or greeting

salute noun
the act of saluting

salvage verb
to salvage something such as a damaged ship is to save or rescue it or parts of it

salvation noun
salvation is saving someone or something

same adjective
not different; exactly equal or alike • *We are the same age.* • *Look, these two leaves are exactly the same.*

samosa noun
a small case of crisp pastry filled with a mixture of spicy meat or vegetables

samosas

sample noun
a small amount that shows what something is like

sample verb
1 to sample something is to take a sample of it • *Scientists sampled the lake water.* **2** to sample something is also to try part of it • *She sampled the cake.*

sanctuary noun (**sanctuaries**)
1 a safe place, especially for someone who is being chased or attacked **2** a place where wildlife is protected • *We visited a bird sanctuary.*

sand noun
sand is the tiny grains of rock that you find on beaches and in deserts

sandal noun
a light shoe with straps that go round your foot

sandpaper noun
sandpaper is strong paper coated with hard grains, rubbed on rough surfaces to make them smooth

sandstone noun
sandstone is rock made of compressed sand

sandwich noun
slices of bread with meat, cheese, or some other filling between them

sandy adjective
(**sandier, sandiest**)
1 made of sand; covered with sand **2** sandy hair is yellowish-red

sane adjective
having a healthy mind; not mad

sanitary adjective
free from germs and dirt; hygienic

sanitation noun
sanitation is arrangements for drainage and getting rid of sewage

sanity noun
sanity is being sane

sap noun
sap is the juice inside a tree or plant

sap verb (**sapping, sapped**)
to sap someone's strength or energy is to use it up or weaken it gradually • *The heat had sapped all my energy.*

sapling noun
a young tree

sapphire noun
a bright blue jewel

sarcastic noun
you are being sarcastic when you mock someone or something by saying the opposite of what you mean • *She said she liked the music I was playing but I think she was being sarcastic.* **sarcastically** adverb **sarcasm** noun when someone is being sarcastic

sardine noun
a small sea fish, usually sold packed tightly in tins

sari noun (*say* **sar**-i)
a long length of cloth worn as a dress, especially by Indian women and girls

sash noun
a strip of cloth worn round the waist or over one shoulder

satchel noun
a bag you wear over your shoulder or on your back, especially for carrying books to and from school

satellite noun
1 a spacecraft sent into space to move in an orbit round a planet, in order to get and send information **2** a moon that moves in orbit round a planet

satellite dish noun
a dish-shaped aerial for receiving television signals sent by satellite

satellite television noun
satellite television is television programmes that are broadcast using a satellite

satin noun
satin is a silky material that is shiny on one side

satire noun
1 satire is using humour or exaggeration to show the faults of a person or thing, especially

the government **2** a satire is a play or piece of writing that does this **satirical** adjective using satire to criticize someone

satirist noun someone who writes satire

satisfaction noun
satisfaction is the feeling of being satisfied

satisfactory adjective
good enough; acceptable

satisfactorily adverb in a satisfactory way

satisfy verb (**satisfies, satisfying, satisfied**)
1 to satisfy someone is to give them what they need or want **2** to be satisfied is to be sure of something • *I am satisfied that you have done your best.*

saturate verb
to be saturated is to be soaking wet • *My clothes are saturated with rain.* **saturation** noun
saturation is being saturated

Saturday noun
the seventh day of the week

sauce noun
a sauce is a thick liquid served with food to add flavour

saucepan noun
a metal cooking pan with a long handle

saucer noun
a small curved plate for a cup to stand on

saucy adjective (**saucier, sauciest**)
rude or cheeky

sauna noun (say **saw**-na or say **sow**-na)
a room filled with steam where people sit and sweat a lot, used as a kind of bath

saunter verb
to saunter is to walk about in a leisurely way

sausage noun
a tube of edible skin or plastic stuffed with minced meat and other ingredients

savage adjective
wild and fierce; cruel **savagely** noun in a violent or cruel way **savagery** noun cruel and violent behaviour

savage verb
an animal savages someone when it attacks them and bites or scratches them fiercely

savannah noun (say sa-**van**-a)
a grassy plain in a hot country, with few trees

save verb
1 to save someone or something is to free them from danger or harm **2** to save something, especially money, is to keep it so that it can be

used later **3** to save computer data is to instruct the computer to keep it on its hard disk **4** in football, to save a ball is to stop it going into your goal

savings plural noun
your savings are the money that you have saved

saviour noun
a person who saves someone

savoury adjective
savoury food is tasty but not sweet

saw noun
a tool with sharp teeth for cutting wood or other hard materials

saw verb (**sawing, sawed, sawn** or **sawed**)
to saw something is to cut it with a saw

sawdust noun
sawdust is powder that comes from wood when it is cut with a saw

saxophone noun
a wind instrument with a tube that curves upward with a wider opening

WORD ORIGIN

The word **saxophone** comes from the name of Adolphe Sax, a Belgian instrument-maker.

say verb (**saying, said**)
1 to say something is to make words with your voice **2** to say something is also to give information or instructions • *The notice said 'Keep Out'.*

saying noun
a well-known phrase or proverb

saxophone

scab noun
a hard covering that forms over a cut or graze while it is healing

scabbard noun
a cover for a sword or dagger

scaffold noun
a platform on which criminals were executed in the past

scaffolding noun
scaffolding is a structure of poles and planks for workers to stand on when they are building or repairing a house

scald verb
to scald your skin is to burn it with very hot liquid or steam

scale¹ noun
1 a series of units or marks for measuring something • *This ruler has one scale in centimetres and another in inches.* **2** the relationship between the size of something on a map or model and the actual size of

the thing in the real world • *The scale of this map is one inch to the mile.*
3 a series of musical notes going up or down in a fixed pattern **4** the relative size or importance of something • *They love organizing parties on a massive scale.*

scale¹ verb
to scale something is to climb up it

scale² noun
one of the thin overlapping parts on the outside of fish, snakes, and other animals **scaly** adjective covered in scales

scales plural noun
a device for weighing things

scalp noun
the skin on the top of your head

scamper verb
to scamper is to run quickly with short steps

scampi plural noun scampi are large prawns eaten in batter or breadcrumbs

scan verb (**scanning, scanned**)
1 to scan something is to look at every part of it **2** to scan a piece of writing is to look over it quickly **3** to scan an area, or a part of the body, is to sweep a radar or electronic beam over it in order to find something **4** poetry scans when it has a fixed rhythm

scan noun
a search or examination using a scanner

scandal noun
1 a scandal is a shameful or disgraceful action **2** scandal is gossip that damages someone's reputation

scandalous adjective shocking or disgraceful

scanner noun
1 a machine used to examine part of the body, using an electronic beam **2** a machine that converts print and pictures into data that can be read by a computer

scanty adjective (**scantier, scantiest**)
hardly big enough; small **scantily** adverb barely; just sufficiently

scapegoat noun
someone who gets all the blame for something that other people have done

scar noun
a mark left on your skin by a cut or burn after it has healed

a
b
c
d
e
f
g
h
i
j
k
l
m
n
o
p
q
r
s
t
u
v
w
x
y
z

scar verb (**scarring, scarred**)
an injury scars you when it
leaves a permanent mark on
your skin

scarce adjective
not enough to supply people
• *Wheat was scarce because
of the bad harvest.* **to make
yourself scarce** (*informal*) is to
go away or keep out of the way

scarcity noun a shortage of
something

scarcely adverb
hardly; only just • *She could
scarcely walk.*

scare verb
to scare someone is to frighten
them

scare noun
a scare is a fright • *You gave me
quite a scare.*

scarecrow noun
a figure of a person dressed in
old clothes, that farmers put
in a field to frighten birds
away from crops

scarf noun (**scarves**)
a strip of material that
you wear round your
neck or head

scarlet adjective ●
bright red

scary adjective
(**scarier,
scariest**)
(*informal*)
frightening

scatter verb
1 to
scatter
things
is to
throw
them in all
directions **2** to scatter
is to move quickly in all
directions • *The crowd
scattered when the police
arrived.*

scarf

scavenge verb
an animal or bird scavenges
when it eats dead animals that
have been killed by another
animal **scavenger** noun an
animal or bird that scavenges

scene noun
1 the place where something
happens • *Here is the scene of
the crime.* **2** a part of a play or
film **3** a view you can see **4** an
angry or noisy outburst • *They
made a scene about the money.*

scenery noun
1 scenery is the natural features
of an area • *We were admiring
the scenery.* **2** scenery is also
the painted panels and other
things put on a stage to
make it look like a place

scent noun (*say* sent)
1 a pleasant smell or perfume
2 an animal's smell, that other
animals can follow **scented**
adjective having a strong
pleasant smell

scent verb
to scent something is to
discover it by its scent

sceptic noun (*say* **skep**-tik)
someone who doesn't believe
things easily or readily

sceptical adjective
(*say* **skep**-tik-al)
you are sceptical when you
don't believe things easily
or readily **scepticism** noun
scepticism is not believing
things easily or readily

schedule noun (*say* **shed**-yool)
a timetable of things that have
to be done **to be on schedule**
is to be on time; not late

scheme noun
a plan of what to do
scheme verb
to scheme is to make
secret plans

scholar noun
1 someone who studies
a subject thoroughly
2 someone who has been
given a scholarship

scholarly adjective
showing knowledge and learning

scholarship noun
1 a scholarship is a grant of
money given to someone for
their education **2** scholarship
is knowledge and learning

school¹ noun
1 a place where children go
to be taught **2** the children
who go there • *The whole
school had a holiday.* **3** a place
where you can learn a skill
• *a driving school*

school² noun
a group of whales or fish
swimming together

schoolchild noun
(**schoolchildren**)
a child who goes to school

schoolteacher noun
a teacher at a school

schooner noun (*say* **skoo**-ner)
a sailing ship with two or more
masts

schooner

science noun
science is the study of objects
and happenings in the world
that can be observed and tested

WORD ORIGIN

The word **science** comes from a Latin
word *scientia* meaning 'knowledge'.

science fiction noun
science fiction is stories about
imaginary worlds, especially
in space and in the future

scientific adjective
1 to do with science **2** studying
things carefully and logically

scientist noun
someone who studies science
or is an expert in science

scissors plural noun
a cutting device made of two
movable blades joined together

scoff verb
to scoff at someone or
something is to make fun
of them

scold verb
to scold someone is to tell them
off harshly

scone noun (*say* skon or skohn)
a small plain cake, usually
eaten with butter and jam

scoop noun
1 a deep spoon for serving
soft food such as ice cream or
mashed potato **2** a deep shovel
3 (*informal*) an important piece
of news that one newspaper
prints before all the others

scoop verb
to scoop something, or to scoop
it out, is to take it out with a
scoop or the palm of your hand

scooter noun
1 a simple type of bicycle for
a child, with two wheels and a
narrow platform. You stand on
the platform and push on the
ground with one foot. **2** a kind of
motor cycle with small wheels

scope noun
1 an opportunity or possibility
for something • *There is scope for
improvement.* **2** what something
deals with or includes • *That
question doesn't come within the
scope of this book.*

scorch verb
to scorch something is to
make it go brown by slightly
burning it

scorching adjective
very hot

score noun
1 the number of points or goals
that are got in a game • *What's
the score?* **2** (*old use*) a score is
twenty • *He reached the age of
four-score (= 80) years.*

score *verb*
1 to score a goal or point in a game is to get it **2** to score is to keep a count of the score in a game • *I thought you were scoring.* **3** to score a surface is to scratch it **scorer** *noun* someone who scores a goal or point

scorn *noun*
scorn is treating a person or thing with contempt

scorn *verb*
to scorn someone or something is to have contempt for them

scornful *adjective* full of contempt and showing no respect **scornfully** *adverb*

scorpion *noun*
an animal related to the spider, with pincers and a poisonous sting in its curved tail

Scot *noun*
a person from Scotland

Scottish *adjective*
to do with Scotland

scorpion

scoundrel *noun*
a wicked or dishonest person

scour *verb*
1 to scour (for example) a pan or bath is to rub it hard with something rough until it is clean and bright **2** to scour an area is to search it thoroughly

Scout *noun*
a member of the Scout Association

scout *noun*
someone sent out ahead of a group in order to collect information

scowl *verb*
to scowl is to look bad-tempered

scowl *noun*
an angry look

scramble *verb*
1 to scramble is to move quickly and awkwardly • *We scrambled up the steep slope.* **2** to scramble eggs is to cook them by mixing them and heating them in a pan **3** to scramble for something is to struggle to do it or get it

scramble *noun*
1 a climb or walk over rough ground **2** a struggle to get something • *There was a scramble for the best seats.* **3** a motorcycle race across rough country

scrap¹ *noun*
1 a scrap is a small piece of something **2** scrap is rubbish, especially unwanted metal

scrap¹ *verb* (**scrapping, scrapped**)
to scrap something is to get rid of it when you do not want it

scrap² *noun*
(*informal*) a fight

scrap² *verb* (**scrapping, scrapped**)
to scrap is to fight or quarrel

scrape *verb*
1 to scrape something is to rub it with something rough, hard, or sharp **2** to scrape past or through is to only just get past or succeed • *She scraped through her exams.* **3** to scrape something together is to collect it with difficulty • *They scraped together enough money for a holiday.* **scraper** *noun* a device for scraping something clean

scrape *noun*
1 a scraping movement or sound **2** a mark made by scraping something **3** (*informal*) an awkward situation • *He's always getting into scrapes.*

scrappy *adjective*
done carelessly or untidily

scratch *verb*
1 to scratch a surface is to damage it by rubbing something sharp over it **2** you scratch your skin when you rub it with your fingers because it itches

scratch *noun*
1 a mark or cut made by scratching **2** the action of scratching • *I need to have a scratch.* **to start from scratch** is to begin at the very beginning **to be up to scratch** is to be up to the proper standard

scrawl *noun*
untidy writing • *Can you read my scrawl?*

scrawl *verb*
to scrawl something is to write it in a hurried or careless way

scream *noun*
a loud high-pitched cry of pain or fear or anger

scream *verb*
to scream is to make a loud high-pitched cry

screech *noun*
a harsh high-pitched sound • *There was a screech of tyres as the car sped off.*

screech *verb*
to screech is to make a harsh high-pitched sound

screen *noun*
1 a surface on which films or television programmes or computer data are shown **2** a movable panel used to hide or protect something **3** a windscreen

screen *verb*
1 to screen a film or television programme is to show it **2** to screen something is to hide it or protect it with a screen **3** to screen people is to test them to find out if they have a disease

screw *noun*
1 a metal pin with a spiral ridge round it, which holds things by being twisted into them **2** a propeller

screw *verb*
1 to screw something is to fix it with screws **2** to screw something in or on is to fit it by turning it • *Screw the lid on to the jar.* • *I screwed in the light-bulb.* **to screw something up** is to twist or squeeze it into a tight ball

screwdriver *noun*
a tool for putting in or taking out screws

scribble *verb*
to scribble is to write untidily or carelessly, or to make meaningless marks

script *noun*
1 the words of a play, film, or broadcast **2** handwriting **3** something you write, especially the answers you write to exam questions

scripture *noun*
the sacred writings of a religion, especially the Bible

scroll *noun*
a roll of paper or parchment with writing on it

scroll *verb*
you scroll up or down on a computer screen when you move the text up or down on the screen to see what comes before or after

scrounge *verb*
(*informal*) to scrounge something is to get it without paying for it • *He scrounged a meal from us.* **scrounger** *noun* someone who tries to get things without paying for them

scrub¹ *verb* (**scrubbing, scrubbed**)
to scrub something is to rub it with a hard brush

scrub¹ *noun*
the action of scrubbing • *You'll need to give your face a good scrub.*

scrub² *noun*
scrub is low trees and bushes, or land covered with them

scruffy *adjective* (**scruffier, scruffiest**)
shabby and untidy

scrum or **scrummage** *noun*
(in rugby football) a group of players from each side who push against each other and try to win the ball with their feet

scuba diving *noun*
scuba diving is swimming underwater, breathing air from a supply carried on your back

scuffle *noun*
a confused struggle or fight

scuffle *verb*
people scuffle when they fight in a confused way

sculptor *noun*
someone who makes sculptures

sculpture *noun*
1 a sculpture is something carved or shaped out of a hard material such as stone, clay, or metal **2** sculpture is the art or work of a sculptor

scum *noun*
scum is froth or dirt on the top of a liquid

scurry *verb*
to scurry is to run or hurry with short steps

scurvy *noun*
scurvy is a disease caused by lack of fresh fruit and vegetables

scuttle¹ *noun*
a container for coal, kept by a fireplace

scuttle² *verb*
to scuttle a ship is to sink it deliberately by making holes in the side or bottom

scuttle³ *verb*
to scuttle is to run with short quick steps

scythe *noun*
a tool with a long curved blade for cutting grass or corn

sea *noun*
1 the salt water that covers most of the earth's surface **2** a large lake or area of water, such as the Mediterranean Sea or the Sea of Galilee **3** a large area of something • I looked down at the sea of faces in the audience. **at sea 1** on the sea **2** unable to understand something or cope with it • He's completely at sea in his new job.

seabed *noun*
the seabed is the bottom of the sea

seafaring *adjective, noun*
travelling or working on the sea

seafarer *noun* someone who travels or works at sea

seafood *noun*
seafood is fish or shellfish from the sea eaten as food

seagull *noun*
a sea bird with long wings

sea horse *noun*
a small fish that swims upright, with a head like a horse's head

seal¹ *noun*
a furry sea animal that breeds on land

seal² *noun*
1 something designed to close an opening and stop air or liquid getting in or out **2** a design pressed into a soft substance such as wax or lead

seal² *verb*
to seal something is to close it by sticking two parts together • He sealed the envelope.

sea level *noun*
sea level is the level of the sea halfway between high and low tide • The mountain rises 1,000 metres above sea level.

sea lion *noun*
a large kind of seal. The male has a kind of mane.

seam *noun*
1 the line where two edges of cloth join together **2** a layer of coal in the ground

seaman *noun* (**seamen**)
a sailor

search *verb*
1 to search for something or someone is to look very carefully for them **2** to search a person or place is to look very carefully for something they may have **searcher** *noun* someone who is trying to find something or someone

search *noun*
1 a very careful look for someone or something **2** when you look for information in a computer database or on the Internet • Let's do a search for 'Roald Dahl'.

search engine *noun*
a computer program that helps you find information on the Internet

searchlight *noun*
a light with a strong beam that can be turned in any direction

seashore *noun*
the seashore is the land close to the sea

seasick *adjective*
someone is seasick when they are sick because of

the movement of a ship
seasickness *noun* feeling sick

seaside *noun*
the seaside is a place by the sea where people go on holiday

season *noun*
1 one of the four main parts of the year: spring, summer, autumn, and winter **2** the time of year when a sport or other activity happens • When does the football season start?

season *verb*
to season food is to put salt, pepper, or other strong-tasting things on it to flavour it

seasonal *adjective*
happening only at certain times of the year • Fruit-picking is seasonal work.

seasoning *noun*
seasoning is something strong-tasting like salt and pepper, used to season food

season ticket *noun*
a ticket that you can use as often as you like for a certain period

seat *noun*
1 something used for sitting on **2** a place in parliament or on a council or a board of a business

seat *verb*
a place seats a certain number of people when it has that many seats for them • The stadium seats 50,000.

seat belt *noun*
a strap to hold a person securely in the seat of a vehicle or aircraft

seaweed *noun*
seaweed is plants that grow in the sea

secateurs *plural noun*
(say sek-a-terz)
a tool used for pruning plants

secluded *adjective*
a secluded place is away from large numbers of people; quiet and hidden • They found a secluded beach for their picnic.

seclusion *noun* seclusion is being private or hidden

second *adjective, noun*
the next after the first **to have second thoughts** is to wonder whether your decision was really right

second *noun*
1 a very short period of time, one-sixtieth of a minute **2** a person or thing that is second **3** someone who helps a fighter in a boxing match or duel

second *verb*
to second a proposal or motion is to support it formally

secondary *adjective*
coming second; not original or essential • *This is of secondary importance.*

secondary school *noun*
a school for children more than about 11 years old

second-hand *adjective, adverb*
bought or used after someone else has used it • *He could only afford a second-hand car.*

secondly *adverb*
as the second thing • *Secondly, I'd like to thank my parents.*

secrecy *noun*
secrecy is being secret

secret *adjective*
1 that must not be told or shown to other people **2** that is not known by many people; hidden • *The house had a secret passage.* **secretly** *adverb* without telling other people

secret *noun*
something that is secret **to do something in secret** is to do it secretly

secretary *noun* (**secretaries**) (*say* **sek**-re-tri)
someone whose job is to type letters, keep files, answer the telephone, and make business arrangements for a person or organization

secrete *verb* (*say* si-**kreet**)
to secrete a substance in the body is to release it • *Saliva is secreted in the mouth.* **secretion** *noun* a substance that is secreted

secretive *adjective* (*say* **seek**-rit-iv)
liking or trying to keep things secret **secretively** *adverb* **secretiveness** *noun*

sect *noun*
a group of people who have special or unusual religious opinions or beliefs

section *noun*
a part of something • *Our school library has a large history section.* • *The tail section of the plane broke off.*

sector *noun*
a part of an area or activity

secure *adjective*
1 firm and safe • *Is that ladder secure?* **2** made safe or protected from attack • *Check that all the doors and windows are secure.* **securely** *adverb*

secure *verb*
to secure something is to make it safe or firmly fixed

security *noun*
1 security is being secure or safe **2** security is also measures taken to prevent theft, spying, or terrorism

sedate *adjective* (*say* si-**dayt**)
calm and dignified **sedately** *adverb*

sedative *noun* (*say* **sed**-a-tiv)
a medicine that makes a person calm or helps them sleep

sediment *noun*
sediment is solid matter that settles at the bottom of a liquid

see *verb* (**seeing, saw, seen**)
1 to see something or someone is to use your eyes to notice them or be aware of them **2** to see someone is to meet or visit them • *See me after class.* **3** to see something is to understand it • *I see what you mean.* **4** to see someone as something is to imagine them being it • *Can you see yourself as a teacher?* **5** to see that something happens is to make sure of it • *See that the windows are shut.* **6** to see someone somewhere is to escort or lead them • *I'll see you to the door.* **to see through something** or **someone** is not to be deceived by them **to see to something** is to deal with it • *Can you see to the lunch?*

seed *noun*
a tiny part of a plant that can grow in the ground to make a new plant

seedling *noun*
a very young plant

seek *verb* (**seeking, sought**)
1 to seek a person or thing is to try to find them **2** to seek something is to try to achieve it • *She is seeking fame.*

seem *verb*
to seem to be something or to have some quality is to appear that way or give that impression • *They seem happy in their new house.*

seep *verb*
a liquid or gas seeps when it flows slowly through or into or out of something • *Water was seeping into the cellar.* **seepage** *noun* when something is seeping

see-saw *noun*
a plank balanced in the middle so that people can sit at each end and make it go up and down

seethe *verb*
1 a liquid seethes when it boils or bubbles **2** you are seething when you are very angry or excited

segment *noun*
a part that is cut off or can be separated from the rest of something • *He ate a few segments of an orange*

segments

segregate *verb* (*say* **seg**-ri-gayt)
to segregate people of different races or religions is to keep them apart and make them live separately **segregation** *noun* when people of different races or religions are kept apart and made to live separately

seize *verb* (*say* seez)
1 to seize someone or something is to take hold of them suddenly or firmly **2** to seize a place is to capture it using force **to seize up** is to become jammed or stuck

seizure *noun*
a seizure is a sudden attack of an illness

seldom *adverb*
not often • *I seldom cry.*

select *verb*
to select a person or thing is to choose them carefully

select *adjective*
small and carefully chosen • *They have a select group of friends.*

self *noun* (**selves**)
the type of person you are; your individual nature • *You'll soon be feeling your old self again.*

self-centred *adjective*
selfish; thinking about yourself too much

self-confident *adjective*
confident in what you can do **self-confidence** *noun* being self confident

self-conscious *adjective*
embarrassed or shy because you know people are watching you

self-control *noun*
self-control is the ability to control your own behaviour or feelings **self-controlled** *adjective* able to control your own behaviour or feelings

self-defence *noun*
1 you act in self-defence when you do something defending yourself against attack **2** self-defence is also skill in defending yourself if someone attacks you

d e f g h i j k l m n o p q r s t u v w x y z

215

self-employed *adjective*
someone who is self-employed works independently and not for an employer

selfish *adjective*
having or doing what you want without thinking of other people **selfishly** *adverb* **selfishness** *noun*

selfless *adjective*
thinking of other people rather than yourself; not selfish

self-service *adjective*
a self-service shop or restaurant is one where customers serve themselves with goods and pay a cashier for what they have taken

sell *verb* (**selling, sold**)
to sell goods or services is to offer them in exchange for money **to sell out** is to sell all your stock of something

semaphore *noun*
semaphore is a system of signalling by holding flags out with your arms in positions to indicate letters of the alphabet

semibreve *noun*
(*say* **sem**-i-breev)
the longest musical note normally used, written ○

semicircle *noun* ▶
half a circle
semicircular *adjective*
in the form of a semicircle

semaphore

semicolon *noun*
a punctuation mark (;), marking a more definite break in a sentence than a comma does

semi-detached *adjective*
a semi-detached house is one that is joined to another house on one side

semi-final *noun*
a match played to decide who will take part in the final **semi-finalist** *noun* a contestant in a semi-final

semitone *noun*
half a tone in music

senate *noun* (*say* **sen**-at)
1 the governing council in ancient Rome **2** the higher-ranking section of the parliament in France, the USA, and some other countries **senator** *noun* a member of a senate

send *verb* (**sending, sent**)
1 to send something somewhere is to arrange for it to be taken there **2** to send someone somewhere is to tell them to go there **to send for something** or **someone** is to ask for them to come to you

senior *adjective*
1 older than someone else **2** higher in rank • *He is a senior officer in the navy.* **seniority** *noun* a person's seniority is how old or high in rank they are

senior *noun*
someone is your senior when they are older or higher in rank than you are

senior citizen *noun*
an elderly person, especially a pensioner

sensation *noun*
1 a feeling • *There's an itchy sensation in my leg.* **2** a very exciting event or the excitement caused by it • *The news caused a great sensation.*

sensational *adjective*
causing great excitement or shock

sense *noun*
1 the ability to see, hear, smell, touch, or taste things **2** the ability to feel or appreciate something • *She has a good sense of humour.* **3** the power to think or make good judgements • *He hasn't got the sense to come in out of the rain.* **4** meaning • *The word 'set' has many senses.* **to make sense** is to have a meaning you can understand

sense *verb*
1 to sense something is to feel it or be aware of it • *I sensed that she did not like me.* **2** to sense something is also to detect it • *This device senses radioactivity.*

senseless *adjective*
1 stupid; not sensible • *I am sick of all this senseless fighting.* **2** unconscious • *He fell senseless to the ground.*

sensible *adjective*
wise; having or showing good sense **sensibly** *adverb*

sensitive *adjective*
1 affected by the sun or chemicals or something else physical • *I have sensitive skin.* **2** easily offended or upset • *He's quite sensitive about being criticized.* **3** aware of other people's feelings **sensitively** *adverb* in a way that shows you are aware of other people's feelings

sensitivity *noun* being sensitive; something you are sensitive about

sensor *noun*
a device or instrument for detecting something physical such as heat or light

sentence *noun*
1 a group of words that express a complete thought and form a statement or question or command **2** the punishment given to a convicted person in a lawcourt

sentence *verb*
to sentence someone is to give them a sentence in a lawcourt • *They were sentenced to two years in prison.*

sentiment *noun*
1 a sentiment is a feeling or opinion **2** sentiment is a show of feeling or emotion

sentimental *adjective*
showing or making you feel emotion, especially too much sad emotion • *The film is a sentimental love story.*
sentimentality *noun*
sentimentality is being too sentimental
sentimentally *adverb*

sentry *noun* (**sentries**)
a soldier guarding something

separate *adjective* (*say* **sep**-er-at)
1 not joined to anything; on its own **2** not together; not with other people • *They lead separate lives.*
separately *adverb* not together • *They arrived together but left separately.*

separate *verb* (*say* **sep**-er-ayt)
1 to separate things or people is to take them away from others **2** to separate is to become separate or move away from each other **3** two people separate when they stop living together as a couple **separation** *noun* when people are apart from each other

September *noun*
the ninth month of the year

septic *adjective*
a wound goes septic when it becomes infected with harmful bacteria

sequel *noun* (*say* **see**-kwel)
a book or film that continues the story of an earlier one

sequence *noun* (*say* **see**-kwenss)
a series of things coming in a particular order

sequin *noun*
(*say* **see**-kwin)
sequins are tiny bright discs sewn on clothes to decorate them

serene *adjective*
calm and peaceful **serenely** *adverb* **serenity** *noun* serenity is being calm and peaceful

sergeant *noun* (*say* **sar**-jent)
a soldier or police officer who is in charge of others

serial *noun*
a story that is presented in separate parts over a period, for example week by week

series *noun* (**series**)
1 a number of things following each other or connected with each other **2** a set of television or radio programmes with the same title

serious *adjective*
1 not funny; important • *We need a serious talk.* **2** thoughtful or solemn • *His face was serious.* **3** very bad • *They've had a serious accident.* **seriously** *adverb* **seriousness** *noun*

sermon *noun*
a talk given by a preacher during a religious service

serpent *noun*
a snake

servant *noun*
a person whose job is to work in someone else's house

serve *verb*
1 to serve people in a shop is to help them find the things they want to buy **2** to serve food or drink is to give it to people at a meal **3** to serve a person or organization is to work for them **4** to serve is to be suitable for a purpose • *This tree stump will serve as a table.* **5** (*in tennis*) to serve is to start play by hitting the ball to your opponent **it serves you right** you deserve it **server** *noun* the player who starts play by serving in tennis

serve *noun*
the action of serving in tennis

service *noun*
1 service is working for someone or something • *He retired after forty years' service.* **2** a service is something that helps people or supplies what they want • *There is a good bus service into town.* **3** a service is also a religious ceremony in a church **4** a service, or dinner service, is a set of plates and crockery **5** a vehicle or machine has a service when someone spends time repairing and maintaining it **6** (*in tennis*) a service is a serve **the services** the armed forces of a country

service *verb*
to service a vehicle or machine is to check it and repair it if necessary

service station *noun*
a place beside the road where you can buy petrol

serviette *noun*
a cloth or paper napkin that you can wipe your hands and mouth on

session *noun*
1 a time spent doing a particular thing • *They were in the middle of a recording session.* **2** a meeting or series of meetings • *The Queen will open the next session of Parliament.*

set *verb* (**setting, set**)
This word has many meanings, depending on the words that go with it: **1** to set something somewhere is to put or place it there • *Set the vase on the table.* **2** to set a device is to make it ready to work • *Have you set the alarm?* **3** to set is to become solid or hard • *The jelly has set now.* **4** the sun sets when it goes down towards the horizon at the end of the day **5** to set someone doing something is to start them doing it • *The news set me thinking.* **6** to set someone a task or problem is to give it to them to do or solve • *I'd better set you some more work.* **to set about something** is to start doing it **to set off** or **set out** is to begin a journey **to set something out** is to display it or make it known • *She set out her reasons for leaving.* **to set something up** is to place it in position or get it started • *We want to set up a playgroup.*

set *noun*
1 a group of people or things that belong together **2** a radio or television receiver **3** a series of games in a tennis match **4** the scenery or furniture on a stage or in a film

setback *noun*
something that causes a difficulty for a while

set square *noun*
a device in the shape of a right-angled triangle, used for drawing parallel lines and to draw angles

settee *noun*
a sofa

setting *noun*
1 the setting of a story is the place and time in which it happens **2** the land and buildings around something • *The house stood in a rural setting.*

settle *verb*
1 to settle a problem, difficulty, or argument is to solve it or decide about it **2** to settle, or settle down, is to become relaxed or make yourself comfortable • *He settled down in the armchair.* **3** to settle somewhere is to go and live there • *The family settled in Canada.* **4** something light such as dust or snow settles when it comes to rest on something • *The dust was settling on the books.* • *A bird flew down and settled on the fence.* **5** to settle a bill or debt is to pay it

settlement *noun*
1 a settlement is a group of people or houses in a new area **2** a settlement is also an agreement to end an argument

settler *noun*
one of the first people to settle in a new area

set-up *noun*
(*informal*) the way that something is organized or arranged

seven *noun*
the number 7

seventeen *noun*
the number 17 **seventeenth** *adjective, noun* 17th

seventh *adjective, noun*
the next after the sixth **seventhly** *adverb* in the seventh place; as the seventh one

seventy *noun* (**seventies**)
the number 70 **seventieth** *adjective, noun* 70th

sever *verb*
to sever something is to cut or break it off

several *adjective*
more than two but not many

severe *adjective*
1 strict or harsh; not gentle or kind **2** very bad or serious • *a severe cold* • *We're in for some severe weather.* **severely** *adverb* harshly or seriously **severity** *noun* being severe, or how severe something is

sew *verb* (**sewing, sewn** or **sewed**) (*say* so)
1 to sew cloth or other soft material is to use a needle and cotton to join it or for it into clothing **2** to sew is to work with a needle and thread or with a sewing machine

sewage *noun* (*say* **soo**-ij)
sewage is waste matter carried away in drains

sewer *noun* (*say* **soo**-er)
an underground drain that carries away sewage

sex *noun*
1 a sex is each of the two groups, male or female, that people and animals belong to **2** sex is the physical act by which people and animals produce offspring
sexual *adjective* to do with sex or the sexes

sexism *noun*
sexism is the unfair or offensive treatment of people of a particular sex, especially women
sexist *adjective* offensive to people of a particular sex, especially women **sexist** *noun* someone who treats people of a particular sex, especially women, in an unfair or offensive way

shabby *adjective* (**shabbier, shabbiest**)
1 very old and worn • *She was wearing a shabby grey coat.* **2** mean or unfair • *What a shabby trick.* **shabbily** *adverb* **shabbiness** *noun*

shack *noun*
a roughly-built hut

shade *noun*
1 shade is an area sheltered from bright sunlight • *We sat down in the shade.* **2** a shade is a colour, or how light or dark a colour is **3** a shade is also a device that reduces or shuts out bright light

shade *verb*
1 to shade something or someone is to shelter them from bright light **2** to shade a drawing is to make parts of it darker than the rest
shading *noun* the parts of a drawing that you make darker than the rest

shadow *noun*
1 a shadow is a dark shape that falls on a surface when something is between it and the light **2** shadow is an area that is dark because the light is blocked • *His face was in shadow.* **shadowy** *adjective* dark or hard to see

shadow *verb*
to shadow someone is to follow them secretly

shady *adjective* (**shadier, shadiest**)
1 giving shade • *We sat under a shady tree.* **2** situated in the shade • *Find a shady spot.* **3** dishonest or suspect • *He's always making shady deals.*

shaft *noun*
1 a long thin rod or straight part of something **2** a deep narrow hole in a mine or building • *They found an old mine shaft.* • *a lift shaft* **3** a beam of light

shaggy *adjective* (**shaggier, shaggiest**)
having long untidy hair

shake *verb* (**shaking, shook, shaken**)
1 to shake something is to move it quickly up and down or from side to side • *Have you shaken the bottle?* **2** to shake is to move in this way **3** to shake someone is to shock or upset them • *The news shook her.* **4** to shake is to tremble • *His voice was shaking.* **to shake hands** is to clasp someone's right hand as a greeting or as a sign that you agree

shake *noun*
a quick movement up and down or from side to side • *Give the bottle a shake.*

shaky *adjective* (**shakier, shakiest**)
shaking or likely to fall down
shakily *adverb*

shall *verb* (past tense **should**)
used with *I* and *we* to refer to the future • *We shall arrive tomorrow.* • *We told them we should arrive the next day.*

shallow *adjective*
not deep • *The stream is quite shallow here.* • *We were playing in the shallow end of the pool.*

sham *noun*
a person or thing that is not genuine or what they claim to be

shambles *noun*
a scene of confusion and chaos; a mess • *The rehearsal was a complete shambles.*

shame *noun*
1 shame is a feeling of great sorrow or guilt because you have done something wrong **2** you say something is a shame when it is something that you regret or are sorry about • *What a shame you won't be able to come.*

shame *verb*
to shame someone is to make them feel ashamed

shameful *adjective* causing shame; disgraceful
shamefully *adverb*

shameless *adjective*
feeling or showing no shame
shamelessly *adverb*

shampoo *noun*
shampoo is liquid soap for washing things, especially your hair or a carpet

shampoo *verb*
to shampoo something is to wash it with shampoo

WORD ORIGIN

The word **shampoo** comes from a Hindi word *campo* meaning 'press!' (as an instruction).

shamrock *noun*
shamrock is a small plant rather like clover, with leaves divided in three

shandy *noun*
shandy is a mixture of beer with lemonade or another soft drink

shanty[1] *noun* (**shanties**)
a sailor's traditional song

shanty[2] *noun* (**shanties**)
a roughly-built hut

shape *noun*
1 the outline of something or the way it looks **2** something that has a definite or regular form, such as a square, circle, or triangle **3** the condition that something is in • *The garden isn't in very good shape.* **to take shape** is to start to develop properly

shape *verb*
to shape something is to give it a shape **to shape up** is to develop well

shapeless *adjective*
having no definite shape

share *noun*
1 one of the parts into which something is divided between several people or things **2** part of a company's money, lent by someone who is then given part of the profits in return

share *verb*
1 to share something, or share it out, is to divide it between several people or things **2** to share something is to use it when someone else is also using it • *She shared a room with me.*

shark *noun*
a large sea fish with sharp teeth

shark

sharp *adjective*
1 a sharp object has an edge or point that can cut or make holes • *This is a sharp knife.* **2** quick to learn or notice things • *She has sharp eyes.* • *It was sharp of you to spot that mistake.* **3** sudden or severe • *We came to a sharp bend in the road.* • *I felt a sharp pain in my side.* **4** slightly sour • *The apples taste sharp.* **5** above the proper musical pitch **sharply** *adverb* **sharpness** *noun*

sharp *adverb*
1 with a sudden change of direction • *Now turn sharp right.* **2** punctually; exactly • *Be there at six o'clock sharp.*

sharp *noun*
the note that is a semitone above a particular musical note; the sign that indicates this

sharpen *verb*
to sharpen something is to make it sharp or pointed
sharpener *noun* a device for sharpening a pencil

shatter *verb*
1 to shatter is to break suddenly into lots of tiny pieces **2** to shatter something is to break it in this way **3** someone is shattered when they are very upset by something or very tired • *We were shattered by the news.*

shave *verb*
1 someone shaves when they scrape hair from their skin with a razor **2** to shave something is to cut or scrape a thin slice off it
shaver *noun* an electric razor

shave *noun*
the act of shaving the face • *Dad was having a shave.*
a close shave (*informal*) a narrow escape

shavings *plural noun*
thin strips that have been shaved off a piece of wood or metal

shawl *noun*
a large piece of material for covering the shoulders or wrapping a baby

she *pronoun*
a female person or animal: used as the subject of a verb

sheaf *noun* (**sheaves**)
1 a bundle of papers **2** a bundle of corn stalks tied together after reaping

shear *verb* (**shearing, sheared, shorn** or **sheared**)
to shear a sheep is to cut the wool from it
shearer *noun*
someone who shears sheep

shears *plural noun*
a tool like a very large pair of scissors for trimming grass and bushes or for shearing sheep

sheath *noun*
a cover for the blade of a sword or dagger

sheathe *verb*
to sheathe a sword is to put it into its sheath

shed¹ *noun*
a simply-made building used for storing things or sheltering animals, or as a workshop

shed² *verb* (**shedding, shed**)
to shed something is to let it fall or flow • *The trees are shedding their leaves.* • *He was so badly hurt he was shedding blood.*

sheen *noun*
a soft shine on a surface

sheep *noun*
a grass-eating animal kept by farmers for its wool and meat

sheepdog *noun*
a dog trained to guard and control sheep

sheepish *adjective*
someone looks sheepish when they look shy or embarrassed
sheepishly *adverb*

sheer *adjective*
1 complete or total • *There was a look of sheer misery on his face.* **2** extremely steep; vertical • *To the right of the road there was a sheer drop.* **3** sheer material is so thin that you can see through it

sheet *noun*
1 a large piece of light material put on a bed **2** a whole flat piece of paper, glass, or metal • *You will need two sheets of newspaper.* **3** a wide area of water, snow, ice, or flame

sheikh *noun* (say shayk)
the leader of an Arab tribe or village

shelf *noun* (**shelves**)
1 a flat piece of hard material fitted to a wall or in a piece of furniture so that you can put things on it **2** a flat level surface that sticks out from a cliff or under the sea

shell *noun*
1 the hard outer covering round a nut or egg, or round an animal such as a snail or tortoise **2** a metal case filled with explosive, fired from a large gun **3** the walls or framework of a building or ship

shell *verb*
1 to shell something is to take it out of its shell **2** to shell a building, ship, town, etc., is to fire explosive shells at it

shellfish *noun* (**shellfish**)
a sea animal that has a shell

shells

shelter *noun*
1 a shelter is a place that protects people from danger or from the weather **2** shelter is being protected from danger or from the weather • *We found shelter from the rain.*

shelter *verb*
1 to shelter somewhere is to stay there because you are protected from danger or from the weather • *We sheltered under the trees.* **2** to shelter something or someone is to protect or cover them • *The hill shelters the house from the wind.*

shelve *verb*
1 to shelve something is to put it on a shelf or shelves **2** to shelve an idea or piece of work is to reject or postpone it

shepherd *noun*
someone whose job is to look after sheep

sherbet *noun*
a fizzy sweet powder or drink

sheriff *noun*
1 in the USA, the chief law officer in a county **2** the chief judge of a Scottish county

sherry *noun*
a kind of strong wine

shield *noun*
1 a large piece of metal or wood a person carries to protect their body in fighting **2** a design or trophy in the shape of a shield **3** a protection from harm • *The spacecraft's heat shield protects it as it enters the planet's atmosphere.*

shield *verb*
to shield someone or something is to protect them • *She shielded her eyes from the sun.*

shift *noun*
1 a change of position or condition **2** a group of workers who start work as another group finishes; the time when they work • *He's on the night shift this month.*

a
b
c
d
e
f
g
i
j
k
l
m
n
o
p
q
r
s
t
u
v
w
x
y
z

219

shift *verb*
1 to shift something is to move it **2** to shift is to change position

shilling *noun*
an old British coin that was worth a twentieth of a pound (now 5 pence)

shimmer *verb*
to shimmer is to shine with a quivering light • *The sea shimmered in the sunlight.*

shin *noun*
the front of your leg between your knee and your ankle

shine *verb* (**shining**, **shone** or, in 'polish' sense, **shined**)
1 to shine is to give out or reflect bright light **2** to shine a torch or light somewhere is to point the light in that direction **3** to shine something is to polish it • *Have you shined your shoes?* **4** to shine is to do well or be excellent • *He does not shine in maths.*

shine *noun*
1 shine is brightness **2** a shine is an act of polishing • *Give your shoes a good shine.*

shingle *noun*
shingle is pebbles on a beach

shiny *adjective* (**shinier**, **shiniest**)
bright or glossy

ship *noun*
a large boat, especially one that goes to sea

ship *verb* (**shipping**, **shipped**)
to ship something is to send it on a ship

shipwreck *noun*
1 when a ship is wrecked in a storm or accident at sea **2** the remains of a wrecked ship
shipwrecked *adjective* left somewhere after your ship has been wrecked at sea

shipyard *noun*
a place where ships are built and repaired

shirk *verb*
you shirk a task or duty when you avoid doing it

shirt *noun*
a piece of clothing you wear on the top half of the body, with a collar and sleeves

shiver *verb*
you shiver when you tremble with cold or fear **shivery** *adjective* unable to stop yourself shivering

shiver *noun*
an act of shivering • *I felt a shiver down my spine.*

shoal *noun*
a large number of fish swimming together

shock[1] *noun*
1 a shock is a sudden unpleasant surprise **2** a shock is also a violent knock or jolt **3** shock is weakness caused by severe pain or injury **4** a shock, or electric shock, is a painful effect caused by a strong electric current passing through your body

shock[1] *verb*
1 to shock someone is to give them a shock **2** to shock someone is also to make them feel disgusted or upset

shock[2] *noun*
a shock of hair is a bushy mass of it

shocking *adjective*
1 horrifying or disgusting **2** very bad • *The weather's been shocking today.*

shoddy *adjective* (**shoddier**, **shoddiest**)
of poor quality; badly made • *This is shoddy work.*

shoe *noun*
1 a strong covering you wear on your foot **2** a horseshoe

shipwreck

shoelace *noun*
a cord for fastening a shoe

shoot *verb*
1 to shoot a gun or other weapon is to fire it **2** to shoot a person or animal is to fire a gun at them **3** to shoot somewhere is to move very fast • *The car shot past.* **4** (*in football*) to shoot is to kick or hit a ball at a goal **5** to shoot a film or scene is to film or photograph it • *The film was shot in Africa.*

shoot *noun*
a young branch or new growth of a plant

shooting star *noun*
a meteor

shop *noun*
a building where people buy things

shop *verb* (**shopping**, **shopped**)
to shop is to go and buy things at shops **shopper** *noun* someone who goes shopping

shopkeeper *noun*
someone who owns or looks after a shop

shoplifter *noun*
someone who steals from shops **shoplifting** *noun* stealing things from shops

shopping *noun*
1 shopping is buying things at shops • *I like shopping.* **2** shopping is also things that you have bought in shops • *Let me help you carry your shopping.*

shore *noun*
1 the seashore **2** the land along the edge of a lake

short *adjective*
1 not long; not lasting long • *I went for a short walk.* **2** not tall • *He is a short man.* **3** not sufficient; scarce • *Water is short.* **4** bad-tempered • *He was rather short with me.* **5** short pastry is rich and crumbly, and contains a lot of fat **for short** as a shorter form of something • *Joanna is called Jo for short.* **short for something** a shorter form of something • *Jo is short for Joanna.* **to be short of something** is to not have enough of it • *We seem to be short of chairs.*
shortness *noun*

short *adverb*
1 before reaching the point aimed at • *My ball landed just short of the hole.* **2** suddenly • *The horse stopped short.*

shortage *noun*
there is a shortage when there is not enough of something

shortbread *noun*
shortbread is a rich sweet biscuit made with butter

shortcake *noun*
1 shortbread **2** a light cake usually served with fruit

shortcoming *noun*
a fault or weakness • *He has many shortcomings.*

short cut *noun*
a route or method that is quicker than the usual one

shorten *verb*
1 to shorten something is to make it shorter **2** to shorten is to become shorter

shorthand *noun*
shorthand is a set of special signs for writing words down as quickly as people say them

shortly *adverb*
soon • *I'll be there shortly.*

shorts *plural noun*
trousers with legs that stop at or above the knee

short-sighted *adjective*
1 unable to see things clearly when they are further away **2** not thinking enough about what may happen in the future

shot¹ *noun*
1 a shot is the firing of a gun or other weapon **2** shot is lead pellets fired from small guns **3** a good or bad shot is a person judged by their skill in shooting • *She is a great shot.* **4** a shot is a stroke in a game with a ball, such as tennis or snooker **5** a shot is also an injection **6** in photography, a shot is a photograph or filmed sequence **7** a shot is a heavy metal ball thrown as a sport **8** a shot at something is an attempt to do it • *Have a shot at this puzzle.*

shot² past tense and past participle of **shoot** *verb*

shotgun *noun*
a gun that fires small lead pellets

should *verb*
used to express **1** what someone ought to do • *You should have told me.* **2** what someone expects • *They should be here soon.* **3** what might happen • *If you should happen to see him, tell him to come.*

shoulder *noun*
the part of your body between your neck and your arm

shoulder blade *noun*
each of the two large flat bones at the top of your back

shout *verb*
to shout is to speak or call very loudly

shout *noun*
a loud cry or call

shove *verb* (*say* shuv)
to shove something is to push it hard

shovel *noun* (*say* **shuv**-el)
a tool like a spade with the sides turned up, for lifting and moving coal, earth, sand, snow, and other things

shovel *verb* (**shovelling, shovelled**)
to shovel (for example) earth or snow is to move it or clear it with a shovel

show *verb* (**showing, showed, shown**)
1 to show something is to let people see it • *She showed me her new bike.* **2** to show something to someone is to explain it to them • *Can you show me how to do it?* **3** to show someone somewhere is to guide or lead them there • *I'll show you to your seat.* **4** to show is to be visible • *That stain won't show.* **to show off** is to try to impress people **to show something off** is to be proud of letting people see it

show *noun*
1 an entertainment • *She loves TV game shows.* **2** a display or exhibition • *Have you been to the flower show?*

show business *noun*
show business is the entertainment business; the theatre, films, radio, and television

shower *noun*
1 a brief fall of light rain • *It's only a shower.* **2** a lot of small things coming or falling like rain • *They were met by a shower of stones.* **3** a device for spraying water to wash your body; a wash in this

shower *verb*
1 to shower is to fall like rain **2** to shower someone with things is to give a lot of them • *He showered her with presents.* **3** to shower is to wash under a shower

showery *adjective*
raining occasionally

showjumping *noun*
showjumping is a competition in which riders make their horses jump over fences and other obstacles

showjumper *noun* someone who takes part in showjumping

show-off *noun*
someone who is trying to impress other people

showy *adjective* (**showier, showiest**)

likely to attract attention; bright or highly decorated

showily *adverb*

showiness *noun*

shrapnel *noun*
shrapnel is pieces of metal scattered from an exploding shell

shred *noun*
1 a tiny strip or piece torn or cut off something • *His cloak had been ripped to shreds.* **2** a very small amount of something *There's not a shred of evidence for what you say.*

shred *verb* (**shredding, shredded**)
to shred something is to tear or cut it into tiny strips or pieces

shrew *noun*
a small animal rather like a mouse

shrewd *adjective*
having common sense and showing good judgement

shrewdly *adverb*

shrewdness *noun*

shriek *noun*
a shrill cry or scream

shriek *verb*
to shriek is to give a shrill cry or scream

shrill *adjective*
a shrill sound is very high and loud • *There was a shrill blast of the whistle.* **shrilly** *adverb*

shrillness *noun*

shrimp *noun*
a small shellfish

shrine *noun*
an altar or chapel or other sacred place

shrink *verb* (**shrinking, shrank, shrunk**)
1 to shrink is to become smaller • *My dress has shrunk.* **2** to shrink something is to make it smaller, usually by washing it • *Their jeans have been shrunk.* **3** to shrink from something is to avoid it because you are afraid or embarrassed • *He shrank from meeting strangers.*

shrivel *verb* (**shrivelling, shrivelled**)
to shrivel is to become wrinkled and dry

shroud *noun*
a sheet in which a dead body is wrapped

shroud *verb*
to shroud something is to cover or conceal it • *The mountain was shrouded in mist.*

shrub *noun*
a bush or small tree

shrubbery *noun* (**shrubberies**)
an area where shrubs are grown

a
b
c
d
e
f
g
h
i
j
k
l
m
n
o
p
q
r
s
t
u
v
w
x
y
z

shrug verb (**shrugging, shrugged**)
you shrug when you raise your shoulders slightly as a sign that you don't care or don't know
shrug noun
the act of shrugging
shrunken adjective smaller than it used to be because it has shrunk
shudder verb
you shudder when you shake because you are cold or afraid
shudder noun
the act of shuddering
shuffle verb
1 to shuffle is to drag your feet along the ground as you walk
2 to shuffle playing cards is to mix them by sliding them over each other several times
shuffle noun
the act of shuffling • *Give the cards a quick shuffle.*
shunt verb
to shunt a railway train or wagons is to move them from one track to another
shut verb (**shutting, shut**)
1 to shut a door or window, or a lid or cover, is to move it so that it blocks up an opening
2 to shut is to become closed • *The door shut suddenly.* **to shut down** is to stop work or business **to shut up** (*informal*) is to stop talking
shut adjective
closed • *Keep your eyes shut.*
shutter noun
1 a panel or screen that can be closed over a window
2 the device in a camera that opens and closes to let light fall on the film
shuttle noun
1 a train or bus or aircraft that makes frequent short journeys between two places **2** a space shuttle **3** the part of a loom that carries the thread from side to side
shuttlecock noun
a small rounded piece of cork or plastic with a ring of feathers fixed to it, that you use in the game of badminton
shy adjective
timid and afraid to meet or talk to other people
shyly adverb
shyness noun
sibling noun
your siblings are your brothers and sisters

shuttlecock

sick adjective
1 ill or unwell • *He looks after sick animals.* **2** you feel sick when you feel that you are going to vomit; you are sick when you vomit **to be sick of something** or **someone** is to be tired of them or fed up with them
sicken verb
1 to sicken someone is to disgust them **2** to sicken is to start feeling ill
sickly adjective (**sicklier, sickliest**)
1 often ill; unhealthy • *a sickly child* **2** making people feel sick • *The drink had a sickly taste.*
sickness noun
an illness or disease
side noun
1 a flat surface, especially one that joins the top and bottom of something **2** a line that forms the edge of a shape • *A triangle has three sides.* **3** the outer part of something that is not the front or the back • *The instructions are on the side of the box.* **4** a position or space to the left or right of something • *There's a window on either side of the door.* **5** your sides are the parts of your body from your armpits to your hips • *I've got a pain down my right side.* **6** a group of people playing, arguing, or fighting against another group • *They are on our side.*
side verb
to side with someone is to support them in a quarrel or argument
sideboard noun
a long heavy piece of furniture with drawers and cupboards and a flat top
sideshow noun
a small entertainment forming part of a large show, especially at a fair
sideways adverb, adjective
1 to or from the side • *Crabs walk sideways.* **2** with one side facing forward • *We sat sideways in the bus.*
siding noun
a short railway line leading off the main line
siege noun (*say* seej)
when an army surrounds a place until the people inside surrender
sieve noun (*say* siv)
a device made of mesh or perforated metal or plastic, used to separate harder or larger parts from liquid or powder

sift verb
1 to sift a fine or powdery substance is to pass it through a sieve **2** to sift facts or information is to examine or select them
sigh noun
a sound you make by breathing out heavily when you are sad, tired, or relieved
sigh verb
to sigh is to make a sigh
sight noun
1 sight is the ability to see • *She has very good sight.* **2** a sight is something that you see • *That sunset is a sight I'll never forget.* **3** the sights of a place are the interesting places worth seeing there • *Visit the sights of Paris.* **4** a sight on a gun is a device that helps you to aim it **to be in sight** is to be able to be seen **to be out of sight** is to be no longer able to be seen
sight verb
to sight something is to see it or observe it
sightseeing noun
sightseeing is going round looking at interesting places
sightseer noun someone who goes sightseeing
sign noun
1 a mark or symbol that stands for something • *a minus sign* **2** a board or notice that tells or shows people something **3** something that shows that a thing exists • *There are signs of rust.* **4** an action or signal giving information or a command • *She made a sign to them to be quiet.*
sign verb
1 you sign your name when you write your signature on something **2** to sign is to make a sign or signal • *He signed to them to follow him.* **3** to sign someone is to give them a contract for a job, especially in a professional sport • *They have signed three new players.*
signal noun
1 a device or gesture or sound or light that gives information or a message **2** a series of radio waves sent out or received
signal verb (**signalling, signalled**)
to signal to someone is to give them a signal
signature noun
your name written by yourself
significant adjective
something is significant when it has a meaning or importance **significance** noun

the significance of something is its meaning or importance **significantly** *adverb* in a way that is important or has a meaning

signify *verb* (**signifying, signified**)
to signify something is to mean it or indicate it

signing or **sign language** *noun*
signing is a way of communicating by using movements of your hands instead of sounds, used by deaf people

signpost *noun*
sign language
a sign at a road junction showing the names and distances of the places that each road leads to

Sikh *noun* (*say* seek)
someone who believes in **Sikhism**, a religion of India having one God and some Hindu and Islamic beliefs

silence *noun*
silence is when no sound can be heard

silence *verb*
to silence someone or something is to make them silent

silencer *noun*
a device designed to reduce the sound made by an engine or a gun

silent *adjective*
without any sound; not speaking **silently** *adverb*

silhouette *noun* (*say* sil-oo-**et**)
a dark outline of something seen against a light background

silicon *noun* (Si)
silicon is a substance found in many rocks and used in making microchips

silk *noun*
1 silk is a fine soft thread produced by silkworms for making their cocoons **2** silk is also smooth shiny cloth made from this thread **silken** *adjective* made of silk **silky** *adjective* soft, smooth, and shiny like silk

silkworm *noun*
a kind of caterpillar that covers itself with a cocoon of fine threads when it is ready to turn into a moth

silk moth and cocoon

sill *noun*
a strip of stone or wood or metal underneath a window or door

silly *adjective* (**sillier, silliest**)
foolish or unwise **silliness** *noun*

silver *noun* (Ag)
1 silver is a shiny white precious metal **2** silver is also coins made of this metal or a metal that looks like it **3** silver is also a greyish-white colour **silvery** *adjective* like silver • *the moon's silvery light*

similar *adjective* one thing is similar to another when it is like it in some ways but not exactly the same **similarity** *noun* the similarity between two things is the fact that they are similar **similarly** *adverb* in a similar way

simile *noun* (*say* **sim**-i-li)
a kind of expression in which you describe something by comparing it with something else, such as *bold as brass* or *as brave as a lion*

simmer *verb*
food simmers when it boils very gently over a low heat
to simmer down is to become calm after being anxious or angry

simple *adjective*
1 easy • *That's a simple question to answer.* **2** not complicated • *It was a simple plan, but it worked.* **3** plain • *She was wearing a simple dress.*
simplicity *noun* how simple something is

simplify *verb* (**simplifies, simplifying, simplified**)
to simplify something is to make it simple or easy to understand
simplification *noun* something that has been made simpler

simply *adverb*
1 in a simple way • *Explain it simply.* **2** completely • *It's simply delicious.* **3** only or merely • *It's simply a question of time.*

simulate *verb*
1 to simulate something is to reproduce the conditions for it • *The machine simulates a space flight.*
2 to simulate a feeling or state is to pretend to have it

• *He simulated illness.*
simulation *noun* when something is simulated or reproduced

simulator *noun* a machine for reproducing the conditions for something, such as flying an aeroplane

simultaneous *adjective* (*say* sim-ul-**tay**-ni-us)
two things are simultaneous when they happen at the same time **simultaneously** *adverb* two things happen simultaneously when they happen at the same time

sin *noun*
something bad a person does that breaks a religious or moral law

sin *verb* (**sinning, sinned**)
to sin is to commit a sin **sinful** *adjective* guilty of sin **sinner** *noun* someone who sins

since *conjunction*
1 from the time when • *Where have you been since I last saw you?* **2** because • *Since we have missed the bus, we must walk home.*

since *preposition*
from a certain time
• *I have been here since Christmas.*

since *adverb*
between then and now
• *He has not been seen since.*

sincere *adjective*
you are being sincere when you mean what you say and express your true feelings • *I gave them my sincere good wishes.*
sincerely *adverb* **sincerity** *noun* sincerity is being sincere

sinew *noun*
strong tissue that joins a muscle to a bone

sing *verb* (**singing, sang, sung**)
1 to sing is to make musical sounds with your voice
2 birds and insects sing when they make musical sounds
singer *noun* someone who sings

singe *verb* (*say* sinj)
to singe something is to burn it slightly

single *adjective*
1 only one; not double
2 designed for one person • *The bedroom had two single beds.* **3** not married **4** for a journey in one direction only

single *noun*
1 a ticket for a journey you make to a place but not back again **2** a record, tape, or CD with one song or short piece of music on it **3** you play singles in tennis when you play against only one other person

single *verb*
to single someone out is to pick them from other people

a b c d e f g h i j k l m n o p q r s t u v w x y z

single file

single file *noun*
in single file in a line, one behind the other

single-handed *adjective*
by your own efforts; without any help

single parent *noun*
a person who is bringing up a child or children without a partner

singular *noun*
the form of a word meaning only one person or thing, such as *cake* and *child*

singular *adjective*
1 in the singular; meaning only one • *'Mouse' is a singular noun.* **2** extraordinary • *She is a woman of singular courage.*

sinister *adjective*
looking or seeming evil or harmful

sink *verb* (**sinking, sank or sunk, sunk**)
1 to sink is to go under water • *The ship sank in a storm.* **2** to sink something is to make it go under water • *They fired on the ship and sank it.* **3** to sink, or to sink down, is to go or fall down to the ground • *He sank to his knees.* **to sink in** is to be gradually understood

sink *noun*
a fixed basin with taps to supply water

sinus *noun* (say **sy**-nus)
your sinuses are the hollows in the bones of your skull, connected with your nose • *My sinuses are blocked.*

sip *verb* (**sipping, sipped**)
to sip a drink is to drink it slowly in small mouthfuls

siphon *noun*
a bent tube used for taking liquid from one container to another at a lower level

siphon *verb*
to siphon liquid is to transfer it with a siphon

sir *noun*
1 a word sometimes used when speaking politely to a man, instead of his name • *Can I help you, sir?* **2** the title given to a knight • *Sir Francis Drake.*

siren *noun*
a device that makes a loud hooting or screaming sound, usually as a warning signal

sister *noun*
1 your sister is a woman or girl who has the same parents as you **2** a senior nurse in a hospital

sister-in-law *noun* (**sisters-in-law**)
a person's sister-in-law is the sister of their husband or wife, or the wife of their brother

sit *verb* (**sitting, sat**)
1 to sit is to rest on your bottom, as you do when you are on a chair **2** to sit someone, or to sit someone down, is to put them in a sitting position **3** to sit an exam or test is to take it **4** to sit somewhere is to be situated or positioned there • *The house sits on top of a hill.* **5** to sit for someone is to act as a babysitter

sitter *noun* someone who is sitting; a babysitter

site *noun*
1 the place where something has been built or will be built • *They crossed a building site.* **2** a place used for something or where something happened • *We stayed at a camping site.* • *This is the site of a famous battle.*

sitting room *noun*
a room with comfortable chairs for sitting in

situated *adjective*
to be situated in a particular place or position is to be placed there • *They lived in a town situated in a valley.*

situation *noun*
1 a place or position; where something is **2** all the things that are happening to someone at a particular time; the way things are • *We're now in a difficult situation because we've run out of money.* **3** a job or employment

six *noun*
the number 6

sixteen *noun*
the number 16
sixteenth *adjective*, *noun* 16th

sixth *adjective*, *noun*
the next after the fifth
sixthly *adverb* in the sixth place; as the sixth one

sixty *noun* (**sixties**)
the number 60 **sixtieth** *adjective*, *noun* 60th

size *noun*
1 how big a person or thing is **2** the measurement something is made in • *I wear a size eight shoe.*

sizzle *verb*
to sizzle is to make a crackling and hissing sound • *The bacon sizzled in the pan.*

skate *noun*
1 a boot with a steel blade attached to the sole, used for sliding smoothly over ice **2** a roller skate

skate *verb*
to skate is to move around on skates **skater** *noun* someone who skates

skateboard *noun*
a small board with wheels, used for standing and riding on as a sport

skeleton *noun*
the framework of bones in a person's or animal's body

sketch *noun*
1 a quick or rough drawing **2** a short amusing play

sketch *verb*
to sketch something or someone is to make a sketch of them

sketchy *adjective* (**sketchier, sketchiest**)
roughly drawn or described, without any detail • *Reports of what happened are sketchy at the moment.*

skeleton

skewer *noun*
a long wooden or metal or plastic pin that you push through meat to hold it together while it is being cooked

ski *noun* (say skee)
a long flat strip of wood or metal or plastic, fastened to each foot for moving quickly over snow

ski *verb* (**skiing, skied or ski'd**)
to ski is to travel on snow wearing skis
skier *noun* someone who skis

skid *verb* (**skidding, skidded**)
to skid is to slide accidentally, especially in a vehicle

skid *noun*
a skidding movement • *The car went into a skid on the icy road.*

skilful *adjective*
having or showing a lot of skill
skilfully *adverb*

skill noun
1 to do something with skill is to do it well **2** a type of work or ability that you learn through training and practice • *He's been learning some new football skills.* **skilled** adjective having a skill or skills

skim verb (**skimming, skimmed**)
1 to skim is to move quickly over a surface **2** to skim something is to remove it from the surface of a liquid, especially to take the cream off milk **skimmed** adjective skimmed milk has had the cream removed

skin noun
1 the outer covering of a person's or animal's body **2** the outer covering of a fruit or vegetable **3** a thin firm layer that has formed on the surface of a liquid

skin verb (**skinning, skinned**)
to skin something is to take the skin off it

skin diving noun
skin diving is swimming under water with flippers and breathing equipment but without a diving suit **skin diver** noun someone who goes skin diving

skinny adjective (**skinnier, skinniest**)
very thin

skip¹ verb (**skipping, skipped**)
1 to skip is to jump or move along by hopping from one foot to the other **2** to skip is also to jump with a skipping rope **3** to skip something is to miss it out or ignore it • *You can skip the last chapter.*

skip¹ noun
a skipping movement

skip² noun
a large metal container for taking away builders' rubbish

skipper noun
the captain of a ship or team

skipping rope noun
a length of rope, usually with a handle at each end, that you swing over your head and under your feet as you jump

skirt noun
a piece of clothing for a woman or girl that hangs down from her waist

skirt verb
to skirt something is to go round the edge of it

skittle noun
a piece of wood or plastic shaped like a bottle, that people try to knock down with a ball in a game of **skittles**

skull noun
the framework of bones in your head which contains your brain

skunk noun
a black and white furry animal from North America that can make an unpleasant smell

sky noun (**skies**)
the space above the earth, where you can see the sun, moon, and stars

skylark noun
a small brown bird that sings as it hovers high in the air

skylight noun
a window in a roof

skyscraper noun
a very tall building

slab noun
a thick flat piece of something hard

slack adjective
1 loose; not pulled tight • *The rope was slack.* **2** lazy; not busy or working hard **slackly** adverb **slackness** noun

slacken verb
1 to slacken something is to loosen it **2** to slacken is to become slower or less busy • *Her pace gradually slackened.*

slam verb (**slamming, slammed**)
1 to slam (for example) a door is to shut it hard or loudly **2** to slam something is to hit it with great force • *He slammed the ball into the net.*

slang noun
slang is a kind of colourful language that you use when speaking to your friends but not in writing or when you want to be polite

slant verb
to slant is to slope or lean

slant noun
a sloping or leaning position • *The caravan floor was at a slant.*

slap verb (**slapping, slapped**)
1 to slap someone is to hit them with the palm of your hand **2** to slap something somewhere is to put it there forcefully or carelessly • *We slapped paint on the walls.*

slap noun
to give someone a slap is to slap them

slapstick noun
slapstick is noisy lively comedy, with people hitting each other, throwing things, and falling over

slash verb
1 to slash something is to make large cuts in it **2** to slash prices or costs is to reduce them a lot

slash noun
1 a large cut **2** a sloping line (/) used to separate words or letters

slat noun
a thin strip of wood or plastic, usually arranged to overlap with others, for example in a blind or screen

slate noun
1 slate is a kind of grey rock that is easily split into flat plates **2** slates are flat pieces of this rock used to cover a roof **slaty** adjective like slate

slaughter verb (say **slor**-ter)
1 to slaughter an animal is to kill it for food **2** to slaughter people or animals is to kill a lot of them

slaughter noun
slaughter is the killing of a lot of people or animals

slave noun
a person who is owned by someone else and has to work for them without being paid

slave verb
to slave over something is to work very hard

slavery noun
slavery is being a slave or the system of having slaves

slay verb (**slaying, slew, slain**)
(*old or poetical use*) to slay someone is to kill them

sledge or **sled** noun
a vehicle for travelling over snow, with strips of metal or wood instead of wheels

sledgehammer noun
a very large heavy hammer

sleek adjective
smooth and shiny • *She has lovely sleek hair.*

sleep noun
1 sleep is the condition in which your eyes are closed, your body is relaxed, and your mind is unconscious • *You need some sleep.* **2** a sleep is a time when you are sleeping • *Did you have a good sleep?*

sleep verb (**sleeping, slept**)
to sleep is to have a sleep

sleeper noun
1 someone who is asleep • *I am a heavy sleeper.* **2** each of the wooden or concrete beams on which a railway line rests **3** a railway carriage equipped for sleeping in

sleeping bag noun
a warm padded bag for sleeping in, especially when you are camping

sleepless adjective
unable to sleep; without sleep • *We've had a sleepless night.*

sleepwalker noun
someone who walks around while they are asleep
sleepwalking noun what a sleepwalker does

sleepy adjective (**sleepier, sleepiest**)
feeling tired and wanting to go to sleep **sleepily** adverb
sleepiness noun

sleet noun
sleet is a mixture of rain with snow or hail

sleeve noun
the part of a piece of clothing that covers your arm
sleeveless adjective not having sleeves

sleigh noun (say slay)
a large sledge pulled by horses

slender adjective
1 slim or thin
2 slight or small • Their chances of winning are slender.

slice noun
a thin flat piece cut off something

slice verb
to slice something is to cut it into slices

slick adjective
done quickly and in a clever way, without obvious effort

slick noun
a large patch of oil floating on water

slide verb (**sliding, slid**)
1 to slide is to move smoothly over a flat or polished or slippery surface • She loved sliding down the bannister.
2 to slide somewhere is to move there quickly or secretly • The thief slid behind a bush.

slide noun
1 a sliding movement
2 a structure for children to play on, with a smooth slope for sliding down 3 a type of photograph that lets light through and that can be shown on a screen 4 a small glass plate on which you can examine things under a microscope 5 a large decorative clip for keeping your hair tidy

slight adjective
very small; not serious or important

slightly adverb
in a slight way; not seriously
• They were slightly hurt.

slim adjective (**slimmer, slimmest**)
1 thin and graceful 2 small; hardly enough • We have a slim chance of winning.

slim verb (**slimming, slimmed**)
to slim is to try to make yourself thinner, especially by dieting **slimmer** noun someone who is slimming

slime noun
slime is unpleasant wet slippery stuff • There was slime on the pond. **slimy** adjective covered in slime

sling verb (**slinging, slung**)
1 to sling something somewhere is to throw it there roughly or carelessly • You can sling your wet clothes into the washing machine. 2 to sling something is also to hang it up or support it so that it hangs loosely • He had slung the bag round his neck.

sling noun
1 a piece of cloth tied round your neck to support an injured arm 2 a device for throwing stones

slink verb (**slinking, slunk**)
to slink somewhere is to move there slowly and quietly because you feel guilty or don't want to be noticed
• He slunk off to bed.

slip verb (**slipping, slipped**)
1 to slip is to slide without meaning to or to fall over
2 to slip somewhere is to move there quickly and quietly • He slipped out of the house before anyone was awake. 3 to slip something somewhere is to put it there quickly without being seen
• She slipped the letter into her pocket. 4 to slip something is to escape from it • The dog slipped its leash. **to slip up** is to make a mistake

slip noun
1 an accidental slide or fall • One slip and you could fall into the river. 2 a small mistake 3 a small piece of paper 4 a piece of women's underwear like a thin dress or skirt **to give someone the slip** is to escape from them or avoid them

slipper noun
a soft comfortable shoe for wearing indoors

slippery adjective
smooth or wet so that it is difficult to stand on or hold

slit noun
a long narrow cut or opening

slit verb (**slitting, slit**)
to slit something is to make a slit in it

slither verb
to slither is to slip or slide along, often unsteadily • The snake slithered away. • We were slithering around on the ice.

sliver noun (say sli-ver)
a thin strip of wood, glass, or other material

slog verb (**slogging, slogged**)
1 to slog something is to hit it hard or wildly 2 to slog is to work hard • I'm slogging away at my essay. 3 to slog is also to walk with effort • We slogged through the snow.

slog noun
a piece of hard work or effort
• Climbing up that hill was a real slog.

slogan noun
a short catchy phrase used to advertise something or to sum up an idea

slop verb (**slopping, slopped**)
1 to slop liquid is to spill it over the edge of its container
2 liquid slops when it spills in this way

slope verb
to slope is to go gradually downwards or upwards or to have one end higher than the other

slope noun
1 a sloping surface 2 the amount by which a surface slopes • The hill has a slope of 30°. 3 the side of a mountain

sloppy adjective (**sloppier, sloppiest**)
1 liquid and spilling easily
2 careless or badly done

• *Their work is sloppy.*
3 (*informal*) too sentimental or romantic • *What a sloppy story.*
sloppily *adverb* **sloppiness** *noun*

slot *noun*
a narrow opening to put things through

sloth *noun* (*rhymes with* **both**)
1 sloth is laziness **2** a sloth is a long-haired South American animal that lives in trees and moves very slowly

slot machine *noun*
a machine that you work by putting a coin in a slot

slouch *verb*
to slouch is to move or stand or sit in a lazy way, especially with your head and shoulders bent forwards

slovenly *adjective*
(*say* **sluv**-en-li)
careless or untidy

slow *adjective*
1 not quick; taking more time than usual **2** a clock or watch is slow when it shows a time earlier than the correct time

slow *adverb*
at a slow rate; slowly • *Go slow.*
slowly *adverb* at a slow rate or speed **slowness** *noun* slowness is being slow

slow *verb*
1 to slow, or to slow down, is to go slower **2** to slow something, or to slow it down, is to make it go slower

sludge *noun*
sludge is thick sticky mud

slug *noun*
a small slimy animal like a snail without its shell

slum *noun*
an area of dirty and crowded houses in a city

slumber *noun*
slumber is peaceful sleep

slumber *verb*
to slumber is to sleep peacefully

slump *verb*
to slump is to fall heavily or suddenly

slush *noun*
slush is snow that is melting on the ground **slushy** *adjective* slushy snow is melting and wet

sly *adjective*
cunning or mischievous
slyly *adverb* **slyness** *noun*

smack *verb*
to smack someone is to slap them with your hand, especially as a punishment

smack *noun*
a slap with your hand

small *adjective*
not large; less than the normal size

smart *adjective*
1 neat and well dressed
2 clever and quick-thinking
3 fast • *We'll need to walk at a smart pace.* **smartly** *adverb*

smart *verb*
to smart is to feel a stinging pain

smarten *verb*
1 to smarten something or someone is to make them smarter • *You need to smarten yourself up a bit.* **2** to smarten is to become smarter

smash *verb*
1 to smash is to break into pieces noisily and violently; to smash something is to break it in this way **2** to smash into something is to hit it with great force • *The lorry left the road and smashed into a wall.*

smash *noun*
1 the act or sound of smashing
2 a collision between vehicles

smear *verb*
to smear something dirty or greasy is to rub it thickly over a surface

smear *noun*
a dirty or greasy mark made by smearing

smell *verb* (**smelling, smelt** or **smelled**)
1 you smell something when you use your nose to sense it
2 to smell is to give out a smell • *The cheese smells funny.*

smell *noun*
1 a smell is something you can smell, especially something unpleasant **2** smell is the ability to smell things • *I have a good sense of smell.*

smelly *adjective* (**smellier, smelliest**)
having an unpleasant smell

smelt *verb*
to smelt ore is to melt it in order to get metal from it

smile *noun*
an expression on your face that shows you are pleased or amused, with your lips stretched and turning upwards at the ends

smile

smile *verb*
to smile is to give a smile

smith *noun*
someone who makes things out of metal

smock *noun*
a loose piece of clothing like a very long shirt

smog *noun*
smog is a mixture of smoke and fog

smoke *noun*
1 smoke is the grey or blue mixture of gas and particles that rises from a fire **2** to have a smoke is to spend time smoking a cigarette • *He wants a smoke.*
smoky *adjective* full of smoke

smoke *verb*
1 something smokes when it gives out smoke • *The fire is smoking.* **2** someone is smoking when they have a lit cigarette in their mouth and are breathing in the smoke from it
smoker *noun* someone who smokes cigarettes

smooth *adjective*
1 having an even surface without any marks or roughness **2** a smooth liquid or substance has no lumps in it **3** moving without bumps or jolts • *We had a smooth ride.*
4 not harsh; flowing easily • *She spoke in a smooth voice.*
smoothly *adverb* in a smooth way; evenly **smoothness** *noun*

smooth *verb*
to smooth something is to make it smooth and flat

smother *verb*
1 to smother someone is to cover their face so that they can't breathe **2** to smother something is to cover it thickly • *He brought in a cake smothered in icing.* **3** to smother a fire is to put it out by covering it

smoulder *verb*
to smoulder is to burn slowly without a flame

smudge *noun*
a dirty or messy mark made by rubbing something

smudge *verb*
to smudge paint or ink is to touch it while it is still wet and make it messy

smug *adjective* (**smugger, smuggest**)
too pleased with yourself
smugly *adverb* **smugness** *noun*

smuggle *verb*
to smuggle something is to bring it into a country secretly and illegally
smuggler *noun* someone who smuggles goods

a
b
c
d
e
f
g
h
i
j
k
l
m
n
o
p
q
r
s
t
u
v
w
x
y
z

snake

snack *noun*
a quick light meal

snag *noun*
an unexpected difficulty or obstacle

snag *verb* (**snagging, snagged**)
to snag something you are wearing is to catch it on something sharp

snail *noun*
a small animal with a soft body in a hard shell

snake *noun*
a reptile with a long narrow body and no legs

snap *verb* (**snapping, snapped**)
1 something snaps when it breaks suddenly with a sharp noise 2 an animal snaps when it bites suddenly or quickly • *The dog snapped at me.* 3 to snap something is to say it quickly and angrily • *There's no need to snap.* 4 to snap your fingers is to make a sharp snapping sound with them 5 to snap something or someone is to take a quick photograph of them

snap *noun*
1 a snap is the act or sound of snapping 2 a snap is also an informal photograph taken quickly 3 snap is a card game in which players shout 'Snap!' when they spot two similar cards

snappy *adjective* (**snappier, snappiest**)
quick and lively

snapshot *noun*
an informal photograph taken quickly

snare *noun*
a trap for catching animals

snare *verb*
to snare an animal is to catch it in a snare

snarl¹ *verb*
an animal snarls when it growls angrily

snarl¹ *noun*
a snarling sound

snarl² *verb*
to be snarled up is to become tangled or jammed • *The motorway was snarled up for several miles.*

snatch *verb*
to snatch something is to grab it quickly
• *He snatched the bag from me.*

sneak *verb*
to sneak somewhere is to move there quietly and secretly

sneak *noun*
(*informal*) a person who tells tales

sneaky *adjective*
dishonest or deceitful

sneer *verb*
to sneer is to speak or behave in a scornful way

sneeze *verb*
you sneeze when you push air through your nose suddenly and uncontrollably

sneeze *noun*
the action or sound of sneezing

sniff *verb*
1 to sniff is to make a noise by drawing air in through your nose 2 to sniff something is to smell it with a sniff

sniff *noun*
the action or sound of sniffing or smelling something

sniffle *verb*
to keep sniffing because you have a cold or are crying

snigger *verb*
to snigger is to give a quiet sly laugh

snigger *noun*
a quiet sly laugh

snip *verb* (**snipping, snipped**)
to snip something is to cut a small piece or pieces off it

snip *noun*
an act of snipping something

sniper *noun*
someone who shoots at people from a hiding place

snippet *noun*
a short piece of news or information

snivel *verb* (**snivelling, snivelled**)
to snivel is to cry or complain in a whining way

snob *noun*
someone who looks down on people who have not got wealth or power or particular tastes or interests

snobbery *noun* snobbery is being a snob **snobbish** *adjective* thinking or behaving like a snob

snooker *noun*
snooker is a game played with long sticks (called *cues*) and 22 coloured balls on a cloth-covered table

snoop *verb*
to snoop is to pry or try to find out about someone else's business **snooper** or **snoop** *noun* someone who snoops

snore *verb*
to snore is to breathe noisily while you are sleeping

snorkel *noun*
a tube with one end above the water, worn by an underwater swimmer to get air

snort *verb*
to snort is to make a loud noise by forcing air out through your nose

snort *noun*
a snorting noise

snout *noun*
an animal's snout is the front part sticking out from its head, with its nose and mouth

snow *noun*
snow is frozen drops of water falling from the sky as small white flakes

snow *verb*
to fall as snow • *It was still snowing when they went out.* • *It might snow later.*

snowball *noun*
snow pressed into the shape of a ball for throwing

snowdrop *noun*
a small white flower that blooms in early spring

snowflake *noun*
a flake of snow

snowman *noun*
a figure of a person made of snow

snowplough *noun*
a vehicle with a large blade at the front for clearing snow from a road or railway track

snowstorm *noun*
a storm with snow falling

snowy *adjective* (**snowier, snowiest**)
1 with snow falling • *We're expecting snowy weather.* 2 covered with snow • *The roofs looked snowy.* 3 brightly white

snub verb (**snubbing, snubbed**)
to snub someone is to treat them in a scornful or unfriendly way

snug adjective (**snugger, snuggest**)
warm and cosy • We found a snug corner by the fire. **snugly** adverb in a snug way • The little ones are tucked up snugly in bed.

snuggle verb
to snuggle is to curl up in a warm comfortable place • She snuggled down in bed.

so adverb
1 in this way; to such an extent • Why are you so cross? **2** very • Cricket is so boring. **3** also • I was wrong but so were you. **and so on** and other similar things • They took food, water, spare clothing, and so on. **or so** or about that number • We need about fifty or so. **so as to** in order to **so far** up to now **so what?** (informal) what does that matter?

so conjunction
for that reason • It was dark, so we took a torch.

soak verb
to soak someone or something is to make them very wet or leave them in water **to soak something up** is to take in a liquid in the way that a sponge does

soap noun
1 soap is a substance you use with water for washing and cleaning things **2** (informal) a soap is a soap opera **soapy** adjective full of soap or covered in soap

soap opera noun
a television serial about the ordinary life of a group of imaginary people

soar verb
1 to soar is to rise or fly high in the air **2** to soar is also to increase a lot • Prices were soaring.

sob verb (**sobbing, sobbed**)
to sob is to cry with gasping noises

sob noun
a sound of sobbing

sober adjective
1 not drunk **2** calm and serious • She had a sober expression. **3** not bright or showy • The room was painted in sober colours.

so-called adjective
having the name but perhaps not deserving it • Even the so-called experts couldn't solve the problem.

soccer noun
soccer is a game played by two teams which try to kick an inflated ball into their opponents' goal

sociable adjective
(say **soh**-sha-bul)
sociable people are friendly and like to be with other people **sociably** adverb
sociability noun

social adjective (say **soh**-shal)
1 to do with people meeting one another in their spare time • Let's join a social club. **2** living in groups, not alone • Bees are social insects. **3** to do with society or a community • They were writing a social history of the area. **socially** adverb in your spare time, not at work

social work noun
social work is work helping people in a community who have problems

social worker noun someone who has a job in social work

society noun (**societies**)
1 a society is a community of people; society is people living together in a group or nation **2** a society is also a group of people organized for a particular purpose • He's joined a dramatic society.

sock noun
a soft piece of clothing that covers your foot and the lower half of your leg **to pull your socks up** (informal) is to try to do better

socket noun
a device or hole that something fits into, especially the place where an electric plug or bulb is put to make a connection

soda noun
1 soda is a substance made from sodium **2** soda is also soda water

soda water noun
soda water is fizzy water used in drinks

sodium noun (say **soh**-di-um) (Na)
sodium is a soft silvery-white metal

sofa noun
a long soft seat with sides and a back

soft adjective
1 not hard or firm; easily pressed or cut into a new shape **2** smooth; not rough or stiff **3** gentle; not loud • He spoke in a soft voice. **softly** adverb in a gentle way; quietly • She closed the door softly behind her. **softness** noun

soft drink noun
a drink that does not contain alcohol

soften verb
1 to soften something is to make it softer **2** to soften is to become softer

software noun
(in computing) software is programs and data, which are not part of the machinery (the hardware) of a computer

soggy adjective (**soggier, soggiest**)
very wet and soft

soil¹ noun
soil is the loose earth that plants grow in

soil² verb
to soil something is to make it dirty

solar adjective
to do with the sun or powered by the sun's energy

solar system noun
the solar system is the sun and the planets that revolve round it

solar system

solder noun
solder is a soft alloy that is melted to join pieces of metal together

solder verb
to solder two pieces of metal is to join them together with solder

soldier noun
a member of an army

sole¹ noun
1 the bottom part of a shoe or foot **2** a flat sea fish used for food

sole² adjective
single or only • She was the sole survivor. **solely** adverb

solemn adjective
serious and dignified **solemnity** noun solemnity is being solemn **solemnly** adverb in a serious and dignified way

solicitor noun
a lawyer who advises clients and prepares legal documents

solid adjective
1 keeping its shape; not a liquid or gas **2** not hollow; with no

space inside • *These bars are made of solid steel.* **3** firm or strongly made • *The house is built on solid foundations.* **4** strong and reliable • *They gave solid support.*
solidly *adverb* something is solidly built when it is firmly and strongly built; to rain solidly is to rain continuously
solidity *noun* how solid something is
solid *noun*
1 a solid thing
2 a three-dimensional shape, such as a cube, sphere, or cone
solitary *adjective*
1 alone; on your own • *He lived a solitary life.*
2 single • *There was a solitary van in the car park.*
solitude *noun* solitude is being on your own
solo *noun* something sung or performed by one person alone
soloist *noun* someone who plays or sings a solo
soluble *adjective* a soluble substance is able to be dissolved
solution *noun*
1 the answer to a problem or puzzle **2** a liquid with something dissolved in it
solve *verb* to solve a problem or puzzle is to find an answer to it
sombre *adjective* gloomy or dark
some *adjective*
1 a few or a little • *I'd like some biscuits and some sugar.*
2 a certain amount of • *Would you like some cake?*
3 an unknown person or thing • *Some fool left the door open.*
some *pronoun* a certain or unknown number or amount • *Some of them were late.*
somebody *pronoun* someone; some person
somehow *adverb* in some way • *We must finish the work somehow.*
someone *pronoun* some person
somersault *noun* (*say* **sum**-er-solt) a movement in which you turn head over heels and land on your feet
something *pronoun* a certain or unknown thing
sometime *adverb* at some time • *I saw her sometime last year.*

sometimes *adverb* at some times but not always • *We sometimes walk to school.*
somewhat *adverb* to some extent; rather • *He was somewhat annoyed.*
somewhere *adverb* in or to some place
son *noun* a boy or man who is someone's child
sonar *noun* sonar is a system using the echo from sound waves to locate objects underwater
song *noun*
1 a song is a tune with words for singing **2** a bird's song is the musical sounds it makes **3** song is singing • *He burst into song.*
songbird *noun* a bird that sings sweetly
sonic *adjective* to do with sound or sound waves
sonnet *noun* a kind of poem with 14 lines
soon *adverb*
1 in a short time from now
2 not long after something • *She became ill, but was soon better.* **3** early or quickly • *You spoke too soon.* **as soon** as willingly • *I'd just as soon stay at home.* **sooner or later** at some time in the future
soot *noun* soot is the black powder left by smoke in a chimney or on a building **sooty** *adjective* covered in soot
soothe *verb*
1 to soothe someone is to make them calm **2** to soothe a pain or ache is to make it hurt less
sophisticated *adjective* (*say* sof-**iss**-ti-kay-tid)
1 someone is sophisticated when they are used to a fashionable or cultured life and have experienced a lot of different things **2** something is sophisticated when it is complicated and highly developed • *It is a sophisticated machine.*
sophistication *noun* sophistication is being sophisticated
sopping *adjective* very wet; soaked
soppy *adjective* (**soppier, soppiest**) (*informal*) sentimental or silly
soprano *noun* (**sopranos**) (*say* so-**prah**-noh) a woman or young boy with a high singing voice
sorcerer *noun* someone who can do magic

sorcery *noun* magic or witchcraft
sorceress *noun* a woman who can do magic
sore *adjective* painful or smarting • *I've got a sore throat.* **soreness** *noun*
sore *noun* a red and painful place on your skin
sorely *adverb* seriously; very • *I was sorely tempted to run away.*
sorrow *noun* sorrow is sadness or regret
sorrowful *adjective* feeling sorrow **sorrowfully** *adverb*
sorry *adjective* (**sorrier, sorriest**)
1 you are sorry that you did something when you regret doing it or want to apologize • *I'm sorry I forgot to send you a birthday card.* **2** you feel sorry for someone when you feel pity for them or are sad that something bad has happened to them • *I'm sorry you've been ill.*
sort *noun* a group of things or people that are similar; a kind • *What sort of fruit do you like?* **sort of** (*informal*) rather; to some extent • *I sort of wanted to go.*
sort *verb* to sort things is to arrange them in groups or kinds **to sort something out** is to organize it or arrange it
SOS *noun* an SOS is an urgent appeal for help from someone whose life is in danger
soul *noun* a person's invisible spirit that some people believe goes on living after the body has died
sound¹ *noun*
1 sound is vibrations in the air that you can detect with your ear **2** a sound is something that you can hear
sound¹ *verb*
1 to sound is to make a sound • *The trumpets sounded.*
2 to sound something is to make a sound with it • *Don't forget to sound your horn.*
3 to sound a certain way is to give that impression when heard • *You sound in a good mood.* • *The car sounds as if it needs a service.*
sound² *verb* **to sound someone out** is to try to find out what they think or feel about something
sound³ *adjective*
1 not damaged; in good condition **2** healthy

3 reasonable or correct • *His ideas are sound.* **4** reliable or secure • *They made a sound investment.* **5** thorough or deep • *She has a sound knowledge of the subject.* • *I am a sound sleeper.* **soundly** *adverb* thoroughly or completely **soundness** *noun* being reliable or sensible

sound effects *plural noun* special sounds produced to make a play or film more realistic

soundtrack *noun* the sound or music that goes with a film or television programme

soup *noun* a liquid food made from vegetables or meat

sour *adjective* **1** having a sharp taste like vinegar or lemons **2** unpleasant or bad-tempered **sourly** *adverb* **sourness** *noun*

source *noun* **1** the place where something comes from **2** the place where a river starts

south *noun* **1** the direction to the right of a person facing east **2** the part of a country or city that is in this direction

south *adjective, adverb* **1** towards the south or in the south **2** coming from the south • *A south wind was blowing.*

south-east *noun, adjective, adverb* midway between south and east

southern *adjective* (*say* **suth**-ern) from or to do with the south

southerner *noun* (*say* **suth**-er-ner) someone who lives in the south of a country

southward or **southwards** *adjective, adverb* towards the south

south-west *noun, adjective, adverb* midway between south and west

souvenir *noun* (*say* soo-ven-**eer**) something that you buy or keep to remind you of a person, place, or event

sovereign *noun* (*say* **sov**-rin) **1** a king or a queen **2** an old British gold coin that was worth £1

sow[1] *verb* (**sowing, sowed, sown** or **sowed**) (*rhymes with* **go**) to sow seeds is to put them into the ground so that they will grow into plants

sow[2] *noun* (*rhymes with* **cow**) a female pig

soya bean *noun* a bean that is rich in protein, used to make kinds of oil and flour

space *noun* **1** space is the whole area outside the earth, where the stars and planets are **2** space is also an area or volume • *There isn't enough space for a car.* **3** a space is an empty area or gap • *There is a space at the back of the cupboard.* • *Leave a space for your name and address.* **4** a space is also a period of time • *They moved house twice in the space of a year.*

space *verb* to space things, or space things out, is to arrange them with gaps or periods of time between them

spacecraft *noun* (**spacecraft**) a vehicle for travelling in outer space

spaceship *noun* a spacecraft

space shuttle *noun* a spacecraft that can travel into space and return to earth

space station *noun* a satellite which orbits the earth and is used as a base by scientists and astronauts

space station

spade *noun* **1** a tool with a long handle and a wide blade for digging **2** a playing card with black shapes like upside-down hearts on it

spaghetti *noun* (*say* spa-**get**-i) spaghetti is pasta made in long strings

span *noun* **1** the length from one end of something to the other **2** the distance between the tips of your thumb and little finger when your hand is spread out **3** a part of a bridge between two supports **4** a period of time

span *verb* (**spanning, spanned**) to span something is to reach from one side or end of it to the other • *A wooden bridge spanned the river.*

spank *verb* to spank someone is to smack them several times on the bottom as a punishment

spaghetti

spanner *noun* a tool for tightening or loosening a nut

spar *verb* (**sparring, sparred**) to spar is to practise boxing • *He was my sparring partner.*

spare *verb* **1** to spare something is to afford it or be able to give it to someone • *Can you spare a moment?* **2** to spare someone is to avoid harming them or making them suffer something unpleasant

spare *adjective* **1** not used but kept ready in case it is needed; extra • *Where's the spare wheel?* • *What do you do in your spare time?* **2** thin or lean

spare *noun* a spare thing or part • *The local garage sells spares.*

spark *noun* **1** a tiny flash of electricity **2** a tiny glowing piece of something hot

spark *verb* to spark is to give off sparks

sparkle *verb* to sparkle is to shine with a lot of tiny flashes of bright light • *The sea sparkled in the sunlight.*

sparkler *noun* a firework that sparkles

sparrow *noun* a small brown bird

sparse *adjective* small in number or amount; thinly scattered • *Vegetation on the island is sparse.* **sparsely** *adverb* a sparsely

h
i
j
k
l
m
n
o
p
q
r
s
t
u
v
w
x
y
z

231

populated area is one with only a few people

spatter *verb*
to spatter something is to splash it or scatter it in small drops or pieces • *The paint spattered all over the page.*

spatter

spawn *noun*
spawn is the eggs of frogs, fish, and other water animals

speak *verb* (**speaking, spoke, spoken**)
1 to speak is to say something • *I spoke to them this morning.* **2** to speak a language is to be able to talk in it • *Do you speak German?* **to speak up** is to say something more clearly or loudly

speaker *noun*
1 a person who is speaking or making a speech **2** the part of a radio, CD player, or computer that the sound comes out of

spear *noun*
a long pole with a sharp point, used as a weapon

spear *verb*
to spear something is to pierce it with a spear or something pointed

special *adjective*
1 different from other people or things; unusual **2** meant for a particular person or purpose • *You'll need special training.*

specialist *noun*
an expert in a particular subject

speciality *noun* (**specialities**)
something that you are especially good at doing

specially *adverb*
for a special purpose • *I came specially to see you.*

species *noun* (**species**)
(*say* spee-shiz)
a group of animals or plants that have similar features and can breed with each other

specific *adjective*
1 definite or precise **2** to do with a particular thing • *The money was given for a specific purpose.*

specifically *adverb*
1 in a special way or for a special purpose • *These scissors are designed specifically for left-handed people.* **2** clearly and precisely • *I specifically said we had to go.*

specify *verb* (**specifies, specifying, specified**)
to specify a person or thing

is to name or mention them precisely • *The recipe specified brown sugar, not white.*

specimen *noun*
1 a small amount or sample of something **2** an example of one kind of plant, animal, or thing • *We saw a fine specimen of an oak.*

speck *noun*
1 a tiny piece of something **2** a tiny mark or spot

speckled *adjective*
covered with small spots

spectacle *noun*
1 an exciting sight or display **2** a ridiculous sight

spectacles *plural noun*
a pair of lenses in a frame, which you wear over your eyes to help improve your eyesight

spectacular *adjective*
exciting to see

spectator *noun*
a person who watches a game or show

spectre *noun* (*say* **spek**-ter)
a ghost

spectrum *noun* (**spectra**)
the band of colours like those in a rainbow

speech *noun*
1 speech is the ability to speak or a person's way of speaking **2** a speech is a talk given to a group of people

speechless *adjective*
unable to speak, especially because you are surprised or angry

speech marks *plural noun*
inverted commas, (" ") used to show that someone is speaking

speed *noun*
1 the speed of something is the rate at which it moves or happens **2** speed is being quick or fast **at speed** fast; quickly

speed *verb* (**speeding, sped** or **speeded**)
to speed is to go very fast or too fast • *Drivers can be fined for speeding.* **to speed up** is to become quicker **to speed something up** is to make it go or happen faster

speedboat *noun*
a fast motor boat

speedboat

speedometer *noun*
(*say* spee-**dom**-it-er)
a gauge in a vehicle that shows its speed

speedy *adjective*
(**speedier, speediest**)
quick or fast • *We need a speedy reply.* **speedily** *adverb* fast or quickly

spell[1] *verb* (**spelling, spelt** or **spelled**)
to spell a word is to give its letters in the right order

spell[2] *noun*
1 a period of time • *We're having a cold spell.* **2** a period of activity • *I must do a spell of work now.*

spell[3] *noun*
a set of words that is supposed to have magic power

spelling *noun*
1 the way in which letters are put together to form words **2** how well someone can spell • *Her spelling is poor.*

spend *verb* (**spending, spent**)
1 to spend money is to use it to pay for things **2** to spend time is to pass it doing something • *He spent the weekend painting his bedroom.* **3** to spend energy or effort is to use it up • *She spends all her spare energy on gardening.*

sphere *noun*
a perfectly round solid shape; a globe or ball **spherical** *adjective* shaped like a ball

spice *noun*
a strong-tasting substance used to flavour food, often made from the dried parts of plants **spicy** *adjective* having a strong flavour; full of spices

spider *noun*
a small animal with eight legs that spins webs to catch insects on which it feeds

spike *noun*
a pointed piece of metal; a sharp point **spiky** *adjective* full of spikes or sharp points • *She has short spiky hair.*

spill *verb* (**spilling, spilt** or **spilled**)
1 to spill something is to let it fall out of a container by accident • *Careful or you'll spill your juice.* **2** to spill is to fall out of a container • *The coins came spilling out.*

spill *noun*
when something gets spilt • *There's been an oil spill at sea.*

spin *verb* (**spinning, spun**)
1 to spin is to turn round and round quickly **2** to spin something is to make it spin **3** to spin is also to make pieces

of wool or cotton into thread by twisting them **4** to spin a web or cocoon is to make it out of threads • *The spider spun a web.*

spinach *noun*
spinach is a vegetable with dark green leaves

spindle *noun*
1 a thin rod on which you wind thread **2** a pin or bar that turns round, or on which something turns round

spine *noun*
1 the line of bones down the middle of your back **2** a sharp point on an animal or plant • *This cactus has sharp spines.* **3** the back part of a book where the pages are joined together

spinal *adjective* to do with your spine **spiny** *adjective* covered in spines

spine-chilling *adjective*
frightening and exciting • *We heard a spine-chilling ghost story.*

spinning wheel *noun*
a machine for spinning thread out of wool or cotton

spinster *noun*
a woman who has not married

spiral *adjective*
going round and round a central point, getting further from it with each turn

spiral *noun*
something with a spiral shape

spire *noun*
a tall pointed part on top of a church tower

spirit *noun*
1 a person's spirit is their soul or their deepest thoughts and feelings **2** a spirit is a ghost or other supernatural being **3** spirit is courage or liveliness **4** a person's spirits are their mood or the way they feel • *She was in good spirits after the exam.* **5** a spirit is also a strong alcoholic drink

spiritual *adjective*
1 to do with the human soul and with a person's deepest thoughts and feelings **2** to do with religious beliefs **spiritually** *adverb*

spiritual *noun*
a religious song originally sung by Black Americans

spit¹ *verb* (**spitting, spat**)
to spit is to shoot drops of liquid out of your mouth • *He spat into the basin.*

spit¹ *noun*
saliva that has been spat out

spit² *noun*
a long thin metal spike put through meat to hold it while it is roasted

spite *noun*
spite is a desire to hurt or annoy someone **in spite of something** although something has happened or is happening • *They went out in spite of the rain.*

spiteful *adjective* wanting to hurt or annoy someone **spitefully** *adverb*

splash *verb*
1 to splash liquid is to make it fly about, as you do when you jump into water **2** to splash is to fly about in drops • *The water splashed all over me.* **3** to splash someone or something is to make them wet by sending drops of liquid towards them • *The bus splashed us as it went past.*

splash *noun*
the action or sound of splashing

splashdown *noun*
the landing of a spacecraft in the sea

splendid *adjective*
magnificent; very fine **splendidly** *adverb*

splendour *noun*
splendour is a brilliant display or appearance

splint *noun*
a straight piece of wood or metal that is tied to a broken arm or leg to hold it firm

splinter *noun*
a small sharp piece of wood or glass broken off a larger piece

splinter *verb*
to splinter is to break into splinters

split *verb* (**splitting, split**)
1 to split is to break into parts **2** to split something is to divide it into parts **to split up 1** is to divide into parts **2** is to separate after being together for some time

split *noun*
a crack or tear in something, where it has split

splutter *verb*
1 to splutter is to make a quick series of spitting or coughing sounds • *The smoke from the bonfire made him splutter.* **2** to splutter is also to speak quickly and unclearly

spoil *verb* (**spoiling, spoilt** or **spoiled**)
1 to spoil something is to damage it and so make it less good or useful • *The rain spoilt our holiday.* **2** to spoil someone is to make them selfish by always letting them have what they want

spoilsport *noun*
someone who spoils other people's fun

spoke *noun*
each of the rods or bars that go from the centre of a wheel to the rim

sponge *noun*
1 a lump of soft material containing lots of tiny holes, used for washing **2** a sea creature from which this kind of material is made **3** a soft lightweight cake or pudding

sponge *verb*
to sponge something is to wash it with a sponge

spongy *adjective* (**spongier, spongiest**)
soft and absorbent like sponge

sponsor *verb*
1 to sponsor someone is to promise to give them money if they do something difficult and give the money to charity **2** to sponsor something or someone is to provide money to support them

sponsor *noun*
someone who provides money to support a person or thing, or who supports someone who sets out to do something for charity **sponsorship** *noun* the money someone provides to support a person or thing

spontaneous *adjective*
(*say* spon-**tay**-ni-us) happening or done without being planned; not forced or suggested by someone else • *Everyone burst into spontaneous applause.* **spontaneously** *adverb* **spontaneity** *noun* behaving in a spontaneous way

spooky *adjective* (**spookier, spookiest**)
(*informal*) frighteningly strange; haunted by ghosts

spool *noun*
a rod or reel for winding on something such as thread or film or tape

spoon *noun*
a piece of metal or wood or plastic consisting of a small bowl with a handle, used for lifting food to your mouth or for stirring or measuring

spoon *verb*
to spoon something is to lift it or take it with a spoon

sport *noun*
1 a sport is a game that exercises your body, especially a game you play out of doors • *What sports do you play?* **2** sport is games of this sort • *Are you keen on sport?*

sporting adjective
1 connected with sport
2 behaving fairly and unselfishly

sportsman or **sportswoman** noun (**sportsmen** or **sportswomen**)
a man or woman who takes part in sport

sportsmanship noun
sportsmanship is behaving fairly and generously in sport

spot noun
1 a small round mark
2 a pimple on your skin
3 a small amount of something • We've had a spot of bother
4 a place • This is a nice spot. **on the spot** immediately; there and then • We can repair your bike on the spot.

spot verb (**spotting, spotted**)
1 to spot someone or something is to notice them or see them • I suddenly spotted my friend Alex in the crowd.
2 to be spotted is to be marked with spots

spotless adjective
perfectly clean **spotlessly** adverb to be spotlessly clean is to be perfectly clean

spotlight noun
a strong light with a beam that shines on a small area

spotty adjective (**spottier, spottiest**)
marked with spots

spout noun
1 a pipe or opening from which liquid can pour
2 a jet of liquid

spout verb
to spout is to come out in a jet of liquid

sprain verb
you sprain your ankle or wrist when you injure it by twisting it

sprain noun
an injury by spraining

sprawl verb
1 you sprawl when you sit or lie with your arms and legs spread out
2 to be sprawled is to be spread out loosely or untidily • There were books and papers sprawled all over the floor.

spray verb
to spray liquid is to scatter it in tiny drops over something; to spray something is to cover it with liquid in this way

spray noun
1 tiny drops of liquid sprayed on something 2 a device for spraying liquid

spread verb (**spreading, spread**)
1 to spread something is to lay or stretch it out to its full size • The bird spread its wings and flew away. 2 to spread something over a surface is to make it cover the surface • He spread a thick layer of jam on his toast. 3 to spread news or information is to make it widely known 4 news or information spreads when it becomes widely known • The story spread quickly round the village.

spread noun
1 something you can spread on bread 2 (informal) a large meal

sprightly adjective (**sprightlier, sprightliest**)
lively and energetic

spring noun
1 spring is the season of the year when most plants start to grow, between winter and summer 2 a spring is a coil of wire that goes back to its original shape when you bend it or squeeze it and let it go 3 a spring is also a sudden upward movement 4 a spring is also a place where water rises out of the ground and becomes a stream

spring verb (**springing, sprang, sprung**)
1 to spring is to move quickly or suddenly • He sprang to his feet. 2 to spring, or spring up, is to develop or come from something • This squabble has sprung from a misunderstanding. 3 to spring something on someone is to surprise them with it

springboard noun
a springy board from which people jump or dive

springtime noun
springtime is the season of spring

springy adjective (**springier, springiest**)
able to spring back to its original position when you bend it or squeeze it and let it go

sprinkle verb
to sprinkle liquid or powder is to make tiny drops or pieces of it fall on something **sprinkler** noun a device for sprinkling liquid

sprint verb
to sprint is to run very fast for a short distance **sprinter** noun someone who sprints

sprint noun
a short fast race

sprout verb
1 a plant sprouts when it starts to produce leaves or shoots
2 to grow or start appearing • Whiskers sprouted from his ears and nose.

sprout noun
a green vegetable like a tiny cabbage

spruce[1] noun
a kind of fir tree

spruce[2] adjective
neat and smart

spud noun
(informal) a potato

spur noun
a sharp spike that a rider wears on the heel of their boot to urge a horse to go faster **on the spur of the moment** on an impulse; without planning

spur verb (**spurring, spurred**)
to spur someone, or to spur someone on, is to encourage them

spurt verb
a liquid spurts when it gushes out or up • Blood was spurting from the cut.

spurt noun
1 a jet of liquid 2 a sudden increase in speed • He put on a spurt and caught us up.

spy noun (**spies**)
someone who works secretly to find out things about another country or person

spy verb (**spies, spying, spied**)
1 to spy is to be a spy or to watch secretly • He was spying on us. 2 to spy someone or something is to see them or notice them • We spied a house in the distance.

squabble verb
people squabble when they quarrel about something unimportant

squabble noun
a minor quarrel or argument

squad noun
a small group of people working or being trained together

squadron noun
part of an army, navy, or air force

squalid adjective
dirty and unpleasant • He lived in a squalid little flat. **squalor** noun squalor is being squalid • They lived in squalor.

squander verb
to squander money or time is to waste it

square noun ■
1 a shape with four equal sides and four right angles
2 in a town, an area surrounded by buildings 3 the result of

multiplying a number by itself • *9 is the square of 3.*

square *adjective*
1 shaped like a square **2** used for units of measurement that give an area, such as a square metre and a square foot. For example, a square metre is the size of a square with each side one metre long. **3** equal or even • *The teams are all square with six points each.* • *If you pay for lunch, we'll be square.*

square *verb*
1 to square a number is to multiply it by itself • *3 squared is 9.* **2** to square with something is to match it or agree with it • *His story doesn't square with yours.*

squarely *adverb*
directly or exactly • *The ball hit him squarely in the mouth.*

square root *noun*
the number that gives a particular number if it is multiplied by itself • *3 is the square root of 9.*

squash *verb*
1 to squash something is to squeeze it so that it loses its shape **2** to squash a person or thing into something is to force them into it when there is not much space • *We squashed ourselves into the minibus.*

squash *noun*
1 a squash is when people or things are pressed together because there is not enough space • *There was a tremendous squash outside the football ground.* **2** squash is a fruit-flavoured drink **3** squash is also a game played with rackets and a small ball in a special indoor court

squat *verb* (**squatting, squatted**)
1 to squat is to sit back on your heels **2** to squat in an unoccupied house is to live there without permission

squatter *noun* someone who squats in a house

squat *adjective* (**squatter, squattest**)
short and fat

squaw *noun*
a Native American woman or wife

squawk *verb*
to squawk is to make a loud harsh cry

squawk *noun*
a loud harsh cry

squeak *verb*
to make a short high-pitched sound or cry

squeak *noun*
a short high-pitched sound or cry **squeaky** *adjective* making squeaks • *a squeaky floorboard*

squeal *verb*
to squeal is to make a long shrill sound

squeal *noun*
a long shrill sound

squeeze *verb*
1 to squeeze something is to press it from opposite sides, especially so that you get liquid out of it **2** to squeeze somewhere is to force a way into or through a place or gap • *We squeezed into the car.*

squeezer *noun* a device for squeezing fruit

squeeze *noun*
1 the action of squeezing **2** a tight fit • *We all got on the bus but it was a bit of a squeeze.*

squelch *verb*
to squelch is to make a sound like someone treading in thick mud

squelch *noun*
a squelching sound

squid *noun*
a sea animal with eight short arms and two long ones

squiggle *noun*
a short curly or wavy line

squint *verb*
1 to squint at something is to peer at it or look at it with half-shut eyes **2** to squint is to have eyes that look in different directions

squint *noun*
a fault in someone's eyesight that makes them squint

squire *noun*
1 the man who owns most of the land in a country district **2** in the Middle Ages, a young nobleman who served a knight

squirm *verb*
to squirm is to wriggle about, especially when you feel awkward or embarrassed

squirrel *noun*
a small animal with grey or red fur and a bushy tail, that lives in trees and eats nuts

squirt *verb*
to squirt something is to send it out in a strong jet of liquid; to squirt is to come out like this • *The orange juice squirted in his eye.*

St. or **St**
short for saint or street

stab *verb* (**stabbing, stabbed**)
to stab someone is to pierce or wound them with something sharp • *She stabbed him with a knife.*

stab *noun*
1 the action of stabbing **2** a sudden sharp pain

stability *noun*
stability is being stable or firm

stabilizer *noun*
a small extra wheel on a bicycle to make it stable

stable[1] *adjective*
steady or firmly fixed **stably** *adverb*

stable[2] *noun*
a building where horses are kept

stack *noun*
1 a neat pile of things **2** a large amount of something • *I've got a stack of work to do.* **3** a single small chimney

stack *verb*
to stack things is to pile them up neatly

stadium *noun* (**stadiums** or **stadia**)
a large sports ground surrounded by seats for spectators

WORD ORIGIN

The word **stadium** comes from a Greek word *stadion*, which originally meant a measure of length of about 185 metres. This was the usual length of a race in an ancient stadium.

staff *noun*
1 the people who work in an office or shop **2** *the teachers in a school or college* **3** a thick stick for walking with

stag *noun*
a male deer

stage *noun*
1 a platform for performances in a theatre or hall **2** the point that you have reached in a process or journey • *The final stage is to paint the model.*

stage *verb*
1 to stage a performance is to present it on a stage **2** to stage an event is to organize it • *They decided to stage a protest.*

stagecoach *noun*
a kind of horse-drawn coach that used to travel regularly along the same route

stagger *verb*
1 to stagger is to walk unsteadily **2** to stagger someone is to amaze or shock them • *I was staggered at the price.* **3** to stagger events is to arrange them so that they do not all happen at the same time • *We stagger our holidays*

so that someone is always here.

staggering *adjective* very surprising or shocking

stagnant *adjective*
stagnant water is not flowin or fresh • *The pond is stagnant.*

stain *noun*
a dirty mark that is difficult to remove

stain *verb*
1 to stain something is to make a stain on it • *The juice has stained my dress.* **2** to stain material or wood is to colour it

stainless steel *noun*
stainless steel is steel that does not rust easily

stair *noun*
each of a series of steps that take you from one floor to another in a building

staircase *noun*
a set of stairs

stake *noun*
1 a thick pointed stick to be driven into the ground **2** the thick post to which people used to be tied for execution by being burnt alive **3** an amount of money you bet on something **to be at stake** is to be at risk of being lost

stake *verb*
to stake money is to use it on a bet **to stake a claim** is to claim something or get a right to it

stalactite *noun*
a stony spike hanging like an icicle from the roof of a cave

stalagmite *noun*
a stony spike standing like a pillar on the floor of a cave

stale *adjective*
no longer fresh • *This bread has gone stale.* • *The air in here smells stale.*

stalk¹ *noun*
the main part of a plant, from which the leaves and flowers grow

stalk² *verb*
to stalk a person or animal is to follow or hunt them stealthily

stall¹ *noun*
1 a table or small open-fronted shop where things are sold, usually in the open air **2** a place for one animal in a stable or shed

stall¹ *verb*
a vehicle stalls when the engine stops suddenly • *The car stalled at the traffic lights.*

stall² *verb*
to stall is to delay or hold things up to give yourself more time

stallion *noun*
a male horse

stalls *plural noun*
the seats on the ground floor of a theatre or cinema

stamen *noun*
(*say* **stay**-men)
the part of a flower that produces pollen

stamina *noun*
(*say* **stam**-in-a)
stamina is the strength and energy you need to keep doing something for a long time • *Does she have the stamina to run a marathon?*

stammer *verb*
to stammer is to keep repeating the sounds at the beginning of words

stammer *noun*
when someone stammers a lot

stamp *noun*
1 a small piece of gummed paper with a special design on it, which you stick on a letter or parcel to show you have paid the postage **2** when you bang your foot on the ground **3** a small block with raised letters for printing words or marks on something; the words or marks made with this

stamp *verb*
1 to stamp is to bang your foot heavily on the ground **2** to stamp an envelope or parcel is to put a postage stamp on it **3** to stamp something is also to put marks on it with a stamp • *The librarian stamped my books.*

stamps

stallion

stampede *noun*
a sudden rush of animals or people

stampede *verb*
animals or people stampede when they rush in a stampede

stand *verb* (**standing, stood**)
1 to stand is to be on your feet without moving • *She stood at the back of the hall.* **2** to stand something somewhere is to put it upright there • *Stand the vase on the table.* **3** something stands somewhere when that is where it is • *The castle stood on the top of a hill.* **4** something stands when it stays unchanged • *My offer still stands.* **5** to stand a difficulty or hardship is to be able to bear it • *I can't stand the heat.* **to stand by** is to be ready for action **to stand for something 1** is to tolerate it or put up with it • *She won't stand for any arguments.* **2** is to mean something • *'Dr' stands for 'Doctor'.* **to stand in for someone** is to take their place **to stand out** is to be clear or obvious **to stand up** is to rise to your feet **to stand up for someone** is to support them or defend them

stand *noun*
1 something made for putting things on • *The statue had fallen off its stand.* **2** a stall where things are sold or displayed **3** a structure at a sports ground with rows of seats for spectators **4** when someone resists an attack or defends their opinion • *She was determined to make a stand for her rights.*

standard noun
1 how good something is
• *They reached a high
standard of work.*
2 a thing used to measure or
judge something else • *The
metre is the standard for length.*
3 a special flag, especially
one used by an army
standard adjective
of the usual or ordinary kind
standard of living noun
(**standards of living**)
the level of comfort and wealth
that a person or country has
standstill noun
a complete stop • *The blizzard
brought traffic to a standstill.*
stanza noun
a group of lines in a poem
staple[1] noun
1 a tiny piece of metal used to
fasten pieces of paper together
2 a U-shaped nail
stapler noun a machine for
putting staples in paper
staple[1] verb
to fasten pieces of paper
together with a staple
staple[2] adjective
main or normal • *Rice is the
staple food in many countries.*
star noun
1 a large mass of burning gas
that you see as a bright speck
of light in the sky at night
2 a shape with five or six points
3 one of the main performers
in a film or show; a famous
entertainer **starry** adjective a
starry sky or night is full of stars
star verb (**starring, starred**)
1 to star in a film or show is to
be one of the main performers
2 a film or show stars someone
when it has them as a main
performer
starboard noun
starboard is the right-hand side
of a ship or aircraft when you
are facing forward
starch noun
1 starch is a white substance
found in bread, potatoes,
and other food, which is an
important part of the human
diet 2 starch is also a form of
this substance used to stiffen
clothes **starchy** adjective like
starch, or containing starch
stare verb
to look hard at someone or
something without moving
your eyes
stare noun
a long fixed look
• *I gave him a hard stare.*

starfish noun
(**starfish** or
starfishes)
a sea animal
shaped
like a star with
five points
starling noun
a noisy black or
brown speckled
bird
start verb
1 to start something is to
take the first steps in doing
it 2 to start, or start out, is to
begin a journey 3 to start is also
to make a sudden movement
of surprise • *They all started
at the noise outside.*
start noun
1 the act of starting • *We
need to make an early start
tomorrow.* 2 the point or
place where something
starts • *Go back to
the start.* • *Saturday
is the start of the new
season.*
3 an advantage that
someone starts with
• *We gave the
young ones 10 minutes' start.*
4 a sudden movement of
surprise • *It gave me quite a start
when the hooter sounded.*
startle verb
to startle a person or animal is
to surprise or alarm them
starve verb
1 someone starves when they
suffer or die because they do
not have enough food 2 to
starve someone is to make
them suffer or die in this
way • *The prisoners had been
starved to death.* 3 (*informal*)
to be starving is to be very
hungry **starvation** noun when
someone does not have enough
food and so dies
state noun
1 the way that someone or
something is, or the condition
that they are in • *The room was
in an untidy state.* 2 a nation
or country 3 a division of a
country • *the state of California*
4 you can refer to a government
and its officials as the state **to
be in a state** (*informal*) is to be
upset
state verb
to state something is to say it
clearly or formally
statement noun
1 words that state something
2 a formal account of
something that happened
• *A witness to the robbery has*

starfish

given a
statement to the
police. 3 a report made
by a bank about the
money in a person's account
statesman or **stateswoman**
noun (**statesmen** or
stateswomen)
someone who is important
or skilled in governing a state
static adjective
not moving or changing
static electricity noun
electricity which is present in
something but does not flow
as a current
station noun
1 a place where people
get on or off trains or buses
2 a building for police, firemen,
or other workers who serve
he public 3 a place from
which radio or television
broadcasts are made
station verb
to station a person
somewhere is to place them
there for a particular purpose
• *He was stationed at the door
to take the tickets.*

WORD ORIGIN

The word **station** comes from a
Latin word *stare* meaning 'to stand',
because a station was originally a
place where someone stood.

stationary adjective
not moving; still
• *The car was stationary
when the van hit it.*

a
b
c
d
h
i
j
m
n
o
p
q
r
s
t
u
v
w
x
y
z

stationery *noun*
stationery is paper, envelopes, and other things used for writing

statistic *noun*
a piece of information expressed as a number • *These statistics show that the population has doubled.* **statistical** *adjective* statistical information is expressed as numbers **statistically** *adverb*

statue *noun*
a model made of stone or metal to look like a person or animal

status *noun*
a person's status is their position or rank in relation to other people • *What is her status in the company?*

staunch *adjective*
firm and loyal • *They are the team's most staunch supporters.*

stave *noun*
a set of five lines on which music is written

stave *verb*
to stave something off is to keep something unwelcome away or delay it • *I ate a banana to stave off my hunger.*

stay *verb*
1 to stay somewhere is to continue to be there or to remain there **2** to stay somewhere or with someone is to spend time as a visitor • *We stayed in a little hotel near the sea.*

stay *noun*
a period of time spent somewhere • *We didn't have time for a long stay.*

steady *adjective* (**steadier, steadiest**)
1 not shaking or moving; firm **2** regular or constant; not changing much • *They kept up a steady pace.* **steadily** *adverb* in a steady way; gradually

steady *verb*
to steady something is to make it steady

steak *noun*
a thick slice of meat or fish

steal *verb* (**stealing, stole, stolen**)
1 to steal something is to take and keep it when it does not belong to you **2** to steal somewhere is to move there quietly without being noticed • *He stole out of the room.*

stealthy *adjective* (**stealthier, stealthiest**)
moving or doing something secretly and quietly so that you are not noticed

stealth *noun* stealth is being stealthy **stealthily** *adverb*

steam *noun*
steam is the gas or vapour that comes from boiling water **steamy** *adjective* full of steam

steam *verb*
1 to steam is to give out steam **2** to steam somewhere is to move using the power of steam • *The boat steamed down the river.* **3** to steam food is to cook it in steam • *Let's have a steamed pudding.* **to steam up** is to be covered with mist or condensation • *The windows have steamed up.*

steam engine *noun*
a railway engine driven by steam

steamer *noun*
a steamship

steamroller *noun*
a heavy vehicle with wide metal wheels, used to flatten surfaces when making roads

steamship *noun*
a ship driven by steam

steed *noun*
(*old or poetical use*) a horse

steel *noun*
steel is a strong metal made from iron and carbon **steely** *adjective* hard, cold, or grey like steel

steel *verb*
to steel yourself is to find the courage to do something difficult

steel band *noun*
a West Indian band of musicians who play instruments made from oil drums

steep *adjective*
rising or sloping sharply **steeply** *adverb* **steepness** *noun*

steeple *noun*
a church tower with a spire

steeplechase *noun*
a race across country or over hedges and fences

steer¹ *verb*
to steer a vehicle is to make it go in the direction you want

steer² *noun*
a young bull kept for its beef

steering wheel *noun*
a wheel for steering a vehicle

stem *noun*
1 the main long thin part of a plant above the ground, that the leaves and flowers grow from; a stalk **2** the thin part of a wine glass

stem *verb* (**stemming, stemmed**)
to stem from something is to start there or come from it • *The problem stems from lack of money.*

stench *noun*
a very unpleasant smell

stencil *noun*
a piece of card or metal or plastic with pieces cut out of it, used to produce a picture or design

step *noun*
1 a movement you make with your foot when you are walking, running, or dancing **2** the sound you make when you put your foot down to walk **3** each of the level surfaces on a stair or ladder **4** each of a series of actions • *The first step is to make a plan.* **to watch your step** is to be careful

step *verb* (**stepping, stepped**)
to step is to tread or walk **to step something up** is to increase it

stepchild *noun*
a child that someone's husband or wife has from an earlier marriage. A boy is a **stepson** and a girl is a **stepdaughter**.

stepfather *noun*
a man who is married to your mother but is not your own father

stepladder *noun*
a folding ladder with flat treads

stepmother *noun*
a woman who is married to your father but is not your own mother

stepping stone *noun*
stepping stones are a line of stones put in a river or stream to help people walk across

steps *plural noun*
a stepladder • *Have you seen my steps?*

stereo *noun*
a system for playing recorded music using two speakers to spread the sound

sterile *adjective*
1 clean and free from germs **2** not able to have children or young **sterility** *noun* sterility is being sterile

sterilize *verb*
1 to sterilize something is to make it free from germs **2** to sterilize a person or animal is to make them unable to bear young **sterilization** *noun* sterilization is sterilizing something or someone

sterling *noun*
sterling is British money • *Tourists paid for their meals in sterling.*

stern¹ *adjective*
strict and severe **sternly** *adverb* **sternness** *noun*

stern² noun
the back part of a ship
stethoscope noun
(say **steth**-o-skohp)
a device used by doctors
for listening to a patient's
heartbeat or breathing
stew verb
to stew food is to cook it slowly
in liquid
stew noun
a dish of meat and vegetables
cooked slowly in liquid
steward noun
1 a man whose job is to look
after the passengers on a ship
or aircraft **2** an official who
looks after the arrangements
at a public event
stewardess noun
a woman whose job is to look
after the passengers on a ship
or aircraft
stick¹ noun
1 a long thin piece of wood
2 a walking stick **3** the long
piece of wood used to hit the
ball in hockey, polo, or other
ball games **4** a long thin piece
of something • I must get a stick
of rock.
stick² verb (**sticking, stuck**)
1 to stick something sharp into
a thing is to push it in roughly
or carelessly • He stuck a pin in
her finger. **2** to stick things is to
fasten or join them **3** something
sticks when it becomes fixed
or jammed • The door keeps
sticking. **4** (informal) you can't
stick something when you
can't bear it • I can't stick it any
longer. **to stick
out** is to come out
from a surface or be
noticeable **to stick
together** is to stay
loyal to one another
to stick up for someone
(informal) is to support
them or defend them **to be
stuck with someone or
something** (informal) is to
be unable to avoid dealing
with them
sticker noun
a label or sign for
sticking on something
stick insect noun
an insect with a long
thin body that looks
like a twig
stickleback noun
a small fish with
sharp spines on its
back
sticky adjective
(**stickier, stickiest**)
able or likely to stick to

things **stickiness** noun
stiff adjective
1 not able to bend
or change its shape
easily **2** difficult
• We had a stiff
examination.
3 formal; not friendly
4 strong or severe
• There's a stiff breeze
outside. **stiffly** adverb
stiffness noun
stiffen verb
1 to stiffen
something is to make it stiff
2 to stiffen is to become stiff
stifle verb
1 to be stifled is to find it
difficult or impossible to
breathe **2** to stifle something
is to stop it happening • She
stifled a yawn.
stile noun
a set of steps or bars for people
to climb over a fence or wall
still adjective
1 not moving **2** quiet and
peaceful • In the night, the
streets are still. **3** not fizzy
stillness noun stillness is being
quiet and not moving
still adverb
1 up to this or that time • He
was still there. **2** even; yet; in a
greater amount • They wanted
still more food. **3** however
• They lost. Still, they have
another game.
still verb
to still something is to make
it still
stilts plural noun
1 a pair of poles on which you
can walk high above the
ground **2** supports for a
house built over water
stimulate verb
1 to stimulate
someone is to
make them excited
or interested **2** to stimulate
something is to encourage
it to develop • His new book
stimulated an interest in wildlife.
stimulation noun being
stimulated or excited
stimulus noun
something that encourages
a thing to develop or
produces a reaction
sting noun
1 the part of an insect
or plant that can
cause pain or a wound
2 a painful area or
wound caused by an insect
or plant
sting verb (**stinging, stung**)
1 an insect or plant stings you

when it wounds or hurts you
with a sting • She was stung
by a wasp. **2** part of your body
stings when you feel a sharp or
throbbing pain there • My back
is stinging from sunburn.
stingy adjective (**stingier,
stingiest**) (say **stin**-ji)
mean; not generous
stink noun
an unpleasant smell
stink verb (**stinking, stank** or
stunk, stunk)
to stink is to have an
unpleasant smell
stir verb
1 to stir something liquid or
soft is to move it round and
round, especially with a spoon
2 to stir is to move slightly or
start to move after sleeping or
being still • She didn't stir all
afternoon. **to stir something
up** is to excite or arouse it
• They are always stirring up
trouble.
stir noun
1 an act of stirring • Give it a stir.
2 a fuss or disturbance • The
news caused a stir.
stirrup noun
a metal loop that hangs down
on each side of a horse's saddle
to support the rider's foot
stitch noun
1 a loop of thread made in
sewing or knitting **2** a sudden
pain in your side caused by
running
stitch verb
to stitch something is to sew it
with stitches
stoat noun
an animal rather like a weasel
stock noun
1 a stock of things is an amount
of them kept ready to be sold
or used **2** stock is a collection
of farm animals, also called
livestock **3** stock is a liquid used
in cooking, made from the juices
you get by stewing meat, fish,
or vegetables **4** stock is also a
number of a company's shares
stock verb
1 a shop stocks goods when it
keeps a supply of them to sell
2 to stock a place is to provide
it with a stock of things • The
explorers stocked their base
camp with tinned food. **to stock
up** is to buy a large supply of
something
stocking noun
a piece of clothing that covers
the whole of someone's leg
and foot
stocks plural noun a wooden
framework with holes for

stick insect

a b c d e f g h i j k l m n o p q r **s** t u v w x y z

239

people's legs and arms, in which criminals were locked as a punishment in the past

stocky adjective (**stockier, stockiest**)
short and solidly built

stodgy adjective (**stodgier, stodgiest**)
thick and heavy; not easy to digest • *The pudding's very stodgy.*

stoke verb
to stoke a furnace or fire is to add fuel to it

stomach noun
1 the part of your body where food starts to be digested **2** the front part of your body that contains your stomach; your abdomen

stomach verb
to stomach something is to tolerate it or put up with it • *I can't stomach their awful jokes.*

stone noun (**stones** or, for the unit of weight, **stone**)
1 stone is the hard solid mineral of which rocks are made **2** a stone is a piece of this mineral **3** a stone is also a jewel **4** a stone is also the hard seed in the middle of some fruits, such as a cherry, plum, or peach **5** a stone is also a unit of weight equal to 14 pounds or about 6.35 kilograms • *She weighs 6 stone.*

stone verb
1 to stone someone is to throw stones at them **2** to stone fruit is to take the stones out of it

stone-deaf adjective
completely deaf

stony adjective (**stonier, stoniest**)
1 stony ground is full of stones **2** hard like stone **3** unfriendly or hostile • *Our question was met by a stony silence.*

stool noun
a small seat without a back

stoop verb
1 to stoop is to bend your body forwards and downwards **2** to stoop to doing something is to lower your standards of behaviour • *I didn't think he'd stoop to cheating.*

stop verb (**stopping, stopped**)
1 to stop something is to finish doing it, or make it finish **2** to stop is to be no longer moving or working or to come to an end **3** to stop something is to prevent it happening or continuing • *I must go out and stop that noise.* **4** to stop a hole

or gap, or stop it up, is to fill it **5** to stop at a place is to stay there briefly

stop noun
1 when something stops or ends • *She brought the car to a stop.* **2** a place where a bus or train stops regularly

stopper noun
something that fits into the top of a bottle or jar to close it

stopwatch noun
a watch that you can start or stop, used for timing races

storage noun
storage is the storing of things

store verb
to store things is to keep them until they are needed

store noun
1 a place where things are stored **2** a supply of things kept for future use **3** a shop, especially a large one **to be in store** is to be waiting to happen soon • *There is a treat in store for you.*

storey noun (**storeys**)
one whole floor of a building

stork noun
a large bird with long legs and a long beak

storm noun
1 a period of bad weather with strong winds, rain or snow, and often thunder and lightning **2** a violent attack or outburst • *There was a storm of protest.*

stork

storm verb
1 to storm is to move or shout angrily • *He stormed out of the room.* **2** soldiers or police storm a place when they attack it suddenly • *They stormed the castle.*

stormy adjective (**stormier, stormiest**)
1 likely to end in a storm • *The weather is stormy today.* **2** loud and angry • *We had a stormy meeting.*

story noun (**stories**)
1 an account of real or imaginary events **2** (*informal*) a lie • *Don't tell stories!*

stout adjective
1 rather fat **2** thick and strong • *She carried a stout stick.*

3 brave • *The defenders put up a stout resistance.* **stoutly** adverb **stoutness** noun

stove noun
a device that produces heat for warming a room or cooking

stow verb
to stow something is to pack it or store it away **to stow away** is to hide on a ship or aircraft so that you can travel without paying

stowaway noun
someone who stows away on a ship or aircraft

straddle verb
1 to straddle something is to sit or stand with your legs either side of it **2** to straddle something is also to be built across it • *A long bridge straddles the river.*

straggle verb
1 to straggle is to walk too slowly and not keep up with the rest of a group **2** to straggle is also to grow or move in an untidy way • *Brambles straggled across the path.*

straggler noun someone who does not keep up with the rest of a group **straggly** adjective growing or hanging untidily

straight adjective
1 going continuously in one direction; not curving or bending **2** level • *Is this picture straight?* **3** tidy; in proper order **4** honest or frank • *Give me a straight answer.*

straight adverb **1** in a straight line • *Go straight on, then turn left.* **2** at once; directly • *I came straight here.*

straightaway adverb
immediately; at once

straighten verb
1 to straighten something is to make it straight **2** to straighten is to become straight

straightforward adjective
1 easy to understand or do; not complicated **2** honest or frank

strain verb
1 to strain something is to stretch it or push it or pull it hard or too hard **2** to strain is to make a great effort to do something **3** to strain liquid is to put it through a sieve to take out any lumps or other things in it

strain noun
1 the strain on something is when it is stretched or pulled too hard • *The rope broke under*

the strain. **2** a strain is an injury caused by straining **3** strain is the effect on someone of too much work or worry

strait *noun*
a narrow stretch of water connecting two seas

strand *noun*
1 each of the threads or wires twisted together to make a rope or cable **2** a lock of hair

stranded *adjective*
1 left on sand or rocks in shallow water • *We could see a stranded ship.* **2** left in a difficult or lonely position • *They were stranded in the desert.*

strange *adjective*
1 unusual or surprising **2** not known or experienced before **strangely** *adverb* in a strange way • *The house was strangely quiet.* **strangeness** *noun*

stranger *noun*
1 a person you do not know **2** a person who is in a place they do not know

strangle *verb*
to strangle someone is to kill them by pressing their throat so they can't breathe

strap *noun*
a flat strip of leather or cloth or plastic for fastening things together or holding them in place

strap *verb* (**strapping, strapped**)
to strap something is to fasten it with a strap or straps

strategy *noun* (**strategies**)
1 a strategy is a plan to achieve or win something **2** strategy is planning a war or military campaign **strategic** *adjective* done as part of a plan to achieve or win something

stratum *noun* (**strata**)
(say **strah**-tum)
a layer or level • *You can see several strata of rock in the cliffs.*

straw *noun*
1 straw is dry cut stalks of corn **2** a straw is a narrow tube that you can drink through

strawberry *noun* (**strawberries**)
a small red juicy fruit, with its

seeds on the outside

stray *verb*
to stray is to wander or become lost

stray *adjective*
1 wandering around lost • *We found a stray cat.* **2** out of place; separated from all the others • *a stray hair*

stray *noun*
a stray dog or cat

streak *noun*
1 a long thin line or mark **2** a streak of something is a trace or sign of it • *He has a cruel streak.* **streaky** *adjective* marked with streaks

streak *verb*
1 to streak something is to mark it with streaks **2** to streak somewhere is to move there very quickly

stream *noun*
1 a narrow river or brook **2** a flow of liquid **3** a number of things moving in the same direction, such as traffic **4** a group in a school containing children of similar ability

stream *verb*
1 to stream is to move in a strong or fast flow • *Traffic streamed across the junction.* **2** to stream is also to produce a flow of liquid • *Blood was streaming from her cut hand.*

streamer *noun*
a long strip of paper or ribbon

streamlined *adjective*
a streamlined vehicle or object has a smooth shape that helps it to move easily through air or water

street *noun*
a road with houses beside it in a city or town

strength *noun*
1 strength is how strong a person or thing is **2** a person's strengths are their good points or the things they are good at • *Patience is your greatest strength.*

strengthen *verb*
1 to strengthen something or someone is to make them stronger **2** to strengthen is to become stronger

strenuous *adjective*
needing or using great effort and determination **strenuously** *adverb*

stress *noun*
1 a stress is a force or pressure that pulls or pushes or twists something **2** stress is the effect on someone of too much work

or worry or pressure **3** stress is also the extra loudness or emphasis you give to a word or part of a word when you say it

stress *verb*
1 to stress a word or part of a word is to pronounce it with extra emphasis **2** to stress a point or idea is to emphasize it • *I must stress that this is an unusual problem.*

stretch *verb*
1 to stretch something is to pull it so that it becomes longer or wider **2** something stretches when it becomes longer or wider when it is pulled **3** you stretch, or stretch out, when you reach out with your arms or extend your arms and legs fully **4** to stretch somewhere is to extend or continue there • *The wall stretches all the way round the park.*

stretch *noun*
1 the action of stretching something • *I got up and had a good stretch.* **2** a continuous period of time or area of land or water

stretcher *noun*
a framework like a light folding bed with handles at each end, for carrying a sick or injured person

strew *verb* (**strewing, strewed, strewn** or **strewed**)
to strew things is to scatter them over a surface • *Flowers were strewn over the path.*

strict *adjective*
1 demanding that people obey rules and behave well • *The teachers are all fairly strict.* **2** complete or exact • *He's not really a hero in the strict sense of the word.* **strictly** *adverb* completely or exactly • *Taking photographs here is strictly forbidden.*

stride *verb* (**striding, strode, stridden**)
to stride is to walk with long steps

stride *noun*
a long step you take when walking or running

strike *verb* (**striking, struck**)
1 to strike something or someone is to hit them **2** to strike people or a place is to attack them suddenly • *A hurricane struck the village.* **3** to strike a match is to light it

streamers

a b c d e f g h i j k l m n o p q r s t u v w x y z

by rubbing it against something rough **4** a clock strikes (for example) seven when it rings seven chimes at seven o'clock **5** workers strike when they stop working as a protest **6** to strike oil or gold is to find it by drilling or mining **7** to strike someone in some way is to make them think that way • *The film struck me as rather violent.*

strike *noun*
1 a hit **2** when workers refuse to work, as a way of making a protest **to go on strike** is to stop working as a protest

striker *noun*
1 a worker who is on strike **2** in football, an attacking player who tries to score goals

striking *adjective*
so impressive, interesting, or attractive that you can't help noticing it

string *noun*
1 string is thin rope or cord for tying things; a string is a piece of thin rope **2** a string is a piece of stretched wire or nylon used in a musical instrument to make sounds **3** a string of things is a line or series of them • *There was a string of buses along the High Street.*

string *verb* (**stringing, strung**)
1 to string something is to hang it on a string **2** to string pearls or beads is to thread them on a string **3** to string a racket or musical instrument is to put strings on it

stringed *adjective*
in music, stringed instruments are ones that have strings, especially members of the violin family

strings *plural noun*
the stringed instruments in an orchestra

stringy *adjective* (**stringier, stringiest**)
1 long and thin like string **2** stringy meat contains tough fibres

strip¹ *verb* (**stripping, stripped**)
1 to strip something is to take a covering off it **2** to strip is to take all your clothes off **3** to strip someone of something is to take it away from them

strip¹ *noun*
the special outfit worn by a sports team

strip² *noun*
a long narrow piece of something

strip cartoon *noun*
a series of drawings telling a story; a comic strip

stripe *noun*
a long narrow band of colour
striped or **stripy** *adjective* having stripes

strive *verb* (**striving, strove, striven**)
to strive to do something is to try hard to do it

strobe *noun*
a light that flickers on and off continuously

stroke¹ *noun*
1 a hit or movement made by swinging your arm **2** a swimming style **3** a line drawn by a pen or brush **4** a sudden illness that often causes someone to be paralysed

stroke² *verb*
to stroke something is to move your hand gently along it

stroll *verb*
to stroll is to walk slowly

stroll *noun*
a short leisurely walk

strong *adjective*
1 having great power, energy, or effect **2** not easily broken or damaged • *The gate was held by a strong chain.* **3** having a lot of flavour or smell • *Do you like your tea strong?*

stronghold *noun*
a fortress or other place that is well defended

strongly *adverb*
1 in a strong way; with strength • *They fought back strongly.* **2** very much • *The room smelt strongly of perfume.*

structure *noun*
1 a structure is something that has been built or put together **2** a thing's structure is the way that it is built or made
structural *adjective* to do with the way that something is built or made

struggle *verb*
1 to struggle is to move your body about violently while you are fighting or trying to get free **2** to struggle to do something is to make strong efforts to do it

struggle *noun*
1 fighting or trying to get free **2** a great effort

strum *verb* (**strumming, strummed**)
to strum a guitar is to sound it by running your finger across its strings

strut *verb* (**strutting, strutted**)
to strut is to walk proudly or stiffly

strut *noun*
1 a strutting walk **2** a bar of wood or metal that strengthens a framework

stub *verb* (**stubbing, stubbed**)
you stub your toe when you knock it against something hard

stub *noun*
a short piece of something left after the rest has been used up or worn down

stubble *noun*
1 stubble is the short stalks of corn left in the ground after a harvest **2** stubble is also the short stiff hairs growing on a man's chin when he has not shaved

stubborn *adjective*
not willing to change your ideas or ways; obstinate
stubbornly *adverb*
stubbornness *noun*

stuck *adjective*
unable to move or make progress • *Is anyone stuck?*

stuck-up *adjective*
(*informal*) unpleasantly proud or snobbish

stud *noun*
a small metal button or knob fixed into something

student *noun*
someone who studies, especially at a college or university

studio *noun*
1 a place where radio or television broadcasts are made **2** a place where cinema or television films are made **3** the room where an artist or photographer works

studious *adjective*
fond of studying; studying hard
studiously *adverb*

study *verb* (**studies, studying, studied**)
1 to study is to spend time learning about something **2** to study something is to look at it carefully

study *noun* (**studies**)
1 study is the process of studying **2** a study is a room used for studying or writing

stuff *noun*
1 stuff is a substance or material • *What's this stuff at the bottom of the glass?* **2** stuff is also a group of things or a person's possessions • *Will you move your stuff off the table?*

stuff *verb*
1 to stuff something is to fill it tightly, especially with stuffing • *She stuffed the turkey.* **2** to stuff one thing inside another is to push it in

carelessly • *He stuffed the paper into his pocket.*

stuffing *noun*
  1 stuffing is material used to fill the inside of something **2** stuffing is also a savoury mixture you put into meat or poultry before cooking it

stuffy *adjective* (**stuffier, stuffiest**)
  1 a stuffy room is badly ventilated, without enough fresh air **2** formal and boring **stuffiness** *noun*

stumble *verb*
  1 to stumble is to lose your balance or fall over something **2** to stumble when you are speaking is to make mistakes or hesitate **to stumble across something or stumble on something** is to find it by chance

stump *noun*
  1 the bottom of a tree trunk left in the ground when the tree has fallen or been cut down **2** (*in cricket*) each of the three upright sticks of a wicket

stump *verb*
  1 (*in cricket*) to stump the person batting is to get them out by touching the stumps with the ball when they are not standing in the correct place **2** something stumps you when it is too difficult for you • *The last question stumped everyone.*

stun *verb* (**stunning, stunned**)
  1 to stun someone is to knock them unconscious **2** something stuns you when it shocks or confuses you • *They were stunned by the news.*

stumps

stunt *noun*
  1 something daring or dangerous done in a film or as part of a performance **2** something unusual done to attract publicity or attention

stupendous *adjective*
  amazing; tremendous

stupid *adjective*
  not sensible; not clever or thoughtful **stupidity** *noun* stupidity is being stupid **stupidly** *adverb*

sturdy *adjective* (**sturdier, sturdiest**)
  strong and solid **sturdily** *adverb* **sturdiness** *noun*

stutter *verb*
  to stutter is to keep repeating the sounds at the beginning of words

stutter *noun*
  a habit of stuttering

sty[1] *noun* (**sties**)
  a pigsty

sty[2] or **stye** *noun* (**sties** or **styes**)
  a sore swelling on your eyelid

style *noun*
  1 a style is the way that something is done, made, said, or written **2** style is being smart and elegant

stylish *adjective*
  fashionable and smart **stylishly** *adverb*

subcontinent *noun*
  a large area of land that forms part of a continent • *the Indian subcontinent*

subdue *verb*
  1 to subdue someone is to overcome them or bring them under control **2** to subdue a person or animal is to make them quieter or gentler

subject *noun* (*say* **sub**-jikt)
  1 the person or thing that is being talked or written about **2** something that you can study **3** (*in grammar*) the person or thing that is doing the action stated by the verb in a sentence, for example *dog* in the sentence *The dog chewed a bone.* **4** someone who must obey the laws of a particular ruler or government

subject *verb* (*say* sub-**jekt**)
  to subject someone to something is to make them experience or suffer it • *They subjected him to a string of questions.*

submarine *noun*
  a type of ship that can travel under water

submerge *verb*
  1 to submerge is to go under water **2** to submerge something

or someone is to put them under water

submit *verb* (**submitting, submitted**)
  1 to submit to someone is to give in to them or agree to obey them **2** to submit something to someone is to hand it in or offer it to be judged or considered

submission *noun* submission is submitting to someone

submissive *adjective* willing to obey

subscribe *verb*
  to subscribe to something is to pay money to receive it regularly or to be a member of a club or society

subscriber *noun* someone who subscribes to something

subscription *noun*
  money you pay to receive something regularly or to be a member of a club or society

subsequent *adjective*
  coming later or after something else • *Subsequent events proved that she was right.*

subsequently *adverb* later

subside *verb*
  1 to subside is to sink • *After a few days the flood water began to subside.* **2** to subside is also to become quiet or normal • *The noise subsided after midnight.*

subsidence *noun* when a building or piece of land sinks into the ground

subsidy *noun* (**subsidies**)
  money paid to keep prices low or to support an industry or activity

subsidize *verb*
  to subsidize someone or something is to help pay the cost of something

substance *noun*
  something that you can touch or see; what something is made of

substantial *adjective*
  1 large or important **2** strong and solid **substantially** *adverb* mostly • *This story is substantially true.*

substitute *verb*
  to substitute one thing or person for another is to use the first one instead of the second • *In this recipe you can substitute oil for butter.* **substitution** *noun* when one thing or person is used instead of another

substitute *noun*
  a person or thing that is used instead of another

subtle *adjective* (*say* **sut**-el)
  1 slight and delicate • *This soup has a subtle flavour.* **2** clever but not obvious • *Your jokes are too*

subtle for me. **subtly** adverb in a subtle way **subtlety** noun subtlety is being subtle or delicate

subtract verb
to subtract one amount from another is to take it away • If you subtract 2 from 7, you get 5. **subtraction** noun the process of taking one amount from another

suburb noun
an area of houses on the edge of a city or large town **suburban** noun a suburban area or street is in a suburb

subway noun
an underground passage for pedestrians

succeed verb
1 to succeed is to do or get what you wanted or intended **2** to succeed someone is to be the next person to do what they did, especially to be king or queen

success noun
1 success is doing or getting what you wanted or intended **2** a success is a person or thing that does well • The plan was a great success.

successful adjective
having success; doing well **successfully** adverb

succession noun
1 a number of people or things coming one after another • The cooks brought in a succession of dishes. **2** the right to be the next person to do something, especially becoming king or queen

successor noun
someone who has a position or does a job after someone else • The headteacher retired and handed over to her successor.

such adjective
1 of that kind; of the same kind • Try not to think about such things. **2** so great or so much • That was such fun!

suck verb
1 to suck liquid or air is to take it in through your mouth • I sucked milk through a straw. **2** to suck something is to move it around inside your mouth so that you can taste it • She was sucking a sweet. **3** to suck something is also to draw it in or absorb it • The boat was sucked into the whirlpool. • He sucked in his cheeks.

suck noun
the action of sucking

suction noun
suction is the process of drawing in liquid or air by creating a vacuum • Vacuum cleaners work by suction.

sudden adjective
happening or done quickly and unexpectedly **suddenness** noun

suddenly adverb
quickly and unexpectedly

suds plural noun
froth on soapy water

sue verb
to sue someone is to start a claim in a lawcourt to get money from them

suede noun (say swayd)
suede is leather with one side soft and velvety

suffer verb
1 to suffer is to feel pain or misery **2** to suffer something unpleasant is to have to put up with it

suffering noun
suffering is pain or misery

sufficient adjective
enough • Have we sufficient food? **sufficiently** adverb to a sufficient degree

suffix noun
a word or syllable joined to the end of a word to change or add to its meaning, as in forget*ful*, lion*ess*, and rust*y*

suffocate verb
1 to suffocate is to suffer or die because you cannot breathe **2** to suffocate someone is to kill them by stopping them breathing **suffocation** noun suffocation is when someone dies because they cannot breathe

sugar noun
sugar is a sweet food obtained from the juices of various plants, such as sugar beet or sugar cane **sugary** adjective full of sugar; sweet

suggest verb
1 to suggest something is to mention it as an idea or possibility **2** to suggest something is also to give an idea or impression of something • Your smile suggests that you agree with me.

suggestion noun
something that you mention to someone as an idea or possibility

suicide noun
suicide is killing yourself deliberately • He committed suicide. **suicidal** adjective wanting to commit suicide

suit noun
1 a matching set of jacket and trousers or jacket and skirt, that are meant to be worn together **2** a set of clothing for a particular activity • He wore a diving suit. **3** each of the four sets in a pack of playing cards: spades, hearts, diamonds, and clubs

suit verb
1 to suit someone or something is to be suitable or convenient for them • What time would suit you? **2** a piece of clothing or hairstyle suits you when it looks good on you

suitable adjective
satisfactory or right for a particular person, purpose, or occasion **suitability** noun how suitable something is **suitably** adverb

suitcase noun
a container with a lid and a handle, for carrying your clothes and other things when you are travelling

suite noun (say sweet)
1 a set of rooms in a hotel **2** a set of matching furniture

suitor noun
a man who wants to marry a particular woman

sulk verb
to sulk is to be silent and bad-tempered because you are not pleased

sulky adjective (**sulkier, sulkiest**)
sulking or moody **sulkily** adverb **sulkiness** noun

sullen adjective
silent and moody **sullenly** adverb **sullenness** noun

sulphur noun Ⓢ
sulphur is a yellow chemical used in industry and medicine

sultan noun
the ruler of certain Muslim countries

sultana noun
a raisin without seeds

sum noun
1 a total, or the amount you get when you add numbers together **2** a problem in arithmetic **3** an amount of money

sum verb (**summing, summed**)
to sum up is to give a summary at the end of a discussion or talk

summarize verb
to summarize something is to give a short statement of its main points

summary noun (**summaries**)
a short statement of the main points of something that someone has said or written

summer *noun*
the warm season between
spring and autumn
summery *adjective*
like summer, or
suitable for summer
summertime *noun*
summertime is the
season of summer
summit *noun*
1 the top of a mountain or hill
2 a meeting between the
leaders of powerful countries
summon *verb*
to summon someone is to order
them to come or appear
sun *noun*
1 the star round which the
earth travels, and from which
it gets warmth and light
2 warmth and light from the
sun • *Shall we sit in the sun?*
sun *verb* (**sunning, sunned**)
to sun yourself is to warm
yourself in the sun
sunbathe *verb*
to sunbathe is to sit or lie in the
sun to get a suntan
sunburn *noun*
sunburn is the redness of the
skin someone gets if they are in
the sun for too long **sunburned**
or **sunburnt** *adjective* affected
by sunburn
sundae *noun* (*say* **sun**-day)
a mixture of ice cream with
fruit, nuts, and cream
Sunday *noun*
the first day of the week
sundial *noun*
a device that shows the
time by a shadow
made by the sun
sunflower *noun*
a tall flower
with a large
round yellow
head
sunglasses
plural noun
dark glasses
you wear to
protect your
eyes from
strong sunlight   sunflowers
sunlight *noun*
sunlight is light from the sun
sunlit *adjective*
lit by sunlight
sunny *adjective* (**sunnier,
sunniest**)
1 having a lot of sunshine
• *It's a sunny day.* **2** full of
sunshine • *What a sunny
room.*
sunrise *noun*
sunrise is the time when the sun
first appears; dawn • *They left
at sunrise.*

sunset *noun*
sunset is the time
when the sun sets
sunshade *noun*
a parasol or other device to
protect people from the sun
sunshine *noun*
sunshine is warmth and light
that come from the sun
sunstroke *noun*
sunstroke is an illness caused
by being in the sun for too long
suntan *noun*
a brown colour of the skin
caused by the sun **suntanned**
adjective having a suntan
super *adjective*
(*informal*) excellent or very
good
superb *adjective*
magnificent or excellent
superbly *adverb*
superficial *adjective*
1 on the surface • *It's only
a superficial cut.* **2** not deep
or thorough • *His knowledge
of French is fairly superficial.*
superficially *adverb*
superintendent *noun*
1 someone who is in charge
2 a police officer above the
rank of inspector
superior *adjective*
1 higher or more important
than someone else **2** better
than another person or thing
3 showing that you think
you are better than other
people **superiority** *noun* being
better than something else;
behaviour that shows you
think you are better than
other people
superior *noun*
someone of higher
rank or position than
another person
supermarket *noun*
a large self-service
shop that sells food
and other goods
supernatural
adjective
not belonging to
the natural world
or having a natural
explanation
supersonic *adjective*
faster than the speed of sound
superstition *noun*
a belief or action that is not
based on reason or evidence
• *It is a superstition that 13 is
an unlucky number.*
superstitious *adjective*
believing in superstitions
supervise *verb*
to supervise someone or
something is to be in charge

of them **supervision** *noun*
being in charge of someone
or something **supervisor**
noun someone who
supervises you
supper *noun*
a meal or snack that you eat
in the evening
supple *adjective*
able to bend easily; flexible,
not stiff **suppleness** *noun*
suppleness is being supple
supplement *noun*
1 something added as an
extra **2** an extra section
added to a book or newspaper
supplementary *adjective*
added as an extra
supply *verb*
1 to supply something is to
give or sell it to people who
need it **2** to supply someone is
to give them what they need
supplier *noun* someone who
supplies something
supply *noun*
1 a supply of something is an
amount of it kept ready to be
used when needed • *We keep a
supply of paper in the cupboard.*
2 supplies are food, medicines,
or equipment needed by an
army or an expedition
• *The truck was carrying
medical supplies.*
support *verb*
1 to support something is to
hold it so that it does not fall
down **2** to support someone or
something is to give them help
or encouragement
3 to support a sports team is to
like them and want them to do
well • *Which football team do
you support?*
support *noun*
1 support is help or
encouragement • *You can rely
on my support.* **2** something
that holds another thing up
supporter *noun*
someone who gives support,
especially to a sports team
suppose *verb*
to suppose something is to
think that it is likely or true **to
be supposed to do something**
is to have to do it as an order
or duty
suppress *verb*
to suppress something is
to keep it hidden or stop it
happening • *He managed to
suppress a smile.*
suppression *noun* suppression
is suppressing something
supreme *adjective*
highest or greatest; most
important **supremacy** *noun*

a
i
j
k
l
m
n
o
p
q
r
s
t
u
v
w
x
y
z

having more power or a higher position than anyone else
supremely *adverb* extremely
sure *adjective*
1 confident about something; having no doubts • *Are you sure you locked the door?*
2 very likely to happen or do something • *Don't worry, we're sure to win.* 3 completely true or known • *One thing is sure: she is not here at the moment.*
4 reliable • *Visiting places is a sure way of getting to know them.* **to make sure of something** is to find out that it is true or right
sure *adverb*
(*informal*) certainly; of course • *Sure I'll come with you.*
surely *adverb*
1 certainly or definitely
2 it must be true; I feel sure • *Surely I met you last year.*
surf *noun*
surf is the white foam of waves breaking on rocks or the seashore
surf *verb*
1 to surf is to go surfing
2 to surf the Internet is to browse through it
surface *noun*
1 the outside of something
2 each of the sides of something, especially the top part
surface *verb*
1 to surface is to come up to the surface from under water • *The submarine slowly surfaced.*
2 to surface a road or path is to give it a hard covering layer
surfboard *noun*
a board used in surfing
surfing *noun*
surfing is the sport of balancing yourself on a board that is carried towards the seashore by the waves **surfer** *noun* someone who goes surfing

surge *verb*
to surge is to move forwards or upwards like waves
surge *noun*
a sudden rush forward or upward
surgeon *noun*
a doctor who deals with disease or injury by cutting or repairing the affected parts of the body
surgery *noun* (**surgeries**)
1 a surgery is a building or room where a doctor or dentist sees patients 2 surgery is the time when patients can see a doctor or dentist • *Surgery will close at 6 o'clock today.*
3 surgery is also the work of a surgeon
surgical *adjective*
to do with a surgeon or surgery
surgically *adverb* by means of surgery
surname *noun*
your last name, which you share with other members of your family
surpass *verb*
to surpass someone is to do better or be better than them
surplus *noun*
an amount left over after you have spent or used what you need
surprise *noun*
1 a surprise is something that you did not expect 2 surprise is the feeling you have when something unexpected happens
surprise *verb*
1 to surprise someone is to be a surprise to them 2 to surprise someone is also to catch or attack them unexpectedly
surrender *verb*
1 to surrender to someone is to stop fighting them and admit that you have been beaten
2 to surrender something to someone is to hand it over to them
surrender *noun*
when someone surrenders
surround *verb*
to surround someone or something is to be or come all round them
surroundings *plural noun*
the things or conditions around a person or place
survey *noun* (*say* **ser**-vay)
1 a general look at a topic or activity 2 a detailed inspection or examination of a building or area
survey *verb* (*say* ser-**vay**)
to survey something is to inspect it or make a survey of it

surveyor *noun*
someone whose job is to survey buildings and land
survive *verb*
1 to survive is to stay alive 2 to survive an accident or disaster is to remain alive in spite of it • *Only two people survived the car crash.* 3 to survive someone is to continue living after they have died **survival** *noun* survival is staying alive
survivor *noun* someone who survives, especially after an accident or disaster
suspect *verb* (*say* su-**spekt**)
1 to suspect something unwelcome is to think that it is likely or possible 2 to suspect someone is to think that they have done something wrong or are not to be trusted
suspect *noun* (*say* **sus**-pekt)
someone who is thought to have done something wrong
suspend *verb*
1 to suspend something that is happening is to stop it for a time 2 to suspend someone is to take away their job or position for a time • *He was suspended from the team for bad behaviour.*
3 to suspend something is to hang it up
suspense *noun*
suspense is an anxious or uncertain feeling you have while you are waiting for something to happen or for news about something • *Don't keep us in suspense – who won?*
suspension *noun*
1 suspension is suspending something or someone 2 a vehicle's suspension is the set of springs and other devices that make the ride more comfortable
suspension bridge *noun*
a bridge supported by cables
suspicion *noun*
1 suspicion is feeling that someone has done something wrong or cannot be trusted
2 a suspicion is a slight or uncertain feeling about something or someone
suspicious *adjective*
1 making you suspect someone or something • *There are suspicious footprints along the path.* 2 suspecting someone or something • *I'm suspicious about what happened.*
suspiciously *adverb*
sustain *verb*
1 to sustain something is to keep it going • *It's difficult to sustain such an effort.*

2 to sustain someone is to give them energy or strength • *We'd packed sandwiches to sustain us on our walk.*

swagger *verb*
to walk or behave in a conceited way

swallow[1] *verb*
to swallow something is to make it go down your throat **to swallow something up** is to cover it or make it disappear • *He was soon swallowed up by the darkness.*

swallow[2] *noun*
a small bird with a forked tail and pointed wings

swamp *verb*
1 to swamp something is to flood it **2** to be swamped is to be overwhelmed with a large number of things • *They have been swamped with complaints.*

swamp *noun*
a marsh **swampy** *adjective* full of swamps

swan *noun*
a large white water bird with a long neck and powerful wings

swap *verb* (**swapping, swapped**)
(*informal*) to swap something is to exchange one thing for another • *After the game they swapped jerseys.*

swap *noun*
1 an act of swapping • *Let's do a swap.* **2** something you swap for something else

swarm *noun*
a large number of bees or other insects flying or moving about together

swarm *verb*
1 bees or other insects swarm when they move in a swarm **2** to be swarming is to be crowded with people • *The town is swarming with tourists in summer.*

swarm

swat *verb* (**swatting, swatted**) (*say* swot)
to swat a fly or other insect is to hit or crush it **swatter** *noun* a device for swatting flies

sway *verb*
to sway is to move gently from side to side

swear *verb* (**swearing, swore, sworn**)
1 to swear is to make a solemn

promise • *She swore to tell the truth.* **2** to swear someone to secrecy is to make them promise not to tell anyone **3** to swear is also to use very rude or offensive words

swear word *noun*
a word that is very rude or offensive, used especially by someone who is very angry

sweat *verb* (*say* swet)
you sweat when you give off moisture through the pores of your skin, especially when you are hot or doing exercise

sweat *noun* (*say* swet)
sweat is moisture that comes out of your skin when you sweat **sweaty** *adjective* covered or damp with sweat

sweater *noun* (*say* **swet**-er)
a jumper or pullover

sweatshirt *noun*
a thick cotton jersey

swede *noun*
a large kind of turnip with purple skin and yellow flesh

sweep *verb* (**sweeping, swept**)
1 to sweep a room or floor is to clean or clear it with a broom or brush • *He swept the floor.* **2** to sweep something away is to move or change it quickly • *The flood has swept away the bridge.* **3** to sweep somewhere is to go there swiftly or grandly • *She swept out of the room.*

sweeper *noun* a machine for sweeping floors

sweep *noun*
1 a sweeping action or movement • *Give this room a sweep.* **2** someone who cleans out a chimney

sweet *adjective*
1 tasting of sugar or honey **2** very pleasant • *There was a sweet smell in the room.* **3** charming or delightful • *What a sweet little cottage.* **sweetly** *adverb* in a very pleasant way • *She smiled sweetly at him.* **sweetness** *noun* sweetness is tasting sweet

sweet *noun*
1 a small piece of sweet food made from sugar or chocolate **2** a pudding; the sweet course in a meal

sweetcorn *noun*
sweetcorn is the juicy yellow seeds of maize

sweeten *verb*
to sweeten something is to make it sweet

sweetener *noun* something used instead of sugar to make food or drink taste sweeter

sweetheart *noun*
a person you love very much

swell *verb* (**swelling, swelled, swollen** or **swelled**)
to swell is to get bigger or louder **swollen** *adjective* having swelled a lot • *My wrist is still very swollen where I bumped it.*

swell *noun*
the rise and fall of the sea's surface

swelling *noun*
a swollen place on your body

swelter *verb*
to swelter is to be uncomfortably hot

swerve *verb*
to swerve is to move suddenly to one side • *The car swerved to avoid the cyclist.*

swerve *noun*
a swerving movement

swift *adjective*
quick; moving quickly and easily **swiftly** *adverb* quickly **swiftness** *noun*

swift *noun*
a small bird rather like a swallow

swill *verb*
to swill something is to rinse or flush it

swill *noun*
swill is a sloppy mixture of waste food given to pigs

swim *verb* (**swimming, swam, swum**)
1 to swim is to move yourself through the water or to be in the water for pleasure **2** to swim a stretch of water is to cross it by swimming • *She has swum the Channel.* **3** to be swimming in liquid or with liquid is to be covered in it or full of it • *Their eyes were swimming with tears.* **4** your head swims when you feel dizzy

swim *noun*
a spell of swimming • *Let's go for a swim.*

swimmer *noun*
someone who swims • *Are you a good swimmer?*

swimming bath or **swimming pool** *noun*
a specially built pool with water for people to swim in

swimming costume *noun*
a piece of clothing for swimming in

swimsuit *noun*
a one-piece swimming costume

a b c d e f g h i j k l m n o p q r s t u v w x y z

swindle *verb*
to swindle someone is to get money or goods from them dishonestly **swindler** *noun* someone who swindles people

swindle *noun*
a trick to swindle someone

swine *noun* (**swine** or **swines**)
a pig

swing *verb* (**swinging, swung**)
1 to swing is to move to and fro or in a curve **2** to swing something is to turn it quickly or suddenly • *He swung the car round to avoid the bus.*

swing *noun*
1 a swinging movement • *He took a swing at the ball.* **2** a seat hung on chains or ropes so that it can move backwards and forwards **to be in full swing** is to be full of activity or working fully

swipe *verb*
1 to swipe someone or something is to give them a hard hit **2** (*informal*) to swipe something is to steal it **3** to swipe a credit card is to pass it through a special reading device when you make a payment

swipe *noun*
a hard hit

swirl *verb*
to swirl is to move around quickly in circles; to swirl something is to make it do this • *The water swirled down the plug hole.*

swirl *noun*
a swirling movement

swish *verb*
to swish is to make a hissing or rustling sound

swish *noun*
a swishing sound

switch *noun*
1 a device that you press or turn to start or stop something working, especially by electricity **2** a sudden change of opinion or methods

switch *verb*
1 to switch a device on or off is to use a switch to make it work or stop working • *Shall I switch the light on?* **2** to switch something is to change it suddenly

switchboard *noun*
a place in a large building or organization where telephone calls are connected

swivel *verb* (**swivelling, swivelled**)
to swivel is to turn round

swoop *verb*
1 to swoop is to dive or come

down suddenly • *The eagle swooped down on its prey.* **2** to swoop is also to make a sudden attack or raid

swoop *noun*
a sudden dive or attack

swop *verb* (**swopping, swopped**)
(*informal*) to swap

sword *noun* (*say* sord)
a weapon with a long pointed blade fixed in a handle

swot *verb*
(*informal*) to swot is to study hard

swot *noun*
(*informal*) someone who swots

sycamore *noun*
a tall tree with winged seeds

syllable *noun*
a word or part of a word that has one separate sound when you say it • *'Cat' has one syllable, 'el-e-phant' has three syllables.*

syllabus *noun* (*say* sil-a-bus)
a list of things to be studied by a class or for an examination

symbol *noun*
1 a mark or sign with a special meaning **2** a thing that stands for something • *The crescent is a symbol of Islam.*

symbolic *adjective*
acting as a symbol of something **symbolically** *adverb*

symmetrical *adjective* (*say* sim-**et**-rik-al)
having two halves which are exactly the same but the opposite way round • *Wheels and butterflies are symmetrical.* **symmetrically** *adverb* in a symmetrical way **symmetry** *noun* symmetry is the quality of being symmetrical

sympathetic *adjective*
feeling sympathy or understanding for someone **sympathetically** *adverb* in a way that shows you feel sympathy for someone • *She smiled at me sympathetically.*

sympathize *verb*
to sympathize with someone is to show or feel sympathy for them

sympathy *noun* (**sympathies**)
1 sympathy is the sharing or understanding of other people's feelings or opinions **2** sympathy is also the feeling of being sorry for someone's unhappiness or suffering

symphony *noun* (**symphonies**)
a long piece of music for an orchestra **symphonic** *adjective* to do with a symphony

symptom *noun*
something wrong with you that is a sign that you have an illness • *Red spots are a symptom of measles.*

synagogue *noun* (*say* **sin**-a-gog)
a building where Jewish people meet to worship

WORD ORIGIN

The word **synagogue** comes from a Greek word *synagoge* meaning 'assembly'.

synonym *noun* (*say* **sin**-o-nim)
a word that means the same or nearly the same as another word, such as *big* and *large* **synonymous** *adjective* two words are synonymous when they have the same, or nearly the same, meaning

synthesizer *noun*
an electronic musical instrument that can make many different sounds

synthetic *adjective*
artificially made; not natural **synthetically** *adverb*

syringe *noun*
a device with a tube and a long needle, used for sucking in liquid and giving injections

syrup *noun*
a thick sweet liquid **syrupy** *adjective* thick and sticky like syrup

system *noun*
1 a set of parts or things or ideas that work together • *the digestive system* • *the Solar System* **2** a well-organized way of doing something • *We have a new system for taking books out of the library.*

systematic *adjective*
using a system; careful and well planned **systematically** *adverb*

Tt

tab *noun*
a small strip or flap that sticks out

tabby *noun* (**tabbies**)
a grey or brown cat with dark streaks in its fur

table *noun*
1 a piece of furniture with a flat top supported on legs **2** a list of facts or numbers arranged in rows and columns

tablecloth *noun*
a cloth for covering a table

tablespoon *noun*
a large spoon used for serving food

tablet *noun*
1 a pill **2** a flat piece of stone or wood with words carved or written on it

table tennis *noun*
table tennis is a game played on a table divided in the middle by a net, over which you hit a small ball with bats

tack *noun*
a short nail with a flat top **to change tack** or **to try a different tack** is to find a different way of doing something

tack *verb*
1 to tack something is to nail it with tacks **2** to tack material is to sew it together quickly with long stitches **3** to tack is to sail a zigzag course to get full benefit from the wind

tackle *verb*
1 to tackle a task is to start doing it **2** in football or hockey, to tackle a player is to try to get the ball from them or (in rugby) to bring them to the ground

tackle *noun*
1 tackle is equipment, especially for fishing **2** a tackle is when you tackle someone in football or rugby or hockey

tacky *adjective* (**tackier, tackiest**)
sticky or not quite dry
• *The paint is still tacky.*

tact *noun*
tact is skill in not offending or upsetting people

tactful *adjective*
careful not to offend or upset people by saying something unkind **tactfully** *adverb* in a way that avoids offending or upsetting someone

tactics *plural noun*
someone's tactics are the methods they use to achieve or win something **tactical** *adjective* done to help you achieve or win something **tactically** *adverb*

tactless *adjective*
likely to offend or upset people by saying the wrong thing; having no tact **tactlessly** *adverb* in a way that offends or upsets someone

tadpole *noun*
a young frog or toad at a stage when it has an oval head and a long tail and lives in water

tag¹ *noun*
a label tied or stuck to something

tag¹ *verb* (**tagging, tagged**)
to tag something is to fix a tag or label on it **to tag along** is to go along with other people

tag² *noun* tag is a game in which one person chases the others

tail *noun*
1 the part that sticks out from the rear end of the body of an animal or bird **2** the part at the end or rear of something, such as an aircraft **3** the side of a coin opposite the head **tailless** *adjective* not having a tail

tail *verb*
to tail someone is to follow them without them seeing you **to tail off** is to become less and less or smaller and smaller

tailback *noun*
a long line of traffic stretching back from an obstruction

tailor *noun*
someone whose job is to make clothes

take *verb* (**taking, took, taken**)
This word has many meanings, depending on the words that go with it: **1** to take something or someone is to get hold of them or bring them into your possession • *He took a cake from the plate.* • *Who do you think took the money?* • *They took many prisoners.* **2** to take someone or something somewhere is to carry or drive them there • *Shall I take you to the station?* • *Take this parcel to the post.* **3** to take something useful or pleasant is to make use of it • *Do you take sugar?* • *You must take a holiday this year.* • *Do take a seat.* **4** to take someone or something is to need them for a purpose • *It will take two people to lift the table.* **5** to take a piece of information is to make a note of it • *Take their names and addresses.* **6** to take a class for a subject is to teach it to them • *Who takes you for English?* **7** to take one number from another is to subtract it • *Take two from ten and you get eight.* **8** to take an exam or test is to do it • *I'm taking my maths exam today.* **9** to take a joke is to accept it well **10** to take a photograph or picture is to produce it with a camera **to take off** is to leave the ground at the beginning of a flight **to take part in something** is to share in doing it **to take place** is to happen **to take someone in** is to fool or deceive them **to take**

something off is to remove it **to take something over** is to take control of it **to take something up** is to start doing it • *I've taken up yoga.*

takeaway *noun*
1 a place that sells cooked food for customers to take away **2** a meal from a takeaway

takings *plural noun*
money that has been received by a shop

talcum powder or **talc** *noun*
talcum powder is a perfumed powder you put on your skin to dry it or make it smell pleasant

tale *noun*
a story

talent *noun*
a natural ability or skill to do something well • *She has a talent for singing.*
talented *adjective* good at doing something

talk *verb*
to talk is to speak or have a conversation **talker** *noun* someone who talks, especially someone who talks a lot

talk *noun*
1 a conversation or discussion **2** a lecture

talkative *adjective*
someone is talkative when they talk a lot

tall *adjective*
1 higher than the average • *They sat under a tall tree.* **2** measured from the bottom to the top • *The bookcase is two metres tall.* **a tall story** is a story that is hard to believe

Talmud *noun*
a collection of writings on Jewish religious law

talon *noun*
a strong claw, especially on a bird of prey

tambourine *noun*
a round musical instrument like a small drum with metal discs fixed around the edge so that it jingles when you shake it or hit it

tambourine

tame *adjective*
1 a tame animal is one that is gentle and not afraid of people **2** something is tame when it is dull or uninteresting **tamely** *adverb* **tameness** *noun*

tame *verb*
to tame a wild animal is to make it used to being with people **tamer** *noun* someone who tames wild animals
• *a lion-tamer*

tamper *verb*
to tamper with something is to interfere with it or change it so that it will not work properly

tan *noun*
1 a tan is a suntan **2** tan is a yellowish-brown colour

tan *verb* (**tanning, tanned**)
1 to tan your skin is to make it brown with a suntan **2** to tan the skin of a dead animal is to make it into leather

tandem *noun*
a bicycle for two riders, one behind the other

tang *noun*
a strong flavour or smell

tangent *noun* (*say* **tan**-jent)
a straight line that touches the outside of a curve or circle

tangerine *noun* (*say* tan-jer-**een**)
a kind of small orange

tangerine

tangle *verb*
1 you tangle something, or it tangles, when it becomes twisted or muddled • *My fishing line has tangled.* **2** something is tangled up when it is twisted together in an untidy mess
• *These computer cables are all tangled up.*

tangle *noun*
a twisted or muddled mass of (for example) hair or wire

tank *noun*
1 a large container for a liquid or gas **2** a large heavy vehicle with guns, used in war

tankard *noun*
a large heavy mug for drinking from

tanker *noun*
1 a large ship for carrying oil **2** a large lorry for carrying a liquid

tantalize *verb*
to tantalize someone is to torment them by showing them something good that they cannot have

tantrum *noun*
an outburst of bad temper

tap¹ *noun* (**taps**)
a device for letting out liquid or gas in a controlled flow

tap¹ *verb* (**tapping, tapped**)
to tap a telephone is to fix a device to it so that you can hear someone else's conversation

tap² *noun*
1 a tap is a quick light hit, or the sound that it makes
• *I gave him a tap on the shoulder.* **2** tap is tap-dancing

tap² *verb* (**tapping, tapped**)
to tap someone or something is to give them a tap or gentle hit • *I tried tapping on the window.*

tap dancing *noun*
tap dancing is dancing in hard shoes that make sharp tapping sounds on the floor **tap dance** *noun* a dance of this kind
tap dancer *noun* someone who does tap-dancing

tape *noun*
1 tape is soft material such as cloth or paper or plastic in a thin strip; a tape is a piece of this **2** tape is also a narrow plastic strip coated with a magnetic substance and used for making recordings; a tape is a cassette • *a video tape*

tape *verb*
1 to tape something is to fasten it by sticking it or tying it with tape **2** to tape music or sound or a television programme is to record it on magnetic tape

tape measure *noun*
a long strip marked in centimetres or inches for measuring things

taper *verb*
something tapers when it gets narrower towards one end

tape recorder *noun*
a machine for recording music or sound on magnetic tape and playing it back
tape recording *noun* a recording made with magnetic tape

tapestry *noun*
(**tapestries**) (*say* **tap**-i-stree)
a piece of strong cloth with pictures or patterns woven or embroidered on it

tapestry

tar *noun*
tar is a thick black sticky liquid made from coal or wood and used in making roads

tar *verb* (**tarring, tarred**)
to tar something is to cover it with tar

tarantula

tarantula *noun*
(*say* ta-**ran**-tew-la)
a large hairy poisonous spider found in warm countries

target *noun*
something that you aim at and try to hit or reach

tarmac *noun*
tarmac is a mixture of tar and broken stone, used for making a hard surface on roads and paths and open areas

tarnish *verb*
1 metal tarnishes when it becomes stained and less shiny **2** to tarnish something is to spoil it • *The scandal tarnished his reputation.*

tarpaulin *noun*
a large sheet of waterproof canvas

tart¹ *noun*
a pie containing fruit or jam

tart² *adjective* (**tarter, tartest**)
sour-tasting • *The apples are tart.*

tartan *noun*
a Scottish woollen cloth with a pattern of squares and stripes in different colours

task *noun*
a piece of work that needs to be done

tassel *noun*
a bundle of threads tied together at the top and used to decorate something

taste *verb*
1 to taste food or drink is to eat or drink a small amount to see what it is like **2** food or drink tastes a certain way when it has a particular flavour • *The milk tastes sour.*

taste *noun*
1 the taste of something is the flavour it has when you taste it • *The milk has a strange taste.* **2** taste is the ability to taste things **3** your tastes are the things you like or prefer • *What are your tastes in music?* **4** you show taste when you are able to choose things that are of good quality or go together well • *The way she dresses shows good taste.* **5** a taste is a tiny amount of food • *Can I have a taste of your pudding?*

tasteful *adjective*
showing good taste
tastefully *adverb*

tasteless *adjective*
showing poor taste
tastelessly *adverb*

tasty *adjective* (**tastier, tastiest**)
tasty food has a strong pleasant taste

tattered *adjective*
tattered clothing is badly torn and ragged

tatters *plural noun*
in tatters badly torn

tattoo¹ *noun*
a picture or pattern made on someone's skin with a needle and dye

tattoo¹ *verb* (**tattooing, tattooed**)
someone is tattooed when they have a tattoo on their skin

tattoo² *noun*
an outdoor entertainment including military music and marching

tatty *adjective* (**tattier, tattiest**)
shabby and worn

taunt *verb*
to taunt someone is to jeer at them or insult them

taunt *noun*
an insulting or mocking remark

taut *adjective*
stretched tightly **tautly** *adverb*
tautness *noun*

tavern *noun*
(*old use*) an inn or pub

tax *noun* (**taxes**)
an amount of money that people and businesses have to pay to the government to pay for things like hospitals and schools

tax *verb*
1 to tax someone is to charge them a tax **2** to tax goods or someone's income is to put a tax on them • *The government taxes alcohol, tobacco, and petrol.* **taxation** *noun* money that has to be paid as taxes

taxi *noun*
a car with a driver which you can hire for journeys

taxi *verb*
an aircraft taxis when it moves slowly along the ground before taking off or after landing

tea *noun*
1 tea is a drink made by pouring hot water on the dried leaves of a shrub grown in Asia **2** tea is also the dried leaves of this shrub **3** tea is also a meal eaten in the late afternoon or early evening

tea

WORD ORIGIN

The word **tea** comes from a Chinese word *te.*

teabag *noun*
a small bag of tea for making tea in a cup

teach *verb* (**teaching, taught**)
1 to teach someone is to show them how to do something or give them knowledge about something **2** to teach a subject is to give lessons in it • *She taught us history last year.*

teacher *noun*
someone who teaches people at a school or college

tea cloth or **tea towel** *noun*
a cloth you use for drying washed dishes and cutlery

teak *noun*
teak is a hard strong wood from Asia

team *noun*
1 a set of players who form one side in a game or sport **2** a group of people who work together

teapot *noun*
a pot with a handle and spout, for making and pouring out tea

tear¹ *verb* (**tearing, tore, torn**)
(*say* tair)
1 to tear something is to make a split in it or to pull it apart **2** to tear something is also to pull or remove it with force • *He tore the picture off the wall.* **3** to tear is to become torn • *Paper tears easily.* **4** to tear somewhere is to move very quickly there • *He tore down the street.*

tear¹ *noun* (*say* tair)
a hole or split made by tearing something

tear² *noun* (*say* teer)
a drop of water that comes from your eye when you cry

tearful *adjective*
in tears; crying easily • *He suddenly became very tearful.*
tearfully *adverb*

tease *verb*
to tease someone is to make fun of them and say things to make them annoyed

teaspoon *noun*
a small spoon for stirring drinks

teat *noun*
1 a nipple through which a baby drinks milk **2** the cap of a baby's feeding bottle

technical *adjective*
1 to do with technology or the way things work **2** using the words that only people who know a lot about a subject will understand • *This article is full of technical terms.*
technically *adverb*

technician *noun*
someone whose job is to look after scientific equipment and do practical work in a laboratory

technique *noun* (*say* tek-**neek**)
a particular method of doing something skilfully

technology *noun* (**technologies**)
technology is using science and machines to help you make things and do things
technological *adjective* to do with technology • *technological developments*

teddy bear *noun*
a soft furry toy bear, **Teddy** is a shortened form of the name *Theodore* and comes from the name of Theodore Roosevelt, who was the American president at the end of the 19th century and was a keen hunter of bears.

teddy bear

tedious *adjective* (*say* **tee**-di-us)
annoyingly slow or long;
boring **tediously** *adverb*
tediousness *noun*

tedium *noun*
tedium is a dull or boring
time or experience • *He
hated the tedium of visiting
his grandparents.*

teem *verb*
1 to teem with something is
to be full of it • *The river was
teeming with fish.* **2** to teem, or
teem down, is to rain very hard

teenage or **teenaged** *adjective*
in your teens; to do with
teenagers

teenager *noun*
a person in their teens

teens *plural noun* the time of
your life between the ages of
13 and 19 • *They started playing
chess in their teens.*

teetotal *adjective*
never drinking alcoholic drink
teetotaller *noun* someone who
is teetotal

telecommunications
plural noun
telecommunications is sending
news and information over
long distances by telephone,
television, radio, and satellite

telegram *noun*
a message sent by telegraph

telegraph *noun*
is a way of sending messages
by using electric current along
wires or by radio

telepathy *noun*
(*say* til-**ep**-a-thee)
telepathy is understanding
another person's thoughts
without them speaking,
writing, or making gestures
telepathic *adjective*
able to know what someone
else is thinking

telephone *noun*
a device using electric
wires or radio to
enable someone
to speak to another
person who is some
distance away

telephone *verb*
to telephone
someone is to speak
to them by telephone

telescope
noun
a tube with lenses at
each end, through
which you can see
distant objects
more clearly
because they
look closer
and larger

telescopic *adjective*
1 to do with telescopes
2 folding into itself like a
portable telescope
• *a telescopic umbrella*

teletext *noun*
teletext is a system for
displaying news and
information on a television
screen

televise *verb*
to televise an event is to film it
and put it on television

television *noun*
1 television is a system using
radio waves to reproduce
pictures on a screen **2** a
television, or a television set,
is a device for receiving these
pictures

tell *verb* (**telling, told**)
1 to tell something to someone
is to give them information
by speaking to them **2** to tell
someone to do something is
to give them instructions to do
it **3** to tell is to reveal a secret
• *Promise you won't tell.* **4** to
tell something is to recognize
it • *Can you tell the difference
between butter and margarine?*
to tell someone off is to tell
them severely that they have
done wrong **to tell tales** is
to report someone else's bad
behaviour

temper *noun*
1 a person's mood • *He is in a
good temper.* **2** an angry mood
• *She was in a temper.* **to lose
your temper** is to become
very angry

temperature *noun*
1 the temperature of
something is how hot or cold
it is **2** an unusually high body
temperature • *She's feverish and
has a temperature.*

tempest *noun*
(*old use*) a violent storm

temple[1] *noun*
a building where a god is
worshipped

temple[2] *noun*
the part of your
head between your
forehead and your ear

tempo *noun*
(**tempos**)
the tempo of a
piece of music is its
speed or rhythm

temporary *adjective*
only lasting or used for a
short time • *They were using
a temporary classroom.*
temporarily *adverb*
for a short
time only

telescope

tempt *verb*
to tempt someone is to try
to make them do something,
especially something they
ought not to do **temptation**
noun when someone is being
tempted **tempting** *adjective*
hard to resist

ten *noun*
the number 10

tenant *noun*
someone who rents a house
or building or a piece of land
from a landlord **tenancy** *noun*
when someone rents a house or
building or a piece of land

tend[1] *verb*
something tends to happen
when it is likely to happen or is
what usually happens • *Prices
tend to rise.*

tend[2] *verb*
to tend something or someone
is to look after them • *She
tended her little garden with care.*

tendency *noun*
the way a person or thing is
likely to behave • *She has a
tendency to be lazy.*

tender *adjective*
1 not tough or hard; easy to
chew **2** delicate or sensitive
• *These are more tender plants.*
3 gentle or loving • *She gave a
tender smile.* **tenderly** *adverb*
gently or lovingly
tenderness *noun*

tendon *noun*
a piece of strong tissue in
the body that joins a muscle
to a bone

tennis *noun*
tennis is a game played with
rackets and a ball on a court
with a net across the middle

tenor *noun*
a male singer with a high voice

tenpin bowling *noun*
tenpin bowling is a game in
which you knock down sets of
ten skittles with a ball

tense[1] *adjective*
1 tightly stretched • *tense
muscles* **2** to be tense is to be
nervous and not able to relax
3 a tense situation makes
people feel nervous and unable
to relax **tensely** *adverb*

tense[2] *noun*
a form of a verb that shows
when something happens. The
past tense of come is *came*, the
present tense is *come*, and the
future tense is *will come*.

tension *noun*
1 tension is a feeling of
anxiety or nervousness about
something about to happen
2 tension is also how tightly

stretched a rope or wire is

tent noun
a shelter made of canvas or cloth supported by upright poles

tentacle noun
a long bending part of the body of an octopus and some other animals

tenth adjective, noun
the next after the ninth
tenthly adverb in the tenth place; as the tenth one

tepid adjective
tepid liquid is only slightly warm; lukewarm

term noun
1 a part of the year when a school or college does its teaching 2 a definite period • *He was sentenced to a term of imprisonment.* 3 a word or expression with a special meaning • *I don't understand these technical terms.* 4 the terms of an agreement are the conditions offered or agreed • *They won't agree to our terms.* **to be on good or bad terms** is to be friendly or unfriendly with someone

terminal noun
1 a building where passengers arrive or depart • *an airport terminal* 2 a place where a wire is connected to a battery or electric circuit 3 a computer keyboard and screen used for sending data to or from the main computer

terminal adjective
a terminal illness is one that cannot be cured and that the person will die from

terminate verb
you terminate something, or it terminates, when it ends or stops • *This train terminates here.* **termination** noun ending or stopping something

terminus noun (**termini**)
the station at the end of a railway or bus route

termite noun
a small insect that eats wood and lives in large groups

termite mound

terrace noun
1 a row of houses joined together 2 a level area on a slope or hillside 3 a paved area beside a house

terrapin noun
a kind of small turtle that lives in water

terrible adjective
awful; very bad

terribly adverb
awfully; badly • *I'm terribly sorry I kept you waiting.* • *He was missing his parents terribly.*

terrific adjective
(*informal*) 1 very good or excellent • *That's a terrific idea.* 2 very great • *They went at a terrific speed.* **terrifically** adverb very; greatly

terrify verb (**terrifies, terrifying, terrified**)
to terrify a person or animal is to make them very frightened

territory noun (**territories**)
an area of land, especially an area that belongs to a country or person **territorial** adjective to do with territory

terror noun
terror is great fear

terrorism noun terrorism is the use of violence, such as setting off bombs, for political purposes

terrorist noun someone who takes part in terrorism

terrorize verb
to terrorize someone is to terrify them with threats

test noun
1 a short set of questions to check someone's knowledge, especially in school 2 a medical examination • *Amy went to have an eye test.* 3 a trial or experiment to find out what something is like • *Tests have shown there is a high level of pollution in the water.* 4 (*informal*) a test match

test verb
1 to test someone is to give them a test 2 to test something is to use it so that you can find out whether it works properly or find out more about it

testament noun
1 a written statement 2 each of the two main parts of the Bible, the **Old Testament** and the **New Testament**

testify verb (**testifies, testifying, testified**)
to testify is to give evidence in a lawcourt

testimony noun (**testimonies**)
evidence; what someone testifies

test match noun
a cricket or rugby match between teams from different countries

test tube noun
a tube of thin glass closed at one end, used for experiments in chemistry

tether verb
to tether an animal is to tie it up so that it cannot move far

tether noun
a rope for tying an animal **to be at the end of your tether** is to be unable to stand something any more

text noun
1 the words of something printed or written 2 a text message

text verb
you text someone when you send them a text message

textbook noun
a book that teaches you about a subject

textiles plural noun
kinds of cloth; fabrics

text message noun
a written message sent using a mobile phone

texture noun
the way that the surface of something feels when you touch it • *Silk has a smooth texture.*

than conjunction
compared with another person or thing • *Claire is taller than David.*

thank verb
to thank someone is to tell them you are grateful for something they have given you or done for you
thank you words that you say when you thank someone

thankful adjective
feeling glad that someone has done something for you
thankfully adverb used to show that you are pleased and relieved about something • *Thankfully no one was hurt.*

thanks plural noun
1 words that thank someone 2 (*informal*) a short way of saying 'Thank you' **thanks to someone or something** because of them • *Thanks to you, we succeeded.*

that adjective
the one there • *Whose is that book?*

that conjunction
used to introduce a fact or statement or result • *I hope that you are well.* • *Do you know that it is one o'clock?* • *The puzzle was so hard that no one could solve it.*

a b c d e f g h i j k l m n o p q r s t u v w x y z

253

that *pronoun*
1 the one there • *Whose book is that?* **2** which or who • *This is the book that I wanted.* • *Are you the person that I saw the other day?*

thatch *noun*
thatch is straw or reeds used to make a roof

thatch *verb*
to thatch a roof is to make it with straw or reeds

thaw *verb*
something thaws when it melts and is no longer frozen • *The snow was beginning to thaw.*

the *adjective* (called the *definite article*)
a particular one; that or those

theatre *noun*
1 a building where people go to see plays or shows **2** a special room where you go to have an operation

theatrical *adjective*
to do with plays or acting

theft *noun*
theft is stealing

their *adjective*
belonging to them • *This is their house.*

theirs *pronoun*
belonging to them • *This house is theirs.*

them *pronoun*
a word used for *they* when it is the object of a verb, or when it comes after a preposition
• *I like them.* • *I gave it to them.*

theme *noun*
1 a main idea or subject of something such as a book or speech **2** a short tune or melody

theme park *noun*
an amusement park with rides and activities connected with a special subject or theme

themselves *plural noun*
them and nobody else, used to refer back to the subject of a verb • *They have hurt themselves.* **by themselves** on their own; alone • *They did the work all by themselves.*

then *adverb*
1 at that time • *I lived in London then.* **2** after that; next • *Then they came home.* **3** in that case; therefore • *If you are going, then I can stay.*

theology *noun*
theology is the study of God and religion **theological** *adjective* to do with theology

theoretical *adjective*
based on theory and not on practice or experience
theoretically *adverb* in theory

theory *noun*
1 a theory is an idea or set of ideas suggested to explain something **2** the theory of a subject is the ideas and principles behind it, rather than the practice
in theory according to what should happen

therapy *noun* (**therapies**)
a way of treating an illness of the mind or the body, usually without using surgery or artificial medicines
therapist *noun* an expert in therapy • *a speech therapist*

there *adverb*
1 in or to that place **2** a word that you say to call attention to someone or something or to refer to them • *There's a spider in the bath.* • *There has been a mistake.*

therefore *adverb*
for that reason; and so

thermal *adjective*
to do with heat; using heat

thermometer *noun*
a device for measuring temperature

thermostat *noun*
a device that automatically controls the temperature of a room or piece of equipment

thesaurus *noun*
(**thesauri** or **thesauruses**)
a kind of dictionary in which words with similar meanings are listed in groups together, instead of one long list in alphabetical order

these *adjective, pronoun*
the people or things here

they *pronoun*
1 the people or things that someone is talking about
2 people in general • *They say it's a very good film.*

thick *adjective*
1 measuring a lot from one side to the other • *He cut himself a thick slice of cake.*
2 measured from one side to the other • *The wall is ten centimetres thick.* **3** dense or closely packed together • *The town was in thick fog.* **4** not very runny • *I love thick gravy.* **5** (*informal*) stupid
thickly *adverb* in thick pieces or in a deep layer **thickness** *noun* how thick something is

thicken *verb*
you thicken something, or it thickens, when it becomes thicker • *As he stirred the sauce, it started to thicken.*

thicket *noun*
a group of trees and shrubs growing close together

thief *noun* (**thieves**)
someone who steals things

thigh *noun*
the part of your leg above your knee

thimble *noun*
a metal or plastic cover that you put on the end of your finger to protect it when you are sewing

thin *adjective* (**thinner, thinnest**)
1 measuring a small amount from one side to the other
2 not fat **3** not dense or closely packed together **4** runny or watery **thinly** *adverb* in thin pieces or in a thin layer
thinness *noun* thinness is being thin

thin *verb* (**thinning, thinned**)
1 to thin something, or thin something out, is to make it less thick or less crowded
2 to thin, or thin out, is to become less dense or less crowded • *The crowds had thinned by late afternoon.*

thing *noun*
an object; anything that can be touched or seen or thought about

think *verb* (**thinking, thought**)
1 to think is to use your mind
2 to think something is to have it as an idea or opinion
• *I think that's a good idea.*
3 to be thinking of doing something is to be planning to do it
thinker *noun* someone who thinks about things

third *adjective, noun*
the next after the second
thirdly *adverb* as the third thing

third *noun*
each of three equal parts into which something can be divided

Third World *noun*
the poor or developing countries of Asia, Africa, and South and Central America

thirst *noun*
thirst is the feeling that you need to drink

thirsty *adjective*
(**thirstier, thirstiest**)
feeling that you need to drink

thirteen *noun*
the number 13
thirteenth *adjective, noun* 13th

thirty *noun* (**thirties**)
the number 30
thirtieth *adjective, noun* 30th

this *adjective, pronoun*
the one here
• *Take this pen.*
• *This is the one.*

thistle *noun*
a wild plant with prickly leaves and purple or white or yellow flowers

thorn *noun*
a sharp point growing on the stem of roses and other plants

thorny *adjective* (**thornier, thorniest**)
1 full of thorns; prickly **2** a thorny problem is a difficult one that causes argument or disagreement

thistle

thorough *adjective*
1 done properly and carefully • *This is a thorough piece of work.* **2** absolute or complete • *Everything was in a thorough mess.* **thoroughly** *adverb* properly and carefully; completely
thoroughness *noun* doing things properly and carefully

those *adjective, pronoun*
the ones there • *Where are those cards?* • *Those are the ones I want.*

though *conjunction*
in spite of the fact that; even if • *It is not true, though he says it is.*

though *adverb*
however; all the same • *She's right, though.*

thought *noun*
1 a thought is something that you think; an idea or opinion **2** thought is thinking • *I'll give the matter some thought.*

thoughtful *adjective*
1 looking or sounding as if you are thinking a lot about something **2** thinking of other people and what they would like **thoughtfully** *adverb*
thoughtfulness *noun*

thoughtless *adjective*
not thinking of other people and what they would like; inconsiderate **thoughtlessly** *adverb* **thoughtlessness** *noun*

thousand *noun*
the number 1,000 **thousandth** *adjective, noun* 1,000th

thrash *verb*
1 to thrash someone is to keep hitting them hard with a stick or whip **2** to thrash a person or team is to defeat them completely in a game or sport **3** to thrash, or thrash about, is to fling your arms and legs about wildly

thread *noun*
1 a long piece of cotton, wool, nylon, or other material used for sewing or weaving **2** a long thin piece of something **3** the spiral ridge round a screw or bolt

thread *verb*
1 to thread a needle is to put a thread through its eye **2** to thread a long and thin material is to put it through or round something **3** to thread a piece of string is to put beads on it

threadbare *adjective*
clothes are threadbare when they are worn thin with threads showing

threat *noun*
1 a warning that you will punish or harm someone if they do not do what you want **2** a danger

threaten *verb*
1 to threaten someone is to warn them that you will punish or harm them if they do not do what you want **2** to threaten is to be a danger to someone or something • *The quarrel threatened to turn violent.*

three *noun*
the number 3

three-dimensional *adjective*
having three dimensions: length, width, and height or depth

thresh *verb*
to thresh corn is to beat it so that you separate the grain from the husks

threshold *noun*
1 a slab of stone or board under the doorway of a building; the entrance **2** the beginning of something important • *We are on the threshold of a great discovery.*

thrift *noun*
thrift is being careful with money and not wasting it

thrifty *adjective* (**thriftier, thriftiest**)
careful with money and not wasting it **thriftily** *adverb*

thrill *noun*
1 a sudden feeling of excitement **2** something that gives you this feeling

thrill *verb*
something thrills you when it gives you a sudden feeling of excitement
thrilling *adjective* very exciting

thriller *noun*
an exciting story or film, usually about crime

thrive *verb*
to thrive is to grow strongly or do well

throat *noun*
1 the front of your neck **2** the tube in your neck that takes food and air into your body

throb *verb* (**throbbing, throbbed**)
to throb is to beat or vibrate with a strong rhythm • *The ship's engines throbbed quietly.* • *He had a throbbing pain in his head.*

throb *noun*
a throbbing sound or feeling

throne *noun*
1 a special chair for a king or queen **2** the position of being king or queen • *The Prince of Wales is heir to the throne.*

throng *noun*
a large crowd of people

throttle *verb*
to throttle someone is to squeeze their throat and strangle them

throttle *noun*
a device to control the flow of fuel to an engine

through *adverb* and *preposition*
1 from one end or side to the other • *I can't get through.* • *Climb through the window.* **2** because of; by means of • *We'll do it through hard work.* **3** (*informal*) finished • *I'm through now.*

throughout *preposition, adverb*
all the way through

throw *verb* (**throwing, threw, thrown**)
1 to throw something or someone is to send them through the air **2** to throw something somewhere is to put it there carelessly • *He came in and threw his coat on the chair.* **3** to throw a part of your body is to move it quickly • *She threw her head back and laughed.* **4** to throw someone into a certain state is to put them in that state • *We were thrown into confusion.*
to throw something away is to get rid of it

throw *noun*
a throwing action or movement • *That was a good throw.*

thrush *noun*
a bird that has a white front with brown spots

thrust *verb*
to thrust something somewhere is to push it there with a lot of force • *He thrust his hands into his pockets.*

thud *noun*
the dull sound of something heavy falling

thud *verb* (**thudding, thudded**)
to fall with a thud

thumb *noun*
the short thick finger at the side of each hand

thump *verb*
1 to thump someone or something is to hit them heavily **2** to thump is to make a dull heavy sound

thump *noun*
an act or sound of thumping

thunder *noun*
thunder is the loud rumbling noise that you hear with lightning during a storm

thunder *verb*
1 to thunder is to make the noise of thunder **2** someone thunders when they speak with a loud booming voice

thunderous *adjective*
extremely loud • *The curtain came down to thunderous applause.*

thunderstorm *noun*
a storm with thunder and lightning

Thursday *noun*
the fifth day of the week

thus *adverb*
1 in this way • *We did it thus.* **2** therefore • *Thus, we must try again.*

tick *noun*
1 a small mark (✓) made next to something when checking it as a sign that it is correct or has been done **2** each of the regular clicking sounds that a clock or watch makes

tick *verb*
1 to tick something is to mark it with a tick • *She ticked the correct answers.* **2** a clock or watch ticks when it makes regular clicking sounds **to tick someone off** (*informal*) is to scold them or tell them off

ticket *noun*
a piece of paper or card that allows you to do something such as see a show or travel on a bus or train

tickle *verb*
1 to tickle someone is to keep touching their skin lightly so that they get a tingling feeling that can make them laugh and wriggle **2** to tickle is to have a tickling or itching feeling • *My throat is tickling.* **3** to tickle

tickets

someone is also to please or amuse them

ticklish *adjective*
someone is ticklish when they are likely to laugh or wriggle if they are tickled

tidal *adjective*
to do with tides or affected by tides

tidal wave *noun*
a huge sea wave moving with the tide

tiddler *noun*
(*informal*) a very small fish

tiddlywink *noun*
a small counter that you flip into a cup with another counter in the game of **tiddlywinks**

tide *noun*
the regular rising or falling of the sea, which usually happens twice a day

tide *verb*
to tide someone over is to give them what they need, especially money, for the time being

tidy *adjective* (**tidier, tidiest**)
1 a tidy place is neat and orderly, with things in the right place • *What a tidy room.* **2** a tidy person keeps things neat and in the right place **3** (*informal*) fairly large • *That's a tidy sum of money.*

tidily *adverb* **tidiness** *noun*

tidy *verb* (**tidies, tidying, tidied**)
to tidy a place is to make it neat by putting things away in the right place

tie *verb* (**ties, tying, tied**)
1 to tie something is to fasten it with string, rope, or ribbon **2** to tie a knot or bow is to make one in a strip of material such as a ribbon **3** two players or teams tie when they finish a game or competition with an equal score or position

tie *noun*
1 a thin strip of material tied round the collar of a shirt with a knot at the front **2** the result of a game or competition in which two players or teams have the same position or score **3** one of the matches in a competition

tiger *noun*
a large wild animal of the cat family, with yellow and black stripes

tight *adjective*
1 fitting very closely or firmly fastened • *These shoes are a bit tight.* **2** fully stretched • *Is this string tight enough?* **tightly** *adverb* **tightness** *noun*

tight *adverb*
1 firmly • *Hold on tight.* **2** fully stretched • *Now pull the string tight.*

tighten *verb*
1 to tighten something is to make it tighter • *These screws need to be tightened.* **2** to tighten is to become tighter

tightrope *noun*
a tightly stretched rope above the ground, for acrobats to perform on

tights *plural noun*
a piece of clothing that fits tightly over the lower parts of the body including the legs and feet

tigress *noun*
a female tiger

tile *noun*
a thin piece of baked clay or other hard material used in rows to cover roofs, walls, or floors **tiled** *adjective* covered with tiles

till[1] *preposition, conjunction*
until

till[2] *noun*
a drawer or box for money in a shop; a cash register

till[3] *verb*
to till soil or land is to plough it ready to grow crops

tiller *noun*
a handle used to turn a boat's rudder

tilt *verb*
1 to tilt is to slope or lean **2** to tilt something is to tip it or make it slope

tilt *noun*
a sloping position

timber *noun*
1 timber is wood used for building or making things **2** a timber is a beam of wood

time *noun*
1 time is a measure of the passing of years, months, days, and other units

tiger

2 you ask the time when you want to know what point in the day it is, as shown on a watch or clock • *What's the time?* **3** a time is a particular moment or period of things existing or happening • *There was a time when I would have agreed with you.* • *Come back another time.* • *There were fields here in past times.* **4** a time is also an occasion • *This is the first time I've been here.* **5** a time is also a period for which something lasts • *She spent a long time in the library.* **6** time is the rhythm and speed of a piece of music **at times** or **from time to time** sometimes or occasionally **in time** or **on time** soon or early enough; not late • *Make sure you get to the station in time.* • *The train left on time.*
time *verb*
1 to time something is to measure how long it takes **2** to time an event or activity is to arrange the time when it will happen • *You timed your arrival perfectly.*
timer *noun*
a device for timing things
times *plural noun*
multiplied by • *5 times 3 is 15 (5 x 3 = 15).*
timetable *noun*
a list of the times when things happen, such as buses and trains leaving and arriving, and when school lessons take place
timid *adjective*
nervous and easily frightened **timidly** *adverb* **timidity** *noun* timidity is being timid
timing *noun*
timing is choosing the right time to do something • *Arriving at lunchtime was good timing.*
tin *noun* Ⓢ
1 tin is a soft white metal **2** a tin is a metal container for preserving food **tinned** *adjective* tinned food is preserved in a tin
tingle *verb*
part of your body tingles when you have a slight stinging or tickling feeling there • *The cold water made my skin tingle.*
tingle *noun*
a tingling feeling
tinker *verb*
to tinker with something is to try to mend or improve it, often without really knowing how to • *He loves tinkering with old clocks.*
tinker *noun*
(old use) someone who travelled around mending pots and pans

tinkle *verb*
something tinkles when it makes a gentle ringing sound
tinkle *noun*
a tinkling sound
tinny *adjective* (**tinnier, tinniest**)
a tinny sound is thin and high-pitched
tinsel *noun*
tinsel is strips of glittering material used for decoration
tint *noun*
a shade of a colour, especially a pale one
tint *verb*
to tint something is to colour it slightly
tiny *adjective*
very small
tip¹ *noun*
the part at the very end of something **tipped** *adjective* having a tip • *The parcel was tied in a ribbon tipped with gold.*
tip² *noun*
1 a small amount of money given to thank someone who has helped you **2** a quick piece of advice or useful information
tip² *verb* (**tipping, tipped**)
1 to tip someone is to give them a small amount of money to thank them for helping you **2** to tip someone or something is to name them as likely to win or succeed
tip³ *verb* (**tipping, tipped**)
to tip something is to turn it upside down or tilt it • *She tipped the water out of the bucket.* • *He tipped his head back and laughed.*
tip³ *noun*
1 a place where rubbish is left **2** a very untidy place
tiptoe *verb*
to tiptoe is to walk on your toes very quietly or carefully
tiptoe *noun*
on tiptoe walking or standing on your toes
tire *verb*
1 to tire someone is to make them tired **2** to tire is to become tired
tired *adjective*
feeling that you need to sleep or rest **to be tired of something** is to have had enough of it
tiresome *adjective*
annoying or tedious
tissue *noun*
1 tissue, or tissue paper, is thin soft paper **2** a tissue is a piece of this, especially one you use for blowing your nose **3** tissue is also the substance of which an

animal or plant is made
tit *noun*
a kind of small bird
title *noun*
1 the name of something such as a book, film, painting, or piece of music **2** a word that shows a person's position or profession, such as • *Sir, Lady, Dr, Mrs.*
titter *verb*
to titter is to giggle or laugh in a silly way
to *preposition*
1 towards • *They set off to London.* **2** as far as; so as to reach • *I am soaked to the skin.* **3** compared with; rather than • *She prefers cats to dogs.* **4** used with a verb to make an infinitive • *I want to see him.* **5** used to show purpose • *He does that to annoy us.*
to *adverb*
to the usual or closed position • *Push the door to.* **to and fro** backwards and forwards
toad *noun*
an animal like a large frog, that lives on land

toad

toadstool *noun*
a fungus that looks like a mushroom, and is often poisonous
toast *verb*
1 to toast food is to cook it by heating it under a grill or in front of a fire **2** to toast someone or something is to have a drink in their honour
toast *noun*
1 toast is toasted bread **2** a toast is when people are asked to toast someone or something with a drink • *Let's drink a toast to the bride and groom.*
toaster *noun*
an electrical device that makes toast
tobacco *noun*
tobacco is the dried leaves of certain plants used for smoking in cigarettes, cigars, or pipes
toboggan *noun*
a small sledge for sliding downhill **tobogganing** *noun* sliding downhill on a toboggan
today *noun*
this day • *Today is Monday.*
today *adverb*
1 on this day • *I saw him today.* **2** nowadays • *Today we don't have slaves.*

toddler *noun*
a young child who is just learning to walk

toe *noun*
1 each of the five separate parts at the end of each foot **2** the part of a shoe or sock that covers your toes

toffee *noun*
1 toffee is a sticky sweet made from butter and sugar **2** a toffee is a piece of this

together *adverb*
with another person or thing; with each other • *They went to school together.* • *Now glue the two parts together.*

toil *verb*
1 to toil is to work hard **2** to toil is also to move slowly and with difficulty • *The old man toiled up the hill.*

toilet *noun*
1 a large bowl with a seat that you use for getting rid of waste from your body **2** a room with a toilet in it

token *noun*
1 a card or voucher that you can exchange for goods in a shop **2** a piece of metal or plastic you use instead of money to pay for something **3** a sign or signal of something • *Please accept these flowers as a small token of my gratitude.*

tolerable *adjective*
able to be tolerated; bearable

tolerant *adjective*
accepting or putting up with other people's behaviour and opinions when you don't agree with them **tolerance** *noun* being willing to accept other people's behaviour and opinions **tolerantly** *adverb*

tolerate *verb*
to tolerate something is to allow it or put up with it although you do not approve of it

toll¹ *noun*
1 a payment charged for using a bridge or road **2** an amount of loss or damage • *The death toll in the earthquake is rising.*

toll² *verb*
to toll a bell is to ring it slowly

tom or **tomcat** *noun*
a male cat

tomahawk *noun*
an axe used by Native Americans

tomato *noun* (**tomatoes**)
a soft round red fruit with seeds inside it, eaten as a vegetable

tomb *noun* (*say* toom)
a place where a dead body is buried; a grave

tomboy *noun*
a girl who enjoys rough noisy games and activities

tombstone *noun*
a memorial stone set up over a grave

tomorrow *noun*, *adverb*
the day after today

ton *noun*
1 a unit of weight equal to 2,240 pounds or about 1,016 kilograms **2** (*informal*) a large amount • *There's tons of room.*

tone *noun*
1 the nature or quality of a sound • *I didn't like the sound of his voice.* **2** a sound in music **3** a shade of a colour **4** the quality or character of something

tone *verb*
to tone something down is to make it softer or quieter **to tone in** is to blend or fit in well, especially in colour

tongs *plural noun*
a tool with two arms joined at one end, used to pick things up or hold them

tongue *noun*
1 the long soft part that moves about inside your mouth **2** a language **3** the flap of material under the laces of a shoe

tongue-tied *adjective*
to be tongue-tied is to feel too shy or embarrassed to speak

tongue-twister *noun*
a sentence or phrase that is very difficult to say

tonic *noun*
something that makes a person healthier or stronger

tonight *adverb*, *noun*
this evening or night

tonne *noun*
a unit of weight equal to 1,000 kilograms

tonsillitis *noun*
tonsillitis is a disease that makes your tonsils extremely sore

tonsils *plural noun*
your tonsils are the two small masses of soft flesh inside your throat

too *adverb*
1 also • *I'd like to come too.* **2** more than is wanted or allowed or wise • *The box is too small.* • *Don't drive too fast.*

tomatoes

tool *noun*
a device that you use to help you do a particular job, such as a hammer or saw

tooth *noun* (**teeth**)
1 each of the hard white bony parts that grow in your gums, used for biting and chewing **2** each in a row of sharp points on a saw or comb
toothed *adjective* having teeth

toothache *noun*
toothache is a pain in one of your teeth

toothbrush *noun*
a small brush on a long handle, for brushing your teeth

toothpaste *noun*
toothpaste is a creamy paste for cleaning your teeth

top¹ *noun*
1 the highest part of something **2** the upper surface of something **3** the covering or stopper of a jar or bottle **4** a piece of clothing you wear on the upper part of your body

top¹ *adjective*
highest or most important • *We live on the top floor.* • *They were travelling at top speed.*

top¹ *verb* (**topping, topped**)
1 to top something is to put a top on it • *The cake was topped with icing.* **2** to top something is also to be at the top of it • *She tops the class in maths.*
to top something up is to fill it to the top when it is already partly full

top² *noun*
a toy that can be made to spin on its point

top hat *noun*
a man's tall stiff black or grey hat worn with formal clothes

topic *noun*
a subject that you are writing or talking or learning about

topical *adjective*
to do with things that are happening or in the news now • *The film we saw was very topical.* **topicality** *noun* topicality is being topical **topically** *adverb*

topping *noun*
food that is put on the top of a cake, pudding, or pizza

topple *verb*
1 to topple, or topple over, is to fall over **2** to topple something is to make it fall over **3** to topple someone in power is to overthrow them

top secret *adjective*
extremely secret

topsy-turvy *adverb, adjective*
upside-down; in a muddle

torch *noun*
1 a small electric lamp that you hold in your hand **2** a stick with burning material on the end, used as a light

torment *verb*
1 to torment someone is to make them suffer or feel pain **2** to torment someone is also to keep annoying them deliberately **tormentor** *noun* the person who is tormenting someone

torment *noun*
torment is great suffering

tornado *noun* (**tornadoes**)
(*say* tor-**nay**-doh)
a violent storm or whirlwind

torpedo *noun*
(**torpedoes**)
a long tube-shaped missile sent under water to destroy ships and submarines

torpedo *verb*
to torpedo a ship is to attack it with a torpedo

torrent *noun*
a very strong stream or fall of water
torrential *adjective* torrential rain pours down very heavily

torso *noun* (**torsos**)
the main part of the human body, not including the head, arms, or legs

tortoise *noun* (*say* tor-tus)
a slow-moving animal with a shell over its body

torture *verb*
to torture someone is to make them feel great pain, especially so that they will give information

torture *noun*
torture is something done to torture a person

toss *verb*
1 to toss something is to throw it into the air **2** to toss a coin is to throw it in the air and see which side is showing when it lands, as a way of deciding something **3** to toss is to move about restlessly in bed • *She*

was tossing and turning all night.

total *noun*
the amount you get by adding everything together

total *adjective*
1 including everything • *What is the total amount?* **2** complete; utter • *There was total darkness outside.* **totally** *adverb* completely • *Now I'm totally confused.*

total *verb* (**totalling, totalled**)
1 to total something is to add it up **2** to total an amount is to reach it as a total • *Sales totalled over £50,000 this month.*

totem pole *noun*
a large pole carved or painted by Native Americans

totter *verb*
to totter is to walk unsteadily or wobble

toucan *noun*
a tropical bird with a large brightly-coloured beak

touch *verb*
1 you touch something when you feel it lightly with your hand or fingers **2** to touch something is to come into contact with it or hit it gently **3** to be touching something is to be next to it so that there is no space in between **4** to touch something is also to interfere or meddle with it • *Don't touch anything in this room.* **5** to touch an amount is to just reach it • *His temperature touched 104 degrees.* **6** to touch someone is to affect their emotions • *We were deeply touched by his sad story.* **to touch down** is to land in an aircraft or spacecraft **to touch something up** is to improve it by making small changes or additions

touch *noun*
1 a touch is an act of touching • *You can find any train timetable you want at the touch of a button.* **2** touch is the ability to feel things by touching them **3** a touch is also a small thing that greatly improves something • *We're just putting the finishing touches to it.*

totem pole

4 touch is also communication with someone • *We have lost touch with them.* **5** touch is also the part of a football or rugby pitch outside the playing area • *He kicked the ball into touch.*

touch and go *adjective*
uncertain or risky

touchy *adjective*
(**touchier, touchiest**)
easily or quickly offended

tough *adjective*
1 strong; hard to break or damage • *You'll need tough shoes for the climb.* **2** tough food is hard to chew **3** rough or violent • *The police were dealing with tough criminals.* **4** firm or severe • *It's time to get tough with football hooligans.* **5** difficult • *It was a tough decision.* **toughly** *adverb*

toughness *noun*

toughen *verb*
to toughen someone or something, or toughen them up, is to make them tougher

tour *noun*
a journey in which you visit several places

tourist *noun*
someone who is travelling or on holiday abroad **tourism** *noun* travelling or being on holiday abroad

tournament *noun*
a competition in which there is a series of games or contests

tow *verb* (*rhymes with* **go**)
to tow a vehicle or boat is to pull it behind you in another vehicle • *They towed our car to a garage.*

tow *noun*
an act of towing

towards or **toward** *preposition*
1 in the direction of • *She walked towards the sea.* **2** in relation to • *He behaved kindly towards his children.* **3** as a contribution to • *Put the money towards a new bicycle.*

towel *noun*
a piece of soft cloth that you use for drying yourself

tower *noun*
a tall narrow building or part of a building

a b c d e f g h i j k l m n o p q r s t u v w x y z

tower *verb*
to tower above or over things is
to be much taller than them
• *The skyscrapers towered above
the city.*
tower block *noun*
a tall building containing
offices or flats
town *noun*
a place with many houses,
shops, schools, offices, and
other buildings
town hall *noun*
a building with offices for the
local council and usually a hall
for public events
towpath *noun*
a path beside a canal or river
toxic *adjective*
poisonous
toy *noun*
something to play with
toy *verb*
to toy with an idea is to think
about it casually or idly
trace *noun*
1 a mark or sign left by a person
or thing • *He vanished without a
trace.* **2** a very small amount of
something • *They found traces of
blood on the carpet.*
trace *verb*
1 to trace someone or
something is to find them after
a search • *Police are trying to
trace one of the witnesses.* **2** to
trace a picture or map is to
copy it by drawing over it on
thin paper you can see through
track *noun*
1 a path made by people or
animals **2** tracks are marks left
by a person or thing **3** a set of
rails for trains or trams to run
on **4** a road or area of ground
prepared for racing **5** a metal
belt used instead of wheels on a
heavy vehicle such as a tank or
tractor **6** one song or item on a
record or CD **to keep track of
something** or **someone** is to
know where they are or what
they are doing
track *verb*
to track a person or animal is
to follow them by following
the signs they leave **to track
something down** is to find it
after it has been lost
tracker *noun* someone who
tracks people or animals
tracksuit *noun*
a warm loose suit of a
kind worn by athletes
for jogging and
warming up
tractor *noun*
a motor vehicle
with large rear

wheels, used for pulling farm
machinery or heavy loads
trade *noun*
1 trade is the business of buying
or selling or exchanging things
2 a trade is a job or occupation,
especially a skilled craft
trade *verb*
to trade is to buy or sell or
exchange things **to trade
something in** is to give it
towards the cost of something
new • *He traded in his
motorcycle for a car.*
trader *noun* someone who
buys and sells things in trade
trademark *noun*
a symbol or name that only
one manufacturer is allowed
to use
tradesman *noun* (**tradesmen**)
someone who sells or delivers
goods
trade union *noun*
an organization of workers in
a particular industry, set up
to help improve pay and work
conditions
tradition *noun*
1 tradition is the passing down
of customs and beliefs from one
generation to the next
2 a tradition is a custom or
belief passed on in this way
traditional *adjective*
1 passed down from one
generation to the next • *It is a
book of traditional stories from
all round the world.* **2** of a kind
that has existed for a long time
• *We go to a very traditional
school.* **traditionally** *adverb*
traffic *noun*
1 traffic is vehicles, ships, or
aircraft moving along a route
2 traffic is also trade, especially
in something illegal or wrong
• *They were involved in traffic in
drugs.*
traffic *verb* (**trafficking,
trafficked**)
to traffic in something is to
trade in it illegally

tractor

traffic lights *plural noun*
a set of coloured lights used
to control road traffic
traffic warden *noun*
an official whose job is to
make sure that vehicles are
parked legally
tragedy *noun* (**tragedies**)
1 a story or play with unhappy
events or a sad ending **2** a very
sad event
tragic *adjective*
1 very sad or distressing
2 to do with tragedy
tragically *adverb* in a way
that is very sad or distressing
trail *noun*
1 a path or track through
the countryside or a forest
2 the scent and marks left
behind by an animal as it
moves **3** marks left behind
by something that has passed
trail *verb*
1 to trail an animal is to follow
the scent or marks it has left
behind **2** you trail something,
or it trails, when it drags along
the ground behind you
3 to trail behind someone is to
follow them more slowly or
at a distance • *A few walkers
trailed behind the others.*
4 to trail is also to hang down
or float loosely • *She wore a
long trailing scarf.*
trailer *noun*
1 a truck or other container that
is pulled along by a car or lorry
2 a short film advertising a film
or television programme that
will soon be shown
train *noun*
1 a group of railway coaches
or trucks joined together and
pulled by an engine **2** a number
of people or animals moving
along together, especially in a
desert • *a camel train* **3** a series
of things • *The train of events
began in London.* **4** a long part
of a dress that trails behind on
the ground
train *verb*
1 to train someone is to give
them skill or practice in
something **2** to train is to learn
how to do a job • *He's training
to be a doctor.* **3** to train is also
to practise for a sporting event
• *She was training for the race.*
4 to train a plant is to make it
grow in a particular direction
• *Roses can be trained up walls.*
5 to train a gun is to aim it at a
target • *He trained his rifle
on the bridge.*
trainer *noun*
1 a person who trains people

or animals **2** a soft shoe with a rubber sole, worn for running and sport

traitor *noun*
someone who betrays their country or friends

tram *noun*
a passenger vehicle that runs along rails set in the road

tramp *noun*
1 a person without a home or job who walks from place to place **2** a long walk **3** the sound of heavy footsteps

tramp *verb*
1 to tramp is to walk with heavy footsteps **2** to tramp is also to walk for a long distance

trample *verb*
to trample something, or to trample on it, is to crush it by treading heavily on it

trampoline *noun*
(*say* **tramp**-o-leen)
a large piece of canvas joined to a frame by springs, used by gymnasts for jumping on

trance *noun*
a dreamy or unconscious state like sleep

tranquil *adjective*
quiet and peaceful **tranquility** *noun* being quiet and peaceful

tranquillizer *noun*
a drug used to make a person feel calm and relaxed

transaction *noun*
a piece of business that involves buying and selling something

transfer *verb* (**transferring, transferred**) (*say* trans-**fer**)
to transfer someone or something is to move them from one place to another

transfer *noun*
(*say* **trans**-fer)
1 the process of moving a person or thing from one place to another **2** a piece of paper with a picture or design that can be transferred to another surface by soaking or heating the paper

transform *verb*
to transform a person or thing is to change their form or appearance to something quite different • *The caterpillar is transformed into a butterfly.*
transformation *noun* a complete change in the form or appearance of something

transfusion *noun*
putting blood taken from one person into another person's body

transistor *noun*
1 a tiny electronic device that controls a flow of electricity **2** a portable radio that uses transistors

transition *noun*
a change from one thing to another

translate *verb*
to translate something said or written in one language is to say or write it in another language **translation** *noun* something translated from another language
translator *noun* someone who translates language

transmission *noun*
1 transmission is transmitting something **2** a transmission is a radio or television broadcast

transmit *verb* (**transmitting, transmitted**)
1 to transmit a broadcast or signal is to send it out **2** to transmit something is to send it or pass it from one person or place to another • *We don't know how the disease is transmitted.*

transmitter *noun*
a piece of equipment for transmitting radio or television signals

transparent *adjective*
something is transparent when you can see through it **transparency** *noun* how transparent something is

transplant *verb*
1 to transplant a body organ is to remove it from one person and put it in the body of a person who is ill **2** to transplant a plant is to move it from one place to another
transplantation *noun* transplantation is transplanting something

transplant *noun*
1 when a body organ is removed from one person and put in another • *a heart transplant* **2** something that is transplanted

transport *verb* (*say* trans-**port**)
to transport people or things is to take them from one place to another

transport *noun* (*say* **trans**-port)
1 transport is the process of transporting people or things **2** transport is also vehicles used to do this

transporter *noun*
a heavy vehicle for transporting large objects, such as cars

trap *noun*
1 a device for catching and holding animals **2** a plan or trick to capture or cheat

someone **3** a two-wheeled carriage pulled by a horse

trap *verb* (**trapping, trapped**)
1 to trap a person or animal is to catch them in a trap **2** to trap someone is to capture or cheat them **3** to be trapped is to be stuck in a dangerous situation you can't escape from • *They were trapped in the burning building.*

trapdoor *noun*
a door in a floor, ceiling, or roof

trapeze *noun*
a bar hanging from two ropes high above the ground, used as a swing by acrobats

trapezium *noun*
a four-sided figure that has only two parallel sides, which are of different length

trapper *noun*
someone who traps animals, especially for their fur

trash *noun*
trash is rubbish or nonsense **trashy** *adjective* worthless or rubbish

travel *verb* (**travelling, travelled**)
to travel is to go from one place to another

travel *noun*
travel is going on journeys • *Do you enjoy travel?*

travel agent *noun*
a person or business whose job is to arrange travel and holidays for people

traveller *noun*
1 someone who is travelling or who often travels **2** a person who lives in a vehicle and does not settle in one place

trawler *noun*
a fishing boat that pulls a large net behind it

tray *noun*
a flat piece of wood or metal or plastic, used for carrying food, cups, plates, and other household things

treacherous *adjective*
1 betraying someone; not loyal **2** dangerous or unreliable • *It's been snowing and the roads are treacherous.*
treacherously *adverb*
treachery *noun* doing something that betrays someone

treacle *noun*
treacle is a thick sweet sticky liquid made from sugar

tread *verb* (**treading, trod, trodden**)
to tread on something is to walk on it or put your foot on it

261

tread *noun*
1 the sound someone makes when they walk • *He had a heavy tread.* **2** the part of a staircase or ladder that you put your foot on **3** the part of a tyre that touches the ground

treason *noun*
treason is betraying your country

treasure *noun*
1 treasure is a collection of valuable things like jewels or money **2** a treasure is a precious thing

treasure

treasure *verb*
to treasure something is to think that it is very precious

treasure hunt *noun*
a game in which people try to find a hidden object

treasurer *noun*
an official who is in charge of the money of an organization or club

treasury (**treasuries**) *noun*
a place where treasure or money is stored **the Treasury** the government department in charge of a country's income

treat *verb*
1 to treat someone or something in a certain way is to behave towards them in that way • *She treats her friends very kindly.* **2** to treat a person or animal is to give them medical care • *He was treated for sunstroke.* **3** to treat something is to put it through a process to improve it • *The woodwork needs treating so that it doesn't rot.* **4** to treat someone is to pay for their food or drink or entertainment • *I'll treat you to an ice cream.*

treat *noun*
1 something special that gives someone pleasure **2** the act of treating someone by paying for them • *This is my treat.*

treatment *noun*
1 your treatment of someone is the way you treat them **2** treatment is medical care

treaty *noun* (**treaties**)
a formal agreement between two or more countries, for example to end a war

treble *adjective*
three times as much or three times as many

treble *noun*
1 treble the amount of something is three times as much or as many **2** a treble is a boy with a high singing voice

treble *verb*
1 to treble something is to make it three times as big **2** to treble is to become three times as big

tree *noun*
a tall plant with leaves, branches, and a thick wooden trunk

trek *verb* (**trekking, trekked**)
to trek is to make a long walk or journey

trek *noun*
a long walk or journey

trellis *noun*
a framework of crossing wooden or metal bars, used to support climbing plants

tremble *verb*
to tremble is to shake gently, especially because you are afraid

tremble *noun*
a trembling movement or sound

tremendous *adjective*
1 very large or very great • *There was a tremendous explosion.* **2** excellent
tremendously *adverb* very much

tremor *noun*
1 a shaking or trembling **2** a small earthquake

trench *noun*
a long hole or ditch dug in the ground

trend *noun*
the general direction in which something is going or developing

trendy *adjective*
(*informal*) fashionable; trying to be up to date **trendily** *adverb* **trendiness** *noun*

trespass *verb*
to trespass is to go on someone's land or property without their permission • *The sign said 'No Trespassing'.*
trespasser *noun* someone who is trespassing • *Trespassers will be prosecuted.*

trestle *noun*
each of a set of supports on

which you place a board to make a table

trial *noun*
1 trying or testing something to see how well it works **2** the process of hearing all the evidence about a crime in a lawcourt to find out whether someone is guilty of it **by trial and error** by trying out different methods until you find one that works **on trial** being tried out, or being tried in a lawcourt

triangle *noun*
1 a flat shape with three straight sides and three angles **2** a musical instrument made from a metal rod bent into a triangle and played by striking it **triangular** *adjective* in the shape of a triangle

tribe *noun*
a group of families living together, ruled by a chief **tribal** *adjective* to do with tribes or a tribe • *a tribal leader*

tributary *noun* (**tributaries**)
a river or stream that flows into a larger river or a lake

tribute *noun*
something you say or do as a mark of respect or admiration for someone

trick *noun*
1 something done to deceive or fool someone **2** a clever or skilful action • *a card trick.* **3** the winning of one round of a card game such as whist

trick *verb*
to trick someone is to deceive or fool them **trickery** *noun* doing something to deceive or fool someone

trickle *verb*
liquid trickles when it flows slowly in small quantities

trickle *noun*
a slow gradual flow

tricky *adjective* (**trickier, trickiest**)
difficult or awkward • *There were a couple of tricky questions in the quiz.*

tricycle *noun*
a vehicle like a bicycle with three wheels

trifle *noun*
1 a pudding made of sponge cake covered with custard, fruit, and cream **2** something that has little importance or is very small

trifling *adjective*
very small or unimportant

trigger *noun*
a lever that is pulled to fire a gun

trillion *noun*
a million million
(1,000,000,000,000),
or sometimes a
million million million
(1,000,000,000,000,000,000)

trilogy *noun*
a group of three books or films
about the same characters

trim *adjective* (**trimmer,
trimmest**)
neat and tidy

trim *verb*
1 you trim something when
you cut the edges or unwanted
parts from it **2** to trim clothing
is to decorate its edges • *The
gown was trimmed with fur.*

trim *noun*
an act of trimming • *My hair
needs a quick trim.*

Trinity *noun*
the Trinity in Christianity, the
union of Father, Son, and Holy
Spirit in one God

trio *noun*
1 three people or things **2** a
group of three musicians

trip *verb* (**tripping, tripped**)
1 to trip, or trip over, is to catch
your foot on something and fall
or stumble **2** to trip someone,
or trip them up, is to make them
fall or stumble **3** to trip, or trip
along, is to move with quick
gentle steps

trip *noun*
1 a short journey or outing
2 the action of tripping or
stumbling

triple *adjective*
1 three times as much or three
times as many **2** consisting of
three parts or involving three
people or groups

triple *verb*
to triple something is to make it
three times as big

triple jump *noun*
an athletics event in which
athletes try to jump as far as
possible with a hop,
step, and jump   triple jump

triplet *noun*
each of three children or
animals born at the same
time to the same mother

tripod *noun* (say **try**-pod)
a stand with three legs, for
supporting a camera or other
instrument

triumph *noun*
1 a triumph is a great success
or victory **2** triumph is a feeling
of victory or success • *They
returned home in triumph.*

triumph *verb*
to triumph is to win or succeed

triumphant *adjective*
enjoying a victory or
celebrating one

triumphantly *adverb*

trivial *adjective*
not important or valuable

trivially *adverb*

triviality *noun* triviality is
being unimportant

troll *noun*
a creature in Scandinavian
mythology, either a dwarf or
a giant

trolley *noun* (**trolleys**)
1 a basket on wheels, used
in supermarkets • *a shopping
trolley* **2** a small table on
wheels, used for serving food
and drink

trombone *noun*
a large brass musical
instrument with a sliding tube

troop *noun*
an organized group of people,
especially soldiers or Scouts

troop *verb*
people troop when they move
along in large numbers

troops *plural noun*
soldiers

trophy *noun* (**trophies**)
a cup or other prize you get
for winning a competition

tropic *noun*
a line of latitude about 23½°
north of the equator (**Tropic
of Cancer**) or about 23½°
south of the equator (**Tropic
of Capricorn**) **the tropics** the
hot regions between these two
latitudes **tropical** *adjective* to
do with the tropics or from the
tropics

trot *verb* (**trotting, trotted**)
1 a horse trots when it runs
gently without cantering or
galloping **2** a person trots
when they run gently with
short steps

trot *noun*
a slow or gentle run

trouble *noun*
trouble is something that
causes worry or difficulty

to be in trouble is to be likely
to get punished because of
something you have done **to
take trouble** is to take great
care in doing something

trouble *verb*
1 to trouble someone is to
cause them worry or difficulty
2 to trouble someone is also to
bother or disturb them • *Sorry
to trouble you, but can you spare
a minute?* **3** to trouble to do
something is to make an effort
to do it • *Nobody troubled to ask
us what we wanted.*

troublesome *adjective*
causing trouble or worry

trough *noun* (say trof)
a long narrow box for animals
to eat or drink from

trousers *plural noun*
a piece of clothing worn over
the lower half of your body,
with two parts to cover your
legs

trout *noun* (**trout**)
a freshwater fish

trowel *noun*
1 a tool for digging small holes
or lifting plants **2** a tool with a
flat blade for spreading cement
or mortar

truant *noun*
a child who stays away from
school without permission
to play truant is to stay away
from school without permission
truancy *noun* being absent
from school without permission

truce *noun*
an agreement to stop fighting
for a while

truck *noun*
1 a lorry **2** an open railway
wagon for carrying goods

trudge *verb*
to trudge is to walk slowly
and heavily

true *adjective*
1 real or correct; telling what
actually exists or happened
• *This is a true story.* **2** genuine
or proper • *He was the true heir.*
3 loyal and faithful • *You are
a true friend.* **to come true** is to
actually happen • *I hope your
dreams come true.*

truly *adverb*
1 truthfully **2** sincerely or
genuinely • *We are truly
grateful.*

trump *noun*
a playing card of a suit that
ranks above the others for one
game or round of play • *Hearts
are trumps this time.*

trump *verb*
to trump a card is to beat it by
playing a trump

a b c d e f g h i j k l m n o p q r s **t** u v w x y z

trumpet noun
a brass musical
instrument with
a narrow tube
that widens
at the end
trumpeter noun
someone who plays   trumpet
the trumpet
trumpet verb
1 an elephant trumpets when
it makes a loud sound **2** to
trumpet something is to shout
it out or announce it loudly
truncheon noun
a short thick stick carried as a
weapon by a police officer
trundle verb
to trundle is to move along
heavily, especially on wheels
• *A lorry trundled across the
bridge.*
trunk noun
1 the main stem of a tree
2 an elephant's long flexible
nose **3** a large box with a
hinged lid, for carrying or
storing clothes and other things
4 the human body except for
the head, legs, and arms
trunks plural noun
shorts worn by men and boys
for swimming, boxing, and
other activities
trust verb
1 to trust someone or
something is to believe that
they are good or truthful
or reliable **2** to trust that
something is so is to hope it
• *I trust that you are well.*
**to trust someone with
something** is to let them use it
or look after it
trust noun
1 trust is the feeling that a
person or thing can be trusted
2 trust is also responsibility or
being trusted • *Our pet dog was
left in the trust of our next-door
neighbour.*
trustworthy adjective
able to be trusted; reliable
trusty adjective
trustworthy or reliable
truth noun
truth is the quality of being
true; the facts about something
truthful adjective
1 telling the truth • *They are
truthful children.* **2** true • *They
gave a truthful account of what
happened.* **truthfully** adverb
truthfulness noun
try verb (**tries, trying, tried**)
1 to try to do something is to
make an effort to do it or to see
if you can do it • *Try to keep still.*
2 to try something is to use it

to see if it
works or
taste it to
see if you
like it • *Try
this can opener.*
3 to try someone in a lawcourt
is to find out whether they are
guilty of a crime, by hearing all
the evidence about it **4** to try
someone is also to annoy them
over a long time • *You really
do try me with your constant
complaining.* **to try something
on** is to put on clothes to see
if they fit or look good **to try
something out** is to use it to
see if it works
try noun (**tries**)
1 a go at trying something;
an attempt • *Have another try.*
2 (*in rugby football*) putting
the ball down on the ground
behind your opponents' goal
to score points
T-shirt noun
a shirt or vest with short sleeves
tub noun
a round container for liquids or
soft stuff such as ice cream
tuba noun (*say* **tew**-ba)
a large brass musical
instrument that makes
a deep sound
tube noun
1 a tube is a long thin hollow
piece of material such as metal,
plastic, rubber, or glass **2** a tube
is also a long hollow container
for something soft such as
toothpaste **3** the tube is the
underground railway in London
• *She goes to work by tube.*
tuber noun
a thick rounded plant root or
stem that produces buds
tubular adjective
shaped like a tube
tuck verb
to tuck something somewhere
is to push a loose edge of
it there so that it is tidy or
hidden • *Now tuck in the flap
of the envelope.* • *She tucked
her hair under her cap.* **to tuck
in** (*informal*) is to eat heartily
to tuck someone up or **in** is
to put the bedclothes snugly
round them
Tuesday noun
the third day of the week
tuft noun
a bunch of soft or fluffy things
such as threads, grass, hair,
or feathers, held or growing
together
tug verb
to tug something is to
pull it hard

tug noun
1 a hard or sudden pull
2 a small powerful boat used
for towing ships
tug-of-war noun
a contest between two teams
pulling a rope from opposite
ends
tulip noun
a large bright cup-shaped
flower that grows on a tall
stem from a bulb
tumble verb
to tumble is to fall over or fall
down clumsily
tumbler noun
1 a drinking glass with no stem
or handle **2** an acrobat
tummy noun (**tummies**)
(*informal*) your stomach
tumour noun (*say* **tew**-mer)
an abnormal growth on or in
your body
tumultuous adjective
noisy and excited • *The
teams came out to tumultuous
applause.*
tuna noun (**tuna** or **tunas**)
(*say* **tew**-na)
a large sea fish used for food
tundra noun
tundra is a large area of
flat land in cold regions
(especially northern Canada
and Siberia) with no trees and
with soil that is frozen for most
of the year
tune noun
a short piece of music; a
pleasant series of musical notes
to be in tune is to be at the
correct musical pitch
tune verb
1 to tune a musical instrument
is to adjust it to be in tune **2** to
tune a radio or television is to
adjust it to receive a particular
broadcasting station **3** to tune
an engine is to adjust it so that
it works smoothly
tuneful adjective
having a pleasant tune
tunefully adverb
tunic noun (*say* **tew**-nik)
1 a jacket that is part of some
uniforms **2** a loose piece of
clothing with no sleeves
tunnel noun
a passage made underground
or through a hill
tunnel verb (**tunnelling,
tunnelled**)
to tunnel is to make a tunnel
turban noun
a covering for the head
made by wrapping a long
strip of cloth round it, worn
especially by Sikh, Hindu,
or Muslim men

turbine noun
a machine or motor that is driven by a flow of water or gas

turbulent adjective
moving violently; heaving • *The seas in March can be turbulent.*

turbulence noun violent and uneven movement of air or water, causing aircraft and ships to be tossed about

turf noun (**turfs** or **turves**)
1 turf is short grass with the soil it is growing in **2** a turf is a piece of grass and soil cut out of the ground

turkey noun
(**turkeys**)
a large bird kept for its meat

turmoil noun
turmoil is a great disturbance or confusion

turn verb
1 to turn is to move round or move to a new direction; to turn something is to make it move in this way **2** to turn (for example) pale is to change appearance and become pale **3** to turn into something is to change into it • *The frog turned into a prince.* **4** to turn something into something else is to change it • *You can turn milk into cheese.* **5** to turn a device on or off is to use a switch to make it work or stop working; to turn (for example) a radio or television up or down is to make it louder or softer **to turn out** is to happen a certain way • *The weather's turned out fine.* **to turn something down** is to refuse it **to turn something out** is to empty it **to turn up** is to appear or arrive suddenly or unexpectedly

turn noun
1 the action of turning; a turning movement • *Give the key three turns.* **2** a place where a road bends; a junction • *Take the next turn on the left.* **3** a task or duty that people do one after the other • *It's your turn to wash up.* **4** a short performance in a show **5** (*informal*) an attack of illness; a nervous shock • *It gave me a nasty turn.* **a good turn** is a favour you do for someone **in turn** first one and then the other; following one after another

turnip noun
a plant with a large round white root used as a vegetable

turnstile noun
a revolving gate that lets one person through at a time

turntable noun
a revolving platform or support, especially the part of a record player that you put the record on

turpentine noun
(*say* **ter**-pen-tyn)
turpentine is a kind of oil used to make paint thinner and to clean paintbrushes

turquoise noun
(*say* **ter**-kwoiz)
1 a sky-blue or greenish-blue colour **2** a blue jewel

turret noun
1 a small tower in a castle **2** a revolving structure containing a gun

turtle noun
a sea animal that looks like a tortoise **to turn turtle** is to capsize

tusk noun
one of a pair of long pointed teeth that stick out of the mouth of an elephant or walrus or boar

tussle noun
a hard struggle or fight

tussle verb
to tussle is to struggle or fight over something

tutor noun
a teacher who teaches one person or a small group at a time

TV
short for television

tweak verb
to tweak something is to twist it or pull it sharply

tweed noun
tweed is a thick rough woollen cloth

tweezers plural noun
a small tool for gripping or picking up small things like stamps and hairs

twelve noun
the number 12

twelfth adjective, noun 12th

twenty noun
the number 20

twentieth adjective, noun 20th

twice adverb
1 two times; on two occasions **2** double the amount

twiddle verb
to twiddle something is to turn it round or over and over in an idle way • *He was twiddling a knob on the radio.*

twig noun
a short thin piece from a branch of a tree

twilight noun
twilight is the time of dim light just after sunset

twin noun
each of two children or animals born at the same time from one mother

twine noun
twine is strong thin string

twinge noun
a sudden sharp pain or unpleasant feeling

twinkle verb
to twinkle is to sparkle or shine with flashes of bright light

twinkle noun
a twinkling light

twirl verb
to twirl is to turn round and round quickly; to twirl something is to make it do this

twirl noun
a twirling movement

twist verb
1 to twist something is to turn its ends in opposite directions **2** to twist is to turn round or from side to side • *The road twisted through the hills.* **3** to twist something is to bend it out of its proper shape • *My bicycle's front wheel is twisted.* • *I think I've twisted my ankle.*

twist noun
a twisting movement or action

twitch verb
to twitch is to jerk or move suddenly and quickly; to twitch something is to make it do this

twitch noun
a twitching movement

twitter verb
birds twitter when they make quick chirping sounds

two noun
the number 2 **to be in two minds** is to be undecided about something

type noun
1 a type is a group or class of similar people or things; a kind or sort • *What type of computer of you got?* **2** type is letters and figures designed for use in printing

type verb
to type something is to write it with a typewriter or computer

typewriter noun
a machine with keys that you press to print letters or figures on a sheet of paper

typewritten adjective written with a typewriter

turkey

typhoon *noun*
a violent tropical storm with strong winds and rain

typical *adjective*
1 usual or normal • *Her typical day would begin with a good breakfast.* **2** as you would expect from a particular person or thing • *She worked with typical thoroughness.*
typically *adverb* usually

typist *noun*
a person who types, especially as their job

tyranny *noun* (**tyrannies**)
(*say* **ti**-ra-nee)
tyranny is a cruel or unjust way of ruling people
tyrannical *adjective* a tyrannical ruler uses their power in a cruel or unjust way

tyrant *noun* (*say* **ty**-rant)
someone who rules people cruelly or unjustly

tyre *noun*
a covering of rubber fitted round the rim of a wheel to make it grip the road and run smoothly

Uu

udder *noun*
the bag-like part of a cow, goat, or ewe, from which milk is taken

UFO *noun*
short for *unidentified flying object*, a flying object that no one can explain

UFO

ugly *adjective* (**uglier, ugliest**)
1 not beautiful; unpleasant to look at **2** threatening or dangerous • *The crowd was in an ugly mood.* **ugliness** *noun*

ulcer *noun*
a sore on the inside or outside of your body

ultimate *adjective*
furthest in a series of things; final **ultimately** *adverb* finally or eventually

ultraviolet *adjective*
ultraviolet light is light beyond the violet end of the spectrum, that causes your skin to tan

umbilical cord *noun*
the tube through which a baby receives nourishment in the mother's womb, connected to the baby's navel

umbrella *noun*
a mushroom-shaped piece of cloth stretched over a folding frame, which you open to protect yourself from rain

WORD ORIGIN

The word **umbrella** comes from an Italian word *ombrella* meaning 'a little shade'.

umpire *noun*
someone who makes sure that people keep to the rules in cricket, tennis, and some other games

unable *adjective*
not able • *She was unable to hear.*

unanimous *adjective*
(*say* yoo-**nan**-i-mus)
a unanimous decision or vote is one where everyone agrees
unanimously *adverb* with everyone agreeing • *She was elected unanimously.*

unarmed *adjective*
without weapons • *unarmed combat.*

unavoidable *adjective*
not able to be avoided; bound to happen **unavoidably** *adverb*

unaware *adjective*
not knowing about something • *She was unaware of the danger ahead.*

unawares *adverb*
unexpectedly; without someone knowing • *His question caught me unawares.*

unbearable *adjective*
something is unbearable when it is so painful or unpleasant that you cannot bear or endure it **unbearably** *adverb* in an unbearable way • *It was unbearably hot.*

unbelievable *adjective*
1 difficult to believe **2** amazing **unbelievably** *adverb*

unblock *verb*
to unblock something is to clear it of a block or obstruction

uncalled for *adjective*
not justified or necessary • *Your rudeness is uncalled for.*

uncanny *adjective* (**uncannier, uncanniest**)
strange and mysterious • *There was an uncanny silence.*

uncertain *adjective*
1 not certain • *He is uncertain about what to do.* **2** not reliable • *The weather is uncertain at the moment.* **uncertainty** *noun*

uncertainty is being uncertain about something

uncle *noun*
1 the brother of your father or mother **2** your aunt's husband

uncomfortable *adjective*
not comfortable
uncomfortably *adverb*

uncommon *adjective*
not common; unusual

unconscious *adjective*
1 not awake or knowing what is happening around you because you have fainted or been knocked out **2** not aware of something • *I was unconscious of doing anything wrong.* **unconsciously** *adverb* without being aware of doing something **unconsciousness** *noun* being unconscious

uncontrollable *adjective*
unable to be controlled **uncontrollably** *adverb*

uncouth *adjective* (*say* un-**koo**th)
rude and rough in manner

uncover *verb*
1 to uncover something is to take the cover or top off it **2** to uncover a secret or something unknown is to discover it • *The police have uncovered a huge fraud.*

undecided *adjective*
you are undecided about something when you have not made up your mind about it

undeniable *adjective*
impossible to deny; certainly true **undeniably** *adverb* something is undeniably true when it is certainly true

under *preposition*
1 lower than; below • *Hide it under the desk.* **2** less than • *They are under 5 years old.* **3** ruled or controlled by • *The army is under his command.* **4** in the process of; undergoing • *The road is under repair.* **5** using; moving by means of • *The machine moves under its own power.*

under *adverb*
in or to a lower place • *Slowly the diver went under.*

underarm *adjective, adverb*
with the arm kept below shoulder level and moving forward and upwards

undercarriage *noun*
an aircraft's undercarriage is its landing wheels and the parts that support them

underclothes *plural noun* or **underclothing** *noun*
underwear

underdog *noun*
the person or team in a contest that is expected to lose

underdone *adjective*
not properly done or cooked

underfoot *adverb*
1 on the ground where you are walking • *It was slippery underfoot.* **2** under someone's feet • *The flag fell to the ground and was trampled underfoot.*

undergo *verb* (**undergoing, underwent, undergone**)
to undergo something is to experience something or have to do it • *He underwent several operations on his leg.*

undergraduate *noun*
a student at a university who has not yet taken a degree

underground *adjective, adverb*
1 under the ground **2** done or working in secret

underground *noun*
a railway that runs through tunnels under the ground

undergrowth *noun*
undergrowth is bushes and other plants growing closely under tall trees

underhand *adjective*
secret and deceitful

underline *verb*
1 to underline something you have written is to draw a line under it **2** to underline a fact is to emphasize it or show it clearly • *This accident underlines the need to be careful all the time.*

undermine *verb*
to undermine someone's efforts or plans is to weaken them gradually

underneath *preposition, adverb*
below or beneath

underpants *plural noun*
a piece of men's underwear worn under trousers

underpass *noun*
a place where one road or path goes under another

underprivileged *adjective*
people who are underprivileged don't have the same opportunities or standard of living as most people

understand *verb* (**understanding, understood**)
1 to understand something is to know what it means or how it works **2** to understand something is also to have heard about it • *I understand you've not been well.*
3 to understand someone is to know what they are like and why they behave the way they

do **understandable** *adjective*
able to be understood; easy to understand

understanding *noun*
1 understanding is the power to understand or think; intelligence **2** an understanding is when people have an agreement • *In the end the two brothers came to an understanding.* **3** understanding is also sympathy or tolerance

understanding *adjective*
sympathetic and helpful
• *He was very understanding when I was ill.*

understudy *noun* (**understudies**)
an actor who learns a part in a play so that they can play the part if the usual actor isn't able to perform

undertake *verb* (**undertaking, undertook, undertaken**)
to undertake something is to agree or promise to do it

undertaker *noun*
someone whose job is to arrange funerals

undertaking *noun*
something that someone agrees to do

underwater *adjective*
placed or used or done below the surface of water

underwater

underwear *noun*
underwear is clothes you wear next to your skin, under your main clothes

underworld *noun*
1 in legends, the underworld is the place for the spirits of the dead; hell **2** the underworld is also people who are regularly involved in crime

undesirable *adjective*
not wanted or liked

undeveloped *adjective*
not yet developed

undo *verb* (**undoing, undid, undone**)
1 to undo something is to unfasten or unwrap it • *Can you undo this knot?* **2** to undo something already done is to cancel the effect of it
• *He has undone all our careful work.*

undoubted *adjective*
definite or certain
undoubtedly *adverb* certainly

undress *verb*
1 to undress is to take your clothes off **2** to undress someone is to take their clothes off

unearth *verb*
1 to unearth something is to dig it up **2** to unearth something is also to find it after searching for it

unearthly *adjective*
supernatural; strange and frightening

uneasy *adjective* (**uneasier, uneasiest**)
anxious or worried **uneasily** *adverb* in a way that shows you are anxious or worried

uneatable *adjective*
not fit for eating

unemployed *adjective*
to be unemployed is to be without a job **unemployment** *noun* being without a job; the number of people without a job

uneven *adjective*
not level, flat, or regular • *The path was uneven.* **unevenly** *adverb* **unevenness** *noun*

unexpected *adjective*
not expected; surprising
unexpectedly *adverb* when you are not expecting it

unfair *adjective*
not fair; unjust **unfairly** *adverb* **unfairness** *noun*

unfaithful *adjective*
not faithful or loyal

unfamiliar *adjective*
not familiar

unfasten *verb*
to unfasten something is to open it when it has been fastened

unfinished *adjective*
not finished

unfit *adjective*
1 someone is unfit when they are not fit or fully healthy **2** to be unfit for something is to be not suitable • *He is unfit for the job.*

unfold *verb*
1 to unfold something is to open it or spread it out • *She unfolded the map.* **2** to unfold a story or plan is to make it known gradually **3** a story unfolds when it becomes known gradually

unforgettable *adjective*
impossible to forget

unforgivable *adjective*
not able to be forgiven

unfortunate *adjective*
1 unlucky **2** you say

something is unfortunate when you wish it hadn't happened; regrettable
• *It was an unfortunate remark.*

unfortunately *adverb* used to say you are sad about something • *Unfortunately he wasn't able to come to the party.*

unfriendly *adjective*
not friendly
unfriendliness *noun*

ungrateful *adjective*
not grateful
ungratefully *adverb*

unhappy *adjective* (**unhappier, unhappiest**)
1 not happy or pleased **2** you say something is unhappy when you wish it hadn't happened; regrettable
• *It was an unhappy choice of words.* **unhappily** *adverb*
unhappiness *noun*

unhealthy *adjective*
(**unhealthier, unhealthiest**)
1 not in good health **2** not good for you • *She has an unhealthy diet.*

unheard-of *adjective*
never known or done before; extraordinary

unicorn *noun* (*say* **yoo**-ni-korn)
an imaginary animal in stories, like a horse with a long straight horn growing out of the front of its head

uniform *noun*
the special clothes worn by members of an army or school or organization

uniform *adjective*
always the same; not changing
uniformly *adverb* in a way that does not change

uniformity *noun*
uniformity is being uniform or the same

unify *verb* (**unifies, unifying, unified**)
to unify several things, especially countries, is to join them into one thing; to unify is to join together **unification** *noun* when several things are joined together into one thing

unimportant *adjective*
not important

uninhabited *adjective*
a place is uninhabited when there is nobody living there

unintentional *adjective*
not done deliberately
unintentionally *adverb* by accident; not on purpose

uninterested *adjective*
not interested

uninteresting *adjective*
not interesting

union *noun*
1 the joining of things together; a united thing
2 a trade union

Union Jack *noun*
the flag of the United Kingdom

unique *adjective* (*say* yoo-**neek**)
something is unique when it is the only one of its kind
• *Everyone's fingerprints are unique.* • *This jewel is unique.*
uniquely *adverb*
uniqueness *noun*

unisex *adjective*
designed to be suitable for either men or women

unison *noun* (*say* **yoo**-ni-son)
in unison said or done by people together at the same time

unit *noun*
1 an amount used in measuring or counting, such as a centimetre or a pound **2** a single person or thing **3** a group of people or things that belong together

unite *verb*
1 to unite several people or things is to form them into one thing or group **2** people or things unite when they join together

unity *noun* (**unities**)
unity is being united or having agreement

universal *adjective*
including everyone and everything **universally** *adverb* by everyone • *This theory is now universally accepted.*

universe *noun*
the universe is everything that exists, including the earth and living things and all the stars and planets

university *noun* (**universities**)
a place where people go to study for a degree after they have left school

unjust *adjective*
not fair or just
unjustly *adverb*

unkind *adjective*
cruel and not kind

unkindly *adverb* **unkindness** *noun*

unless *conjunction*
except when; if not • *We cannot go unless we are invited.*

unlike *preposition*
not like • *unlike me, she enjoys sport.*

unlike *adjective*
not alike; different • *The two children are very unlike.*

unlikely *adjective*
(**unlikelier, unlikeliest**)
not likely to happen or be true

unload *verb*
to unload a container or vehicle is to take off the things it carried

unlock *verb*
to unlock a door or container is to open it with a key

unlucky *adjective* (**unluckier, unluckiest**)
not lucky **unluckily** *adverb*

unmistakable *adjective*
not likely to be mistaken for something or someone else; clear and definite
unmistakably *adverb* in a way that is unlikely to be mistaken for something else
• *His accent was unmistakably French.*

unnatural *adjective*
not natural or normal
unnaturally *adverb*

unnecessary *adjective*
not needed **unnecessarily** *adverb* when it is not needed

unoccupied *adjective*
a house is unoccupied when it is empty, with no one living there

unpack *verb*
to unpack a suitcase or bag is to take out the things in it

unpleasant *adjective*
not pleasant **unpleasantly** *adverb* **unpleasantness** *noun*

unplug *verb* (**unplugging, unplugged**)
to unplug an electrical device is to disconnect it by taking its plug out of the socket

unpopular *adjective*
not liked or enjoyed by people
unpopularity *noun* the fact that a person or thing is unpopular

unravel *verb* (**unravelling, unravelled**)
1 to unravel something is to unwind it or disentangle it **2** to unravel a problem or mystery is to investigate it and solve it

unreal *adjective*
not real; existing only in the imagination

unreasonable *adjective*
not reasonable or fair

unrest *noun*
unrest is trouble caused by people feeling unhappy

unroll *verb*
to unroll something is to open it when it has been rolled up

unruly *adjective* (**unrulier**, **unruliest**) (*say* un-**roo**-lee)
badly behaved and difficult to control **unruliness** *noun*

unsafe *adjective*
not safe; dangerous

unscrew *verb*
to unscrew something is to undo it by turning it or by removing screws

unseen *adjective*
not seen or noticed
• *He managed to slip out of the room unseen.*

unselfish *adjective*
not selfish; not thinking only about yourself **unselfishly** *adverb* **unselfishness** *noun*

unsightly *adjective*
not pleasant to look at; ugly

unsteady *adjective* (**unsteadier**, **unsteadiest**)
shaking or wobbling or likely to fall **unsteadily** *adverb* **unsteadiness** *noun*

unsuccessful *adjective*
not successful
unsuccessfully *adverb*

unsuitable *adjective*
not suitable **unsuitably** *adverb*

unthinkable *adjective*
too bad or unlikely to be worth thinking about

untidy *adjective* (**untidier**, **untidiest**)
messy and not tidy
untidily *adverb* **untidiness** *noun*

untie *verb* (**unties**, **untying**, **untied**)
to untie something is to undo it when it has been tied

until *preposition, conjunction*
up to a particular time or event
• *The shop is open until 8 o'clock.*
• *We will stay with you until the train comes.*

untold *adjective*
too great to be counted or measured • *The hurricane caused untold damage.*

untrue *adjective*
not true

untruthful *adjective*
not telling the truth
untruthfully *adverb*

unused *adjective* (*say* un-**yoozd**)
not yet used **unused to something** (*say* un-**yoost**)
not familiar with something
• *He is unused to eating meat.*

unusual *adjective*
different from what is usual or normal; strange or rare
unusually *adverb*

unwanted *adjective*
not wanted

unwell *adjective*
not well; ill

unwilling *adjective*
you are unwilling to do something when you don't want to do it **unwillingly** *adverb* **unwillingness** *noun*

unwind *verb* (**unwinding**, **unwound**) (*rhymes with* **find**)
1 to unwind something is to unroll it **2** to unwind is to become unrolled **3** (*informal*) to unwind is also to relax after you have been working hard

unwrap *verb* (**unwrapping**, **unwrapped**)
to unwrap something is to take it out of its wrapping

unzip *verb* (**unzipping**, **unzipped**)
to unzip something is to undo it when it is zipped up

up *adverb*
1 in or to a standing or upright position • *Stand up.*
2 in or to a high or higher place or level • *Put it up on the shelf.*
• *Prices are going up.*
3 completely
• *Eat up your carrots.* **4** out of bed • *It's time to get up.*
5 finished • *Your time is up.*
6 (*informal*) happening
• *Something is up.* **ups and downs** changes of luck, sometimes good and sometimes bad **to be up to something** is to be doing something mysterious or suspicious • *What are they up to?* **up to date 1** modern or fashionable **2** having the latest information

up *preposition*
in or to a higher position on something • *Let's climb up the mountain.*

upbringing *noun*
your upbringing is the way you have been brought up

update *verb*
to update something is to bring it up to date

upgrade *verb*
to upgrade a machine is to improve it by installing new parts in it

upheaval *noun*
a sudden violent change or disturbance

uphill *adjective, adverb*
1 sloping upwards; going up a slope **2** difficult • *It was an* uphill struggle.

uphold *verb* (**upholding**, **upheld**)
to uphold a decision or belief is to support it or agree with it

upholstery *noun*
upholstery is covers and padding for furniture

upkeep *noun*
the upkeep of something is the cost of looking after it and keeping it in good condition

uplands *plural noun*
the highest part of a country or region

upon *preposition*
on

upper *adjective*
higher in position or rank

upright *adjective*
1 standing straight up; vertical **2** honest

upright *noun*
an upright post or support

uprising *noun*
a rebellion or revolt against the government

uproar *noun*
uproar is a loud or angry noise or disturbance • *The room was in uproar.*

upset *adjective* (*say* up-**set**)
unhappy or anxious about something

upset *verb* (**upsetting**, **upset**) (*say* up-**set**)
1 to upset someone is to make them unhappy or anxious
2 to upset something is to knock it over and spill its contents

upset *noun* (*say* **up**-set)
a slight illness • *He's got a stomach upset.*

upside down *adjective, adverb*
1 with the upper part underneath instead of on top; the wrong way up
2 in disorder or confusion
• *The thieves turned the place upside down.*

upstairs *adverb, adjective*
to or on a higher floor in a house or other building

upstream *adjective, adverb*
in the direction opposite to the flow of a river or stream

uptight *adjective*
(*informal*) upset or nervous about something

up-to-date *adjective*
1 modern or fashionable
2 having the latest information

upward *adjective, adverb*
going towards what is higher

upwards *adverb*
towards what is higher

a
b
c
d
e
f
g
h
i
j
k
l
m
n
o
p
q
r
s
t
u
v
w
x
y
z

uranium noun Ⓤ
(say yoor-**ay**-ni-um)
uranium is a radioactive metal
used as a source of atomic
energy

urban adjective
to do with a town or city

Urdu noun
Urdu is a language related to
Hindi, spoken in northern India
and Pakistan

urge verb
1 to urge someone to do
something is to try to persuade
them to do it **2** to urge people
or animals is to drive them
forward

urge noun
a sudden strong desire or wish
• *She felt an urge to go for a
swim.*

urgent adjective
needing to be done or dealt
with immediately **urgency**
noun urgency is when
something needs to be done
or dealt with immediately
urgently adverb

urinate verb (say **yoor**-i-nayt)
to urinate is to pass urine out
of your body **urination** noun
urination is passing urine

urine noun (say **yoor**-in)
urine is the waste liquid that
collects in your bladder and is
passed out of your body

urn noun
1 a large metal
container with
a tap, in which
water is heated
2 a kind of large
vase for holding
the ashes of a
person who has
been cremated

us pronoun
a word used for
we, usually when
it is the object
of a sentence, or
when it comes
after a preposition
• *She likes us.*
• *She gave it to us.*

usage noun
(say **yoo**-sij)
the way that
something is used, especially
the way that words and
language are used

use verb (say yooz)
to use something is to perform
an action or job with it • *Are
you using my pen?* **used to**
did in the past • *I used to live
in Glasgow.* **to be used to
something** or **someone** is to
know them well or be familiar

urn

with them • *We're used to hard
work.* **to use something up** is to
use all of it, so that none is left

use noun (say yooss)
1 the action of using something
or being used **2** the purpose or
value of something • *Can you
find a use for this box?* • *This
knife is no use to us.*

used adjective (say yoozd)
not new; second-hand
• *We're buying a used car.*

useful adjective
able to be used a lot or do
something that needs doing
usefully adverb
usefulness noun

useless adjective
1 not having any use
2 (informal) not very good
at something • *I'm useless
at drawing.* **uselessly** adverb
uselessness noun

user noun
someone who uses something

user-friendly adjective (**user-
friendlier, user-friendliest**)
designed to be easy to use

usher noun
someone who shows people
to their seats in a church or
cinema or theatre

usher verb
to usher someone is to lead
them in or out of a place

usherette noun
a woman who shows
people to their seats
in a cinema or
theatre

usual adjective
as happens often
or all the time;
expected • *He sat
in his usual chair
by the fire.* • *She
was late as usual.*
usually adverb on
most occasions;
normally

utensil noun
(say yoo-**ten**-sil)
a tool or device,
especially one you
use in the house

utmost adjective
greatest • *Look after it
with the utmost care.*

utter[1] verb
to utter something is to say
it clearly, or to make a sound
with your mouth • *He uttered
a loud yell.* **utterance** noun
something that someone says

utter[2] adjective
complete or absolute • *It was
utter misery.* **utterly** adverb
completely • *You look utterly
ridiculous.*

Vv

vacancy noun (**vacancies**)
a job, or a room in a guest
house, that is available and
not taken

vacant adjective
1 empty; not filled or occupied
• *There were no vacant seats.*
2 not showing any expression
• *He gave a vacant stare.*

vacate verb
to vacate a place is to leave
it empty

vacation noun
(say vay-**kay**-shon)
a holiday, especially between
the terms at a university

vaccinate verb (say **vak**-si-nayt)
to vaccinate someone is to
protect them from a disease by
injecting them with a vaccine
vaccination noun when you
are vaccinated against a
disease

vaccine noun (say **vak**-seen)
a type of medicine injected into
people to protect them from
disease

WORD ORIGIN

It is called **vaccine** from the Latin
word *vacca* meaning 'cow', because
the first vaccine was taken from cows.

vacuum noun
a completely empty space;
a space without any air in it

vacuum verb
to clean something using a
vacuum cleaner

vacuum cleaner noun
an electrical device that sucks
up dust and dirt from the floor

vacuum flask noun
a container with double walls
that have a vacuum between
them, for keeping liquids hot
or cold

vagina noun (say va-**jy**-na)
the passage in a woman's
female body that leads from
the outside of her body to her
womb

vague adjective
not definite or clear • *I only
have a vague memory of his face.*
vaguely adverb not clearly
vagueness noun

vain adjective
1 too proud of yourself,
especially of how you look
2 unsuccessful or useless • *They
made vain attempts to save him.*
in vain with no result; without
success • *I tried in vain to call for*

help. **vainly** *adverb*
without success

valentine *noun*
1 a card sent on St Valentine's Day (14 February) to someone you love **2** the person you send a valentine to

valentine card

valiant *adjective*
brave or courageous
valiantly *adverb*
in a brave or courageous way

valid *adjective*
able to be used or accepted; legal • *My passport is no longer valid.* **validity** *noun* the validity of something is the fact that it is acceptable or legal

valley *noun* (**valleys**)
an area of low land between hills

valour *noun*
valour is bravery, especially in a battle

valuable *adjective*
1 worth a lot of money **2** very useful or important • *She gave me valuable advice.*

valuables *plural noun*
things that are worth a lot of money

value *noun*
1 the amount of money that something could be sold for **2** how useful or important something is

value *verb*
1 to value something is to think that it is important or worth having • *I value her friendship.* **2** to value something is also to work out how much it could be sold for • *The estate agent is coming to value the house.*

valuation *noun* an estimate of what something is worth **valuer** *noun* someone who values something

valve *noun*
a device used to control the flow of gas or liquid

vampire

vampire *noun*
in stories, a creature that sucks people's blood

van *noun*
1 a small lorry with a covered area for goods at the back **2** a railway carriage used for goods or for the train's guard

vandal *noun*
someone who deliberately breaks or damages things, especially buildings **vandalism** *noun* doing deliberate damage to something, especially a building

vanilla *noun*
vanilla is a flavouring made from the pods of a tropical plant

vanish *verb*
to vanish is to disappear completely

vanity *noun*
vanity is being too proud of yourself, especially of how you look

vanquish *verb*
to vanquish someone is to win a victory over them

vapour *noun*
a visible gas, such as mist or steam, which some liquids and solids can be turned into by heat

variable *adjective*
able or likely to change

variation *noun*
1 a change in something • *There have been slight variations in temperature.* **2** a different form of something

varied *adjective*
of various kinds; full of variety • *She has varied interests.*

variety *noun*
1 a variety is a number of different kinds of the same thing • *There was a variety of cakes to choose from.* **2** a variety is a particular kind of something • *There are many rare varieties of butterfly.* **3** variety is a situation where things are not always the same • *We have a life full of variety.*

various *adjective*
1 of different kinds • *They came for various reasons.* **2** several • *We met various people.*

variously *adverb* in several different ways

varnish *noun*
a liquid that dries to form a hard shiny surface on wood or other surfaces

varnish *verb*
to varnish wood or another surface is to put varnish on it

vary *verb* (**varies, varying, varied**)
1 to vary is to keep changing • *The weather varies a lot here.* **2** things vary when they are different from each other • *The cars are the same, although the colours vary.* **3** to vary something is to make changes to it

vase *noun* (*say* vahz)
a jar used for holding flowers or as an ornament

vast *adjective*
very large or wide **vastly** *adverb* greatly; very • *They are from vastly different backgrounds.* **vastness** *noun* being very large or wide

VAT
short for *value-added tax*, a tax on goods and services

vat *noun*
a very large container for holding liquid

vault *verb*
you vault something, or vault over it, when you jump over it, using your hands to support you or with the help of a pole

vault *noun*
1 a jump done by vaulting **2** an underground room for storing money and valuables

VDU
short for *visual display unit*

veal *noun*
veal is the meat from a calf

vector *noun*
(*in mathematics*) a quantity that has size and direction, such as velocity (which is speed in a certain direction)

Veda *plural noun*
the ancient writings of the Hindu religion

veer *verb*
to veer is to swerve or change direction suddenly • *The cyclist veered off to the left*

vegan *noun* (*say* **vee**-gan)
someone who does not use or eat any products made from animals

vegetable *noun*
a plant that can be used as food

vegetarian *noun* (*say* vej-i-**tair**-i-an)
someone who does not eat meat

vegetation *noun*
vegetation is plants that are growing

vehicle *noun*
a means of carrying people or things, especially on land. Cars, buses, trains, and lorries are vehicles.

veil *noun*
a piece of thin material to cover a woman's face or head
veiled *adjective* covered with a veil; partially hidden

vein *noun*
1 your veins are the tubes in your body that carry blood towards your heart **2** a line or streak on a leaf or rock or insect's wing **3** a long deposit of a mineral in the middle of rock

velocity *noun* (**velocities**)
(*say* vil-**os**-i-tee)
velocity is speed in a particular direction

velvet *noun*
velvet is a soft material with short furry fibres on one side
velvety *adjective* soft, like velvet

vendetta *noun*
a long-lasting quarrel or feud

WORD ORIGINS

Vendetta is an Italian word, which comes from a Latin word *vindicta* meaning 'vengeance'.

vending machine *noun*
a machine that you can buy food, drinks, or other things from, which you operate by putting in coins

venerable *adjective*
worthy of respect or honour because of being so old

venetian blind *noun*
a blind for a window, made of thin horizontal slats which you can move to control the amount of light that comes through

vending machine

vengeance *noun*
vengeance is harming or punishing someone because they have done harm to you
vengeful *adjective* a vengeful person wants to punish someone who has harmed them

venison *noun*
venison is the meat from a deer

Venn diagram *noun*
(*in mathematics*) a diagram using circles to show how sets of things relate to one another

venom *noun*
1 venom is the poison of snakes **2** venom is also a feeling of bitter hatred for someone

venomous *adjective* poisonous

vent *noun*
an opening in something, especially to let out smoke or gas

ventilate *verb*
to ventilate a place is to let fresh air come into it and move around it **ventilation** *noun* letting fresh air move freely around a place **ventilator** *noun* a machine that breathes for someone in hospital

ventriloquist *noun*
(*say* ven-**tril**-o-kwist)
an entertainer who speaks without moving their lips, so that it looks as though a dummy is speaking
ventriloquism *noun* what a ventriloquist does

venture *noun*
something new that you decide to do that is risky or daring

venture *verb*
to venture somewhere is to go there even though you know it might be difficult or dangerous • *Shall we venture out into the snow?*

veranda *noun* (*say* ver-**an**-da)
an open terrace with a roof along the outside of a house

verb *noun*
a word that shows what someone or something is doing, such as *be, go, sing, take*

verbal *adjective*
spoken rather than written • *We had a verbal agreement.*
verbally *adverb* in spoken words, not in writing

verdict *noun*
the decision reached by a judge or jury about whether someone is guilty of a crime

verge *noun*
a strip of grass beside a road or path **on the verge of** about to do something • *She was on the verge of leaving.*

verge *verb*
to verge on something is to be nearly something • *His remark verged on the absurd.*

verify *verb* (**verifies, verifying, verified**)
to verify something is to find or show whether it is true or correct
verification *noun* verification is verifying something

vermin *noun*
vermin are animals or insects that damage crops or food or carry disease, such as rats and fleas

verruca *noun* (**verrucas**)
(*say* ver-**oo**-ka)
a kind of wart on the sole of your foot

versatile *adjective*
(*say* **ver**-sa-tyl)
able to do or be used for many different things
versatility *noun* versatility is being able to do or be used for many different things

verse *noun*
1 verse is writing in the form of poetry **2** a verse is a group of lines in a poem or song **3** a verse is also each of the short numbered sections of a chapter in the Bible

version *noun*
1 someone's account of something that has happened • *His version of the accident is different from mine.* **2** a different form of a thing • *I don't like their version of the song.*

versus *preposition*
against or competing with, especially in sport • *The final will be Brazil versus Germany.*

vertebra *noun* (**vertebrae**)
(*say* **ver**-ti-bra)
each of the bones that form your backbone

vertebrate *noun* (*say* **ver**-ti-brit)
an animal with a backbone

vertical *adjective*
going directly upwards, at right angles to something level or horizontal **vertically** *adverb* in a vertical direction

vertigo *noun*
vertigo is feeling dizzy because you are high up

very *adverb*
to a great amount; extremely • *It is very cold.*

very *adjective*
1 exact or actual • *That's the very thing we need!* **2** extreme • *We've reached the very end.*

Vesak *noun* (*say* **ves**-ak)
Vesak is an important festival of Buddhism, held in April to May

vessel noun
1 a boat or ship
2 a container for liquids 3 a tube inside an animal or plant, carrying blood or some other liquid

vest noun
a piece of underwear you wear on the top half of your body

vestment noun
a piece of outer clothing worn by the clergy or choir at a church service

vet noun
a person trained to treat sick animals

blood vessels

veteran noun
1 a person with long experience of something 2 a soldier who has returned from a war

veterinary adjective (say **vet**-rin-ree)
to do with the medical treatment of animals

veto noun (say **vee**-toh)
1 a refusal to let something happen 2 the right to stop something from happening

veto verb (**vetoes, vetoing, vetoed**)
to veto something is to refuse to let it happen

vex verb
to vex someone is to annoy or worry them **vexation** noun
vexation is vexing someone

via preposition (say **vy**-a)
going through; stopping at
• This train goes from Edinburgh to London via York.

viaduct noun (say **vy**-a-dukt)
a long bridge with many arches, carrying a road or railway over low ground

vibrate verb
to vibrate is to move quickly from side to side and with small movements • Every time a train went past the walls vibrated. **vibration** noun when something moves quickly from side to side and with small movements

vicar noun
a minister of the Church of England who is in charge of a parish

vicarage noun
the house of a vicar

vice¹ noun
1 a vice is a bad or evil habit

2 vice is evil or wickedness
vice² noun
a device with jaws for holding something tightly in place while you work on it

vice-president noun
a deputy to a president
vice versa adverb
(say vys-**ver**-sa)
the other way round • 'We need them and vice versa' means 'We need them and they need us'.
vicinity noun
(**vicinities**)
the area near or surrounding a particular place • Are there any parks in the vicinity?

vicious adjective (say **vish**-us)
1 cruel and aggressive 2 severe or violent **viciously** adverb
viciousness noun

victim noun
1 a person who suffers from something • He is a polio victim. 2 someone who is killed, injured, or robbed
• The murderer lay in wait for his victim.

victimize verb
to victimize someone is to treat them unfairly

victor noun
the winner of a battle or contest

victory noun (**victories**)
winning a battle or contest or game **victorious** adjective
someone is victorious when they win a battle or contest or game

video noun (say **vid**-i-oh)
1 video is the recording on tape of pictures and sound 2 a video is a video recorder 3 a video is also a television programme or a film recorded on a video cassette

WORD ORIGIN

The word **video** comes from a Latin word videre meaning 'to see'. The -o ending is based on audio in audiovisual.

video verb
to video something is to record it on videotape
video recorder or **video cassette recorder** noun
a machine for recording television programmes and playing them back
videotape noun
videotape is magnetic tape used for video recording
view noun
1 what you can see from one place • There's a fine view from the top of the hill. 2 someone's

opinion • She has strong views about smoking. **on view** shown for people to see
view verb
1 to view something is to look at it carefully 2 to view something or someone in a certain way is to think about them in that way • They seemed to view us with suspicion.

viewer noun
someone who watches something, especially a television programme

vigilant adjective (say **vij**-i-lant)
someone is vigilant when they are watching carefully for something
vigilantly adverb **vigilance** noun vigilance is watching carefully for something

vigorous adjective
full of strength and energy
vigorously adverb

vigour noun
vigour is strength and energy
Viking noun
a Scandinavian pirate or trader in the 8th to 10th centuries

vile adjective
disgusting or bad • What a vile smell.

villa noun
a house, especially a large one in its own grounds, or one used for holidays abroad

village noun
a group of houses and other buildings in the country, smaller than a town
villager noun someone who lives in a village

villain noun
a wicked person or criminal
villainous adjective wicked
villainy noun wicked behaviour

vine noun
a plant on which grapes grow
vinegar noun
vinegar is a sour liquid used to flavour food

vineyard noun (say **vin**-yard)
an area of land where vines are grown to produce grapes for making wine

vintage noun
1 all the grapes that are harvested in one season, or the wine made from them 2 the period from which something comes • The furniture is of 1920s vintage.

vinyl noun (say **vy**-nil)
vinyl is a kind of plastic
viola noun (say vee-**oh**-la)
a stringed instrument rather like a violin but slightly larger and with a lower pitch

273

violate verb
1 to violate a rule or law is to break it 2 to violate a person or place is to treat them without respect **violation** noun the breaking of a rule or law

violence noun
1 violence is when someone uses force to hurt or kill people 2 violence is also force that damages things • *We weren't prepared for the violence of the storm.* **violent** adjective using violence; strong and forceful **violently** adverb with violence or great force

violet noun
1 a bluish-purple colour 2 a small plant that usually has purple flowers

violin noun
a musical instrument with four strings, played with a bow **violinist** noun someone who plays a violin

violin

VIP
short for *very important person*

viper noun
a small poisonous snake

virtual adjective
1 almost the same as the real thing • *His silence was a virtual admission of guilt.* 2 using virtual reality • *Click here to go on a virtual tour of the gallery.*

virtually adverb
in effect; nearly • *She comes here so often she's virtually a member of the family.*

virtual reality noun
virtual reality is an image or environment created by a computer that imitates the real world and that you can be part of

virtue noun
1 a virtue is a good quality in a person's character • *Honesty is a virtue.* 2 virtue is moral goodness **virtuous** adjective behaving in a very good way

virus noun (say **vy**-rus)
1 a microscopic creature that can cause disease 2 a disease caused by a virus • *The doctor said I had a virus.* 3 a hidden set of instructions in a computer program that is designed to destroy data

visa noun
an official mark put on someone's passport to show that the person has permission to enter a country

visibility noun
visibility is how far you can see clearly • *Visibility is down to 20 metres.*

visible adjective
able to be seen • *The ship was visible on the horizon.*

vision noun
1 vision is the ability to see 2 a vision is something that you see or imagine, especially in a dream 3 vision is also imagination and understanding • *They need a leader with vision.*

visit verb
to visit a place or person is to go to see them or stay there

visit noun
a short stay at a place or with a person **visitor** noun someone who is visiting or staying at a place

visor noun (say **vy**-zer)
the clear part of a helmet that closes over the face

visual adjective
to do with seeing; used for seeing **visually** adverb in a way that is connected with your ability to see

visual display unit noun
a screen on which a computer displays information

vital adjective
1 extremely important; essential • *It is vital that we get there on time.* 2 connected with life; needed in order to live **vitally** adverb

vitality noun
vitality is liveliness or energy

vitamin noun
each of several substances which are present in some foods and which you need to stay healthy

vivid adjective
bright and clear • *The colours are very vivid.* • *She gave a vivid description of the storm.* **vividly** adverb **vividness** noun

vixen noun
a female fox

vocabulary noun (vocabularies)
1 the vocabulary of a language is all the words used in it 2 a person's vocabulary is the words that they know and use

vocal adjective
to do with the voice; using your voice

vocation noun
a job or activity that you feel strongly you want to do

vodka noun
vodka is a strong alcoholic drink especially popular in Russia

voice noun
1 the sound you make when you speak or sing 2 the ability to speak or sing • *She has lost her voice.*

volcano noun (**volcanoes**)
a mountain with a hole at the top formed by molten lava which has burst through the earth's crust **volcanic** adjective caused or produced by a volcano

WORD ORIGIN

The word **volcano** is Italian and comes from Vulcan, the name of the Roman god of fire.

vole noun
a small animal rather like a rat

volley noun
1 a number of bullets or shells fired at the same time 2 in ball games, hitting or kicking the ball back before it touches the ground

volleyball noun
volleyball is a game in which two teams hit a large ball to and fro over a net with their hands

volt noun
a unit for measuring the force of an electric current

voltage noun
voltage is electric force measured in volts

volume noun
1 the amount of space filled by something 2 the strength

volca

or power of sound • *Turn down the volume!* **3** an amount • *The volume of traffic has increased.* **4** a book, especially one of a set

voluntary *adjective*
done or doing something because you want to, not for pay **voluntarily** *adverb* because you want to

volunteer *verb*
1 to volunteer is to offer to do something that you do not have to do **2** to volunteer information or time is to provide it willingly without being asked for it • *Several people generously volunteered their time.*

volunteer *noun*
someone who volunteers to do something

vomit *verb*
to vomit is to bring food back from the stomach through your mouth

vote *verb*
1 to vote for someone or something is to show which you prefer by putting up your hand or making a mark on a piece of paper **2** to vote to do something is to say that you want to do it • *I vote we go away this weekend.*

vote *noun*
1 a way of choosing someone or something by getting people to put up their hand or make a mark on a piece of paper **2** a choice you make by voting **3** the right to vote

voter *noun*
someone who votes, especially in an election

voucher *noun*
a piece of paper showing that you are allowed to pay less for something or that you can get something in exchange

vow *verb*
to vow is to make a solemn promise to do something

vow *noun*
a solemn promise

vowel *noun*
any of the letters a, e, i, o, u, and sometimes y

voyage *noun*
a long journey by ship or in a spacecraft

vulgar *adjective*
rude; without good manners or good taste

vulgar fraction *noun*
a fraction shown by numbers above and below a line (such as ½ and ⅞), not a decimal fraction

vulnerable *adjective*
able to be harmed or attacked easily

vulture *noun*
a large bird that eats the flesh of dead animals

Ww

vulture

wad *noun*
a pad or bundle of soft material or pieces of paper

waddle *verb*
to waddle is to walk with short steps, rocking from side to side, like a duck

wade *verb*
to wade through water or mud is to walk through it

wafer *noun*
a thin kind of biscuit, often eaten with ice cream

waffle *noun*
1 a waffle is a crisp square pancake with a pattern of squares on it **2** waffle is talking for a long time without saying anything important or interesting

wag *verb* (**wagging, wagged**)
1 a dog wags its tail when it moves it quickly from side to side because it is happy or excited **2** you wag your finger when you move it up and down or from side to side

wag *noun*
a wagging movement

wage *noun* or **wages** *plural noun*
the money paid to someone for the job they do

wage *verb*
to wage a war or campaign is to fight it

wager *noun* (*say* **way**-jer)
a bet

wager *verb*
to wager someone is to make a bet with them

waggle *verb*
to waggle something is to move it quickly from side to side or up and down • *Can you waggle your ears?*

wagon *noun*
1 a cart with four wheels, pulled by a horse or ox **2** an open railway truck

wagon

wail *verb*
to wail is to make a long sad cry

wail *noun*
a sound of wailing

waist *noun*
the narrow part in the middle of your body

waistcoat *noun*
a close-fitting jacket without sleeves, worn over a shirt and under a jacket

wait *verb*
1 to wait, or to wait for someone or something, is to stay in a place or situation until something happens **2** to wait is also to be a waiter

wait *noun*
a time spent waiting • *We had a long wait for the bus.*

waiter *noun*
a man who serves people with food in a restaurant or hotel

waitress *noun*
a woman who serves people with food in a restaurant or hotel

wake[1] *verb* (**waking, woke, woken**)
1 you wake, or wake up, when you stop sleeping **2** to wake someone, or wake them up, is to make them stop sleeping • *You have woken the baby.*

wake[2] *noun*
the trail left on the water by a ship or boat

waken *verb*
to waken someone is to wake them

walk *verb*
to walk is to move along on your feet at an ordinary speed

a
b
c
d
e
f
g
h
i
j
k
l
m
n
o
p
q
r
s
t
u
v
w
x
y
z

walk noun
1 a journey on foot 2 the way that someone walks • *He has a funny walk.* 3 a path or route for walking • *There are some lovely walks near here.*

walker noun
someone who goes for a walk, especially a long one

walkie-talkie noun
a small portable radio transmitter and receiver

walking stick noun
a stick a person carries or uses as a support while walking

wall noun
1 a structure built of brick or stone and forming one of the sides of a building or room, or going round a garden or other space 2 the outer surface of something, such as the stomach

wall verb
to wall something, or wall it in, is to surround or enclose it with a wall

wallaby noun (**wallabies**)
(*say* **wol**-a-bee)
a kind of small kangaroo

wallet noun
a small flat folding case for holding paper money, credit cards, and small documents

wallflower noun
a sweet-smelling garden plant

wallow verb
1 to wallow is to roll about in water or mud 2 to wallow in something is to get great pleasure from it • *They are wallowing in luxury.*

wallpaper noun
wallpaper is paper used to cover the walls of rooms

walnut noun
a kind of nut with a wrinkled surface

walrus noun
a large Arctic sea animal that looks like a large seal and has two long tusks

waltz noun
a dance with three beats to a bar

waltz verb
to waltz is to dance a waltz

wand noun
a short thin rod used by a magician, wizard, or fairy

wander verb
1 to wander is to go about without trying to reach a particular place
2 to wander, or wander off, is to stray or get lost • *Don't let the sheep wander.*

wanderer noun someone who

keeps travelling from place to place

wane verb
1 the moon wanes when its bright area gets gradually smaller 2 to wane is to become less or smaller or less strong • *His popularity was waning.*

want verb
1 to want something is to feel that you would like to have it or do it 2 to want something is also to need it • *Your hair wants cutting.*

want noun
1 a want is a wish to have something 2 want of something is a lack of it • *They died for want of water.*

wanted adjective
someone is wanted when they are being looked for by the police as a suspected criminal • *He was a wanted man.*

war noun
1 war is fighting between nations or armies; a war is a period of fighting 2 a war is also a serious struggle or effort against an evil such as crime or disease

warble verb
to warble is to sing gently, the way some birds do

warble noun
a warbling sound

ward noun
1 a long room with beds for patients in a hospital 2 a child looked after by a guardian 3 an area of a town or city represented by a councillor

ward verb
to ward something off is to keep it away • *He put his arms up to ward off the blows.*

warden noun
an official in charge of a hostel, college, or other building

warder noun
an official who guards prisoners in a prison

wardrobe noun
1 a cupboard to hang your clothes in 2 a stock of clothes or costumes

warehouse noun
a large building where goods are stored

wares plural noun
goods offered for sale

warfare noun
warfare is fighting or waging war

warhead noun
the part of a missile that explodes

warlike adjective

warlike people are fond of fighting or are likely to start a war

warm adjective
1 fairly hot; not cold or cool 2 warm clothes are thick and keep you warm 3 a warm person is enthusiastic or friendly • *They gave us a warm welcome.* 4 (*informal*) close to the right answer, or to something hidden • *You're getting warm now.*
warmly adverb

warm verb
1 to warm something or someone is to make them warm 2 to warm, or warm up, is to become warm **to warm up** is to do gentle exercises to prepare yourself before playing sport

warm-blooded adjective
having blood that does not change temperature according to the surroundings

warmth noun
1 warmth is being warm or keeping warm • *The cattle huddled together for warmth.* 2 warmth is also being friendly and enthusiastic • *She was touched by the warmth of their welcome.*

warn verb
to warn someone is to tell them about a danger or difficulty that might affect them

warning noun
something that tells someone about a danger

warp verb (*say* worp)
to warp, or be warped, is to become bent or twisted out of shape because of dampness or heat

warrant noun
a document that gives the police the right to arrest someone or search a place

warren noun
a piece of ground where there are many rabbit burrows

warrior noun
someone who fights in battles; a soldier

warship noun
a ship designed for use in war

wart noun
a small hard lump on your skin

wary adjective (**warier, wariest**)
cautious and careful • *I gave the tiger a wary glance.*
warily adverb cautiously
wariness noun

wash verb
1 to wash something is to clean it with water 2 you wash when you clean yourself with

water 3 to wash is to flow over or against something • *Waves washed over the beach.* **4** to be washed somewhere is to be carried along by the force of moving water • *The boxes were washed overboard.* **to wash up** is to wash the dishes and cutlery after a meal

wash *noun*
1 the action of washing **2** the disturbed water behind a moving ship **3** a thin coating of colour or paint

washbasin *noun*
a small basin with taps, holding water for washing your hands and face

washer *noun*
a small ring of metal or rubber placed between two surfaces so that they fit tightly together

washing *noun*
washing is clothes that need to be washed or have been washed

washing-up *noun*
washing the dishes and cutlery after a meal; the things that need to be washed

wasp *noun*
a stinging insect with black and yellow stripes across its body

wastage *noun*
wastage is losing something by waste

waste *verb*
1 to waste something is to use more of it than you need to, or to use it without getting much value from it **2** to waste something is also to fail to use it • *You are wasting a good opportunity.* **to waste away** is to become thinner and weaker

waste *adjective*
1 left over or thrown away because it is not wanted • *What shall we do with all this waste paper?* **2** not used or usable • *We came to an area of waste land.*

waste *noun*
1 a waste is wasting something or not using it well • *It's a waste of time.* **2** waste is things that are not wanted or used **3** a waste is also an area of desert or frozen land • *We flew over the wastes of Alaska.*

wasteful *adjective*
wasting things or not using them well **wastefully** *adverb*

watch *verb*
1 to watch someone or something is to look at them for some time **2** to watch, or watch out, is to be on guard or ready for something to happen

• *Watch for the lights to change.* **3** to watch something is also to take care of it • *His job is to watch the sheep.* **to watch out** is to be careful about something

watcher *noun* someone who watches something

watch *noun*
1 a device like a small clock, usually worn on a person's wrist **2** a period of being on guard or on duty

watchdog *noun*
a dog kept to guard buildings

watchful *adjective*
alert and watching carefully **watchfully** *adverb*
watchfulness *noun*

watchman *noun* (**watchmen**)
someone whose job is to guard a building at night

water *noun*
1 water is a transparent colourless liquid that falls as rain and is found in seas, rivers, and lakes **2** a water is a sea or lake **to pass water** is to urinate

water *verb*
1 to water a plant is to sprinkle water over it • *Have you watered the flowers?* **2** to water an animal is to give it water to drink **3** your eyes or mouth water when they produce tears or saliva • *The smell of toast makes my mouth water.* **to water something down** is to dilute it or make it weaker

watercolour *noun*
1 a paint that can be mixed with water **2** a painting done with this kind of paint

watercress *noun*
a kind of cress that grows in water

waterfall *noun*
a place where a river or stream flows over a cliff or large rock

watering can *noun*
a container with a long spout, for watering plants

waterlogged *adjective*
waterlogged ground is so wet it cannot soak up any more water

watermark *noun*
a faint design in some types of paper, which you can see if you hold it up to the light

waterproof *adjective*
able to keep water out • *a waterproof jacket*

water-skiing *noun*
the sport of skimming over the surface of water on flat boards (**water-skis**) while being towed by a motor boat

watertight *adjective*
1 made so that water cannot get into it **2** so

carefully prepared that it has no mistakes or weaknesses • *He has a watertight alibi.*

waterway *noun*
a river or canal that ships or boats can travel on

waterworks *noun*
a place with pumping machinery for supplying water to a district

watery *adjective*
1 like water • *The paint is too watery.* **2** full of water • *You have watery eyes.*

watt *noun*
a unit of electric power

wave *verb*
1 to wave is to move your hand from side to side, usually to say hello or goodbye **2** you wave something, or it waves, when it moves from side to side or up and down • *Flags were waving in the wind.* **3** to wave hair is to make it curl

wave *noun*
1 a moving ridge on the surface of water, especially on the sea **2** a curling piece of hair **3** (*in science*) one of the to-and-fro movements in which sound and light and electricity travel **4** the action of waving your hand • *He gave us a little wave.* **5** a sudden increase in something strong • *She felt a wave of anger.*

wavelength *noun*
the size of a sound wave or electric wave

waver *verb*
1 to waver is to hesitate or be uncertain • *They wavered between two choices.* **2** to waver is also to be unsteady or move unsteadily

wavy *adjective* (**wavier, waviest**)
full of waves or curves

wax¹ *noun*
wax is a soft substance that melts easily, used for making candles, crayons, and polish **waxy** *adjective* looking or feeling like wax

wax¹ *verb*
to wax something is to cover it with wax

wax² *verb*
the moon waxes when its right area gets gradually larger

waxwork *noun*
a model made of wax, especially a full-size model of a person

way *noun*
1 how something is done; a

method or manner **2** the way to a place is how you get there **3** a road or path leading from one place to another **4** a distance • *Is it a long way?* **5** a respect • *It's a good idea in some ways.* **6** a condition or state • *Things are in a bad way.* **to get your own way** is to make people let you have what you want **in the way** blocking your path so that you can't move or see properly **no way** (*informal*) that is impossible; that is not true

we *pronoun*
a word used by someone to mean 'I and someone else' or 'I and others'

weak *adjective*
1 without much strength or energy **2** easy to break, bend, or defeat **3** poor at doing something **weakly** *adverb* **weakness** *noun* weakness is being weak; a weakness is a fault you have or something you don't do well

weaken *verb*
1 to weaken something is to make it weaker **2** to weaken is to become weaker

weakling *noun*
a weak person

wealth *noun*
1 wealth is a lot of money or property **2** a wealth of something is a lot of it • *The book has a wealth of illustrations.*

wealthy *adjective* (**wealthier, wealthiest**)
someone is wealthy when they have a lot of money or property

weapon *noun*
something used to harm or kill people in a battle or fight

wear *verb* (**wearing, wore, worn**)
1 to wear something is to be dressed in it **2** to wear something is to damage it by rubbing or using it; to wear is to become damaged like this • *The carpet has worn thin.* **3** to last • *This cloth wears well.* **to wear off** is to become less strong or intense **to wear out** is to become weak or useless **to wear someone out** is to make them very tired

wear *noun*
1 wear is clothes • *Where can I find men's wear?* **2** wear is gradual damage done by rubbing or using something

weary *adjective* (**wearier, weariest**)
very tired **wearily** *adverb* in a way that shows you are very tired **weariness** *noun*

weasel *noun*
a small fierce animal with a slender body

weather *noun*
weather is the rain, snow, wind, sunshine, and temperature at a particular time or place **to be under the weather** is to feel ill or depressed

weather *verb*
1 to weather is to become worn because of being exposed to the weather **2** to weather something is to make it suffer the effects of the weather • *The wind and rain have weathered the cliffs.* **3** you weather a difficulty when you come through it successfully • *They weathered the storm.*

weathercock or **weathervane** *noun*
a pointer, often shaped like a cockerel, that turns in the wind and shows which way the wind is blowing

weave *verb* (**weaving, wove, woven**)
1 to weave material or baskets is to make them by crossing threads or strips over and under each other **2** to weave is to twist and turn • *He wove skilfully through the traffic.*

weaver *noun* someone who weaves material

web *noun*
1 a net of thin sticky threads that spiders spin to catch insects **2** something complicated • *We were caught up in a web of lies.* **3** a computer network, especially the Internet

webbed or **web-footed** *adjective*
webbed feet have toes joined by pieces of skin, as ducks' feet do

website *noun*
a place on the Internet where you can get information

wed *verb* (**wedding, wedded** or **wed**)
to wed someone is to marry them

wedding *noun*
the ceremony when a man and woman get married

wedge *noun*
1 a piece of wood or metal or plastic that is thick at one end and thin at the other, pushed between things to force them apart or to hold them tight **2** something shaped like a wedge • *a wedge of cheese*

wedge *verb*
to wedge something is to hold

it in place, especially with a wedge

Wednesday *noun*
the fourth day of the week

weed *noun*
a wild plant that grows where it is not wanted

weed *verb*
to weed the ground is to remove weeds from it

weedy *adjective* (**weedier, weediest**)
1 full of weeds **2** thin and weak

week *noun*
1 a period of seven days, especially from Sunday to the following Saturday **2** the part of the week that doesn't include the weekend

weekday *noun*
any day except Saturday and Sunday

weekend *noun*
Saturday and Sunday

weekly *adjective, adverb*
every week

weep *verb* (**weeping, wept**)
to weep is to cry or shed tears

weigh *verb*
1 to weigh something is to find out how heavy it is **2** to weigh a certain amount is to have that as its weight • *How much do you weigh?* **to weigh anchor** is to raise the anchor and start a voyage **to weigh something down** is to hold it down with something heavy **to weigh something up** is to think about it carefully before deciding what to do

weight *noun*
1 weight is the measure of how heavy something is **2** a weight is a piece of metal that you know the weight of, used on scales to weigh things **3** a weight is also a heavy object, used to hold things down

weights

weightless *adjective*
astronauts are weightless when they float around because there is no gravity

weightlifting *noun*
weightlifting is the sport or exercise of lifting heavy weights

weighty adjective (**weightier, weightiest**)
1 heavy **2** important or serious • *These are weighty matters.*

weir noun (say weer)
a small dam across a river or canal to control the flow of water

weird adjective (say weerd)
very strange or unnatural
weirdly adverb
weirdness noun

welcome noun
a kind or friendly greeting or reception

welcome adjective
1 that you are glad to get or see • *This is a welcome surprise.* **2** allowed or free to do or take something • *You are welcome to use my bicycle.*

welcome verb
to welcome someone or something is to show that you are pleased when they arrive

weld verb
to weld pieces of metal or plastic together is to join them by using heat or pressure **welder** noun
someone who welds things together

welfare noun
welfare is people's health, happiness, and comfort

well[1] noun
a deep hole dug or drilled to get water or oil out of the ground

well[2] adverb (**better, best**)
1 in a good or successful way • *He can play the piano quite well now.* **2** thoroughly • *Wash your hands well.* **3** actually; probably • *It may well be our last chance.* **as well** also
to be well off is to be fairly rich or fortunate

well[2] adjective
1 in good health • *She is not well.* **2** good or satisfactory • *All is well.*

well-being noun
well-being is health or happiness

wellington boots or
wellingtons plural noun
rubber or plastic waterproof boots

WORD ORIGIN

The word **wellingtons** comes from the name of the Duke of Wellington, the British statesman and soldier who defeated Napoleon at the Battle of Waterloo in 1815.

well-known adjective
known to many people; famous

werewolf noun (**werewolves**)
in stories, a person who sometimes changes into a wolf

west noun
1 the direction where the sun sets **2** the part of a country or city that is in this direction

west adjective, adverb
1 towards the west or in the west **2** coming from the west • *There was a west wind blowing.*

western adjective
from or to do with the west

western noun
a film or story about American cowboys

westward or **westwards** adjective, adverb
towards the west

wet adjective (**wetter, wettest**)
1 covered or soaked in water or other liquid **2** not yet set or dry • *Watch out for wet paint.* **3** rainy • *It's been wet here all day.* **wetness** noun

wet verb
to wet something is to make it wet

wet suit noun
a rubber suit that clings to the skin, worn by skin divers and windsurfers to keep them warm and dry

whack verb
to whack someone or something is to hit them hard

whack noun
a hard hit or blow

whale noun
a very large sea animal **to have a whale of a time** (informal) is to enjoy yourself

whaling noun
whaling is hunting whales

wharf noun (**wharves** or **wharfs**) (say worf)
a quay where ships are loaded or unloaded

what adjective
1 used to ask questions about something • *What kind of bike have you got?* **2** used to say how strange or great a person or thing is • *What a fool you are!*

what pronoun
1 what thing or things • *What did

you say?* **2** the thing that • *This is what you must do.*

whatever pronoun
1 anything or everything • *Do whatever you like.* **2** no matter what • *I'll be there whatever happens.*

whatever adjective
of any kind or amount • *Get whatever help you can.*

wheat noun
wheat is a cereal plant from which flour is made

wheel noun
a round device that turns on an axle passing through its centre. Wheels are used to move vehicles or work machinery.

wheel verb
1 to wheel a bicycle or cart is to push it along on its wheels **2** to wheel is to move in a curve or circle • *The column of soldiers wheeled to the right.*

wheelbarrow noun
a small cart with one wheel at the front and two handles at the back

wheelchair noun
a chair on wheels for a person who cannot walk

wheeze verb
to wheeze is to make a whistling or gasping noise as you breathe

whales

whelk noun
a shellfish that looks like a snail

when adverb
at what time • *When can you come to tea?*

when conjunction
1 at the time that • *The bird flew away when I moved.* **2** because; considering that • *Why are you wearing a coat when it's so hot?*

whenever conjunction
at any time; every time • *Whenever I see him, he's smiling.*

wellington boots

279

where *adverb, conjunction*
1 in or to what place • *Where have you put the glue?* **2** in or to that place • *Leave it where it is.*

whereabouts *adverb*
roughly where; in what area • *Whereabouts is Timbuktu?*

whereabouts *noun*
the place where something is • *Have you any idea of her whereabouts?*

whereas *conjunction*
but on the other hand • *Some people like sailing, whereas others hate it.*

whereupon *adverb*
after that; and then

wherever *adverb, conjunction*
in or to whatever place; no matter where

whether *conjunction*
used to introduce more than one possibility • *I don't know whether they are here or not.*

whey *noun* (*say* way)
whey is the watery liquid left when milk forms curds

which *adjective*
what particular • *Which way did he go?*

which *pronoun*
1 what person or thing • *Which is your desk?* **2** the person or thing just mentioned • *Here's my book, which you asked me to bring.*

whichever *pronoun, adjective*
that or those which; any which • *Take whichever you like.*

whiff *noun*
a slight smell of something • *He caught a whiff of perfume as she walked past him.*

while *conjunction*
1 during the time that; as long as • *She was singing while she worked.* **2** but; although • *She is fair, while her sister is dark.*

while *noun*
a period of time • *We have waited all this while.*

while *verb*
to while away time is to pass it doing something leisurely

whilst *conjunction*
while

whim *noun*
a sudden desire to do or have something

whimper *verb*
to whimper is to cry with a low trembling voice

whimper *noun*
a sound of whimpering

whine *verb*
1 to whine is to make a long high piercing sound **2** to whine is also to complain in an annoying way

whine *noun*
a whining sound

whinny *verb* (**whinnies, whinnying, whinnied**)
a horse whinnies when it neighs gently

whip *noun*
a cord or strip of leather fixed to a handle and used for hitting people or animals

whip *verb* (**whipping, whipped**)
1 to whip a person or animal is to beat them with a whip **2** to whip cream is to beat it until it becomes thick and frothy **3** (*informal*) to whip something is to steal it **to whip something out** (*informal*) is to take it out quickly or suddenly **to whip something up** is to stir up people's feelings • *They quickly whipped up support for the idea.*

whirl *verb*
you whirl something round, or it whirls, when it turns or spins very quickly

whirl *noun*
when something turns or spins very quickly

whirlpool *noun*
a strong current of water going round in a circle and pulling things towards it

whirlwind *noun*

whirlpool

a very strong wind that whirls around or blows in a spiral

whirr *verb*
to whirr is to make a continuous buzzing sound

whirr *noun*
a continuous buzzing sound

whisk *verb*
1 to whisk cream or eggs is to beat them until they are thick or frothy **2** to whisk something somewhere is to move it there very quickly • *A waiter whisked away my plate.*

whisk *noun*
1 a device for whisking eggs or cream **2** a whisking movement

whisker *noun*
1 whiskers are the long stiff hairs on the face of a cat or other animal **2** you can refer to the hair growing on a man's face as his whiskers

whisky *noun*
a kind of very strong alcoholic drink

whisper *verb*
to whisper is to speak very softly or secretly

whisper *noun*
a very soft voice or sound

whist *noun*
whist is a card game for four people

whistle *verb*
1 you whistle when you make a shrill or musical sound by blowing through your lips **2** something whistles when it makes a shrill sound • *The kettle was whistling away.*

whistle *noun*
1 a whistling sound **2** a device that makes a shrill sound when you blow into it

white *adjective*
1 of the very lightest colour, like snow or milk **2** having light-coloured skin **3** white coffee is coffee with milk
whiteness *noun*

white *noun*
1 a white colour **2** the substance round the yolk of an egg, which turns white when it is cooked

whitewash *noun*
whitewash is a white liquid made from lime and chalk and painted on walls and ceilings

whitewash *verb*
to whitewash a wall or ceiling is to coat it with whitewash

whizz *verb*
1 to whizz is to move very quickly **2** to whizz is also to sound like something rushing through the air

who *pronoun*
1 which person or people • *Who threw that?* **2** the person or people spoken about • *These are the boys who did it.*

whoever *pronoun*
any person who • *Whoever comes is welcome.*

whole *adjective*
1 all of something; without anything missing • *Could you eat a whole pizza?* **2** not broken or damaged

whole noun
a complete thing; all the parts of something **on the whole** considering everything; mainly

wholefood noun
wholefood is food that has been produced without using artificial fertilizers

wholemeal adjective
wholemeal flour or bread is made from the whole grain of wheat

whole number noun
a number without a fraction

wholesale adjective, adverb
1 sold in large quantities to be sold again by others
2 on a large scale; including everybody or everything • There has been wholesale destruction.

wholesome adjective
healthy and good for you • We all need wholesome food.

wholly adverb
completely or entirely • He's not wholly to blame.

whom pronoun
a word used for who when it is the object of a verb or comes after a preposition, as in the boy whom I saw or the boy to whom I spoke

whooping cough noun
(say **hoop**-ing-kof)
whooping cough is an illness that makes you cough and gasp

who's
short for who has or who is

whose adjective, pronoun
1 belonging to what person • Whose bike is that? 2 of which; of whom • The girl whose party we went to.

why adverb
for what reason or purpose • Why have you come?

wick noun
the string that goes through the middle of a candle, which you light to give a flame

wicked adjective
1 very bad or cruel; doing things that are wrong
2 mischievous • He gave a wicked smile. 3 (slang) very fine or good • That's a wicked goal! **wickedly** adverb in a cruel or mischievous way **wickedness** noun doing bad things

wicker or **wickerwork** noun
wicker or wickerwork is reeds or canes woven together to make baskets and furniture

wicket noun
1 in cricket, each set of three stumps with two bails on top

of them 2 the part of a cricket ground between or near the wickets

wicketkeeper noun
the fielder in cricket who stands behind the batsman's wicket

wide adjective
1 measuring a lot from one side to the other • The river was wide.
2 from one side to the other • The room is 4 metres wide.
3 covering a large range • She has a wide knowledge of birds.

wide adverb
1 you are wide awake when you are completely or fully awake 2 to open or spread something wide is to open or spread it as far as possible
3 far from the target • The shot went wide.

widely adverb
commonly; among many people • They are widely admired.

widen verb
to widen something is to make it wider; to widen is to become wider

widespread adjective
existing or found in many places; common

widow noun
a woman whose husband has died

widower noun
a man whose wife has died

width noun
the width of something is how much it measures from one side to the other

wield verb (say weeld)
to wield a weapon or tool is to hold it and use it • a picture of a knight wielding a sword

wife noun (**wives**)
the woman that a man is married to

WORD ORIGIN

The word **wife** comes from an Anglo-Saxon word wif meaning 'woman'.

---

wig noun
a covering of false hair worn on the head

wiggle verb
to wiggle something is to move it from side to side

wiggle noun
a wiggling movement

wigwam noun
the tent of a Native American

wild adjective
1 wild animals and plants live or grow in their natural state and are not looked after by people 2 wild land is in its

natural state and has not been changed by people
3 not controlled; violent or angry • His behaviour became more and more wild. • She went wild when she saw the mess. 4 very foolish or unreasonable • They do have wild ideas. **wildly** adverb in a way that is not controlled • My heart was beating wildly. **wildness** noun

wild noun
animals live in the wild when they live in their natural environment

wilderness noun
an area of wild country; a desert

wildlife noun
wildlife is wild animals in their natural setting

wilful adjective
1 someone is wilful when they are determined to do exactly what they want • What a wilful child. 2 something is wilful when it is done deliberately • This is wilful disobedience. **wilfully** adverb **wilfulness** noun

will¹ verb (past tense **would**)
used to refer to the future • I will be there at 12 o'clock.

will² noun
1 will is the power to use your mind to decide and control what you do 2 someone's will is what they choose or want • He was forced to write the letter against his will. 3 someone's will to do something is their determination to do it • She has a strong will to succeed.
4 a will is a legal document saying what is to be done with someone's possessions after they die

willing adjective
ready and happy to do what is wanted • Are you willing to help? **willingly** adverb **willingness** noun

willow noun
a tree with long thin branches, often growing near water

wilt verb
a plant wilts when it loses freshness and droops

wily adjective (**wilier, wiliest**)
crafty or cunning **wiliness** noun

win verb (**winning, won**)
1 to win a contest or game or battle is to do better than your opponents 2 to win something is to get it by using effort or in a competition • She won second prize.

a
b
c
d
e
f
g
h
i
j
k
l
m
n
o
p
q
r
s
t
u
v
w
x
y
z

a
b
c
d
e
f
g
h
i
j
k
l
m
n
o
p
q
r
s
t
u
v
w
x
y
z

win noun
a success or victory

wince verb
to wince is to make a slight movement because you are in pain or embarrassed

winch noun
a device for lifting or pulling things, using a rope or cable that goes round a wheel or drum

winch verb
to winch something is to lift it or pull it with a winch

wind[1] noun (rhymes with **tinned**)
1 wind, or a wind, is a current of air **2** wind is gas in the stomach or intestines that makes you uncomfortable **3** wind is also breath used for a purpose, such as running **4** in an orchestra, the wind is the wind instruments

wind[2] verb (**winding, wound**) (rhymes with **find**)
1 something like a road or river winds when it twists and turns • *The river winds down the valley.* **2** to wind something is to wrap or twist it round something else • *She wound her scarf round her neck.* **3** to wind, or wind up, a watch or clock is to tighten its spring so that it works

windfall noun
1 a fruit blown down from a tree **2** a piece of unexpected good luck, especially a sum of money

wind instrument noun
a musical instrument played by blowing, such as a flute or clarinet

windmill noun
a mill with four long arms called *sails* which are turned by the wind

window noun
1 an opening in a wall or roof to let in light and air, usually filled with glass **2** (*in computing*) an area on a computer screen used for a particular purpose

windpipe noun
the tube through which air reaches your lungs

windscreen noun
the window at the front of a motor vehicle

windmill

windsurfing noun
windsurfing is surfing on a board with a sail fixed to it

windsurfer noun someone who goes windsurfing

windy adjective
with a lot of wind • *It's a windy day today.*

wine noun
an alcoholic drink made from grapes or other plants

wing noun
1 a bird's or insect's wings are the parts it uses for flying **2** an aircraft's wings are the long flat parts that stick out from its sides and support it in the air **3** a part of a building that is built at the side and is joined to the main part **4** each side of a theatre stage, out of sight of the audience **5** the part of a car's body above a wheel **6** each of the players in football and other ball games whose place is at the side of the field **on the wing** flying **to take wing** is to fly away **winged** adjective having wings • *Pegasus was a mythical winged horse.*

wingspan noun
the distance across the wings of a bird or aeroplane

wink verb
1 you wink when you close and open one of your eyes quickly **2** a light winks when it flickers or twinkles

wink noun
1 when you close and open one of your eyes quickly **2** a short period of sleep • *I didn't sleep a wink.*

winkle noun
a shellfish that is used for food

winner noun
1 a person who wins something **2** (*informal*) something very successful • *Her new book is a winner.*

winnings plural noun
the money someone wins in a game or by betting

winter noun
the coldest season of the year, between autumn and spring **wintry** adjective cold, like winter

wintertime noun
wintertime is the season of winter

wipe verb
to wipe something is to rub it gently to dry it or clean it **to**

wires

wipe something out is to destroy it or cancel it • *He's wiped out his debt.*

wipe noun
when you wipe something • *Give it a quick wipe.*

wire noun
a thin length of metal used to carry electric current or for making fences

wire verb
to wire something, or wire it up, is to connect it with wires to carry electricity

wireless adjective
something that is wireless can send and receive signals without using wires • *You can get a wireless Internet connection for your computer.*

wireless noun
(*old use*) a radio set

wiring noun
wiring is the system of wires carrying electricity in a building or in a device • *The fire was caused by faulty wiring.*

wiry adjective (**wirier, wiriest**)
1 a wiry person is lean and strong **2** wiry hair is tough and stiff

wisdom noun
1 wisdom is being wise **2** wisdom is also wise sayings or writings

wisdom tooth noun (**wisdom teeth**)
a tooth that may grow at the back of your jaw much later than the other teeth

wise adjective
knowing or understanding many things and so able to make sensible decisions **wisely** adverb when it is the sensible thing to do • *He wisely decided to tell the truth.*

wish verb
1 to wish something, or wish to do something, is to think or say that you would like it **2** to wish someone something is to say that you hope they will get it • *They wished us luck.*

wish noun
1 something you want **2** when you wish for something • *Make a wish.* • *We send you our best wishes.*

wishbone noun
a forked bone from the breast of a chicken or other bird

wisp *noun*
a thin piece or line of something light or fluffy, such as hair or smoke **wispy** *adjective* thin and fluffy

wistful *adjective*
thinking sadly about something you can no longer have **wistfully** *adverb*
wistfulness *noun*

wit *noun*
1 wit is intelligence or cleverness **2** wit is also a clever kind of humour **3** a wit is a witty person **to keep your wits about you** is to stay alert

witch *noun*
a woman who is believed to use magic

witchcraft *noun*
witchcraft is using magic, especially to make bad things happen

with *preposition*
there are many meanings, of which the most important are:
1 having • *I saw a man with a wooden leg.* **2** in the company of or accompanied by • *I came with a friend.* **3** using • *Hit it with a hammer.* **4** against • *They fought with each other.* **5** because of • *He shook with laughter.*

withdraw *verb* (**withdrawing, withdrew, withdrawn**)
1 to withdraw something is to take it away or take it back • *She withdrew her offer.*
2 to withdraw is to retreat or drop out of something • *The troops have withdrawn from the frontier.* • *His injury meant he had to withdraw from the race.* **withdrawal** *noun*
when someone withdraws something or withdraws from a place

wither *verb*
a plant withers when it shrivels or wilts

withhold *verb* (**withholding, withheld**)
to withhold something is to refuse to give it to someone • *He has withheld his permission.*

within *preposition, adverb*
inside; not beyond something • *Is the top shelf within your reach?*

without *preposition*
not having; free from • *It is difficult to live without money.*

withstand *verb* (**withstanding, withstood**)
to withstand something is to resist it or put up with it successfully • *The bridge is designed to withstand high winds.*

witness *noun*
1 a person who sees something happen and can describe it • *There were no witnesses to the accident.* **2** a person who gives evidence in a lawcourt

witty *adjective* (**wittier, wittiest**)
clever and amusing
wittily *adverb*

wizard *noun*
1 a man who has magic powers **2** a person who is very good at something • *He's a wizard on the accordion.*

wizardry *noun* the clever and impressive things that a computer or other machine can do

wizard

wobble *verb*
to wobble is to move unsteadily from side to side
wobble *noun*
a wobbling movement
wobbly *adjective* moving unsteadily from side to side

woe *noun*
1 someone's woes are their troubles and misfortunes
2 woe is great sorrow
woeful *adjective* very sad; very bad or serious
woefully *adverb*

wok *noun*
a deep round-bottomed frying-pan used in Chinese cookery

wolf *noun*
a wild animal like a large fierce dog

woman *noun* (**women**)
a grown-up female human being

womb *noun* (*say* woom)
the part of a female's body where babies develop before they are born

wonder *verb*
1 to wonder about something is to be trying to decide about it or to be curious about it • *I wonder what we should do next.* • *I wonder what's for dinner.*
2 to wonder at something is to feel surprise and admiration about it

wonder *noun*
1 wonder is a feeling of surprise and admiration **2** a wonder is something that makes you feel surprised and admiring
no wonder it is not surprising

wonderful *adjective*
marvellous or excellent
wonderfully *adverb*
extremely; very well

won't
short for *will not*

wood *noun*
1 wood is the substance that trees are made of **2** a wood is a lot of trees growing together

wooded *adjective*
a wooded area is covered with growing trees

wooden *adjective*
made of wood

woodland *noun*
land covered with trees

woodlouse *noun* (**woodlice**)
a small crawling creature with seven pairs of legs, living in rotten wood or damp soil

woodpecker *noun*
a bird that taps tree trunks with its beak to find insects

woodwind *noun*
in an orchestra, the woodwind is the wind instruments that are usually made of wood or plastic, such as the clarinet and oboe

woodwork *noun*
1 woodwork is making things with wood **2** woodwork is also things made out of wood

woodworm *noun* (**woodworm** or **woodworms**)
the larva of a beetle that bores into wood

woody *adjective* (**woodier, woodiest**)
1 like wood or made of wood
2 full of trees

wool *noun*
1 wool is the thick soft hair of sheep or goats **2** wool is also thread or cloth made from this hair

woollen *adjective*
made of wool

a b c d e f g h i j k l m n o p q r s t u v **w** x y z

woolly *adjective* (**woollier, woolliest**)
1 covered with wool **2** made of wool or like wool **3** vague and not clear • *He has woolly ideas.*
woolliness *noun*

word *noun*
1 a set of sounds or letters that has a meaning and is written with a space before and after it **2** a brief talk with someone • *Can I have a word with you?* **3** your word is when you promise to do something • *He gave me his word.* **4** a command or signal to do something • *Run when I give the word.* **5** a message or piece of news • *We sent word that we had arrived safely.*

word *verb*
to word something is to express it in words • *I'm not sure how to word this question.*

word class *noun*
each of the groups (also called **parts of speech**) into which words can be divided in grammar: noun, adjective, pronoun, adverb, preposition, conjunction, interjection

wording *noun*
the wording of something is the words used to say it

word processing *noun*
word processing is using a computer for writing and editing letters and documents, and for printing them out
word processor *noun* a computer used for word processing

work *verb*
1 to work is to spend time doing something that needs effort or energy **2** to work is also to have a job or be employed • *She works in a bank.* **3** something works when it operates correctly or successfully • *Is the lift working?* **4** to work something is to make it act or operate • *Can you work the lift?* **5** to work loose is to become gradually loose • *The screw had worked loose.* **to work out** is to succeed or happen in a certain way • *Things have worked out well for her.* **to work something out** is to find the answer to it

work *noun*
1 work is something that you have to do that needs effort or energy • *Digging is hard work.* **2** a person's work is their job • *What work do you do?* **3** at school, your work is something you write or produce • *Please*

get on with your work quietly. **4** a work is a piece of writing or music or painting • *The book has all the works of Shakespeare.*
to be at work is to be working

worker *noun*
1 someone who does work **2** a bee or ant that does the work in a hive or colony but does not produce eggs

workman *noun* (**workmen**)
a man who does manual work

workmanship *noun*
workmanship is skill in making something

works *plural noun*
1 the moving parts of a machine **2** a factory or industrial site

worksheet *noun*
a sheet of paper with a set of questions about a subject for students

workshop *noun*
a place where things are made or mended

world *noun*
1 the world is the earth with all its countries and peoples **2** a world is a planet • *The film is about creatures from another world.* **3** everything to do with a particular subject or activity • *He knows a lot about the world of sport.*

worldly *adjective* (**worldlier, worldliest**)
1 to do with life on earth **2** only interested in money and possessions

worldwide *adjective, adverb*
over the whole world

World Wide Web *noun*
the system of keeping information on computers all over the world so that people can use it by using the Internet

worm *noun*
1 a small thin wriggling animal without legs, especially an earthworm **2** (*informal*) an unimportant or unpleasant person

worm *verb*
to worm your way somewhere is to move along slowly when people or things are in your way • *He wormed his way through the crowd.*
to worm something out of someone is to get them to tell you something secret

worn *adjective*
damaged because it has been rubbed or used so much **to be worn out** is to be very tired

worry *verb* (**worries, worrying, worried**)
1 to worry is to feel anxious or troubled about something **2** to worry someone is to make them feel anxious or troubled about something
worried *adjective* anxious or troubled about something
worrier *noun* someone who worries a lot

world

worry noun
1 worry is worrying or being anxious 2 a worry is something that makes you anxious

worse adjective, adverb
more bad or more badly; less good or less well

worsen verb
1 to worsen is to become worse 2 to worsen something is to make it worse

worship verb
(**worshipping, worshipped**)
1 to worship God or a god is to give them praise or respect 2 to worship someone is to adore them or have great respect for them **worshipper** noun someone who worships

worship noun
worship is worshipping; religious ceremonies or services

worst adjective, adverb
most bad or most badly; least good or least well

worth adjective
1 having a certain value
• This stamp is worth £100.
2 deserving something; good or important enough for something • That book is worth reading.

worth noun
a thing's worth is its value or usefulness

worthless adjective
having no value; useless

worthwhile adjective
important or good enough to be worth doing

worthy adjective (**worthier, worthiest**)
deserving respect or support
• The sale is for a worthy cause.
to be worthy of something is to deserve or be good enough for something
• This charity is worthy of your support.
worthily adverb **worthiness** noun worthiness is being deserving or good enough for something

would verb
1 past tense of the verb **will**[1]
• We said we would do it.
• He said he would come if he could. 2 used in polite questions or requests • Would you like some tea?

wound noun (say woond)
an injury done to a part of a person's or animal's body, especially one in which the skin is cut

wound verb
to wound a person or animal is to give them a wound

wrap verb (**wrapping, wrapped**)
to wrap something is to put paper or some other covering round it

wrapper noun
a piece of paper or plastic that something is wrapped in

wrapping noun
wrapping is material used to wrap something, especially a present

wrath noun
(rhymes with **cloth**)
(old-fashioned use) anger
wrathful adjective angry

wreath noun
(say reeth)
flowers and leaves and branches bound together to make a circle

wreathe verb (say reeth)
to be wreathed in something is to be covered in it or decorated with it • Her face was wreathed in smiles.

wreck verb
to wreck something is to damage or ruin it so badly that it cannot be used again
wrecker noun
someone who wrecks something

wreck noun
a badly damaged ship or car

wreckage noun
wreckage is the pieces of something that has been wrecked

wren noun
a very small brown bird

wrench verb
to wrench something is to pull or twist it suddenly or violently • He wrenched the door open.

wrench noun
1 a wrenching movement 2 a tool for gripping and turning bolts or nuts

wrestle verb
1 to wrestle with someone is to fight them by grasping them and trying to throw them to the ground 2 to wrestle with a problem or difficulty is to struggle to solve it **wrestler** noun someone who wrestles for sport **wrestling** noun

wretch noun
someone who is unhappy, poor, or disliked

wretched adjective (say rech-id)
1 poor and unhappy • a wretched beggar 2 not satisfactory or pleasant • This wretched car won't start.

wriggle verb
to wriggle is to twist and turn your body **to wriggle out of something** is to avoid doing something you do not like

wriggle noun
a wriggling movement
wriggly adjective wriggling a lot

wring verb (**wringing, wrung**)
1 to wring something wet, or to wring it out, is to squeeze or twist it to get the water out of it 2 to wring something is to squeeze it violently • I'll wring your neck! **wringing wet** very wet; soaked

wrinkle noun
1 wrinkles are the small lines and creases that appear in your skin as you get older 2 a small crease or line on the surface of something

wrinkle verb
something wrinkles when wrinkles appear in or on it
wrinkled adjective wrinkled skin or clothing has wrinkles

wrist noun
the joint that connects your hand to your arm

wristwatch noun
a watch that you wear on your wrist

write verb (**writing, wrote, written**)
1 to write words or signs is to put them on paper or some other surface so that people can read them 2 to write a story or play or a piece of music is to be the author or composer of it 3 to write to someone is to send them a letter **to write something off** is to think it is lost or useless

writer noun
a person who writes; an author

writhe verb (say ryth)
to writhe is to twist your body about because you are in pain or discomfort

writing noun
1 writing is something you write 2 your writing is the way you write

wrong adjective
1 not fair or morally right
• It is wrong to cheat.
2 incorrect • That's the wrong answer. 3 not working properly
• There's something wrong with the engine. **wrongly** adverb in a way that is unfair or incorrect

a
b
c
d
e
f
g
h
i
j
k
l
m
n
o
p
q
r
s
t
u
v
w
x
y
z

a
b
c
d
e
f
g
h
i
j
k
l
m
n
o
p
q
r
s
t
u
v
w
x
y
z

wrong *adverb*
wrongly • *You guessed wrong.*

wrong *noun*
something that is wrong
to be in the wrong is to
have done or said something
wrong

wrong *verb*
to wrong someone is to do
wrong to them

wry *adjective*
slightly
mocking
or
sarcastic
• *He gave a
wry smile.*

Xx

Xmas *noun*
(*informal*)
Christmas

X-ray *noun*
a photograph of the inside
of something, especially
a part of the body, made
by a kind of radiation that
can pass through something
solid

X-ray *verb*
to X-ray something is to make
an X-ray of it

xylophone *noun*
(*say* **zy**-lo-fohn)
a musical instrument made
of wooden bars of different
lengths, that you
hit with small
hammers

X-ray

WORD ORIGINS
The word **xylophone** comes from
Greek words *xylon* meaning 'wood'
and phone meaning 'sound' (the
same word as in telephone).

Yy

yacht *noun* (*say* yot)
1 a sailing boat used
for racing or
cruising
2 a private
ship

yam *noun*
a tropical
vegetable
that
grows
underground

yank *verb*
to yank
something is to
pull it strongly and
suddenly

yap *verb* (**yapping,
yapped**)
a small dog yaps when it makes
a shrill barking sound

yap *noun*
a shrill barking sound

yard¹ *noun*
a measure of length, 36 inches
or about 91 centimetres

yard² *noun*
a piece of ground beside a
building, or one used for a
special purpose, such as a
railway yard

yarn *noun*
1 yarn is thread spun by
twisting fibres together
2 (*informal*) a yarn is a tale
or story

yashmak *noun*
a veil covering most of the face,
worn by some Muslim women

yawn *verb*
you yawn when you open your
mouth wide and breathe in
deeply because you are tired
or bored

yawn *noun*
an act of yawning

year *noun*
the time that the earth takes
to go right round the sun,
about 365¼ days or twelve
months

yearly *adjective, adverb*
every year

yearn *verb*
to yearn for something is to
long for it

yeast *noun*
yeast is a substance used in
baking bread and in making
beer and wine

yell *noun*
a loud cry or shout

yell *verb*
to yell is to cry or shout loudly

yellow *noun*
the colour of ripe lemons
and buttercups

yellow *adjective*
1 yellow in colour
2 (*informal*) cowardly

yelp *verb*
to yelp is to make a shrill bark
or cry, as a dog does when it is
hurt

yelp *noun*
a yelping sound

yachts

yes *exclamation*
a word used for agreeing to something

yesterday *noun, adverb*
the day before today

yet *adverb*
1 up to now; by this time • *Has the postman called yet?* **2** eventually; still • *I'll get even with him yet.* **3** in addition; even • *She became yet more excited.*

yet *conjunction*
nevertheless • *It is strange, yet it is true.*

yeti *noun* (**yetis**) (*say* **yet**-ee)
a very large hairy creature that some people think lives in the Himalayas

yew *noun*
an evergreen tree with red berries and dark leaves like needles

yield *verb*
1 to yield is to surrender or give in • *He yielded to persuasion.* **2** to yield a crop or profit is to produce it • *These trees yield good apples.*

yield *noun*
an amount produced by something • *What is the yield of wheat per acre?*

yodel *verb* (**yodelling, yodelled**)
to yodel is to sing or shout with your voice going rapidly from low to high notes

yoga *noun*
yoga is a Hindu system of exercise and meditation

yoghurt *noun* (*say* **yog**-ert)
yoghur is milk made thick by the addition of bacteria, giving it a sharp taste

yoke *noun*
a curved piece of wood put across the necks of animals pulling a cart

yoke *verb*
to yoke animals is to harness them or link them by means of a yoke

yolk *noun*
(*rhymes with* **coke**)
the yellow part of an egg

Yom Kippur *noun*
the Day of Atonement, an important Jewish religious festival

Yorkshire pudding *noun*
a pudding made of batter and usually eaten with roast beef

you *pronoun*
1 the person or people someone is speaking to • *Who are you?* **2** people; anyone • *You can never be too sure.*

young *adjective*
having lived or existed only a short time; not old

young *plural noun*
an animal's or bird's young are its babies

youngster *noun*
a young person or child

your *adjective*
belonging to you

yours *pronoun*
belonging to you • *Is this house yours?* **Yours faithfully, Yours sincerely, Yours truly** formal ways of ending a letter before you sign it

yourself *pronoun* (**yourselves**)
you (referring to one person) and nobody else, used to refer back to the subject of a verb • *Have you hurt yourself?* **by yourself** or **yourselves** on your own • *Did you do the work all by yourself?*

youth *noun*
1 youth is being young, or the time when you are young **2** a youth is a young man **3** youth also means young people • *The youth of today are much more serious.*

youthful *adjective* looking young or behaving like a young person

youth club *noun*
a club providing leisure activities for young people

youth hostel *noun*
a hostel where young people can stay cheaply when they are on holiday

yo-yo *noun* (**yo-yos**)
a round wooden or plastic toy that moves up and down on a string which you hold

Zz

zany *adjective* (**zanier, zaniest**)
funny in a crazy kind of way

WORD ORIGIN
The word **zany** comes from the Italian name Gianni, a shortening of Giovanni, which is the name often used for 'clown' in an old form of Italian comedy.

zap *verb* (**zapping, zapped**)
(*slang*) **1** to zap something or someone is to attack or destroy them, especially in a computer game **2** to zap between television channels is to use a remote control to quickly change from one to another

zapper *noun*
a remote control for changing television channels

zeal *noun*
zeal is enthusiasm or eagerness, especially in doing what you believe to be right

zealous *adjective* (*say* **zel**-us)
very enthusiastic or keen
zealously *adverb* very enthusiastically

zebra *noun*
an African animal like a horse with black and white stripes

zebra crossing *noun*
part of a road marked with broad white stripes for pedestrians to cross

zebra

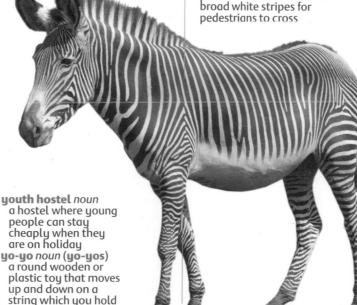

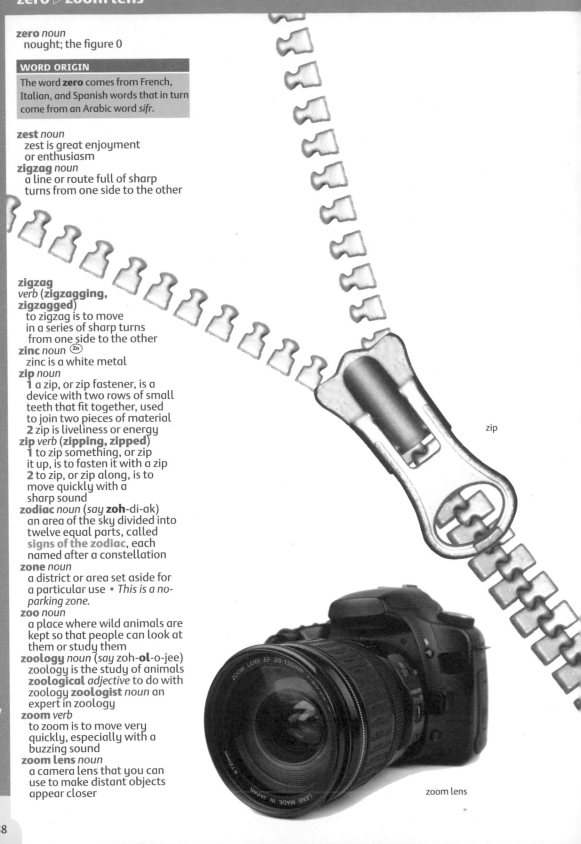

zero *noun*
nought; the figure 0

WORD ORIGIN

The word **zero** comes from French,
Italian, and Spanish words that in turn
come from an Arabic word *sifr*.

zest *noun*
zest is great enjoyment
or enthusiasm

zigzag *noun*
a line or route full of sharp
turns from one side to the other

zigzag
verb (**zigzagging,
zigzagged**)
to zigzag is to move
in a series of sharp turns
from one side to the other

zinc *noun* ⓩ
zinc is a white metal

zip *noun*
1 a zip, or zip fastener, is a
device with two rows of small
teeth that fit together, used
to join two pieces of material
2 zip is liveliness or energy

zip *verb* (**zipping, zipped**)
1 to zip something, or zip
it up, is to fasten it with a zip
2 to zip, or zip along, is to
move quickly with a
sharp sound

zodiac *noun* (*say* **zoh**-di-ak)
an area of the sky divided into
twelve equal parts, called
signs of the zodiac, each
named after a constellation

zone *noun*
a district or area set aside for
a particular use • *This is a no-
parking zone.*

zoo *noun*
a place where wild animals are
kept so that people can look at
them or study them

zoology *noun* (*say* zoh-**ol**-o-jee)
zoology is the study of animals
zoological *adjective* to do with
zoology **zoologist** *noun* an
expert in zoology

zoom *verb*
to zoom is to move very
quickly, especially with a
buzzing sound

zoom lens *noun*
a camera lens that you can
use to make distant objects
appear closer

zip

zoom lens